European VAT and the Sharing Economy

EUCOTAX Series on European Taxation

VOLUME 65

Series Editors

Introduction

EUCOTAX (European Universities Cooperating on Taxes) is a network of tax institutes currently consisting of eleven universities: WU (Vienna University of Economics and Business) in Austria, Katholieke Universiteit Leuven in Belgium, Corvinus University of Budapest, Hungary, Université Paris-I Panthéon-Sorbonne in France, Universität Osnabrück in Germany, Libera, Università Internazionale di Studi Sociali in Rome (and Università degli Studi di Bologna for the research part), in Italy, Fiscaal Instituut Tilburg at Tilburg University in the Netherlands, Universidad de Barcelona in Spain, Uppsala University in Sweden, Queen Mary and Westfield College at the University of London in the United Kingdom, and Georgetown University in Washington DC, United States of America. The network aims at initiating and coordinating both comparative education in taxation, through the organization of activities such as winter courses and guest lectures, and comparative research in the field, by means of joint research projects, international conferences and exchange of researchers between various countries.

Contents/Subjects

The EUCOTAX series covers a wide range of topics in European tax law. For example tax treaties, EC case law, tax planning, exchange of information and VAT. The series is well-known for its high-quality research and practical solutions.

Objective

The series aims to provide insights on new developments in European taxation.

Readership

Practitioners and academics dealing with European tax law.

Frequency of Publication

2-3 new volumes published each year.

The titles published in this series are listed at the end of this volume.

European VAT and the Sharing Economy

Giorgio Beretta

Wolters Kluwer

Published by:
Kluwer Law International B.V.
PO Box 316
2400 AH Alphen aan den Rijn
The Netherlands
E-mail: international-sales@wolterskluwer.com
Website: lrus.wolterskluwer.com

Sold and distributed in North, Central and South America by:
Wolters Kluwer Legal & Regulatory U.S.
7201 McKinney Circle
Frederick, MD 21704
United States of America
Email: customer.service@wolterskluwer.com

Sold and distributed in all other countries by:
Air Business Subscriptions
Rockwood House
Haywards Heath
West Sussex
RH16 3DH
United Kingdom
Email: international-customerservice@wolterskluwer.com

ISBN 978-94-035-1435-2

e-Book: ISBN 978-94-035-1442-0
web-PDF: ISBN 978-94-035-1445-1

European VAT and the Sharing Economy

Giorgio Beretta

Wolters Kluwer

Published by:
Kluwer Law International B.V.
PO Box 316
2400 AH Alphen aan den Rijn
The Netherlands
E-mail: international-sales@wolterskluwer.com
Website: lrus.wolterskluwer.com

Sold and distributed in North, Central and South America by:
Wolters Kluwer Legal & Regulatory U.S.
7201 McKinney Circle
Frederick, MD 21704
United States of America
Email: customer.service@wolterskluwer.com

Sold and distributed in all other countries by:
Air Business Subscriptions
Rockwood House
Haywards Heath
West Sussex
RH16 3DH
United Kingdom
Email: international-customerservice@wolterskluwer.com

ISBN 978-94-035-1435-2

e-Book: ISBN 978-94-035-1442-0
web-PDF: ISBN 978-94-035-1445-1

In memory and praise of Professor Dr Dr h.c. Ben J.M. Terra
(2 September 1947 – 30 June 2019)

Table of Contents

About the Author

Dr Giorgio Beretta is a PhD in Management, Finance, and Law for Business at LIUC University (Italy), where he defended his doctoral thesis on 'European VAT and the Sharing Economy' in December 2018. The thesis was prepared under the joint supervision of Prof. Dr Mariken van Hilten and Prof. Dr Dr h.c. Ben Terra. Prof. Dr Rita de la Feria and Prof. Dr Pasquale Pistone acted as external referees.

Giorgio was educated at the University of Milano-Bicocca (Italy), where he graduated in law (five years) with full marks in 2014. He obtained an Advanced Master's (Postgraduate) in Corporate Tax Law from Bocconi University (Italy) in 2015 and an Advanced Master's (LLM) in International Tax Law jointly organized by the University of Amsterdam (UvA) and International Bureau of Fiscal Documentation (IBFD) (Netherlands) in 2017, both with full marks. During 2018, he was scholarship holder at the Max Planck Institute for Tax Law and Public Finance (Germany) and visiting researcher at IBFD (Netherlands).

Giorgio regularly participates and speaks in international and national conferences, seminars, and other events. He is an author of several publications on issues of European VAT, as well as International, European, and Italian tax laws.

In parallel to his academic activities, Giorgio was research associate at the International Fiscal Association (IFA) for the 2017-2018 term and worked as a tax advisor in Milan from 2014 to 2016.

List of Abbreviations

AG	Advocate General
Art.	Article
ATO	Australian Taxation Office
B2B	Business-to-Business (transactions made between two taxable persons)
B2C	Business-to-Consumer (transactions made between a taxable person and a non-taxable person)
BEPS	Base Erosion and Profit Shifting
C2B	Consumer-to-Business (transactions made between a non-taxable person and a taxable person)
C2C	Consumer-to-Consumer (transactions made between two non-taxable persons)
CBR	Cross-Border Ruling
CFREU	Charter of Fundamental Rights of the European Union
CJEU/ECJ	Court of Justice of the European Union
Commission	European Commission
Council	European Council
EC	European Community
EEC Treaty	Treaty establishing the European Economic Community
EU	European Union
EU VAT	European Value Added Tax
FCA	Federal Court of Appeal
G20	Group of Twenty
GAFA	Acronym for Google, Apple, Facebook, and Amazon
GDP	Gross Domestic Product
GPS	Global Positioning System
GST	Goods and Services Tax

HMRC	Her Majesty's Revenue and Customs
IBFD	International Bureau of Fiscal Documentation
ICJ	International Court of Justice
ICT	Information and Communication Technology
IFA	International Fiscal Association
IPO	Initial Public Offering
MOSS	Mini-One-Stop-Shop
MTC	Model Tax Convention on Income and on Capital
OECD	Organisation for Economic Co-operation and Development
OECD Model	Model Tax Convention on Income and on Capital 2017
OECD VAT/GST Guidelines	OECD International VAT/GST Guidelines
OECD WP9	OECD Working Party No. 9 on Consumption Taxes
OJ	Official Journal
OSS	One Stop Shop
Ottawa Framework Conditions	OECD, Electronic Commerce: Taxation Framework Conditions. A Report by the OECD Committee on Fiscal Affairs, as presented to Ministers at the OECD Ministerial Conference 'A Borderless World: Realizing the Potential of Electronic Commerce' on 8 October 1998 (OECD Publishing 1998)
Para.	Paragraph
RST	Retail Sales Tax
SC	Supreme Court
SME	Small and Medium Enterprise
TAG	Technical Advisory Group
TEU	Treaty on the European Union
TFEU	Treaty on the Functioning of the European Union
TOMS	Tour Operators' Margin Scheme
UK	United Kingdom
US	United States
VAT	Value Added Tax
VAT Committee	European Commission – Value Added Tax Committee
VAT Directive	Council Directive 2006/112/EC of 28 November 2006 on the Common System of Value Added Tax, OJ L 347/1 of 11 December 2006
First VAT Directive	First Council Directive 67/227/EEC of 11 April 1967 on the Harmonisation of Legislation of Member States concerning Turnover Taxes, OJ 71/1301 of 14 April 1967
Second VAT Directive	Second Council Directive 67/228/EEC of 11 April 1967 on the Harmonisation of Legislation of Member States concerning Turnover Taxes – Structure and Procedures for Application of the Common System of Value Added Tax, OJ 71/1303 of 14 April 1967

Sixth VAT Directive	Sixth Council Directive 77/388/EEC of 17 May 1977 on the Harmonisation of the Laws of the Member States relating to Turnover Taxes - Common System of Value Added Tax: Uniform Basis of Assessment, OJ L 145/1 of 13 June 1977
VAT Directive	Council Directive 2006/112/EC of 28 November 2006 on the Common System of Value Added Tax, OJ L 347/1 of 11 December 2006
VAT Implementing Regulation	Council Implementing Regulation (EU) No 282/2011 of 15 March 2011 laying down Implementing Measures for Directive 2006/112/EC on the Common System of Value Added Tax, OJ L 77/1 of 23 March 2011
VoIP	Voice over Internet Protocol

List of Figures

List of Tables

Acknowledgements

This book is based on my doctoral thesis, which was the ultimate fruit of my employment as PhD researcher at the Department of Law of LIUC University (Italy) between September 2015 and December 2018 (however, cases and materials produced up to 31 March 2019 were taken into consideration for the purposes of this book). The thesis was defended on 17 December 2018 in the fulfilment of the requirements for the degree of Doctor of Laws. I also received the additional label of 'Doctor Europaeus' awarded by the European University Association in consideration of the pan-European relevance of my dissertation and studies.

Several people, in various ways, have inspired and supported my efforts during the three years of PhD pursuit (2015-2018), whose valuable assistance was deeply appreciated and at least deserves to be acknowledged here. My primary thanks go to my two exceptional supervisors, Prof. Dr Mariken van Hilten and Prof. Dr Dr h.c. Ben Terra, who guided me through an understanding of European VAT and steered my whole academic research. I am particularly grateful to them for the depth of knowledge, wisdom, and expertise generously shared as well as for the wealth of patience, persistence, and perseverance eagerly demonstrated while reading and commenting footnote-by-footnote the innumerable drafts of the present study. I cannot fully express my appreciation for the time and constant attention that both have dedicated to me, despite their several commitments and undertakings. I am even more indebted to them considering their highly liberal gesture of supervising my academic research although I was affiliated with another university. Such joint support was indeed crucial to bring my academic *voyage* farther – I would even dare to say – *au bout de la nuit*.

I would also express my deepest sense of gratitude to the two outstanding academic referees who have positively assessed my work, Prof. Dr Rita de la Feria and Prof. Dr Pasquale Pistone, who, with their insightful comments, incisive remarks, and valuable suggestions, have contributed to greatly enhance the present study. Considering their incredibly jam-packed agendas, their time and efforts were even more welcome and at least deserve to be acknowledged here.

A special note of thanks goes to Prof. Dr Dr h.c. Wolfgang Schön, managing director of the Max Planck Institute for Tax Law and Public Finance, who generously allowed me to undertake a considerable part of my research at the institute during 2018. I would also express my deepest appreciation to Mr Piet Battiau, head of the Consumption Taxes Unit in the Centre for Tax Policy and Administration of the Organisation for Economic Co-operation and Development (OECD), who liberally granted me the sensational opportunity to attend the OECD Working Party No. 9's meetings during 2018.

I also found extremely beneficial for my overall academic research and understanding of tax law to collaborate with Prof. Scott Wilkie, vice-chair of the Permanent Scientific Committee of the International Fiscal Association (IFA), and with Prof. Jan de Goede, senior principal and director of the Knowledge Centre at IBFD. During the same period, it was also fruitful the assistance of Ms Fabiola Annacondia, editor of the IBFD's International VAT Monitor journal and the EU VAT Compass book.

I also owe thanks to Prof. Dr Raffaella Manzini, director of the PhD Program in Management, Finance, and Law for Business at LIUC University, who constantly supported all my activities throughout the years as a PhD researcher. I am equally grateful to Prof. Dr Giuseppe Marino, professor of Tax Law at the University of Milan, and Prof. Dr Giuseppe Zizzo, professor of Tax Law at LIUC University, who kindly accompanied my PhD and tax journeys, as well as to Prof. Dr Nicola Rondinone, professor of Commercial Law at LIUC University, who willingly assumed the inconvenient role of home university's supervisor while my PhD was already ongoing.

I would also like to praise Mr Francesco de Lillo, associate at IBFD, who friendly helped me in searching and retrieving several materials valuable to my work. A similar kind of appreciation goes to Mr René Offermanns, principal associate at IBFD, who patiently assisted me with various administrative matters during my permanence in the Netherlands, and to Mr Matteo Manzinello, tech expert and app creator, who carefully drafted the figures enclosed in the present study.

I would like to thank, without specifically mentioning but having all of them in my heart and soul, all the professors, researchers, PhD, LLM, and other fellows who I had the privilege to meet at the several conferences, seminars, and other events that I have attended all around the world during these years.

On a more personal note, I finally wish to thank my parents, family, and friends for their unrelenting support, both in person and from a distance.

Milan, March 2019
Giorgio Beretta

Part I Introduction and Background

CHAPTER 1
Introduction

§1.01 PRELUDE AND SUBJECT OF THE RESEARCH

The past few years have seen the sensational rise of new models of production, distribution, and consumption of goods and services, which have been synthetically captured under the umbrella definition of 'sharing economy'.[1] Billed by Time Magazine as one of the '10 Ideas That Will Change the World'[2], the sharing economy has a profound impact on individuals, businesses, and institutions alike.[3] The ascent of digital platforms – including renowned companies headquartered in the Silicon Valley like Airbnb and Uber, or the French unicorns HomeExchange and BlaBlaCar, just to name few of 'the Upstarts'[4] that are now familiar to everyone – expands, in fact, dramatically the range of possibilities for businesses and consumers alike to exchange with each other anything, from accommodation to rides. In the virtual marketplaces shaped and ruled by those novel matchmakers, rather than from a combination of several, distinct operations carried out by a single centralized entity, value is created through the granular interaction of many dispersed individuals. In economics jargon, markets such as those created by sharing economy platforms are usually referred to as 'two-sided markets', since two distinct groups of participants, i.e., individual suppliers and individual customers, directly interact through an intermediary, i.e., the platform, which provides its own services to both sides.[5]

1. T.L. Friedman, *Welcome to the 'Sharing Economy'*, The New York Times (20 Jul. 2013).
2. B. Walsh, *Today's Smart Choice: Don't Own. Share*, Time Magazine (17 Mar. 2011).
3. For a survey on individual perceptions, attitudes, and practices in relation to the sharing economy in the European Union (EU), *see* European Commission, *Report: The Use of the Collaborative Economy. Survey Requested by the European Commission, Directorate-General for Internal Market, Industry, Entrepreneurship and SMEs and Co-ordinated by the Directorate-General for Communication* (2018), Flash Eurobarometer 467 – TNS Political & Social.
4. B. Stone, *The Upstarts. How Uber, Airbnb and the Killer Companies of the New Silicon Valley Are Changing the World* (Little, Brown & Co. 2017).
5. J.C. Rochet & J. Tirole, *Platform Competition in Two-Sided Markets*, 1 J. Eur. Econ. Ass. 4 (2003), at 990-1029.

The rise of the sharing economy has spawned a great deal of attention in recent times. Indeed, several publications have been released, many conferences have been held, and dedicated research units have been set up on this specific subject in many universities and research centres all around the world, whereas the phenomenon itself has been investigated from the perspective of various social sciences, including economics, sociology, and law. Notably, in this latter field only, studies having the sharing economy as a narrow subject have been carried out in areas as different as competition, consumer, insurance, intellectual property, labour, and privacy law.[6] Legal disruption, in fact, is not an accident, rather it is a core feature of the sharing economy. In the sharing economy, foundational dichotomous categories, such as those between suppliers and customers, business and private spheres, employees and self-employed, are largely no longer viable as organizational legal structures, whereas new legal 'hybrids' are being created.[7] As vividly explained by US District Court Judge Chhabria in a case involving the US-based sharing economy platform operating a network of taxi, Lyft, 'in this case will be handed a square peg and asked to choose between two round holes', in the sense that the jury in its decision had to figure out how a 'square peg' business model such as that of Lyft could be inserted into the 'round holes' of existing legal categories, where none of them was a perfect fit.[8]

Tax law issues have been investigated as well. Notably, with regard to an indirect, consumption-type tax such as European Value Added Tax (hereinafter, EU VAT), the Value Added Tax Committee (hereinafter, VAT Committee) – an advisory body inside the European Commission (hereinafter, Commission) – has discussed certain issues specifically related to the treatment of sharing economy activities.[9] The OECD Working Party No. 9 on Consumption Taxes (hereinafter, WP9), in close consultation with the business community through the Technical Advisory Group (hereinafter, TAG), is also working actively on the role of digital and sharing economy platforms in relation to the collection of Value Added Tax (hereinafter, VAT) and Goods and Services Tax (hereinafter, GST).[10] The phenomenon has equally caught the

6. For an overview of the main challenges that the sharing economy poses in different areas of EU law (although neither EU tax nor EU VAT law), *see* V. Hatzopoulos, *The Collaborative Economy and EU Law* (Hart Publishing 2018).
7. O. Lobel, *The Law of the Platform*, 101 Minn. L. Rev. 1 (2016), at 143-144. Such kind of legal disruption occurs also in the tax field, in so far as taxation is 'a form of governmental regulation that classifies attributes and relationships into existing patterns and forms' and, indeed, 'the menu of such possible categories under tax law is limited'. *See* T. Dagan, *Itemizing Personhood*, 29 Va. Tax Rev. 1 (2009), at 111.
8. US: Northern California District Court, 11 Mar. 2015, *Patrick Cotter et al. v. LYFT Inc.*, No. 13-cv-04065-VC, 60 F.Supp.3d 1067 (N.D. Cal. 2015), at para. 7.
9. European Commission, Value Added Tax Committee, *Working Paper No. 878. VAT Treatment of Sharing Economy* (taxud.c.1(2015)4370160); *Working Paper No. 947. Services Provided by an Electronic Platform Connecting for Remuneration, by means of a Smartphone Application, a Driver Using His Own Vehicle with Persons Who Wish to Make Urban Journeys. The Significance of the VAT Identification Number* (taxud.c.1(2018)1735106).
10. OECD, *The Role of Digital Platforms in the Collection of VAT/GST on Online Sales* (OECD Publishing 2019). Noteworthy, the terms 'Value Added Tax' (VAT) and 'Goods and Services Tax' (GST) are used interchangeably in the present study.

attention of VAT scholars[11], practitioners[12], governments[13], and, to an extent, even of the general public[14]. Despite a growing spark of interest, until now no comprehensive analysis, neither from a perspective of EU VAT nor from that of other VAT/GST systems, has been carried out concerning the treatment of the sharing economy. Neither specific policies concerning the VAT/GST treatment of the sharing economy have been discussed at the international level. The existence of such gap in the literature, besides the keen interest of the author as well as of the general public on this topic, is what motivates the present research.

§1.02 VAT/GST SYSTEMS AND EU VAT

This section provides some background information on the basic design and functioning of an indirect, consumption-type tax such as the VAT/GST. In particular, the main properties and features of EU VAT are summarized below.

Albeit consumption taxes have in the past been associated with war and crises[15] and despite its allegedly low capacity in terms of progressivity and redistribution effects[16], the VAT is now widely seen as a well-designed[17] and relatively growth-friendly[18] tax. The initiation of a VAT by an increased number of countries has indeed been considered as one of the most remarkable achievements in the development of tax systems during the second half of the twentieth century.[19] Beginning from the late 1960s onwards, VAT has in fact become the main consumption tax and an important

11. M. Lamensch, *The Scope of the EU VAT System: Traditional & Digital Economy Related Questions*, in *CJEU – Recent Developments in Value Added Tax 2017*, at 118-124 (M. Lang et al. eds, Linde 2018); M. Álvarez Suso, *Comments on CJEU Case-Law on Taxable Transaction 2017: The Anti-Abuse Doctrine (Cussens) and the Sharing Economy (UBER)*, in *CJEU – Recent Developments in Value Added Tax 2017*, at 233-249 (M. Lang et al. eds, Linde 2018); H.A. Kogels & M.E. van Hilten, *Never a Dull Moment*, 28 Intl. VAT Monitor 2 (2017), Journals IBFD; R. Millar, *UberX Drivers Supply Taxi Travel and So Must Be Registered for GST*, 6 World J. VAT/GST L. 1 (2017), at 47-54. The author would also like to mention his article published in the IBFD's World Tax Journal. *See* G. Beretta, *VAT and the Sharing Economy*, 10 World Tax J. 3 (2018), Journals IBFD.
12. Ernst & Young (EY), *Key Indirect Tax Issues in the Sharing Economy*, http://www.ey.com/gl/en/services/tax/vat--gst-and-other-sales-taxes/ey-managing-indirect-taxes-in-the-digital-age-ch7-key-indirect-tax-issues-in-the-sharing-economy (accessed 31 Mar. 2019).
13. AU: Australian Taxation Office (ATO), *The Sharing Economy and Tax*, https://www.ato.gov.au/General/The-sharing-economy-and-tax/ (accessed 31 Mar. 2019).
14. *Sharing Economy Shows Up Outdated Tax Rules*, Financial Times (3 Jan. 2017).
15. B.J.M. Terra, *Sales Taxation. The Case of Value Added Tax in the European Community* at 1-2 (Kluwer Law International 1988).
16. OECD, *The Distributional Effects of Consumption Taxes in OECD Countries* at 37-38 (OECD Publishing 2014).
17. J. Mirlees et al., *Tax by Design* Ch. 9 (Oxford University Press 2011).
18. OECD, *Consumption Tax Trends 2018* at 16 (OECD Publishing 2018).
19. A.A. Tait, *Value Added Tax – International Practice and Problems* at 3 (International Monetary Fund 1988), describes the rise of the VAT as an 'unparalleled tax phenomenon', whereas A. Schenk, V. Thuronyi & W. Cui, *Value Added Tax: A Comparative Approach* at 33 (Cambridge University Press 2015) claim that 'the VAT has been the most pervasive tax reform throughout the world during the second half of the twentieth century and into the twenty-first century and has proved to be a major source of government revenue'.

source of revenues for more than 168 countries worldwide.[20] At present, nearly all OECD countries have a VAT, the only exception being the United States (US).[21] Despite its popularity and an increasing interaction between different VAT/GST systems due to the expansion of cross-border trade, no international organization is currently responsible for supervising and monitoring the operation of the tax across different jurisdictions.[22]

Although the palm of 'modern VAT' – in the sense of constituting an international best practice as featuring an allegedly neutral system – is usually attributed to the Australian and New Zealand GSTs[23], EU VAT can boast about being the first 'modern VAT' to have been enacted. EU VAT was in fact implemented as early as 1967[24], as a result of the sudden awareness of the potential negative impact that the application of several turnover taxes across Member States could have had.[25] As from its original intent and that of a supranational institution like the EU, national VAT laws are largely harmonized across Member States. Presently, EU VAT rules are laid down in the Sixth Directive, recast in 2006, i.e., the VAT Directive.[26] To ensure a smooth application of the VAT Directive across Member States, the Implementing Regulation was enacted in 2011.[27] Uniformity of interpretation and application of VAT provisions in all EU countries is also sought through the extensive case law of the Court of Justice of the

---

20. VAT is in fact a high-yield tax. It enables governments to smoothly collect additional revenue by simply raising its rate(s). In the accounts of S. Cnossen, *Global Trends and Issues in Value Added Taxation*, 5 Intl. Tax & Pub. Fin. 3 (1998), at 413, 'the VAT is a revenue workhouse'. Among OECD countries, revenue generated by VAT represented 6.8% of GDP and 20.2% of total revenue on average in 2016, while standard VAT rates have reached a record level of 19.3% in average in 2015 and have remained stable since. *See* OECD, *supra* n. 18, at 11.
21. OECD, *supra* n. 18, at 16.
22. Against this background, it should be observed that the OECD has taken a much more active role in the international administration of VATs/GSTs, especially after the issuance of the OECD International VAT/GST Guidelines in 2015-2017, which were endorsed by over 100 jurisdictions and several international organizations sitting at the Global Forum on VAT and by G20 leaders in 2015.
23. L. Ebrill et al. (eds), *The Modern VAT* (International Monetary Fund 2001).
24. First Council Directive 67/227/EEC of 11 April 1967 on the Harmonisation of Legislation of Member States concerning Turnover Taxes, OJ 71/1301 of 14 Apr. 1967 [hereinafter, First Directive]; Second Council Directive 67/228/EEC of 11 April 1967 on the Harmonisation of Legislation of Member States concerning Turnover Taxes – Structure and Procedures for Application of the Common System of Value Added Tax, OJ 71/1303 of 14 Apr. 1967 [hereinafter, Second Directive].
25. As R. de la Feria, *VAT and the EC Internal Market: The Shortcomings of Harmonization* at 2 (Working Paper Series, University of Oxford 2009), highlights, EU VAT is, in principle, 'a tax at the centre of internal market policy'. The same author, however, warns that the current EU VAT system is, in effect, 'an obstacle to the establishment of the internal market', as it is 'vast, complex, and extremely detailed'. *See* R. de la Feria, *The EU VAT System and the Internal Market* Ch. 3 (IBFD 2009).
26. Sixth Council Directive 77/388/EEC of 17 May 1977 on the Harmonisation of the Laws of the Member States relating to Turnover Taxes – Common System of Value Added Tax: Uniform Basis of Assessment, OJ L 145/1 of 13 Jun. 1977 [hereinafter, Sixth Directive]; Council Directive 2006/112/EC of 28 November 2006 on the Common System of Value Added Tax, OJ L 347/1 of 11 Dec. 2006 [hereinafter, VAT Directive].
27. Council Implementing Regulation (EU) No 282/2011 of 15 March 2011 laying down Implementing Measures for Directive 2006/112/EC on the Common System of Value Added Tax, OJ L 77/1 of 23 Mar. 2011 [hereinafter, Implementing Regulation]. An earlier version of the Implementing Regulation was enacted in 2005. *See* Council Regulation (EC) No 1777/2005 of 17 October 2005

European Union (hereinafter, CJEU), the legal opinions of the Advocates General to the Court, as well as by means of soft-law instruments in the form of guidelines drafted by the VAT Committee and explanatory notes issued by the Commission.

The VAT aims to be a broad-based tax levied on final consumption. The scope of EU VAT is clearly set forth in Article 1(2) of the VAT Directive, which stipulates that EU VAT is 'a general tax on consumption'.[28] The term 'consumption', however, is not defined anywhere in the VAT Directive or in the Implementing Regulation. Nevertheless, the author concurs that the expression ought to be understood as EU VAT being a tax on everything a private individual or, even, a taxable person acting in a private capacity consumes.[29] And yet, the tax is not concerned with the 'adventures' of the sold product. Thus, the circumstance that certain goods or services are consumed immediately, like a ride on a taxi, whereas others, like a rental of immovable property, can be exploited over a long period is, by itself, immaterial.[30]

Although no tax could reasonably claim not distorting economic decisions anyhow, VAT is intended to remain as far as possible neutral for businesses. The basic premise is that VAT shall not be a cost for economic operators – under EU VAT termed as 'taxable persons'. To this end, taxable persons are entitled to deduct the VAT paid on their purchases from the VAT due in relation to the furtherance of their own economic activities. The ultimate result is that each taxable person has to collect and remit the net balance – and only that – between the VAT charged to his customers on his outputs and the VAT paid to his suppliers on his inputs. In so far as the tax only applies on the margin, which in a way reflects the 'value added' by each taxable person, EU VAT is non-cumulative. In simple terms, VAT is not levied on VAT. This avoids cascading of the tax and ensures that the amount aggregately collected by tax authorities remains always proportional to the final price paid by the end consumer. By 'flowing through the business' till the end consumer, EU VAT can thus claim leaving business decisions unaffected.[31]

As stated, the overarching purpose of EU VAT is to tax – only – final consumption.[32] As a proxy for that, expenditures made by private households are used.[33] In so

---

laying down Implementing Measures for Directive 77/388/EEC on the Common System of Value Added Tax, OJ L 288/1 of 29 Oct. 2005.

28. On VAT being a tax on consumption, *see* J. Englisch, *VAT/GST and Direct Taxes: Different Purposes*, in *Value Added Tax and Direct Taxation – Similarities and Differences*, at para. IV (M. Lang, P. Melz & E. Kristoffersson eds, IBFD 2009).
29. M.E. van Hilten, *The Legal Character of VAT*, in *Selected Issues in European Tax Law: The Legal Character of VAT and the Application of General Principles of Justice: Summary of an EFS Seminar in Honour of Fons Simons*, at 3 (D. Albregtse & H. Kogels eds, Kluwer Law International 1999).
30. B.J.M. Terra & J. Kajus, *Introduction to European VAT (Recast)* at para. 7.2.2. (IBFD Tax Research Platform 2019).
31. OECD, *International VAT/GST Guidelines* at 20 (OECD Publishing 2017).
32. J. Reugebrink, *The Sixth Directive for Harmonization of Value Added Tax*, 15 Comm. Mkt. L. Rev. 3 (1978), at 309-319.
33. All VAT/GST systems in the world adopt an indirect system for taxing final consumption. For a theoretical conceptualization of alternative consumption taxes, in which the taxpayer instead coincides with the end consumer, *see* N. Kaldor, *An Expenditure Tax* (Allen & Unwin 1955) and S-O. Lodin, *Progressive Expenditure Tax – An Alternative? A Report of the 1972 Government Commission on Taxation* (LiberFörlag 1978).

far as EU VAT is structurally designed to be passed on to the end consumer[34], it is only him who ultimately bears the full burden of the tax.[35] Although achieving the same economic effects as it follows from the application of a retail sales tax (hereinafter, RST) levied only at the last stage of the supply chain, EU VAT is administratively levied on a transaction-by-transaction basis and its collection takes place through a system of fractional payments made by taxable persons at each stage of the supply chain. Importantly, the tax is remitted by a person different than the end consumer.[36] This explains the inner paradox of VAT: 'the VAT is a tax in which those who believe themselves exempt are taxed, and those who believe themselves taxed, are generally exempt'.[37]

Ratione loci, EU VAT is governed by the 'territoriality principle'[38], whereas, for allocating taxing rights across different jurisdictions, like nearly all VAT/GST systems, EU VAT generally follows the 'destination principle', meaning that substantive jurisdiction to tax is attributed only to the country where final consumption ultimately takes place.[39] Pursuant to such rule, imported products are generally taxed, whereas exports are exempted (*rectius*: zero-rated with a right for the supplier to deduct the related input VAT).

§1.03 SETTING THE SCENE: TRADITIONAL VERSUS PLATFORM BUSINESS MODEL

The present age can essentially be described as 'the age of the platform'.[40] The last decade has in fact seen the exponential rise of a new type of intermediaries, i.e., digital platforms, with the largest among them, Google, Apple, Facebook, and Amazon – colloquially known with the acronym of 'GAFA' – reaching sensational valuation heights.[41] Although intermediaries have also existed in a pre-digital era, e.g., in the form of shopping centres bringing together retailers and shoppers, credit card companies linking merchants to cardholders, or newspaper magazines matching advertisers

34. AT: Opinion of the Advocate General, 6 Sep. 2018, Case C-531/17, *Vetsch Int. Transporte GmbH Interveniente: Zollamt Feldkirch Wolfurt*, para. 64.
35. NL: ECJ, 1 Apr. 1982, Case C-89/81, *Staatssecretaris van Financiën v. Hong-Kong Trade Development Council*, para. 9.
36. As repeatedly observed by the CJEU, a supplier of goods or services indeed acts as a 'mere tax collector for the state and in the interest of the public exchequer'. *See* e.g., DE: ECJ, 21 Feb. 2008, Case C-271/06, *Netto Supermarkt GmbH & Co. OHG v. Finanzamt Malchin*, para. 21.
37. J. Reugebrink & M.E. van Hilten, *Omzetbelasting* at 40 (Deventer 1997).
38. Title II of the VAT Directive (Arts 5-8) sets out the 'territorial scope' of EU VAT. In some instances (e.g., Art. 52 of the VAT Directive), a country may however be allowed to levy VAT even on services provided partially outside its own territory. *See* IT: ECJ, 23 Jan. 1986, Case C-283/84, *Trans Tirreno Express SpA v. Ufficio Provinciale IVA*, para. 21.
39. For a discussion of the territoriality and destination principles, *see* B.J.M. Terra, *The Place of Supply in European VAT* at 3-4 (Kluwer Law International 1998). In this connection, *see also* Chapter 7.
40. P. Simon, *The Age of the Platform: How Amazon, Apple, Facebook, and Google Have Redefined Business* (BookBaby 2011).
41. *See* e.g., P.C. Evans & A. Gawer, *The Rise of the Platform Enterprise: A Global Survey* (2016), https://www.thecge.net/app/uploads/2016/01/PDF-WEB-Platform-Survey_01_12.pdf (accessed 31 Mar. 2019).

with readers[42], due to recent advances in information and communication technology (ICT), which are capable of rendering physical infrastructures rather superfluous, nowadays it has become much easier, faster, and cheaper to build a marketplace where suppliers and customers can meet.[43]

But what exactly is a digital platform and, in particular, a multisided digital platform, which constitutes the focus of the present research? In a nutshell, a multisided digital platform is an online intermediary that facilitates interaction between two or more distinct, and yet interdependent, groups of users, either supplying or consuming goods and services. Importantly, not only users supply or consume goods and services among themselves, but also each group is indeed a customer of the multisided digital platform. As such, the business model of a multisided digital platform differs in several respects from that according to which a traditional firm operates.[44]

A traditional firm, in fact, usually operates along a linear supply chain: inputs at one side of the chain are processed, through a series of internal consecutive operations by various manufacturing or distributing businesses, and thus they are transformed into outputs which are valuable to end consumers.[45] Pursuant to such business model, as originally established during the Industrial Revolution and further refined by Taylor's economic theories at the inception of the twentieth century[46], value is created by an undertaking internally, through the marshalling of capital and labour resources, and then it flows from the original producer to the end consumer along the supply chain. Value accumulation throughout the chain occurs by way of each business simply repeating a series of operations all over again.[47] Figure 1.1 below captures the basic structure and functioning of what it can be termed as 'traditional business model'.

42. For these and other 'real-world' examples of two-sided markets, *see* e.g., T. Eisenmann, G. Parker & M.W. van Alstyne, *Strategies for Two-Sided Markets*, 84 Harv. Bus. Rev. 10 (2006), at 92-101.
43. *See* e.g., M.W. van Alstyne, G.G. Parker & S.P. Choudary, *Pipelines, Platforms, and the New Rules of Strategy*, 94 Harv. Bus. Rev. 4 (2016), at 54-62.
44. *See* e.g., D.S. Evans (ed.), *Platform Economics: Essays on Multi-Sided Businesses* (Competition Policy International 2011).
45. A. Das, *An Introduction to Operations Management: The Joy of Operations* at 4 (Routledge 2015).
46. F.W. Taylor, *The Principles of Scientific Management* (Harper & Brothers 1919).
47. For a more detailed description, *see* D. Ivanov, A. Tsipoulanidis & J. Schönberger, *Global Supply Chain and Operations Management in Business and Economics: A Decision-Oriented Introduction to the Creation of Value* Ch. 1 (Springer 2017).

Figure 1.1 Traditional Business Model

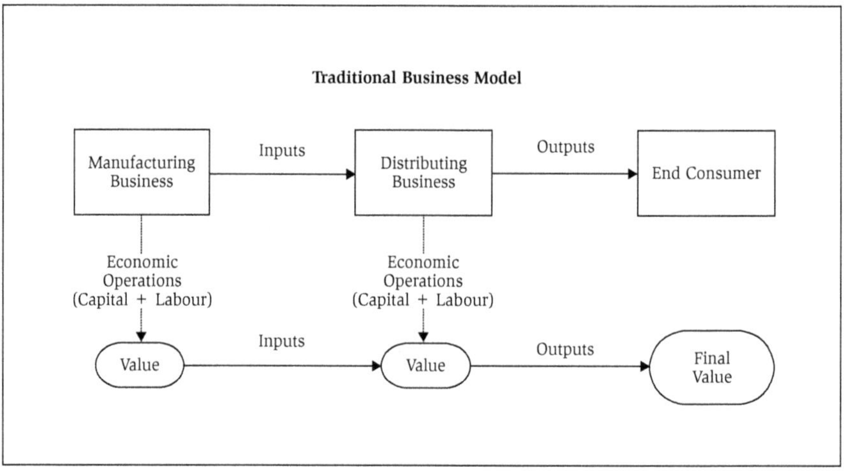

Rather than along a linear supply chain, multisided digital platforms operate according to a circular supply chain. In particular, while in a linear supply chain value is created aggregately by several businesses which transform inputs into outputs, multisided digital platforms generate value by building virtual marketplaces and facilitating transactions among two or more groups of users, who, otherwise, would fail to interact by their own forces mainly due to high transaction costs.[48] Pursuant to such business model, value is thus created directly by users via technological, commercial, and legal infrastructures set up by the platform, i.e., the 'market maker'.[49] And indeed, value delivered to each user in one group increases as the number in another, interdependent group grows: this creates what economists term as 'indirect network effects'.[50] The ability to build a large network among different groups of users and to leverage from such critical mass is what, in the end, determines the fortune of a platform.[51] In order to reach critical mass more rapidly, digital platforms may even exploit 'non-neutral pricing' strategies, namely platforms can charge one group of users less – or even

48. G.G. Parker, M.W. Van Alstyne & S.P. Choudary, *Platform Revolution: How Networked Markets Are Transforming the Economy and How to Make Them Work for You* at Ch. 1 (W.W. Norton & Company 2016).
49. I. Grinberg, *User Participation in Value Creation*, Brit. Tax Rev. 4 (2018), at 415.
50. D. Evans & R. Schmalensee, *Matchmakers: The New Economics of Multisided Platforms* at 25 (Harvard Business School 2016). Noteworthy, 'indirect network effects' can be either positive or negative, thus functioning according to either a mutual attraction spiral or an attraction/repulsion pendulum.
51. In the context of two-sided markets, such as those operated by digital platforms, 'critical mass' is intended as a minimal set of individuals (i.e., suppliers and customers) on each side, in a way that each side is large enough to attract more individuals and results in sustainable positive feedbacks. *See* D.S. Evans & R. Schmalensee, *Failure to Launch: Critical Mass in Platform Businesses*, 9 Rev. Net. Econ. 4 (2010), at 1-26.

decide not to charge them at all[52]–, whereas imposing a fare on another group of users at a price higher than the cost-compensating one. The net result is that one group of users, in fact, subsidizes the activity of another group of users, from which the platform is thus capable of monetizing.[53] Figure 1.2 below captures the basic structure and functioning of what it can be termed as 'platform business model'.

Figure 1.2 Platform Business Model

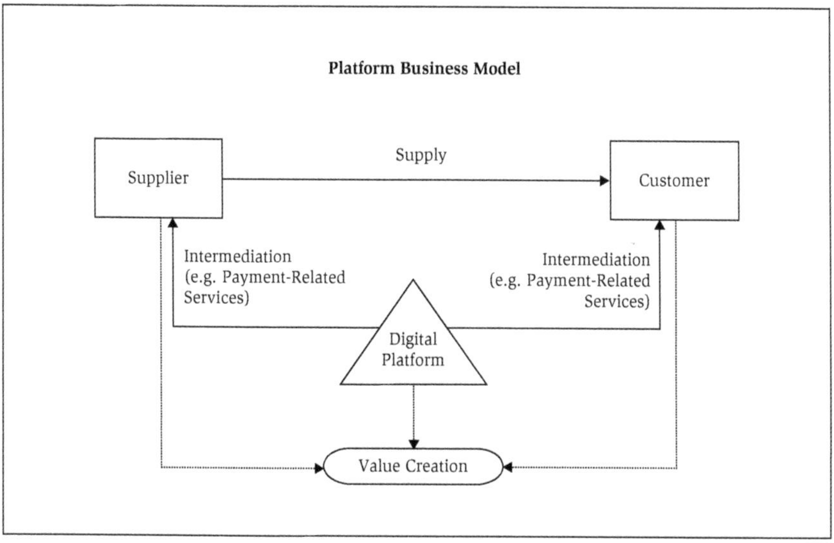

By connecting two or more interdependent groups of persons in a way that aims to benefit all sides, multisided platforms have ushered in a fundamentally new mode of doing business.[54] As such, it is no wonder that platform business models have come under close scrutiny by many institutions and governments all around the world.

52. Thus, effectively operating based on a so-called 'freemium' pricing strategy. *See* e.g., V. Kumar, *Making 'Freemium' Work*, 92 Harv. Bus. Rev. 5 (2014), at 27-29. In this context, the maximum amount of money that a firm should spend on a 'free' customer must, arguably, be set equal to the indirect economic returns that the company is able to obtain from that customer over its economic lifetime. For a perspective on this, *see* S. Gupta & C.F. Mela, *What Is a Free Customer Worth? Armchair Calculations of Nonpaying Customers' Value Can Lead to Flawed Strategies*, 86 Harv. Bus. Rev. 11 (2008), at 102-109.
53. D.S. Evans & M. Noel, *Defining Antitrust Markets When Firms Operate Two-Sided Platforms*, Colum. Bus. L. Rev. 3 (2005), at 680-681. Interestingly, in 2018, in a landmark decision the US Supreme Court ruled that non-neutral pricing strategies adopted by credit card companies are not per se anticompetitive and, thus, do not violate US antitrust laws. US: Supreme Court, 25 June 2018, *Ohio et al. v. American Express Co. et al.*, No. 16-1454, 138 S.Ct. 2274 (2018).
54. As firstly highlighted by J.A. Schumpeter, *Capitalism, Socialism, and Democracy* (Routledge 2010), capitalism, in itself, is in fact an evolutionary process, which can never be stationary. It incessantly revolutionizes the economic structure from within, destroying the old one and creating a new one. Based on such understanding, the rise of multisided digital platforms can arguably be seen as just another (the last) phase of capitalism evolution.

Indeed, under EU law, a comprehensive assessment of the role of online platforms, including those of the sharing economy, have been carried out by the Commission in recent years[55], whereas, in the specific field of tax law, a proposal to impose a 'special' turnover levy on certain digital services offered by multisided digital platforms to their users was tabled by the Commission in 2018.[56]

And indeed, the main challenge that the platform business model poses to EU VAT does not much relate to the fact that such a tax was developed in 1960s – at a time when trades mainly involved tangible goods and cross-border commerce was relatively limited, rather than in the digital economy flourished as from the 2000s, which has enabled products to be supplied across jurisdictions even from a distance[57] – but rather to the circumstance that EU VAT was conceived having the 'traditional business model' in mind, i.e., a business model where value is created aggregately by each business internally, through the exploitation of capital and labour resources, and then it flows along the supply chain till reaching the end consumer. Although the enactment of EU VAT was intended as a means to achieve competitive neutrality between businesses regardless where they find themselves along the supply chain and whatever the length of such chain is, express reference – as from the First Directive enacted in 1967 – to the 'length' of the production and distribution chain, in fact, suggests that the business model that the original EU legislator had in mind is best represented, precisely, by a linear supply chain.

Indeed, it strikes that no indication can be found – even in the current VAT Directive – to other features of the supply chain, i.e., how complex or wide it is, in the sense of entailing the participation at the same stage of the supply chain of several undertakings performing only a discrete operation of what – once combined – constitutes the good or the service that is valuable to the end consumer.[58] Matching, combining, and dispatching: this is, in a nutshell, the 'magic' of the 'platform business model'. It is the ability of multisided digital platforms, by allowing instantaneous and smooth interaction among millions of individuals, to transform otherwise economically inconvenient activities into fully feasible and profitable services. It is, in fact, the action of the platform, rather than the mere relationship established between users, what ultimately creates value in those kinds of business models.[59]

55. European Commission, *Communication from the Commission to the European Parliament, the Council, The European Economic and Social Committee and the Committee of the Regions. Online Platforms and the Digital Single Market Opportunities and Challenges for Europe*, COM(2016) 288 final.
56. European Commission, *Proposal for a Council Directive on the Common System of a Digital Services Tax on Revenues resulting from the Provision of Certain Digital Services*, COM(2018) 148 final.
57. For a discussion of several EU VAT issues in relation to advent of the digital economy, *see* M. Lamensch, *European Value Added Tax in the Digital Era* (IBFD 2015).
58. On a side note, however, it ought to be observed that, despite its name, VAT is not a tax on the 'value added', since the jurisdiction taxing the final supply toward the end consumer gets the entire tax revenue, rather than only the portion connected with the 'value added' before the final supply is made. *See* Ebrill et al. (eds), *supra* n. 23, at 1.
59. In the accounts of a US district court's decision (US: Southern New York District Court, 31 Mar. 2016, *Meyer v. Kalanick*, No. 15 Civ, 9796, 174 F. Supp. 3d 817 (S.D. New York 2016)), with a reference to Uber's business model, 'the capacity of orchestrating such an agreement is the

The pivotal role played by a multisided digital platform as an intermediary party in the homonymous business model contributes to explain the difference with the phenomenon of electronic commerce. Notably, while, in this latter, suppliers and customers normally enter into contact only by means of the Internet, without the need to rely on any type of intermediary, on the contrary, in the platform business model, interaction among users is – to a large extent – only viable thanks to the intervention of a digital platform, which, indeed, assumes a pivotal role in the supply chain. Accordingly, from a tax perspective, while in the case of electronic commerce the main challenge is to ensure a fair level of competition between online and offline supplies without, at the same time, imposing unfeasible administrative constraints on online suppliers, in the case of platform business models the nodal issue is somehow more radical, being that of ensuring fair competition and administrative easiness even between undertakings supplying exclusively online and, yet, operating along a supply chain as different as the linear or circular one.

More specifically with regard to EU VAT, while, in the case of electronic commerce, the main issues concern the categorization and itemization of digital products, the determination of the place of taxation for cross-border trade, as well as the establishment of appropriate mechanisms to secure registration and collection of VAT on remote supplies of digital products by foreign suppliers[60], in the case of platform business models, instead, the main challenges relate to the concepts themselves of suppliers and supplies, the scope and boundaries of transactions entailing the joint provision of several services by distinct undertakings, the correct classification of supplies for place of supply purposes, as well as the allocation of liabilities for collection and remittance of VAT among the various parties within the supply chain.[61] Overall, those kinds of challenges instantly reflect the reality that, through the years, the 'digital frontier' has been pushed farther and farther[62], so as to include within it even services once not capable of direct delivery from a remote location such as accommodation and passenger transport services[63], undoubtedly the most prominent services in the sharing economy. As a result of this continuous shift, not only the boundaries between the analogical and digital worlds are becoming increasingly fluid,

"genius" of Mr. Kalanick [Uber's founder] and his company, which, through the magic of smartphone technology, can invite hundreds of thousands of drivers in far-flung locations to agree to Uber's terms'.

60. In a nutshell, those issues attain, respectively, to 'character and source', 'physical presence', and 'allocation of taxing rights' across different jurisdictions. *See* C.I. Kingston, *Taxing the Future*, 51 Tax L. Rev. 4 (1996), at 641-653.
61. *See* section §1.04.
62. OECD/G20, *Tax Challenges Arising from Digitalisation – Interim Report 2018* at 15 and 207 (OECD Publishing 2018).
63. OECD, *Consumption Taxation of Cross-Border Services and Intangible Property in the Context of E-Commerce* at 2 (OECD Publishing 2001). *See also* European Commission, *Communication from the Commission to the European Parliament, the Council and the European Economic and Social Committee on the Future of VAT: Toward a Simpler, More Robust and Efficient VAT System Tailored to the Single Market*, at 11, COM(2011) 851 final, considering that 'similar goods and services should be subject to the same VAT rate and progress in technology should be taken into account in this respect, so that the challenge of convergence between the online and the physical environment is addressed'.

but also 'the "unity of action, time and place", to refer to the categories of classical theatre, is thus upset'.[64]

§1.04 PURPOSE AND SCOPE OF THE RESEARCH

The aim of this book is to understand whether the current EU VAT system is sufficiently equipped to deal with the ongoing transformation of the supply chain as well as the increasing digitalization of the economy ushered in by the rise of multisided digital platforms. In particular, the present contribution intends to examine and evaluate some of the main issues that the sharing economy poses to the EU VAT system, as well as to advance solutions wherever and in so far relevant shortcomings in the application of the current EU VAT provisions to the sharing economy are found.

This study, therefore, has two purposes. The first of these is to make an inventory of the main issues arising in the context of applying EU VAT to the sharing economy, as well as to assess the practical feasibility to shoehorn the main sharing economy business models, i.e., those available in the accommodation and passenger transport sectors, into the framework of existing EU VAT provisions. To this end, formulations of statements *de lege lata* are provided. As a second purpose, the study seeks to evaluate the opportunity for some reform of the current EU VAT system and proposes solutions to that effect, in the form of incremental and targeted amendments to the current EU VAT provisions. To this end, formulations of statements *de lege ferenda* are provided.

The ensuing analysis focuses on various legal propositions underpinning the EU VAT system. In particular, the study analyses basic concepts such as those of 'taxable persons'[65] and 'taxable transactions'[66], reviews the CJEU's doctrine on 'composite supplies' and other alternative approaches to it'[67], considers the interpretation and application of 'place of supply' rules[68] and, lastly, examines the current and potential role of sharing economy platforms in relation to a 'liability for collection and remittance of VAT' in lieu of individual suppliers[69].

The aforementioned sets of propositions, essentially, are meant to respond to the following – basic and, yet, challenging – five dogmatic questions:

(1) Who to tax?
(2) What to tax?
(3) How many – both suppliers and supplies – to tax?
(4) Where to tax?
(5) Who, when, and to which extent shall be responsible for collecting and remitting the tax?

64. NL: Opinion of the Advocate General, 12 Feb. 2019, Case C-568/17, *Staatssecretaris van Financiën, L.W. Geelen*, para. 17 [author's unofficial translation].
65. *See* Chapter 4.
66. *See* Chapter 5.
67. *See* Chapter 6.
68. *See* Chapter 7.
69. *See* Chapter 8.

The author submits that answering these five questions is essential to the central queries of this book, which seeks to evaluate how the sharing economy actually fits into the current EU VAT system and, further, to advance solutions wherever and in so far relevant shortcomings in the application of the current EU VAT provisions to the sharing economy are found.

The exploratory purpose of this study is, however, limited. The research, in fact, does not aim to develop brand new theories as regards the theoretical design of EU VAT. Rather, tentative solutions and possible recommendations are only advanced with an aim of reforming the current EU VAT system, without the (false?) pretence to revolutionize the main properties and features of a tax which, despite the inevitable shortcomings of every piece of legislation, can boast fifty years of more than egregious application. Indeed, it is firm conviction of the author that incremental and targeted reforms are a better aim to be pursued and, ultimately, can yield better results.[70]

Lastly, and from a broader perspective, the present contribution intends to provide a theoretical framework for future studies in the tax field on a recent and ever-expanding phenomenon such as the sharing economy, which is shaping and – the author believes – will continue moulding society and the economy during the twenty-first century.

§1.05 METHODOLOGY

The two purposes of this study, i.e., first, to assess the practical feasibility to apply the current EU VAT rules to the sharing economy and, second, to formulate tentative solutions and possible recommendations for improving the current EU VAT system, are pursued using a qualitative method of research. In particular, the method used in the present study entails a compounded rule-based and principle-based approach.

The point of departure of the ensuing analysis entails a description of the law as it stands.[71] Notably, the study seeks to clarify the meaning and interpretation of the five EU VAT propositions detailed in the previous section. To this end, the dogmatic method of legal analysis, which includes a literal, historical, contextual, and teleological interpretation, is used.[72] With an aim of depicting the state of art of the current EU VAT system in a more accurate fashion, a thorough review of the aforementioned five

70. For a similar approach in relation to tax challenges of the digital economy, *see* A. Turina, *Which 'Source' Taxation for the Digital Economy?*, 46 Intertax 6&7 (2018), at 495-519. Advocating for more radical changes to the EU VAT system in relation to digital supplies, *see instead* Lamensch, *supra* n. 57. For more radical solutions, such as reliance on blockchain technology and crypto tax currency, to address fundamental issues in VAT/GST matters, *see* e.g., R. Azam & O. Mazur, *Cloudy with a Chance of Taxation*, 22 Flo. Tax. Rev. 2 (2019), at 500-570.
71. The description of the law as it stands is part of the 'expository' tradition in legal research, i.e., the applied form of doctrinal research concerned with the systematic presentation and explanation of a particular legal doctrine. *See* P. Chynoweth, *Legal Research*, in *Methodologies of Legal Research: Which Kind of Method for What Kind of Discipline?* at 31 (M. van Hoecke ed., Hart Publishing 2011).
72. Under EU law, the traditional four methods of interpretation (literal, historical, contextual, and teleological) have originally been laid down by the CJEU in *CILFIT*. *See* IT: ECJ, 6 Oct. 1982, Case C-283/81, *Srl CILFIT and Lanificio di Gavardo SpA v. Ministry of Health*.

propositions based on *travaux preparatoires* publicly available, as well as their understanding by the CJEU, the Advocates General to the Court, the VAT Committee, the Commission, and the VAT doctrine, is provided.[73]

Reflecting an increasing need for a more adaptable legal thinking, the research further seeks to test the aforementioned five EU VAT propositions against a framework of selected legal principles, i.e., the principles of equality, neutrality, simplicity, flexibility, and proportionality, which serve as normative standards and which, in the author's understanding, might help test the 'reflexes'[74] of the current EU VAT system in the appraisal of a recent and ever-expanding phenomenon such as the sharing economy.[75] In the study, these principles are thus used as theoretical groundwork for amending or, even, introducing new rules.[76]

The legal analysis, conducted through such compounded rule-based and principle-based approach, further aims to fulfil the second scope of this study, which entails the formulation of a series of tentative solutions and possible recommendations for improving the current EU VAT system in relation to the issues identified in the research.

§1.06 (DE)LIMITATIONS

The scope of the research has been (de)limited as follows.

A first delimitation - or, if the reader wishes, a first limitation - of the research attains to a preliminary definitional issue. As will be explained later in Chapter 2, in assessing the EU VAT treatment of the sharing economy, this study adopts the definition provided by the Commission in its Communication of 2 June 2016 titled *A European Agenda for the Collaborative Economy*[77], despite the author plainly acknowledges that such a definition is certainly not exempt from criticism and, indeed, many and mostly inconsistent descriptions of the sharing economy can be found in the literature.

73. As the work of H.L.A. Hart, *The Concept of Law*. 3rd ed. at 124-154 (Clarendon Law Series 2012) highlights, law is essentially an interpretative venture and the doctrines which can be used for interpreting legal provisions are then various.
74. In a similar context, other researchers might have used the word 'rationality'. *See* P. Rendahl, *Cross-Border Consumption Taxation of Digital Supplies* at para. 1.2 (IBFD 2009).
75. As underlined by previous doctoral researches (*see* e.g., M. Papis-Almansa, *Insurance in European VAT: Current and Preferred Treatment in the Light of the New Zealand and Australian GST Systems* at 5 (Kluwer Law International 2017)), the correlation between a rule-based and a principle-based analysis is profound, given that it reflects the broader relationship existing between positive law and theoretical justice, in the sense that a departure from the principles underpinning a tax constitutes also a deviation from the fairness - and, hence, the inner justification - of its imposition by a jurisdiction.
76. J. Raz, *Legal Principles and the Limits of Law*, 81 Yale. L. J. 5 (1972), at 839-842.
77. European Commission, *Communication from the Commission to the European Parliament, the Council, the European Economic and Social Committee and the Committee of the Regions on a European Agenda for the Collaborative Economy*, COM(2016) 356 final.

The second (de)limitation attains to the subject matter of the research, i.e., the sharing economy, which is often perceived as just a corner of the digital economy[78] and, thus, from which arguably should not be ring-fenced[79]. Despite the unquestionable merits of having a broader conversation on the various issues arising from the digitalization of the economy, with an aim of maintaining the research sufficiently focused, the ensuing analysis is limited to the specific challenges surrounding the application of EU VAT to the sharing economy.

As a third note of caution, the research is not meant to be comparative. Although the sharing economy is undoubtedly a global phenomenon, due to time and publication length constraints, the analysis is restricted to EU VAT, which, indeed, was the first type of 'modern VAT' to be enacted and by now can boast an extensive case law.[80] Only a micro-comparison examination, then, is occasionally carried out. Implemented or proposed solutions to similar issues under other VAT/GST systems, in fact, are only discussed wherever and in so far as those measures might provide effective remedies to specific shortcomings in the application to the sharing economy of the current EU VAT provisions.

As a fourth point, it ought to be stressed that the study carves out the various standstill clauses[81], facultative norms[82], delegating rules[83], and derogations[84] contained in the VAT Directive. The same occurs for national provisions, judgements, and interpretative guidelines. Indeed, in light of the current state of (non-)harmonization of EU VAT, it would not have been feasible to carry out a separate analysis, for each Member State, of its own VAT system. Therefore, excursions into national VAT laws are conducted on an *impromptu* basis, i.e., only when it is considered relevant for the ultimate purposes of the research.[85]

The fifth (de)limitation relates to the five legal propositions that the author has specifically considered as the most relevant to assess the EU VAT treatment of the sharing economy. Other issues - arguably - equally relevant are instead carved out from the present contribution. In particular, the study does not discuss issues concerning either the 'chargeable event' and 'chargeability of VAT'[86], or the determination of the 'taxable amount'[87] to be subject to VAT. Other prominent issues equally left out of the research attain to the potential operation, with regard to specific transactions in the

78. The expression 'digital economy' is usually traced back to a 1996 book by D. Tapscott titled '*The Digital Economy: Promise and Peril in the Age of Networked Intelligence*' (McGraw-Hill 1996).
79. OECD/G20, *supra* n. 62, at 18, 166-167 and 212.
80. Based on Curia.europe.eu, together with a separate survey made by the law firm Law Square, as to 31 December 2017, 992 cases have been dealt with by the CJEU, 849 of which are preliminary rulings, while 143 infringement proceedings. *See* I. Lejeune & E. Peters, *Trends in the VAT Case-Law of the CJEU (2017)*, in *CJEU – Recent Developments in Value Added Tax 2017*, at 363-381 (M. Lang et al. eds, Linde 2018).
81. For example Arts 175(2), 176, 284(1) and 394 VAT Directive.
82. For example Art. 194 VAT Directive.
83. For example Art. 3(2)(a) VAT Directive.
84. Article 395 VAT Directive.
85. For a similar approach, *see* F.J.G. Nellen, *Information Asymmetries in EU VAT* at 21 (Kluwer Law International 2017).
86. Articles 62-71 VAT Directive.
87. Articles 72-92 VAT Directive.

sharing economy, of different VAT rates (e.g., for passenger transport services)[88], of certain exemptions (e.g., in relation to leasing or letting of immovable property)[89], or of any of the six special schemes contained in the VAT Directive.[90]

Sixth and lastly, a (de)limitation also exists with regard to the linguistic sources utilized for the present research. Although a limited number of contributions written in Italian, French, and other languages have been examined, most of the sources used are in fact in English. Further from a linguistic point of view, EU VAT terms have been considered, out of the twenty-four authentic languages in the EU, only in their English, Italian, and French versions.

§1.07 OUTLINE

This book comprises four parts. This introduction, setting forth the purpose and scope of the research as well as the legal methodology based on which the ensuing analysis is conducted, is Chapter 1 of Part I. Chapter 2, which continues Part I, contains the definition of the sharing economy as intended in the present study. Notably, this chapter is meant to provide a general background of the main features of the sharing economy. In particular, the main factors behind the surge of the various business models clutched under the umbrella term of 'sharing economy' are laid down and the main characteristics of the four sharing economy platforms specifically examined in the study, i.e., Airbnb, Uber, HomeExchange, and BlaBlaCar, are described.

Part II, composed of Chapter 3 only, proposes a framework of selected legal principles for evaluating whether and to which extent the current EU VAT treatment of the sharing economy could be improved. Importantly, the five selected principles, i.e., the principles of equality, neutrality, simplicity, flexibility, and proportionality, also provide the normative standards based on which tentative solutions and possible recommendations for reform are then formulated.

Part III contains the analysis of the five legal propositions, which, in the author's understanding, are of most relevance to assess the EU VAT treatment of the sharing economy. These five legal propositions are discussed, in turn, in separate chapters. In particular, following the VAT Determination scheme, whose steps reflect the structure of the VAT Directive, Chapter 4 analyses the notion of 'taxable persons'. Chapter 5, instead, focuses on the concept of 'taxable transactions'. Chapter 6 deals with 'composite supplies' and reviews the related doctrine developed by the CJEU as well as other alternative approaches to it. Next, Chapter 7 considers the interpretation and

88. Article 98 and point 5 of Annex III VAT Directive.

89. Article 135(1)(l) VAT Directive. However, not every economic activity concerning the rental of immovable property is necessarily exempt. *See* e.g., Arts 135(2)(a) and 137(1)(d) of the VAT Directive.

90. The six special schemes are laid down in Title XII of the VAT Directive and concern respectively: (1) small and medium-sized enterprises (SMEs), (2) farmers, (3) travel agents and tour operators (the so-called 'Tour Operators' Margin Scheme' or 'TOMS'), (4) second-hand goods, works of art, collectors' items, and antiques, (5) investment gold, and (6) non-established taxable persons supplying electronic services to non-taxable persons (the so-called 'One Stop Shop Scheme' or 'OSS'). Of these special schemes, only the SMEs and OSS schemes are briefly discussed, respectively, in Chapters 4 and 7.

application of 'place of supply' rules to sharing economy services. Lastly, Chapter 8 examines the current and potential role of sharing economy platforms in relation to a 'liability for collection and remittance of VAT' in lieu of individual suppliers.

Part IV, composed of Chapter 9 only, concludes the study and provides a summary of the main findings of the research. Building on the analysis conducted throughout the study, a series of tentative solutions and possible recommendations for improving the current EU VAT system is also formulated.

CHAPTER 2

The Sharing Economy

§2.01 INTRODUCTION

The advent of the sharing economy is promoting entirely new models of production, distribution, and consumption. Sharing economy platforms – including giant companies like Airbnb[1] and Uber[2] as well as less-known players like HomeExchange[3] and BlaBlaCar[4] – have dramatically expanded the range of possibilities for businesses and consumers alike, providing new wage-earning opportunities to the former and increasing the number of services available to the latter. In the sharing economy, businesses can in fact exploit the idling capacity[5] of their resources with an unprecedented scale of flexibility both in terms of timing and means, whereas consumers, in turn, have access to a wider band of services, from accommodations to rides[6], often in a more convenient way in terms of timing and pricing. By enabling the marketization of nearly every personal resource[7], the matchmaking action of these multisided platforms functions, in

1. *See* section §2.07[A].
2. *See* section §2.07[B].
3. *See* section §2.08[A].
4. *See* section §2.08[B].
5. The term 'idling capacity' defines the extent to which an object is not being used at its full capacity. *See* Y. Benkler, *'Sharing Nicely': On Sharable Goods and the Emergence of Sharing as a Modality of Economic Production*, 114 Yale L. J. 2 (2004), at 273-358.
6. Although accommodation (Airbnb, HomeExchange, Couchsurfing) and rides (Uber, Lyft, BlaBlaCar) are, by far, the most common examples of resources 'shared' among platform users, items exchanged on sharing economy platforms can include nearly everything, from household tools and vehicles (Open Shed, Getaround), office spaces and parking lots (Rubberdesk, JustPark), used clothes and other stuff (Tulerie, NeighborGoods), everyday errands and household tasks (TaskRabbit, Handy), home restaurant services and surplus food (EatWith, Olio), to package and grocery delivery (Postmates, Instacart).
7. The commercialization of nearly everything reflects a broader – and perhaps worrying – trend in society and the economy. For a perspective on this, *see* M.J. Sandel, *What Money Can't Buy: The Moral Limits of Markets* (Macmillan 2012).

effect, as lubricant for exchanges among peers[8], leapfrogging traditional middlemen[9], and trimming down transaction costs[10].

The sharing economy is even contributing to transform many long-established categories and paradigms at the centre of the traditional capitalist economy.[11] With the advent of the sharing economy, conventional dividing lines between suppliers and consumers[12] or between employees and self-employed[13] are in fact progressively blurring, whereas the spatial divides of private and business[14] and of leisure and market[15] activities are simply fading away. Besides, for suppliers, return might come in the form of monetary or non-monetary benefits, as well as in a combination of the two. Indeed, in the sharing economy, transactions span the whole market-to-gift spectrum.[16] The 'hybrid' nature of the sharing economy is also reflected in that, rather than being driven by the mere logic of profit-making, economic actors are moved by selfish insomuch as more altruistic aims.[17] The sharing economy has equally a wider impact on society in general, contributing to orient consumer base's mindset toward more responsible and environmentally conscious spending behaviours[18] as well as to restore

8. M. Bauwens, *Peer to Peer and Human Evolution. On 'the P2P Relational Dynamic' as the Premise of the Next Civilizational Stage* at 11 (2005), http://z.agoravox.fr/IMG/P2PandHumanEvolV2.pdf (accessed 31 Mar. 2019), defines 'peer-to-peer' (P2P) as 'a specific form of relational dynamic, based on the assumed equipotency of its participants, organized through the free cooperation of equals in view of the performance of a common task, for the creation of a common good, with forms of decision-making and autonomy that are widely distributed throughout the network'.
9. Intermediation, however, remains crucial also in the realm of the sharing economy. As R. Dyal-Chand, *Regulating Sharing: The Sharing Economy as an Alternative Capitalist System*, 90 Tul. L. Rev. 2 (2015), at 278-284, observes, the sharing economy can actually be seen as an innovative type of 'coordinated market economy', in which 'coordination', rather than via conventional means, is accomplished through technological infrastructures.
10. Economists have traditionally considered transaction costs as one of the most prominent reasons behind the formation of companies. *See* e.g., R.H. Coase, *The Nature of the Firm*, 16 Economica New Series 4 (1937), at 386-405.
11. O. Lobel, *The Law of the Platform*, 101 Minn. L. Rev. 1 (2016), at 90.
12. S. Kreiczer-Levy, *Consumption Property in the Sharing Economy*, 43 Pepp. L. Rev. 1 (2015), at 61-124. In truth, in the sharing economy 'consumers may have a far more active role not only as consumers, but also as producers and reviewers'. *See* OECD, *Protecting Consumers in Peer Platform Markets. Exploring the Issues* at 4 (OECD Publishing 2016).
13. V. de Stefano, *The Rise of the 'Just-in-Time Workforce': On-Demand Work, Crowdwork and Labour Protection in the 'Gig Economy'*, Intl. Lab. Off., Condition of Work and Employment Series, No. 71 (2016).
14. C. Koopman, M. Mitchell & A.D. Thierer, *The Sharing Economy: Issues Facing Platforms, Participants, and Regulators* (2015), https://papers.ssrn.com/sol3/papers.cfm?abstract_id=2610875 (accessed 31 Mar. 2019).
15. M.A. Cherry, *The Gamification of Work*, 40 Hofstra L. Rev. 4 (2012), at 851-858.
16. As J. Schor, *Debating the Sharing Economy*, 4 J. Self-Gov. & Man. Econ. 3 (2016), at 4, highlights, the character of digital platforms depends both on their market orientation (for-profit versus non-profit) and their market structure (peer-to-peer versus business-to-peer). On the gift economy, *see* D. Cheal, *The Gift Economy* (Routledge 2015).
17. A. Sundararajan, *The End of Employment and the Rise of Crowd-Based Capitalism* at 44 (MIT Press 2016); L. Lessig, *Remix: Making Art and Commerce Thrive in the Hybrid Economy* at 145 (Penguin 2008). A perfect example of the continuum existent between 'selfish' and 'altruistic' motivations is represented by the idea of 'indirect reciprocity', best epitomized by the expression 'I will help you, someone else helps me'.
18. C.J. Martin, *The Sharing Economy: A Pathway to Sustainability or a Nightmarish Form of Neoliberal Capitalism?*, Ecol. Econ. 121 (2016), at 149-159.

mutual trust among people[19]. All these factors combined generate the 'creative destruction' or the 'disruptive innovation' against which traditional businesses often struggle to compete on equal terms and which existing regulations usually fail to capture in a satisfactory manner.[20]

§2.02 THE SHARING ECONOMY AND THE SIX SHARING PILLARS

Although it is clear enough that a radical shift is underway in today's society and economy, nobody seems to know how exactly to name such ongoing transformation.[21] Equally referred to as 'collaborative economy'[22], 'collaborative consumption'[23], 'peer-to-peer economy'[24], 'gig economy'[25], 'on-demand economy'[26], 'platform economy'[27], '1099 economy'[28], 'the Uberization of everything'[29], or with a handful of other imaginative synonyms[30], the sharing economy actually lacks a 'shared' definition.[31] Various proposals have been advanced in this regard, but none has reached general consensus.[32]

---

19. J. Hamari, M. Sjöklint & A. Ukkonen, *The Sharing Economy: Why People Participate in Collaborative Consumption*, 67 Ass'n Info. Sci. & Tech. 9 (2015), at 2047-2059.
20. H. Schneider, *Creative Destruction and the Sharing Economy* (Edward Elgar Publishing 2017).
21. R. Botsman, *The Sharing Economy: Dictionary of Commonly Used Terms*, https://rachelbotsman.com/blog/the-sharing-economy-dictionary-of-commonly-used-terms/ (accessed 31 Mar. 2019). Noteworthy, in 2015 the term 'sharing economy' was included in the Oxford Dictionary, under which it is defined as 'an economic system in which assets or services are shared between private individuals, either free or for a fee, typically by means of the Internet'.
22. J. Owyang & A. Samuel, *The New Rules of the Collaborative Economy: 2015 Data on the Growth of Sharing* (2015), http://www.web-strategist.com/blog/2015/10/05/report-the-new-rules-of-the-collaborative-economy-2015-data-on-the-rise-of-sharing/ (accessed 31 Mar. 2019).
23. R. Botsman & R. Rogers, *What's Mine Is Yours. How Collaborative Consumption Is Changing the Way We Live* (HarperCollinsPublishers 2010).
24. S. Scanlon, *Peer-to-Peer Rental: The Rise of the Sharing Economy*, The Economist (9 Mar. 2013).
25. G. Friedman, *Workers Without Employers: Shadow Corporations and the Rise of the Gig Economy*, 2 Rev. Keynesian Econ. 2 (2014), at 171-188.
26. D. Farrell & F. Greig, *Paychecks, Paydays and the On-Demand Platform Economy: Big Data on Income Volatility* (JP Morgan Chase & Co. Institute 2016).
27. C. Busch et al., *The Rise of the Platform Economy: A New Challenge for EU Consumer Law?*, 5 J. Eur. Consumer & Mkt L. 1 (2016), at 3-10.
28. The term '1099 economy' is particularly popular in the United States, as it refers to the 1099-MISC, which is the form that businesses, non-profits, and government agencies must fill out when they pay someone USD 600 or more in non-employee compensation during a fiscal year. *See* e.g., E. Dourado & C. Koopman, *Evaluating the Growth of the 1099 Workforce* (Mercatus Center, George Mason University 2015), https://www.mercatus.org/publication/evaluating-growth-1099-workforce (accessed 31 March 2019).
29. S. Freeman, *'Uberization' of Everything Is Happening, but Not Every 'Uber' Will Succeed*, Huffington Post (1 Apr. 2015).
30. *See* e.g., L. Gansky, *The Mesh: Why the Future of Business Is Sharing* (Penguin 2010).
31. R. Botsman, *The Sharing Economy Lacks a Shared Definition* (2013), http://www.fastcoexist.com/3022028/the-sharing-economy-lacks-a-shared-definition#8 (accessed 31 March 2019); S. Greenhouse, *The Whatchamacallit Economy*, New York Times (16 Dec. 2016).
32. *See* e.g., Rachel Botsman's four quadrants, dividing up the sharing economy according to four broad activities (production, consumption, finance, and education), or Jeremiah Owyang's honeycomb, mapping out an industry-sector-based classification of the different kinds of collaborative economy activities. *See* Botsman, *supra* n. 31; J. Owyang, *Honeycomb 3.0: The*

For the purposes of the present study, the author equates the notion of 'sharing economy' with the definition of 'collaborative economy' spelt out by the Commission in its Communication of 2 June 2016 titled *A European Agenda for the Collaborative Economy*. Notably, in its communication the Commission considered that

> the term 'collaborative economy' refers to business models where activities are facilitated by collaborative platforms that create an open marketplace for the temporary usage of goods or services often provided by private individuals. The collaborative economy involves three categories of actors: (1) service providers who share assets, resources, time and/or skills – these can be private individuals offering services on an occasional basis ('peers') or service providers acting in their professional capacity ('professional services providers'); (2) users of these; and (3) intermediaries that connect – via an online platform – providers with users and that facilitate transactions between them ('collaborative platforms'). Collaborative economy transactions generally do not involve a change of ownership and can be carried out for profit or not-for-profit.[33]

In the author's opinion, the above definition is sufficiently accurate, in so far as it avoids either a too loose or too narrow appraisal of the new phenomenon.[34] All the relevant elements at the gist of the sharing economy, and, yet, without any further 'odd' ingredient, are in fact included in the definition set forth above. As such, the definition of the 'sharing economy' used in the present study remains limited to its 'most important applications'.[35] From its wording, the author contends that it is possible to extract six key propositions, which – in a way – constitute the six 'pillars' on which the legal construction of the sharing economy is built. Each of these pillars is singled out and explained below.

First, the sharing economy entails innovative and, yet, divergent business models, all 'sharing' some common traits and distancing themselves significantly from more traditional businesses, but, at the same time, with 'fifty shades of grey' at their inside, which render quite hard to position all of them in a single, straightforward

Collaborative Economy Market Expansion (2016), http://www.web-strategist.com/blog/2016/03/10/honeycomb-3-0-the-collaborative-economy-market-expansion-sxsw/ (accessed 31 March 2019).

33. European Commission, *Communication from the Commission to the European Parliament, the Council, the European Economic and Social Committee and the Committee of the Regions on a European Agenda for the Collaborative Economy*, at 3, COM(2016) 356 final. Noteworthy, although the Commission used the term 'collaborative economy' in its Communication, the VAT Committee instead preferred to employ the term 'sharing economy'. *See* European Commission, Value Added Tax Committee, *Working Paper No. 878. VAT Treatment of Sharing Economy*, at 10 (taxud.c.1(2015)4370160).
34. The preference attributed in the present study to the definition given by the Commission in its Communication on *A European Agenda for the Collaborative Economy* is motivated by the cross-pollination that frequently occurs under EU law, where a term used in one area of law is later transplanted into another legal area. For instance, the CJEU has made reference to the definition contained in the directive on insurance in order to define insurance services for EU VAT purposes. *See* UK: ECJ, 25 Feb. 1999, Case C-349/96, *Card Protection Plan Ltd (CPP) v. Commissioners of Customs & Excise*, paras 17-18.
35. For a similar approach, *see* Y. Brauner & A. Báez, *Withholding Taxes in the Service of BEPS Action 1: Address the Tax Challenges of the Digital Economy* at 11 (IBFD White Paper 2015).

category. Indeed, the sharing economy is not a black and white phenomenon. Rather, it is a spectrum and, as such, it is crucial to understand all its various shades.

Second, sharing transactions take place in large-sized marketplaces intermediated by digital platforms, where users allow or obtain temporary access to goods or services, whereas no change of ownership occurs.[36]

Third, three distinct economic actors are involved: a digital platform operating a virtual marketplace, an individual supplier providing assets and resources, and an individual customer receiving temporary access to those products.

Fourth, while digital platforms are generally professionals, both individual suppliers and customers may instead act either in a business or a private capacity. Likewise, services provided could entail the exploitation of business or private assets as well as involve the expeditious inclusion of the latter into the former category.

Fifth, individual suppliers in the sharing economy remain at liberty to perform their own activities either on a habitual or an occasional basis.

Sixth and lastly, sharing economy activities can be carried out either for a profit or for free, but most often in a continuum between the two.

At this juncture, it is useful to complement the analysis above with some 'real-world' examples. Considering the accommodation sector, the author finds that platforms like Airbnb, where users rent out their spared residential premises in return for a fee, HomeExchange, where accommodation providers receive credits from the platform which can later be used for being hosted by other peers of the same community, and Couchsurfing, a platform on which users conclude accommodation exchanges for free, are all part of the domain of the sharing economy. On the contrary, virtual marketplaces like Booking.com or Hotels.com do not belong to the sharing economy, in so far as accommodation availabilities are listed therein mostly by hotel brands or similar professional ventures.

Likewise, considering the passenger transport industry, both Uber, where taxi rides are provided in return for a fee, and BlaBlaCar, where instead users merely 'share up' the costs of a journey, are part of the sharing economy, whereas car-sharing services directly operated by large-sized companies like Car2go or Zipcar, which in fact manage their own fleet of vehicles, clearly are not.

Despite having certain traits in common with markets in the sharing economy, namely the circumstance that their users may act either in a business or a private capacity, on a habitual or an occasional basis, for monetary consideration or in return for other goods, also virtual marketplaces like Alibaba or eBay must be placed outside the domain of the sharing economy, as long as exchanges of ownership rather than of services take place on those marketplaces.

Lastly, content- and video-sharing websites like Wikipedia or YouTube, in which new content is created by users but it is marketized by these websites either in return for a fee or for free, are not part of the sharing economy, since no direct interaction occurs among visitors of those websites.

---

36. On the increased preference of consumers for access to rather than ownership of a property, *see* J. Rifkin, *The Age of Access: The New Culture of Hypercapitalism* (Penguin 2001).

§2.03 MAIN DRIVERS OF SHARING ECONOMY BUSINESS MODELS

The rise of the sharing economy is fuelled by a cocktail of technological, economic, and societal factors.

Technological advances lower market entry barriers for services providers, thus dramatically reducing costs and time for peers to secure transactions among themselves. At the same time, by allowing ubiquitous connectivity, ICT devices such as the smartphones greatly enhance allocation efficiency and competitiveness in the market.[37]

From an economic standpoint, sharing economy markets defy the traditional business model whereby goods and services are supplied by a single central player, typically taking the form of an enterprise. On the contrary, in the sharing economy, services are provided through the interaction of many dispersed individuals, albeit purposely coordinated by a platform. And yet, the role of sharing economy platforms is, in reality, much more pervasive than that of a traditional intermediary. By setting the terms and conditions of participation in their own marketplaces, sharing economy platforms are in fact able to control key features of the underlying transactions taking place among their users.[38]

Importantly, thanks to the advent of sharing economy platforms like HomeExchange or BlaBlaCar, the sharing economy also brings a revival of 'barter'. By matching in a cost- and time-efficient way supply and demand of services, sharing economy platforms in fact have managed to solve one of the most ticklish problems of bartering, that is the so-called 'double coincidence of wants', meaning that each party needs to find another party who has to offer what he exactly wants to receive and, at the same time, is prepared to receive what he exactly has to offer in return.[39]

Lastly, an important thrust in the sharing economy comes from certain underlying movements occurring in society, such as the rapid advent of social media platforms like Facebook or Twitter, the ongoing shift in consumer preferences due to an increasing desire for variety and authenticity of experiences, as well as the dramatic fallouts of the 2008 financial crisis that have induced many individuals to search for other disposable sources of income.[40]

---

37. Advances in ICT are at the origin of what has been termed as 'the death of the distance'. *See* F. Cairncross, *The Death of Distance: How the Communications Revolution Is Changing Our Lives* (Harvard Business Press 1997).
38. *See* S.A. Donovan, D.H. Bradley & J.O. Shimabukuru, *What Does the Gig Economy Mean for Workers?* at 3 (2016), https://digitalcommons.ilr.cornell.edu/cgi/viewcontent.cgi?article=2512&context=key_workplace (accessed 31 Mar. 2019), noting that platforms collect a portion of job-earning, own the brand, and control the provider-client relationship.
39. On the legal implications of bartering, *see* A. Kocourek & J.H. Wigmore, *Primitive and Ancient Legal Institutions* at 435-439 (Little, Brown & C. 1915).
40. As R. Belk, *Sharing*, 36 J. Consum. Res. 5 (2010), at 715-734, recalls from a sociological perspective, 'sharing is the most universal form of human economic behaviour, distinct from and more fundamental than reciprocity'.

§2.04 ECONOMIC ACTORS IN THE SHARING ECONOMY

The sharing economy involves three economic actors.

The leading role in the sharing economy is certainly played by digital platforms. Platforms essentially act as brokers, which, through their technological, commercial, and legal infrastructures, facilitate trusted transactions among users willing to provide or receive certain services. Eventually, platforms may also offer users a series of ancillary services, e.g., payment processing and insurance coverage. And indeed, platforms may well take advantage of their pivotal intermediary position. By controlling virtually every aspect of user interaction and by tracking consumer habits in close detail, platforms are in fact capable of exploiting several cognitive biases of their users, thus potentially inducing them to undertake an activity or purchase a service.[41]

The second category of economic actors is composed of individual suppliers who dispense resources, e.g., assets, skills, or simply their own time, through a virtual marketplace. Individual suppliers may seemingly act in a business or a private capacity, as well as either on a habitual or an occasional basis. The Commission itself acknowledges that distinguishing when a service provider is acting in a business or a private capacity is not always clear-cut, as long as 'EU legislation does not establish at what point a peer becomes a professional services provider in the collaborative economy'.[42] Moreover, it ought to be recalled that the status of a person can change over time.[43]

The third and last category of economic actors includes individual customers. Those are mostly private individuals who receive services from both individual suppliers and the platform. Although service recipients are usually consumers only, in certain instances they may provide certain services as well. This indeed happens if a user concludes a barter exchange with another user, e.g., in case of accommodation swaps on HomeExchange, or with the platform itself, e.g., where a user allows a platform to access his own personal data in return for services used in the furtherance of his business activity[44].

---

41. In this connection, *see* R. Calo & A. Rosenblat, *The Taking Economy: Uber, Information, and Power*, 117 Colum. L. Rev. 6 (2017), at 1623-1690, describing the Uber's practice to display icons of available 'taxi' cars nearby to potential passengers, when actually those vehicles are not there (a practice colloquially called as 'phantom cars'), or not to disclose the final destination (and, thus, the remunerative value) of the ride to drivers, which impede them to make completely informed choices (a practice mostly referred to as 'blind ride acceptance'), as prominent examples of 'digital market manipulation' by sharing economy platforms against their users.
42. *See* European Commission, *supra* n. 33, at 5. With an aim of shedding some light on this matter, the European Economic and Social Committee has pledged for the introduction of minimum income thresholds. *See* European Economic and Social Committee, *Taxation of the Collaborative Economy – Analysis of Possible Tax Policies Faced with the Growth of the Collaborative Economy (Exploratory Opinion Requested by the Estonian Presidency)*, at para. 5.8 (ECO/434-EESC-2017 -02946-00-00-ac-tra).
43. With regard to the evolving concept of 'consumer' in relation to the use of a Facebook account, *see* AT: Opinion of the Advocate General, 14 Nov. 2017, Case C-498/16, *Maximilian Schrems v. Facebook Ireland Limited*, paras 35-41.
44. Notoriously, 'personal data is the new oil of the Internet and the new currency of the digital world'. *See* M. Kuneva (European Consumer Commissioner), *Keynote Speech. Roundtable on Online Data Collection, Targeting and Profiling* (2009), http://europa.eu/rapid/press-release_

§2.05 TYPES OF SHARING ECONOMY BUSINESSES

The sharing economy groups together different business models and spans across several industries. Two main types of businesses, which can ultimately be traced back to the two key components of economic production, i.e., capital and labour, may notably be distinguished. For the sake of simplicity, more elaborated taxonomies are hereinafter avoided.[45]

Capital platforms are those which link customers with individuals willing to rent or swap their own assets. Assets used can range from residential premises (Airbnb, HomeExchange, Couchsurfing), vehicles (Getaround), household (Open Shed) or other spared items (NeighborGoods). Labour platforms, instead, purport to connect customers with a contingent workforce performing a series of discrete tasks. Assignments may equally consist in the provision of passenger transport (Uber, Lyft, BlaBlaCar), delivery operations (Postmates), household tasks (Handy) or a wealth of other services (TaskRabbit).

Admittedly, the above distinction is overly simplistic. Notably, in case of 'capital platforms', suppliers can provide services together with assets. Airbnb and HomeExchange hosts may, in fact, prepare breakfast for their guests or clean their own apartments at the end of each rental period. Likewise, companies labelled as 'labour platforms' may well require the exploitation by individual suppliers of their own personal assets. As matter of fact, both Uber and BlaBlaCar drivers use their own cars in the furtherance of their business activities.

§2.06 TYPES OF SHARING ECONOMY TRANSACTIONS

The sharing economy is not a single-sided phenomenon. Rather, the term presides over a wide array of economic activities.

Pursuant to a consumerist classification, transactions among platform users can in fact be categorized either as business-to-consumer (B2C), if only the individual supplier is a business, or consumer-to-business (C2B), if only the individual customer is a business. However, business-to-business (B2B) and consumer-to-consumer (C2C) relationships might also be established if neither the individual supplier nor the individual customer acts in a business or a consumer capacity. For classification

SPEECH-09-156_en.htm (accessed 31 Mar. 2019). As for the concept of 'personal data', in the author's opinion, the formulation contained in the General Data Protection Regulation (GDPR) provides a valid definition. Pursuant to Art. 4 point 1) of the GDPR '"personal data" means any information relating to an identified or identifiable natural person', i.e., 'one who can be identified, directly or indirectly, in particular by reference to an identifier such as a name, an identification number, location data, an online identifier or to one or more factors specific to the physical, physiological, genetic, mental, economic, cultural or social identity of that natural person'.

45. For instance, PricewaterhouseCoopers (PwC) subdivides the sharing economy into five economic sectors, i.e., peer-to-peer accommodation, peer-to-peer transportation, on-demand household services, on-demand professional services, and collaborative finance. *See* PricewaterhouseCoopers (PwC), *The Sharing Economy: How Will It Disrupt Your Business* (2014), http://pwc.blogs.com/files/sharing-economy-final_0814.pdf (accessed 31 Mar. 2019).

purposes, a case-by-case approach is then to be followed. In all evidence, it does not appear convenient to merely rely on the legal clauses inserted in the terms and conditions set up by a sharing economy platform, which frequently claim that a service is only available for personal, non-commercial use.[46]

Different types of activities, such as sharing, bartering, lending, trading, renting, swapping, and gifting, do equally pertain to the realm of the sharing economy. Four types of transactions can in particular be distinguished, based on whether they involve cash, barter, cost-sharing, or gratuitous arrangements. The accommodation sector constitutes a perfect typification to illustrate each of them. Access to available accommodation, in fact, can be provided either in return for monetary consideration – both on a transaction (Airbnb) or a subscription basis (HomeExchange), as result of a barter exchange – both through a direct reciprocal swap and by means of multiple indirect exchanges among members of the same community (HomeExchange), or simply for free (Couchsurfing). Likewise, rides can be provided for a price (Uber), on a cost-sharing basis (BlaBlaCar), or merely by asking passengers to submit a 'donation' (Lyft until 2013).[47]

The following sections are meant to provide some background information on the business models of the four sharing economy platforms specifically examined in the present study. Notably, two of these platforms operate in the accommodation sector, whereas the other two are active in the passenger transport industry. The four companies distinctly examined are divided across the two main sections below based on their significantly different business structure and market orientation. In close detail, section §2.07 describes, first, the business model of Airbnb, the most famous specimen of sharing economy platform active in the accommodation sector, and, then, that of Uber, the world-known sharing economy platform operating a network of taxies. Section §2.08 instead describes, first, the business model of HomeExchange, the leading sharing economy platform for barter accommodation exchanges, and, then, that of BlaBlaCar, the popular French company for ridesharing.

§2.07 'SHARING' BUT FOR A FEE: AIRBNB AND UBER

[A] Airbnb: The Hotel Chain That Does Not Own a Single Property

Founded by Brian Chesky, Joe Gebbia, and Nathan Blecharczyk in San Francisco in late 2007, Airbnb is a US-based company operating a multisided digital platform which allows individuals, named hosts, to rent out their spared residential premises to other peers, named guests, usually for a limited period of time. In the EU, the company started its operation in mid-2011, first, in Germany and, then, rapidly spreading across

46. Notably, such types of legal provisions are inserted in their terms and conditions, for both hosts and guests, by HomeExchange and BlaBlaCar, whereas only for passengers by Uber. For its part, Airbnb has instead developed a specific strategy for targeting business travellers, to whom the platform now offers dedicated accommodation listings.
47. For a more elaborated taxonomy, *see* G. Beretta, *The Taxation of the 'Sharing Economy'*, 70 Bull. Intl. Taxn. 11 (2016), Journals IBFD.

the whole continent as to reach main cities like London, Paris, Milan, and Barcelona.[48] According to the most recent financial estimates valued at USD thirty-one billion[49], as to March 2019 Airbnb counts on its platform more than six million properties located in over 191 countries.[50] Inside the EU, Airbnb facilitates accommodation services among its users through a subsidiary located in Ireland, whereas a United Kingdom (UK) and, as of 2019, also a Luxembourg subsidiary are tasked with payment processing (the situation, instead, differs for bookings made by residents of Australia, mainland China, India, and the US). In addition to its Irish subsidiary, Airbnb maintains other subsidiaries in some of the countries in which it operates (e.g., in France, Italy, and Spain). However, these companies are mostly tasked only with advertising and marketing activities. Alongside its accommodation listing services, through the years, Airbnb has significantly expanded the range and types of services offered to its users, both to hosts and guests. Notably, the company now allows both hosts and guests to partner with other individuals who take over hosting or guesting responsibilities (called, respectively, 'co-hosts' and 'organizers'). Beside the provision of accommodation, Airbnb enables hosts to offer their guests a number of other local 'experiences' (e.g., equitation lessons or wine-tasting itineraries). Remarkably, the platform is even committed to support various cultural, community, or non-profit initiatives and events.

The business model of Airbnb can be summarized as follows. In order to access the booking accommodation services, both hosts and guests need to register and create a profile on Airbnb. Online registration requires the provision of a valid email address, first and last name and date of birth. Alternatively, individuals can use their own Facebook account to log in. Individuals who are active both as hosts and guests do not need to keep two separate accounts for listing and renting, since the two functions are merged into one. Airbnb may conduct identity checks and information screenings or, even, require users the provision of official documents. Upon listing of their own properties, hosts are asked to determine the type of listing, add photos, title and a summary of the accommodation, as well as to set rental prices, calendar availabilities, and reservation criteria. Guests can surf over the listings and filter them by type, price, features, and location. Importantly, both hosts and guests may act in a business or a private capacity. Airbnb, in fact, promotes accommodation listings by boutique hotels and bed&breakfasts, as well as it allows bookings by business and professional travellers.

The booking process, which is the same over all countries, follows two alternative routes. While, under the 'ordinary' booking procedure guests are asked to submit a booking request with hosts having twenty-four hours to approve it before the booking can be completed and payment to the platform can be processed, in the 'instant' booking procedure there is no need of any host's prior approval to complete the

48. For a story full of anecdotes about the company, *see* L. Gallagher, *The Airbnb Story: How Three Ordinary Guys Disrupted an Industry, Made Billions … and Created Plenty of Controversy* (Houghton Mifflin Harcourt 2017).
49. K. Gmelich, *Airbnb Says It Made a Profit Again in 2018*, Bloomberg (15 Jan. 2019).
50. *Airbnb Fast Facts*, https://press.airbnb.com/fast-facts/ (accessed 31 Mar. 2019).

transaction in question.[51] Under both procedures, when a listing is selected, a legally binding agreement is formed, with the system automatically displaying the total price and a breakdown of all fares, which includes the rental price, the service fees charged by the platform, as well as any other kind of fares, such as those for cleaning services. Further, in case of late checkouts, guests may be charged with an overstay fee.

Upon confirmation of the booking request, guests make payments to the host through the platform, which retains a commission fee of between 0%-20% (VAT excluded) of the booking price, i.e., the nightly rate, plus cleaning and additional guest fees, but excluding fees charged by Airbnb to the other party and local taxes. The actual rate charged by the platform to the guests depends on a variety of factors, such as the reservation subtotal, the length of the stay, as well as the characteristics of the listing. For 'experiences', Airbnb instead always charges guests with a flat 20% fee. For every successful booking, Airbnb also charges each host usually with a 3% transaction fee (again, VAT excluded) of the booking price, i.e., the nightly rate, plus cleaning and additional guest fees, but excluding fees charged by Airbnb to the other party and local taxes.[52] Figure 2.1 below depicts graphically the business model of Airbnb.

Figure 2.1 Airbnb's Business Model

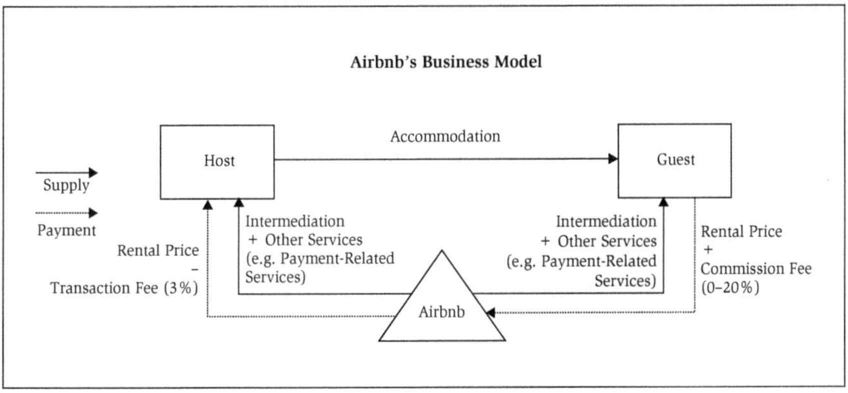

In its legal terms and conditions (last modified on 21 January 2019)[53], Airbnb clearly states that it neither owns, manages, or supplies any listings or related accommodation services, nor the digital platform is to be considered as an organizer or a retailer of travel packages. Airbnb, in fact, does not become a party to any contractual relationship between hosts and guests. Accordingly, hosts alone remain responsible for their own listings and for the related accommodation services. This includes the fact that, in many cities, hosts may be required to register and/or obtain a permit or a licence before

51. *What Is Instant Book?*, https://www.airbnb.com/help/article/523/what-is-instant-book (accessed 31 Mar. 2019).
52. *What Is the Airbnb Service Fee*, https://www.airbnb.com/help/article/1857/what-is-the-airbnb-service-fee (accessed 31 Mar. 2019).
53. *Terms of Service*, https://www.airbnb.com/terms (accessed 31 Mar. 2019).

being allowed to provide certain services (e.g., preparing food, serving alcohol for sale, or guiding tours). The platform further claims to merely be a limited payment collection agent acting on behalf and in the name of hosts, so that payments received by the platform in such capacity shall be considered the same as payments made directly by guests to hosts.

Nevertheless, besides obtaining information on user profiles (e.g., name, surname, date of birth, email, phone number, and profile picture) and listed properties (e.g., characteristics, location, description, and images), Airbnb's algorithm automatically collects a series of other information, such as geo-localization, calendar availabilities, usage, log, device and payment transaction data. According to its privacy policy (last modified on 21 January 2019)[54], Airbnb uses all these pieces of information not only to provide, improve, and develop its own platform or to create and maintain a trusted and safer environment, but it also conducts profiling on user characteristics and preferences with an aim of forwarding to those users promotional messages, marketing, advertising, and other information which may be of interest to them. Upon user consent, the company may also decide to share collected information with third parties, including commercial partners and advertising companies.

The platform also sets some standards for user interaction. These standards include obligations such as 'do not offer any accommodation that you do not yourself own or have permission to make available as residential or other property', 'do not contact any other user for any purpose other than asking a question related to a booking or a listing', 'do not request, make or accept any booking or payment independent of the platform', 'do not discriminate against or harass anyone', 'do not violate or infringe anyone else's rights or otherwise cause harm to anyone'.

It also ought to be recalled that, other than by guests, the performance of hosts is rated by Airbnb based on a series of indicators, including the average response rate, the proportion of bookings confirmed without cancelling, and interaction with guests.[55] In case of multiple poor ratings and reviews or cancellations of booking requests, Airbnb can either temporarily or permanently restrict access to or suspend a host's account.[56] Further, in case of misbehaviours or other hazards, both hosts and guests can submit a complaint to a dispute resolution centre set up by the company and some insurance coverage, in the form of either a host guarantee or a guest refund policy, is provided up to a limit by the platform to both parties.[57]

---

54. *Airbnb Privacy Policy*, https://www.airbnb.com/terms/privacy_policy (accessed 31 Mar. 2019).
55. *How Does My Experience's Rating or Reviews Affect My Ability to Host?*, https://www.airbnb.com/help/article/2159/how-does-my-experience-s-rating-or-reviews-affect-my-ability-to-host (accessed 31 Mar. 2019).
56. *Why Was My Listing Deactivated?*, https://www.airbnb.com/help/article/489/why-was-my-listing-deactivated (accessed 31 Mar. 2019); *Why Was My Listing Paused or Suspended?*, https://www.airbnb.com/help/article/1303/why-was-my-listing-paused-or-suspended (accessed 31 Mar. 2019).
57. *Airbnb's Host Guarantee*, https://www.airbnb.com/guarantee (accessed 31 Mar. 2019); *What Is Airbnb's Guest Refund Policy for Homes?*, https://www.airbnb.com/help/article/544/what-is-airbnb-s-guest-refund-policy-for-homes?q=Airbnb%20Guest%20Refund%20Policy (accessed 31 Mar. 2019).

Importantly, although the price of the rental is determined by hosts alone, Airbnb offers, on an optional basis, a dynamic pricing algorithm, called 'Smart Pricing', which automatically adjusts, from a minimum to a maximum set by hosts, rental prices based on changes in demands due to seasonality or other events.[58] Further, upon request, the platform offers for a price to hosts the possibility to have a professional photographer taking photograph shoots of their residential properties to include in their listings, called 'verified images', and which Airbnb may also use for advertising, marketing, and other business purposes.[59]

Coming to its obligations under EU VAT, the platform charges VAT on top of the service fees demanded to both hosts and guests. Price quotation is inclusive of VAT. Since the booking accommodation services provided by Airbnb are characterized, by the platform, as electronically supplied services, the place of supply of those services is where the users (either hosts or guests) are established, have their permanent address, or usually reside.[60] On the contrary, both hosts and guests remain the sole responsible for their respective VAT obligations.[61]

As for other taxes, Airbnb has sealed several voluntary cooperation agreements with local authorities of many cities and regions all around the world for collection and remittance of hotel, tourist, lodging, and occupancy taxes. Notably, in the EU, agreements have been concluded with, *inter alia*, Amsterdam, Frankfurt, Lisbon, Milan, and many French cities.[62] In Italy, as from mid-2017, Airbnb is even required to collect and remit the taxes due by hosts on the income made through the rental of their own residential properties (for which a substitute tax of 21 % of the total amount of the rental applies) and to share data on housing rentals with tax authorities.[63] In Estonia, Airbnb has instead a collaboration agreement in place with tax authorities pursuant to which hosts, on a voluntary basis, are enabled to automatically report their earnings through the platform to the tax authorities, which use those data to pre-fill a taxpayer's income tax return.[64]

58. *How Do I Turn Smart Pricing On or Off?*, https://www.airbnb.com/help/article/1168/how-do-i-turn-smart-pricing-on-or-off (accessed 31 Mar. 2019).
59. *Does Airbnb Provide Professional Photography Services?*, https://www.airbnb.com/help/article/297/does-airbnb-provide-professional-photography-services?q=photo (accessed 31 Mar. 2019).
60. *What Is VAT and How Does It Apply to Me?*, https://www.airbnb.com/help/article/436/what-is-vat-and-how-does-it-apply-to-me (accessed 31 Mar. 2019). For a discussion on place of supply rules, *see* Chapter 7.
61. *How Do Taxes Work for Hosts?*, https://www.airbnb.com/help/article/481/how-do-taxes-work-for-hosts (accessed 31 Mar. 2019); *How Do Taxes Work for Guests?*, https://www.airbnb.com/help/article/318/how-do-taxes-work-for-guests (accessed 31 Mar. 2019).
62. *In What Areas Is Occupancy Tax Collection and Remittance by Airbnb Available*, https://www.airbnb.com/help/article/2509/in-what-areas-is-occupancy-tax-collection-and-remittance-by-airbnb-available (accessed 31 Mar. 2019).
63. For a discussion, *see* G. Beretta, *Il Regime Fiscale delle Locazioni Brevi*, Diritto e Pratica Tributaria 3 (2018), at 1011-1056.
64. *New Agreements Make Host Income Tax Simple*, https://press.airbnb.com/new-agreements-make-host-income-tax-simple/ (accessed 31 Mar. 2019).

[B] Uber: A Worldwide Taxi Fleet at the Push of a Button

Founded in San Francisco by Travis Kalanick and Garrett Camp in 2009, and with an expected valuation of as much as USD 120 billion in an Initial Public Offering (IPO) to be launched in 2019[65], from many perspectives Uber represents the 'poster child' of the sharing economy. Uber operates a multisided digital platform, accessible through a smartphone app, which connects individual drivers with prospective passengers, handles transaction payments, and ensures the smooth operation of the overall passenger transport services. After having spread across several cities in the US, such as New York and Chicago, Uber started operating in EU major cities during 2011-2012, first, in Paris and, then, in London.[66] As to March 2019, Uber operates in sixty-five countries and more than 600 cities worldwide, with the company presiding over an average of fifteen million trips completed every day and its platform counting three million drivers, and seventy-five million riders.[67] Intermediary services related to passenger transport, of several types, available for different fares, and provided under various brands, are offered throughout the world (except for Brazil, mainland China, and the US) by a Dutch subsidiary of the US parent company. Other ancillary activities, such as booking services, are instead carried out by a few controlled companies located in the UK. Moreover, Uber maintains other subsidiaries nearly in every country in which it operates, which are tasked with a series of supporting operations, but mainly related to advertising and marketing activities. Although, through the years, the company has significantly broadened the range of its own activities, e.g., Uber now provides food delivery services, offers bike rides, and invests billions in self-driving technologies, passenger transport has remained at the core of its own business.

The business model of Uber can be summarized as follows. Prospective drivers register online through the Uber app – a process which Uber wittily calls 'on-boarding'. A driving licence, a national insurance number, and a vehicle above the set minimum standard are all requirements to complete registration. Once 'on-board', drivers can access the Uber app by using their own smartphones. Although even fleet partners that do own and operate multiple vehicles can sign up for Uber, generally Uber drivers provide their own vehicles and remain the sole responsible for all the costs incidental to owning and running the vehicle (Uber, however, has arranged partnerships with a few car leasing companies). As for prospective passengers, fundamentally their only hassle consists in downloading the Uber app – which is provided to them for free – on to their own smartphones and logging on. In this regard, the sole limitations are that a passenger must be aged, at least, eighteen, or have the age of legal majority in a jurisdiction, and must provide at least one valid payment method, in the form of either credit card or another accepted payment partner.

65. A. Barinka & E. Newcomer, *Uber Valued at $120 Billion in an IPO?*, Bloomberg (17 Oct. 2018).
66. For a behind-the-scenes story about Uber's inception and expansion, see A. Lashinsky, *Wild Ride: Inside Uber's Quest for World Domination* (Portfolio 2017).
67. *Uber – Company Info*, https://www.uber.com/en-IT/newsroom/company-info/ (accessed 31 Mar. 2019).

The process of requesting a ride is very easy and runs extremely smoothly. A passenger can request a ride by simply logging on the Uber app which locates the nearest available driver (instead, it is not possible to make a request for a specific driver), who is informed of the passenger's first name and rating (even passengers, in fact, get rated). Then, the driver has as little as ten seconds to accept the ride. In case of no response, the Uber app assumes that the requested driver is not available and, thus, locates another driver. If, instead, the driver accepts the request, the app confirms the booking by the passenger and allocates the ride to the driver. Noteworthy, if a passenger cancels a ride more than two minutes after a request is accepted by a driver, the passenger is charged with a cancellation fee which takes the place of the fare for the cancelled ride.[68]

Importantly, drivers are unaware of the final destination until the passenger is eventually picked up. The final destination, in fact, is disclosed to them only when the passenger sits in the car and, thus, the driver presses the 'start trip' button on the Uber app. As the trip commences, the Uber app provides the driver with detailed directions using satellite navigation technology. Drivers are not bound to follow those directions, but Uber highly recommends drivers usage of its own app and an adjustment of the ride fare may apply in case the followed route was not 'ideal'.[69] Upon arrival, the driver presses the 'complete trip' button on the Uber app and the fare amount is automatically calculated by the Uber's algorithm, based on distances and time recorded by Global Positioning System (GPS) data obtained from the driver's smartphone, plus any additional charges, such as tolls, surcharges, or other fees. At 'surge times', a multiplier is applied, resulting in a charge above the standard level. It is open to drivers to agree lesser, but not greater sums with passengers.[70] In case of damages to the vehicle, passengers may be charged with an additional repair or cleaning fee. For their own account, passengers are free to provide additional payment as a gratuity to drivers, although under no obligation to do so.[71] Notwithstanding in some cities payment of a fare can be made in cash, passengers usually pay the ride fare to Uber using a credit or a debit card and, then shortly after, a receipt is emailed to them.[72] Separately, Uber generates an invoice, on behalf of the driver, addressed to the passenger, simply using the driver's first name and providing no other contact details. The invoice is not directly sent to the passenger, rather it is available to him for download through the Uber app.

Payment to drivers is made by Uber on a weekly period and it is calculated on the basis of the fare charged for the rides undertaken by the driver less a service fee which Uber normally sets at 25%. Such a fee is meant to cover costs for Uber software's usage,

---

68. *Cancelling an Uber Ride*, https://help.uber.com/riders/article/cancelling-an-uber-ride-?nodeId =56270015-1d1d-4c08-a460-3b94a090de23 (accessed 31 Mar. 2019).
69. *My Fare Was Adjusted*, https://help.uber.com/partners/article/my-fare-was-adjusted-?nodeId =5f9a6dc9-0357-41b7-be1b-912cb883ee46 (accessed 31 Mar. 2019).
70. *How Are Fares Calculated?*, https://help.uber.com/riders/article/how-are-fares-calculated?nodeId=d2d43bbc-f4bb-4882-b8bb-4bd8acf03a9d (accessed 31 Mar. 2019).
71. *Can I Tip My Driver with the App?*, https://help.uber.com/riders/article/can-i-tip-my-driver-with-the-app--?nodeId=8459a496-5ed2-4f9d-b15c-d8afd9ccf34f (accessed 31 Mar. 2019).
72. *Getting a Trip Receipt*, https://help.uber.com/riders/article/getting-a-trip-receipt?nodeId=846f6cad-6f27-492a-9e0b-d2f056e1298e (accessed 31 Mar. 2019).

collection and transfer of fares, credit card commission, and distribution of invoices to clients.[73] As stated, for passengers the use of Uber app is, instead, free of any charge (in the terms and conditions, it is however stated that Uber 'reserves the right to introduce a fee for the provision of the Booking Services'). Figure 2.2 below depicts graphically the business model of Uber.

Figure 2.2 Uber's Business Model

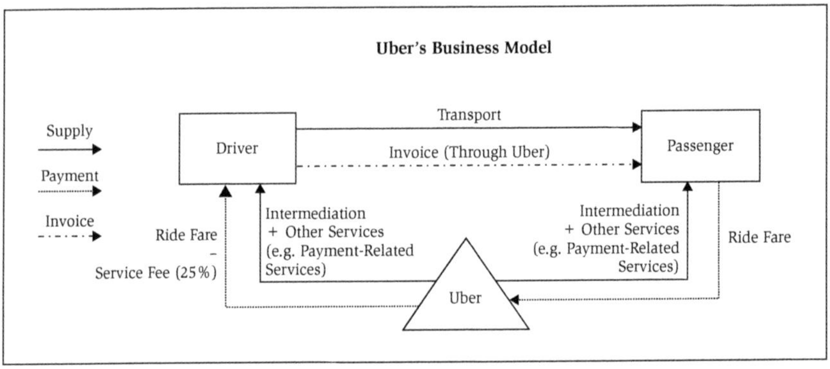

In its legal terms and conditions (last modified on 14 March 2018), Uber clearly states that it neither provides transport, nor the digital platform is to be considered as a transport provider or a carrier. Allegedly, passenger transport is provided only by 'third-party contractors', i.e., drivers who are not employed by Uber or any of its many affiliates. As such, drivers remain fully responsible for arranging everything which is necessary to supply passenger transport services. As for payment handling, the platform claims to merely act as a limited payment collection agent on behalf of drivers (i.e., the principal) and, in such capacity, only to deliver passengers receipts related to transport services, which, instead, are performed by drivers alone. In this connection, Uber also maintains that payments made in such a manner shall be considered the same as payments made directly by passenger to drivers.

Nevertheless, besides obtaining information on user profiles (e.g., name, surname, date of birth, address, email, phone number, driver licence, and social security number) and vehicles used (e.g., brand, model, and insurance information), Uber's algorithm automatically collects a series of other information, such as geo-localization, usage, log, device, and payment transaction data. According to its privacy policy (last modified on 25 May 2018)[74], Uber uses all these pieces of information not only to provide, personalize, and improve its own products and services or to enhance the safety and security of its users, but it also analyses and processes those data with a view of identifying trends and tailoring marketing messages to user needs. Upon user

73. *Payments and Earnings*, https://www.uber.com/en-GH/drive/resources/payments/ (accessed 31 Mar. 2019).
74. *Uber Privacy Policy*, https://privacy.uber.com/policy (accessed 31 Mar. 2019).

consent, the company may also decide to share information collected with third parties, including car suppliers, vehicle solution vendors, and insurance and financing companies.

Indeed, Uber's characterization of its own business model is hotly debated. Notably, it is argued by many that the 'real' nature of Uber is not so much that of an intermediary, rather that of a blunt passenger transport company. The main points of concern in this regard are hereinafter summarized.

As a first point, it is observed that, despite both drivers and passengers are free to decide if, when, and where using Uber, interaction between the two parties is heavily regulated by the 'Uber Community Guidelines', which includes a list of recommendations, such as 'treat your fellow riders and drivers as you would like to be treated yourself', 'respect differences', 'it's common courtesy not to shout, swear or slam the car door', 'tide up after yourself', 'respect driver's or rider's privacy', 'not to contact the driver or rider after the trip has ended', and 'not to tolerate acts of sexual harassment, aggressive or threatening behaviour and violence'. Repetitive failure to comply with any of those recommendations or other misbehaviours can lead both drivers and passenger to a deactivation of their own account.[75]

Moreover, although, in principle, free to accept or decline rides, Uber demands drivers to accept at least a minimum number of ride requests in order to retain their own account status. A 'cancellation rate', based on the percentage of ride requests accepted and then cancelled, is in fact calculated for each driver. Every city has its own maximum cancellation rate, but in the US version of the 'Uber Community Guidelines' the company submits that 'high-quality drivers typically have a cancellation rate lower than 5%'.[76] If a driver's cancellation rate is above the set maximum, Uber may deactivate that driver's account.

A further critical point in Uber's business model concerns ratings, which both drivers and passengers are shortly requested to provide at the end of each ride. This two-way rating system is based on a five-star scale and calculated on an average number of post-ride reviews. A minimum rating is set for each city. Therefore, for both parties it is crucial to maintain a good rating. If a driver's or a passenger's rating drops below that minimum, Uber may in fact take action and, in case of a driver, also deactivate the account. The account may eventually be reactivated once the driver has successfully completed a specific reactivation process.[77]

As an additional point of concern, drivers are not able to set their own fare for each ride. As stated, the ride fare is instead calculated automatically by the Uber's algorithm based on a series of elements, such as distances and time recorded by GPS data obtained from the driver's smartphone and, further, taking into account additional charges, such as tolls, surcharges, or other fees.

75. *United Kingdom – Uber Community Guidelines*, https://www.uber.com/legal/community-guidelines/uk-en/ (accessed 31 Mar. 2019).
76. *United States – Uber Community Guidelines*, https://www.uber.com/legal/community-guidelines/us-en/ (accessed 31 March 2019).
77. *Understanding Ratings*, https://help.uber.com/partners/article/understanding-ratings?nodeId=fa1eb77f-ad79-4607-9651-72b932be30b7 (accessed 31 Mar. 2019).

Concerns also exist in tax matters. Although Uber actively participates in the OECD ongoing debate on taxation of the digital economy[78] and it has even a specific tax policy in place, pursuant to which the platform commits to 'comply with applicable tax laws and regulations in all jurisdictions' where it operates[79], there is a question on whether the ride-hailing company actually pays its 'fair share' of taxes.[80]

Indeed, controversies relate not only to corporate taxes, but also to VAT matters.[81] In this connection, two kinds of concern are prominently flagged. The first relates to the fact that, as stated, in all countries where it operates (except for Brazil, mainland China, and the US) Uber provides its own services through a Dutch subsidiary. As a result, services provided by the company in all EU countries (obviously, apart from services related to passenger transport taking place in the Netherlands) constitute cross-border and, in general, also business-to-business (B2B) transactions in respect of which the mandatory reverse charge mechanism of Article 196 of the VAT Directive applies. Pursuant to such mechanism, the liability for the VAT due on these transactions shifts from the supplier to the recipient of the services in question. This implies that it is the driver and not Uber who must collect and remit the VAT due on such services to the competent tax authorities. If, however, the driver's annual turnover is below the registration threshold set in a Member State, then no VAT is, in practice, due.[82] The second issue relates to the taxable status of Uber drivers. As stated, in its terms and conditions, the company claims that drivers are third-party contractors. In so far as Uber does not collect and remit VAT on behalf of them[83], VAT on passenger transport services is to be paid by drivers alone. Should, instead, drivers be characterized as employees of the platform as some courts all around the world have ruled, then VAT on passenger transport services would have to be collected and remitted by Uber itself.[84]

78. OECD, *Public Comments Received on the Possible Solutions to the Tax Challenges of Digitalisation* (2019), http://www.oecd.org/tax/beps/public-comments-received-on-the-possible-solutions-to-the-tax-challenges-of-digitalisation.htm (accessed 31 March 2019).
79. *UK Tax Strategy*, https://www.uber.com/legal/other/uk-tax/ (accessed 31 Mar. 2019).
80. B. O'Keefe & M. Jones, *How Uber Plays the Tax Shell Game*, Fortune (22 Oct. 2015).
81. T. Bergin, *Exclusive – Loophole Allows Uber to Avoid UK Tax, Undercut Rivals*, Reuters (7 June 2017); J. Croft & M. Murgia, *Uber Faces Legal Challenge on Paying VAT*, Financial Times (20 Mar. 2017).
82. *How to Do Your VAT Registration*, https://www.uber.com/en-GB/drive/tax-information/ (accessed 31 Mar. 2019). For a discussion of registration thresholds, *see* Chapter 4. For a description of the operation of the reverse charge mechanism, *see* Chapter 8.
83. The situation is instead different with regard to certain sales taxes (e.g., those applicable in the Canadian state of Quebec) or other levies (e.g., a 4% assessment imposed by the US State of New York, as from 29 June 2017, on the gross amount of the fare of each ride that is prearranged by transportation network companies), which are collected and remitted to the competent tax authorities by Uber on behalf of the drivers. *See* CA: Revenu Québec, *Uber Drivers*, https://www.revenuquebec.ca/en/businesses/sector-specific-measures/uber-drivers/ (accessed 31 Mar. 2019); US: New York State. Department of Taxation and Finance, *Transportation Network Company Assessment*, https://www.tax.ny.gov/bus/tnc/assessment.htm (accessed 31 Mar. 2019).
84. *See e.g.*, UK: Employment Tribunals, 28 Oct. 2016, No. 2202551/2015 & Others, *Aslam, Farrar & Others v. Uber BV, Uber London Ltd and Uber Britannia Ltd* [2017] IRLR 4, [2016], at paras 89-92, which was upheld on appeal (*see* UK: Employment Appeal Tribunal, 10 Nov. 2017, Appeal No. UKEAT/0056/17/DA, *Uber B.V et al. v. Aslam et al.* [2018] RTR 14, [2017] WLR(D)

§2.08 THE OTHER SIDE OF 'SHARING': HOMEEXCHANGE AND BLABLACAR

[A] HomeExchange: Bartering Has Never Been So Cool

Founded with the name of GuestToGuest in France in 2011 by Charles-Edouard Girard and Emmanuel Arnaud, together with twenty-two families of various nationalities, the leading platform for barter exchanges of accommodation turned its name into Home-Exchange after the acquisition of the homonymous US-based company in 2017.[85] Subsequent to the merger, the French company relocated its legal seat in the US.[86] The platform operates a virtual marketplace offering its users a series of services to connect with other peers and to conclude home exchanges among themselves. More specifically, the platform allows host members to post advertisements offering residential properties, which they own or of which they are tenants, for exchange and guest members to respond to such offerings. The company also arranges for some special accommodation schemes, i.e., family, senior, disabled, and pet-friendly exchanges. As to March 2019, the platform counts over 400,000 listed properties located in 187 countries with 10,000 new properties added on average per month.[87] Other than being just a company, HomeExchange regards itself as a community of people committed to social values such as 'welcoming, sharing, caring, and discovering'.[88]

The business model of HomeExchange can be summarized as follows. After registering with the platform and creating an account by providing personal information as requested, each member gains access to the messaging service provided by the platform, as well as to other details necessary to contact the other party. Arrangements concerning the exchange (e.g., number of nights or guests) are made directly by members through the messaging service provided by the platform. During exchanges, hosts can be present or not. In any event, members are encouraged to provide each other practical information and travel advices or, even, to create a 'home guide'. Both hosts and guests are requested to rate their own exchange experiences using a five-star scale. Exchanges between members of the community are usually concluded free-of-charge, based on a gratuitous loan for use agreement. Hosts, however, are permitted to charge guests with cleaning fees. Even the messaging service is provided by the platform to its members free-of-charge. For its other services, the company instead charges guests with a fixed fee of EUR 10 per night. An alternative form of payment is

809, at paras 103-126). Considering Uber drivers truly as third-party contractors, *see* e.g., AU: Fair Work Commission, 11 May 2018, App. No. 2017/13448, *Janaka Namal Pallage v. Rasier Pacific Pty Ltd* [2018] FWC 2579; FR: Conseil de Prud'hommes de Paris, Commerce Division No. 4 (Paris Industrial Tribunal), 29 Jan. 2018, No. F 16/11460, *Florian Menard v. Sas Uber France & Societé Uber BV*.

85. *HomeExchange Acquires HomeExchange*, https://www.homeexchange.com/blog/guesttoguest-acquires-homeexchange/ (accessed 31 Mar. 2019).
86. *Legal Notice*, https://www.homeexchange.com/p/legal-notice (accessed 31 Mar. 2019).
87. *We Are Home-Exchangers*, https://www.homeexchange.com/p/about-us (accessed 31 Mar. 2019).
88. *Welcome to the HomeExchange Community*, https://www.homeexchange.com/p/community (accessed 31 Mar. 2019).

also provided. Users can in fact subscribe to an annual membership for a one-time payment of EUR 130 and, thus, benefit from accessing to an unlimited number of exchanges over a twelve-month period.[89]

Undoubtedly, the main feature – and the one that likely contributes the most to the enduring success of the platform – is constituted by GuestPoints. GuestPoints are credits issued by the platform to its users in order to enable them to conclude non-reciprocal and deferred exchanges, rather than requiring them to necessarily arrange for reciprocal and simultaneous swaps. In a sense, GuestPoints are the currency for home exchanges, whereas the platform essentially performs the role of a central bank. The attribution of GuestPoints to a member varies depending on a valuation operated independently by HomeExchange of the listed residential property, according to its size, comfort, and location. However, members can modify such valuation to some extent.[90] Moreover, several activities made by the member on the platform, i.e., completing a profile, verifying an account with official documents and a residence address, subscribing an annual membership, or introducing a new member, allows him/her to earn a certain number of points which can later be used by him/her to be hosted by another member. GuestPoints can also be earned as a result of an exchange. Notably, there are two ways for a member to earn GuestPoints via an exchange. A first possibility is that the member concludes an exchange with another member whose residential property is valued less. A second possibility is instead through a unilateral exchange, i.e., where accommodation is provided free-of-charge only by one party to the other.[91] However, with an aim of rendering the conclusion of home exchanges smoother, GuestPoints can also be bought. The cost of GuestPoints varies, also depending on geographical areas. As to March 2019, in the EU, each GuestPoint is priced EUR 0.10 up to 20% of the totality of the GuestPoints that are required for concluding an accommodation exchange. Above that limit, GuestPoints instead cost EUR 1 each.[92] It is important to note that GuestPoints are neither refundable nor transferable.[93] It is also worth mentioning that in no event GuestPoints can be redeemed for cash, even in case of cancellation of a member account.[94] Figure 2.3 below depicts graphically the business model of HomeExchange.

89. *Pricing*, https://www.homeexchange.com/choose-plan (accessed 31 Mar. 2019).
90. *Reciprocal and Non-Reciprocal Exchanges*, https://homeexchangehelp.zendesk.com/hc/en-us/articles/360000601998-Reciprocal-and-non-reciprocal-exchanges (accessed 31 Mar. 2019).
91. *GuestPoints*, https://www.homeexchange.com/p/guestpoints-en (accessed 31 Mar. 2019).
92. *Can I Purchase GuestPoints?*, https://homeexchangehelp.zendesk.com/hc/en-us/articles/360000622018-Can-I-purchase-GuestPoints- (accessed 31 Mar. 2019).
93. *Do GuestPoints Expire?*, https://homeexchangehelp.zendesk.com/hc/en-us/articles/360001002358-Do-GuestPoints-expire- (accessed 31 Mar. 2019).
94. *Can I Redeem My GuestPoints for Cash?*, https://homeexchangehelp.zendesk.com/hc/en-us/articles/360000631297-Can-I-redeem-my-GuestPoints-for-cash- (accessed 31 Mar. 2019).

Figure 2.3 HomeExchange's Business Model

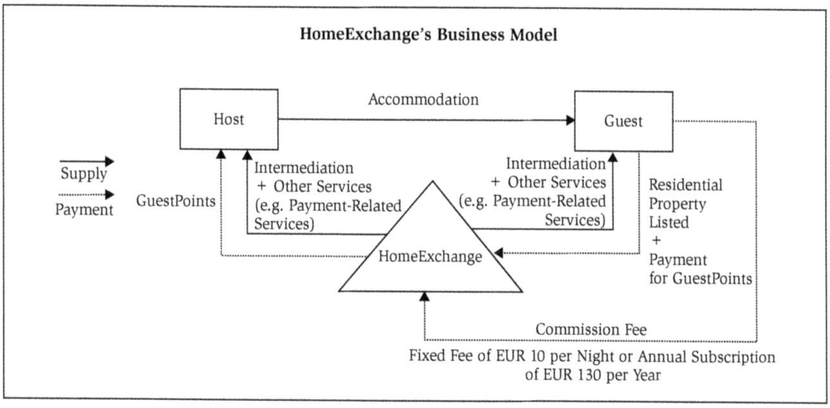

In its legal terms and conditions (last modified on 19 December 2018), HomeExchange declares to operate an 'exchange management service' and, in such capacity, to be a mere 'platform provider', not instead a 'real-estate broker'. Accordingly, members are intended to enter directly into contact with each other and to act exclusively on their own behalf. This further implies that members have complete discretion on whether and when to list a property or to conclude an exchange. Users, in fact, remain solely responsible for providing description, location, and availability dates, for setting rules and restrictions on use of their listed property, as well as for determining any laws or regulations that apply to them. Equally, ratings and reviews are submitted by users alone. Moreover, in so far as no money is either provided or received by any party while concluding an exchange, the platform does not act as a limited payment collection agent.

Nevertheless, besides obtaining information on user profiles (e.g., name, surname, date of birth, mini-biograph, email, phone number, and profile picture) and listed properties (e.g., characteristics, location, surface area, description, and images), HomeExchange's algorithm automatically collects a series of other information, such as geo-localization, calendar availabilities, search-related data, GuestPoints earned and used, response rate and time, usage, log, device and payment transaction data. According to its privacy policy (last modified on 19 December 2018)[95], HomeExchange uses all these pieces of information not only to provide, improve, and develop its own services or to allow users to share information among themselves, socialize, and enter into contact with other members, but it also conducts profiling on user characteristics and preferences with a view of recommending listings which might be of interest to users and of improving the order of listing appearance in its own search engine. Upon user consent, the company may also decide to share collected information with third parties, including social networks and research centres.

95. *HomeExchange Privacy Policy*, https://www.homeexchange.com/p/privacy-policy (accessed 31 Mar. 2019).

A certain degree of interaction is also exerted by HomeExchange over exchanges among its users. Several considerations can be advanced in this regard.

First, the order in which the properties listed are displayed is constantly updated by the platform through its own search algorithm, which takes into account a series of criteria, such as the response rate of a host, photos and descriptions of the listed property, recent activity undertaken on the website, or, even, the other party's preference for a destination where the searcher has a listed property. Ratings also matter. Notably, the platform rates members based on the number and readiness of responses which they are able to provide.[96]

Second, both hosts and guests are made subject by the platform to a series of obligations and prohibitions, such as 'not to create fake accounts', 'not to provide false or misleading information', 'not to use the platform to violate any applicable law and not to post or send any content or engage in any conduct resulting in civil or criminal penalties', 'not to advertise to or solicit other members to buy or sell any products or services', 'not to impersonate any person or entity or falsely state or misrepresent an affiliation with any person or entity', as well as 'not to offer or solicit any property for rent'. In case of non-compliance with any of those recommendations or other misbehaviours, HomeExchange can either limit user access to the platform, remove any user content from its own website, or close a member account, even without prior warning or formal notice.

It also ought to be considered that, in case a host cancels an exchange, the platform provides the guest with the option of staying in another listed property having similar kinds of amenities.[97] In case of damage, loss or theft, the platform instead allows users to file a claim before it and handles complaints.[98] Further, in case of damages or other unforeseen circumstances, insurance is provided to both hosts and guests.[99]

While, for taxes in general, there are no noticeable issues, HomeExchange's obligations under EU VAT differ substantially depending on the platform's service considered. As stated, the messaging service is provided by HomeExchange to its members for free. Therefore, no VAT needs to be charged in this regard. However, the platform also provides its members with several optional services, namely a verification service, which consists in checking the consistency of information related to a listing or the identity of a member, a deposit service, providing hosts with a guarantee in case of damages to the property exchanged with a guest, as well as various types of assistance services for guest members, including an email supporting line active 24/7, for all of which users either pay-as-you-go or retain an annual subscription. In both

96. *What Is the Order that the Listings Appear in Search Results?*, https://homeexchangehelp.zendesk.com/hc/en-us/articles/360000730577-What-is-the-order-that-the-listings-appear-in-search-results- (accessed 31 Mar. 2019).
97. *What Happens if My Host Cancels?*, https://homeexchangehelp.zendesk.com/hc/en-us/articles/360000609918-What-happens-if-my-host-cancels- (accessed 31 Mar. 2019).
98. *What Happens in the Case of Damages or Disagreements?*, https://homeexchangehelp.zendesk.com/hc/en-us/articles/360000626478-What-happens-in-the-case-of-damages-or-disagreements- (accessed 31 Mar. 2019).
99. *Conditions and Details of HomeExchange's Guarantees*, https://www.homeexchange.com/p/service-plus-termsofuse-en (accessed 31 Mar. 2019).

cases, VAT applies on top of the price of those services. In principle, the characterization of such services under EU VAT should differ. While, in fact, messaging and verification services are provided by the platform via the Internet and, therefore, are completely automated, the platform explicitly acknowledges that other types of services, such as the deposit service, do instead require some level of human intervention. Nevertheless, the platform assumes that all the services in question are indivisible and, thus, that they fall under Article 45 of the VAT Directive, which means that for all of those services the place of supply is to be found where the company has established its own business (i.e., the US).[100]

As regards platform members, in its terms and conditions, HomeExchange maintains that use of the platform is 'for your sole, personal use' and that 'companies and businesses may not be members'. Pursuant to such a rule, no VAT should in principle be charged on accommodation exchanges, since the supplier is not a taxable person either. It is not clear, however, whether any checks and verification are actually made to ensure compliance by users with such a rule.[101]

[B] BlaBlaCar: The Added Value of Sharing the Costs of a Journey

Started by Frédéric Mazzella, a computer scientist, together with co-founders Nicolas Brusson and Francis Nappez in France in 2004, BlaBlaCar is the leading long-distance ridesharing (or carpooling) platform, which connects individuals who need to travel across cities with peers going in the same direction and having empty seats in their own car. Based on the latest financial estimates, the company is valued at USD 1.6 billion.[102] As of March 2019, the platform counts more than seventy million members across twenty-two countries and over twenty-five million travellers every quarter worldwide.[103] In the EU, the platform is available in sixteen countries, including, beside the native France, Germany, Italy, Spain, and the UK. Through the years, as a result of a geographical expansion of its own activities, the French platform has acquired other carpooling companies operating locally across different jurisdictions. Meanwhile, BlaBlaCar has also launched other lines of services, e.g., BlaBlaLines, a carpooling app for daily commuting. Remarkably, the company is even committed to making travel more social, affordable, efficient, as well as environmentally friendly for millions of people.

The business model of BlaBlaCar can be summarized as follows. The company operates a website, accessible also through a smartphone app, which allows users, after registering with it (for this purpose, they may also use their own Facebook account), to post advertisements showing information about a trip (e.g., date, time, pick-up/drop-off location points, number of seats available, and amount of the cost contribution). By accessing the platform, other users interested in the same journey can

100. For a discussion of place of supply rules, *see* Chapter 7.
101. For a discussion of taxable persons, *see* Chapter 4.
102. A. Thomson, *BlaBlaCar Value Hits $1.6 Billion after Latest Funding Round*, Bloomberg (17 Sep. 2015).
103. *About Us – BlaBlaCar*, https://www.blablacar.com/about-us (accessed 31 Mar. 2019).

file a request for a seat in the vehicle in question, for them or even for third parties. On the contrary, availability of trips can be viewed also by non-registered persons. Every member has an experience level attached to his/her own profile. Members are also allowed to indicate their own preferences regarding the driver and the trip (e.g., a non-smoking person or a music genre). BlaBlaCar may verify information submitted by users while completing their own profile. The booking request is either automatically or manually accepted by the driver. Upon acceptance, the passenger is required to make a payment, using a credit or debit card, through the platform, in order to contribute to the costs of the journey[104] as well as in return for BlaBlaCar's own services. For its own services, the company normally charges users with a fee which is largely variable, but generally spans from 10% up to 30% of the cost contribution asked by the driver to each passenger, inclusive of VAT.[105] In Italy, as of 2018, BlaBlaCar instead adopts a subscription-based model, where passengers can purchase either a seven-day or a monthly pass in return for a flat fee, respectively equal to EUR 4 and EUR 6 VAT-inclusive.[106] Both the contribution cost and the service fee are collected by BlaBlaCar, which however remits the former to the driver. A booking receipt, showing the amount paid to the driver as well as the service fee charged by the platform, is issued by the platform to the passenger immediately afterwards. Figure 2.4 below depicts graphically the business model of BlaBlaCar.

104. In *Uber Systems Spain*, Advocate General Szpunar defined 'ride sharing' as an activity consisting in 'sharing a common journey, determined by the driver and not the passenger, in return for, at the most, for the driver, reimbursement of part of the travel costs. … It is therefore a sort of "hitchhiking 2.0". In any case, it is not a gainful activity'. *See* ES: Opinion of the Advocate General, 11 May 2017, Case C-434/15, *Asociación Profesional Elite Taxi v. Uber Systems Spain SL*, at note 14.
105. For BlaBlaCar's service fee in the United Kingdom, *see Service Fees*, https://blog.blablacar.co.uk/blablalife/lp/service-fees (accessed 31 Mar. 2019). Noteworthy, for journeys not benefiting from the online system to book available seats, BlaBlaCar offers a free service enabling the passenger to send a message to the driver for a trip which he may be interested in.
106. *Pass e Abbonamento: Ecco le Tariffe*, https://blog.blablacar.it/blablalife/lp/costo-servizio (accessed 31 Mar. 2019).

Figure 2.4 BlaBlaCar's Business Model

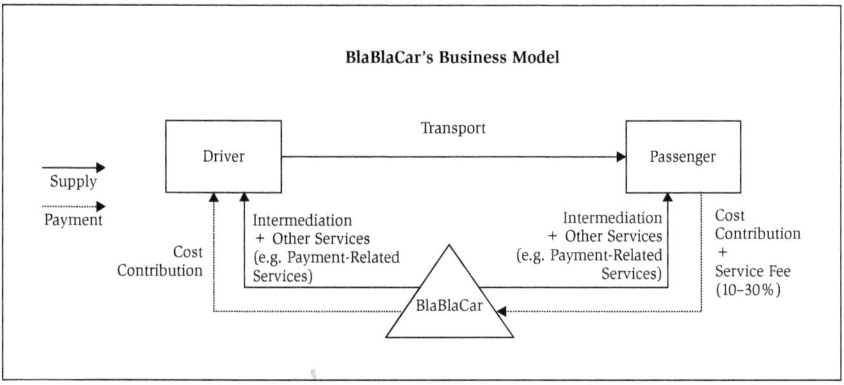

In its legal terms and conditions (last modified on 24 April 2017), BlaBlaCar declares to operate solely an online networking platform which members can use for ridesharing purposes, nor the company is to be considered as either a supplier of any trip or an owner of any vehicle. In its capacity of an intermediary, in fact, BlaBlaCar is not a party to any agreement entered into among users with a view of sharing the costs relating to a common trip. Accordingly, both drivers and passengers are considered to act under their sole and full responsibility. In particular, the driver with his vehicle's insurance is the sole responsible for the effective occurrence of the trip as well as for every belonging transported in the vehicle, such as a passenger's own luggage. Moreover, with regards to payment handling of cost contribution, the platform claims to operate under a 'collection mandate' in the name and on behalf of drivers (however, in Italy cost contribution to the driver can be paid by the passenger also in cash).

Nevertheless, besides obtaining information on user profiles (e.g., name, surname, date of birth, a mini-biography, email, phone number, profile picture, and driver licence) and vehicle used (e.g., brand, model, and insurance information), BlaBlaCar's algorithm automatically collects a series of other information, such as geo-localization, usage, log, device, and payment transaction data. According to its privacy policy (last modified on 25 May 2018)[107], BlaBlaCar uses all these pieces of information not only to provide, improve, and develop the service or to enable users to communicate and interact among themselves, but also to send users marketing materials or to make suggestions and recommendations about products which might be of interest to users. Upon user consent, the company may also decide to share collected information with third parties, including social media platforms and insurance companies.

The platform also sets some standards for user interaction. These standards include obligations such as 'to hold a valid driving licence', 'to have a third-party insurance for the vehicle', 'to post advertisements only with respect to vehicle that the

107. *BlaBlaCar Privacy and Data Protection Policy*, https://blog.blablacar.co.uk/about-us/privacy-policy (accessed 31 Mar. 2019).

driver owns or uses with the express permission of the owner', 'to use a vehicle in good working order and which complies with the applicable legal provisions and customs', 'to arrive on schedule at pick/drop-off location points', 'not to negotiate the price that has already been agreed', as well as 'not to use the platform for professional, commercial or profit-making purposes'.

A certain degree of interaction is also exerted by BlaBlaCar over ridesharing arrangements among its users. Several considerations can be advanced in this regard.

First, although in principle available trips are displayed in chronological order, using the date and the time which a user enter when looking for a ride, BlaBlaCar highlights one ride – termed as 'the best ride' – at the top of the search results.[108]

Second, eligibility for a trip to both drivers and passengers remains at the sole discretion of BlaBlaCar, which may even suspend a user's account. Notably, an account can be suspended if a user has received, on average, poor reviews by other users. It also ought to be recalled that BlaBlaCar exerts 'moderation' powers in relation to reviews made by drivers to passengers and vice versa – in this connection, a five-level rating is employed, which goes from 'outstanding' to 'very disappointing'[109]–, notably by reserving a right not to publish or delete any review non-compliant with its own terms and conditions. In addition, a driver's account can be suspended, if it is discovered that the driver uses a taxi for his own passenger transport activities and, due to this, is capable of making a profit through ridesharing.

It also worth mentioning that, in case a passenger cancels a booking request less than twenty-four hours before departure or does not show up, BlaBlaCar also arranges for a refund to the driver.[110] If, instead, it is the driver who cancels the trip, passengers are notified via SMS or email. The driver is not penalized for calling off, but, if a driver cancels regularly or at the last minute, his account might be suspended.[111] Further, although for ridesharing no specific car insurance is required beyond the mandatory third-party liability insurance, BlaBlaCar offers its members a free-of-charge additional insurance, which covers adverse events such as a flat tyre, motor breakdown, accidents, vandalism, or theft.[112]

And yet, the most important type of interaction exerted by BlaBlaCar over arrangements made by platform users arguably entails the setting of the cost contribution amount. Notably, the company requires drivers to limit the cost contribution – a fixed price per seat[113] – asked to passengers to the costs actually incurred to provide

108. *How Do We Order Rides in the Search Results?*, https://www.blablacar.co.uk/faq/question/how-do-we-order-rides-in-the-search-results (accessed 31 Mar. 2019).
109. *Ratings*, https://www.blablacar.co.uk/member-ratings (accessed 31 Mar. 2019).
110. *What If a Passenger Cancels Before Departure or Doesn't Show Up?*, https://www.blablacar.co.uk/faq/question/what-if-a-passenger-cancels-before-departure-or-doesn-t-show-up (accessed 31 Mar. 2019).
111. *How Do I Cancel a Ride?*, https://www.blablacar.co.uk/faq/question/how-do-i-cancel-a-ride (accessed 31 Mar. 2019).
112. *Who Is Covered by the Free of Charge Additional Insurance Cover Offered by BlaBlaCar?*, https://www.blablacar.co.uk/faq/question/who-is-covered-by-the-free-of-charge-additional-insurance-offered-by-blablacar (accessed 31 Mar. 2019).
113. *Why Is There a Fixed Price per Passenger?*, https://www.blablacar.co.uk/faq/question/why-is-there-a-fixed-price-per-passenger (accessed 31 Mar. 2019).

the trip. BlaBlaCar even suggests the driver an amount for the cost contribution, based on the nature of the trip and the distances travelled. The driver can increase or decrease such an amount. However, the possibility for a driver to operate adjustments to the cost contribution is fairly limited.[114] It should also be noted that, although BlaBlaCar allows the use of a company car for ridesharing purposes, the platform also prescribes that the trip should not be part of a business trip.[115]

Besides participating in the OECD ongoing debate on taxation of the digital economy[116], pursuant to its own obligations under EU VAT, the company (or one of its local subsidiaries) charges VAT on top of its service fee. Price quotation is inclusive of VAT. In case of a cross-border trip, there is an issue of the allocation of VAT across different Member States. Notably, until 2018, the method for allocating the VAT on the service fee among different Member States depended on the collection point and/or to the destination of the trip. Recently, the platform has instead changed its own policy and, at present, its terms and conditions provide that the allocation of VAT follows the residence of the passenger.[117] Lastly, it ought to be noted that, as long as drivers are inhibited from using the platform for commercial, business, or profit-making purposes, in principle they are not taxable persons and, therefore, no VAT is charged by them with regard to payments made by passengers for cost contribution.[118]

114. *How Do I Set the Passenger Contribution for My Ride?*, https://www.blablacar.co.uk/faq/question/how-do-i-set-my-price (accessed 31 Mar. 2019).
115. *Can I Offer a Ride on BlaBlaCar with My Company Car?*, https://www.blablacar.co.uk/faq/question/my-car-is-a-professional-a-company-or-a-service-vehicle-can-i-offer-trips-on-blablacar-using-that-vehicle (accessed 31 Mar. 2019).
116. OECD, *supra* n. 78.
117. For a discussion of place of supply rules, *see* Chapter 7.
118. For a discussion of taxable persons, *see* Chapter 4.

Part II Legal Principles

CHAPTER 3

Principles for Assessing the Sharing Economy under EU VAT

§3.01 INTRODUCTION

The sharing economy is a new and ongoing phenomenon. Indeed, due to its sheer novelty and rapid evolution, every legal rule which supranational or national institutions might enact is likely to become obsolete in the span of few years. As many new issues arise and will probably continue cropping up, the author submits that, rather than just relying on legislative or regulatory provisions, it is more convenient to establish a framework of legal principles based on which the treatment of the sharing economy under EU VAT can be constantly monitored and targeted solutions to address its specific challenges can be developed and eventually modified later on.[1] This reflects the idea that, as long as regulated phenomena become more complex and, thus, also more difficult to handle, principles deliver more consistency than rules.[2] As a first thing, however, it is necessary to clarify what exactly is a rule and what, instead, is a principle.

The distinction between legal rules and principles is well-established in the literature and widely acknowledged among scholars. In a nutshell, it is stipulated that legal rules are definitive commands, that is norms which can only be complied with or not. Legal principles are instead optimization standards, which can only be fulfilled to the highest possible degree. Although far from uncontroversial[3], this distinction further

1. On the need to 'resort to principles of law' rather than to statutory provisions, *see* T. Koopman, *Judicial Activism and Procedural Law*, 1 Eur. Rev. Priv. L. 1/2 (1993), at 78.
2. J. Braithwaite, *Rules and Principles: A Theory of Legal Certainty*, 27 Austl. J. Leg. Phil. (2002), at 47.
3. For instance, N. MacCormick, *Reconstruction after Deconstruction: A Response to CLS*, 10 Oxford J. Legal Stud. 4 (1990), at 545, argues that 'standards are not something apart from rules, but one possible component of rules'.

stipulates that rules are decisional, whereas principles are directional.[4] The difference between legal rules and principles is, thus, a difference in quality.[5] Such qualitative difference can be appreciated, in particular, by comparing how a conflict between divergent legal rules and that between opposing legal principles is solved. A conflict between divergent legal rules, in fact, is solved by means of a standard of judgment, that is by introducing an exception or invalidating one of the two or more rules in conflict. In a sense, legal rules are applicable in an all-or-nothing fashion. A conflict between opposing legal principles, instead, is settled in a rather different way, notably by assessing the relative weight of each principle in each individual case.[6] As such, the application of legal principles is much less straightforward than that of legal rules.[7]

Despite the qualitative difference existing between legal rules and principles is theoretically clear, whether a legal provision is actually a rule or a principle is, in practice, not always plain to determine.[8] A first reason for such lack of clarity is that a legal provision can be formally construed as a rule and, yet, substantially functions as a principle.[9] Such an eventuality is most likely to occur where a rule covers a wide variety of situations.[10] Indeed, the VAT Directive itself contains some provisions which demand to be treated more like principles than as rules. Notably, this is the case with terms such as 'negligible'[11] or 'small'[12], whose inherently undefined nature permits that the application of EU VAT would remain flexible enough to potentially accommodate a wide array of situations.[13] A second reason that renders rather controversial distinguishing a rule from a principle is that the two terms themselves, especially the latter, are hard to define with sufficient precision.[14] Indeed, the terminology used by the same CJEU while referring to legal principles is not entirely consistent. As recalled by Advocate General Trstenjak in *Audiolux and Others*, in order to determine when a principle is used, reference is normally made only to the words employed by the Court or the Advocates General, which, however, may equally refer to 'generally accepted rules of law', 'principles generally accepted', 'basic principles of law', 'fundamental

4. C. Brokelind, *Chapter 1: Introduction*, in *Principles of Law: Function, Status and Impact in EU Tax Law* (C. Brokelind ed., IBFD 2014).
5. R. Alexy, *On the Structure of Legal Principles*, 13 Ratio Juris 3 (2000), at 295.
6. R. Dworkin, *Taking Rights Seriously* at 26 (Harvard University Press 1977) observes that, contrary to positive norms, legal principles always require a certain degree of discretion in their own application, in so far as they do not imply 'an exact measurement, and the judgment that a particular principle ... is more important than another will often be a controversial one'.
7. *See* F.J.G.M. Vanistendael, *Chapter 3: The Role of (Legal) Principles*, in *Principles of Law: Function, Status and Impact in EU Tax Law*, at para. 3.1 (C. Brokelind ed., IBFD 2014), arguing that 'principles, including legal principles, are rather soft and flexible, not immediately dictating any specific answer to a legal question and certainly not pointing to the payment of a precise amount of cold cash'.
8. Dworkin, *supra* n. 6, at 27.
9. *Id.*, at 28.
10. Vanistendael, *supra* n. 7, at para. 3.3.1.
11. Articles 13(1) Third Indent, 38(2), 191 and 395(1) Second Indent VAT Directive.
12. Articles 13(1) Third Indent, 16(2) and 185(2) VAT Directive.
13. K. Lenaerts & J.A. Gutiérrez-Fons, *The Constitutional Allocation of Powers and General Principles of EU Law*, 47 Comm. Mkt. L. Rev. 6 (2010), at 1651.
14. J.R. Muñiz, *Legal Principles and Legal Theory*, 10 Ratio Juris 3 (2010), at 267-287.

principles', or simply to 'principles'.[15] Third and lastly, the classification of a legal provision as a rule or a principle is far from immutable. Indeed, it could well happen that a legal rule is transformed, through interpretive action, especially by courts, into a principle or the other way around. Notably, under EU VAT, the former type of transformation seems to have occurred to third-party liability for VAT fraud.[16]

Since the distinction between legal rules and principles is not, by itself, Cartesian, less so it is to provide an answer to whether, in legal matters, it would be preferable to rely on the former or the latter.[17] What should appear rather clear at this juncture, however, is that principles are indispensable ingredients of a 'good' legal and tax system. Based on such assumption, the following section provides a tentative elaboration on some legal principles of tax, EU, and VAT law, with an aim of forming an evaluation model for assessing the sharing economy under EU VAT.

§3.02 TAX, EU AND VAT LAW PRINCIPLES

Legal principles are generally listed among the sources of law.[18] As for tax matters, although no 'Generally Accepted Taxation Principles' have been formulated so far[19], the principles of equity (or equality), certainty (which includes legal certainty), convenience (or simplicity), and economy (or efficiency), are the first legal principles that spring to mind.[20] Indeed, those are the four canons of taxation famously spelt out by Adam Smith.[21] In particular, according to Smith, the principle of equity demands that the tax imposed on a taxpayer corresponds to his ability to pay. Certainty, instead, requires that the amount which each taxpayer has to remit to the tax authorities is clear and plain to him. Such principle also includes that of legal certainty, which serves to shelter taxpayers from arbitrary requests filed by governments. The canon of convenience, instead, stipulates that it should be simple and also convenient for taxpayers to comply with their own tax obligations. Lastly, the principle of economy purports an efficient administration and collection of taxes by the competent authorities.

Other tax principles have been identified as well by various parties through the years. Notably, in 1978, a UK report of a committee chaired by James Meade epitomized 'the desirable characteristics of a tax structure', in the sense of representing valuable standards for the legislator in designing a tax system, in the following six propositions: (1) incentives and economic efficiency, (2) distributional effects, (3)

15. LU: Opinion of the Advocate General, 30 Jun. 2009, Case C-101/08, *Audiolux SA e.a v. Groupe Bruxelles Lambert SA (GBL) and Others and Bertelsmann AG and Others*, para. 67.
16. R. de la Feria, *Tax Fraud and the Rule of Law* at 26-27 (Working Paper Series, University of Oxford 2018).
17. J. Avery Jones, *Tax Law: Rules or Principles?*, 17 Inst. Fiscal Stud. 3 (1996), at 75.
18. *See* e.g., Art. 38(1)(c) of the Statute of the International Court of Justice (ICJ).
19. However, an attempt in that direction was made by J.R. Shelton, *Emerging Issues in Taxing Business in a Global Economy*, in *Taxing International Business. Emerging Trends in APEC and OECD Economies*, at 15 (R. Venn ed., OECD Publishing 1997).
20. For a discussion of various tax principles, *see* B. Westberg, *Cross-Border Taxation of E-Commerce* Ch. 4 (IBFD 2002).
21. A. Smith, *An Inquiry into the Nature and Causes of the Wealth of Nations*, Part Three 'Of Taxes' (R.H. Campbell, A.S. Skinner & W.B. Todd eds, Oxford University Press 1976).

international aspects, (4) simplicity and cost of administration and compliance, (5) flexibility and stability, and (6) transitional problems.[22] In 2005, the US Tax Foundation recommended the US government, for its own legislative action, as many as *Ten Principles of Sound Tax Policy*, that is: (1) transparency is a must, (2) be neutral, (3) maintain a broad base, (4) keep it simple, (5) stability matters, (6) no retroactivity, (7) keep tax burdens low, (8) don't inhibit trade, (9) ensure an open process, and (10) state and local taxes matter.[23]

A series of legal principles have also been identified in the specific realm of consumption taxes. Notably, in 1963, in his influential book titled *Government Finance*, John Due spelt out the four attributes of a 'good' sales tax, that is: (1) taxation of all consumption, (2) exemption of all sales to business, (3) taxation by the state of destination, and (4) simplicity.[24] Having regard to tax issues arising in the context of electronic commerce, another set of tax principles were laid down by the OECD in the so-called Ottawa Framework Conditions in 1998, namely: (1) neutrality, (2) efficiency, (3) certainty and simplicity, (4) effectiveness and fairness, and (5) flexibility.[25] The same principles endorsed at Ottawa in 1998 are also recalled in the OECD International VAT/GST Guidelines finally approved in 2017, which set forth a series of principles for the VAT/GST treatment of the most common types of cross-border transactions, although mainly focusing on trades in services and intangibles.[26]

A different string of principles stems directly from EU VAT being part of EU law.[27] Notably, the Treaties establishing, first, the European Communities and, later, the European Union have created a legal system with its own terminology and underlying principles[28], which takes priority over the national laws of Member States.[29] Indeed, under EU law it did not take many years to the CJEU to establish the need for both Member States and persons to comply with 'the general principles of law'[30], as well as to accord constitutional status to most of them.[31]

Principles have come into EU law in a rather haphazard way.[32] Most of them are contained in primary EU law, that is in the founding Treaties, their Protocols, as well

22. J. Meade, *The Structure and Reform of Direct Taxation* at 7 (Institute for Fiscal Studies 1978).
23. US Tax Foundation, *Ten Principles of Sound Tax Policy* (2005).
24. J.F. Due, *Government Finance: An Economic Analysis* at 23-24 (RD Irwin 1963).
25. OECD, *Electronic Commerce: Taxation Framework Conditions. A Report by the OECD Committee on Fiscal Affairs, as presented to Ministers at the OECD Ministerial Conference 'A Borderless World: Realizing the Potential of Electronic Commerce' on 8 October 1998* at 4 (OECD Publishing 1998).
26. OECD, *International VAT/GST Guidelines* at 17-18 (OECD Publishing 2017).
27. For an overview of the main EU principles, *see* e.g., T. Tridimas, *The General Principles of EU Law*. 3rd ed. (Oxford University Press 2013).
28. For a discussion of EU law principles in the EU VAT-specific context, *see* B.J.M. Terra & J. Kajus, *Introduction to European VAT (Recast)* Ch. 2 (IBFD Tax Research Platform 2019).
29. *See* e.g., IT: ECJ, 15 Jul. 1964, Case C-6/64, *Flaminio Costa v. E.N.E.L.*
30. DE: ECJ, 17 Dec. 1970, Case C-11/70, *Internationale Handelsgesellschaft mbH v. Einfuhr- und Vorratsstelle für Getreide und Futtermittel*, para. 4.
31. Not every principle, however, enjoys constitutional status. For instance, under EU VAT, constitutional status is not granted to the principle of neutrality or to the right to deduct. *See* DE: ECJ, 19 Jul. 2012, Case C-44/11, *Finanzamt Frankfurt am Main V-Höchst v. Deutsche Bank AG*, para. 45.
32. Vanistendael, *supra* n. 7, at para. 3.3.8.

as in the so-called *Acquis Communautaire*, i.e., the applicable primary and secondary EU law which Candidate States for accession to the EU must comply with.[33] At the level of primary EU law, direct reference is made, *inter alia*, to the principles of sincere cooperation[34], reconciliatory interpretation[35], conferral[36], subsidiarity[37], and proportionality[38]. Of particular relevance for tax matters, it is the principle of non-discrimination.[39] As known, the prohibition of double taxation, formerly included in Article 293 of the European Community Treaty (hereinafter, EC Treaty), was instead removed from the consolidated version of the EU treaties as recast after the entering into force of the Treaty of Lisbon in 2009.[40]

Important principles are also contained in the Charter of Fundamental Rights of the European Union (hereinafter, CFREU), which, after the Treaty of Lisbon, enjoys the same legal status of the founding Treaties.[41] Among the principles contained in the Charter, those of equal treatment[42], non-discrimination[43], equality of arms[44], respect for the rights of the defence[45], legality, proportionality of criminal offences and penalties[46], and *ne bis in idem*[47] are especially worth mentioning.

33. Notably, with 'primary EU law' reference is made to the Treaty on the European Union (TEU), the Treaty on the Functioning of the European Union (TFEU), their respective Protocols, the EURATOM Treaty, as well as the Charter of Fundamental Rights of the European Union (CFREU), which has the same legal value as the Treaties.
34. Article 4 TEU. In the field of EU VAT, *see* e.g., LU: ECJ, 4 May 2017, Case C-274/15, *European Commission v. Grand Duchy of Luxembourg*, paras 33-41.
35. Article 4(3) TEU. In the field of EU VAT, *see* e.g., HU: ECJ, 6 Jul. 2017, Case C-254/16, *Glencore Agriculture Hungary Kft., Formerly Glencore Grain Hungary Kft. v. Nemzeti Adó- és Vámhivatal Fellebbviteli Igazgatóság*, para. 34.
36. Articles 5(1-2) and 7 TFEU.
37. Articles 5(3) TEU and 69 TFEU. In the field of EU VAT, *see* e.g., PL: ECJ, 29 Sep. 2015, Case C-276/14, *Gmina Wrocław v. Minister Finansów*, para. 41.
38. Articles 5(4) TEU, 69, and 269 TFEU. In the field of EU VAT, *see* e.g., FR: ECJ, 19 Sep. 2000, Joined Cases C-177/99 and C-181/99, *Ampafrance SA v. Directeur des services fiscaux de Maine-et-Loire and Sanofi Synthelabo v. Directeur des services fiscaux du Val-de-Marne*, paras 41-70.
39. Article 18 TFEU. In the field of EU VAT, *see* e.g., AT: ECJ, 26 Oct. 2010, Case C-97/09, *Ingrid Schmelz v. Finanzamt Waldviertel*, paras 44-45.
40. Signally, Art. 293 of the EC Treaty (applicable as until 1 December 2009) imposed an obligation upon EU Member States to eliminate double taxation, *inter alia*, through the conclusion of international tax treaties.
41. Article 6(1) First Indent TEU. For a discussion on the increased relevance of the CFREU in the field of EU VAT, *see* K.K. Egholm Elgaard, *The Impact of the Charter of Fundamental Rights of the European Union on VAT Law*, 2 World J. VAT/GST L. 2 (2016), at 63-91.
42. Article 20 CFREU. In the field of EU VAT, *see* e.g., PL: ECJ, 7 Mar. 2017, Case C-390/15, *Proceedings brought by Rzecznik Praw Obywatelskich (RPO)*, paras 37-72.
43. Article 21 CFREU. In the field of EU VAT, *see* e.g., SL: ECJ, 26 Oct. 2017, Case C-534/16, *Finančné Riaditeľstvo Slovenskej Republiky v. BB Construct S.r.o.*, paras 30 and 43-46.
44. Article 47 CFREU. In the field of EU VAT, *see* e.g., BE: ECJ, 28 Jul. 2016, Case C-543/14, *Ordre des Barreaux Francophones et Germanophone and Others v. Conseil des Ministres*, paras 39-47.
45. Article 48 CFREU. In the field of EU VAT, *see* e.g., HU: ECJ, 17 Dec. 2015, Case C-419/14, *WebMindLicenses kft v. Nemzeti Adó- és Vámhivatal Kiemelt Adó- és Vám Főigazgatóság*, para. 83.
46. Article 49 CFREU. In the field of EU VAT, *see* e.g., IT: ECJ, 8 Sep. 2015, Case C-105/14, *Criminal Proceedings against Ivo Taricco and Others*, paras 54-58.
47. Article 50 CFREU. In the field of EU VAT, *see* e.g., SW: ECJ, 26 Feb. 2013, Case C-617/10, *Åklagaren v. Hans Åkerberg Fransson*, paras 16-42.

A further bunch of principles is contained in secondary EU law, which is composed of regulations, directives, decisions, recommendations, and opinions from EU institutions. Notably, principles contained in the VAT Directive and generally recalled in its Preamble, such as those of general[48], uniform[49], harmonized[50], non-discriminatory[51], neutral[52], and simple[53] application of VAT, prevention of double taxation[54], distortion of competition[55], and tax evasion or avoidance[56], as well as taxation at place of consumption[57], fall under such grouping.

Lastly, a lengthy series of principles can be derived from the CJEU's case law as well as from Advocates General's opinions, most of which, however, found a due parallel in positive norms of the Treaties or of the Charter, viz. the principles of equal treatment[58], fiscal neutrality[59], legal certainty[60], protection of legitimate expectations[61],

48. Point 5 of the Preamble of the VAT Directive. In the CJEU's case law, *see* e.g., PT: ECJ, 8 Mar. 2012, Case C-524/10, *European Commission v. Portuguese Republic*, para. 31.
49. Points 8, 22, 28, 35, 45, 58, and 61 of the Preamble of the VAT Directive. In the CJEU's case law, *see* e.g., NL: ECJ, 4 Oct. 2001, Case C-326/99, *Stichting 'Goed Wonen' v. Staatssecretaris van Financiën*, para. 47.
50. Points 4, 6, 7, 24, 25, 38, 39, 45, 46 and 49 of the Preamble of the VAT Directive. In the CJEU's case law, *see* e.g., UK: ECJ, 6 Oct. 2005, Case C-291/03, *MyTravel plc v. Commissioners of Customs & Excise*, para. 33.
51. Point 13 of the Preamble of the VAT Directive. In the CJEU's case law, *see* e.g., BG: ECJ, 13 Jun. 2013, Case C-62/12, *Galin Kostov v. Direktor na Direktsia 'Obzhalvane I upravlenie na izpalnenieto' – Varna pri Tsentralno upravlenie na Natsionalnata agentsia za prihodite*, para. 29.
52. Points 5, 7, 30, and 34 of the Preamble of the VAT Directive. In the CJEU's case law, *see* e.g., BE: ECJ, 27 Mar. 2019, Case C-201/18, *Mydibel SA v. État belge*, paras 44-48.
53. Points 5, 16, 38, 42, 48, and 59 of the Preamble of the VAT Directive. In the CJEU's case law, *see* e.g., NL: ECJ, 27 May 2004, Case C-68/03, *Staatssecretaris van Financiën v. D. Lipjes*, para. 15.
54. Points 19, 37, 51 and 62 of the Preamble of the VAT Directive. A referral to the CJEU, which might eventually help clarify the scope of this principles, was made in 2018. *See* HU: *Request for a preliminary ruling from the Fővárosi Közigazgatási és Munkaügyi Bíróság (Hungary) lodged on 24 April 2018 – KrakVet Marek Batko sp. K. v. Nemzeti Adó- és Vámhivatal Fellebbviteli Igazgatósága (Case C-276/18)*.
55. Points 4, 7, 11, 20, 22, 23, 29, and 51 of the Preamble of the VAT Directive. In the CJEU's case law, *see* e.g., DE: ECJ, 29 Nov. 2018, Case C-264/17, *Harry Mensing v. Finanzamt Hamm*, para. 35.
56. Points 27, 42, 55, and 59 of the Preamble of the VAT Directive. In the CJEU's case law, *see* e.g., PT: ECJ, 6 Dec. 2018, Case C-672/17, *Tratave – Tratamento de Águas Residuais do Ave SA v. Autoridade Tributária e Aduaneira*, para. 33.
57. Points 19 and 22 of the Preamble of the VAT Directive. In the CJEU's case law, *see* e.g., DE: ECJ, 6 Dec. 2007, Case C-401/06, *Commission of the European Communities v. Federal Republic of Germany*, para. 24.
58. In the field of EU VAT, *see* e.g., DE: ECJ, 20 Dec. 2017, Case C-462/16, *Finanzamt Bingen-Alzey v. Boehringer Ingelheim Pharma GmbH & Co. KG*, para. 46.
59. In the field of EU VAT, *see* e.g., DK: ECJ, 18 Jun. 2009, Case C-174/08, *NCC Construction Danmark A/S v. Skatteministeriet*, paras 36-47.
60. In the field of EU VAT, *see* e.g., LV: ECJ, 21 Sep. 2017, Case C-326/15, *DNB BANKA' AS v. Valsts Ienemumu Dienests*, paras 42-43.
61. In the field of EU VAT, *see* e.g., IR: ECJ, 22 Nov. 2017, Case C-251/16, *Edward Cussens and Others v. T.G. Brosman*, paras 39-44.

transparency[62], proportionality[63], equivalence and effectiveness[64], the right of defence[65], as well as the prohibition of *bis in idem*[66], abusive practices[67], tax fraud[68] or any alternative general tax on turnover[69].

Many - sometimes conflicting - principles equally govern the functioning of EU VAT.[70] Among those 'system principles'[71], the territoriality[72] and destination principles[73], which set forth the jurisdictional scope of EU VAT, indeed play a prominent role. Notably, the territoriality principle sets the 'limits of the geographical scope'[74] of the EU VAT system, by prescribing that only transactions taking place in the territories of the Member States - however, with some exclusions[75] and exceptions[76] - shall be subject to EU VAT. In line with this principle, foreign transactions are not subject to tax even if carried out by domestic businesses, whereas domestic transactions are taxed irrespective of whether the supplier is domestic- or foreign-based.[77] The destination principle, instead, mandates that no VAT is levied on exports (*rectius*: the VAT due is rebated, since exports are zero-rated, i.e., the supplier maintains the right to deduct his input VAT), whereas imports are fully taxed. Thus, all the revenues generated by a taxable transaction accrue only to the jurisdiction where the final supply to the end consumer actually takes place.[78]

62. In the field of EU VAT, *see* e.g., NL: ECJ, 8 Nov. 2001, Case C-338/98, *Commission of the European Communities v. Kingdom of the Netherlands*, para. 22.
63. In the field of EU VAT, *see* e.g., IT: ECJ, 23 Nov. 2017, Case C-246/16, *Enzo Di Maura v. Agenzia delle Entrate*, paras 25-27.
64. In the field of EU VAT, *see* e.g., IT: ECJ, 15 Mar. 2007, Case C-35/05, *Reemtsma Cigarettenfabriken GmbH v. Ministero delle Finanze*, para. 37.
65. In the field of EU VAT, *see* IT: ECJ, 21 Nov. 2018, Case C-648/16, *Fortunata Silvia Fontana v. Agenzia delle Entrate - Direzione Provinciale di Reggio Calabria*, paras 43-46.
66. In the field of EU VAT, *see* e.g., SL: ECJ, 26 Oct. 2017, Case C-534/16, *Finančné Riaditeľstvo Slovenskej Republiky v. BB Construct S.r.o.*, paras 30-31.
67. In the field of EU VAT, *see* e.g., UK: ECJ, 21 Feb. 2006, Case C-255/02, *Halifax plc, Leeds Permanent Development Services Ltd and County Wide Property Investments Ltd v. Commissioners of Customs & Excise*, para. 70.
68. In the field of EU VAT, *see* e.g., BG: ECJ, 6 Dec. 2012, Case C-285/11, *Bonik EOOD v. Direktor na Direktsia 'Obzhalvane i upravlenie na izpalnenieto' - Varna pri Tsentralno upravlenie na Natsionalnata agentsia za prihodite*, para. 38.
69. In the field of EU VAT, *see* e.g., FR: ECJ, 3 Mar. 1988, Case C-252/86, *Gabriel Bergandi v. Directeur Général des Impôts*, para. 11.
70. B.J.M. Terra, *The Place of Supply in European VAT* at 1 (Kluwer Law International 1998).
71. A. van Doesum, H.W.M. van Kesteren & G.J. van Norden, *Fundamentals of EU VAT Law* at 35 (Kluwer Law International 2016).
72. Articles 5-8 VAT Directive. For a discussion, *see* Terra, *supra* n. 70, at 4.
73. Articles 44-59a VAT Directive. For a discussion, *see* Terra, *supra* n. 70, at 5.
74. FR: ECJ, 25 Jan. 2001, Case C-429/97, *Commission of the European Communities v. French Republic*, para. 52.
75. EU VAT, in fact, does not apply to certain territories, even if forming part of the EU Customs territory, listed in Art. 6(1) of the VAT Directive.
76. Notably the CJEU has permitted taxation by a Member State of a transport operation taking place partially outside its territory, provided this does not encroach upon the tax jurisdiction of other Member States. *See* IT: ECJ, 23 Jan. 1986, Case C-283/84, *Trans Tirreno Express v. Ufficio Provinciale IVA*, para. 21.
77. Terra, *supra* n. 70, at 3.
78. Terra, *supra* n. 70, at 6.

The CJEU and the Advocates General to the Court have also resorted to a series of other principles, namely the right to deduct[79], the common system of VAT[80], VAT uniformity[81], elimination of distortion in competition[82], and liability for tax[83]. Importantly, since EU VAT rules, being contained in the VAT Directive, are part of secondary EU law, these specific VAT principles must comply with the rules and principles set forth by EU primary law as detailed above. For its part, the principle of fiscal neutrality has somehow a mixed nature, as long as, apparently, it constitutes a specification in the field of taxation of a general EU law principle such as that of equal treatment.[84]

§3.03 A FRAMEWORK OF PRINCIPLES AS AN EVALUATION MODEL

A full elaboration on all the aforementioned legal principles would obviously stretch well beyond the purpose and scope of the present study. It is therefore inevitable to select only those principles which are of most relevance for assessing the sharing economy under EU VAT. Indeed, if it is true that the character of a tax is determined by its underlying principles, then those principles ought to be considered not only for interpretative purposes, but also in the context of designing, implementing, and applying future legal provisions.[85]

From the many tax, EU, and VAT law principles listed above, the author has identified five legal principles, i.e., the principles of equality, neutrality, simplicity, flexibility, and proportionality, which can be used for the ensuing analysis. Based on their main function, i.e., whether they concern the theoretical design, the practical implementation or, rather, the methodological application of law, these five principles can be further divided into three distinct groups: (1) theoretical principles (equality and neutrality), (2) practical principles (simplicity and flexibility), and (3) methodological principles (proportionality).[86]

79. DK: ECJ, 29 Oct. 2009, Case C-174/08, *NCC Construction Danmark A/S v. Skatteministeriet*, paras 27 and 40.
80. RO: ECJ, 19 Oct. 2017, Case C-101/16, *SC Paper Consult SRL v. Direcţia Regionala a Finanţelor Publice Cluj-Napoca and Administraţia Judeţeana a Finanţelor Publice Bistriţa Nasau*, para. 37.
81. FR: ECJ, 3 May 2001, Case C-481/98, *Commission of the European Communities v. French Republic*, paras 19 and 22.
82. UK: ECJ, 28 June 2007, Case C-363/05, *JP Morgan Fleming Claverhouse Investment Trust plc, The Association of Investment Trust Companies*, para. 47.
83. DK: Opinion of the Advocate General, 25 Mar. 2004, Case C-382/02, *Cimber Air A/S v. Skatteministeriet*, para. 24.
84. BG: ECJ, 19 Dec. 2012, Case C-549/11, *Direktor na Direktsia 'Obzhalvane i Upravlenie na Izpalnenieto' – Grad Burgas pri Tsentralno Upravleniena Natsionalnata Agentsia za Prihodite v. Orfey Balgaria EOOD*, para. 33.
85. T. Ecker, *A VAT/GST Model Convention: Tax Treaties as Solution for Value Added Tax and Goods and Services Tax Double Taxation* Ch. 6 (IBFD 2013).
86. Importantly, although distinct, these three groups of principles are not 'ring-fenced', rather reinforce their understanding from each other. The author submits that, in a sense, 'we can become conscious of pure practical [principles] … just as we are conscious of pure theoretical principles'. *See* I. Kant, *Critique of Practical Reason* at 43 (Hackett Publishing 2002).

Admittedly, both the selection and the classification of the principles above are very much 'political'[87] and, as such, may well be questioned.[88] Nevertheless, the author submits that the selected principles generally accord with the theoretical design, the practical implementation, as well as the methodological application of EU VAT. Mimicking the overall and balanced approach adopted in the Ottawa Framework Conditions in relation to electronic commerce, the evaluation model as conceptualized in the present study in fact assumes that, while tax principles that guide governments in relation to conventional economic activities should also steer their action in relation to the sharing economy, new legislative or administrative measures, or changes to existing measures, relating to the sharing economy are not precluded, in so far as those innovations are intended to assist in the application of existing tax principles.[89] More narrowly, while commitment to the 'theoretical principles' of equality and neutrality ensures that the EU VAT treatment of the sharing economy would not be 'ring-fenced' from that accorded to more conventional economic activities, the 'practical principles' of simplicity and flexibility, instead, avoid that strict adherence to the former principles would ultimately translate into a sort of inconvenient straitjacket.[90]

Importantly, in assessing the EU VAT treatment of the sharing economy, no single principle is intended to take priority as a more important standard of review over any other. Instead, a careful trade-off is made in case of a conflict between opposing principles, so that the evaluation framework proposed always applies to the sharing economy based on an overall and balanced consideration of all the principles captured under it. Such a mediating function, indeed, is fulfilled by the principle of proportionality, which in the present study precisely serves as methodological rule to weigh up opposing principles. It also ought to be observed that such an approach does not make the use of principles any less worthwhile, in so far as, in setting priorities in their own application, all principles are considered and, thus, transparency in the evaluation process is ensured.[91] In a sense, if the assessment made is discretionary, it is a kind of discretion not astray from some guidance.[92] Figure 3.1 below depicts graphically the framework of principles which form the evaluation model for assessing the sharing economy under EU VAT and outlines the methodology used in its application.

---

87. *See* K.C. Messere, *Tax Policy in OECD Countries: Choices and Conflicts* at 109 (IBFD 1993), arguing that principles themselves are based on value judgments.
88. However, as observed by H.L.A. Hart, *The Concept of Law*. 3rd ed. at 124-154 (Clarendon Law Series 1994), given the open-texture of (legal) language, a margin of uncertainty and discretion in the identification of the relevant legal principles ought to be tolerated.
89. OECD, *supra* n. 25, at 3; Ecker, *supra* n. 85, at Ch. 6.
90. Indeed, such a risk is far from unlikely, especially considering – as acknowledged by European Commission, Value Added Tax Committee, *Working Paper No. 947, Services Provided by an Electronic Platform Connecting for Remuneration, by means of a Smartphone Application, a Driver Using His Own Vehicle with Persons Who Wish to Make Urban Journeys. The Significance of the VAT Identification Number*, at 8 (taxud.c.1(2018)1735106) – that in the sharing economy 'different business models are possible' and, further, that 'these [business models] may be modified over time'.
91. C. Alley & D. Bentley, *A Remodelling of Adam Smith's Tax Design Principles*, 20 Austl. Tax F. 4 (2005), at 582.
92. *See* J. Raz, *Legal Principles and the Limits of Law*, 81 Yale. L. J. 5 (1972), at 846, reflecting that courts' 'discretion may be, and usually is, guided by principles'.

Figure 3.1 A Framework of Principles as an Evaluation Model

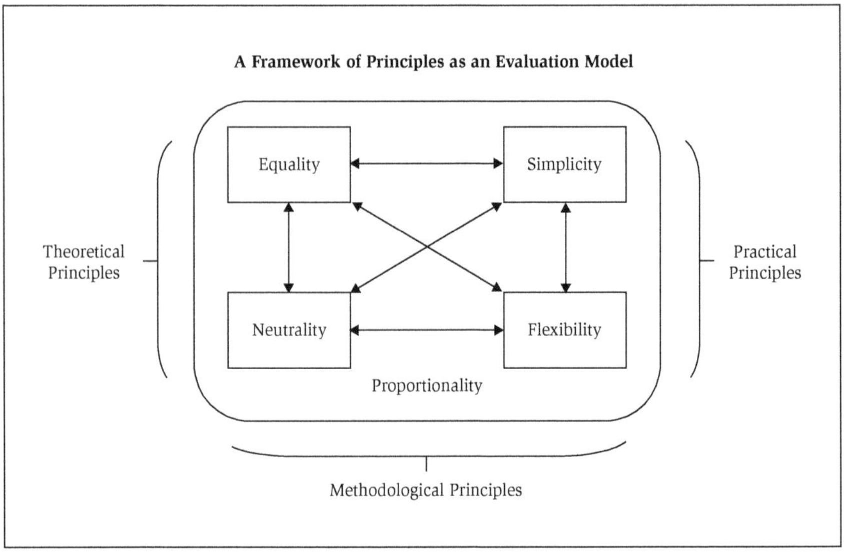

The next sections discuss, in turn, each of the five legal principles which form the evaluation model depicted above. Importantly, the ensuing examination provides the framework for evaluating whether and to which extent the current EU VAT treatment of the sharing economy may be improved in relation to the five EU VAT propositions discussed in the following chapters.

§3.04 EQUALITY

Equality is a milestone of law.[93] It is also a general principle of EU law.[94] Sometimes also termed as principle of non-discrimination, even in the field of taxation it responds to the general demand for fairness.[95] Notably, the notion of equality splits into two directions: horizontal and vertical.

Horizontal equality mandates that people at the same level of well-being shall face the same tax burden.[96] Under EU VAT, this objective is achieved by means of its design structure, i.e., the fact that all products, either goods or services, are subject to

93. The principle of equality is enshrined in many international treaties, such as the European Convention of Human Rights (Art. 14) and the International Covenant on Civil and Political Rights (Art. 26).
94. Articles 2 TEU and 20 CFREU.
95. Only in Art. 3 TEU, as well as in the Preamble and Art. 102 of the TFEU, however, EU primary law makes explicit reference to 'fairness'.
96. According to J. Englisch, *Chapter 11 – VAT and General Principles of EU Law*, in *Traditional and Alternative Routes to European Tax Integration: Primary Law, Secondary Law, Soft Law, Coordination, Comitology and Their Relationship*, at para. 11.3.2 (D. (Dennis) Weber ed., IBFD 2010), in the field of EU VAT the principle of equality translates into that 'people with the same

tax, and that the levy is exactly proportional to the final price of the product paid by the end consumer. In such way, horizontal equality is achieved at the level of both taxable persons and taxable transactions.

Although the principle of horizontal equality can somehow be equated to that of legal neutrality[97] discussed in the next section, apparently the latter is narrower in scope, since it aims to compare only businesses or products which are in competition with one another.[98] Notably, for two or more activities being in competition with each other, the CJEU refers to the decision of the average consumer to choose one product over the other and, indeed, such a choice is even susceptible to 'vary according to the different degree of penetration of new technologies in each national market'.[99] By itself, the principle of equality instead involves a broader comparison, not necessarily restricted to an economic dimension, but which may well serve to fend off other kinds of discrimination.[100] Notably, for determining whether businesses and transactions are similar and, therefore, should receive the very same treatment, the OECD International VAT/GST Guidelines make reference, respectively, to the right to deduct which businesses under comparison have and to the characterization of the services or intangibles in comparison, whereas 'the way the supply was made, the person from whom it was acquired within the supply chain, or the terms under which the services or intangibles were acquired are not relevant'.[101]

Vertical equality, instead, mandates that people in different situations should pay a correspondingly different amount of taxes, as a heavier tax burden on people who are better placed to bear it.[102] Consumption taxes, however, are levied irrespective of personal circumstances. This makes those taxes be intended as 'regressive'[103], precisely because, moving up the income scale, the proportion between the tax burden

expenditure should also bear the same tax burden, and the tax burden of people with different expenditure should also differ correspondingly'.

97. *See* section §3.05. Indeed, the two concepts are paired in both the VAT Directive (*see* point 7 of the Preamble) and the OECD Ottawa Framework Conditions (which refer to a single idea of 'neutral and equitable' taxation).
98. FR: ECJ, 3 May 2001, Case C-481/98, *Commission of the European Communities v. French Republic*, paras 21-22. In this connection, M. Lamensch, *European Value Added Tax in the Digital Era* at para. 3.3. (IBFD 2015), notes that the CJEU, quite logically, in case two supplies are similar, does not further verify whether the supplies at stake are also in competition. In such event, the criterion of competition is, thus, somehow stifled. For an example in this regard, *see* UK: ECJ, 10 Nov. 2011, Joined Cases C-259/10 and C-260/10, *Commissioners for Her Majesty's Revenue and Customs v. The Rank Group plc*, para. 33.
99. FI: ECJ, 11 Sep. 2014, Case C-219/13, *K Oy*, para. 30.
100. DE: ECJ, 20 Dec. 2017, Case C-462/16, *Finanzamt Bingen-Alzey Gegen Boehringer Ingelheim Pharma GmbH & Co. KG*, para. 28. *See also* AT: ECJ, 23 Apr. 2009, Case C-460/07, *Sandra Puffer v. Unabhängiger Finanzsenat, Außenstelle Linz*, paras 52-57, where the CJEU ruled that placing different VAT burdens on similar private expenditure amounts to a discrimination.
101. OECD, *supra* n. 26, at 30.
102. *See* Meade, *supra* n. 22, at 12, who, considering the 'distributional effects' of a tax system, argues that 'a modern tax system must be so constructed as to be capable of use for vertical redistribution between rich and poor'.
103. For a comprehensive discussion of the regressive nature of VAT – or otherwise, *see* G.N. Carlson & M.K. Patrick, *Addressing the Regressivity of a Value-Added Tax*, 42 National Tax J. 3 (1989), at 339-351.

and income falls.[104] A solution against regressivity of VAT might then consist in introducing reduced tax rates[105] or exemptions[106] for products that are meant to satisfy the most basic human needs (e.g., foods and houses) and, thus, are presumably purchased also by poorest households. Those kinds of policies, however, have a few noticeable drawbacks, not least that of distorting competition.[107]

Moreover, it s not always feasible to implement the principle of equality free from any constraint.[108] Indeed, it occurs frequently that measures aimed at making an indirect tax system, supposedly, more equitable are to be traded off with other principles, such as those of simplicity and flexibility. The VAT Directive itself sometimes allows a difference in treatment between persons in similar situations or between comparable products. By way of example, Member States are permitted to treat bodies governed by public law as non-taxable persons provided that their own activities are carried out 'on such a small scale as to be negligible'[109] or, even, a country may grant taxable persons the possibility to deduct their non-deductible input VAT provided that such amount is 'insignificant'[110].

§3.05 NEUTRALITY

Although not part of primary EU law[111], the principle of neutrality is undoubtedly the leading principle of EU VAT[112], as constantly recalled by the CJEU[113] and also affirmed

104. S. Cnossen, *The Value-Added Tax: Key to a Better Tax Mix*, 6 Austl. Tax F. 3 (1989), at 272-273, however, objects that VAT is regressive only in relation to income, not necessarily in relation to consumption.
105. A.A. Tait, *Value Added Tax: International Practice and Problems* at 42-44 (International Monetary Fund 1988).
106. J. Creedy, *Indirect Tax Reform and the Role of Exemptions*, 22 Fiscal Stud. 4 (2001), at 457-486.
107. For a perspective on this and other pitfalls, especially in relation to the EU VAT treatment of activities by public bodies, *see* R. de la Feria, *The EU VAT Treatment of Public Sector Bodies: Slowly Moving in the Wrong Direction*, 37 Intertax 3 (2009), at 148-165.
108. By way of example, in *Eurodental*, the CJEU ruled – despite the opposite opinion of Advocate General Ruiz-Jarabo Colomer (LU: Opinion of the Advocate General, 22 Jun 2006, Case C-240/05, *Administration de l'Enregistrement et des Domaines v. Eurodental Sàrl*, para. 36) – that a Member State is not permitted to subject to tax a transaction, contrary to what EU VAT legislation prescribes, even if it does so with a view of restoring an equal treatment with another transaction. *See* LU: ECJ, 7 Dec. 2006, Case C-240/05, *Administration de l'Enregistrement et des Domaines v. Eurodental Sàrl*, para. 55.
109. Article 13(1) Third Indent VAT Directive.
110. Article 173(2)(e) VAT Directive.
111. DE: CJEU, 19 Jul. 2012, Case C-44/11, *Finanzamt Frankfurt am Main V-Höchst v. Deutsche Bank AG*, para. 45.
112. R. de la Feria, *The EU VAT System and the Internal Market* at para. 3.1.1.1. (IBFD 2009) argues that the principle of fiscal neutrality 'is probably the most important principle of the EU VAT system and the one on which the Court has relied more heavily as a basis for its decisions. It is essentially a fall-back principle, conveying the idea of neutrality where other principles such as VAT as a tax on consumption or the principle of the right to deduct do not apply'.
113. *See* e.g., RO: ECJ, 7 Mar. 2018, Case C-159/17, *Întreprinderea Individuala Dobre M. Marius v. Ministerul Finanţelor Publice – A.N.A.F. – D.G.R.F.P. Galaţi – Serviciul Soluţionare Contestaţii and A.N.A.F – D.G.R.F.P. Galaţi – A.J.F.P. Constanţa – Serviciul Inspecţie Fiscala Persoane Fizice 2 Constanţ*, para. 31.

in the Preamble of the VAT Directive[114]. Indeed, the principle of fiscal neutrality has inspired a purposive construction of the EU VAT system in several matters, such as the treatment of 'taxable persons'[115], the notion of 'taxable transactions'[116], the determination of the 'taxable amount'[117], the scope of 'tax exemptions'[118], the extent of 'the right to deduct'[119], as well as the possibility to apply different 'tax rates'[120]. The CJEU has also maintained that double taxation constitutes an infringement of the principle of fiscal neutrality.[121]

Nevertheless, the VAT Directive, by itself, does not explain the exact meaning of the term 'neutrality'. Scholars mostly agree that neutrality has at least two dimensions, which reflect its external and internal orientation.[122] Based on such understanding, the concept can further be divided into external and internal neutrality.[123]

External neutrality relates to the international aspect of levying EU VAT. It mandates a neutral functioning of the tax frontiers, by prescribing, on the one hand, that the tax on foreign products shall not exceed that levied internally on comparable domestic products, and by requiring, on the other hand, a refund on exported products of the same amount of the tax that was levied domestically.[124] Indeed, external neutrality not only concerns foreign and domestic supplies, but also foreign and domestic suppliers, who, in this regard, should neither be advantaged nor disadvantaged.[125]

Internal neutrality, instead, relates to the domestic aspects of levying EU VAT. From such a perspective, it can be grossly divided into legal and economic neutrality.[126]

---

114. *See*, in particular, point 5 of the Preamble of the VAT Directive.
115. *See* e.g., PT: ECJ, 28 Feb. 2018, Case C-672/16, *Imofloresmira – Investimentos Imobiliários SA v. Autoridade Tributária e Aduaneira*, para. 44.
116. *See* e.g., RO: ECJ, 21 Sept. 2017, Case C-441/16, *SMS Group GmbH v. Direcția Generala Regionala a Finanțelor Publice București*, para. 40.
117. *See* e.g., UK: ECJ, 14 Dec. 2017, Case C-305/16, *Avon Cosmetics Ltd v. Commissioners for Her Majesty's Revenue and Customs*, para. 54.
118. *See* e.g., PL: ECJ, 16 Nov. 2017, Case C-308/16, *Kozuba Premium Selection sp. z o.o., v. Dyrektor Izby Skarbowej w Warszawie*, para. 43.
119. *See* e.g., PT: ECJ, 12 Apr. 2018, Case C-8/17, *Biosafe – Indústria de Reciclagens SA v. Flexipiso – Pavimentos SA*, para. 44.
120. *See* e.g., PL: ECJ, 9 Nov. 2017, Case C-499/16, *AZ v. Minister Finansów*, para. 36.
121. *See* e.g., SL: ECJ, 2 Jul. 2015, Case C-209/14, *NLB Leasing d.o.o. v. Republika Slovenija*, para. 40.
122. Terra & Kajus, *supra* n. 28, at para. 7.3.
123. In addition to 'internal' and 'external' neutrality, P. Rendahl, *Cross-Border Consumption Taxation of Digital Supplies* at para. 3.2.5 (IBFD 2009), identifies also a third dimension, which she calls 'intra-external neutrality' and relates to the international aspects of neutrality in a common market (such as the EU), whereas 'external neutrality' is reserved to cross-border situations in non-common markets.
124. B.J.M. Terra, *Sales Taxation. The Case of Value Added Tax in the European Community* at 15 (Kluwer Law International 1988).
125. *See* OECD, *supra* n. 26, at 22, prescribing that, 'with respect to the level of taxation, foreign businesses should not be disadvantaged or advantaged compared to domestic businesses in the jurisdiction where the tax may be due or paid'.
126. Terra & Kajus, *supra* n. 28, at paras 7.3.1-7.3.1.3, subdivide the concept of 'internal neutrality' into 'legal', 'competition', and 'economic' neutrality. Based on their understanding, while 'competition neutrality' is a concept linked to the idea of the price paid by the end consumer as being unaffected by the extent of vertical and horizontal integration, 'economic neutrality'

Legal neutrality is tightly clinched to the normative character of EU VAT, which requires the tax being applied equally to similar products and its amount reflecting a set percentage of the retail price. Economic neutrality, instead, demands that the levying of VAT shall not interfere with the optimal allocation of overall wealth, but rather it is a means to promote growth in the overall economy.[127] As such, the application of EU VAT is neither to affect the amount of the tax paid by the end consumer nor to lead to a concentration of businesses in the production and distribution chain.[128] Further, economic neutrality implies that the tax should remain as technologically neutral as possible.[129]

The principle of neutrality is also used for interpreting EU VAT provisions and, in particular, exemptions.[130] For determining the scope of exemptions, through the years, the CJEU has indeed developed a 'neutrality test', whereby the different treatment accorded to two or more supplies is evaluated from the perspective of the average consumer.[131] However, the principle of neutrality is not absolute. Rather, it must be traded off with other interpretative principles, notably those which demand strict[132], contextual[133], or uniform[134] interpretation of exemptions. As such, the principle of neutrality cannot serve to extend the scope of an exemption in the absence of a clear provision to that effect.[135] VAT exemptions, in fact, are to be interpreted strictly, 'since they constitute exceptions to the general principle that turnover tax is to be levied on all services supplied for consideration by a taxable person'.[136] And yet, 'for obvious reasons of impartiality', the CJEU maintains that a share transaction which,

instead relates to the idea of leaving business choices unaffected. According to the author, the two concepts can ultimately be reconnected to the idea of leaving both business and consumer choices unaffected.

127. As from the original intent of EU VAT. *See* C. Herbain, *VAT Neutrality* at 50 (Larcier Promoculture 2015).

128. *See* OECD, *supra* n. 26, at 15, mandating VAT/GST to remain neutral 'whatever the nature of the product, the structure of the distribution chain, and the means used for its delivery (e.g., retail stores, physical delivery, Internet downloads)'.

129. Rendahl, *supra* n. 123, at para. 7.6.2.6.

130. R. de la Feria, *EU VAT System as Interpretative Aids to EU VAT Rules*, in *CJEU – Recent Developments in Value Added Tax 2015*, at 3-19 (M. Lang et al. eds, Linde 2016) considers that two main principles are used as interpretative principles in the field of EU VAT, i.e., the principle of EU VAT as a general consumption tax and, indeed, the principle of fiscal neutrality.

131. *See* e.g., UK: ECJ, 10 Nov. 2011, Case C-259/10, *Commissioners for Her Majesty's Revenue and Customs v. The Rank Group plc*, para. 58.

132. *See* e.g., UK: ECJ, 23 Feb. 1988, Case C-353/85, *Commission of the European Communities v. United Kingdom of Great Britain and Northern Ireland*, para. 26.

133. *See* e.g., DE: ECJ, 10 Sep. 2002, Case C-141/00, *Ambulanter Pflegedienst Kügler GmbH v. Finanzamt für Körperschaften I in Berlin*, para. 28.

134. *See* e.g., UK: ECJ, 4 May 2006, Case C-169/04, *Abbey National plc and Inscape Investment Fund v. Commissioners of Customs & Excise*, para. 38.

135. *See* e.g., FR: ECJ, 5 Mar. 2015, Case C-479/13, *European Commission v. French Republic*, para. 43.

136. DK: ECJ, 5 June 1997, Case C-2/95, *Sparekassernes Datacenter (SDC) v. Skatteministeriet*, para. 20.

economically speaking, is equivalent to a supply of immovable property shall be exempt from VAT under the same terms of a direct transfer of immovable property.[137]

Although achieving neutrality, under its manifold acceptations[138], is highly desirable, in practice it might be necessary to reconcile such principle with other ones.[139] Notably, 'since practically every activity overlaps to some extent with another', it is not conceivable to require that, as to reach neutrality, all activities partly in competition with each other are to receive the same VAT treatment.[140]

§3.06 SIMPLICITY

Only three years after the enactment of VAT (*rectius*: *'taxe sur la valeur ajoutée'* or 'TVA') in France, its putative father, Maurice Lauré, pointed to the complexity of VAT as one of the intrinsic evils of the then new tax: *'la TVA … est rongée par un mal sournois: la complexité'*.[141] The concept of complexity naturally recalls that of its contrary, i.e., simplicity, a principle which is also perceived as a means to achieve economic neutrality.[142] Unfortunately, accomplishing such a goal is far from simple.[143] And indeed, opinions split on how an allegedly complex tax system should be simplified - if anything.[144] Thus, it is no wonder that a tax system's overhaul may, ultimately, fail to simplify that system[145] or may, actually, render it even more complex[146], in a way that only a hollow appearance of simplicity is achieved.[147]

137. NL: ECJ, 5 July 2012, Case C-259/11, *DTZ Zadelhoff vof v. Staatssecretaris van Financiën*, para. 42.
138. M.E. van Hilten, *Over Neutraliteit van de Omzetbelasting en Het Hellend Vlak van de Uitzonderingen* at 47 (Kluwer Deventer 2010), cited by C. Amand, *VAT Neutrality: A Principle of EU Law or a Principle of the VAT System?*, 2 World J. VAT/GST L. 3 (2013), at 164 note 8, after analysing more than one hundred and forty CJEU's cases, concludes that, while the Court always refers to 'the' neutrality, fiscal neutrality is a broad concept, i.e., there is no single fiscal neutrality, but instead one for competition and another for the interpretation of VAT exemptions.
139. *See* e.g., UK: ECJ, 12 Oct. 2017, Case C-262/16, *Shields & Sons Partnership v. The Commissioners for Her Majesty's Revenue and Customs*, para. 41.
140. DE: Opinion of the Advocate General, 8 May 2012, Case C-44/11, *Finanzamt Frankfurt am Main V-Höchst v. Deutsche Bank AG*, para. 60.
141. 'VAT … is consumed by an insidious evil: complexity' [author's unofficial translation]. *See* M. Lauré, *Au Secours de la TVA* at 48 (Presses Universitaires de France 1957).
142. Van Doesum et al., *supra* n. 71, at 38.
143. S. James, *The Complexity of Tax Simplification: The UK Experience*, in *The Complexity of Tax Simplification*, at 229-246 (S. James, A. Sawyer & T. Budak eds, Palgrave Macmillan 2016).
144. *See* PL: Opinion of the Advocate General, 5 Sep. 2018, Case C-422/17, *Szef Krajowej Administracji Skarbowej v. Skarpa Travel sp. z o.o. w Krakowie*, para. 79, in which Advocate General Bobek refers - certainly not without a veil of irony - to the existence of a 'diversity in simplification'.
145. R. Vann, *Improving Tax Law Improvement: An International Perspective*, 12 Austl. Tax F. 2 (1995), at 193-246.
146. *See* DE: Opinion of the Advocate General, 5 Sep. 2018, Case C-552/17, *Alpenchalets Resorts GmbH v. Finanzamt München Abteilung Körperschaften*, para. 65, where Advocate General Bobek maintained that, 'despite the heralded objective of simplification', the Tour Operators' Margin Scheme (i.e., 'TOMS', Arts 306-310 of the VAT Directive) 'has become one of the most complex areas of VAT'.
147. Such appearance of simplicity has been termed 'simplexity' by some. *See* J.D. Blank & L. Osofsky, *Simplexity: Plain Language and the Tax Law*, 66 Emory L. J. 2 (2016), at 189-264.

Simplicity is measured in two distinct ways, notably by looking at compliance efforts for taxpayers as well as at administrative costs for tax authorities.[148] Indeed, both forms of savings resulting from a commitment to simplicity ensure the fulfilment of the Smithian endeavour to an 'economy of tax collection'.[149]

Compliance costs measure the resources, in terms of time and money, wasted by taxpayers to meet their own obligations within a tax system. Notably, compliance costs are low when tax rules are plain and simple, so that taxpayers are able to understand in advance and in full the tax consequences of their own activities.[150] Inasmuch as it affects the predictability of tax consequences for taxable persons, simplicity also relates to legal certainty. In the field of EU VAT, the introduction of legal presumptions, generalizing classification, or lump-sum rules could indeed represent a viable solution to lower compliance costs.[151] This is the case of all those indicia which can be used by a supplier to determine the status of a customer.[152] Another way to simplify the application of EU VAT could be the enactment of a simplified registration and collection regime.[153] Indeed, measures like the One-Stop-Shop (OSS) scheme[154] or those concerning 'intra-Community trade'[155] intend to fulfil, precisely, this scope.

Administrative costs, instead, measure the resources, in terms of time and money, spent by tax authorities to implement and operate a tax system. Notably, administrative costs are low when tax rules facilitate the collection of the amount due with little or no controversies between taxable persons and tax authorities.[156] In the field of VAT, a significant reduction of administrative costs could be pursued by

148. J. Slemrod & J. Bakija. *Taxing Ourselves: A Citizen's Guide to the Debate over Taxes* at 159-188 (MIT Press 2008).
149. Smith, *supra* n. 21, at Part Three 'Of Taxes'.
150. As a well ago maintained by the Italian philosopher Tommaso Campanella (1568-1639), 'excellent laws are those few and short, as they accord with people's habits and the common good. Tyrannical laws instead trap with strings that are useful only to one or a few persons, as they do not accord with people's habits but benefit only those few who made them'. ['Le leggi ottime sono le poche e brevi che si accordano al costume del popolo e al bene comune. Le leggi tiranniche sono molti lacciuoli che ad uno o a pochi sono utili, e non si accordano col costume pubblico, purché crescano gli pochi autori di esse'.] [author's unofficial translation]. *See* T. Campanella, *Aforismi Politici [Political Aphorisms]* (1601).
151. Englisch, *supra* n. 96, at para. 11.3.3.
152. OECD, *Mechanisms for the Effective Collection of VAT/GST When the Supplier Is Not Located in the Jurisdiction of Taxation* at 31-32 (OECD Publishing 2017), listing a series of indicia to identify the status of a customer, such as a VAT registration number, a certificate issued by the customer's competent tax authority, information available in commercial registers, as well as a cluster of commercial indicia.
153. *Id.*, at 35-53, listing various simplification measures, such as online registration, simplified VAT returns, electronic payment methods, record keeping, and invoicing.
154. Council Directive 2002/38/EC of 7 May 2002 amending and amending temporarily Directive 77/388/EEC as regards the Value Added Tax Arrangements Applicable to Radio and Television Broadcasting Services and Certain Electronically Supplied Services, OJ L 128/41 of 15 May 2002.
155. Council Directive (EU) 2018/1910 of 4 December 2018 amending Directive 2006/112/EC as regards the Harmonisation and Simplification of Certain Rules in the Value Added Tax System for the Taxation of Trade between Member States, OJ L 311/3 of 5 Dec. 2018.
156. Due, *supra* n. 24, at 312, epitomizes such concept as follows: 'the tax must be feasible of administration, with tolerable levels of enforcement attained at reasonable costs of collection and taxpayer compliance'.

increasing registration thresholds and, thus, reducing the number of taxable persons that tax authorities need to monitor and audit.[157]

The principle of simplicity may equally serve other equally desirable ends. For one thing, the principle of simplicity is used for tax design reasons. Notably, a simplicity argument lies behind the historical inclusion in the VAT Directive of a provision like Article 16(1), concerning the application or the disposal free-of-charge by a taxable person of goods forming part of his business assets for his private use or for that of his own staff.[158]

Simplicity is also of importance in the application of the VAT Directive, for instance in order to determine the place of supply in each individual case. Notably, in *Aro Lease*, concerning the determination of the place of supply in case of the hiring-out of forms of transport, the CJEU concluded that neither the physical placing of vehicles at customer disposal under leasing agreements nor the place at which those vehicles were actually used could be regarded as 'a clear, simple and practical criterion' for place of supply purposes.[159]

Simplicity may also assist the application of a far-flung doctrine like that on composite supplies. Notably, in *Dudda*, Advocate General Fennelly maintained that 'to seek unnecessarily to separate the various elements of the plaintiff's business, in order to define for each one a distinct place of supply' would have gone against 'the practical interest in simplicity of administration and collection'.[160]

Simplicity can even serve to extend the application of EU VAT provisions. Notably, the VAT Committee has warmly recommended the application of Article 9a of the Implementing Regulation 'as widely as possible in the interest of simplicity'.[161]

And yet, despite having all the allure of being the opposite of complexity, simplicity is not an absolute aim. Rather, it should be carefully balanced out with a series of other equally important principles. Thus, for all its evils, complexity is not always a tenable justification for simplicity.[162]

---

157. OECD, *supra* n. 26, at 77; OECD, *supra* n. 152, at 29.
158. European Commission, *Proposal for a Sixth Council Directive on the Harmonization of Member States concerning Turnover Taxes Common System of Value Added Tax: Uniform Basis of Assessment (submitted to the Council by the Commission on 29 June 1973)*, at 10, COM(73) 950, Bulletin of the European Communities No. 11 (1973).
159. NL: ECJ, 17 Jul. 1997, Case C-190/95, *ARO Lease BV v. Inspecteur van de Belastingdienst Grote Ondernemingen te Amsterdam*, paras 20 and 26.
160. DE: Opinion of the Advocate General, 25 Apr. 1996, Case C-327/94, *Jürgen Dudda v. Finanzgericht Bergisch Gladbach*, para. 35.
161. European Commission, Value Added Tax Committee, *Working Paper No. 885. VAT 2015: Harmonized Application of the Presumption; Article 9a of the VAT Implementing Regulation*, at 3 (taxud.c.1(2015)4659331).
162. For instance, in *MacDonald* (UK: ECJ, 16 Dec. 2010, Case C-270/09, *Macdonald Resorts Ltd v. The Commissioners for Her Majesty's Revenue & Customs*, paras 35-37), the Court did not follow the method of apportionment, for the purposes of attributing taxing rights over a supply between two Member States, suggested in his opinion by Advocate General Trstenjak, since the only justification of the proposed method was to simplify the administrative tasks required to the taxpayer.

§3.07 FLEXIBILITY

The principle of flexibility describes the thorough ability and readiness of a tax system to respond to changes in societal and economic circumstances.[163] Based on such understanding, the Ottawa Framework Conditions stipulate that 'the systems for the taxation should be flexible and dynamic to ensure that they keep pace with technological and commercial developments'.[164] Flexibility is, thus, a principle intrinsically driven by a societal and an economic purpose, which essentially reflects the need to adjust the tax system to the transformation of society and the economy.[165]

Flexibility was indeed crucial for the development of EU law through the years. As the CJEU observed quite early on in *CILFIT*, 'every provision of Community [now EU] law must be placed in its context and interpreted in the light of the provision of Community [EU] law as a whole, regard being had to the objectives thereof and to its state of evolution at the date which the provision in question is to be applied'.[166]

Flexibility is also an instrument to evaluate legislative drafting. In this connection, the more specific legal provisions are, the less flexible those provisions would be.[167] In the EU, soft law measures, such as the guidelines drafted by the VAT Committee or the explanatory notes issued by the Commission, respond precisely to a demand of flexibility in legislative drafting.[168] And indeed, although neither of the above instruments is binding, the importance of 'soft tax coordination' in our globalized era can by no means be underestimated.[169]

Nevertheless, the principle of flexibility is not the Holy Grail. Legal stability, its exact opposite, is in fact an equally important aim to safeguard. A sufficient level of legal stability, indeed, needs to be maintained as to allow taxable persons to take reasonably far-sighted economic decisions. In this connection, the more openly written legal provisions are, the less legally stable those provisions would be.[170] In the EU, hard law measures such as regulations and directives respond precisely to a demand of legal stability.[171] And indeed, although neither infinite flexibility nor changeless legal

163. J.E. Stiglitz, *Economics of the Public Sector.* 3rd ed. at 466-467 (W.W. Norton & Company Inc. 2000).
164. OECD, *supra* n. 25, at 4.
165. Meade, *supra* n. 22, at 21.
166. IT: ECJ, 6 Oct. 1982, Case C-283/81, *Srl CILFIT and Lanificio di Gavardo SpA v. Ministry of Health*, para. 20.
167. Rendahl, *supra* n. 123, at para. 7.4.6.
168. Advocate General Kokott has emphasized the importance of the guidelines issued by the VAT Committee, by describing them as a valid 'aid to interpretation'. *See* PL: Opinion of the Advocate General, 31 Jan. 2013, Case C-155/12, *Minister Finansów v. RR Donnelley Global Turnkey Solutions Poland Sp. z.o.o.*, paras 46-51. For a discussion, *see* M. Lamensch, *The Use of Soft Law by the European VAT Legislator, and What the CJEU Makes of It*, in *CJEU – Recent Developments in Value Added Tax 2015*, at 21-50 (M. Lang et al. eds, Linde 2016).
169. P. Pistone, *Soft Tax Coordination: A Suitable Path for the OECD and the European Union to Address the Challenges of International Double (Non-)Taxation in VAT/GST Systems*, in *Value Added tax and Direct Taxation – Similarities and Differences*, at 8 (M. Lang, P. Melz & E. Kristoffersson eds, IBFD 2009).
170. Rendahl, *supra* n. 123, at para. 7.4.6.
171. *See* points 4 and 5 of the Preamble of the Implementing Regulation, recalling the need 'to ensure uniform application of the current VAT system ... in particular in respect of taxable persons, the

stability are desirable as outcomes, it is clear enough that a proper balance between the two is to be sought.[172]

The idea of flexibility as that of a principle which allows a tax system to keep pace with changes occurring in society and the economy is also acknowledged in the CJEU's case law. Notably, such understanding is well displayed in the opinion rendered by Advocate General Kokott in *Solleveld*, where it was reasoned that the definition of 'medical care' contained in Article 132(1)(c) of the VAT Directive should be 'sufficiently flexible to allow alternative and interdisciplinary methods of treatment recognized as care'.[173]

The principle of flexibility was even recalled by the CJEU in the context of interpreting and applying certain vague and undefined expressions included in the VAT Directive.[174] One of those expressions relates to the concept of 'gift of small value' contained in Article 16(2) of the VAT Directive. Notably, in *EMI Group*, Advocate General Jääskinen reasoned that, although disregarding the quantitatively fixed threshold established by a Member State for the application of that rule would contradict the requirement to provide a uniform treatment to all taxable persons, 'the implementation measures undertaken by Member States should [however] allow for some flexibility, in exceptional cases, in relation to the application of quantitative limits set'.[175]

The principle of flexibility also plays a role in a few administrative matters. Notably, in the CJEU's case law, flexibility was invoked in relation to the possibility for a transaction to be exempt[176], the choice of the most appropriate apportionment method to deduct input VAT[177], the imposition of a VAT liability on a taxable person[178], as well as the collection of VAT debts from a taxable person in financial distress[179].

supply of goods and services, and the place of taxable transactions' and 'to bring uniform treatment throughout the Union'. For a discussion, *see* I. Lejeune, E. Cortvriend & D. Accorsi, *Implementing Measures Relating to EU Place-of-Supply Rules: Are Business Issues Solved and Is Certainty Provided?*, 22 Intl. VAT Monitor 3 (2011), Journals IBFD.

172. D. (Dennis) Weber & T. Sirithaporn, *Chapter 11: Legal Certainty, Legitimate Expectations, Legislative Drafting, Harmonization and Legal Enforcement in EU Tax Law*, in *Principles of Law: Function, Status and Impact in EU Tax Law*, at para. 11.1.1. (C. Brokelind ed., IBFD 2014).
173. NL: Opinion of the Advocate General, 15 Dec. 2005, Joined Cases C-443/04 and C-444/04, *H.A. Solleveld and J.E. van den Hout-van Eijnsbergen v. Staatssecretaris van Financiën*, para. 69.
174. In this connection, R. de la Feria, *Chapter 12 – VAT and the EU Internal Market: The Paradoxes of Harmonization*, in *Traditional and Alternative Routes to European Tax Integration: Primary Law, Secondary Law, Soft Law, Coordination, Comitology and Their Relationship*, at para. 12.4.2. (D. (Dennis) Weber ed., IBFD 2010) distinguishes between 'macro-flexibility' and 'micro-flexibility'. The former is achieved by the inclusion within the VAT Directive of general exceptions, options and, in some areas of the EU VAT system, a high degree of discretion as regards the implementation of provisions. Micro-flexibility, instead, is the result of the numerous authorizations granted to Member States to derogate from the provisions of the VAT Directive.
175. UK: Opinion of the Advocate General, 15 Apr. 2010, Case C-581/08, *EMI Group Ltd v. The Commissioners for Her Majesty's Revenue and Customs*, para. 95.
176. SW: Opinion of the Advocate General, 6 May 2010, Case C-84/09, *X v. Skatteverket*, para. 53.
177. DE: Opinion of the Advocate General, 26 Apr. 2012, Case C-511/10, *Finanzamt Hildesheim v. BLC Baumarkt GmbH & Co. KG*, para. 42.
178. PL: Opinion of the Advocate General, 15 May 2014, Case C-605/12, *Welmory sp. Z.o.o. v. Dyrektor Izby Skarbowej w Gdańsku*, paras 27 and 30.
179. IT: Opinion of the Advocate General, 14 Jan. 2016, Case C-546/14, *Proceedings brought by Degano Trasporti Sas di Ferrucio Degano & C.*, para. 37.

At times, flexibility can even support the application of other principles. Notably, in relation to the principle of neutrality, Member States are obliged to take into account changes in the degree of private use of an input by a business for determining the proportion of deductible input VAT.[180]

In sum, although advances in ICT might hold in favour of adopting a more flexible approach in drafting, interpreting, and applying legal provisions, it is quite indisputable that too much flexibility breeds legal instability. Thus, in a 'good' tax system, a proper balance between flexibility and legal stability is to be sought.[181]

§3.08 PROPORTIONALITY

Historically, the principle of proportionality passed into EU legislation and case law from the French and German legal traditions.[182] Notably, under those legal systems, the principle was meant to regulate the maximum level of intervention of public powers in the context of a federal state. As a principle of public law, proportionality was further understood as an 'expression of the general right of the citizen toward the state that his freedom should be limited by the public authorities only to the extent indispensable for the protection of public interest'.[183]

Similarly, in tax matters, the principle of proportionality is used to justify the competence of a state to impose taxes and, further, to limit the scope of that competence. Moreover, the principle of proportionality is used to determine the ways in which the tax burden should be distinctly allocated among taxpayers, even in a cross-border dimension.[184]

Indeed, the role of proportionality in the field of EU VAT is overwhelming.[185] For instance, the principle of proportionality is used to assess the actual liability of a person participating in a VAT fraud[186], in so far as there is a need to strike an appropriate balance between the protection of neutrality and that of tax revenues.[187] A rule of

---

180. DE: Opinion of the Advocate General, 16 May 2002, Case C-269/00, *Wolfgang Seeling v. Finanzamt Starnberg*, para. 28.
181. Rendahl, *supra* n. 123, at para. 3.6.5.
182. T. Tridimas, *The Principle of Proportionality*, in *Oxford Principles of European Union Law*, at 243-264 (R Schütze & T. Tridimas eds, Oxford University Press 2018).
183. J. Schwarze, *European Administrative Law* at 690 (Sweet & Maxwell 1992).
184. D. Freyer, *The Proportionality Principle under EU Tax Law: General and Practical Problems Caused by Its Extensive Application – Part 1*, 57 Eur. Taxn. 9 (2017), Journals IBFD; D. Freyer, *The Proportionality Principle under EU Tax Law: General and Practical Problems Caused by Its Extensive Application – Part 2*, 57 Eur. Taxn. 10 (2017), Journals IBFD.
185. J.D. Rolim, *Proportionality and Fair Taxation*, 43 Intertax 5 (2015), at 405-409.
186. M.T. Soler Roch, *The Principle of Proportionality and the Prevention of Fraud in VAT*, in *VAT in an EU and International Perspective: Essays in Honor of Han Kogels*, at 81-90 (H. van Arendonk, S. Jansen, R. van der Paardt eds, IBFD 2011).
187. *See* e.g., UK: ECJ, 27 Sep. 2007, Case C-409/04, *The Queen, on the Application of Teleos plc and Others v. Commissioners of Customs & Excise*, paras 45, 47, 52 and 58.

proportionality is also observed for determining the extent to which a taxable person should be entitled to deduct his input VAT.[188]

Other than a principle of its own right, the principle of proportionality represents an important instrument of legal methodology, which is used to evaluate the opportunity to deviate from other principles, viz. the principles of equality, neutrality, and simplicity, as well as a rule of reason to solve conflicts between opposing principles. Notably, proportionality is the main methodological rule that the CJEU adopts in its decision-making process.[189] It helps the Court maintain a sufficiently broad approach in its legal appraisal and, further, it serves to reconcile opposing principles. And indeed, proportionality is the condition for accepting an override of other EU law principles, that is for prescribing how, in each individual case, a conflict between two or more EU law principles must be brought to an end.[190]

In the evaluation framework proposed in the present study, the principle of proportionality is used precisely in this latter acceptation, i.e., as an instrument of legal methodology to solve conflicts between opposing principles through an assessment of their relative weight in each individual case. Indeed, the role of proportionality in this regard is particularly significant, as long as no principle in the evaluation framework is more important than any other and, further, since, assumedly, no hierarchy between the selected principles exists.[191]

188. *See* e.g., FR: ECJ, 19 Sep. 2000, Joined Cases C-177/99 and C-181/99, *Ampafrance SA v. Directeur des services fiscaux de Maine-et-Loire and Sanofi Synthelabo v. Directeur des services fiscaux du Val-de-Marne*, para. 69.
189. Tridimas, *supra* n. 182, at 243.
190. Englisch, *supra* n. 96, at para. 11.2.
191. For a different appraisal, *see* Rendahl, *supra* n. 123, at paras 3.7.2.-3.8, who instead puts the principle of 'place of consumption' at the centre of her 'Spider's Web' evaluation framework, based on the assumption that 'the other criteria in the evaluation model could be seen as a means for reaching the goal of achieving taxation in the place of consumption'. At the same time, however, she plainly admits that 'the place of consumption principle may ... be affected by other criteria'.

Part III Selected European VAT Propositions

CHAPTER 4
Taxable Persons

§4.01 INTRODUCTION

As a first condition to apply EU VAT on a transaction, the person making the transaction in question must be a 'taxable person'. The present chapter aims to filter out the main characteristics of the concept of 'taxable persons'. More specifically, the ensuing analysis seeks to explore whether all persons in the sharing economy, in particular platforms and individual suppliers, shall be considered as taxable persons or not.

The concept of 'taxable person' (in French, *'assujetti'*; in Italian, *'soggetto passivo'*) marks out the external boundaries of EU VAT, as it defines the subjective or personal scope of the tax. Importantly, the attribution to a person of the status of 'taxable person' must not be confused to the actual maintenance by that person of an 'objective liability to tax', resulting in a requirement for that person to collect and remit the tax.[1] As will be explained later in Chapter 8, although these two statuses may be – and, indeed, frequently are – attributed to the same person[2] and, further,

1. *See* NL: Opinion of the Advocate General, 2 Mar. 1982, Case C-89/81, *Staatssecretaris van Financiën v. Hong-Kong Trade Development Council*, para. 2, considering that 'since the provisions of the directive on objective liability to tax and on exemptions make it possible that taxable persons are nevertheless not liable to tax ..., the concept of "taxable person" ... clearly covers a wider group of persons than those who are actually liable to tax'.
2. *See* Art. 193 of the VAT Directive. Under such provision, the supplier, in fact, is both a taxable person and the person who is responsible for collection and remittance of VAT. Noteworthy, attribution to the same person of the two aforementioned statuses might also arise if the reverse charge mechanism applies, so that the customer is designated as both the taxable person and the person liable for collection and remittance of VAT. *See*, in particular, Arts 194 and 196 of the VAT Directive.

notwithstanding the relevant provisions in this connection should arguably be read in parallel[3], several exceptions to such an overlap are laid down in the VAT Directive.[4]

EU VAT has always provided a definition of the concept of 'taxable person'. Notably, Article 4 of the Second Directive defined a taxable person as 'any person who independently and habitually engages in transactions pertaining to the activities of producers, traders or persons providing services, whether or not for gain'. Under Article 4 of the Sixth Directive, in the text as finally adopted, a taxable person was instead defined as 'any person who independently carries out in any place any economic activity specified in paragraph 2, whatever the purpose or results of that activity'. To that effect, paragraph 2 of the same article stipulated that 'the economic activities referred to in paragraph 1 shall comprise all activities of producers, traders and persons supplying services including mining and agricultural activities and activities of the professions. The exploitation of tangible or intangible property for the purpose of obtaining income therefrom on a continuing basis shall also be considered an economic activity'.

This latter definition has passed substantially unchanged in the text of the VAT Directive. Pursuant to Article 9(1) of the VAT Directive, a taxable person in fact is currently described as anyone 'who independently carries out in any place any economic activity, whatever the purpose or result of that activity'. From the definition of Article 9(1) of the VAT Directive, it appears that four distinctive elements are of importance for a person to be regarded as a 'taxable person', that is:

(1) any person;
(2) in any place;
(3) economic activity;
(4) independently.

All these four elements make reference to the fulfilment by a person of substantial conditions rather than just to formal requirements, such as the maintenance by a person of a legal personality[5] or a separate tax identification number[6]. Notably, in excluding that a marital community could constitute a taxable person for EU VAT purposes, the CJEU took account not only of the formal circumstance that the community formed by the spouses did not in effect possess any legal personality, but,

3. European Commission, *Proposal for a Sixth Council Directive on the Harmonisation of Member States concerning Turnover Taxes Common System of Value Added Tax: Uniform Basis of Assessment (submitted to the Council by the Commission on 29 June 1973)*, at 8, COM(73) 950, Bulletin of the European Communities No. 11 (1973).
4. *See*, in particular, Arts 204 and 205 of the VAT Directive, laying down specific liability regimes for, respectively, tax representatives and persons who are held jointly and severally liable for payment of VAT.
5. *See* UK: ECJ, 22 Dec. 2010, Case C-277/09, *The Commissioners for Her Majesty's Revenue & Customs v. RBS Deutschland Holdings GmbH*, para. 53, considering that taxable persons 'are generally free to choose the organizational structures and the form of transactions which they consider to be most appropriate for their economic activities and for the purposes of limiting their tax burdens'.
6. PT: ECJ, 7 Aug. 2018, Case C-16/17, *TGE Gas Engineering GmbH – Sucursal em Portugal v. Autoridade Tributária e Aduaneira*, paras 42-43.

from a more substantial standpoint, the Court also considered the fact that such a community 'did not itself carry out an economic activity either as a civil law partnership with its own legal personality or in a form which, although without legal personality, was in fact able to act independently'.[7] It follows that the status of taxable person cannot be achieved in the absence of substantive requirements. Lastly, it should also be recalled that, in certain instances, the VAT Directive provides that 'anyone' must be considered as a taxable person. Notably, this occurs with regard to occasional suppliers of new means of transport in another Member State[8], as well as in relation to importation of goods from third countries or territories[9].

Other than the extension of scope entailed in the above situations, it seems that even the concept of 'taxable person' as meant in Article 9(1) of the VAT Directive must receive a broad understanding and that, to that effect, the four conditions laid down therein shall be interpreted widely. Notably, this circumstance could have already been assumed from a reading of the Proposal for a Second Directive, which, in this connection, stipulated that 'should a Member State propose ... not to tax certain activities, it will be better to provide for exemptions rather than to exclude the persons exercising these activities from the scope of the tax'.[10] Such statement found a confirmation in the text of the Second Directive as finally adopted.[11] Certainly, a broad interpretation of the concept of 'taxable person' better complies, *inter alia*, with the principles of equality and neutrality underpinning EU VAT. In this connection, the Explanatory Memorandum accompanying the Proposal for a Sixth Directive maintained that 'the new definition of taxable persons demonstrates the concern which exists that the field of application of value added tax, in keeping with its character as a general tax on consumption, should be extended to cover all economic activities, whenever they take place, and all transactions which are in the nature of such economic activities but which may be carried out separately or occasionally. Such transactions should be taxed in order to ensure impartial application of the tax, particularly as regards supplies of immovable property'.[12]

An extension of the concept of 'taxable persons' is also entailed in its geographical reach, which indeed is not limited to the territorial scope of application of EU VAT. This simple fact can be derived from a plain reading of Article 9(1) of the VAT Directive, stipulating that an economic activity can be carried out by a person 'in any place'. In this connection, the Explanatory Memorandum accompanying the Proposal for a Sixth Directive stipulated that 'the definition of a taxable person, although applicable only in the Member State, is not confined to the boundaries of the

7. DE: ECJ, 21 Apr. 2005, Case C-25/03, *Finanzamt Bergisch Gladbach v. HE*, paras 54-55.
8. Article 9(2) VAT Directive.
9. Articles 2(1)(d) and 30 VAT Directive.
10. European Commission, *Proposal for a Second Directive for the Harmonisation among Member States of Turnover Tax Legislation, concerning the Form and Methods of Application of the Common System of Taxation on Value Added*, at Annex A 2 Second Indent, COM(65) 144 final, Supplement to the Bulletin of the European Economic Community No. 5 (1965).
11. Annex A 2 of the Second Directive.
12. European Commission, *supra* n. 3, at 8.

Community; this is in order to make the tax more impartial with regard to the place where undertakings may be carrying on business'.[13]

Out of the four elements laid down in Article 9(1) of the VAT Directive for a person to be regarded as a 'taxable person', two in particular deserve closer attention in the context of the sharing economy. The first element relates to whether the activity performed, respectively, by the platform and by the individual supplier can indeed be considered as an 'economic activity' in full EU VAT terms. The second element, instead, concerns whether the activity in question is effectively carried out by those undertakings 'independently' or not. An analysis of these two elements is provided in the following sections. Instead, the two other elements of 'any person' and 'any place' laid down above are not specifically discussed, since the broad subjective and geographical scope entailed in those expressions is not sufficiently determinative of the taxable status of a person.

§4.02 ECONOMIC ACTIVITY

Article 9(1) of the VAT Directive refers to the concept of 'economic activity' (in French, '*activité économique*'; in Italian, '*attività economica*') as a requirement for an activity to be subject to EU VAT. Apparently, the CJEU equates such expression to that of 'taxable transactions' (in French, '*opérations imposables*'; in Italian, '*operazioni imponibili*')[14], which is used in other provisions of the VAT Directive[15]. Terra and Kajus, however, maintain that the expression 'economic activity' should be distinguished from that of 'taxable transactions', as long as the term 'activity' includes both 'transactions' and other operations which directly or indirectly are necessary to conclude taxable transactions.[16] In their opinion, this circumstance can in particular be inferred from *Rompelman*, a case in which the CJEU affirmed that even preparatory acts, in the form of an initial investment made by a taxable person with the intention to carry out an 'economic activity', gave rise for that person to a right to deduct input VAT, despite no output transaction was, in effect, subsequently made.[17] Whether these considerations are ultimately persuasive or not, it seems clear enough that the two concepts eventually overlap in case of output transactions, i.e., in the context of levying VAT on the activities carried out by a taxable person.[18] Rather than the concept of 'activity', however, it is the adjective 'economic' whose assessment is far more engaging.

13. *Ibid.*
14. *See* HU: ECJ, 2 Jun. 2016, Case C-263/15, *Lajvér Meliorációs Nonprofit Kft. and Lajvér Csapadékvízrendezési Nonprofit Kft. v. Nemzeti Adó- és Vámhivatal*, paras 21-24, where the two expressions are used interchangeably.
15. In particular, in Titles IV and V of the VAT Directive. With regard to the concept of 'taxable transactions', *see* Chapters 5 and 6.
16. B.J.M. Terra & J. Kajus, *Commentary on European VAT* at para. 3.2.3. (IBFD Tax Research Platform 2019).
17. NL: ECJ, 14 Feb. 1985, Case C-268/83, *D.A. Rompelman and E.A. Rompelman-Van Deelen v. Minister van Financiën*, paras 22-23. *See also* IR: ECJ, 17 Oct. 2018, Case C-249/17, *Ryanair Ltd v. The Revenue Commissioners*, para. 31.
18. *See* e.g., PL: ECJ, 16 Nov. 2017, Case C-308/16, *Kozuba Premium Selection sp. z o.o., v. Dyrektor Izby Skarbowej w Warszawie*, paras 24-27.

[A] Economic

Article 9(1), second paragraph, of the VAT Directive lists a series of activities – 'any activity of producers, traders or persons supplying services, including mining and agricultural activities and activities of the professions' – which shall be considered as 'economic activities', and notes, at the third paragraph, that the 'exploitation of tangible or intangible property for the purposes of obtaining income therefrom on a continuing basis' shall – 'in particular'[19] – be regarded as such.

In principle, activities of an economic nature alone are subject to EU VAT.[20] Nevertheless, the CJEU has attributed to such expression a very wide meaning.[21] Indeed, several elements hold in favour of an extensive interpretation of this concept.

First, for being 'economic', not necessarily an activity shall be profitable. Article 9(1) of the VAT Directive in fact stipulates that a person who, independently, carries out an economic activity, must be considered as a taxable person 'whatever the purpose or result of that activity' (in French, '*quells que soient les buts ou les résultats de cette activité*'; in Italian, '*indipendentemente dallo scopo o dai risultati di detta attività*'). In this connection, the wording of Article 4 of the Second Directive was even more open, since it considered as a taxable person any person engaged in an economic activity, 'whether or not for gain'. It follows that the expression 'economic activity' is 'objective in character, in the sense that the activity is considered *per se* and without regard to its purpose or results' (emphasis original).[22] As further reasoned by the CJEU in *BLP Group*, it would in fact be contrary to the objectives of ensuring legal certainty and facilitating the application of EU VAT if the tax authorities, 'save in exceptional cases', instead of making reference to 'the objective character of the transaction in question', 'would have to carry out inquiries to determine the intention of the taxable person' concerned.[23]

The broad interpretation attributed to the expression 'economic activities', however, does not also imply that all sort of activities must necessarily be considered as such. Notably, activities performed free-of-charge remain well outside the scope of EU VAT. In *Hong Kong Trade Development Council*, the CJEU indeed clarified that, 'where a person's activity consists exclusively in providing services for no direct consideration ... the person providing services must be assimilated to a final consumer because he is at the final stage of the production and distribution chain'.[24] From this,

19. As used in this context, the expression 'in particular' apparently means 'also but not only', thus suggesting that even activities other than those involving the exploitation of tangible or intangible property might be regarded as economic activities under EU VAT. For a similar understanding, *see* DE: Opinion of the Advocate General, 28 Mar. 1996, Case C-230/94, *Renate Enkler v. Finanzamt Homburg*, para. 14.
20. *See* e.g., FR: ECJ, 11 July 1996, Case C-306/94, *Régie dauphinoise – Cabinet A. Forest SARL v. Ministre du Budget*, para. 15.
21. *See* e.g., PT: ECJ, 29 Oct. 2015, Case C-174/14, *Saudaçor – Sociedade Gestora de Recursos e Equipamentos da Saúde dos Açores SA v. Fazenda Pública*, para. 31.
22. NL: ECJ, 26 Mar. 1987, Case C-235/85, *Commission v. Netherlands*, para. 8.
23. UK: ECJ, 6 Apr. 1995, Case C-4/94, *BLP Group plc v. Commissioners of Customs & Excise*, para. 24.
24. NL: ECJ, 1 Apr. 1982, Case C-89/81, *Staatssecretaris van Financiën v. Hong-Kong Trade Development Council*, para. 10.

and having specific regard to the expression 'whatever the purpose or result of that activity', Terra and Kajus derive that a hobby should not be considered as an 'economic activity' in full EU VAT terms.[25]

Nevertheless, it should be recalled that, in certain instances, even the performance of an activity free-of-charge might assume relevance for EU VAT purposes. Notably, this occurs when a entailing some form of affiliation, exists between two or more parties to a transaction. In this connection, Article 26(1)(b) of the VAT Directive provides that EU VAT shall apply in case of 'services carried out free of charge by a taxable person for ... his staff or, more generally, for purposes other than those of his business', unless those services are 'provided for strictly business-related purposes', as found by the CJEU in *Danfoss and AstraZeneca*.[26] Further, in *Iberdrola Inmobiliaria Real Estate Investments*, the CJEU concluded that a taxable person is entitled to deduct input VAT relating to certain free-of-charge activities, in so far as those activities are carried out by that person in the furtherance of his economic activity as a whole.[27] Drawing inspiration from the old maxim '*donatio non praesumitur*', EU VAT therefore does not appear to take 'gratuitous transactions at their face value'.[28]

It is also important to recall that the CJEU has constantly ruled that no 'true' economic activity exists where only a symbolic payment is made.[29] Notably, in *Weald Leasing*, the CJEU held that 'unusually low payments' or – situation which apparently the Court paired to that – even payments 'not reflecting any economic reality' shall not be subject to the tax.[30] First, in *Lajver* and, then, in *Gemeente Borsele* the Court further extended the scope of such carveout, by including within it also the situation of transactions carried out for a fee other than *qua* (i.e., as for) consideration, although without providing any guidance in this regard.[31] Despite these latter protestations, the CJEU has repeated time and again that the circumstance that the price paid by the

25. Terra & Kajus, *supra* n. 16, at para. 3.2.5.
26. DK: ECJ, 11 Dec. 2008, Case C-371/07, *Danfoss A/S and AstraZeneca A/S v. Skatteministeriet*, para. 65.
27. BG: ECJ, 14 Sep. 2017, Case C-132/16, *Direktor na Direktsia 'Obzhalvane i danachno-osiguritelna praktika' – Sofia v. 'Iberdrola Inmobiliaria Real Estate Investments' EOOD*, para. 29.
28. UK: Opinion of the Advocate General, 15 Apr. 2010, Case C-581/08, *EMI Group Ltd v. The Commissioners for Her Majesty's Revenue and Customs*, para. 2. *See also* DE: Opinion of the Advocate General, 6 Mar. 2001, Case C-380/99, *Bertelsmann AG v. Finanzamt Wiedenbrück*, para. 37, where Advocate General Stix-Hackl observed that, 'for in the commercial world, it must generally be assumed that supplies are not provided gratuitously'.
29. *See* e.g., FR: ECJ, 21 Sep. 1988, Case C-50/87, *Commission v. France*, para. 21, considering the possibility that, 'because of the amount of the rent, the lease must necessarily be regarded as involving a concession and not as constituting an economic activity within the meaning of the directive'.
30. UK: ECJ, 22 Dec. 2010, Case C-103/09, *Commissioners for Her Majesty's Revenue & Customs v. Weald Leasing*, para. 39.
31. HU: ECJ, 2 June 2016, Case C-263/15, *Lajvér Meliorációs Nonprofit Kft. and Lajvér Csapadékvízrendezési Nonprofit Kft. v. Nemzeti Adó- és Vámhivatal*, para. 49. In *Gemeente Borsele*, the Court instead maintained that the contribution paid by pupils' parents to a Dutch municipality were to be regarded 'more as a fee than as consideration'. *See* NL: ECJ, 12 May 2016, Case C-520/14, *Gemeente Borsele v. Staatssecretaris van Financiën and Staatssecretaris van Financiën v. Gemeente Borsele*, para. 33.

customer is higher or lower than the cost price is, per se, irrelevant.[32] The amount on which VAT is charged, in fact, is set equal to the price effectively paid, whereas the possibility to refer to an 'open market value' within the meaning of Articles 73 and 80 of the VAT Directive is rather constrained.[33] Moreover, for the purposes of input VAT deduction, it does not count whether a taxable person makes supplies for a price 'considerably lower than the cost price', unless such price is 'purely symbolic'.[34]

Considering, first, the activity of a sharing economy platform, from *Hong Kong Trade Development Council* it follows that, where a platform does not charge anything to its users for all its services, the activity in question does not constitute an 'economic activity' under EU VAT and, therefore, the platform cannot be regarded as a taxable person for EU VAT purposes either.[35] Hence, platforms exclusively maintaining a not-for-profit orientation shall not be considered as taxable persons. Noteworthy, this is not the case of a platform like HomeExchange, where only some services (i.e., the messaging service) are provided to users for free.

A few considerations need to be made with regard to the provision of services by a platform to its users 'for free' but in return for user personal data. Should one take the view that personal data do not amount to a 'true' consideration[36] or, even, that a direct link between the provision of services by a platform and personal data provided to it by users is missing[37], then a question might arise on whether a sharing platform, which for its own services receives only personal data in return, carries out an economic activity for EU VAT purposes - or otherwise. From *Hong Kong Trade Development Council*, it might be assumed that such an activity cannot be regarded as an 'economic activity' for EU VAT purposes and, therefore, the platform is not a taxable person under EU VAT either. However, the non-linear functioning of new business models constantly

---

32. *See* e.g., SW: ECJ, 20 Jan. 2005, Case C-412/03, *Hotel Scandic Gåsabäck AB v. Riksskatteverket*, para. 22.
33. *See* e.g., BG: ECJ, 26 Apr. 2012, Joined Cases C-621/10 and C-129/11, *Balkan and Sea Properties ADSITS and Provadinvest OOD v. Direktor na Direktsia 'Obzhalvane i upravlenie na izpalnenieto' – Varna pri Tsentralno upravlenie na Natsionalnata agentsia za prihodite*, para. 51. Pursuant to Art. 72(1) of the VAT Directive, '"open market value" shall mean the full amount that, in order to obtain the goods or services in question at that time, a customer at the same marketing stage at which the supply of goods or services takes place, would have to pay, under conditions of fair competition, to a supplier at arm's length within the territory of the Member State in which the supply is subject to tax'. Point 2 of the Second Indent of Art. 72(2) of the VAT Directive further stipulates that 'where no comparable supply of goods or services can be ascertained, "open market value" shall mean ... in respect of services, an amount that is not less than the full cost to the taxable person of providing the service'.
34. NL: ECJ, 22 Jun. 2016, Case C-267/15, *Gemeente Woerden v. Staatssecretaris van Financiën*, para. 41. Noteworthy, in *Campsa Estaciones de Servicio*, the CJEU used the expression 'patently lower' rather than 'considerably lower'. However, it is not clear whether any distinction between the two expressions eventually exists or not. *See* ES: ECJ: 9 June 2011, Case C-285/10, *Campsa Estaciones de Servicio SA v. Administración del Estado*, para. 27.
35. European Commission, Value Added Tax Committee, *Working Paper No. 878. VAT Treatment of Sharing Economy*, at 10 (taxud.c.1(2015)4370160).
36. Certainly, this does not reflect the view held by the Commission, which indeed estimates that the value of EU citizens' personal data has the potential to grow to nearly EUR 1 trillion annually by 2020. *See* European Commission, *Questions and Answers – Data Protection Reform Package* (2017), http://europa.eu/rapid/press-release_MEMO-17-1441_en.htm (accessed 31 March 2019).
37. For a discussion of the concepts of 'consideration' and 'direct link', *see* Chapter 5.

emerging in the digital economy[38] might suggest a less narrow appraisal of the concept of 'economic activity'[39]. Indeed, in the author's opinion, such an issue has already been tackled by the CJEU to some extent. As recalled above, in *Iberdrola Inmobiliaria Real Estate Investments*, the CJEU has in fact affirmed that there is an economic activity, from which a right for a taxable person to deduct his input VAT arises, where the person in question carries out a free-of-charge activity, in so far as this is done by that person in the furtherance of his economic activity as a whole. Similar considerations can be applied to the situation of a sharing economy platform offering services to its users free-of-charge, provided that such an activity is necessary for that platform's economic activity as a whole, meaning that the platform is able to make a profit in another way, e.g., by offering its users the possibility to purchase products from third parties, which pay the platform a commission in return.

Similar observations can be advanced with regard to the activity of platform users. Where a user provides a service or his personal data to another party free-of-charge, neither the activity thereof indeed constitutes an 'economic activity' nor the user in question can be considered as a taxable person for EU VAT purposes. As stated, however, EU VAT requires not to take gratuitous transactions at their face value.[40] Thus, if those free-of-charge supplies, rendered either to another user or to the platform, are made by a user for strictly business-related purposes, as found by the CJEU in *Danfoss and AstraZeneca*, EU VAT shall be applied on those supplies and the person in question shall be regarded as a taxable person. Further, as ruled by the Court in *Iberdrola Inmobiliaria Real Estate Investments*, whether those free-of-charge supplies are made by a user in the furtherance of his economic activity as a whole, input VAT paid on acquisitions used for making those supplies can be deducted. Eventually, a different appraisal might be required in case a payment for a service is unusually low or does not reflect any economic reality, as maintained by the CJEU in *Weald Leasing*, or if a fee other than *qua* (i.e., as for) consideration is provided in return for a service, in light of the Court's decisions, first, in *Lajver* and, then, in *Gemeente Borsele*.

[B] Market Participation

Another condition, albeit not expressed in the wording of Article 9(1) of the VAT Directive, which must be fulfilled for an activity to be regarded as an 'economic activity' for EU VAT purposes, is that the person carrying out such activity shall take

38. In particular, in light of the possibility for a digital company to make a profit in various ways, at a different stage, and even from parties other than their users (e.g., offering its users the opportunity to readily purchase products through a link to a third party's website).
39. Indeed, a broader definition of the concept of 'economic activity' was favoured by a few delegations during the discussions taking place at a meeting of the VAT Committee in 2018. *See* European Commission, Value Added Tax Committee, *Minutes 111th Meeting – 30 November 2018*, at 7 (taxud.c.1(2019)1709500).
40. Whether a service is effectively provided 'for free', in fact, is a condition which must be ascertained extremely carefully. For a discussion in this regard, *see* S. Pfeiffer, *VAT on 'Free' Electronic Services?*, 27 Intl. VAT Monitor 3 (2016), Journals IBFD.

part in a market.[41] Notably, in *SPÖ Landesorganization Kärnten*, the CJEU concluded that the activity carried out by a section of a political party could not be regarded as an 'economic activity', because the political party in question did not eventually participate in any kind of market.[42] The Court has found likewise in other instances, notably where a public body did not ultimately carry out an economic activity because there was not enough evidence either of its participation in the relevant market or, even, of the existence of a market to participate into.[43] As to assess whether there is an 'economic activity' or not, especially in the public sector, the Court often takes a look at whether that activity is carried out in the same way as a comparable activity is carried out in the private field. More specifically, the Court compares the activity at stake with usual activities of the trades and professions referred to in the first sentence of the second subparagraph of Article 9(1) of the VAT Directive.[44]

There is little or no doubt that sharing economy platforms do participate in a market. Indeed, on closer inspection, it might even be argued that those platforms themselves contribute to create the market where their users meet. In this connection, it is useful to recall that the sharing economy is a dual-sided market, where two distinct groups of users interact via technological, commercial, and legal infrastructures set up by the platform, i.e., the 'market maker'.[45]

More elaboration, instead, requires providing an answer to the question whether, in every single instance, users do participate in a market. Notably, in case users provide a platform only with their own personal data, it might be argued that, as a matter of fact, they do not intend to participate in any kind of market and that permission for using personal data merely constitutes the price paid by those users to obtain services from the platform in question.[46] However, the author ultimately disagrees with this

41. NL: Opinion of the Advocate General, 23 Dec. 2015, Case C-520/14, *Gemeente Borsele v. Staatssecretaris van Financiën and Staatssecretaris van Financiën v. Gemeente Borsele*, paras 62-69. C. Heber, *Recent CJEU Case-Law on Public Bodies – A Comment*, in *ECJ – Recent Developments in Value Added Tax 2016*, at 182 (M. Lang. et al. eds, Linde 2017), however contends that reference to 'market participation' by Advocate General Kokott in *Gemeente Borsele* is 'unclear'.
42. AT: ECJ, 6 Oct. 2009, Case C-267/08, *SPÖ Landesorganisation Kärnten v. Finanzamt Klagenfurt*, paras 24-25.
43. Since Art. 13(1) First Indent of the VAT Directive stipulates that public bodies are not taxable persons in relation to 'the activities or transactions in which they engage as public authorities', as to evaluate fulfilment of this condition, indeed the Court is often required to determine whether a transaction takes place in a market or, instead, is outside the scope of any kind of market. *See* e.g., IR: ECJ, 19 Jan. 2017, Case C-344/15, *National Roads Authority v. The Revenue Commissioners*, paras 41-44.
44. *See also* A.A. Tait, *Value Added Tax: International Practice and Problems* at 368-369 (International Monetary Fund 1988), who lays down some tests to determine whether an economic activity must be subject to VAT. Among them, he includes a test relating to the 'appearance of business', meaning that 'the activities should have the characteristics of a normal commercial undertaking with some acceptable method of record keeping in place'.
45. *See* section §1.03.
46. *See* European Commission, Value Added Tax Committee, *Working Paper No. 958. Conditions for There Being a Taxable Transaction When Internet Services Are Provided in Exchange for User Data*, at 4-5 (taxud.c.1(2018)6248826), where the Commission argued that 'if individuals were given the possibility of paying a monetary price instead of granting that permission [to access and use their personal data] they might agree to pay that monetary price'. For quite similar considerations, *see* J. Kollmann, *Taxable Supplies and Their Consideration in European VAT* –

view and believes that the relevant question is not whether users, i.e., the customers of platform services, intend to participate in a market, rather only the factual circumstance that those users do participate in a market where, like in any kind of market, a number of services are thoroughly offered to customers by economic operators, as it evidently occurs on virtual marketplaces operated by sharing economy platforms.

As for individual suppliers, it is indisputable that activities such as those carried out by an Airbnb host or by an Uber driver do indeed involve the participation, respectively, in the accommodation and passenger transport markets. Only apparently, it might be found otherwise with regard to other sharing economy platforms. Notably, one might think that there is no such thing as a market for a spot on another person's sofa or for a seat on another person's car.[47] And yet, the sheer fact that sharing economy platforms like HomeExchange and BlaBlaCar, precisely providing those kinds of services to their users, exists demonstrates that in the sharing economy nearly everything, even a spot on another person's sofa or a seat on another person's car, can be marketized and that this can be done almost readily.[48] It also ought to be recalled that, in legal fields other than EU VAT – in particular, in the area of competition law –, the CJEU apparently considers the existence of 'a market' as amounting to anything more than the factual offering by a person of goods and services to potential customers.[49]

All in all, market participation does not appear the 'killer' factor for demonstrating the existence of an 'economic activity' in the context of the sharing economy.

[C] On a Continuing Basis

The concept of 'economic activity' further demands supplies to be made 'on a continuing basis'. Accordingly, occasional suppliers should, in principle, be excluded from the subjective or personal scope of the tax. Indeed, the need of a certain degree of continuity for having an economic activity in full EU VAT terms can be inferred from various provisions enshrined in the VAT Directive. Notably, Article 12(1) of the VAT

With Selected Examples of the Digital Economy at para. 6.2.3 (IBFD 2018). Such line of reasoning seems to be premised on the so-called 'active choice' models, i.e., models which refer to an active choice for users between paying for a digital service with money, but without any consent given to the service provider to access their own personal data, or rather accessing the service for free, but with a full disclosure of their own personal data. For a discussion in this regard, *see* P. Hacker & B. Petkova, *Reining in the Big Promise of Big Data: Transparency, Inequality, and New Regulatory Frontiers*, 15 Nw. J. Tech. & Intell. Prop. 1 (2017), at 1-42.

47. Worth mentioning, in *EDM*, Advocate General Léger argued that, in order to constitute an economic activity for EU VAT purposes, loans made by a holding company 'must be agreed on conditions which are comparable to the relevant market conditions, as though they had been agreed between a financial institution and its customers'. *See* PT: Opinion of Advocate General, 12 Sep. 2002, Case C-77/01, *Empresa de Desenvolvimento Mineiro SGPS SA (EDM) v. Fazenda Pública*, para. 45.
48. As O. Lobel, *The Law of the Platform*, 101 Minn. L. Rev. 1 (2016), at 90, observes, in the sharing economy 'what has been non-commodifiable is being brought into the market – whether it be a ride share, a spare bedroom, a pot on a waitlist, or a lawnmower loan'.
49. *See* e.g., ES: ECJ, 27 Jun. 2017, Case C-74/16, *Congregación de Escuelas Pías Provincia Betania Ayuntamiento de Getafe*, para. 45.

Directive grants Member States an option to treat certain occasional suppliers – 'in particular'[50] – of 'a building or parts of a building and of the land on which the building stands' as well as of 'building land' as taxable persons. Arguably, this provision would be rather superfluous if also incidental supplies were to be considered as economic activities by default.[51] And indeed, in this connection, recital 13 of the VAT Directive states that, 'in order to enhance the non-discriminatory nature of the tax, the term "taxable person" should be defined in such a way that the Member States may use it to cover persons who occasionally carry out certain transactions'.

Nevertheless, in the author's view, the idea of 'continuity', by no means, can be intended as absolute. Rather, the concept needs to be closely related to the peculiar nature of the activity at stake, which indeed might even consist in the mere exploitation of a tangible or intangible property. The second period of the second indent of Article 9(1) of the VAT Directive, in fact, stipulates that the 'exploitation of tangible or intangible property', such as the granting of loans, the leasing of immovable or movable property, and the licensing of patents, 'for the purposes of obtaining income therefrom on a continuing basis shall in particular be regarded as an economic activity'.[52] From this statement, it can be inferred that the exploitation of tangible or intangible property is usually regarded as an economic activity for EU VAT purposes, albeit subject to the relevant conditions that: (1) the purpose of the activity is 'to obtain income therefrom', and (2) income therefrom is derived by a person 'on a continuing basis'.[53]

50. By using the expression 'in particular', apparently, Art. 12 of the VAT Directive allows a Member State to consider as taxable persons for EU VAT purposes even occasional operators of supplies other than those listed therein. Noteworthy, it would no longer be possible to assume this standpoint under the new wording of Art. 12 of the VAT Directive, as proposed by the Commission, given that the expression 'in particular' is set to be removed. *See* European Commission, *Proposal for a Council Directive amending Directive 2006/112/EC as regards the Introduction of the Detailed Technical Measures for the Operation of the Definitive VAT System for the Taxation of Trade between Member States*, Art. 1(6), COM(2018) 329 final.
51. *See* A. van Doesum, H.W.M. van Kesteren & G.J. van Norden, *Fundamentals of EU VAT Law* at 61 (Kluwer Law International 2016). Similarly, DE: Opinion of the Advocate General, 25 Sep. 1990, Case C-186/89, *W.M. van Tiem v. Staatssecretaris van Financiën*, para. 12. B.J.M. Terra & J. Kajus, *Introduction to European VAT (Recast)* at para. 9.2.2. (IBFD Tax Research Platform 2019), however, contend that, from the provision of Art. 12 of the VAT Directive, it cannot be derived 'a contrario that activities must have a certain frequency in order to be qualified as relevant economic activities'.
52. Noteworthy, Art. 4(3)(a) of the Proposal for a Sixth Directive used the expression 'on a permanent basis', rather than 'on a continuing basis'. In this connection, Terra & Kajus, *supra* n. 16, at para. 3.3.2., note the 'anomaly' that 'the exploitation of tangible or intangible property for the purpose of obtaining income therefrom on a *permanent* basis' was included among the activities that might be *occasionally* carried out. Art. 4 of the Sixth Directive as finally adopted, however, employed the expression 'on a continuing basis' and, further, removed the aforesaid 'anomaly' (emphases original).
53. *See* Terra & Kajus, *supra* n. 51, at 9.2.1., arguing that 'the concept of "continuing" used in Article 9 cannot ... be construed as excluding the imposition of VAT on activities carried out on an occasional basis' and, further, noting that such term 'is used in the VAT Directive only in relation to a specific example of economic activity, i.e., the exploitation of tangible or intangible property, and is applied not to the activity itself but to the income obtained from that particular activity'.

The concept of 'exploitation' (in French, '*exploitation*'; in Italian, '*sfruttamento*') has been dealt with by the CJEU in a number of occasions. Notably, in *Van Tiem*, the CJEU ruled that, in light of the very wide scope of EU VAT, which is meant to cover all stages of production and distribution of services, the grant of building rights, whereby the grantee was authorized to use the immovable property for a specified period of time in return for consideration, entails a form of 'exploitation' and, as such, it does constitute an 'economy activity' for EU VAT purposes.[54] Also, in *Enkler*, a case concerning the exploitation of a tangible property – in the form of the hiring-out of a motor caravan by a private individual to third parties for a limited number of days, whereas for the remainder of the time the motor caravan was used for private purposes only –, the CJEU considered such an activity as an economic activity, whether carried on for the purpose of obtaining income on a continuing basis, this latter condition to be determined by the referring court in relation to the actual length of the period for which the property was hired, the number of customers, and the amount of earnings.[55] Based on the specific facts at stake in *Enkler*, involving the exploitation of a tangible property for a limited period of time, to a few customers, and in return for small earnings, one may well agree that 'the threshold for taxability is fairly low as regards services carried out on a continuous basis'.[56]

The author, however, submits that the concepts of 'economic activity' and 'exploitation' are neither synonyms nor interchangeable. Although both terms require an activity to be somehow repetitive, the 'continuity' requirement is, in fact, less important for blunt forms of exploitation of tangible or intangible property, such as indeed it was the purchase and immediate granting of building rights in *Van Tiem*, in so far as for those forms of economic activities 'regularity', rather than from the existence of a flow of transactions, stems from income being obtained on a continuing basis.[57] In a sense, it could be maintained that, as for the 'continuity' requirement, the activity, the income therefrom, or both must be provided 'on a continuing basis'.[58]

'Regularity' of an economic activity is certainly less important, and yet not bluntly irrelevant under EU VAT. Notably, in *Slaby and Others*, the Court considered that 'the simple acquisition and the mere sale of an asset' cannot amount to an exploitation of a property, intended to produce income on a continuing basis within the meaning of Article 9(1) of the VAT Directive, in so far as the sole consideration for

---

54. NL: ECJ, 4 Dec. 1990, Case C-186/89, *W.M. van Tiem v. Staatssecretaris van Financiën*, paras 16-20.
55. DE: ECJ, 26 Sep. 1996, Case C-230/94, *Renate Enkler v. Finanzamt Homburg*, paras 28-29.
56. P. Melz, *Who Is a Taxable Person to VAT?*, in *International Studies in Taxation, Liber Amicorum Sven-Olof Lodin*, at 164 (K. Andersson, P. Melz & C. Silfverberg eds, Kluwer London 1991). *See also* M. van de Leur, *Watch Out, You May Be a Taxable Person!*, 24 Intl. VAT Monitor 5 (2013), Journals IBFD, who notes that, as soon as they 'derive some form of regular income from their private assets, private individuals run the risk of qualifying as taxable persons. Their intention to be engaged in economic activities is less important and the question of whether they make a profit is irrelevant'.
57. Van Doesum et al., *supra* n. 51, at 63-64.
58. *See* AT: ECJ, 20 June 2013, Case C-219/12, *Finanzamt Freistadt Rohrbach Urfahr v. Unabhängiger Finanzsenat Außenstelle Linz*, paras 27-28, where the 'continuity' requirement was equally referred by the CJEU to the activity and the income therefrom.

those transactions consisted in a potential profit on the sale of that asset.[59] Also, according to Advocate General Kokott, 'the purely occasional commercial exploitation of property' is not to be regarded as an 'economic activity', which, however, the Advocate General maintained was not the case in *Hutchison 3G UK and Others*.[60] Indeed, it was not also the case in *Rēdlihs*, where the CJEU ruled that an economic activity takes place even in case of a sale of a property made with a view of alleviating the consequence of a situation of force majeure.[61]

In the author's opinion, the 'killer' factor as regards the 'continuity' requirement rather relates to whether a person takes active steps to marketize his own property by mobilising resources similar to those deployed by a producer, a trader, or a person supplying services, within the meaning of the second paragraph of Article 9(1) of the VAT Directive. This was also the approach adopted by the CJEU, first, in *Slaby and Others*[62] and, then, in *Rēdlihs*[63]. Further in this connection, in *EDM*, concerning whether a holding company had a business or commercial purpose in the management of its participations, Advocate General Léger considered that 'the business purpose ... involves a holding company introducing permanent human and logistical resources arranged in the same way as the resources of a credit institution and on a greater scale than the resources belonging to a private investor which are used merely for his own needs'.[64] On the contrary, in *Wellcome Trust*, the CJEU maintained the mere management of personal property does not amount to an economic activity for EU VAT purposes, even where it does involve a large volume of sales.[65] Whether or not resources mobilized by a person effectively exceed those belonging to a private investor is, indeed, a hard judgment call to make.[66] In any event, it should be observed that, in *Kostov*, the Court held that a natural person, who is already a taxable person for EU VAT purposes, must be regarded as a taxable person in respect of any other

59. PL: ECJ, 15 Sep. 2011, Joined Cases C-180/10 and C-181/10, *Jarosław Słaby v. Minister Finansów and Emilian Kuć and Halina Jeziorska-Kuć v. Dyrektor Izby Skarbowej w Warszawie*, para. 45. Noteworthy, in that case, Advocate General Mazák considered that there was an economic activity based on the 'repeated nature' of the transactions, rather than based on the 'volume' of sales concluded by the person in question. *See* PL: Opinion of the Advocate General, 12 Apr. 2011, Joined Cases C-180/10 and C-181/10, *Jarosław Słaby v. Minister Finansów and Emilian Kuć and Halina Jeziorska-Kuć v. Dyrektor Izby Skarbowej w Warszawie*, para. 24.
60. UK: Opinion of the Advocate General, 7 Sep. 2006, Case C-369/04, *Hutchison 3G UK Ltd and Others v. Commissioners of Customs and Excise*, paras 63-64.
61. LV: ECJ, 19 Jul. 2012, Case C-263/11, *Ainars Redlihs v. Valsts Ieņemumu Dienests*, para. 37.
62. *Slaby and Others* (C-180/10 & C-181/10), para. 39.
63. *Redlihs* (C-263/11), para. 36.
64. Opinion *EDM* (C-77/01), para. 44.
65. UK: ECJ, 20 June 1996, Case C-155/94, *Wellcome Trust Ltd v. Commissioners of Customs and Excise*, paras 36-37. In a similar vein, *see* NL: ECJ, 20 June 1991, Case C-60/90, *Polysar Investments Netherlands BV v. Inspecteur der Invoerrechten en Accijnzen*, para. 13.
66. Noteworthy, such an assessment is also difficult because, at times, the 'private investment' criterion is mixed up with that of a person not carrying out an activity on an occasional basis and/or not having a business or commercial purpose. *See* BE: ECJ, 14 Nov. 2000, Case C-142/99, *Floridienne SA and Berginvest SA v. Belgian State*, para. 28; UK: Opinion of the Advocate General, 7 Dec. 1995, Case C-155/94, *Wellcome Trust Ltd v. Commissioners of Customs and Excise*, para. 19.

economic activity, even if this latter activity is carried out occasionally.[67] As rightly noted, '*Kostov* thus makes it clear that the status of taxable person has knock-on effects', i.e., the status of taxable person makes other occasional supplies carried out by that person fall within the scope of EU VAT, provided those other occasional supplies constitute 'economic activities'.[68]

Based on the above exposition, the 'continuity' requirement seems to be met by all actors in the sharing economy, i.e., both by platforms and individual suppliers. In particular, it seems rather clear that sharing economy platforms do act 'on a continuing basis', in so far as their own activities are carried out and income therefrom is obtained, both, on a continuing basis.

As for individual suppliers, apparently, this condition is fulfilled as well. Indeed, in the author's opinion, the mere act of joining a platform by a user can well amount to an 'active step', i.e., a mobilization of resources similar to those deployed by a producer, a trader, or a person supplying services, as maintained by the CJEU, first, in *Slaby* and, then, in *Rēdlihs*.[69] In this connection, the opinion that the possibility for an individual supplier to provide his own services through a platform cannot be equated to the marketing of similar services by a professional trader does not seem sufficiently grounded.[70] On the contrary, it can be argued that the mere act of joining a sharing economy platform on which various services are regularly and readily traded implies, by itself, a certain degree of at least potential 'continuity'.[71] In this connection, the author concurs that the 'continuity' requirement cannot be understood as meaning that, in order to qualify as a taxable person, an individual must necessarily enter into a series of transactions, otherwise it would be fairly simple for a taxable person to circumvent his own obligation to pay VAT by completing all his economic activities in a single day.[72] The author further submits that, in light of the principles of equality and neutrality underpinning EU VAT, the VAT Directive does not - and, in any event, should not - contain any exemption for occasional activities, unless, based on an examination of all the facts and circumstances of the case, it emerges that those activities remain within the very narrow scope of the mere management of an individual's personal property.[73]

67. BG: ECJ, 13 June 2013, Case C-62/12, *Galin Kostov v. Direktor na Direktsia 'Obzhalvane I upravlenie na izpalnenieto' - Varna pri Tsentralno upravlenie na Natsionalnata agentsia za prihodite*, para. 31.
68. O. Henkow, *Taxable Persons*, in *ECJ – Recent Developments in Value Added Tax 2014*, at 81 (M. Lang. et al. eds, Linde 2015). Interestingly, for consumer law purposes, the CJEU instead maintained that it cannot be assumed sic et simpliciter that a trader has concluded a transaction in a business capacity, since 'one and the same person can act as a consumer in certain transactions and as a seller or suppliers in others'. *See* RO: ECJ, 3 Sep. 2015, Case C-110/14, *Horaţiu Ovidiu Costea v. SC Volksbank România SA*, para. 20.
69. European Commission, Value Added Tax Committee, *supra* n. 35, at 6.
70. I. Grlica, *How the Sharing Economy Is Challenging the EU VAT System*, 28 Intl. VAT Monitor 2 (2017), Journals IBFD.
71. European Commission, Value Added Tax Committee, *supra* n. 35, at 6.
72. In this connection, *see* Opinion *Wellcome Trust* (C-155/94), para. 32. Concurring with this statement, *see also* Terra & Kajus, *supra* n. 51, at para. 9.2.2.; A.M. Bal, *The Vague Concept of 'Taxable Person' in EU VAT Law*, 24 Intl. VAT Monitor 5 (2013), Journals IBFD.
73. For similar considerations, *see* BG: Opinion of the Advocate General, 28 Feb. 2013, Case C-62/12, *Galin Kostov v. Direktor na Direktsia 'Obzhalvane I upravlenie na izpalnenieto' – Varna*

[D] Acting as Such

Only supplies made by a taxable person 'acting as such' (in French, '*agissant en tant que tel*'; in Italian, '*che agisce in quanto tale*') in light of Article 2(1) of the VAT Directive fall within the scope of EU VAT.[74] It follows that a taxable person concluding a transaction exclusively in his private capacity is not a taxable person in respect of that transaction.[75] This also implies the need to draw a line between supplies which a taxable person makes in the furtherance of his business and, instead, those pertaining to a non-business domain.

Such a distinction, indeed, carries several implications. The most relevant one concerns the determination of whether and, eventually, the extent to which a taxable person shall be entitled to deduct the VAT paid on his inputs. From EU VAT being a tax on private consumption, it can in fact be maintained that, where a taxable person incurs expenditures which are not business-related, he acts as an end consumer rather than as a trader and, as such, he should bear the cost of VAT in full.[76]

It is not necessary, however, that a person decides whether an expenditure is business-related or not early on, i.e., at the time of making it.[77] Indeed, in relation to the possibility for a person to deduct the input VAT paid on an asset privately acquired, but used for economic activities only on a later date, in *Gmina Ryjewo*, Advocate General Kokott observed that, although the VAT Directive does not contain any specific provision in this regard, a denial of such a possibility would appear rather difficult to justify in light of the principles of equality and neutrality underpinning EU VAT.[78] This interpretation was confirmed – although apparently restricted only to situations in which the intention about how to use a capital item is not yet clearly expressed by the person in question[79] – by the Court in its decision, which also upheld the view expressed by the Advocate General that the concept of acquisition 'as a taxable person' must receive 'a generous interpretation'.[80]

The CJEU has constantly maintained that the determination of a person's status is a question of fact, which therefore must be settled in light of all the facts and circumstances of the case, including the nature of an asset used for business purposes and the time period which elapses between the acquisition of that asset and its use in the furtherance of that person's economic activity.[81] As regards the nature of an asset,

pri Tsentralno upravlenie na Natsionalnata agentsia za prihodite, paras 53-54. It should however be noted that, as recalled, in *Kostov*, the person in question was already a 'taxable person' and not, instead, a private individual up to carrying out an economic activity.

74. Interestingly, this condition was added to Art. 2 of the Sixth Directive without having previously been proposed elsewhere, not even in the Proposal for a Sixth Directive.
75. DE: ECJ, 4 Oct. 1995, Case C-291/92, *Finanzamt Uelzen v. Dieter Armbrecht*, para. 17.
76. R. de la Feria, *The EU VAT System and the Internal Market* at para. 3.2.2.1.1. (IBFD 2009).
77. DE: ECJ, 11 Jul. 1991, Case C-97/90, *Hansgeorg Lennartz v. Finanzamt München III*, para. 16.
78. PL: Opinion of the Advocate General, 19 Apr. 2018, Case C-140/17, *Szef Krajowej Administracji Skarbowej v. Gmina Ryjewo*, paras 32-34.
79. PL: ECJ, 25 Jul. 2018, Case C-140/17, *Szef Krajowej Administracji Skarbowej v. Gmina Ryjewo*, para. 59.
80. *Gmina Ryjewo* (C-140/17), paras 54-55; Opinion *Gmina Ryjewo* (C-140/17), para. 55.
81. *See* e.g., LT: ECJ, 22 Oct. 2015, Case C-126/14, *UAB 'Sveda' Gegen Valstybine Mokesčių Inspekcija Prie Lietuvos Respublikos Finansų Ministerijos*, para. 21.

the fact that a property is suitable only for economic exploitation normally suffices. Whether, instead, the nature of a property is such that it may be used either for business or private purposes, a more careful examination of all the facts and circumstances of the case is required in order to evaluate in which capacity the person in question actually acts.[82] And indeed, such an examination can go as further and deeper as entailing even a close inspection of a person's private house.[83]

Where an asset is used by a person for his business as well as his private activities, an apportionment rule must be followed. As regards the most appropriate method in this regard, although ultimately left to the discretion of national legislations and subject to a review by domestic courts, some guidance can be gleaned from *Armbrecht*, where the Court notably reasoned that the 'apportionment between the part allocated to the taxable person's business activities and the part retained for private use must be based on the proportions of private and business use in the year of acquisition and not on a geographical division'.[84]

The actual application scope of 'private activities' under EU VAT is quite unclear. Nevertheless, some examples of activities carried out by a person acting in a private capacity can be drawn from the CJEU's case law. Notably, in *Wellcome Trust*, the CJEU concluded that a person confining its own undertaking to the management of an investment portfolio does carry out an economic activity. In this connection, the Court further submitted that neither the scale of a share sale, nor the involvement of consultancy firms might constitute, by themselves, sufficient criteria for distinguishing between the activities of a private investor, which fall outside the scope of the VAT Directive, and those of a professional investor, which instead are fully subject to the tax.[85] Along the same lines, in *Slaby and Others*, the CJEU considered that 'a natural person who carried out an agricultural activity on land that was reclassified, following a change to urban management plans which occurred for reason beyond his control, as land designated for developments must not be regarded as a taxable person for VAT ... when he begins to sell that land if those sales fall within the scope of the management of the private property of that person'.[86] A further example in this regard might be constituted by the payment of a tax debt effectuated in kind, which, in *Posnania Investment*, Advocate General Kokott indeed considered amounting to nothing more than 'the discharge of a personal duty under public law'.[87]

---

82. *See* e.g., *Redlihs* (C-263/11), para. 34.
83. *See HE* (C-25/03), para. 67, a case concerning a room within a private house which was used as office by a self-employed specialist writer (even if working on a part-time basis, so that such business activity constituted only an ancillary activity for him).
84. *Armbrecht* (C-291/92), para. 21.
85. *Wellcome Trust* (C-155/94), paras 36-37. Interestingly, in his opinion, Advocate General Lenz argued that, 'so far as the scale of the share sale is concerned, a very wealthy private investor can also carry out extensive sales of shares' and, further, 'it is unclear what scale or volume would be required before there would be an assumption of an economic activity within the meaning of the Sixth VAT Directive', whereas, with regard to the involvement of some consultancy firms, he pointed out that 'it is today no longer possible even for a private investor to exercise his activity entirely without advice, albeit minimal'. *See* Opinion *Wellcome Trust* (C-155/94), para. 22.
86. *Slaby and Others* (C-180/10 & C-181/10), para. 50.
87. *See* PL: Opinion of the Advocate General, 16 Feb. 2017, Case C-36/16, *Minister Finansów v. Posnania Investment SA*, para. 26. Showing a disagreement with the Advocate General's opinion

In any event, the application scope of all those kinds of 'private activities' seems quite narrow. It follows, *inter alia*, from *Kezić* that, where the person concerned has taken active steps to marketize a private property, notably by carrying out preparatory works on a land to make building development on it possible, that person would act as a taxable person at the point of sale.[88] A similar submission can be found in *Rēdlihs*, where the Court observed that the fact that a person had acquired a forest solely for his own private needs did not preclude that he subsequently used it for carrying out an economic activity, also taking into account that forests, by their own nature, are very much suitable to be exploited on a commercial basis.[89] All in all, for determining whether a person acts in a business capacity, it seems decisive, as it is for the 'continuity' requirement, whether that person takes active steps to mobilize resources similar to a producer, a trader, or a person supplying services, within the meaning of the second paragraph of Article 9(1) of the VAT Directive.

Nevertheless, apparently, a person does not need to 'walk' too many steps to become a taxable person. This emerges quite starkly from *Fuchs*. In *Fuchs*, the question was whether the operation of solar panels by an individual, Mr Fuchs, installed on the roof of his private house and plugged into the electricity network, constituted an economic activity in full EU VAT terms. The Court ruled in the affirmative, despite all the electricity produced in such a manner by the individual in question was supplied back to the electricity network and notwithstanding the fact that, under the contract granting access to that network, no monetary remuneration was provided as a consideration for that supply.[90] The CJEU's ultimate findings are even more surprising, given that the amount of electricity produced through solar panels was always lower than the amount consumed by Mr Fuchs. The operation of such photovoltaic instalments, in fact, was carried out only to make that individual energy self-sufficient and to decrease the overall costs of his own personal consumption of electricity. From previous CJEU's case law, one might have assumed that an activity structurally designed to barely cover expenses, in no event, could be regarded as an economic activity for EU VAT purposes.[91] Apparently, as from *Fuchs*, this assumption no longer holds true.

Importantly, the capacity in which a person acts must be assessed not only with regard to the supplier, but also in relation to the customer.[92] As for a business customer to deduct his input VAT, inputs must be supplied to him by another taxable person.[93]

in the case, Terra & Kajus, *supra* n. 16, at para. 3.2.5.1, observe that 'the statement that "the payment of tax is simply the discharge of a personal duty under public law" may be correct for a natural person/entrepreneur (in the sense of it also being a "personal" duty) but is difficult to personalize, in the sense of "non-economic", when talking about legal persons'. The author of this book, however, does not find this latter line of reasoning particularly convincing.

88. SL: ECJ, 9 Jul. 2015, Case C-331/14, *Petar Kezić s.p. Trgovina Prizma v. Republika Slovenija*, para. 24.
89. *Redlihs* (C-263/11), paras 37 and 39.
90. *Fuchs* (C-219/12), para. 37.
91. *SPÖ Landesorganisation Kärnten* (C-267/08), para. 23.
92. *See* Art. 17 of the Implementing Regulation, stipulating that, for place of supply purposes, the status of the customer shall be determined on the basis of Arts 9-13 of the VAT Directive.
93. *See* e.g., RO: ECJ, 19 Oct. 2017, Case C-101/16, *SC Paper Consult SRL v. Direcţia Regionala a Finanţelor Publice Cluj-Napoca and Administraţia Judeţeana a Finanţelor Publice Bistriţa Nasaud*, para. 39.

If the supplier is not a taxable person, a customer acting in a business capacity, instead, would not be able to deduct any input VAT.[94] This circumstance helps explain the rationale underpinning the special scheme on second-hand goods contained in Articles 311-343 of the VAT Directive, pursuant to which VAT is remitted by the supplier only on the difference between the price charged for his outputs (i.e., its 'profit margin') and that paid on his inputs (i.e., 'the amount of VAT relating to the profit margin').[95] As explained by the CJEU in *Commission versus Netherlands*, a case discussed prior the introduction of the special scheme in question[96], in fact, 'second-hand goods which are reintroduced into commercial circulation are ... taxed once again, whereas second-hands goods which pass directly from one consumer to another remain burdened solely by the tax imposed on the occasion of the first sale to a non-taxable consumer'.[97]

Based on the above exposition, determining in which capacity – a business or a private one – a sharing economy platform actually acts appears quite straightforward. In relation to services provided to its users, clearly a platform acts in a business capacity. Against this conclusion, the considerations made by the CJEU in *Wellcome Trust* do not in fact hold up, since the situation examined by the Court in that case concerned a rather passive activity such as the management of an investment portfolio, which, obviously, is not the case of a platform's activity.

More challenging, instead, is to determine in which capacity platform users actually act. Indeed, the answer depends on a careful examination of all the facts and circumstances of the case. From the CJEU's case law, one might fairly conclude that the possibility for a person to carry out an activity in a private capacity is quite constrained. And yet, according to the Commission, this situation occurs precisely with regard to the provision to a digital company of personal data by its users. The Commission, for its part, takes the view that personal data in fact pertain to the private sphere of an individual, so that the permission granted by an individual to a digital company to use his own personal data falls within the scope of the management of a private property.[98] Ultimately, the conclusion reached by the Commission does not convince the author. In this connection, it should in fact be recalled that, under EU VAT, subjective intentions are immaterial and, further, as found by the CJEU in *Fuchs*, for carrying out an economic activity a person is not required to mobilize so many resources.

Similar kinds of considerations apply to transactions among platform users. In this connection, distinguishing between business and private spheres might not be feasible, in so far as the two domains in the sharing economy are increasingly

94. As a matter of fact, a penalty equal to the non-deductible input tax occurs for any transfer from the private to the business sphere. *See* AT: Opinion of the Advocate General, 11 Dec. 2008, Case C-460/07, *Sandra Puffer v. Unabhängiger Finanzsenat, Außenstelle Linz*, para. 50.
95. *See*, in particular, Art. 315 of the VAT Directive.
96. Council Directive 94/5/EC of 14 February 1994 supplementing the Common System of Value Added Tax and amending Directive 77/388/EEC – Special Arrangements Applicable to Second-Hand Goods, Works of Art, Collectors' Items and Antiques, OJ L 60/16 of 3 Mar. 1994.
97. NL: ECJ, 10 Jul. 1985, Case C-16/84, *Commission of the European Communities v. Kingdom of the Netherlands*, para. 18.
98. European Commission, Value Added Tax Committee, *supra* n. 46, at 3-5.

intertwined.[99] Perhaps, only activities carried out by a BlaBlaCar driver or a HomeExchange host could be seen as involving the mere management of private properties. And yet, based on *Fuchs*, it can well be maintained that even activities such as rendering an apartment available for a single holiday exchange on HomeExchange or becoming an occasional driver on BlaBlaCar to barely cover travel expenses do amount to economic activities in EU VAT terms. In this connection, it should also be considered that treating an individual supplier as a non-taxable person might be detrimental for a business customer, in so far as, in such event, no input VAT can be deducted by the latter party.

Although, in the sharing economy, the capacity in which both individual suppliers and individual customers act remains difficult to concretely ascertain, an examination of the assets used in the provision of the services in question might eventually simplify such an assessment. Notably, with regard to activities like accommodation and passenger transport services, it is useful to consider whether the relevant asset, such as a residential property or a car, can be used for business purposes only, as it occurs, for instance, with a building earmarked as business property under cadastral rules or with a company car. In case of mixed-used assets, an apportionment rule must instead be followed.

Despite this, it remains ultimately unclear whether, in light of CJEU's decision in *Gmina Ryjewo*, an individual supplier (e.g., an Airbnb host or an Uber driver) is entitled to deduct the input VAT paid on expenditures incurred (e.g., for the renovation of a residential property or for purchasing a car), even if those expenditures are initially borne for private purposes only. Indeed, the lack of clear indication on how to determine the amount of deductible input VAT might cause individual suppliers to claim a higher or lower amount in this regard than the right one.

§4.03 INDEPENDENTLY

For being a 'taxable person', Article 9(1) of the VAT Directive requires a person to carry out an activity 'independently' (in French, '*d'une façon indépendante*'; in Italian, '*in modo indipendente*'). The meaning of this adverb is further detailed in Article 10 of the VAT Directive, according to which employed and other persons are excluded at the outset from EU VAT, 'in so far as they are bound to an employer by a contract of employment or by any other legal tie creating the relationship of employer and employee as regards working conditions, remuneration and the employer's liability'.[100] Indeed, the exclusion of employees from the subjective or personal scope of EU VAT is

99. For a case concerning the use of a Facebook account as a 'consumer' or, instead, as an 'economic operator', *see* AT: ECJ, 25 Jan. 2018, Case C-498/16, *Maximilian Schrems v. Facebook Ireland Limited*. paras 25-41.

100. Indeed, already the Proposal for a Second Directive stipulated that 'the expression "on his own account" [the term then used for "independently"] is intended particularly to preclude taxation of wage and salary earners bound to their employer by a labour contract, including person working in their own home'. This statement was then confirmed by the wording of the Second Directive, which specifically provided that 'the expression "independently" is intended in particular to exclude from taxation wage-earners who are bound to their employer

motivated by practical reasons, relating to the need to reduce the sheer number of persons subject to VAT liabilities and obligations, as well as the amount of administrative work for tax authorities.[101]

The notion of 'employee', however, is not defined anywhere in the VAT Directive. The concept has instead received a specification in the CJEU's case law. Notably, in *Lawrie-Blum* – admittedly, not a case on EU VAT –, the CJEU considered that 'the term "worker" covers any person performing for remuneration work the nature of which is not determined by himself for and under the control of another, regardless of the legal nature of the employment relationship'. More precisely, the Court submitted that an employee is a person that, for a certain period of time, 'performs services for and under the direction of another person in return for which he receives remuneration'.[102] Further, in the field of competition law, it was observed that for an employee to be considered as an undertaking separate from his employer, i.e., a separate 'economic unit', the person in question must be capable of exerting sufficient competitive significance and retaining 'a certain degree of – essentially economic – autonomy'.[103]

In any event, excluding employees from the reach of EU VAT is not, by itself, sufficient. Rather, from a more substantial standpoint, it is necessary to establish whether a person effectively acts 'independently'.[104] The existence of such substantial requirement can be inferred from the wording of Article 10 of the VAT Directive, which, first, assimilates to a contract of employment 'any other legal ties creating the relationship of employer and employee'[105], and, then, assumes that a relationship akin to that of employment exists whether the 'working conditions, remuneration and the employer's liability' are those normally established under a contract of employment. While interpreting those elements, the CJEU specifically considered that an activity is carried out independently if: (1) it is exercised by a person who is not organically integrated into an undertaking or an administration, (2) the person in question has appropriate organizational freedom with regard to the human and material resources used in the exercise of the relevant activity, and (3) the person concerned bears the economic risk entailed in the relevant activity.

---

by a contract of service', and later in the Sixth Directive, which contained a provision with a wording identical to that of Art. 9 of the VAT Directive actually in force.

101. *See* Melz, *supra* n. 56, at 160, who also observes that excluding employees from the EU VAT system implies that 'the value added produced by them will be taxed when their employers charge VAT on the sales of goods and services produced by them'.

102. DE: ECJ, 3 Jul. 1986, Case C-66/85, *Deborah Lawrie-Blum v. Land Baden-Württemberg*, paras 12 and 17. Noteworthy, the same criteria laid down by the CJEU in *Lawrie-Blum* are used for establishing employment status at EU level under the proposed directive regarding, *inter alia*, platform workers. *See* European Commission, *Proposal for a Directive of the European Parliament and of the Council on Transparent and Predictable Working Conditions in the European Union*, at 11, COM(2017) 797 final.

103. BE: Opinion of the Advocate General, 25 Mar. 1998, Case C-22/98, *Criminal Proceedings Against Jean Claude Becu, Annie Verweire, Smeg NV and Adia Interim NV*, para. 47.

104. NL: Opinion of the Advocate General, 20 May 1999, Case C-23/98, *Staatssecretaris van Financiën v. J. Heerma*, paras 18-19.

105. This condition was also reaffirmed by the Commission during a meeting of the VAT Committee. *See* European Commission, Value Added Tax Committee, *Working Paper No. 786. Services Provided to Companies by Their Shareholders*, at 3 (taxud.c.1(2014)201835).

Those criteria have been applied consistently by the CJEU in a series of cases. Notably, in *Commission versus Netherlands*, the Court considered Dutch notaries and bailiffs as carrying out an activity 'independently' for EU VAT purposes, in so far as those persons were not integrated in the public administration, carried out their activities on their own account and responsibility, were essentially free, even if subject to the limitations imposed by their statute, to arrange how to perform their own work and, lastly, received from themselves the remuneration which made up their income. The existence of disciplinary control by the public authorities and, further, the fact that their remuneration was statutorily determined did not suffice, in the Court's view, to reach an opposite conclusion.[106] Similarly, in *Ayuntamiento de Sevilla*, the CJEU found that, although tax collectors were appointed by and subject to the control of a municipality, they remained taxable persons for EU VAT purposes, as long as those persons maintained their own offices, were responsible for recruiting their own staff and, lastly, their remuneration exclusively depended on the amount collected. Instead, the circumstance that the municipality was liable for the actions of the tax collectors was not enough, in the Court's view, to establish an employer-employee relationship.[107] Similar to those in the aforementioned cases were the CJEU's findings in *Nigl and Others*, concerning whether civil law partnerships, which supplied agricultural products under a joint trading name and through a limited company, were to be regarded as carrying out an economic activity independent from each other, question to which the Court eventually responded in the affirmative. Importantly, the CJEU concluded that the existence of a cooperation agreement between, on the one hand, those partnerships and, on the other hand, the limited company could not call into question the independence of the former vis-à-vis the latter.[108] Thus, for the CJEU, apparently 'cooperation' is not equal to 'subordination'.[109]

Importantly, a person can be regarded as 'truly' carrying out an economic activity independently for EU VAT purposes only if he bears the 'economic risk' entailed in that activity. Notably, in *Van der Steen*, a sole director/shareholder of a company was found to be in an employment relationship with his own company, and therefore not a taxable person for EU VAT purposes, precisely on the ground that he did not bear any economic risk but, instead, he received a fixed monthly salary and an annual holiday payment from his own company, regardless of his company's actual financial situation.[110] In its decision, the CJEU took some time to distinguish *Van der Steen* from

106. *Commission v. Netherlands* (C-235/85), para. 14.
107. ES: ECJ, 25 Jul. 1991, Case C-202/90, *Ayuntamiento de Sevilla v. Recaudadores de Tributos de las Zonas primera y segunda*, paras 11-16. As observed by Advocate General Tesauro in that case, 'the tax collector bears the entire economic risk in so far as any taxes he fails to collect translates into a loss of earnings, which would not be the case if he were bound to the commune by a contract of employment since in that case he would still be paid whether or not he collected the taxes'. *See* ES: Opinion of the Advocate General, 4 Jun. 1991, Case C-202/90, *Ayuntamiento de Sevilla v. Recaudadores de Tributos de las Zonas primera y segunda*, para. 6.
108. DE: ECJ, 12 Oct. 2016, Case C-340/15, *Christine Nigl and Others v. Finanzamt Waldviertel*, paras 30-34.
109. DE: Opinion of the Advocate General, 30 Jun. 2016, Case C-340/15, *Christine Nigl and Others v. Finanzamt Waldviertel*, para. 21.
110. NL: ECJ, 18 Oct. 2007, Case C-355/06, *J.A. van der Steen v. Inspecteur van de Belastingdienst Utrecht-Gooi/kantoor Utrecht*, paras 22-26.

Heerma, a case concerning the letting of property by a person to the partnership – not regarded as a legal person under Dutch law, but still as a de facto company capable of carrying out economic activities independently – of which he was a member, where, instead, it was found that the partner acted in his own name, on his own behalf, and under his own responsibility, even if, eventually, he was at the same time manager of the lessee partnership.[111]

§4.04 INDIVIDUAL SUPPLIERS: BETWEEN CONTRACTUAL FICTION AND ECONOMIC REALITY

Pursuant to the legal terms and conditions of most sharing economy platforms, the relationship between the platform and its individual suppliers is not one of employment. Under nearly all contractual arrangements in the sharing economy, in fact, individual suppliers are characterized as third parties. The platform does not employ any of them. Rather, it provides those suppliers with a number of intermediary services. The underlying services, i.e., the accommodation or passenger transport services, are instead supplied to individual customers by those individual suppliers alone. Therefore, based on contractual arrangements among parties, three transactions usually occur in the sharing economy: the first – a supply of intermediary services – between the platform and the individual supplier, the second – another supply of intermediary services – between the platform and the individual customer, and the third – the underlying supply of accommodation or passenger transport services – between the individual supplier and the individual customer.[112]

Economic reality – which constitutes a fundamental criterion for the application of EU VAT and, as such, should always take precedence over contractual documentation[113] – might however change the actual state of play, whether this latter would appear no more than a contractual fiction.[114] Notably, if the actual relationship between the platform and its individual suppliers resembles more closely the one existing between an employer and its employees, then those individual suppliers would no longer be considered as taxable persons for EU VAT purposes.[115] And indeed,

111. NL: ECJ, 27 Jan. 2000, Case C-23/98, *Staatssecretaris van Financiën v. J. Heerma*, para. 18. More recently, *see also* NL: *Request for a Preliminary Ruling from the Gerechtshof's-Hertogenbosch (Netherlands) lodged on 26 June 2018 – IO, Other Party: Inspecteur van de Rijksbelastingdienst (Case C-420/18)*, concerning whether 'a member of the Supervisory Board of a foundation, who is in a subordinate position in regard to that Board for his employment and remuneration conditions, but who is otherwise not in a subordinate position in regard to the Supervisory Board or the foundation, carries out his economic activities independently', within the meaning of Arts 9 and 10 of the VAT Directive. It remains to be seen whether the CJEU will confirm its findings in *Van der Steen* or whether, instead, it will revert back to its previous decision in *Heerma*.
112. *See* Chapter 2.
113. *See* e.g., PT: ECJ, 22 Nov. 2018, Case C-295/17, *MEO – Serviços de Comunicações e Multimédia SA v. Autoridade Tributária e Aduaneira*, para. 61.
114. European Commission, Value Added Tax Committee, *supra* n. 35, at, at 7.
115. *See* European Commission, Value Added Tax Committee, *Working Paper No. 947, Services Provided by an Electronic Platform Connecting for Remuneration, by means of a Smartphone Application, a Driver Using His Own Vehicle with Persons Who Wish to Make Urban Journeys.*

both the findings of the CJEU and the conclusions of Advocate General Szpunar, first, in *Uber Systems Spain* and, then, in *Uber France* point in that direction.[116] Notably, in *Uber Systems Spain*, the Advocate General observed that, although Uber's 'control is not exercised in the context of a traditional employer-employee relationship, one should not be fooled by appearances'.[117] In particular, he reasoned that, as a matter of fact, 'drivers who work on the Uber platform do not pursue an independent activity that exists independently [*sic*] of the platform. On the contrary, the activity exists solely because of the platform, without which it would have no sense', which ultimately leads to conclude that 'Uber is therefore not a mere intermediary between drivers willing to offer transport services occasionally and passengers in search of such services'.[118]

Although - admittedly - the two aforementioned cases do not specifically concern EU VAT, but rather the freedom to provide services in the internal market[119], as well as the application of the Directive on Electronic Commerce[120], potential fallouts on EU VAT matters as a result of the CJEU's findings and the Advocate General's conclusions cannot be entirely ruled out. Indeed, the Commission itself has hinted at such an eventuality and reasoned that, although no automatic conclusions for EU VAT purposes can be derived from the analysis of those cases, the examination provided therein 'can be helpful for the reflections on the possible VAT consequences of the relevant supplies' and can even be applied to 'supplies of any other electronic platforms, whose main features are comparable to those characterizing the platform referred to in that judgment [i.e. *Uber Systems Spain*]'.[121]

The CJEU's findings as well as the Advocate General's conclusions, first, in *Uber Systems Spain* and, then, in *Uber France*, therefore, do not provide ultimate guidance on this matter. It should in fact be considered that, unlike a traditional employee, an individual supplier in the sharing economy is usually remunerated based on the number of transactions concluded, he often owns all the assets and resources used to make the underlying supply, and, further, he is not prevented from carrying out his

---

The Significance of the VAT Identification Number, at 9 (taxud.c.1(2018)1735106), considering that 'perhaps the features of the relationship between the platform and the driver are such that in fact the employer-employee dependence is in reality present'.

116. ES: ECJ, 20 Dec. 2017, Case C-434/15, *Asociación Profesional Elite Taxi v. Uber Systems Spain SL*, paras 33-41; ES: Opinion of the Advocate General, 11 May 2017, Case C-434/15, *Asociación Profesional Elite Taxi v. Uber Systems Spain SL*, paras 39-66; FR: ECJ, 10 Apr. 2018, Case C-320/16, *Uber France SAS*, paras 15-28; FR: Opinion of the Advocate General, 4 Jul. 2017, Case C-320/16, *Uber France SAS*, paras 15-22.
117. Opinion *Uber Systems Spain* (C-434/15), para. 52.
118. *Id.*, paras 56 and 61.
119. Articles 56 and 58(1) TFEU; Directive 2006/123/EC of the European Parliament and of the Council of 12 December 2006 on Services in the Internal Market, OJ L 376/36 of 27 Dec. 2006; Directive 98/34/EC of the European Parliament and of the Council of 22 June 1998 laying down a Procedure for the Provision of Information in the field of Technical Standards and Regulations, OJ L 204/37 of 21 Jul. 1998, now repealed and replaced by Directive (EU) 2015/1535 of the European Parliament and of the Council of 9 September 2015 laying down a Procedure for the Provision of Information in the field of Technical Regulations and of Rules on Information Society Services, OJ L 241/1 of 17 Sep. 2015.
120. Directive 2000/31/EC of the European Parliament and of the Council of 8 June 2000 on Certain Legal Aspects of Information Society Services, in particular Electronic Commerce, in the Internal Market ('Directive on Electronic Commerce'), OJ L 178/1 of 1 Jul. 2000.
121. *See* European Commission, Value Added Tax Committee, *supra* n. 115, at 4.

own economic activity through various sharing economy platforms or, even, by using more conventional means. It also ought to be acknowledged the need to assess each sharing economy business model on its own merits[122], notably by considering all the elements which – if cumulatively taken – might indicate whether individual suppliers effectively carry out their own economic activity independent from a platform or otherwise.[123] As a result, a 'functional analysis' of the business model specifically adopted by a sharing economy platform is – largely – unavoidable on this matter.[124]

A functional analysis of the business model specifically adopted by the four sharing economy platforms examined in the present study is tentatively made hereinafter. Notably, Table 4.1 below contains a schematic summary of the various conditions, extrapolated from the CJEU's case law analysed above, which could be useful for establishing whether individual suppliers effectively carry out their own economic activity independent from the platform or otherwise. Those conditions were tentatively related to the four sharing economy platforms specifically examined in the present study, i.e., Airbnb, Uber, HomeExchange, and BlaBlaCar. Notably, 'V' indicates that the specific condition under assessment, showing a certain level of independence from the platform, is met by the individual suppliers concerned, whereas ' × ' states that the condition assessed is not, or not entirely, fulfilled by those suppliers. Where the majority of the conditions are met, the author submits that an assumption can be made that the individual suppliers in question effectively carry out an economic activity 'independent' from the platform and, therefore, that they are taxable persons for EU VAT purposes.

---

122. Indeed, what has been found for Uber is not necessarily applicable to other sharing economy platforms. Notably, two Spanish Commercial Courts ruled that Airbnb and BlaBlaCar are mere intermediaries, since it was found that those platforms do not take part in the supply of the underlying services. *See* ES: Juzgado Contencioso-Administrativo 11 de Barcelona, 29 Nov. 2016, Sentencia No. 309/2016, *Airbnb Online Services Spain, SL v. Direcció General de Turisme – Administración de la Generalitat de Catalunya*; ES: Juzgado de lo Mercantil No. 02 de Madrid, 2 Feb. 2017, Sentencia No. 30/2017, *Confederación Española* de *Transportes en Autobús (Confebus) v. Comuto Iberia SL and Comuto S.A.* Noteworthy, this latter decision was also confirmed on appeal. *See* ES: Audencia Provincial de Madrid Sección 28, 22 Feb. 2019, Sentencia No. 86/2019, *Confederación Española* de *Transportes en Autobús (Confebus) v. Comuto Iberia SL and Comuto S.A.*

123. *See* European Commission, *Communication from the Commission to the European Parliament, the Council, the European Economic and Social Committee and the Committee of the Regions on a European Agenda for the Collaborative Economy*, at 6, COM(2016) 356 final, considering that 'whether a collaborative platform also provides the underlying service will normally have to be established on a case-by-case basis'. For a possible approach on how to conduct such an assessment, *see* J. Prassl & M. Risak, *Uber TaskRabbit, & Co: Platforms as Employers? Rethinking the Legal Analysis of Crowdwork*, 37 Comp. Lab. L. & Pol'y J. 3 (2016), at 604-619.

124. As regards the need to resort to a 'functional analysis' in EU VAT matters, *see* IR: Opinion of the Advocate General, 3 May 2018, Case C-249/17, *Ryanair Ltd v. The Revenue Commissioners*, para. 35.

Table 4.1 Conditions to Check for an Individual Supplier to Independently Carry Out an Economic Activity Pursuant to Article 9 of the VAT Directive

Conditions	*Airbnb*	*Uber*	*HomeExchange*	*BlaBlaCar*
Non-exclusionary Membership	v	v	v	v
Organizational Autonomy	v	v	v	v
Economic Risk	v	v	v	v
Regulatory Autonomy	v/x	x	v	v/x
Remuneration Independence	v	x	v/x	v/x
Personal Liability	x	x	v	v

As expected, Table 4.1 above reveals that the assessment varies significantly according to the specific sharing economy platform on which the individual suppliers operate. Nevertheless, a number of conditions seem to be fulfilled by all individual suppliers. Namely, those conditions relate to the fact that: (1) the individual suppliers are not organically integrated in the sharing economy platform on which they operate, neither they are obliged to operate only through a single platform but multiple affiliation is permitted, (2) they enjoy a sufficient degree of organizational autonomy, in terms of human and material resources for carrying out the economic activity in question (e.g., with regard to employment of auxiliary staff and assets used), and (3) they generally bear the economic risk entailed in the provision of the underlying service (e.g., in case of damages to residential properties or car breakdowns). As for other conditions, notable differences among the individual suppliers under assessment instead exist. Notably, the regulatory autonomy enjoyed by those individual suppliers varies to a great extent: while HomeExchange hosts are bound by a limited number of regulations enacted by that platform (e.g., requirements to comply with existing laws and regulations or to act in good faith), the activities of Airbnb hosts as well as those of Uber and BlaBlaCar drivers instead appear - to a different degree - subject to more constraints (e.g., deactivation or suspension of accounts in case of multiple poor ratings and/or refusal of booking/ride requests). To similar outcomes it leads the assessment of the condition concerning personal liability of the individual suppliers in the furtherance of their own economic activities. In particular, while Airbnb and Uber provide certain insurance coverage to individual suppliers, the same does not occur in case of activities carried out by individual suppliers through HomeExchange and BlaBlaCar (insurance coverage offered by BlaBlaCar to its drivers, in fact, is only additional to the mandatory third-party liability insurance which each driver is bound to have). Lastly, with regard to the possibility to set their own remuneration, the situation among the individual suppliers of the sharing economy platforms examined above is equally, although differently, split. Airbnb hosts, in fact, are allowed to set the price of their own activities basically without any constraint from the platform, for HomeExchange hosts and BlaBlaCar drivers such a possibility is quite limited, whereas on Uber price setting is made automatically by the company's algorithm.

Based on the functional analysis tentatively conducted in Table 4.1, it appears that only Uber drivers might eventually be recharacterized as employees of the platform, as long as there is an equal split on the number of conditions fulfilled and disregarded by those persons. Should a similar recharacterization indeed occur, then Uber would have to account for VAT also on the underlying supply. More specifically, under such scenario, there would be two transactions only, both between Uber and the individual passenger: the first concerning the intermediary service (i.e., the use of Uber app), the second regarding the underlying service (i.e., passenger transport). On the contrary, no supply would exist between Uber and the driver, in so far as the establishment of an employment relationship between these two parties concerned would make the transaction in question irrelevant for EU VAT purposes. Figure 4.1 below depicts this scenario graphically.

Figure 4.1 Uber: Driver as an Employee (1)

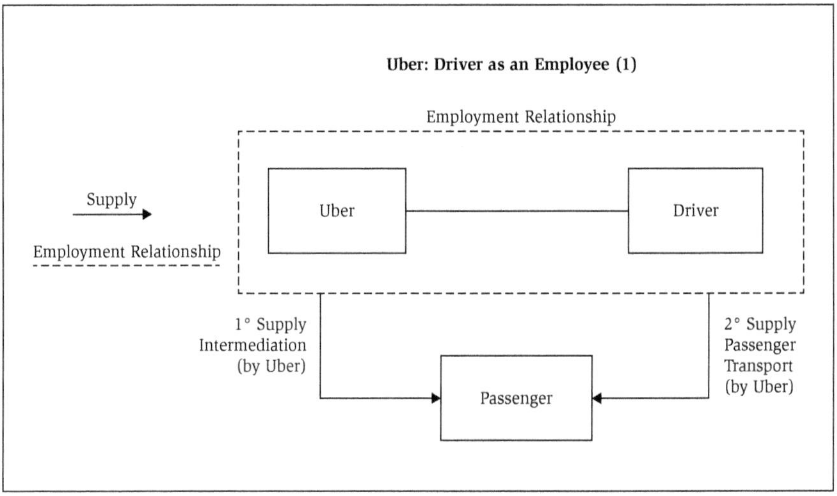

Alternatively, it might be assumed that the platform would make a single supply to the passenger, in a way that the intermediary and the passenger transport services would be jointly provided to the individual passenger by Uber itself.[125] Figure 4.2 below depicts this scenario graphically.

Figure 4.2 Uber: Driver as an Employee (2)

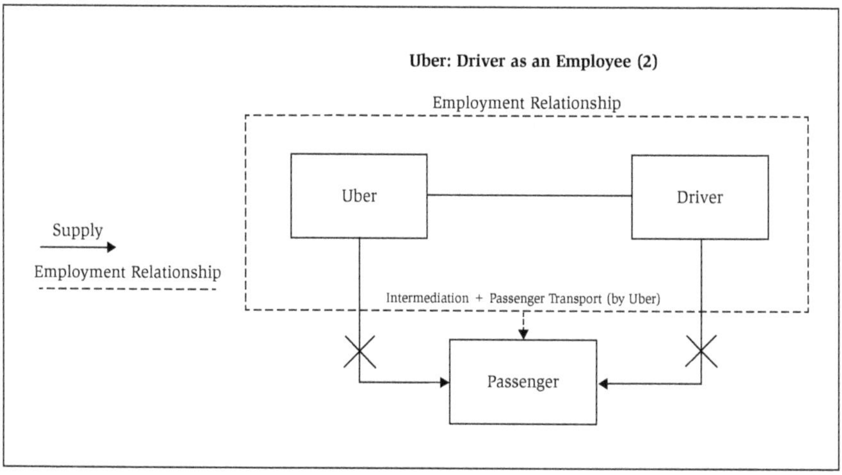

In the event of any of the aforementioned possible recharacterizations, two distinct issues would have to be addressed. Notably, a first issue would arise in relation to the VAT originally charged by Uber to the driver for its own intermediary services, since in light of Articles 9 and 10 of the VAT Directive the related supply is to be disregarded for EU VAT purposes. Only the underlying supply must in fact be subject to VAT, in so far as it entails the sole economic activity carried out toward a truly independent party. Another drawback resulting from a recharacterization of Uber drivers as employees of the platform relates to the circumstance that the company would be factually unable to deduct the VAT paid by the drivers on their inputs. Actually, being recharacterized as employees, drivers would no longer be considered as taxable persons and, thus, they would not also be allowed to deduct any input VAT. Both these circumstances generate tax cascading, an occurrence which contradicts a central tenet of EU VAT, i.e., that the tax should remain neutral for businesses.[126] As to avoid tax cascading, Uber might eventually provide its drivers with the vehicles used for their own economic activities

125. For a discussion about composite supplies, *see* Chapter 6.
126. *See* e.g., NL: ECJ, 8 Mar. 1988, Case C-165/86, *Leesportefeuille 'Intiem' CV v. Staatssecretaris van Financiën*, para. 14, considering that the 'deduction system must be applied in such a way that its scope corresponds as far as possible to the sphere of the taxable person's business activity'.

and, in the long run, the company might even be induced to dispense with drivers altogether and veer toward fully autonomous vehicles.[127]

Due to these and other possible shortcomings, the author submits that it would be preferable not to recharacterize Uber drivers as employees of the platform and, thus, as non-taxable persons for EU VAT purposes. In the author's view, in fact, the shortcomings highlighted above are not fully compensated by the reduction on the number of taxable persons which such a recharacterization would bring. Should this latter be a truly desirable aim, then the author contends that it would be much better to narrow the broad application scope of the concept of 'taxable person'. This result could be achieved in various ways, either by raising the fairly low requirement for an activity to be regarded as an 'economy activity', by reducing the broad interpretation scope of the term 'independently', or by excluding a greater number of individual suppliers from the scope of EU VAT through an increase of registration thresholds. Indeed, this latter concept is the subject matter of the next section.

§4.05 REGISTRATION THRESHOLDS AND THE SPECIAL SCHEME FOR SMES

Although, stricto sensu, registration is not a requirement for qualifying as a taxable person under EU VAT[128], due to their practical relevance, the operation of registration thresholds as well as the special scheme for SMEs are certainly worthy of examination in the context of the sharing economy.[129] Registration thresholds essentially set the minimum level of economic activity which is deemed relevant for EU VAT purposes. Indeed, a person not exceeding the threshold does not need to register, although he may opt to do so if this is favourable to him from a financial point of view.[130] In a sense, the person in question is considered an 'exempt' or 'out-of-scope' supplier, with the relevant consequence that both his output and input supplies would be disregarded for EU VAT purposes.[131] Although, undoubtedly, entailing a reduction of the amount of

127. Notably, such an anticompetitive strategy, consisting in a firm assuming control and presiding over business operations normally operated by distinct undertakings, is usually referred to as 'vertical integration'.
128. The possession of a VAT identification number, in fact, is not a requirement needed as to be a taxable person and the lack of such a number does not mean automatically that a person is not a taxable person. In other words, the fact that a taxable person has or not a VAT identification number does not change his status. *See*, to that effect, LV: ECJ, 14 Mar. 2013, Case C-527/11, *Valsts ieņemumu dienests v. Ablessio SIA*, paras 16-39.
129. Title XII, Chapter 1, section 2, Arts 282-292 of the VAT Directive. Worth mentioning, a special scheme for SMEs was envisaged both in the Second Directive (Art. 14) and in the Sixth Directive (Art. 24). It also ought to be noted that, as entailed in Art. 292 of the VAT Directive, the scheme was originally intended to provisionally apply only until the transitional regime would have been replaced by the definitive arrangements for taxation in the Member State of origin. Since, meanwhile, the transactional regime has become the definitive one, it is clear enough that such an original intent would no longer be pursued.
130. Article 290 VAT Directive.
131. Article 289 VAT Directive. R. de la Feria & R. Krever, *Ending VAT Exemptions: Toward a Post-Modern VAT*, in *VAT Exemptions: Consequences and Design Alternatives*, at 14-16 (R. de la Feria ed., Kluwer Law International 2013). As J. Englisch, *EU Perspectives on VAT Exemptions* at 6 (Working Paper Series, University of Oxford 2011) puts it, the special scheme

taxes collected[132], the main scope of registration thresholds and of the special scheme for SMEs is to lower the costs for businesses, especially small ones, to comply with the EU VAT system.[133] As economists have long shown, compliance costs in fact tend to be distributed regressively with respect to income, in the sense that small businesses incur, on average, higher costs for tax compliance reasons than large ones.[134]

As a yardstick for measuring the level of economic activity, a person's annual turnover - exclusive of VAT - is generally used.[135] Despite having the calculation method in common, registration thresholds vary greatly across Member States and, further, their implementation by a country is optional.[136] Indeed, high registration thresholds are hard to justify in light of the equality and neutrality principles.[137] Although, arguably, contributing to reduce compliance and administrative costs for taxpayers and tax authorities alike, registration thresholds - especially if set particularly high - in fact create a 'bunching' effect, in so far as a business holds an incentive to ensure that its annual turnover remains just below the set registration threshold in order to obtain VAT savings from this.[138] It also ought to be observed that the revenue forgone by the public exchequer only partially might be recouped by savings resulting from a reduction of administrative costs for tax authorities.[139] Lastly, it should not be underestimated the distortive effects entailed in the special scheme for SMEs, due to the circumstance that registration thresholds and the special schemes for Small and Medium Enterprises (SMEs) only apply to businesses trading domestically[140] and, further, that those measures tend to favour those making B2C transactions[141]. Indeed,

for SMEs constitutes 'a personal or subjective exemption', whereas the CJEU has described such scheme as a 'personal exemption scheme'. *See* HU: ECJ, 17 May 2018, Case C-566/16, *Dávid Vámos v. Nemzeti Adóés Vámhivatal Fellebbviteli Igazgatósága*, para. 31.

132. Notwithstanding it is claimed otherwise in Art. 281 of the VAT Directive.
133. AT: ECJ, 28 Sep. 2006, Case C-128/05, *Commission of the European Communities v. Republic of Austria*, para. 25.
134. *See* e.g., C. Evans, *Taxation Compliance and Administrative Costs: An Overview*, in *Tax Compliance Costs for Companies in an Enlarged European Community*, at 447-470 (M. Lang et al. eds, Kluwer Law International 2008).
135. Article 288 VAT Directive. The only notable exception in this respect is constituted by the Netherlands, whose VAT national act provides for a different method of calculation.
136. For an overview of VAT registration thresholds in EU Member States, *see* F. Annacondia, *VAT Registration Thresholds in Europe*, 29 Intl. VAT Monitor 6 (2018), Journals IBFD.
137. Notably, this is the case of the United Kingdom, which, as for 2018, had a general threshold for SMEs of GBP 85,000 (approximately EUR 98,000), and of France, which set an equally high threshold (EUR 82,800) for suppliers in the hotel accommodation sector.
138. *See* UK: Office of Tax Simplification, *Value Added Tax: Routes to Simplification. Presented to Parliament pursuant to Section 186(4)(b) of Finance Act 2016* at 6-7 (2017), https://www.gov.uk/government/uploads/system/uploads/attachment_data/file/657213/Value_added_tax_routes_to_simplification_web.pdf (accessed 31 March 2019).
139. In this connection, economists generally observe that VAT registration thresholds should be set precisely balancing out collection costs against the marginal value of additional tax revenues. *See* e.g., M. Keen & J. Mintz, *The Optimal Tax Threshold for Value-Added Tax*, 88 J. Publ. Econ. 3-4 (2004), at 559-576.
140. Article 283(1)(c) of the VAT Directive, which, in *Schmelz* (AT: ECJ, 26 Oct. 2010, Case C-97/09, *Ingrid Schmelz v. Finanzamt Waldviertel*, para. 71), the CJEU ultimately found compliant with the principle of equal treatment.
141. A small business, in fact, might find convenient to register if he mainly operates in a B2B context, i.e., he mostly makes supplies to registered taxpayers, since these latter usually limit their own acquisitions to those supplied by taxable persons in respect of which input VAT can

the strict territorial limitation of the current special regime for SMEs is highly problematic, given the ongoing shift of the EU VAT system toward the principle of taxation at destination[142], which was anticipated, as from 2015, by changes to place of supply rules for telecommunication, broadcasting, and electronically supplied services.[143]

In the sharing economy, the ability of individual suppliers, whose annual turnover usually falls below the statutory registration threshold for national VAT, to make - de facto - exempt supplies is highly critical, in so far as this circumstance enables those suppliers to obtain VAT savings vis-à-vis more conventional businesses active in the same economic sector. Indeed, this is the situation of many Airbnb hosts - especially in the UK, where the registration threshold is set particularly high - who, from this, are likely to end up VAT-advantaged compared to traditional hotels.[144]

Similar advantages over competitors active in the same industry are gained by a sharing economy platform like Uber, which, by treating its drivers as taxable persons for EU VAT purposes, is not required to account for VAT on the fees charged to them in relation to its intermediary services, since the supplies in question are regarded as B2B supplies to which the reverse charge mechanism as provided for in Article 196 of the VAT Directive applies.[145] On the contrary, in a purely domestic scenario, a comparable sharing economy platform would have to collect and remit to the competent tax authorities the tax charged in relation to its own intermediary services pursuant to Article 193 of the VAT Directive.[146] Arguably, this circumstance grants Uber an (unfair?) advantage over its domestic competitors, at least in terms of reduced administrative obligations, not to mention the benefits resulting from a likely lower final price charged by drivers to passengers.[147]

be claimed. The situation is exactly opposite where a small business mainly operates in a B2C context, i.e., he mostly makes supplies to end consumers, since these latter do not have the possibility to claim any input VAT deduction in relation to their purchases.

142. European Commission, *Proposal for a Council Directive amending Directive 2006/112/EC as regards the Introduction of the Detailed Technical Measures for the Operation of the Definitive VAT System for the Taxation of Trade between Member States*, COM(2018) 329 final.

143. For a discussion about electronically supplied services, *see* section §7.07.

144. *See* V. Houlder, *Airbnb's Edge on Room Prices Depends on Tax Advantages*, Financial Times (2 Jan. 2017), highlighting that 'VAT and property taxes account for up to 17 per cent of the price of a typical London hotel room after the recovery of VAT paid on costs. The VAT on most Airbnb stays can be as little as 0.6 per cent because the UK only levies the tax when businesses sell more than GBP 83,000 [as of 2019, GBP 85,000] per year - a threshold reached by very few Airbnb hosts'.

145. For a discussion of the reverse charge mechanism contained in Art. 196 of the VAT Directive, *see* section §8.02. The circumstance that for, for determining the scope of Art. 44 of the VAT Directive, whether a taxable person falls under the special scheme for SMEs or not is, in itself, immaterial also gains confirmation in the guidelines drafted by the VAT Committee. *See* European Commission, Value Added Tax Committee, *Guidelines resulting from the 88th Meeting of 13-14 July 2009* (taxud.d.1(2009)358416 - 634).

146. For a discussion of the liability rule contained in Art. 193 of the VAT Directive, *see* section §8.02.

147. T. Bergin, *Exclusive - Loophole Allows Uber to Avoid UK Tax, Undercut Rivals*, Reuters (7 Jun. 2017); T. Worstall, *Reuters' Tom Bergin Wrong Again - Uber Does Not Avoid VAT, Rather It Does Not Charge VAT*, Forbes (8 Jun. 2017).

Indeed, in light of the equality and neutrality principles underpinning EU VAT, one might well question the rationale behind leaving sharing economy platforms nearly at liberty to exploit such kinds of opportunities for eroding their own VAT liabilities and obligations.[148] In this connection, a better level playing field would certainly be achieved by removing or lowering significantly registration thresholds[149], or if Uber drivers would be recharacterized as employees of the US-based platform – solution which, however, the author does not find desirable[150] –, since, in this latter event, the company would easily exceed the registration threshold established by any Member State and, thus, would be obliged to account for VAT under normal rules. Indeed, a departure from the equality and neutrality principles underpinning EU VAT should be permissible only if and in so far as it is capable of rendering simpler and more flexible the application of EU VAT through an overall reduction of both compliance and administrative costs. Admittedly, striking an appropriate balance between these two conflicting needs is not an easy task. A step in that direction might be represented by the Commission's proposal suggesting the introduction, for SMEs, of an EU-wide maximum registration threshold of EUR 85,000 or the equivalent in national currency.[151] There are, however, at least two noticeable pitfalls in the Commission's current proposal. First, the enactment of an EU-wide registration threshold for SMEs would remain an option for a Member State. Second, each Member State would remain at liberty to set its own registration threshold, provided that such threshold does not exceed EUR 85,000 or the equivalent in national currency. Thus, under the Commission's current proposal, divergent treatments are likely to remain, depending on whether a Member State has established a registration threshold or not and, further, due to the different national registration thresholds in place. Ultimately, an EU-wide scheme with a single, common, and mandatory threshold seems the obvious solution for ensuring a better level playing field in the single market, as well as for reducing compliance and administrative costs for small businesses and tax authorities alike.[152]

148. In truth, the practice of splitting-up a single economic operation among several taxable persons, in a way that each of them would benefit from a special scheme, has long been acknowledged in the EU VAT literature. *See* e.g., European Commission, *supra* n. 3, at 8.
149. *See* AU: Federal Court of Australia, 17 Feb. 2017, *Uber B.V. v. Commissioner of Taxation* [2017] FCA 110, which, by equating Uber drivers to taxi drivers, has de facto inhibited the former from using the general registration turnover threshold (equal to AUD 75,000) to escape their own GST obligations. Under Australian GST, businesses operating taxi travel, in fact, are required to register under all circumstances, even if their annual turnover remains below the statutory registration threshold.
150. *See* section §4.04.
151. European Commission, *Proposal for a Council Directive amending Directive 2006/112/EC on the Common System of Value Added Tax as regards the Special Scheme for Small Enterprises*, COM(2018) 21 final.
152. European Commission, *Commission Staff Working Document. Impact Assessment accompanying the Document Proposal for a Council Directive amending Directive 2006/112/EC on the Common System of Value Added Tax as regards the Special Scheme for Small Enterprises*, at 38-48, SWD(2018) 9 final; European Commission, *Green Paper on the Future of VAT: Toward a Simpler, More Robust and Efficient VAT System*, at 17, COM(2010) 695 final.

§4.06 CHAPTER CONCLUSIONS AND RECOMMENDATIONS FOR IMPROVEMENT

[A] Main Findings

The concept of 'taxable person' defines the subjective or personal scope of EU VAT. The relevant definition contained in Article 9(1) of the VAT Directive, as further complemented by Articles 2(1) and 12(1) of the VAT Directive, has a wide scope and, indeed, the concept has also received a broad understanding in the *travaux preparatoires* as well as by the CJEU. As a matter of fact, it is quite easy for a person to fulfil all the four elements laid down in the relevant statutory definition, even those referring to the exercise by a person of an 'economic activity' and the carrying out of this activity 'independently', given that those elements are premised on substantial rather than formal conditions. Several considerations can be advanced in this regard.

As for the concept of 'economic activity', in order to be 'economic', it is neither necessary that the activity in question is profitable, nor it is relevant the subjective intention of the person carrying out such an activity. The sole exceptions in this regard relate to activities performed free-of-charge, those for which only a symbolic, unusually low, or not reflecting any economic reality payment is provided, as well as activities carried out for a fee other than *qua* (i.e., as for) consideration. It is, however, important to recall that free-of-charge activities still need to be considered as 'economic activities' under EU VAT if they are provided by a person for strictly business-related purposes or, also, in the furtherance of his economic activity as a whole.

As for two further specifications of the concept of 'economic activity', i.e., those of 'market participation' and 'on a continuing basis', both these notions do not seem quite decisive for establishing whether a person is a taxable person or not, given the broad scope of interpretation and application of those expressions made by the CJEU. Indeed, with regard to the 'continuity' requirement, it is remarkable that an economy activity can also entail the mere 'exploitation of tangible or intangible property' and, further, be concluded even in a single day.

Whether or not, by carrying out an economic activity, a person acts in a business rather than a private capacity is, instead, a condition to examine extremely carefully in light of all the facts and circumstances of the case. A taxable person exclusively making or receiving a supply in his private capacity, in fact, is not entitled to charge and deduct any VAT on those activities. Ultimately, even this condition seems quite easy to be fulfilled, in so far as a person is not required to mobilize so many resources to become a taxable person and, further, the application scope of private activities under EU VAT is quite narrow. What, rather, is much more difficult to assess is the extent to which a taxable person should be entitled to deduct the VAT paid on the inputs used in the furtherance of his economic activity, especially if an asset privately acquired is used for business purposes only on a later date.

As for the requirement that a person carries out an economic activity 'independently', it is pretty clear that not only employees, but also those having a relationship similar to the one of employment, shall not be considered as taxable persons under EU VAT. Despite its apparently broad wording, such condition is quite hard to be met.

Based on the CJEU's case law, even a person under some disciplinary control, subject to limitations as for his remuneration and responsibility, or acting under a cooperation agreement with other persons, can in fact qualify as a taxable person under EU VAT. Only where a person does not bear any economic risk a different conclusion might eventually be reached.

Although, stricto sensu, not being a requirement to qualify as a taxable person under EU VAT, registration thresholds and the special scheme for SMEs have a practical relevance in this regard, in so far as a person, whose annual turnover does not exceed the registration threshold established by a Member State, is considered as an exempt or out-of-scope supplier, with the relevant consequence that both his output and input supplies are disregarded for EU VAT purposes. There are, however, several problems with registration thresholds, mainly due to the fact that they vary greatly across Member States and, further, that their implementation by a country is optional. Other drawbacks relate to the fact that the operation of registration thresholds and the special scheme for SMEs is only available to businesses trading domestically and, further, that those measures tend to favour those making B2C transactions.

In light of the above, it can be maintained that, nearly in all situations, sharing economy platforms qualify as taxable persons under EU VAT. Normally, platforms in fact carry out an activity which is economic, participate in a market, provide their own services on a continuing basis and, further, act in a business capacity as well as independently. The only exception in this regard might be constituted by those platforms which exclusively carry out free-of-charge activities or act in a private capacity, situations which, however, do not occur for any of the four platforms examined in the present study and, in the author's opinion, neither this is the case of the provision by a platform of its own services only in return for user personal data.

The circumstance that, nearly in all situations, sharing economy platforms qualify as taxable persons for EU VAT purposes is also consistent with the five legal principles which compose the evaluation model as conceptualized in the present study. Indeed, the author does not find any compelling reason, in light of either the equality, neutrality, simplicity, flexibility, or proportionality principles, for excluding sharing economy platforms from the subjective or personal scope of EU VAT, besides situations in which more conventional undertakings would be excluded too. Platforms engaging in personal data transactions, certainly, are not an exception.

Even individual suppliers generally qualify as taxable persons under EU VAT. Apparently, all the conditions laid down in Article 9(1) of the VAT Directive are fulfilled: individual suppliers independently carry out an economic activity, whatever the purpose or results of that activity. The sole exceptions might entail situations in which individual suppliers carry out an economic activity free-of-charge, receive only a symbolic, unusually low, or not reflecting any economic reality payment, or, further, if individual suppliers provide a service for a fee other than *qua* (i.e., as for) consideration.

In so far as EU VAT requires not to take gratuitous transactions at their face value, the provision of personal data by a user to a platform could well amount to an 'economic activity' and, therefore, the user can be considered as a taxable person for EU VAT purposes, if the activity in question is carried out by that person for strictly business-related purposes or, also, in the furtherance of his economic activity as a whole. It is equally indisputable that, although, at first glance, it might seem odd that there is such a thing as a market for another person's sofa or for a seat on another person's car, users of sharing economy platforms like HomeExchange and BlaBlaCar do factually participate in a market. Further, the author submits that, under current EU VAT rules, no carveout for occasional activities exists, whereas the possibility for a person to act in a private capacity appears quite narrow. Rather, a difficulty attains to the need to concretely determine the amount of input VAT that an individual supplier should be effectively entitled to deduct, given the lack of a clear indication in this regard.

Equally narrow it appears the possibility to recharacterize, looking at economic reality rather than contractual documentation, individual suppliers as employees of a sharing economy platform for EU VAT purposes. As shown by the functional analysis tentatively conducted in Table 4.1, this eventuality might in fact be open only to Uber drivers, in which event Uber would have to account for VAT in respect of both its own intermediary services and the underlying supply of passenger transport. Should this recharacterization indeed occur, then issues would arise with respect to the VAT originally charged by Uber to its drivers for its own intermediary services and, further, with regard to the possibility for the platform to deduct the VAT paid by the drivers on their inputs, in so far as tax cascading generated by both these circumstances runs counter the principle of neutrality underpinning EU VAT.

An event which might occur more often is that an individual supplier's annual turnover remains below the registration threshold for EU VAT purposes, especially if the relevant threshold is set particularly high in a Member State. In such event, the individual supplier is not required to charge any VAT on his supplies, although he is not entitled to deduct any input VAT either. Despite being warranted by simplification reasons, this circumstance could give sharing economy platforms like Airbnb and Uber an (unfair?) advantage over competitors active in the same industry. An EU-wide scheme for SMEs with a single, common, and mandatory registration threshold seems the obvious solution in this regard.

The circumstance that individual suppliers generally qualify as taxable persons for EU VAT purposes is also consistent with the five legal principles which compose the evaluation model as conceptualized in the present study. As it was reasoned above with regard to sharing economy platforms, the author does not find any compelling reason, in light of either the equality, neutrality, simplicity, flexibility, or proportionality principles, for excluding individual suppliers from the subjective or personal scope of EU VAT, besides situations in which comparable suppliers in the traditional economy would be excluded too. As a matter of fact, it accords with the principles of equality and neutrality considering the provision of personal data by a user to a platform as a full-fledged 'economic activity' and, hence, the user in question as a full-fledged taxable person for EU VAT purposes, in so far as a user may equally obtain a service used as an input in the furtherance of his economic activity either by paying in money or in kind, i.e., by using his own personal data. The principles of equality and neutrality also impede considering underlying activities in the sharing economy as not entailing the participation in any kind of market, in so far as sharing economy services are similar and in competition with more conventional services, in the sense that the individual customer may choose one service over another. The principles of equality and neutrality can also be recalled in the context of a possible recharacterization of individual suppliers as employees of the platform, especially in light of the issues arising from such a recharacterization. As regards the possibility for individual suppliers to deduct their input VAT, the application of the equality and neutrality principles might instead be softened by the intervention of the principles of simplicity and flexibility, given that distinguishing between business and private spheres is not always feasible in the sharing economy and, further, that an individual supplier may even decide to use a privately acquired asset in the furtherance of his economic activities only on a later date. Lastly, it has already been stressed that the application of registration thresholds across the European Union is not in line with the principles underpinning the EU VAT system, especially the equality and neutrality principles, in so far as registration thresholds create opportunities for platforms and their users to erode their own VAT liabilities and obligations.

[B] Recommendations

In terms of possible recommendations for improving the current EU VAT system in relation to the issues identified in this chapter, the author submits that no amendment of the definition of 'taxable person', as provided in Articles 9(1), 2(1), and 12(1) of the VAT Directive, is required. The application scope of this concept is, in fact, wide and equally broad it is its interpretation by the CJEU, in a way as to include within it both sharing economy platforms and individual suppliers. In this connection, it is sufficient to recall that even occasional activities - such as those carried out by individual suppliers in the sharing economy might eventually be - shall be regarded as economic activities subject to VAT. Equally difficult it is to claim that individual suppliers in the sharing economy act in a private capacity. Given the broad but consistent interpretation of the concept of 'taxable person' made by the CJEU, the author further believes that it is also not necessary to introduce any measure or guidelines to clarify the interpretation of such concept.[153] Should it be decided not to tax certain activities, such as the provision of personal data by users to a platform in return for 'free' services, then it would be better to introduce, as suggested in the Proposal for a Second Directive, a specific exemption in the VAT Directive - solution which the author, however, does

153. In this connection, F. Cannas, *Sharing Economy: Everyone Can Be an Entrepreneur for Two Days ... But What about a VAT Taxable Person?*, 6 World J. VAT/GST L. 2 (2018), at 82-99, argues that the scope of the concept of 'taxable person' should be enlarged in a way to include also services supplied discontinuously, as it frequently occurs in the sharing economy. The author of this book, however, submits that there is no need to make such an amendment, since both the current definition and the interpretation of the concept of 'taxable persons' are broad enough as to include within it even activities carried out discontinuously. Noteworthy, also the Commission is against any legislative changes or interpretative clarification with regard to the definition of 'taxable persons' in relation to occasional suppliers. *See* European Commission, *Commission Staff Working Document*, *supra* n. 152, at 68-69.

not endorse[154]–, or to rely on the 'personal exemption' entailed in the application of a registration threshold, rather than excluding the persons carrying those economic activities altogether from the subjective or personal scope of the tax.[155] Even the assessment conducted through the evaluation model as conceptualized in the present study, indeed, provides no ground for reviewing the current definition of 'taxable persons'.

Rather, solutions need to be found in order to concretely determine the amount of input VAT that an individual supplier shall be effectively entitled to deduct. In the sharing economy, in fact, assets are frequently and seamlessly used by an individual supplier for both business and private purposes. As a result, it is quite problematic for such supplier to establish the actual extent of his entitlement to input VAT deduction, not least because the business use of an asset, e.g., a residential property for an Airbnb and a HomeExchange host or a car for an Uber and a BlaBlaCar driver, may well change over time. In this connection, a solution aimed at simplifying this assessment would be to compile a list of assets normally utilized in the provision of accommodation and passenger transport services (e.g., a residential property and a car), and, for each of those assets, to establish a fixed percentage of deductible input VAT. Eventually, the relevant percentage may vary depending on the effective use of an asset in the furtherance of a person's own economic activities. Thus, for instance, different percentages may apply depending on the number of days a residential premise is rented out or based on the time a car is used for passenger transport services, information which are readily collected by and could be easily retrieved from a platform's algorithm.

The use of fixed percentages for input VAT deduction certainly is not a novelty, as, indeed, many national VAT systems currently employ them. However, the proposal submitted here differs in that such fixed percentages would be determined at the EU level, so as to remain the same for each Member State and, thus, to ensure a better level playing field for businesses competing in the internal market. Obviously, those fixed percentages also need to be the same for all businesses in the same industry, irrespective of whether those businesses concern sharing economy or more conventional activities. On a more practical note, the fixed percentages might be calculated on the basis of macro-economic statistics related to the specific economic sector concerned, averaged for a certain number of years, as similarly provided with regard to the flat-rate compensation scheme available to small farmers pursuant to Articles 295-305 of the VAT Directive. The author submits that, overall, the introduction of fixed percentages for input VAT deduction would contribute to greatly enhance legal certainty for individual suppliers in the sharing economy, thus also avoiding potential litigations with tax authorities. Also, the proposed solution appears consistent with the five legal principles which compose the evaluation model as conceptualized in the

154. *See* section §5.06[B].
155. *See infra*. In this connection, the author further submits that the possibility for a platform user to opt out from the 'personal exemption' entailed in the application of a registration threshold and, thus, to account for VAT under normal rules would achieve neutrality and efficiency, inasmuch as it would enable the person in question to evaluate his actual convenience of being included or not into the EU VAT system.

present study. As a matter of fact, the introduction of fixed percentages for input VAT deduction would amount to a relevant simplification measure for individual suppliers and tax authorities alike, which would enable them to reduce their respective compliance and administrative costs. In parallel, the circumstance that such fixed percentages would be the same for all businesses in the same industry, irrespective of whether those businesses concern sharing economy or more conventional activities, would bring the simplification measure in question into line with the principles of equality and neutrality. Operatively, the best legislative course would be to insert the various fixed percentages, calculated differently based on the asset and the economic sector concerned, in an Annex of the Implementing Regulation.

At the same time, it would be opportune to allow an individual supplier to opt out from such flat-rate compensation scheme, in so far as that person might find financially more convenient to account for VAT under normal rules. It is also important that the person in question would have the possibility to deduct his input VAT even if it relates to an asset that that person did not initially intend to expressly use in the furtherance of his own economic activities, since the principles of equality and neutrality underpinning EU VAT would otherwise be impaired. Indeed, such a possibility complies not only with these two principles, but also with those of flexibility and proportionality, since it would be a measure exactly reflecting, from both a temporal and quantitative perspective, the variable use of an input by a taxable person in the furtherance of his own economic activities. Eventually, a specification in this regard might be inserted in the wording of the VAT Directive and, in particular, in the second paragraph of Article 187(2), which obliges Member States to allow a taxable person to make adjustments to the initial percentage of input VAT deduction on the basis of the variations in the deduction entitlement in subsequent years in relation to that for the year in which the asset was used for the first time. In detail, the specification to be inserted in the text of the VAT Directive might clarify that a person is entitled to an adjustment of his initial deduction of input VAT, even if it relates to an asset that the person in question did not initially intend to expressly use in the furtherance of his own economic activities, but it was used for such purpose only at a later date. Overall, the proposed solution appears consistent with the five legal principles which compose the evaluation model as conceptualized in the present study. In particular, the possibility for a taxable person to make adjustments to the initial percentage of input VAT deduction would be a measure consistent with the principle of flexibility, which describes the thorough ability and readiness of a tax system to respond to changes in societal and economic circumstances. The amended provision of Article 187(2) of the VAT Directive might then read as follows (additions in italics):

> Article 187
>
> [...]
>
> 2. [...] The adjustment referred to in the first subparagraph shall be made on the basis of the variations in the deduction entitlement in subsequent years in relation to that for the year in which the goods were acquired, manufactured or, where applicable, used for the first time, *even if, at the time in which the goods were acquired, manufactured or, where applicable, used for the first time, the person*

using them had not yet declared any intention to use those items for the purposes of his taxable transactions.

As regards registration thresholds, it would instead be recommendable to introduce some harmonization measures in order to establish a sufficiently level playing field in the internal market. A first step in that direction would consist in removing the current prohibition for SMEs to benefit from the exemption regime in a Member State other than the country in which the VAT is due, as stipulated by Article 283(1)(c) of the VAT Directive. As stated, in fact, the current prohibition generates relevant market distortions, to the extent that it discourages SMEs from carrying out cross-border activities and, further, it favours B2C over B2B trades. The Commission's current proposal to introduce an EU-wide maximum registration threshold of EUR 85,000, or the equivalent in national currency, might partially achieve such a harmonization goal and, therefore, should be implemented. However, rather than remaining a mere option, the introduction of a registration threshold should be made mandatory for every Member State. In particular, in order to achieve a better level playing field and avoid distortions in the internal market, due to the fact that one Member State has a very low registration threshold (e.g., Sweden), whereas another has set a very high registration threshold (e.g., the UK), it would be desirable to introduce also a minimum registration threshold, below which no business would be required to account for any VAT.[156] From an administrative standpoint, it might be opportune to set up an online portal through which SMEs can complete VAT registration, as well as an OSS mechanism available to SMEs for complying with their own cross-border VAT obligations, such as filing VAT returns, if their annual turnover is above the EU-wide threshold.[157] Nevertheless, the current possibility for an individual supplier to opt out and account for VAT under normal rules ought to be retained, if this is favourable to that person from a financial point of view. Overall, the recommendation in question appears consistent with the five legal principles which compose the evaluation model as conceptualized in the present study. In particular, the introduction of both maximum and minimum registration thresholds common to all Member States accords with principles of equality and neutrality. In parallel, the enactment of an online portal for registration and an OSS mechanism for complying with cross-border VAT obligations are measures which achieve simplicity and flexibility. As long as both types of measures were implemented, the principle of proportionality would also be respected. Operatively, the provisions relating to the new EU-wide registration threshold and the administrative simplification measures might be inserted in Article 284 of the VAT

156. Against this position, *see*, however, European Parliament, *Report on the Proposal for a Council Directive amending Directive 2006/112/EC on the Common System of Value Added Tax as regards the Special Scheme for Small Enterprises*, COM(2018)0021 - C8-0022/2018 - 2018/0006(CNS), at 9, A8-0260/2018, stipulating that, 'for the sake of flexibility and to ensure that it is possible for Member States to set appropriate lower thresholds proportional to the size and the needs of their economy, only maximum thresholds should be set at Union level'.

157. Indeed, the introduction of these two specific measures was suggested by the European Parliament in its review of the Commission's proposal concerning the special scheme for SMEs. *See* European Parliament, *supra* n. 156, at 10-11.

Directive, as redrafted according to the Commission's current proposal and the recommendations made above:

Article 284

1. *Member States shall exempt the supply of goods and services made within their territory by small enterprises established in that territory whose Member State annual turnover, attributable to such supplies, does not exceed a threshold fixed by those Member States for the application of this exemption.*

   Member States may fix varying thresholds for different business sectors based on objective criteria. However, those thresholds shall be no higher than EUR 85 000 or the equivalent in national currency.

   In any event, Member States shall exempt taxable persons whose annual turnover is lower than EUR … [number] *or the equivalent in national currency.*

   […]

4. *Prior to availing themselves of the exemption in other Member States, small enterprises shall register through an online portal set up by the Commission. The Commission shall also establish a one-stop-shop through which small enterprises can file VAT returns for each Member State of consumption in which VAT is due.*

CHAPTER 5
Taxable Transactions

§5.01 INTRODUCTION

As a second condition to apply EU VAT on a transaction, the transaction in question must be a 'taxable transaction'. The present chapter aims to filter out the main characteristics of the concept of 'taxable transactions'. More specifically, the ensuing analysis seeks to explore whether all transactions in the sharing economy, both those made by platforms and individual suppliers, shall be considered as taxable transactions or not.

The concept of 'taxable transactions' (in French, '*opérations imposables*'; in Italian, '*operazioni imponibili*') marks out the external boundaries of EU VAT, as it defines the objective or substantive scope of the tax. In general, unless otherwise prescribed[1], for a transaction to exist there must be two identifiable parties, i.e., a supplier and a customer.[2] Moreover, under EU VAT, only certain transactions are subject to tax. Importantly, the term 'transaction' must not be equated to that of 'supply'. As will be explained later in Chapter 6, although these two terms may be - and frequently are - used interchangeably, even in the text of the VAT Directive, a transaction can in fact be constituted either by a single supply or by two or more supplies.

---

1. *See* e.g., Arts 16 and 26 of the VAT Directive, stipulating that the application or use of business assets by a taxable person for purposes other than those of his business, shall be treated as a taxable transaction under EU VAT.
2. *See* e.g., DE: ECJ, 18 Dec. 1997, Case C-384/95, *Landboden-Agrardienste GmbH & Co. KG v. Finanzamt Calau*, para. 23. In this connection, *see also* M.E. van Hilten, *The Legal Character of VAT*, in *Selected Issues in European Tax Law: The Legal Character of VAT and the Application of General Principles of Justice: Summary of an EFS Seminar in Honour of Fons Simons*, at 6 (D. Albregtse & H. Kogels eds, Kluwer Law International 1999), considering that a taxable transaction exists even if, rather than a single individual, it aims to benefit a group of 'limited and, therefore, identifiable' persons.

EU VAT has always provided a specification of the concept of 'taxable transactions'. Notably, Article 2 of the Second Directive listed three types of taxable transactions, i.e., 'the supply of goods', 'the provision of services', and 'the importation of goods'. Article 2 of the Sixth Directive adopted almost the same wording, although referring to 'the supply of services' rather than to 'the provision of services'. Pursuant to Article 2(1) of the VAT Directive, instead, four types of transactions are relevant for EU VAT purposes:

(1) the supply of goods for consideration;
(2) the supply of services for consideration;
(3) the intra-Community acquisition of goods;
(4) the importation of goods.

Each of these four taxable events - being manifestations of expenditure, which itself is a proxy for consumption[3] - finds a specification in Articles 14-30 of the VAT Directive. Importantly, all the terms defining taxable transactions under EU VAT are objective in nature, meaning that they apply without any regard to the results of the activity concerned[4] or the purpose of the taxable persons making them, even if their sole purpose is ultimately to obtain a tax advantage[5]. Whether the customer effectively makes use of his purchases or not[6] and, further, whether the supplier is unaware of factually performing a supply[7] is also immaterial. It follows that only fictitious transactions, as long as they have never taken place, cannot be considered as taxable

3. J. Englisch, *VAT/GST and Direct Taxes: Different Purposes*, in *Value Added Tax and Direct Taxation: Similarities and Differences*, at para. 4.1. (M. Lang, P. Melz & E. Kristoffersson eds, IBFD 2009). As regards 'consumption' by a business, *see however* W. Hellerstein & M. Keen, *Interjurisdictional Issues in the Design of a VAT*, 63 Tax L. Rev. 2 (2010), at 366, reasoning that, 'as economists understand and use the term, only people consume. Businesses buy and use capital goods, office supplies and the like, but they do not consume them in this sense. Indeed, even to talk about business consumption is something of an oxymoron'. Thus, strictly speaking, businesses 'expend' but not indeed 'consume'. Ultimately, the author submits that, for businesses, it might be more appropriate to talk about 'productive consumption'.
4. UK: ECJ, 12 Jan. 2006, Joined Cases C-354/03, C-355/03 and C-484/03, *Optigen Ltd, Fulcrum Electronics Ltd and Bond House Systems Ltd v. Commissioners of Customs & Excise*, para. 44.
5. UK: ECJ, 21 Feb. 2006, Case C-255/02, *Halifax plc, Leeds Permanent Development Services Ltd and County Wide Property Investments Ltd v. Commissioners of Customs & Excise*, para. 59.
6. FR: ECJ, 23 Dec. 2015, Joined Cases C-250/14 and C-289/14, *Air France-KLM and Hop!-Brit Air SAS v. Ministère des Finances et des Comptes Publics*, para. 50.
7. *See* e.g., BE: ECJ, 14 Jul. 2005, Case C-435/03, *British American Tobacco International Ltd and Newman Shipping & Agency Company NV v. Belgische Staat*, para. 36, considering a theft of goods as not being a 'taxable transaction' under EU VAT, yet not based on the subjective intention shown by the supplier/thief, rather only based on the objective circumstance that a thief is not the owner but the mere possessor of the stolen goods and, therefore, neither he can transfer any ownership of those goods to another party. *Contra see* J. Kollmann, *Taxable Supplies and Their Consideration in European VAT – With Selected Examples of the Digital Economy* at para. 4.2.2.2.1 (IBFD 2018), first contending that 'supplies relevant for the purposes of VAT need to be covered by the supplier's knowledge and consent regarding the performance of the supply', but then plainly admitting that 'the willingness to perform a supply only needs to include the performance in practice'.

transactions for EU VAT purposes.[8] Lastly, it also ought to be recalled that, in order to facilitate intergenerational transfers of undertakings in full or in part, Member States are allowed to treat a transfer of a going concern as a non-taxable transaction for EU VAT purposes.[9]

Given the narrower application scope of operations such as 'the intra-Community acquisition of goods' and 'the importation of goods', the next section only focuses on 'the supply of goods' and 'the supply of services', which happen to be the most important taxable events under EU VAT. In particular, the relevance of the concept of 'supply of goods' relates to the definition of 'supply of services', which, as will be explained in the following section, is derived on a residual basis from the former.[10] Although, in fact, supplies of goods and services do not differ as regards the general conditions for a taxable transaction to exist for EU VAT purposes[11], the determination of a supply as entailing the provision of goods, services, or both[12] is not devoid of importance under EU VAT. Whether a supply consists in the provision of goods or services might, in fact, lead to the application of different rules as regards the place of supply,[13] the chargeable event and chargeability of VAT[14], as well as the applicable rates[15] and exemption[16].

§5.02 SUPPLIES OF GOODS AND SUPPLIES OF SERVICES

The supply of goods is defined by Article 14(1) of the VAT Directive as 'the transfer of the right to dispose of tangible property as owner'.[17] As regards the concepts of 'transfer' and 'right to dispose', in *Shipping and Forwarding Enterprise Safe*, the CJEU clarified that 'the right to dispose of tangible property as owner' is an EU law's concept, which, as such, must not depend on criteria established by national laws, but rather should be understood as including any transfer of tangible property giving the recipient thereof the power to dispose of that property as if he were the owner, whether legal or

8. BE: ECJ, 6 July 2006, Joined Cases C-439/04 and C-440/04, *Axel Kittel v. Belgian State and Belgian State v. Recolta Recycling SPRL*, para. 53.
9. Articles 19 and 29 VAT Directive.
10. B.J.M. Terra & J. Kajus, *Commentary on European VAT* at para. 4.1. (IBFD Tax Research Platform 2019).
11. *See* sections §5.03 and §5.04.
12. DE: ECJ, 2 May 1996, Case C-231/94, *Faaborg-Gelting Linien A/S v. Finanzamt Flensburg*, paras 11-20. For a discussion of 'composite supplies', *see* Chapter 6.
13. *See*, respectively, Arts 31-39 and 43-59a VAT Directive.
14. *See* e.g., Art. 67 VAT Directive, concerning 'goods dispatched or transported to a Member State other than that in which dispatch or transport of the goods begins'.
15. *See* e.g., Art. 98(2) First Indent and Point 1 of Annex III, allowing Member States to apply a reduced rate to the supply of 'foodstuffs' 'for human and animal consumption', but not also to the supply of restaurant and catering services.
16. *See* e.g., Art. 132(1)(b) of the VAT Directive, exempting the provision of a service consisting in 'medical care', but not also the supply of a drug by a doctor.
17. Notably, Art. 3 of the Proposal for a Second Directive referred to 'delivery' rather than 'supply' of goods. Instead, reference to the 'supply of goods' is made both in Art. 5 of the Second Directive, in the text as finally adopted, and in Art. 5(1) of the Sixth Directive.

mere economic ownership is transferred.[18] Accordingly, even a 'de facto' ownership transfer of a tangible property suffices for having a supply of goods in full EU VAT terms.[19] Further, pursuant to Article 14(2)(a) of the VAT Directive, a transfer can also be mandatory, i.e., 'by order made by or in the name of a public authority or in pursuance of the law', if payment or compensation is provided in return.[20]

Still, a question remains on what exactly can be considered as 'tangible property' (in French, '*bien corporel*'; in Italian, '*bene materiale*'). Based on the Latin origin of the expression ('*res quae tangi possunt*'), it appears that this term should comprise any physically touchable thing, including animals.[21] This understanding, however, does not entirely reconcile with the fact that also non-physical things, such as 'electricity, gas, heat or cooling energy and the like'[22], shall be treated as 'tangible property'[23] and, further, that not every physically touchable thing is also a 'tangible property' within the meaning of Article 14 of the VAT Directive (e.g., 'the supply of staff'[24]), especially if such physically touchable thing is of little or no value compared to the service component attached to it (e.g., a ticket for admission to 'cultural, artistic, sporting, scientific, educational, entertainment or similar activities, such as fairs or exhibitions'[25]).

It also ought to be recalled that, pursuant to Article 15(2) of the VAT Directive, Member States may also regard as tangible property certain rights relating to immovable property, namely: (1) 'certain interests in immovable property', (2) 'rights in rem giving the holder thereof a right of use over immovable property', and (3) 'shares or interest equivalent to shares giving the holder thereof de jure or de facto rights of ownership or possession over immovable property or part thereof'.[26]

The supply of services, instead, is defined by Article 24(1) of the VAT Directive only in the negative, that is as 'any transaction which does not constitute a supply of goods'.[27] In this connection, only a few examples of supplies of services are provided in Article 25 of the VAT Directive, which, to that effect, lists in particular 'the assignment of intangible property'.

---

18. NL: ECJ, 8 Feb. 1990, Case C-320/88, *Staatssecretaris van Financiën v. Shipping and Forwarding Enterprise Safe BV*, paras 6-10.
19. BG: ECJ, 18 Jul. 2013, Case C-78/12, *'Evita-K' EOOD v. Direktor na Direktsia 'Obzhalvane i upravlenie na izpalnenieto' – Sofia pri Tsentralno upravlenie na Natsionalnata agentsia za prihodite*, para. 35.
20. PL: ECJ, 13 June 2018, Case C-665/16, *Minister Finansów v. Gmina Wrocław*, paras 26-51.
21. UK: ECJ, 21 June 1988, Case C-10/87, *The Queen v. Commissioners of Customs and Excise Ex Parte Tattersalls Ltd*, para. 10.
22. Article 15(1) VAT Directive.
23. *See* A. van Doesum, H.W.M. van Kesteren & G.J. van Norden, *Fundamentals of EU VAT Law* at 106 (Kluwer Law International 2016), reasoning that Art. 15(1) of the VAT Directive, indeed, expands the application scope of the concept of 'goods'.
24. Article 59(1)(f) VAT Directive.
25. Article 54(1) VAT Directive.
26. *See* Kollmann, *supra* n. 7, at para. 3.2.1.1., reasoning that Art. 15(2) of the VAT Directive, indeed, extends the meaning of 'tangible property'.
27. The definition of services as a residual category, rather than through itemization, seems to be premised on the fact that services are less easily identifiable than goods. *See* A.A. Tait, *Value Added Tax – International Practice and Problems* at 387 (International Monetary Fund 1988).

A more extensive list of services was instead drawn up in the Proposal for a Second Directive, notably in Annex B. The services listed in that Annex included, *inter alia*, 'assignment of patents, trademarks and similar rights', 'commercial advertising', 'transport of goods and their storage, together with ancillary services', 'leasing of movable tangible goods to a taxpayer', 'making personnel available to a taxpayer', 'banking transactions on behalf of a taxpayer', 'services of consultants, engineers, planning bureaux and similar offices, in the technical, economic and scientific field', 'fulfilment of an obligation not to exercise, wholly or partly, a professional activity or a right enumerated in this list', as well as 'services of brokers, independent intermediaries, commercial agents and forwarding agents in connection with transactions involving goods or services enumerated in this list'.

The positive list included in the Proposal for a Second Directive was also maintained in the text of the Second Directive as finally adopted, but it was then repealed by the Sixth Directive, whose Article 6(1), in fact, only contained the negative definition which is identically reproduced in Article 24 of the current VAT Directive. As observed by the Explanatory Memorandum attached to the Proposal for a Sixth Directive, the repeal of the list implied that 'all supplies of services are henceforth taxable, with the exception of those covered by exemptions contained in this Directive'[28], a statement that, in the author's opinion, should be considered equally valid for the negative definition contained in Article 24 of the current VAT Directive.

From this negative definition, it follows that a supply of services necessarily consists of something other than 'the transfer of the right to dispose over tangible property as owner'. It further derives that the terms 'supply of goods' and 'supply of services' are not only mutually exclusive, but also all-comprehensive, in the sense that the two expressions in question are meant to cover any foreseeable transaction carried out for consideration.[29] This impression gains additional force from a reading of Article 25(1)(b) of the VAT Directive, stipulating that a supply of services also includes 'the obligation to refrain from an act, or to tolerate an act or situation'.[30] Indeed, a supply of service can even be made on a continuous or a permanent basis[31] and, further, can well take place where a person is paid for not performing an activity or for surrendering a contract.[32] The situation, instead, differs where a transaction is declared null or void, since this might also imply that there was no supply within the meaning of the VAT

28. European Commission, *Proposal for a Sixth Council Directive on the Harmonization of Member States concerning Turnover Taxes Common System of Value Added Tax: Uniform Basis of Assessment (submitted to the Council by the Commission on 29 June 1973)*, at 11, COM(73) 950, Bulletin of the European Communities No. 11 (1973).
29. Indeed, as meant in Art. 1(2) of the VAT Directive, which defines EU VAT as 'a general tax on consumption' of all goods and services.
30. In the CJEU's case-law, *see* e.g., BG: ECJ, 3 Sep. 2015, Case C-463/14, *Asparuhovo Lake Investment Company OOD v. Direktor na Direktsia 'Obzhalvane i danachno-osiguritelna praktika' Varna pri Tsentralno upravlenie na Natsionalnata agentsia za prihodite*, paras 32-43.
31. NL: ECJ, 21 Mar. 2002, Case C-174/00, *Kennemer Golf & Country Club v. Staatssecretaris van Financiën*, para. 40.
32. UK: ECJ, 15 Dec. 1993, Case C-63/92, *Lubbock Fine & Co. v. Commissioners of Customs and Excise*, paras 8-9.

Directive and, therefore, that no VAT was ever due.[33] In a sense, being the scope of supplies of services almost endless[34], the related definition of Article 24(1) of the VAT Directive functions as a sort of 'catch-all provision'.[35]

Given the definition of sharing economy as used in the present study[36], both transactions between a sharing economy platform and its users and among users themselves fall within the scope of the negative definition laid down in Article 24 of the VAT Directive and, therefore, should be characterized as 'supplies of services'. More specifically, transactions made by a platform to its users constitute supplies of services, as long as in those circumstances no transfer of right to dispose of tangible property as owner pursuant to Article 14(1) of the VAT Directive occurs. Transactions made by users among themselves also constitute supplies of services, as long as they entail only a temporary usage of goods (i.e., short-term accommodation) or the provision of services (i.e., passenger transport). In case of barter transactions, such as those occurring between a platform and its users and involving the provision of 'free' services in return for personal data or, also, those among users themselves on a platform like HomeExchange, instead, there are two supplies of services rather than just one.[37]

The circumstance that both transactions between a sharing economy platform and its users and among users themselves constitute, in principle, supplies of services under EU VAT, however, does not absolve from the need to verify whether the supplies in question meet the general conditions for a taxable transaction to exist for EU VAT purposes. Two, in particular, are the general conditions for a taxable transaction to exist under EU VAT. The first condition demands that the transaction is carried out 'for consideration'. The second condition, instead, requires that a 'direct link' between the supply and the consideration for it is established. An analysis of these two conditions, with specific regard to supplies of services, is provided in the following sections.

§5.03 FOR CONSIDERATION

Article 2(1)(a) and (c) of the VAT Directive limits the application of EU VAT to supplies of goods and services made 'for consideration' (in French, '*à titre onéreux*'; in Italian, '*a titolo oneroso*').[38]

---

33. BG: ECJ, 27 Jun. 2018, Case C-364/17, '*Varna Holideis' EOOD v. Direktor na Direktsia 'Obzhalvane i danachno-osiguritelna praktika'– Varna pri Tsentralno upravlenie na Natsionalnata agentsia za prihodite*, para. 14.
34. Van Doesum et al., *supra* n. 23, at 123.
35. Kollmann, *supra* n. 7, at para. 3.2.2.
36. *See* section §2.02.
37. A distinct and, indeed, much more complicated issue, instead, concerns the characterization of those services under EU VAT, a question of importance given that, based on such characterization, different place of supply rules might apply. Notably, this specific issue will be dealt with only later, in Chapter 7.
38. Article 2 of the Second Directive, in its English version, used the expression 'against payment' rather than 'for consideration', which was adopted only from the Sixth Directive onward. The wording of the French and Italian versions has, instead, remained unchanged. As stipulated by Advocate General Slynn in *Apple and Pear Development Council*, such a change was likely made

The term 'consideration', however, is not defined in the VAT Directive or elsewhere. In the absence of a statutory definition of 'consideration', the CJEU strove to find one. Notably, in *Coöperatieve Aardappelenbewaarplaats*, the Court explained that a 'consideration' is everything which is received in return for the supply of goods or services and, further, it entails an amount which must be capable of being expressed in money.[39]

It was also reasoned that a supply made otherwise than for consideration falls outside the scope of EU VAT.[40] Notably, in *Hong Kong Trade Development Council*, the CJEU held that supplies carried out free-of-charge are not subject to EU VAT.[41] Moreover, as already recalled in Chapter 4, first, in *Lajver*, and then, in *Gemeente Borsele*, the Court further extended the scope of the carveout for free-of-charge services, by including within it also the situation of transactions carried out for a fee other than *qua* (i.e., as for) consideration.[42] Further, in *Coöperatieve Aardappelenbewaarplaats*, the Court maintained that an unascertained reduction in the value of the shares held by members of a cooperative did not qualify as a consideration under EU VAT, in so far as such a loss of share value could not be regarded as a payment received by the cooperative in return for the supply of services to its members.[43] Along the same lines, it might also be argued that providing a mere 'reward' (e.g., a key chain or a sticker), as a result of a donation, by no means can be seen as a supply for which a consideration is paid.[44]

Despite these latter protestations, the CJEU has repeated time and again that the circumstance that the price paid by the customer is higher or lower than the cost price is, per se, irrelevant.[45] Under EU VAT, in fact, the consideration represents a 'subjective value', meaning a value assessed according to the amount actually received by the

as to clarify that a consideration not necessarily is to be paid in cash. *See* UK: Opinion of the Advocate General, 28 Oct. 1987, Case C-102/86, *Apple and Pear Development Council v. Commissioners of Customs and Excise*.

39. NL: ECJ, 5 Feb. 1981, Case C-154/80, *Staatssecretaris van Financiën v. Association coopérative 'Coöperatieve Aardappelenbewaarplaats GA'*, paras 10 and 13.
40. A supply not made for any type of consideration can be seen as an 'out-of-scope supply'. *See* R. de la Feria & R. Krever, *Ending VAT Exemptions: Toward a Post-Modern VAT*, in *VAT Exemptions: Consequences and Design Alternatives*, at 12-13 (R. de la Feria ed., Kluwer Law International 2013).
41. NL: ECJ, 1 Apr. 1982, Case C-89/81, *Staatssecretaris van Financiën v. Hong-Kong Trade Development Council*, para. 10.
42. HU: ECJ, 2 Jun. 2016, Case C-263/15, *Lajvér Meliorációs Nonprofit Kft. and Lajvér Csapadékvízrendezési Nonprofit Kft. v. Nemzeti Adó- és Vámhivatal*, para. 49; NL: ECJ, 12 May 2016, Case C-520/14, *Gemeente Borsele v. Staatssecretaris van Financiën and Staatssecretaris van Financiën v. Gemeente Borsele*, para. 33.
43. *Coöperatieve Aardappelenbewaarplaats* (C-154/80), para. 12.
44. *See* M.M.W.D. Merkx, *The VAT Consequences of Crowdfunding*, 27 Intl. VAT Monitor 1 (2016), Journals IBFD, arguing that a reward only aims to render a donation more attractive for the donor and, therefore, cannot qualify as a consideration for EU VAT purposes, since it serves a purpose other than the 'real' intention of the donor, i.e., to financially support an activity, which he believes in, carried out by the supplier. A 'particular scenario' for rewards of a symbolic value is also envisaged by the Commission while discussing reward-based crowdfunding models. *See* European Commission, Value Added Tax Committee, *Working Paper No. 836. VAT Treatment of Crowdfunding*, at 8-14 (taxud.c.1(2015)576037).
45. *See* e.g., SW: ECJ, 20 Jan. 2005, Case C-412/03, *Hotel Scandic Gåsabäck AB v. Riksskatteverket*, para. 22. For a discussion, *see also* section §4.02[A].

supplier and not, instead, a value determined according to objective criteria.[46] In case no amount is agreed between the parties to a transaction, the consideration must be set equal to the value which the customer attributes to the supply which he seeks to obtain and, thus, corresponds to the amount which he is prepared to spend for that purpose.[47] Indeed, according to the same Court, even a mere reimbursement of expenses by one party to another constitutes a consideration, with the relevant consequence that the transaction in question falls within the scope of EU VAT in full.[48] Further, in *Bertelsmann*, the CJEU found a consideration in that a good was paid by a customer simply through the provision to the supplier of information and contact details relating to other potential customers.[49]

A consideration can also be paid by means of a subscription. The VAT Directive, in fact, does not contain any provision stipulating a different treatment, on the one hand, for periodic, flat-rate payments and, on the other hand, for one-time, proportional payments.[50] This circumstance was also clarified by the CJEU, *inter alia*, in *Kennemer Golf*, in *La Rayon d'Or*, and in *Asparuhovo Lake Investment Company*, where the fact that the services performed were neither defined in advance, nor personalized, and that the amount paid was fixed and payment made in the form of a membership fee, a lump sum, or a subscription fee, did not impede the Court from establishing the existence of a consideration for EU VAT purposes.[51]

Not always a payment, however, amounts to a consideration under EU VAT. Notably, a payment, not being the counterpart of a reciprocal obligation, must remain

46. Pursuant to Art. 80 of the VAT Directive, in fact, there is only a narrow possibility for Member States to rely on objective rather than subjective criteria, that is only in specific cases and in order to prevent tax evasion or avoidance.
47. *See* e.g., BG: ECJ, 19 Dec. 2012, Case C-549/11, *Direktor na Direktsia 'Obzhalvane i Upravlenie na Izpalnenieto' – Grad Burgas pri Tsentralno Upravleniena Natsionalnata Agentsia za Prihodite v. Orfey Balgaria EOOD*, para. 44.
48. LU: ECJ, 4 May 2017, Case C-274/15, *European Commission v. Grand Duchy of Luxembourg*, paras 83 and 89.
49. DE: ECJ, 3 Jul. 2001, Case C-380/99, *Bertelsmann AG v. Finanzamt Wiedenbrück*, para. 18. Similarly, in *Empire Stores*, Advocate General van Gerven found a consideration in 'the obtaining of personal ... information concerning the customer'. *See* UK: Opinion of the Advocate General, 16 Mar. 1994, Case C-33/93, *Empire Stores Ltd v. Commissioners of Customs and Excise*, para. 15. Against these conclusions, P. Farmer & R. Lyal, *EC Tax Law* at 123 (Clarendon Press 1994) argue that, 'in the absence of other factors, the mere fact of agreeing to be a customer cannot constitute additional consideration over and above the price paid for any supplies'. Along the same lines, although specifically discussing the case of 'free Internet services', *see also* M. Lamensch, *The Scope of the EU VAT System: Traditional & Digital Economy Related Questions*, in *CJEU – Recent Developments in Value Added Tax 2017*, at 128 (M. Lang et al. eds, Linde 2018).
50. C. Trenta, *Rethinking EU VAT for P2P Distribution* at 162 (Kluwer Law International 2015). The situation of pre-payments, instead, might require a different appraisal. *See* e.g., UK: ECJ, 21 Feb. 2006, Case C-419/02, *BUPA Hospitals Ltd and Goldsborough Developments Ltd v. Commissioners of Customs & Excise*, para. 51, concerning lump sums 'paid for goods referred to in general terms in a list which may be altered at any time by agreement between the buyer and the seller and from which the buyer may possibly select articles, on the basis of an agreement which he may unilaterally resile from at any time'.
51. *Kennemer Golf* (C-174/00), para. 40; FR: ECJ, 27 Mar. 2014, Case C-151/13, *Le Rayon d'Or SARL v. Ministre de l'Économie et des Finances*, paras 36-37; *Asparuhovo Lake Investment Company* (C-463/14), para. 39.

outside the scope of EU VAT.[52] An example in this regard can be found in *Posnania Investment*, a case concerning the payment of a tax debt effectuated in kind, namely by means of an ownership transfer of an immovable property from the taxpayer to the state, where the CJEU concluded that, although a legal relationship existed between the two parties, i.e., the taxpayer and the state, the related obligation was not reciprocal but 'unilateral', in so far as payment of the amount due by the taxpayer resulted only in the 'statutory discharge of its tax debt'.[53]

Indemnities constitute another prominent example of payments made in the absence of a supply. Although the VAT Directive does not contain any specific provision in this regard, compensatory damages have been the subject matter of a few cases dealt with by the CJEU.[54] Notably, in *Société Thermale d'Eugénie-les-Bains*, a case concerning the characterization under EU VAT of deposits provided by clients for reserving hotel rooms and retained by the hotelier as fixed compensation for the loss suffered as a result of a client's cancellation, the CJEU ruled that such advanced payments did not amount to a consideration for EU VAT purposes.[55] Nevertheless, in *Air France – KLM*, a case concerning the VAT treatment of advanced payments for flight tickets in the event of passenger no-shows, the Court, taking an opposite stance, concluded that such payments were, actually, to be subject to VAT, being the consideration for a full-fledged service (i.e., flight passenger transport) already identifiable at the time of the purchase of the flight tickets by the passengers.[56] Similarly, in *MEO – Serviços de Comunicações e Multimédia*, the CJEU found that a predetermined sum, corresponding to the basic monthly amount payable by customers in the event of termination, for reasons attributable to them, of a contract containing an obligation to be bound for a defined term before its end (i.e., the so-called tie-in period), amounted to a consideration under EU VAT, given that the predetermined sum was set equal to the consideration for services supplied to those customers.[57]

It is also important to note that, as explained by the CJEU in *Marcandi*, a payment can constitute the consideration provided for a transaction only. This means that a payment made for a transaction cannot constitute the consideration for another transaction or, even, a payment on account in respect of the consideration to be paid

---

52. NL: ECJ, 20 Jun. 1991, Case C-60/90, *Polysar Investments Netherlands BV v. Inspecteur der Invoerrechten en Accijnzen*, para. 13.
53. PL: ECJ, 11 May 2017, Case C-36/16, *Minister Finansów v. Posnania Investment SA*, paras 32-33.
54. For a discussion of compensatory damages under EU VAT, *see* J. Swinkels, *Cancellation Charges and Compensations under EU VAT*, 19 Intl. VAT Monitor 6 (2008), Journals IBFD.
55. FR: ECJ, 18 Jul. 2007, Case C-277/05, *Société Thermale d'Eugénie-les-Bains v. Ministère de l'Économie, des Finances et de l'Industrie*, paras 16-36. Noteworthy, a different conclusion on this point was reached in the case by Advocate General Poiares Maduro, who argued that, indeed, deposits were paid so that hoteliers accepted the obligation to have a room available to the clients on an agreed date. *See* FR: Opinion of the Advocate General, 13 Sep. 2006, Case C-277/05, *Société Thermale d'Eugénie-les-Bains v. Ministère de l'Économie, des Finances et de l'Industrie*, paras 15-16.
56. FR: ECJ, 23 Dec. 2015, Joined Cases C-250/14 and C-289/14, *Air France-KLM and Hop!-Brit Air SAS v. Ministère des Finances et des Comptes Publics*, para. 35.
57. PT: ECJ, 22 Nov. 2018, Case C-295/17, *MEO – Serviços de Comunicações e Multimédia SA v. Autoridade Tributária e Aduaneira*, para. 44.

for another transaction.[58] On the contrary, as regards the person receiving the payment, the Court maintained that a consideration can also be paid to a person by allowing him to deduct the amount due from a payment made through him.[59]

The above exposition shows that, for a transaction to be subject to EU VAT, a consideration needs to be paid. As for services provided by a sharing platform to its users, a consideration indeed exists in nearly all cases. As a matter of fact, since a consideration can also be provided by means of periodic, flat-rate payments, this condition is even fulfilled in case an annual subscription rather than a transaction fee is paid, which indeed is a further possibility of payment for users on a platform like HomeExchange.[60] Also, in light of the CJEU's case law, it is irrelevant the fact that the consideration for its own services is deducted by the platform from the amount that the individual customer pays to the individual supplier, situation which, indeed, occurs for all the four sharing economy platforms examined in the present study.

It follows that, only if a sharing economy platform does not charge anything for its own services, a different conclusion might eventually be reached. As clarified by the CJEU in *Hong Kong Trade Development Council*, if a supplier provides his services exclusively free-of-charge, those transactions, in fact, do not fall within the scope of EU VAT. And yet, none of the four sharing economy platforms examined in the present study provides all its services exclusively free-of-charge.[61]

In light of the CJEU's most recent decisions – in particular, *Air France – KLM*, and *MEO – Serviços de Comunicações e Multimédia* – it also appears no longer tenable to claim that cancellation fees, such as those imposed by Uber in certain instances, do not amount to a consideration in full EU VAT terms, as instead found by the Court, previously, in *Société Thermale d'Eugénie-les-Bains*.

Last but not least, recalling the findings of the CJEU in *Bertelsmann*, the author believes that personal data do indeed constitute a consideration for EU VAT purposes.[62] Admittedly, not everyone agrees with this contention.[63] In any event, the

58. UK: ECJ, 5 July 2018, Case C-544/16, *Marcandi Limited, Agissant Sous le Nom Commercial 'Madbid' v. Commissioners for Her Majesty's Revenue & Customs*, para. 53.
59. BE: ECJ, 25 May 1993, Case C-18/92, *Chaussures Bally SA v. Belgian State, Minister for Finance*, para. 16.
60. *See* section §2.08[A]. A subscription-based model is also available, for BlaBlaCar passengers, in Italy. *See* section §2.08[B].
61. As recalled in section §2.08[A], however, a messaging service is offered by HomeExchange to its users free-of-charge.
62. Indeed, making an excursion outside EU VAT, it might also be recalled that the draft of the Digital Economy Directive stipulates that a remuneration does exist even where 'a price is to be paid or the consumer actively provides counter-performance other than money in the form of personal data or any other data'. *See* European Commission, *Proposal for a Directive of the European Parliament and of the Council on Certain Aspects Concerning Contracts for the Supply of Digital Content*, at 24-25, COM(2015) 634 final.
63. *See* e.g., F.S. Zawodsky, *Value Added Taxation in the Digital Economy*, Brit. Tax Rev. 5 (2018), at 614-615, contending that the extension of the expression 'for consideration' as to include within it also 'non-monetary data or the right to utilize data is arguably asking too much'. He further maintains that 'the fact that the amount of consideration is too uncertain could hinder taxation'. Admittedly, these considerations might well find a parallel in the CJEU's case-law. *See* CZ: ECJ, 10 Nov. 2016, Case C-432/15, *Odvolací finanční ředitelství contro Pavlína Baštová*, para. 35, where the Court missed to find a consideration in the supply of a horse by its owner to the organizer of a horse race, on the ground that 'although the horse owner could possibly derive a

author strongly rejects the view that the consideration for platform services, in reality, is not paid immediately by users, but rather by a third party (e.g., an advertising company) only at a later stage.[64] This is because, as explained by the CJEU in *Marcandi*, a payment can constitute the consideration provided for a transaction only, whereas, clearly, the payment made by a third party (e.g., an advertising company) at a later stage constitutes the consideration paid for another transaction, resulting in that the platform enables such third party to access personal data of its users.[65]

Based on the above exposition, apparently also transactions among platform users are to be considered as taxable transactions for EU VAT purposes. This can be maintained not only in case of a monetary consideration, but also where a consideration for a service is paid in kind, i.e., with an individual customer providing another service in return, as it occurs among users on a platform like HomeExchange.[66] As a matter of fact, from *Hong Kong Trade Development Council*, it follows that, only if a supply is made free-of-charge, the transactions in question must not be subject to EU VAT. Indeed, as confirmed by the CJEU, even a mere reimbursement of expenses by one party to another, as provided by the passenger to the driver on a platform like BlaBlaCar, shall be seen as a consideration for EU VAT purposes. Lastly, as regards cancellation charges, such as those which might be paid to an individual supplier in case of a late cancellation by an individual customer, considerations similar to those submitted above with regard to platform services apply.

§5.04 DIRECT LINK BETWEEN SERVICE AND CONSIDERATION

For a transaction to be subject to EU VAT, the existence of a consideration alone, however, does not suffice. Rather, a direct link between the service supplied and the consideration provided for it must also be established.[67] The VAT Directive, by itself, does not explain what a 'direct link' is. Indeed, such concept is only mentioned in passim in Article 73 of the VAT Directive, containing a reference to subsidies 'directly linked' (in French, '*directement liées*'; in Italian, '*direttamente connesse*') to the price of the supply, with a view of determining the relevant taxable amount.

Despite a lack of any reference to it, the need to establish a direct link between the service supplied and the consideration provided for it has been confirmed by the CJEU

---

benefit from that participation as a result of the increase in the value of the horse in the event that it is placed or the publicity gained by the horse from its participation, that benefit is difficult to quantify and uncertain, since it essentially depends on the result of the race'.

64. Zawodsky, *supra* n. 63, at 616-617.
65. Supporting this view, *see* Kollmann, *supra* n. 7, at para. 5.3.2.3.2. Further, as duly considered even by those proposing the interpretation in question, accepting third-party consideration as the 'right' scenario for personal data exchanges would have the non-negligible, detrimental effect to place the right to deduct input VAT in the hands of users of 'free' services, who, in most events, are end consumers and, therefore, neither have the right to deduct any input VAT. Indeed, such non-deductibility of input VAT would create VAT cascading, with the relative burden of the tax most likely being shifted on to the third-party business. *See* Zawodsky, *supra* n. 63, at 619.
66. For a discussion of barter transactions, *see* section §5.05.
67. For a discussion, *see* C. Amand, *When Is a Link Direct?*, 7 Intl. VAT Monitor 1 (1996), Journals IBFD.

in numerous occasions.[68] Notably, in *Apple and Pear Development Council*, a case concerning activities carried out by a council funded by mandatory charges imposed upon commercial growers of apples and pears, the CJEU affirmed that there was no direct link between the benefits received by the individual apple and pear growers and the benefits accrued generally to the industry as a whole.[69] In particular, in his opinion, Advocate General Slynn found two indications – in his own words, 'pointers' – that such a levy was not, in any real sense, a payment directly linked to the service supplied. The first indication related to the lack of any consensual element in the payment of the levy by the individual growers to the council. The second indication, instead, stemmed from the lack of any control shown by the individual growers over the activity of the council.[70] Ultimately, it was established that the council was not in the position to ensure that those who did not pay did not also benefit from its own activity, even though the same council was instead able to demand payment from those persons.[71]

The concept of 'direct link' was further refined, and a new dimension was added to it, by the CJEU in *Tolsma*. Notably, in that case, the Court affirmed that a supply is effected 'for consideration' in full EU VAT terms only if there is a legal relationship between the supplier and the customer, in a way that a direct link can be established between the supply made and the consideration paid in return.[72] Apparently, the CJEU added a 'subjective dimension', relating to the existence of a legal relationship between the parties to a transaction, to the 'objective dimension', relating to the existence of a direct link between the supply and the consideration for it, so that both conditions are necessary for a transaction to be subject to EU VAT.[73] In the Court's account, none of those conditions was notably fulfilled in case of a musician performing on the public highway and receiving donations from passers-by. In particular, the CJEU reasoned that (1) no agreement between the organ grinder and the passers-by existed and, further, that (2) no direct (*rectius*: 'necessary') link between the musical service and the payments to which it gave rise could be established. The Court also specified that the fact that the organ grinder solicited money from the passers-by and, quite understandably, could expect to receive money by playing music on the public highway could not alter the aforementioned conclusions, as long as those payments were entirely voluntary and uncertain, whereas their amount was practically impossible to determine.[74]

Indeed, the decision rendered by the CJEU in *Tolsma* was heavily criticized by scholars. For instance, Simons considered that, in so far as the national VAT systems have the objective

68. For a discussion, *see* R. Pincher, *Is There a Link?*, Brit. Tax Rev. 3 (1995), at 306-316.
69. UK: ECJ, 8 Mar. 1988, Case C-102/86, *Apple and Pear Development Council v. Commissioners of Customs and Excise*, para. 14.
70. Opinion *Apple and Pear Development Council* (C-102/86).
71. D. Butler, *The Usefulness of the 'Direct Link' Test in Determining Consideration for VAT Purposes*, 13 EC Tax Rev. 3 (2004), at 94.
72. NL: ECJ, 3 Mar. 1994, Case C-16/93, *R.J. Tolsma v. Inspecteur der Omzetbelasting Leeuwarden*, para. 14.
73. CZ: ECJ, 22 Jun. 2016, Case C-11/15, *Odvolací finanční ředitelství v. Český rozhlas*, paras 23-28.
74. *Tolsma* (C-16/93), paras 16-19.

> to tax all facets of an economic society with all its complexity ..., the more one approximates the idea to tax the whole economic community, the better the legal instruments will have to be adapted to achieve that aim. ... It is clear that in general a tax on consumption in an economic society on the music of an organ-grinder should be taxable, irrespective of whether he collects on the street or that he is – as it is common – contracted to play both on and off the street.[75]

Eventually, a looser stand in relation to the concept of 'direct link' was taken by the CJEU itself later on. Notably, in *Town & County Factors*, the Court reasoned that making the existence of a legal relationship in the *Tolsma* sense – i.e., based on the so-called '*Tolsma* test'[76] – depend on the obligations of the supplier of the service being enforceable would undermine the effectiveness of EU VAT, in that it would cause the subjection to VAT of that transaction to vary from one Member State to another, due to a different legal appraisal of the concept of reciprocal performance. Moreover, this approach would enable a taxable person to avoid paying VAT by simply including in a contract a 'binding in honour only' clause. It follows that even an obligation which is binding in honour only, such as a natural obligation, entails a legal relationship between two parties, not least because also the impossibility of seeking enforcement of that obligation derives from a specific agreement between the two parties.[77]

Despite this interpretative rift, apparently, the existence of a legal relationship between the supplier and the customer is still a requirement for a transaction to be subject to EU VAT.[78] Notably, in *Cibo Participations*, the CJEU considered as missing the direct link between a dividends distribution and the exercise of shareholding rights, which was necessary for a dividends distribution to be regarded as a consideration for EU VAT purposes, due to the fact that entitlement to dividends is not premised on a legal relationship, but rather it is a mere function of shareholding. More specifically, in the Court's view, three features of dividends account for their exclusion from EU VAT, that is: (1) the payment of dividends entirely depends on a company actually making a profit, (2) the amount of dividends is solely determined by reference to the type and class of the shares held, and (3) dividends are merely the result of ownership in a company.[79] On the contrary, as affirmed by the CJEU in *Régie Dauphinoise*, interest payments cannot be excluded from the scope of EU VAT, being the consideration paid to a party for placing capital at the disposal of another party, which, obviously, implies

75. A.L.C. Simons, *Neutrality in VAT and the Organ-Grinder*, 3 EC Tax Rev. 2 (1994), at 45. *See also* F. Vanistendael, *Neutrality and the Limits of VAT*, in *Selected Issues in European Tax Law: The Legal Character of VAT and the Application of General Principles of Justice: Summary of an EFS Seminar in Honour of Fons Simons*, at 15-16 (D. Albregtse & H. Kogels eds, Kluwer Law International 1999), considering that the 'killer' factor, for a transaction to be subject to EU VAT, 'is whether or not the transaction can be deemed to constitute an economic activity from the perspective of the supplier of the goods and/or services'.
76. UK: Opinion of the Advocate General, 27 Sep. 2001, Case C-498/99, *Town & County Factors Ltd v. Commissioners of Customs & Excise*, para. 19.
77. UK: ECJ, 17 Sep. 2002, Case C-498/99, *Town & County Factors Ltd v. Commissioners of Customs & Excise*, paras 16-24.
78. PT: Opinion of the Advocate General, 3 May 2018, Case C-16/17, *TGE Gas Engineering GmbH – Sucursal em Portugal v. Autoridade Tributária e Aduaneira*, paras 42-46.
79. FR: ECJ, 27 Sep. 2001, Case C-16/00, *Cibo Participations SA v. Directeur Régional des Impôts du Nord-Pas-de-Calais*, paras 42- 43.

the existence of a legal relationship between the two parties in question.[80] Further, from *Serebryannay vek*, it can be inferred that, for a direct link to exist, a timing difference between the supply of a service and the related payment is, per se, irrelevant.[81]

Nevertheless, there are instances in which, although a legal relationship between the supplier and the customer undeniably exists, a direct link between the service provided and the consideration received ultimately lacks. EU VAT, in fact, is based on the 'quid pro quo' principle[82], i.e., it presupposes a direct reciprocity between the service provided and the consideration received in return.[83] A relationship of direct reciprocity lacks, in particular, where no correlation exists between the amount of the service supplied and the consideration provided in return.[84] Notably, in *Apple and Pear Development Council*, the Court found that no relationship existed between the level of the benefits which individual growers obtained from the services provided by the council and the mandatory charges which they were obliged to pay.[85] The CJEU followed a similar strand of reasoning in *Commission versus Finland*, where no direct link was found between the legal aid services provided by public offices and the payment effectuated by the recipients, since, although such payment represented a portion of the overall fees, its amount was not calculated solely and exclusively on the basis of those fees, but it also depended upon the recipient's income and assets.[86] A similar string of arguments can be found in *Gemeente Borsele*, where the Court excluded the existence of a sufficiently direct link between the fees paid by parents of

80. FR: ECJ, 11 Jul. 1996, Case C-306/94, *Régie dauphinoise – Cabinet A. Forest SARL v. Ministre du Budget*, para. 17.
81. BG: ECJ, 26 Sep. 2013, Case C-283/12, *Serebryannay vek EOOD v. Direktor na Direktsia 'Obzhalvane i upravlenie na izpalnenieto' – Varna pri Tsentralno upravlenie na Natsionalna agentsia za prihodite*, para. 41.
82. *See* e.g., PL: Opinion of the Advocate General, 22 Feb. 2018, Case C-665/16, *Minister Finansów v. Gmina Wrocław*, para. 87, equating the concept of 'direct link' to 'the basic "quid pro quo" logic inherent in any transaction'.
83. UK: ECJ, 3 May 2012, Case C-520/10, *Lebara Ltd v. Commissioners for Her Majesty's Revenue & Customs*, para. 31.
84. According to H. van Kesteren, *Taxable Transactions*, in *CJEU – Recent Developments in Value Added Tax 2017*, at 211-212 (M. Lang et al. eds, Linde 2018), based on an overall analysis of the CJEU's case law, there are four situations in which a direct link cannot be recognized, that is: (1) the number of supplies is fixed and known in advance, but the consideration is variable, (2) the consideration is fixed and known in advance, but the number of supplies is variable, (3) both the supply and the consideration for it fluctuate in an independent and uncoordinated manner, so that they are not known and cannot be calculated in advance, or (4) both the supply and the consideration for it are fixed, but the consideration does not stem from the supply.
85. *Apple and Pear Development Council* (C-102/86), para. 15. Along the same lines, in *Julius Fillibeck Söhne*, the Court considered that, 'since the work to be performed and the wages received are independent of the use or otherwise by employees of the transport provided to them by their employer, it is not possible to regard a proportion of the work performed as being consideration for the transport services'. *See* DE: ECJ, 16 Oct. 1997, Case C-258/95, *Julius Fillibeck Söhne GmbH & Co. KG v. Finanzamt Neustadt*, para. 16.
86. FI: ECJ, 29 Oct. 2009, Case C-246/08, *Commission of the European Communities v. Republic of Finland*, paras 48-49. Noteworthy, in his opinion, Advocate General Ruiz-Jarabo Colomer held that 'there is therefore a certain connection between the service and the amounts' paid by the recipient of the legal aid, 'but that link is neither direct nor does it have the intensity which the case-law requires in order to identify a service effected for consideration, because it is "contaminated" by the taking account of the client's income and assets. The more modest the

pupils to a municipality for the operation a common schooling transport system and the transport service that such municipality provided in return, given that, by means of those contributions, the municipality was able to recover only a small fraction of the overall costs incurred in the provision of the service in question, which for the remainder was entirely financed through public funds.[87]

In light of all the above, ultimately, it does not seem hard to establish a direct link between the services supplied by a sharing economy platform and the consideration paid in return by its users. Access to services by a platform, in fact, is made conditional upon a payment, either on a transaction or a subscription basis, by users.

More elaboration, instead, requires verifying whether a direct link can indeed be established in case no payment is provided by users in return for platform services, other than by providing their own personal data. Notably, in case users either (1) do not share personal information on a social media platform, (2) do not upload pictures or, even, (3) restrict the use of personal data by technical means, it might be maintained - along the lines of the CJEU's decisions in *Apple and Pear Development Council*, in *Commission versus Finland*, and in *Gemeente Borsele* - that no such thing as a direct link exists, in so far as the consideration paid (i.e., user personal data) is not calculated on the basis of the services provided (i.e., the platform services).[88]

Indeed, this was also the conclusion reached by the Commission in a Working Paper released by the VAT Committee in 2018. Despite recognizing that user data do have 'an economic value', since they constitute the 'raw material' used, directly or after processing, by digital companies to carry out their own economic activities and, therefore, those data can well constitute a consideration in full EU VAT terms, in that document the Commission objects that a direct link between the provision of 'free' services by a digital company and the personal data given by users in return is missing.[89] Notably, in the Commission's account, this is due to the circumstance that

person's income, the less direct the aforementioned link will be'. *See* FI: Opinion of the Advocate General, 7 Jul. 2009, Case C-246/08, *Commission of the European Communities v. Republic of Finland*, para. 49.

87. *Gemeente Borsele* (C-520/14), paras 33-35.
88. *See* S. Pfeiffer, *VAT on 'Free' Electronic Services?*, 27 Intl. VAT Monitor 3 (2016), Journals IBFD. Apparently, the author mentioned above in this note has, however, changed his mind on this point. *See* S. Pfeiffer, *Comment on 'Free' Internet Services*, in *CJEU – Recent Developments in Value Added Tax 2017*, at 136 (M. Lang et al. eds, Linde 2018), where he argues that 'the consideration is substantiated because the right to use the data is provided in the service provider's terms and conditions' and, indeed, it is such a right, 'rather than the actual data set, which must be seen as the consideration'. *See also* Zawodsky, *supra* n. 63, at 614, who centres his criticism against the concept of data barter transactions on the fact that, in his opinion, personal data do not amount to a consideration, rather than on the circumstance that a direct link between the services provided and the personal data received in return can hardly be established.
89. European Commission, Value Added Tax Committee, *Working Paper No. 958. Conditions for There Being a Taxable Transaction When Internet Services Are Provided in Exchange for User Data*, at 5-7 (taxud.c.1(2018)6248826). The Commission's position was also shared by the German delegation, which had submitted the question before the VAT Committee. Delegations of other Member States, instead, stipulated that they had not yet arrived at a definitive position in this regard, as long as discussions on this matter were still ongoing. *See* European Commission, Value Added Tax Committee, *Minutes 111th Meeting – 30 November 2018*, at 7, (taxud.c.1(2019)1709508).

digital companies 'provide their services in the same way irrespective of the amount of data provided by the users or the quality of such data', especially considering that users can even provide the supplier with fake data, block the use by the company of cookies, or utilize 'disposable' email addresses for registration purposes. In this connection, the Commission further observed that the provision of services by digital companies does not depend on the quantity[90] or quality[91] of personal data provided by users. As a matter of fact, one user might utilize the services provided by a digital company continuously, whereas another user might barely access to the same types of services, so that the amount of data provided by each user to the digital company would, eventually, differ greatly.[92]

As regards transactions among users themselves on most sharing economy platforms, establishing a direct link between the services provided and the consideration paid for it does not appear, indeed, a difficult exercise. Access to services provided by an individual supplier, in fact, is usually made conditional upon payment - submitted through the platform - by an individual customer.

However, a few considerations need to be advanced with regard to accommodation exchanges among users on a platform like HomeExchange. Notably, in case of reciprocal and simultaneous home exchanges among users, clearly, a direct link between the two supplies in question can be established. And yet, such a direct link might eventually be broken where - along the lines of the CJEU's decisions in *Apple and Pear Development Council*, in *Commission versus Finland*, and in *Gemeente Borsele* - the benefits provided by users to each other are not evenly balanced, as it is in case of a holiday exchange relating to homes for which the market renting fees clearly do not match.[93]

Even in case of non-reciprocal and deferred exchanges, which indeed constitute a further possibility for users to conclude an exchange on a platform like HomeExchange, other than through reciprocal and simultaneous swaps, a direct link might ultimately be considered as missing. As explained in Chapter 2, those kinds of exchanges are settled by means of GuestPoints, which are credits issued by HomeExchange and that the recipients can later use to be hosted by other members of the same community.[94] In relation to such arrangements, it might be concluded that no legal

---

90. Notably, some users might access services provided by a digital company on a continuous basis and, thus, supply a large amount of their personal data to that company, whereas other users might access those services only on an occasional basis and, thus, supply only a small amount of their personal data to that company.
91. Notably, it might be maintained that users having a lower propensity to consume and lower income, presumably, have also less valuable personal data than other users.
92. European Commission, Value Added Tax Committee, *Working Paper No. 958, supra* n. 89, at 6. Nevertheless, the Commission established the existence of a direct link where a user agrees to pay to a digital company a periodical fee in order not to be exposed to advertising while accessing the company's services. In such event, the direct link, in fact, is no longer between the supply of services by the company and the provision of personal data by the user, but rather between the payment made by the user and the obligation of the company to refrain from sending him any kind of advertisement. *Id.*, at 7.
93. European Commission, Value Added Tax Committee, *Working Paper No. 878. VAT Treatment of Sharing Economy*, at 9-10 (taxud.c.1(2015)4370160).
94. *See* section §2.08[A].

relationship - stricto sensu, as held by the CJEU in *Tolsma* - between the individual supplier and the individual customer actually exists. Against this conclusion, however, it ought to be observed that, in line with the considerations laid down by the CJEU in *Town & County Factors*, making the existence of a legal relationship depend on the obligations of the service supplier being legally enforceable would, ultimately, undermine the effectiveness of EU VAT. Arguably, for each user on HomeExchange, credits issued by the platform, in fact, represent nothing less than the possibility to access services provided not just by a single user, but potentially by all members of the same community. From this perspective, therefore, a direct link between the supply and the consideration for it is to be considered existent.

§5.05 BARTER TRANSACTIONS

Barter, inasmuch as trades for money, is 'a means by which commercial life is carried on'.[95] Indeed, payment in return for a supply does not need to be made in money. Rather, it could well be provided in kind, although the CJEU has explained that a consideration must necessarily be capable of being expressed in monetary terms.[96] Thus, in order to avoid leaving the door open to lawful tax avoidance as well as creating distortions in the tax treatment of situations which are, from an economic or a commercial standpoint, substantially identical, under EU VAT a consideration for a supply could well be constituted in full or in part by another supply made by the recipient of the first one.[97] Besides, both those reciprocal supplies might involve the provision of either goods, services, or a mixture of both.[98]

After all, barter involves expenditure, which under EU VAT is a proxy for consumption. As such, from a tax standpoint, it is rational to treat every barter exchange in the same manner as its economically and commercially equivalent monetary transaction.[99] A distinction between these two types of transactions would, arguably, restrict the possibility for a business to choose the arrangement best suited to satisfying his own economic interests.[100] It is no wonder, therefore, that the CJEU has long maintained that the principle of neutrality would be impaired if a barter payment was not to qualify as a consideration under EU VAT.[101] And yet, barter has its own peculiarities, which may warrant the following considerations.

The first peculiarity relates to the fact that, in a barter transaction, there are simultaneously two supplies and two acquisitions, rather than just a single supply and

95. UK: Opinion of the Advocate General, 27 Feb. 1997, Case C-330/95, *Goldsmiths (Jewellers) Ltd v. Commissioners of Customs & Excise*, para. 29.
96. UK: ECJ, 23 Nov. 1988, Case C-230/87, *Naturally Yours Cosmetics Limited v. Commissioners of Customs and Excise*, para. 16.
97. UK: Opinion of the Advocate General, 14 Jul. 1988, Case C-230/87, *Naturally Yours Cosmetics Limited v. Commissioners of Customs and Excise*, para. 19.
98. B.J.M. Terra & J. Kajus, *Introduction to European VAT (Recast)* at para. 13.2.1 (IBFD Tax Research Platform 2019).
99. R.I. Keller, *The Taxation of Barter Transactions*, 67 Minn. L. Rev. 2 (1983), at 444-445.
100. Van Hilten, *supra* n. 2, at 7.
101. UK: ECJ, 3 Jul. 1997, Case C-330/95, *Goldsmiths (Jewellers) Ltd v. Commissioners of Customs & Excise*, para. 25.

a single acquisition, as it occurs in a monetary transaction.[102] Accordingly, for EU VAT purposes, these two supplies – the direct and the reverse supply – must be considered and subject to tax separately.[103] This further implies that both supplies part of a barter transaction must necessarily fulfil all the requirements for being supplies in EU VAT terms, notably they must be provided 'for consideration' and a 'direct link' between each supply and the consideration for it must be established.[104]

The rationale for splitting, for EU VAT purposes, a single barter transaction into two separate supplies is, perhaps, best explained by the need to grant each party the full opportunity to deduct his input VAT. Notably, this circumstance is particularly relevant if both parties to a transaction are taxable persons. In case of a barter transaction between two taxable persons, the VAT on the non-monetary consideration charged by each party, in fact, is ultimately cancelled out by the input VAT deduction which the other party is entitled to. Thus, should the output VAT charged by one party be excessive, so it would be the input VAT deduction which the other party is entitled to. The same 'fortunate' circumstance, however, does not occur in case of a transaction where one party is a non-taxable person, since such person neither can charge VAT on his outputs nor he can deduct VAT on his inputs. This leads to VAT cascading, i.e., the situation in which VAT is charged on an amount which already incorporates a 'hidden' or 'sticking' VAT.[105]

The second peculiarity of barter transactions relates to how a consideration in kind should be valued. As stated, under EU VAT, the consideration actually received by a party to a transaction represents a 'subjective value', i.e., not a value determined according to objective criteria, but rather the value which the recipient of that supply specifically attributes to what he receives. As Advocate General Fennelly explained in his opinion in *Argos Distributors*, 'the word "subjective" is not used ... in its normal sense, but rather to describe the value placed by the parties on key elements in a transaction .... The effect ... is to distinguish and exclude, for the purpose of assessing the consideration for a sale, any supposed independent valuation, different from that adopted by the parties'.[106] Notably, this circumstance implies that the value of the supply made by each party has to be determined only with a reference to the value placed by each party in receiving the supply by the other party.

In practice, however, it is nearly impossible for the supplier to determine such a value, especially if each supply has a different value or, further, if one or both supplies have no clear value. In order to solve this valuation issue, the CJEU has developed two different methods. The first method refers to the market valuation of the goods or services supplied. Notably, this approach was used by the CJEU in *Naturally Yours*

102. AT: Opinion of the Advocate General, 24 Feb. 2005, Case C-465/03, *Kretztechnik AG v. Finanzamt Linz*, note 19.
103. PL: ECJ, 13 June 2018, Case C-421/17, *SZEF Krajowej Administracji Skarbowej v. Polfarmex Spółka Akcyjna w Kutnie*, para. 41.
104. Kollmann, *supra* n. 7, at para. 4.1.1.2.
105. For a discussion, *see* R. Millar, *Illusory Supplies and Unacknowledged Discounts: VAT and Valuation in Consumer Transaction*, Brit. Tax Rev. 2 (2003), at 154; Pfeiffer, *Comment on 'Free' Internet Services*, *supra* n. 88, at 137.
106. UK: Opinion of the Advocate General, 27 Jun. 1996, Case C-288/94, *Argos Distributors Ltd v. Commissioners of Customs & Excise*, para. 21.

Cosmetics, a case concerning some beauty consultants who arranged parties at which the products furnished by a manufacturing company were sold and who received for this purpose a pot of cream at a discounted price from that company. In that case, following a market valuation methodology, the CJEU equated the value of the service rendered by the beauty consultants to the company to the difference between the normal wholesale price (GBP 10.14) and the price paid by the beauty consultants to the company for each pot of cream (GBP 1.50).[107]

The second method, instead, refers to the price or the cost for one party to supply goods or services to the other party. Notably, this approach was used by the CJEU, first, in *Empire Stores* and, then, in *Bertelsmann*.[108] *Empire Stores* concerned a catalogue company which offered products free-of-charge to prospective customers as well as to existing customers in return for the introduction to it of new customers. In that case, following a price or cost methodology, the CJEU equated the value of the products offered free-of-charge to prospective and existing customers to the price or the cost for the company to supply its own products to those parties.[109] A similar approach was later adopted by the CJEU in *Bertelsmann*, a case concerning a company which offered existing customers bonuses in kind, such as books, records, and bicycles, in return for the introduction to it of new customers. In that case, following a price or cost methodology, the CJEU equated the value of the bonuses offered to its customers to the price or the cost for the company to supply those bonuses to them.[110] Importantly, this method – which refers to the price or the costs for one party to supply goods or services to the other party – is also the one favoured among scholars, who specifically suggest applying Article 75 of the VAT Directive, concerning the taxable amount of goods part of the business assets used for private purposes or of services carried out free-of-charge, analogously to the case of barter transactions.[111]

In the realm of the sharing economy, barter comes into prominence quite frequently. Notably, the author submits that a first type of barter transactions occurs between a sharing economy platform and its users in case a service is provided by the platform to its users in return for no monetary consideration other than personal data of those users.[112] Indeed, in the author's opinion, the transaction in question constitutes a taxable transaction for EU VAT purposes. As a matter of fact, holding otherwise would run counter the principle of neutrality underpinning EU VAT, in so far as it would distort business choices as regards concluding monetary or, instead, barter exchanges using personal data. Since, for EU VAT purposes, a single barter transaction needs to be split into two, in case of a barter exchange between a platform and its users

107. *Naturally Yours Cosmetics* (C-230/87), paras 17-18.
108. For a discussion, *see* G. Morse, *Identifying the Taxable Amount for Value Added Tax of a Supply of Goods at a Reduced Cash Price: A Question of Analysis or Principle*, Brit. Tax Rev. 3 (2002), at 181; A. van Doesum, *Taxable Amount*, in *CJEU – Recent Developments in Value Added Tax*, at 177-222 (M. Lang, et al. eds, Linde 2014).
109. UK: ECJ, 2 June 1994, Case C-33/93, *Empire Stores Ltd v. Commissioners of Customs and Excise*, para. 19.
110. *Bertelsmann* (C-380/99), paras 23-25.
111. *See* e.g., Terra & Kajus, *supra* n. 98, at para. 13.2.1.; Van Doesum et al., *supra* n. 23, at 131.
112. Against considering services provided by digital companies in return for user personal data as barter transactions, *see* Zawodsky, *supra* n. 63, at 606-627.

there are simultaneously two supplies and two acquisitions, which must, accordingly, be considered and subject to tax separately.

As for the determination of the value of the services supplied by the platform to its users free-of-charge, unfortunately, both the method referring to a market valuation and the one referring to the price or the cost for the supplier are not easily applicable in this situation, in so far as either of the two approaches laid down above entails a value difficult to ascertain with sufficient precision by anyone other than the platform itself, which would presumably hold an incentive to conceal the 'real' value of its own supply.

Barter transactions may also take place among users themselves. Notably, this occurs on a sharing economy platform like HomeExchange. As it was in case of barter exchanges among a platform and its users, in light of the principle of neutrality, EU VAT shall apply to each of the two supplies which are part of a barter transaction. There is, however, an additional hurdle in relation to those transactions, which relates to the taxable status of the parties involved in them. Notably, three scenarios can be distinguished in this regard. If both parties to a barter transaction are taxable persons, the transaction in question is B2B and, thus, each of the parties involved must account for his own output and input VAT. Under this first scenario, the VAT on the non-monetary consideration charged by each party is, ultimately, cancelled out by the input VAT deduction which the other party is entitled to. In this way, the principle of neutrality is respected. If, instead, only one party to a barter transaction is a taxable person, whereas the other is a non-taxable person, the transaction in question is a B2C or C2B transaction and, thus, only the taxable person must account for his own output and input VAT. Under this second scenario, the non-taxable person neither can charge VAT on his outputs nor can he deduct VAT on his inputs, situation which eventually leads to VAT cascading. As seen, this is problematic for the principle of neutrality. Lastly, if both parties to a barter transaction are non-taxable persons or, even, taxable persons, but their annual turnover falls below the registration threshold set by the Member State in which they are established, the transaction in question is a C2C transaction and, thus, neither of the two parties must account for his own output and input VAT. Under this third scenario, the barter transaction is placed completely outside the scope of EU VAT and, thus, no problem in relation to the principle of neutrality arises. Figures 5.1, 5.2 and 5.3 below depict each of these three distinct scenarios graphically.[113]

113. N.B.: in the figures, in order to distinguish the two parties to the barter transaction, users are called, respectively, 'host' and 'guest', although each party actually performs, simultaneously, the role of host and guest.

Figure 5.1 HomeExchange: Direct Barter Exchanges (B2C)

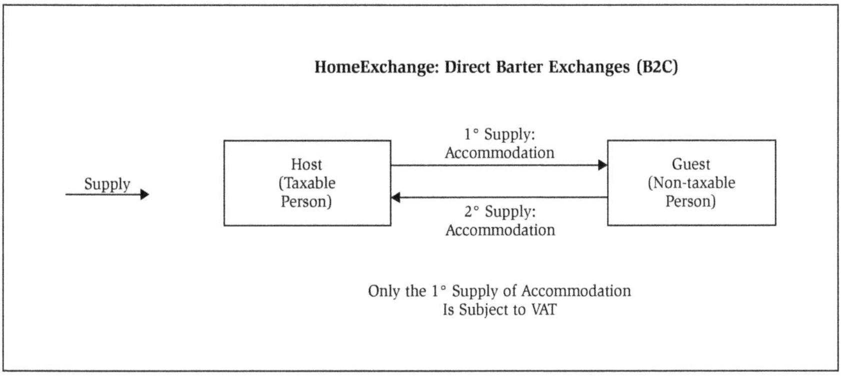

Figure 5.2 HomeExchange: Direct Barter Exchanges (C2B)

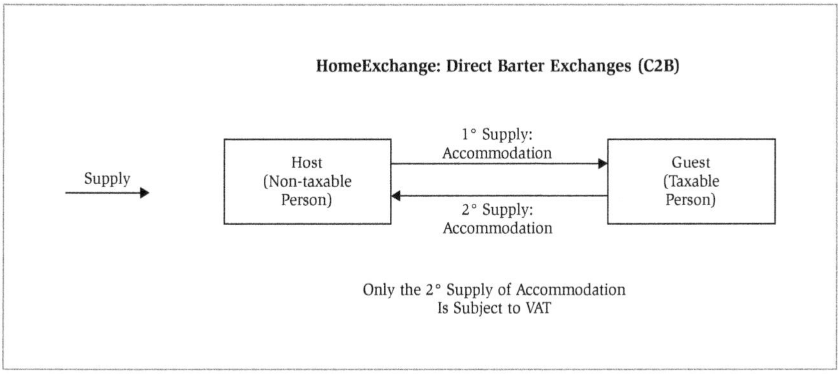

Figure 5.3 HomeExchange: Direct Barter Exchanges (C2C)

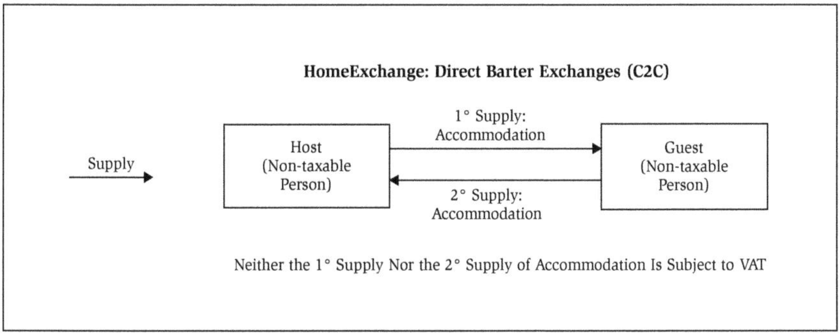

As stated, rather than reciprocal and simultaneous exchanges, hosts and guests on a platform like HomeExchange might also conclude non-reciprocal and deferred exchanges settled by using GuestPoints. As seen, in this situation, the existence of a direct link between the two supplies which are part of the same barter transaction could well be questioned.[114] Should a direct link be considered as missing, then one might argue that, rather than a single barter transaction composed of two reciprocal supplies, indeed there are two distinct barter transactions, taking place between each of the two users and the platform. In particular, it might be considered that a first barter transaction takes place when a first user renders available his home on HomeExchange to a second user in return for the issuance to him by the platform of GuestPoints. Along the same lines, it might be maintained that a second barter transaction takes place when the second user books the first user's house on HomeExchange by remitting part of his GuestPoints to the platform. The relevant question, then, is whether all the supplies composing those two barter transactions shall be subject to EU VAT or not. In light of the CJEU's decision in *Hedqvist*, concerning mutual exchanges of traditional currencies for the 'bitcoin' virtual currency and vice versa, it might be assumed that, as regards the first barter transaction, while the provision of accommodation by the first user to HomeExchange is subject to VAT, the issuance by the platform of GuestPoints in return is an exempt supply pursuant to Article 135(1)(e) of the VAT Directive, involving, *inter alia*, transactions 'concerning currency, bank notes and coins used as legal tender'.[115] As a matter of fact, although not designated as legal tender in any country, GuestPoints – like bitcoins in *Hedqvist* – are nothing more than a direct means of payment which users on HomeExchange accept as an alternative to money, of which indeed they perform the same function.[116] The situation is exactly reverse with regard to the second barter transaction, in which the second user books the first user's house on HomeExchange by remitting part of his GuestPoints to the platform. In such event, the exempt supply, in fact, relates to the supply of GuestPoints by the second user to the platform, whereas the supply of accommodation by the platform to the first user is fully subject to VAT. Figure 5.4 below depicts this scenario graphically.[117]

114. *See* section §5.04.
115. *See* SW: ECJ, 22 Oct. 2015, Case C-264/14, *Skatteverket v. David Hedqvist*, para. 53. *See also* UK: ECJ, 16 Dec. 2010, Case C-270/09, *Macdonald Resorts Ltd v. The Commissioners for Her Majesty's Revenue & Customs*, para. 21, with regard to 'Points Rights' reflecting the entitlement of a member to some temporary accommodation in holiday resorts.
116. *Hedqvist* (C-264/14), para. 42.
117. N.B.: in the figures, in order to distinguish the two parties to the barter transaction, users are called, respectively, 'host' and 'guest', although each party actually performs, simultaneously, the role of host and guest.

Figure 5.4 HomeExchange: Indirect Barter Exchanges

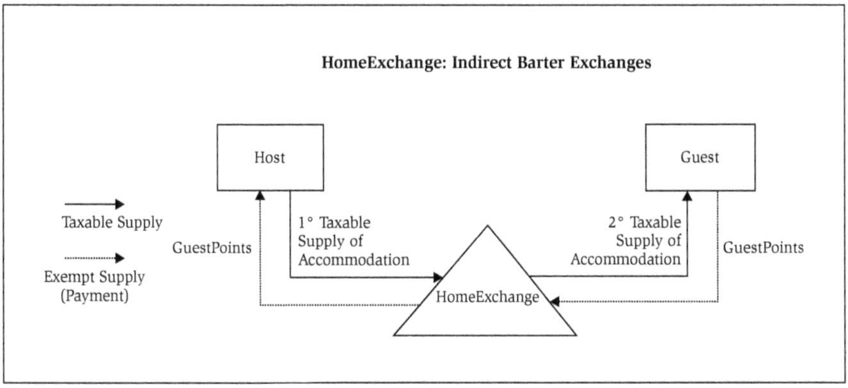

Lastly, as for the determination of the value of the services supplied by platform users in a barter transaction among themselves, both the methods used by the CJEU, on the one hand, in *Naturally Yours Cosmetics*, and, on the other hand, in *Empire Store* and in *Bertelsmann*, appear fairly inadequate in the context of the sharing economy. If, in fact, a market valuation methodology is followed, no market value is likely to be found for those kinds of services (indeed, which may it be the market value of a spot on another person's sofa or of a seat in another person's car?). Similarly, if a price or cost methodology is followed, a price or a cost might not exist where the services in question are generated internally by the individual supplier and, in any event, the cost of the services supplied could not be easy to determine where an individual supplier makes use of his private assets in order to supply the services in question (indeed, which exact costs should be attributed to a room rental or an occasional ride?).

§5.06 CHAPTER CONCLUSIONS AND RECOMMENDATIONS FOR IMPROVEMENT

[A] Main Findings

The concept of 'taxable transactions' defines the objective or substantive scope of EU VAT. Out of the four types of transactions listed in Article 2(1) of the VAT Directive, which are all objective in nature, the supply of goods and the supply of services are the most important taxable events under EU VAT. While Article 14(1) of the VAT Directive defines the supply of goods as 'the transfer of the right to dispose of tangible property as owner', the supply of services is defined only in the negative under Article 24(1) of the VAT Directive, that is as 'any transaction which does not constitute a supply of goods'. From this negative definition, which functions as a sort of 'catch-all provision', it follows that the terms 'supply of goods' and 'supply of services' are not only mutually exclusive, but also all-comprehensive, in the sense that the two expressions are meant to cover any foreseeable transaction carried out for consideration. However, for being taxable transactions under EU VAT, both supplies of goods and supplies of services must meet two general conditions.

As a first general condition for a transaction to be subject to EU VAT, a consideration in return for which the supply is made must exist. A supply made otherwise than for consideration, in fact, falls outside the scope of EU VAT. Thus, supplies made free-of-charge, for a fee other than *qua* (i.e., as for) consideration, in return for an unascertained reduction in value, or for a mere 'reward', are not subject to EU VAT. Although not defined in the VAT Directive or elsewhere, the expression 'for consideration' has been interpreted broadly by the CJEU, as entailing everything received in return for a supply, provided it is capable of being expressed in money. Indeed, a consideration may also be provided for a lower price than the cost price, consist in a mere reimbursement of expenses, or be paid by a customer simply through the provision to the supplier of information and contact details relating to other potential customers. Moreover, payment of a consideration can be made in the form of a membership fee, a lump sum, or a subscription fee, or by deducting the relevant amount from another payment. On the contrary, only unilateral payments, indemnities, or payments related to a transaction other than the one in question might not qualify as a consideration for EU VAT purposes.

As a second general condition for a transaction to be subject to EU VAT, a direct link between the supply and the consideration for it must be established. Notably, despite a lack of any reference to it in the VAT Directive, the CJEU has clarified that such a direct link cannot be established when the benefits of a supply accrue not only to an individual customer, but instead to an industry as a whole. The concept of 'direct link' has a subjective and an objective dimension. The subjective dimension presupposes the existence of a legal relationship between the supplier and the customer. Notably, although heavily criticized by scholars and, to an extent, revisited by the CJEU itself, apparently, the existence of a legal relationship between the supplier and the customer is still a requirement for a transaction to be subject to EU VAT. The objective dimension, instead, presupposes a direct reciprocity between the service provided and the consideration received in return. Notably, a relationship of direct reciprocity lacks where no correlation exists between the amount of the service supplied and the consideration provided in return.

Barter transactions are also subject to EU VAT, inasmuch as their economically and commercially equivalent monetary transactions. And yet, barter transactions have two main peculiarities. The first peculiarity relates to the fact that, in a barter transaction, there are two supplies for EU VAT purposes, both of which must be provided for consideration and fulfil the direct link requirement. The rationale for splitting, for EU VAT purposes, a single barter transaction into two separate supplies relates to the need to grant each party the full opportunity to deduct his input VAT. In case of a barter transaction between a taxable person and a non-taxable person, however, such possibility is precluded to the latter party, situation which, ultimately, leads to VAT cascading. The second peculiarity relates to the value to be attributed to the consideration in kind. Although representing a subjective value, i.e., the value that each recipient of each supply specifically attributes to what he receives, in practice, it is nearly impossible for the supplier to determine such a value, especially if each supply has a different value or, further, if one or both supplies have no clear value. The CJEU has developed two different methods in order to solve this valuation issue. The first method refers to the market valuation of the goods or services supplied. The second method – which is the one favoured among scholars –, instead, refers to the price or the cost for one party to supply goods or services to the other party.

In light of all the above, it can easily be maintained that both transactions between a sharing economy platform and its users and among users themselves constitute supplies of services under EU VAT. Notably, as regards transactions between a platform and its users, clearly, no transfer of the right to dispose of tangible property occurs, whereas transactions among users themselves entail only the temporary usage of goods (i.e., short-term accommodation) or the provision of service (i.e., passenger transport). None of the principles included in the evaluation model as conceptualized in the present study, indeed, suggests a different appraisal.

It also indisputable that, nearly in all situations, sharing economy platforms provide their own services for consideration. A consideration, indeed, exists even if paid by means of an annual subscription, which is a further possibility of payment for users on a platform like HomeExchange. Further, it is irrelevant that the consideration is deducted by the platform from the amount that the individual customer pays to the individual supplier or, even, the circumstance that, at times, a cancellation fee rather than a full-fledged compensation is paid. The author also submits that, given the broad interpretation attributed to the term 'consideration', personal data do indeed constitute a consideration for EU VAT purposes.

A consideration also exists in case of transactions among users themselves, irrespective of whether payment is made in money or in kind, that is with the individual customer providing another service in return, as it occurs among users on a platform like HomeExchange. Indeed, even the mere reimbursement of expenses provided by the passenger to the driver on a platform like BlaBlaCar must be seen as a consideration for EU VAT purposes. Lastly, in so far as cancellation charges take the place of full-fledged compensation, those payments must also be regarded as a consideration under EU VAT.

The five legal principles which compose the evaluation model as conceptualized in the present study uphold the above conclusions. Indeed, the author does not find any compelling reason, in light of either the equality, neutrality, simplicity, flexibility, or proportionality principles, for excluding transactions made by sharing economy platforms or those among users themselves from the objective or substantive scope of EU VAT, besides situations in which similar kinds of transactions in the traditional economy would be excluded too. Transactions made by platforms only in return for user personal data are not to be seen as an exception in this regard.

In general, it does seem hard to establish a direct link between the services supplied by a sharing economy platform and the consideration paid in return by its users, in so far as access to platform services is made conditional upon payment by users. The Commission, however, maintains that a direct link is ultimately missing between the services provided by a digital company to its users free-of-charge and the personal data given by users in return, particularly in light of the fact that the provision of services by a digital company does not depend on the quantity or the quality of personal data provided by users.

In the author's view, however, this Commission's contention is at odds with the economic reality that, rather than the quantity or the quality of personal data collected from the single user, it is by means of the combination and processing of personal data from all its users that a digital platform is able to obtain a remuneration for its own economic activities. Based on such understanding, for a digital company user personal data are just another way to carry out its own economic activities and, eventually, to make a profit out of it. An interpretation more in line with the principles of neutrality and flexibility would, therefore, suggest broadening the concept of 'direct link', as to include within it also services provided by a platform to its users free-of-charge, but in return of user personal data.

It does not also appear a difficult exercise to establish a direct link between the services provided and the consideration paid for it in case of transactions among users themselves. And yet, a direct link might eventually be broken where, in relation to a reciprocal and simultaneous barter transaction on HomeExchange, the benefits provided by users to each other are not evenly balanced, as it is in the case of a holiday exchange relating to homes for which the market renting fees clearly do not match. A direct link might ultimately be considered as missing, due to the lack of a legal relationship between the individual supplier and the individual customer, also in case of non-reciprocal and deferred exchanges, which constitute a further possibility for users to conclude an exchange on a platform like HomeExchange, other than through reciprocal and simultaneous swaps.

This latter conclusion, however, conflicts with the principles of equality and neutrality underpinning EU VAT, in so far as one perceives that the fact that two users agree to conclude an accommodation exchange is, per se, sufficient to establish a legal relationship between these two parties and, further, that a direct link is to be considered existent where a user has the possibility to access services provided not just by a single user, but potentially by all the members of the same community. Indeed, there is no sound policy rationale, in light of the principles of simplicity and flexibility, for having a different treatment in both these situations.

In the realm of the sharing economy, barter comes into prominence quite frequently. Notably, there is a barter transaction where a service is provided by a platform to its users in return for no monetary consideration other than personal data of those users. In such event, the single barter transaction needs to be split into two supplies, which must be considered and subject to tax separately. However, determining the value of the services supplied by the platform to its users free-of-charge is not straightforward, in so far as such a value is difficult to ascertain with sufficient precision by anyone else than the platform itself.

Barter transactions may also take place among users themselves, notably on a sharing economy platform like HomeExchange. Besides the need to split the single barter transaction into two separate supplies, an additional hurdle arises where one party is a non-taxable person, resulting from the fact that the non-taxable person neither can charge VAT on his outputs, nor can he deduct VAT on his inputs, situation which, ultimately, leads to VAT cascading. A further complication arises in case of non-reciprocal and deferred exchanges, settled by using GuestPoints, among users on a platform like HomeExchange. In such situation, one might argue that, rather than a single barter transaction composed of two reciprocal supplies, indeed there are two distinct barter transactions, taking place between each of the two users and the platform. In relation to both these barter transactions, however, only the supply of accommodation is subject to tax, whereas the supply of GuestPoints is exempt under EU VAT. Lastly, as for the determination of the value of the services supplied by platform users in a barter transaction among themselves, both the methods developed by the CJEU in this regard, following a market valuation and a price or cost methodology, appear fairly inadequate in the context of the sharing economy.

In light of the principles of equality and neutrality, as also considered by the CJEU, it is rational to treat every barter exchange in the same manner as its economically and commercially equivalent monetary transaction. At the same time, in light of the principles of simplicity and flexibility, it might however be opportune to introduce some derogations and simplification measures for the application of EU VAT to barter transactions where one party is a non-taxable person and, further, in relation to the determination of the value of the services supplied by platform users in a barter transaction among themselves.

[B] Recommendations

In terms of possible recommendations for improving the current EU VAT system in relation to the issues identified in this chapter, the author submits that, although not defined in the VAT Directive or elsewhere, no specification of the expression 'for consideration', as provided in Article 2(1) of the VAT Directive, or, even, a clarification for assisting its application in an individual case is required. The application scope of this expression is, in fact, wide and, indeed, equally broad it is its understanding by the CJEU, in a way as to include within it both transactions between a sharing economy and its users and those among users themselves. In this connection, it is sufficient to recall that also a mere reimbursement of expenses or a cancellation fee shall be regarded as a consideration under EU VAT. Indeed, even the assessment conducted through the evaluation model as conceptualized in the present study provides no ground for changing or introducing new rules in relation to the expression 'for consideration'.

Nevertheless, in certain instances, especially in cases in which the application of EU VAT can ultimately discourage the carrying out of certain sharing economy activities, it might be convenient to narrow down the scope of the expression 'for consideration'. Notably, a provision to that effect might be inserted in the VAT Directive and/or in the Implementing Regulation, containing a carveout, in the form of an exemption from VAT, for transactions among sharing economy users where a mere reimbursement of expenses is paid by the individual customer to the individual supplier.[118] More specifically, such an exemption should operate where the individual supplier obtains a mere reimbursement of expenses in return for his own services, provided the individual customer is a non-taxable person. However, it might be that the individual supplier finds financially more convenient to deduct the VAT paid on the inputs used in the furtherance of his own economic activities, even if, conversely, he must charge VAT on output supplies for which he obtains a mere reimbursement of expenses. Taking this eventuality into account, the author submits that a right of option for taxation in respect of those transactions should be rendered available to those individual suppliers. Overall, the author believes that the exemption in question would contribute to simplify the application of EU VAT, whereas the possibility for a taxable person to opt-out from such an exemption, if this is financially more convenient to him, is a measure to achieve flexibility. Operatively, the exemption in question, together with the related 'opt-out' provision, could be inserted in the wording of Article 132(1) of the VAT Directive, notably at point (f-*bis*), immediately after the exemption concerning 'the supply of services by independent groups of persons, who are carrying on an activity which is exempt from VAT or in relation to which they are not taxable persons, for the purpose of rendering their members the services directly necessary for the exercise of that activity, where those groups merely claim from their members exact reimbursement of their share of the joint expenses, provided such exemption is not likely to cause distortion of competition'. Importantly, usage of this latter safeguard also in the proposed provision would contribute to maintain the exemption in question sufficiently narrow and, therefore, also more in line with the principles of equality and neutrality. The new point (f-*bis*) of Article 132(1) of the VAT Directive might then read as follows (additions in italics):

> Article 132
>
> 1. Member States shall exempt the following transactions:
>
> [...]
>
> *f*-bis. *The supply of tangible services, such as those consisting in the provision of accommodation or passenger transport, personally rendered by individuals, where those individuals merely claim from the other party exact reimbursement of their*

---

118. In the author's opinion, instead, the introduction of a legal provision, as to exclude from the scope of EU VAT barter transactions concerning the supply of 'free' services by a platform to its users in return for personal data of those users or vice versa, would ultimately be an overreaching measure in light of the principles governing the EU VAT system, in so far as those platform activities are indeed full-fledged economic activities, which, as such, should be fully subject to EU VAT. Should it be decided not to tax those transactions, especially the provision of personal data to a platform by its users, then it would be better to rely on the 'personal exemption' entailed in the application of a registration threshold, rather than excluding the transactions in question altogether from the objective or substantive scope of the tax. For a discussion, *see* section §4.06[B]. Against this background, *see however* Kollmann, *supra* n. 7, at para. 5.3.4., pleading for the introduction of a new provision in the VAT Directive or in the Implementing Regulation, as to exclude from the scope of EU VAT barter transactions having personal data as a consideration. Notably, according to Kollmann, a measure to that effect is needed in order to improve the administrability of the EU VAT system in relation to those transactions, especially in light of the difficulty to determine the taxable amount as well as the liquidity issues for the platform, which, in the absence of a monetary consideration, would have to pay a monetary amount of VAT – so to speak – 'out of its own pocket'.

share of the joint expenses and the individual recipients of those services are non-taxable persons, provided that such exemption is not likely to cause distortion of competition. Member States shall however allow taxable persons a right of option for taxation in respect of the transactions referred to in the above;

[...]

As regards the existence of a direct link between the supply and the consideration for it, which is the second general condition for a transaction to be subject to EU VAT, the related assessment, as seen, might not always be straightforward. Accordingly, it would be recommendable to develop some guidelines for making such determination easier. Notably, specific indications in this regard could be inserted in the guidelines drafted by the VAT Committee or in the explanatory notes issued by the Commission. Those indications, offered through non-binding (for taxable persons, tax authorities, and courts), and yet, precisely for this reason, more flexible instruments, might be derived from the CJEU's decisions, in particular from *Apple and Pear Development Council*, *Tolsma*, *Town & County Factors*, *Commission versus Finland*, and *Gemeente Borsele*. Notably, if inserted in the guidelines drafted by the VAT Committee, such indications might read as follows:

GUIDELINES RESULTING FROM THE ... [NUMBER] *MEETING OF ...* [DATE]

DOCUMENT ... [NUMBER] – *TAXUD...(...)...–...* [NUMBER AND YEAR]

QUESTIONS CONCERNING THE APPLICATION OF EU VAT PROVISIONS

Origin: Commission

Reference: Article 2(1)(c)

Subject: Establishment of a direct link between a supply of services and the consideration for it

(Document taxud ...) [NUMBER]

1. *In accordance with the settled case-law of the Court of Justice of the European Union, for a supply of services to be carried out 'for consideration' on the basis of Article 2(1)I of the VAT Directive, a direct link must be established between the supply of services provided and the consideration received.*
2. *The VAT Committee ...* [unanimously/almost unanimously/by large majority] *recognises that the assessment of whether such a direct link exists shall be done on a case-by-case basis.*
3. *However, an assumption can reasonably be made that a direct link between a supply of services and the consideration for it does not exist where:*
   - *(i) No relationship of direct reciprocity between the service provided and the consideration received in return exists, in the sense that the supplier and the customer can decide freely, without being contractually bound, on all the factors which are of importance for their own relationship. This might in particular occur where the supplier can terminate the provision of his own services at any time, whereas, conversely, the customer can decide freely for how long he wishes to receive the services in question;*
   - *(ii) No legally recognisible tie between the parties is created, in the sense of a clearly defined transaction with a 'quid pro quo', whether such tie is based on enforceable obligations or not. This might in particular occur where no components of the reciprocal performance are exchanged in the framework of the agreements between the parties to a transaction;*

(iii) Payment for a supply of service is entirely voluntary and uncertain, in the sense that it depends on subjective motives of the customer and originates in voluntary decisions by the customer to pay an amount of his own choice. This might in particular occur where, first, there is no necessary link between the supply of the services and the payment to which it gives rise and, second, the amount of the consideration is determined by the customer as he wishes;

(iv) The services supplied relate to the common interests of the recipients, in the sense that the benefits of the services in question do not accrue to the individual customer only, but instead to the industry as a whole. This might in particular occur where the supplier is not in the position to ensure that those who do not pay do not also benefit from his own activity;

(v) No correlation exists between the level and the amount of the services supplied and the consideration provided in return, in the sense that the payment made by the customer only partially covers the costs for the supplier to provide the services in question. This might in particular occur where the consideration is not solely and exclusively calculated on the basis of the services supplied, but it also depends upon other factors, such as the customer's income and assets.

As regards barter transactions among users of a sharing economy platform, in particular barter exchanges in which only one party is a taxable person, as it occurs among users on a platform like HomeExchange, a possible solution against VAT cascading might be to exempt (*rectius*: zero-rate) those transactions. Indeed, this measure would enable the non-taxable person to receive the services in question from the taxable person free of VAT. As a result, the non-taxable person would not also pass any 'hidden' or 'sticking' VAT – equal to the input VAT which the person in question would not otherwise be entitled to deduct – in the price of the services which he, in turn, supplies in the course of the barter exchange with the taxable person, whereas this latter would not lose the possibility to deduct the input VAT related to the supply of his own services. Operatively, a specific provision might be inserted in the VAT Directive, perhaps in the wording of Article 169, allowing the taxable person to deduct the input VAT incurred in the furtherance of certain exempt transactions. Overall, the author submits that the exemption in question would contribute to greatly simplify the application of EU VAT. Once again, however, it is important that the application scope of such exemption would be maintained sufficiently narrow, so as to have 'negligible' effects and, thus, be more in line with the principles of equality and neutrality. The new paragraph of Article 169 of the VAT Directive might then read as follows (additions in italics):

> Article 169
>
> In addition to the deduction referred to in Article 168, the taxable person shall be entitled to deduct the VAT referred to therein in so far as the goods and services are used for the purposes of the following:
>
> [...]
>
> *d. transactions relating to the reciprocal supply of services by a taxable person to a non-taxable person, provided that the open market value of the services exchanged is equal and that such a measure remains limited in its scope and is not likely to cause distortion of competition.*

Lastly, as for the determination of the value of the services supplied in case of barter exchanges, either between a sharing economy platform and its users or among users themselves, the author submits that such a value should be appraised in light of market mechanisms, as long as only reference to a market valuation could, arguably, ensure equal treatment between transactions concluded in money and those made in kind. For this purpose, it would be recommendable to statutorily establish - as a clear departure from the principle that, under EU VAT, the consideration represents a subjective value - that the value of the services exchanged in those situations is equal to the 'open market value'.[119] More specifically, it could be provided that, in case of certain barter exchanges, the value of the services supplied shall be determined according to a series of fixed, predetermined and, possibly, objective criteria and indices to be laid down in the text of the Implementing Regulation. Operatively, a new paragraph could be added to the wording of Article 77 of the VAT Directive, providing a reference to the Implementing Regulation, where a list of barter transactions, including the supply of personal data to a sharing economy platform by its users[120], as well as a series of criteria and indices used to determine the value of the services exchanged, are to be precisely detailed. Arguably, this measure would amount to a simplification, as such consistent with the principles of simplicity and flexibility. Moreover, in so far as the value of the services relating to those barter exchanges would be determined according to a series of fixed, predetermined and, possibly, objective criteria and indices, the principles of equality and neutrality would not be impaired. As for the principle of proportionality, it ought to be relied upon with a view of establishing the relative weight of those two sets of principles in each individual case. The new paragraph 2 added to the wording of Article 77 of the VAT Directive might then read as follows:

> Article 77
>
> [...]
>
> *2. In respect of the reciprocal supply, by two persons, of services specified in ...* [Article or Annex] *of the Implementing Regulation 282/2011, the taxable amount*

119. It ought to be recalled, however, that the possibility for Member States to make reference to the open market value for the determination of the taxable amount in situations other than those narrowly prescribed in Art. 80 of the VAT Directive was specifically denied by the CJEU. *See Orfey Balgaria* (C-549/11), paras 41-49.

120. As a matter of fact, several methodologies to 'price' personal data have, already, been tentatively explored. *See* e.g., OECD, *Exploring the Economics of Personal Data: A Survey of Methodologies for Measuring Monetary Value* (OECD Publishing 2013); G. Malgieri & B. Custers, *Pricing Privacy – The Right to Know the Value of Your Personal Data*, 34 Comp. L. & Sec. Rev. 2 (2018), at 289-303. Indeed, the Financial Times has even developed a calculator for what a person's personal data presumably are worth. *See How Much Is Your Personal Data Worth*, https://ig.ft.com/how-much-is-your-personal-data-worth/ (accessed 31 Mar. 2019). Admittedly, the actual possibility to 'price' personal data has however been considered as 'not realistic to implement within a short period of time' by the Commission. *See* European Commission, Commission Staff Working Document, *Impact Assessment accompanying the Document Proposal for a Council Directive laying down Rules relating to the Corporate Taxation of a Significant Digital Presence and Proposal for a Council Directive on the Common System of a Digital Services Tax on Revenues resulting from the Provision of Certain Digital Services*, at 56, SWD(2018) 81 final.

shall be the open market value of the services supplied as determined according to the criteria and indices laid down therein.

CHAPTER 6
Composite Supplies

§6.01 INTRODUCTION

Although targeting final consumption, EU VAT is administratively levied on each transaction, which is taken as a proxy for expenditure and, ultimately, for consumption. Defining what exactly constitutes a transaction is therefore crucial, especially where a transaction entails the joint provision to the same customer of several goods and/or services, possibly by distinct undertakings. The present chapter aims to filter out the main characteristics of the doctrine on 'composite supplies' developed by the CJEU as well as other alternative approaches to make such a determination. More specifically, the ensuing analysis seeks to explore how the doctrine on 'composite supplies', as well as other alternative approaches to it, shall be related to the sharing economy, which entails the joint provision to the same individual customer of several services by two distinct undertakings, namely the platform and the individual supplier.

Defining the tax object is of profound importance under EU VAT, as, in general, it is in tax law.[1] Notably, under EU VAT, the taxing point is constituted by each single transaction. As stipulated by Article 1(2) Second Indent of the VAT Directive, in fact, EU VAT is levied 'on each transaction' (in French, '*à chaque opération*'; in Italian, '*a ciascuna operazione*'). Therefore, in the context of EU VAT, it is crucial to determine whether an economic operation, which may entail the joint provision of several goods and/or services, possibly by distinct undertakings, constitutes a single transaction or not.

In the author's view, the term 'transaction' (in French, '*opération*'; in Italian, '*operazione*') is not to be equated to that of 'supply' (in French, '*prestation*'; in Italian, '*prestazione*'). A transaction, in fact, can be constituted either by a single supply of goods and/or services or, instead, by two or more supplies of goods and/or services. In

1. O. Henkow, *Chapter 15: Accessorium Sequitur Principale – The Issue of Defining the Tax Object for VAT Purposes*, in *Principles of Law: Function, Status and Impact in EU Tax Law*, at para. 15.1. (C. Brokelind ed., IBFD 2014).

other terms, the notion of 'transaction' is, by definition, unitary, in so far as it does not give any consideration either to how many supplies are involved in it or, even, to the nature of those supplies, i.e., whether they entail the provision of goods, services, or a mixture of both.[2]

Clearly, if a single supply of goods and/or services is made, there is also a single transaction. This scenario, however, is almost only theoretical. In general, economic operations are, in fact, much more complex and entail the joint provision to the same customer of several goods and/or services. As explained by the CJEU in *Talacre Beach Caravan Sales*, the problem is that there is no 'set rule' for determining the scope of a supply under EU VAT. Rather, for this purpose, all the facts and circumstances of a case, including the specific legal framework, must be taken into account.[3]

It also ought to be observed that even the supply of a single good or a single service often requires a taxable person to perform several deeds. This cluster of acts is not necessarily treated separately under EU VAT. On the contrary, following a *reductio ad unum* approach, these acts are treated, whenever feasible, as part of a single supply toward the same customer.[4] As explained by the CJEU in *BGZ Leasing*, the problem is that there is no 'absolute rule' for determining the extent of a service and, hence, for determining the extent of a supply of a service under EU VAT.[5]

Ultimately, the reality is that where a transaction includes several supplies, a supply entails the provision of several goods and/or services or, even, the provision of a single good or service comprises a bundle of features and acts, the application of EU

2. *See* DE: ECJ, 10 Mar. 2011, Joined Cases C-497/09, C-499/09, C-501/09 and C-502/09, *Finanzamt Burgdorf v. Manfred Bog, CinemaxX Entertainment GmbH & Co. KG v. Finanzamt Hamburg-Barmbek-Uhlenhorst, Lothar Lohmeyer v. Finanzamt Minden, and Fleischerei Nier GmbH & Co. KG v. Finanzamt Detmold*, para. 56, where the CJEU considered the following: 'in each of the disputes in the main proceedings, there is a combination of a supply of goods or several goods and a supply of various service elements, and the referring court considers that those supplies of goods and services form a single transaction for the purposes of VAT'. Admittedly, the use of the two terms, i.e., 'transaction' and 'supply', in the VAT Directive is not entirely consistent. *See* e.g., Art. 168(1)(b) of the VAT Directive, which enables a taxable person to deduct 'the VAT due in respect of *transactions treated as supplies of goods or services* pursuant to Article 18(a) and Article 27', or Art. 199(3)(a) of the VAT Directive, which imposes a liability for VAT upon 'a taxable person who also carries out activities or *transactions that are not considered to be taxable supplies of goods or services* in accordance with Article 2' (emphases added).
3. UK: ECJ, 6 July 2006, Case C-251/05, *Talacre Beach Caravan Sales Ltd v. Commissioners of Customs & Excise*, para. 25.
4. *See* DE: ECJ, 2 May 1996, Case C-231/94, *Faaborg-Gelting Linien A/S v. Finanzamt Flensburg*, para. 14, considering that 'restaurant transactions are characterized by a cluster of features and acts, of which the provision of food is only one component and in which services largely predominate'.
5. PL: ECJ, 17 Jan. 2013, Case C-224/11, *BGŻ Leasing sp. z o.o. v. Dyrektor Izby Skarbowej w Warszawie*, para. 32. In this connection, *see also* European Commission, Value Added Tax Committee, *Guidelines resulting from the 52nd Meeting of 28-29 May 1997* (XXI/97/1.566), considering that where a taxable person, in the context of a fair or similar exhibition, supplies another person 'a complex package of services, comprising, in addition to the provision of a stand, a number of other, related services, the whole package is to be regarded as a single service comprising various components which cannot and need not to be itemized according to their own place of taxation'.

VAT is likely to become a rather difficult exercise.[6] And indeed, defining what exactly constitutes a transaction, a supply or, even, a single good or service neither is a theoretical exercise nor certainly is devoid of any practical importance. As from this determination, a different sets of rules may in fact apply, e.g., with regard to the classification of a transaction, the place of supply, the chargeable event and chargeability of VAT, the taxable amount, the deduction of VAT, the applicable rates and exemptions, as well as the liability for payment of VAT.[7] Indeed, in case of a cross-border trade, the determination of whether or not an economic operation is to be considered as a unitary transaction for EU VAT purposes could also lead to situations of double taxation or non-taxation, should the Member States concerned take opposing views in this regard.[8]

Defining what exactly constitutes a transaction, a supply or, even, a single service is also crucial in the context of the sharing economy, which, indeed, entails the joint provision to the individual customer of several services by distinct undertakings, namely at least two, i.e., an intermediary service provided by the platform and an underlying service provided by the individual supplier. In order to make such a determination, all the facts and circumstances of a sharing economy economic operation as a whole must be duly taken into account. An analysis in this regard, in light of the CJEU's doctrine on 'composite supplies' as well as of the other potential approaches to it, is provided in the following sections.

§6.02 THE CJEU'S DOCTRINE ON COMPOSITE SUPPLIES

The VAT Directive does not contain any rule on how to deal with transactions, supplies, goods, or services composed of several elements, in short 'composite supplies'. Some guidance in this regard has nevertheless been provided by the CJEU. Through the years, the Court has in fact developed a specific doctrine on 'composite supplies'.

Card Protection Plan is rightly regarded as the founding stone in the development of such doctrine. Notably, the case concerned a company, Card Protection Plan ('CPP'), offering holders of credit cards a protection plan, which included certain services that, if assessed on an individual basis, were to be classified as insurance services and, therefore, exempt from EU VAT, pursuant to Article 135(1)(a) of the VAT

6. A. van Doesum, H.W.M. van Kesteren, & G.J. van Norden, *Fundamentals of EU VAT Law* at 135 (Kluwer Law International 2016).
7. For a limited sample collection of the various issues in this regard, *see* e.g., UK: ECJ, 25 Feb. 1999, Case C-349/96, *Card Protection Plan Ltd (CPP) v. Commissioners of Customs & Excise*; NL: ECJ, 27 Oct. 2005, Case C-41/04, *Levob Verzekeringen BV and OV Bank NV v. Staatssecretaris van Financiën*; PL: ECJ, 27 June 2013, Case C-155/12, *Minister Finansów v. RR Donnelley Global Turnkey Solutions Poland sp. z o.o.*; UK: ECJ, 5 Jul. 2018, Case C-544/16, *Marcandi Limited, Agissant Sous le Nom Commercial 'Madbid' v. Commissioners for Her Majesty's Revenue & Customs*; UK: ECJ, 28 Oct. 2010, Case C-175/09, *Commissioners for Her Majesty's Revenue and Customs v. AXA UK plc*; NL: ECJ, 18 Jan. 2018, Case C-463/16, *Stadion Amsterdam CV v. Staatssecretaris van Financiën*.
8. OECD, *The Application of Consumption Taxes to the Trade in International Services and Intangibles: Progress Report and Draft Principles* at 7 (OECD Publishing 2005).

Directive, plus a series of other services that, if assessed on an individual basis, were to be classified as card registration services and, therefore, fully subject to EU VAT. The CJEU, in particular, was asked to determine whether the various services composing the credit card protection plan were to be treated as a single composite supply or, instead, as several distinct supplies and, following this determination, whether the services in question were to be exempt or not from VAT.

The CJEU commenced its analysis by considering that, having regard to the sheer diversity of commercial operations, all the facts and circumstances of a case must be taken into account as to make an appropriate determination on this point.[9] In particular, the Court emphasized the need to ascertain the 'essential features'[10] - in other cases, instead, referred to as 'characteristic elements'[11] - of the transaction concerned.

As better clarified in later decisions, while doing such an assessment, the CJEU looks, in particular, at the 'economic purpose'[12] - equally described as 'economic reason'[13] or 'economic objective'[14] - of the operation at stake.[15] And yet, the economic purpose of the operation is not the sole perspective considered by the Court. Rather, in its assessment, the CJEU equally takes into account the actual interest displayed by the individual customer in receiving a certain supply.[16] In practice, the Court endeavours to put itself in the shoes of the recipient of a supply[17], as to determine which, actually, is his 'ultimate intention'.[18] To be more precise: it is not the intention of the immediate customer which matters, but instead that of the end consumer.[19]

In the author's opinion, such an assessment is not very much different from the test developed by the CJEU in *The Rank Group*, as to determine whether two activities are comparable and, thus, shall receive the same treatment in light of the neutrality principle underpinning EU VAT. The 'neutrality test' developed by the CJEU in *The Rank Group*, in fact, looks at (1) whether the supplies at stake are identical or similar from the perspective of the end consumer, and (2) whether those supplies meet the same needs of the end consumer.[20] And indeed, as it is in relation to composite

9. *Card Protection Plan* (C-349/96), para. 28.
10. *Id.*, para. 29.
11. *BGŻ Leasing* (C-224/11), para. 32.
12. NL: ECJ, 19 Nov. 2009, Case C-461/08, *Don Bosco Onroerend Goed BV v. Staatssecretaris van Financiën*, para. 39.
13. UK: ECJ, 27 Sep. 2012, Case C-392/11, *Field Fisher Waterhouse LLP v. Commissioners for Her Majesty's Revenue and Customs*, para. 23.
14. HU: ECJ, 8 Dec. 2016, Case C-208/15, *Stock '94 Szolgáltató Zrt. v. Nemzeti Adóés Vámhivatal Dél-dunántúli Regionális Adó Főigazgatósága*, para. 29.
15. *AXA UK* (C-175/09), para. 23.
16. UK: ECJ, 2 Dec. 2010, Case C-276/09, *Everything Everywhere Ltd v. Commissioners for Her Majesty's Revenue and Customs*, para. 27.
17. PL: ECJ, 16 Apr. 2015, Case C-42/14, *Minister Finansów v. Wojskowa Agencja Mieszkaniowa w Warszawie*, para. 35.
18. UK: ECJ, 16 Dec. 2010, Case C-270/09, *Macdonald Resorts Ltd v. The Commissioners for Her Majesty's Revenue & Customs*, para. 22.
19. UK: ECJ, 15 May 2001, Case C-34/99, *Commissioners of Customs & Excise v. Primback Ltd*, para. 43.
20. UK: ECJ, 10 Nov. 2011, Case C-259/10, *Commissioners for Her Majesty's Revenue and Customs v. The Rank Group plc*, para. 36.

supplies, while doing such an assessment, the Court looks 'in the eyes of the consumer, in terms of the satisfaction of his own needs'.[21]

Despite the undeniable similarities with the 'neutrality test' highlighted above, the doctrine on 'composite supplies' developed by the CJEU as from *Card Protection Plan* follows a different, rather schematic, step-by-step approach. An analysis of this approach and of its various steps is provided in the following sections.

[A] The Main Rule: Splitting

The doctrine on composite supplies has a main rule, which is pretty straightforward to explain. This rule mandates that every transaction shall be considered as fully distinct and independent. This entails that the treatment accorded to each transaction under EU VAT must be kept separate, which inevitably implies that their VAT treatment may potentially diverge. This primary course is usually termed as 'splitting', precisely because it demands that each of the various elements composing a transaction is examined on its own merits.

Indeed, the above 'splitting' rule stems directly from the 'principle of singularity' enshrined in Article 1(2) Second Indent of the VAT Directive, which prescribes that EU VAT, calculated on the final price of all the goods and services supplied at the rate applicable to such goods and services, shall be charged on each single transaction.[22]

This main 'splitting' rule, however, has two relevant exceptions. Notably, two or more supplies need to be treated as a single, indivisible composite supply, (1) if they constitute 'a single supply from an economic point of view', or (2) if one supply is ancillary to the other. An examination of both these two exceptions is provided in the following sections.

[B] The First Exception: A Single Supply from an Economic Point of View

As a first exception to the foregoing main course, two or more supplies need to be considered as a single, indivisible composite supply if such supplies constitute 'a single supply from an economic point of view', which should not be artificially split, so as not to distort the functioning of the EU VAT system.[23] Should each of the supplies in question have 'a distinct, self-contained, economic rationale'[24], then this first exception would not come into consideration and the main 'splitting' rule would, instead, apply.

21. DE: ECJ, 27 Feb. 2014, Joined Cases C-454/12 and C-455/12, *Pro Med Logistik GmbH v. Finanzamt Dresden-Süd and Eckard Pongratz v. Finanzamt Würzburg mit Außenstelle Ochsenfurt*, para. 56.
22. *See* e.g., UK: ECJ, 18 Oct. 2018, Case C-153/17, *Commissioners for Her Majesty's Revenue and Customs v. Volkswagen Financial Services (UK) Ltd.*, para. 30.
23. *Levob Verzekeringen and OV Bank* (C-41/04), para. 20.
24. FR: Opinion of the Advocate General, 4 Feb. 2015, Case C-584/13, *Directeur Général des Finances Publiques v. Mapfre Asistencia Compañia Internacional de Seguros y Reaseguros SA and Mapfre Warranty SpA v. Directeur Général des Finances Publiques*, para. 42.

It is not quite clear, however, what exactly the CJEU intends by using the expression 'from an economic point of view' in this context. Notably, the Court has failed to explain whether, for this purpose, primacy should be attributed to the 'objective' economic purpose of the transaction or if, instead, the 'subjective' intention shown by the individual customer ought to be, first and foremost, taken into account.[25]

Apparently, in *Aktiebolaget NN*, the CJEU attributed primacy to the 'objective' economic purpose of the transaction. Notably, *Aktiebolaget NN* concerned a company installing an undersea fibre-optic cable and carrying out operational tests after that installation. In this connection, in order to dismiss the operation of the main rule about composite supplies, i.e., the 'splitting' approach, the Court considered that 'all the elements of the transaction at issue in the main proceedings appear to be necessary to its completion and, secondly, they are all closely linked'.[26] The conclusions of Advocate General Léger, however, were clearer on this point. Notably, the Advocate General reasoned that, 'given that the right to dispose of the cable is transferred only when installation is complete and operational tests have been carried out, it would not be in keeping with the commercial reality of that transaction to consider that the client has first purchased the undersea fibre-optic cable and subsequently the services relating to its installation'.[27] Reference to 'commercial reality' was also made by the Court in *Levob Verzekeringen and OV Bank*, where the CJEU even argued that taking an opposite stance would have implied entering 'the realms of the artificial'.[28]

RRLE Tellmer Property is another case in which, apparently, the Court has adopted an objective approach for determining the economic purpose of the transaction. Notably, the question put before the CJEU concerned whether separately invoiced sums for the cleaning of the common parts of a building could be considered accessory to the leasing or letting, exempt from VAT, of that building. In this connection, the Court found that the cleaning services in question did not necessarily fall within the concept of leasing or letting of immovable property, on the ground that, despite the cleaning services were supplied to the tenants by the landlord himself, under other commercial practices, those services could well have been supplied by a third party directly to the tenants, without the landlord being anyhow involved.[29]

25. Indeed, both these two approaches, i.e., the 'objective' and the 'subjective' one, have emerged, quite early on, in the CJEU's case law on composite supplies, namely as from *Card Protection Plan*, a case in which the taxpayer argued in favour of a more analytical approach, which took into account its subjective intentions, rather than for an approach focusing on the average consumer's perspective, as instead proposed by the Commission. *See* UK: Opinion of the Advocate General, 11 Jun. 1998, Case C-349/96, *Card Protection Plan Ltd (CPP) v. Commissioners of Customs & Excise*, para. 44.
26. SW: ECJ, 29 Mar. 2007, Case C-111/05, *Aktiebolaget NN v. Skatteverket*, para. 25.
27. SW: Opinion of the Advocate General, 14 Sep. 2006, Case C-111/05, *Aktiebolaget NN v. Skatteverket*, para. 45.
28. *Levob Verzekeringen and OV Bank* (C-41/04), para. 24.
29. CZ: ECJ, 11 Jun. 2009, Case C-572/07, *RLRE Tellmer Property sro v. Finanční Ředitelství v. Ústí nad Labem*, paras 14-25.

In light of the case law recalled above, the author concurs that, ultimately, the way in which the services are normally presented on the market is of importance for determining what exactly a typical customer requests.[30]

The second approach, instead, follows a 'subjective' pattern, in the sense that it looks at what an individual customer, from an economic point of view, intends to achieve in a specific situation. The 'subjective' intention of an individual customer in receiving a supply can, most notably, emerge from the contractual arrangements between the parties.[31] For instance, in *Field Fisher Waterhouse*, a case concerning a contract for the rent of offices by a law firm, the CJEU found that a single supply of services existed between the landlord and his tenant, in so far as the contract in question required that, in addition to the leasing or letting of those premises, the landlord provided the tenant (i.e., the law firm) with a number of other services and, therefore, the 'economic reason' for the individual customer (i.e., the tenant) to secure that arrangement was not to merely obtain the right to occupy the premises concerned, but also that of receiving those other services.[32]

The contractual arrangements also played a decisive role in *Régie Communale Autonome du Stade Luc Varenne* for the Court to conclude that the lease of a football stadium, along with the provision of several other services, such as the maintenance, cleaning, repair, and upgrading of such building, which represented 80% of the overall charge agreed upon in a contract, did not constitute, as a general rule, a 'letting of immovable property', but rather a composite supply of various services, given the importance attached to those services, as to ensure that the football stadium was suitable for the use to which it was devoted, i.e., to host football matches.[33]

A similar line of reasoning was displayed by the Court in *Wojskowa Agencja Mieszkaniowa w Warszawie*, concerning a company which let immovable property together with the provision of certain utilities, including electricity, heating, water, and waste disposal. Notably, according to the rental agreement between the parties, the company charged tenants in advance, using the tax rate specifically applicable to each

30. O. Henkow, *Financial Activities in European VAT: A Theoretical and Legal Research of the European VAT System* at 207 (Kluwer Law International 2008).
31. Nevertheless, the CJEU has duly emphasized the need that, with regard to 'the VAT liability of a transaction', 'the declared intention of the parties ... is supported by objective evidence'. *See* NL: ECJ, 12 Jul. 2012, Case C-326/11, *J.J. Komen en Zonen Beheer Heerhugowaard BV v. Staatssecretaris van Financiën*, para. 33. *See also* DK: Opinion of the Advocate General, 19 Mar. 2019, Case C-71/18, *Skatteministeriet v. KPC Herning*, paras 50-51, where Advocate General Bobek held that, for the application of EU VAT, 'mere statements of the parties, unsupported by any concrete evidence, can play no role' and, further, that 'the intention and plans of the parties can [only] colour or confirm a certain reading of the reality ... unless tax law assessment is to become an instance of metaphysical voluntarism, in which, to paraphrase Schopenhauer, the transaction is just will and representation'.
32. *Field Fisher Waterhouse* (C-392/11), para. 23. *See also* CZ: Opinion of the Advocate General, 14 Jun. 2016, Case C-432/15, *Odvolací finanční ředitelství contro Pavlína Baštová*, paras 46-50, where Advocate General Wahl reasoned that customers concluding a contract relating to the 'operation of racing stables' sought precisely 'a combination of various services such as training of the horse, use of sports equipment, all-day accommodation in stables, feeding of and other care for the horse'.
33. BE: ECJ, 22 Jan. 2015, Case C-55/14, *Régie Communale Autonome du Stade Luc Varenne v. État Belge*, paras 20-39.

utility and then, at the end of each year, adjusting the amounts collected to reflect the actual consumption of utilities by the tenant concerned. Considering this mode of operation, the CJEU ruled that the circumstance that 'the tenant is free to determine his own levels of consumption', by means of 'the existence of individual meters and billing according to the amount of the goods used', implied that the provision of utilities constituted a separate supply from the letting.[34]

Based on the above exposition, it can fairly be maintained that the ability of a customer to determine his own level of consumption, i.e., to make choices in relation to the products supplied to him, is a factor of importance while assessing whether there is a single composite supply or not.[35]

Ultimately, the two approaches above, i.e., the 'objective' and the 'subjective' one, can be reconciled where the economic purpose considered is that of the 'typical'[36] or 'average'[37] customer. As a matter of fact, such a reconciliatory approach seems to represent the best course of action, in so far as it avoids the risk of establishing the existence of a single composite supply on a too abstract analysis of the economic operation or, even, to separate a single transaction into two or more supplies pursuant to 'artificial distinctions based on insignificant differences'.[38] Notably, such middle-ground approach was followed by the CJEU in *Levob Verzekeringen and OV Bank*, in which the Court was asked to determine whether the supply of a customized software constituted a single supply of services, comprising both the provision of the software and its customization, or, vice versa, two fully distinct supplies of services, which included the supply of the software plus a separate supply of its customization. The Court, ultimately, stood for the former position, precisely based on the assumption that the two services in question were so closely linked that they formed, objectively, a single, indivisible economic supply from the point of view of the 'typical consumer'.[39]

[C] The Second Exception: The Ancillary Principle

The second exception to the aforementioned main 'splitting' rule relates to what could be termed as 'ancillary principle' or 'principle of absorption'.[40] In a nutshell, this

34. *Wojskowa Agencja Mieszkaniowa w Warszawie* (C-42/14), paras 29-47.
35. *See* e.g., UK: Opinion of the Advocate General, 7 Mar. 2018, Case C-544/16, *Marcandi Limited, Trading as 'Madbid' v. Commissioners for Her Majesty's Revenue and Customs*, para. 58.
36. *Levob Verzekeringen and OV Bank* (C-41/04), paras 20, 22 and 30.
37. UK: ECJ, 19 Jan. 2012, Case C-117/11, *Purple Parking Ltd and Airparks Services Ltd v. Commissioners for Her Majesty's Revenue and Customs*, para. 38.
38. *Pro Med Logistik and Pongratz* (C-454/12 & C-455/12), para. 53.
39. *Levob Verzekeringen and OV Bank* (C-41/04), para. 22. *See also* DE: ECJ, 19 Jul. 2012, Case C-44/11, *Finanzamt Frankfurt am Main V-Höchst v. Deutsche Bank AG*, para. 25, referring, in the context of certain banking and financial operations, to the 'average client investor'.
40. Based on its ordinary meaning, the author submits that, with the expression 'ancillary', it should be intended something that is 'subordinate', 'secondary' or 'subservient' to something else. *See* English Oxford Dictionary, *Ancillary*, https://en.oxforddictionaries.com/definition/ancillary (accessed 31 March 2019). For an examination of the term in the CJEU's case law on EU VAT, *see* DE: Opinion of the Advocate General, 25 Apr. 1996, Case C-327/94, *Jürgen Dudda v. Finanzgericht Bergisch Gladbach*, para. 38, also making reference to the ordinary meaning of the term.

principle stipulates that a single composite supply exists also if one or more elements of a transaction constitute a principal supply, whereas another or more other elements constitute an ancillary supply, which, as such, must share the treatment of the principal supply. In particular, a supply must be regarded as ancillary to another principal supply if it does not constitute for a customer an end in itself, but simply a means of better enjoying the principal supply.[41]

The 'ancillary principle', indeed, constitutes a specification of the so-called principle of the 'unity of the supply'[42], which demands not breaking a transaction into its various components, with a view of applying EU VAT separately to each of them, but instead to maintain the focus on 'the whole' of what the end consumer receives. This principle is best epitomized in the Latin maxim '*accessorium sequitur principale*', a rule which has been developed and borrowed to EU VAT by the CJEU from other areas of EU law.[43]

The application of the 'ancillary principle' has been at stake in several CJEU's decisions. Perhaps the best illustration of a situation in which a supply ought to be regarded as ancillary to another principal supply is when a physical connection exists between the elements of the two supplies in question. Notably, this was the situation at stake in *Henriksen*, where the CJEU was asked to determine whether the 'letting of premises and sites for parking vehicles' also encompassed closed garages connected with an immovable property, whose letting was exempt under EU VAT. Precisely based on the physical connection existing between these two spaces, the Court answered to that question in the affirmative.[44]

Whether or not a supply should be considered as ancillary to another principal supply requires a case-by-case evaluation, which must take into account all the facts and circumstances of a case. And yet, the exact course of action for conducting such an evaluation is anything but crystal clear. In particular, it is far from plain whether such evaluation should be premised on the qualitative or, rather, the quantitative contribution made by a supply to an economic operation as a whole. Notably, in *Madgett and*

41. Notably, a formulation of the 'ancillary principle' was firstly laid down by Advocate General Léger and subsequently confirmed by the CJEU in *Madgett and Baldwin*. *See* UK: Opinion of the Advocate General, 30 Apr. 1998, Case C-308/96, *Commissioners of Customs and Excise v. T.P. Madgett, R.M. Baldwin and The Howden Court Hotel*, para. 36; UK: ECJ, 22 Oct. 1998, Case C-308/96, *Commissioners of Customs and Excise v. T.P. Madgett, R.M. Baldwin and The Howden Court Hotel*, para. 24.
42. This expression was used, for the first time, by Advocate General Ruiz-Jarabo Colomer in *Hotel Scandic* and, then, by Advocate General Trstenjak in *RCI Europe*. *See* SW: Opinion of the Advocate General, 23 Nov. 2004, Case C-412/03, *Hotel Scandic Gåsabäck AB v. Riksskatteverket*, para. 21; UK: Opinion of the Advocate General, 2 Apr. 2009, Case C-37/08, *RCI Europe v. Commissioners for Her Majesty's Revenue and Customs*, para. 81.
43. DE: ECJ, 15 Jan. 1987, Case C-266/85, *Hassan Shenavai v. Klaus Kreischer*, para. 19.
44. DK: ECJ, 13 Jul. 1989, Case C-173/88, *Skatteministeriet v. Morten Henriksen*, paras 7-18. Along the same lines, *see* RO: ECJ, 19 Dec. 2018, Case C-17/18, *Criminal Proceedings Against Virgil Mailat and Others*, paras 31-41, where the supply of equipment and kitchen appliances was considered ancillary to the supply of a restaurant, being the former movable objects incorporated in the latter immovable property.

Baldwin, Advocate General Léger made reference both to qualitative and quantitative criteria.[45] The same course of action was ultimately taken by the CJEU in later cases.[46]

It also seems that the method of balancing these two approaches, referring to the qualitative or the quantitative contribution made by a supply to an economic operation as a whole, could vary in each specific situation. For instance, a predominantly qualitative-based approach was followed by the CJEU in *Purple Parking and Airparks Services*. Notably, in that case, the Court found that services related to the parking of vehicles in an 'off-airport' car park and for transport of passengers of those vehicles between that car park and the airport terminal concerned constituted a single composite supply, in which the parking service was predominant, whereas the transport service was merely ancillary to it. For reaching such conclusion, it was decisive, *inter alia*, the observation that 'the customer seeks, first and foremost, parking at an advantageous price', whereas 'the transport service is only the inevitable consequence of the fact that the car park is located at a certain distance from the airport, a location accepted by the customer given that that distance allows him to pay less for the parking service'.[47]

A qualitative criterion, making specific reference to the business model as adopted by a taxable person in an individual case, was also employed by the CJEU in *Město Žamberk*. Notably, the case concerned a company operating an aquatic park, in which various sporting facilities were jointly offered to customers for a single entrance price. Although the ultimate factual reconstruction was left to the referring court, in that case, the CJEU concluded that a single complex service was provided to the customers, based on the consideration that 'the only type of entrance ticket offered for the aquatic park gives access to all of the facilities, without any distinction according to the type of facility actually used and to the manner and to the duration of its use during the period of the entrance ticket's validity'.[48]

Apparently, the approach referring to the qualitative contribution made by a supply to an economic operation as a whole is also the one preferred by the CJEU. And yet, the approach referring to a quantitative contribution is not completely disregarded by the Court. Notably, a quantitative criterion was adopted by the CJEU in *Régie Communale Autonome du Stade Luc Varenne*, where the circumstance that the

45. *See* Opinion *Madgett and Baldwin* (C-308/96), para. 36, where Advocate General Léger observed the following: 'I consider that a service is ancillary if, first, it contributes to the proper performance of the principal service and, second, it takes up a marginal proportion of the package price compared to the principal service'.

46. *See* e.g., *Bog and Others* (C-497/09, C-499/09, C-501/09 and C-502/09), para. 62, where the Court observed the following: 'it should also be pointed out that the predominant element must be determined … having regard, in an overall assessment, to the qualitative and not merely quantitative importance of the elements of supply of services in relation to the elements of supply of goods'.

47. *Purple Parking and Airparks Services* (C-117/11), para. 35. Along the same lines, *see Stock '94* (C-208/15), para. 35, where loans granted by a company to farmers, in order to purchase the assets needed in their own activity, were considered by the CJEU as an ancillary supply in respect of the supply of those assets, based on the assumption that such loans constituted merely a means for the farmers to acquire the assets concerned.

48. CZ: ECJ, 21 Feb. 2013, Case C-18/12, *Město Žamberk v. Finanční ředitelství v. Hradci Králové, now Odvolací finanční ředitelství*, para. 32.

economic value of certain services represented 80% of the economic operation as a whole led the Court to treat those services as the principal element of what, overall, was supplied to the customer.[49]

The price attributed to a specific service in the context of a composite supply was also decisive in *ISt*, a case concerning a company that offered customers, in return for the payment of an all-inclusive sum, travel facilities as well as language training and education services. Notably, in that case, the CJEU reasoned that, in so far as the provision of travel facilities had a substantial effect on the overall price charged to the customer, the service in question did not represent 'a marginal share' in relation to the language training and education services and, therefore, could not be considered as merely ancillary to these latter services.[50]

All the three rules constituting the CJEU's doctrine on composite supplies as outlined in the above may well find an application in the context of the sharing economy. In this connection, the author submits that none of these three rules should, in principle, be favoured over any other.

As a first possible scenario, a single sharing economy operation, which entails both the supply made by the platform and that made by the individual supplier, can be split into two or more supplies for EU VAT purposes. At first glance, it could perhaps be assumed that this is, indeed, the 'ordinary' course of action in the sharing economy, as long as this phenomenon entails the provision to the same individual customer of two different supplies, i.e., the intermediary and the underlying supply, by two distinct undertakings, i.e., the platform and the individual supplier. This scenario, however, might not ultimately hold up. Notably, besides the possibility to apply the doctrine on composite supplies also to the case of an economic operation carried out jointly by two distinct undertakings - situation which will be illustrated in the following[51]-, the scenario above might not materialize where a platform provides both the intermediary and the underlying service to the individual customer - in a sense, the platform acts as a 'double service provider' -, situation which occurs when the individual supplier is not 'truly' independent from the platform, as some courts might find especially in the case of Uber drivers.[52]

All the three rules constituting the CJEU's doctrine on composite supply may equally come into prominence in relation to, on the one hand, the possibly various supplies made by the platform to its users, and, on the other hand, the possibly various supplies made by the individual supplier to the individual customer. Rather than the main 'splitting' rule, both the exceptions to it, however, show a much more promising ground of application in the context of the sharing economy.

As regards platform services, a platform can in fact provide two or more supplies to its users, either to the individual supplier, the individual customer, or both. Such supplies can be viewed as a single composite supply from an economic point of view

49. *Régie Communale Autonome du Stade Luc Varenne* (C-55/14), para. 34.
50. DE: ECJ, 13 Oct. 2005, Case C-200/04, *Finanzamt Heidelberg v. ISt internationale Sprach- und Studienreisen GmbH*, para. 28.
51. *See* section §6.03[B].
52. *See* section §4.04.

or, alternatively, as a single composite supply in which one supply is ancillary to the other. In this connection, payment handling services, possibly including other instrumental activities such as invoicing, are the first types of services which spring to mind. Indeed, it would imply entering 'the realms of the artificial' to maintain that those services constitute a separate supply from the service of intermediation provided by the platform, in so far as, clearly, a payment cannot be considered as independent from the service which it refers to. As regards other types of services offered by a platform to its users, such as those relating to profile verification, security deposit, and damage protection offered by HomeExchange to its users, or those relating to insurance coverage offered by Airbnb, Uber, and BlaBlaCar to their respective users, instead, it might be necessary to look at the specific circumstances of the economic operation at stake, which could entail an evaluation of the way in which the services in question are normally presented on the market, the contractual arrangements between the parties and, even, the ability of the individual customer to determine his own level of consumption.[53]

As for services among platform users, instead, the doctrine on composite supplies does not appear to come into prominence, as long as, in most instances, those services entail the provision to the individual customer of a 'unitary service', i.e., accommodation or passenger transport. Nevertheless, there might be instances in which a series of services are jointly provided by the individual supplier to the individual customer. Notably, this is the case of an Airbnb host who, together with short-term accommodation, provides a guest with a number of 'experiences' (e.g., equitation lessons or wine-tasting itineraries).[54] In such event, the CJEU's doctrine on composite supply and, in particular, the two exceptions to the main rule, could indeed kick in. The main 'splitting' rule, instead, is harder to apply in such scenario, as long as 'experiences' constitute merely ancillary supplies to the principal supply of short-term accommodation or if, from an economic point of view, what the guest primarily seeks to obtain happens to be bare accommodation. Nevertheless, 'splitting' might remain the best course of action where those 'experiences' maintain an autonomous relevance in relation to the overall supply to the individual customer, in the sense of having 'a different status and weight'.[55]

53. Indeed, as maintained by Advocate General Szpunar in *Uber Systems Spain*, the possibility to classify a service as an information society service under EU law requires a careful examination of whether such service does not form, instead, 'an inseparable whole' with another, not dematerialised service. *See* ES: Opinion of the Advocate General, 11 May 2017, Case C-434/15, *Asociación Profesional Elite Taxi v. Uber Systems Spain SL*, para. 35.

54. *See* section §2.07[A].

55. *See* DE: Opinion of the Advocate General, 5 Sep. 2018, Case C-552/17, *Alpenchalets Resorts GmbH v. Finanzamt München Abteilung Körperschaften*, para. 44, where Advocate General Bobek reasoned that, although services such as cleaning and laundry are normally considered as ancillary to the provision of accommodation, 'there may be exceptional cases in which ... those normally ancillary services would have a different status and weight. Examples which might spring to mind could include an exceptional breakfast in the bucolic setting of the Austrian Tyrol, tailored for romantic souls, or various types of gastronomic retreats. Or accommodation in a medieval castle with the special offer of "do-your-own laundry" in historic laundries using traditional methods and promising the "genuine feel for the life of a fifteenth century launderer"'. What a fantasy for a man of law!

§6.03 ALTERNATIVE APPROACHES TO COMPOSITE SUPPLIES

The three rules, i.e., the main rule and its two exceptions, constituting the CJEU's doctrine on composite supply, however, do not exhaust the full spectrum of possible approaches in this regard. This circumstance was expressly recognized by Advocate General Kokott in *Levob Verzekeringen and OV Bank*. Notably, after finding that neither of the two supplies at stake in that case was ancillary to the other, the Advocate General observed that 'the principal/ancillary supply arrangement is only *one* scenario already recognized in case law' (emphasis original).[56] According to the Advocate General, in fact, the CJEU's doctrine on composite supplies presupposes a broader evaluation than the one entailed in the three rules so far delineated by the Court, i.e., an evaluation in which 'the essential issue is still to determine the substance of the supplies', in particular whether the two supplies 'are so closely linked that, in isolation, from the perspective of the average consumer, they do not have the necessary practical benefit for customers'.[57] From this, the author derives that, for having a single composite supply, what ultimately matters is that the two supplies are 'closely interlinked'[58] or 'inextricably interlinked'[59]. Alternative approaches to composite supplies, especially those of particular relevance in the context of the sharing economy, are examined in the following sections.

[A] Two-Step and Preliminary Transactions

In the previous sections, only situations in which two or more related supplies are made by a taxable person to the same customer simultaneously, i.e., at the same point in time, have been considered. However, it is well possible that two or more related supplies are made by a taxable person to the same customer at different points in time. In such event, one may wonder whether the supplies in question are, indeed, fully distinct supplies or if, instead, a different course is to be taken, in the sense that either the first supply needs to be considered as a mere preliminary step toward the making of the second supply or, alternatively, the latter supply is to be regarded as necessary to the completion of the former supply. Based on the CJEU's case law illustrated below, the author refers to this situation as entailing 'two-step transactions', i.e., transactions composed of supplies in which one supply is merely preliminary to the other.

To the author's knowledge, such an issue first came close to the attention of the CJEU in *Ludwig*, a case concerning the provision of advisory services by a financial consultant to clients prior the entering of those clients into credit arrangements with a

56. Opinion *Levob Verzekeringen and OV Bank* (C-41/04), para. 68. For similar considerations, *see* UK: House of Lords, 20 Oct. 2005, *College of Estate Management v. Her Majesty's Commissioners of Customs and Excise* [2005] UKHL 62, at para. 10, considering that 'in cases where there is no ancillary supply, a single supply may still be made up of more than one element'.
57. Opinion *Levob Verzekeringen and OV Bank* (C-41/04), para. 69.
58. FR: ECJ, 11 Feb. 2010, Case C-88/09, *Graphic Procédé v. Ministère du Budget, des Comptes Publics et de la Fonction Publique*, paras 19 and 23.
59. DE: Opinion of the Advocate General, 14 Jul. 2011, Case C-93/10, *Finanzamt Essen-NordOst v. GFKL Financial Services AG*, para. 91.

bank. Notably, in that case, the CJEU found that the activity carried out by the consultant was ancillary to the credit arrangements concluded by the clients in question with the bank at a later stage. More specifically, the Court reasoned that, as a matter of fact, the negotiation of credit by the bank was the relevant service for the clients, whereas the prior advisory activity carried out by the financial consultant was a mere preliminary step to it, as long as such activity only aimed at helping the bank's clients to choose, from the wealth of financial products offered by that credit institution, the most suitable for their own needs.[60]

Situations involving two-step transactions, i.e., two related supplies made by a taxable person to the same customer at two distinct points in time, have indeed grown significantly in recent years, especially with the advent of the so-called 'subscription economy', i.e., the increasing tendency of customers to access goods and services by way of an initial or periodic subscription, rather than by paying a straight transaction fee for each single good or service received.[61] Notably, the most relevant and recent cases concerning two-step transactions under EU VAT precisely relate to the payment of membership fees, i.e., situations in which customers are required to pay a price as a condition to enter into a market or to join a community. An analysis of this line of cases is provided in the following.

The first case, in chronological order, of this series of CJEU's decisions is *RCI Europe*. Notably, RCI Europe was a UK company, whose business consisted in organizing and facilitating the exchange of timeshare usage rights held by its members in holiday accommodation located outside the UK, mainly in Spain. In order to conclude such kinds of exchanges among themselves, holiday resort developers were invited to become affiliates of RCI Europe by paying an initial enrolment fee, which covered a period from one up to five years, plus an annual subscription fee. In this connection, the question put before the CJEU was whether, for place of supply purposes, those fees related to the mere participation in the exchange of timeshare rights or, rather, to the actual provision of holiday accommodation, a point on which the intervening UK and Spanish governments had opposite views as well as conflicting fiscal interests. Despite the findings of the Advocate General Trstenjak in this regard, who considered both enrolment and subscription fees as a mere 'preliminary step' for members toward the actual provision of holiday accommodation[62], the CJEU ultimately adhered to the latter of the two hypotheses, on the ground that the supply of membership services by the company followed by the actual exchange of timeshare usage rights among its members constituted a single composite supply taking place in two steps. This was found despite the fact that, in return for payment of the enrolment and subscription fees, a member initially received only a right to access to the exchange scheme operated by RCI, but not also an entitlement to any holiday accommodation. And yet, the Court reasoned that, for a participant, membership of such a scheme

60. DE: ECJ, 21 June 2007, Case C-453/05, *Volker Ludwig v. Finanzamt Luckenwalde*, para. 19.
61. For a quick overview on the 'subscription economy', *see Subscribers Are the New, New Thing in Business*, The Economist (7 Apr. 2018).
62. Opinion *RCI Europe* (C-37/08), paras 63-90.

would be 'pointless' if he had no intention of exchanging his own timeshare usage rights for those of another member at a later stage.[63]

The line of CJEU's decisions on membership fees continued with *Macdonald Resorts*, a case concerning a UK (*rectius*: Scottish) company operating a quite similar business to that of RCI Europe. As it was in *RCI Europe*, the question put before the Court concerned the correct classification and, hence, the determination of the place of supply of certain services relating to timeshare usage rights provided by the company to its own members. Remarkably, different positions in this regard were taken by the taxable person (Macdonald Resorts), the national governments involved (the UK, Portuguese, and Greek governments), the Commission, the Advocate General, and the Court.

Advocate General Trstenjak, in particular, released a very articulated opinion. He essentially reasoned that, in that case, two fully distinct and independent supplies existed, the first supply consisting in the granting by the company to its own members of the possibility to exchange among themselves timeshare usage rights relating to listed immovable properties - which, as the Advocate General elegantly put it, constituted the 'condition of entry to a virtual exchange platform'[64]-, whereas the second supply entailing 'the procuring of timeshare properties'[65], which each member could access only upon redeeming previously acquired timeshare usage rights, although, ultimately, for both transactions the place of supply was to be found where the properties concerned were located.[66]

The Advocate General, however, also examined other approaches alternative to the one which he ultimately adhered to. In this connection, he reasoned that, as a matter of fact, members completed the first transaction not just for the sake of obtaining usage timeshare rights, but rather with the more meaningful intention to access the residential properties concerned. Indeed, from the perspective of individual members, the purchase of timeshare usage rights did not have, in itself, 'any intrinsic value', so that, more realistically, the purchase and the redemption of timeshare usage rights ought to have been regarded, rather, as '*interim* stages which have to be completed in order to be able to exercise the timeshare usage right in the property in

63. UK: ECJ, 3 Sep. 2009, Case C-37/08, *RCI Europe v. Commissioners for Her Majesty's Revenue and Customs*, paras 26-35. At a closer inspection, the actual reasoning adopted by the Court in its decision, however, was not that crystal clear. In particular, the CJEU appeared quite undecided on how to exactly characterize the relationship existing between the two supplies at stake. On the one hand, the Court in fact acknowledged that the service provided by RCI Europe was 'certainly not immediate', as long as it occurred only at a later stage. On the other hand, the Court considered the two supplies in question as fully distinct and independent. Ultimately, the Court settled its indecisiveness by holding that access to the accommodation exchange pool was meant to serve an ancillary purpose to the principal scope of the economic operation as a whole and that, notably, such ancillary purpose was represented by the possibility for a member to participate into an exchange of timeshare usage rights to be concluded only at a later stage.
64. UK: Opinion of the Advocate General, 7 Sep. 2010, Case C-270/09, *Macdonald Resorts Ltd v. The Commissioners for Her Majesty's Revenue & Customs*, para. 55.
65. *Id.*, para. 70.
66. *Id.*, paras 115-116.

question' (emphasis added). Thus, it was only at this latter point that the chargeable event occurred and the VAT became chargeable.[67]

The doctrine on 'preliminary transactions'[68] formulated, although in the specific case excluded, by Advocate General Trstenjak was eventually picked up by the Court in its decision. Notably, the CJEU observed that it was only at time of the conversion of usage timeshare rights that the purchaser of those rights received the consideration for his initial payment of the membership fees, so that it could not be maintained that the service was fully supplied until the rights in question were indeed converted. In its findings, the Court in particular attributed importance to the circumstance that, at the time of becoming a member, a person neither knew exactly which accommodation or other services would have received in a year, nor indeed was able to determine the value of the services to be supplied to himself.[69]

Since the question concerning the VAT treatment of 'membership fees' was decided in an opposite manner by the CJEU in the two aforementioned cases, it is no wonder that the issue came to the fore once again in *Marcandi*. Notably, the case concerned a UK company (Marcandi Ltd), operating an online shopping business as well as an online platform where registered users could participate in online penny auctions to bid for, and possibly win, goods, in short 'a pay-to-bid auction website'.[70] Under a different scheme, however, the company enabled customers to purchase goods directly from its online shop.

The business model of the platform operated as follows. In order to bid in an online auction or to purchase goods online, customers had to register online with the company and specifically agree to the company's contractual terms. Once registered, users could buy so-called credits, whereby they were allowed to place bids in online auctions. Noteworthy, Marcandi's website included a button feature allowing users to immediately access a page on which those credits were readily sold. While those credits could neither be used to purchase goods directly from the company's shop, nor could they be converted back into cash, as stated, the platform also operated an alternative scheme, which enabled a user to purchase, during the course of an auction, goods identical to those for which he was bidding. Importantly, while, in the first case, the price was equal to the auctioned price, in the second instance, the price of the goods was usually set equal to the recommended retail price. Importantly, the customer was however entitled to reduce such a price by the value of the credits spent in placing bids during the penny auction.

The company, in its submission supported by the German government, argued that the circumstance that credits spent in bidding could later be used to purchase goods directly from its online shop demonstrated that the issuance of those credits

67. *Id.*, para. 74.

68. Arguably, the doctrine of 'preliminary transactions' received some prior formulations in both *RCI Europe* and *Societé Thermale d'Eugénie-les-Bains*. *See RCI Europe* (C-37/08), paras 28-29; FR: ECJ, 18 Jul. 2007, Case C-277/05, *Société Thermale d'Eugénie-les-Bains v. Ministère de l'Économie, des Finances et de l'Industrie*, paras 21-26.

69. *Macdonald Resorts* (C-270/09), paras 16-42.

70. UK: ECJ, 5 July 2018, Case C-544/16, *Marcandi Limited, Agissant Sous le Nom Commercial 'Madbid' v. Commissioners for Her Majesty's Revenue & Customs*, para. 38.

constituted a mere preliminary transaction of the kind identified by the CJEU in *MacDonald Resorts*. An opposite stance was eventually taken by both the UK government and the Commission, which contended that the possibility for a member to participate in the online auction marketplace in return for the payment of a subscription fee constituted a full-fledged supply, distinct and independent from the purchase by users of goods from the company's online shop. This latter position was then upheld by Advocate General Tanchev.[71] Notably, the Advocate General observed that, by registering with the company's website and purchasing the bid credits, users made 'a decision to buy the chance of acquiring the goods on offer *for less – often much less* – than their shop price', i.e., 'the chance of a *discount* through winning the auction, which the straightforward shoppers do not have' (emphases original), and, indeed, such grant of a right to participate in online auctions constituted a fully distinct and independent supply.[72]

The Advocate General, however, took also some time to examine possible alternatives to the conclusion he finally supported, among which the CJEU's doctrine on composite supplies. In this connection, he maintained that the issuance of credits and the subsequent supply of goods could not be regarded as a single composite supply, due to the fact that, first, customers might purchase goods directly from the company's shop without any need to participate in online auctions and, second, the possibility to buy the auctioned goods under the alternative scheme and to settle the credits spent in placing bids could not be considered as the principal supply to which the supply of goods was ancillary.[73]

In its decision, the CJEU essentially agreed with the line of reasoning which the Advocate General finally adhered to. Notably, the Court maintained that, for users, the grant of a right to participate in online auctions, through the acquisition of credits issued by the company, was 'an autonomous interest', compared with the purchase by those users of goods in the company's website.[74] Notably, it was reasoned that, as a matter of fact, credits represented nothing less than a consideration for the chance granted to users to purchase goods at a price below their market value. Based on those assumptions, the CJEU concluded that the issuance of credits by the company amounted to a separate transaction from the subsequent – and indeed, merely eventual – purchase of products made by users from the company's online shop.[75]

In principle, the CJEU's case law recalled in this section also comes into prominence in the context of the sharing economy. In particular, a question arises with regard to the grant of a right to participate in the virtual marketplace operated by a sharing economy platform. Apparently, the VAT Committee considers such a service as a fully distinct and independent service supplied by that platform to its users. Notably, in the context of assessing the EU VAT treatment of crowdfunding, the VAT Committee observed that 'online crowdfunding platforms provide an opportunity for contributors

71. Opinion *Marcandi* (C-544/16), paras 28-37.
72. *Id.*, para. 39.
73. *Id.*, para. 58.
74. *Marcandi* (C-544/16), para. 30.
75. *Marcandi* (C-544/16), paras 26-49.

and entrepreneurs to interact, and in exchange the platform perceives a fee usually borne by the entrepreneur. This service would typically constitute intermediation to the extent that the crowdfunding platform does not act in its own name'.[76] A similar stance was maintained by the VAT Committee in a later document concerning the treatment of sharing economy platforms under EU VAT. Notably, it was reasoned therein that, 'just like online crowdfunding platforms, the sharing economy platforms provide an opportunity for customers and individual service providers to interact'.[77] Based on those considerations, the doctrine on two-step or preliminary transactions recalled above does not seem applicable, as such, to the grant of a right to participate in the virtual marketplace operated by a sharing economy platform.

These considerations seemingly apply to the payment of a subscription fee to a sharing economy platform by its users, which, indeed, constitutes an alternative form of payment available to users on a platform like HomeExchange.[78] As a matter of fact, the doctrine on two-step or preliminary transactions recalled above can hardly apply to the case of HomeExchange, in a way that the subscription fee paid, immediately, by a user in order to participate in the virtual marketplace operated by the platform, and the sums paid, at a later moment, by that user, in order to receive an accommodation service, are seen as a single supply of services. In case of a subscription-based platform like HomeExchange, in fact, it cannot be maintained that such a platform is also involved in the provision of the underlying service of accommodation. Possibly, a different stance could be taken where a sharing economy platform supplies - de facto, although not de iure - not only the intermediary service, but also the underlying service, as some courts might find especially in the case of Uber.[79]

Even without specifically mentioning it, the doctrine on two-step or preliminary transactions was evoked, instead, in a recent working paper of the VAT Committee, concerning whether the provision of services by a digital company in return for user personal data constitutes a taxable transaction or not under EU VAT. Although ultimately taking the view that, in such situation, there is no taxable transaction, in so far as a direct link between the services in question and the consideration for them is missing, the Commission meaningfully observed that, also 'from an economic point of view', it makes sense not to consider the transaction in question as a taxable transaction. This is because, in the Commission's account, the provision of 'free' services by a digital company is merely a means for the company to obtain personal data, which the company can later sell to advertising businesses, but it is not the

76. European Commission, Value Added Tax Committee, *Working Paper No. 836. VAT Treatment of Crowdfunding*, at 17 (taxud.c.1(2015)576037).
77. European Commission, Value Added Tax Committee, *Working Paper No. 878. VAT Treatment of the Sharing Economy*, at 10 (taxud.c.1(2015)4370160).
78. *See* section §2.08[A]. A subscription-based model is also available for BlaBlaCar passengers in Italy. *See* section §2.08[B].
79. *See* section §4.04. Indeed, in *Uber Systems Spain*, Advocate General Szpunar hinted at the possibility to envisage the intermediary service provided by Uber as a sort of 'preliminary transaction', by submitting that 'the connection stage is merely preparatory in order to enable the main supply to be performed in the best possible conditions'. The suggestion, however, was not further developed by the Advocate General in his opinion. *See* Opinion *Uber Systems Spain* (C-434/15), para. 64.

activity or, in itself, the purpose of the company. Based on those assumptions, the Commission concluded that better it would be to levy EU VAT at a later stage, i.e., at the time when the digital company sells user personal data to advertising businesses.[80]

The author, however, is not persuaded by the Commission's aforementioned line of reasoning. Whether EU VAT is levied at the time when the digital company sells user personal data to advertising businesses, in fact, cannot obstruct the fact that the digital company provides services for which a consideration in kind, i.e., personal data, is immediately paid. Moreover, it is rather undeniable that the digital company attributes an economic value to the personal data which it receives from its users and that, indeed, such a value is well taken into account by the company, not only in the price that it charges to advertising businesses at a later stage, but also in relation to the quantity and the quality of the services that the company is willing to provide to its users 'for free' at an earlier stage. The circumstance that the subjective value that the digital company attributes to the personal data obtained is not openly disclosed to its users is not preclusive in this regard, as long as such a disclosure neither is mandated to apply EU VAT. In any event, such value would likely be equal to the amount of the price that the digital company charges to advertising businesses at the time of selling user personal data to them.[81]

Indeed, quite similar considerations were advanced by the CJEU in *A.*, a case concerning whether a supply of demolition services by a company, in addition to a monetary payment, was also carried out in exchange for a supply of goods, namely the supply by the customer of recyclable scrap metal contained in the waste and used materials, which the company was eventually able to sell on to third parties at a later moment. The CJEU ruled in the affirmative, precisely on the ground that an economic value was attributed by the demolition company to the supply of recyclable scrap metal obtained from the customer. Notably, according to the Court, the value of recyclable scrap metal was taken into account, although not specifically agreed upon in the demolition contract, but only presumptively estimated by the demolition company, in the calculation of the price charged by the company for the provision of its own demolition works and, indeed, such value was set equal to the amount of the price reduction granted by the company to the customer for carrying out its own activities.[82]

80. European Commission, Value Added Tax Committee, *Working Paper No. 958. Conditions for There Being a Taxable Transaction When Internet Services Are Provided in Exchange for User Data*, at 7 (taxud.c.1(2018)6248826).
81. Indeed, as Facebook founder Marc Zuckerberg explained during a quite revealing testimony hearing before the US Senate, a digital company, actually, may not sell personal data of its users to third-party advertisers, rather it may allow them to select those users who are most likely interested in their products and to which the digital company then forwards their 'targeted' adverts. *See Transcript of Mark Zuckerberg's Senate Hearing*, The Washington Post (10 Apr. 2018).
82. FI: ECJ, 10 Jan. 2019, Case C-410/17, *Proceedings brought by A Oy*, paras 34-45.

[B] Two Suppliers for a Single Composite Supply

In all the situations illustrated in the previous sections, a single composite supply was made to the same customer by a single supplier. The question tackled in the present section, instead, is whether the doctrine on composite supplies and, in particular, the two exceptions to the main 'splitting' rule, i.e., whether there is a single composite supply from an economic point of view or through 'absorption' of the ancillary into the principal supply, might also apply to the situation in which two distinct undertakings jointly supply a good and/or a service to the same customer. In this connection, the CJEU's case law still appears in full development. Notably, a similar possibility was envisaged by the Court in two cases, first, in *Part Service*[83] and, then, in *Mapfre Asistencia and Mapfre Warranty*[84]. This latter case, in particular, seems to have marked quite a turning point in the CJEU's case law.

Mapfre Asistencia and Mapfre Warranty concerned a Spanish (Mapfre Asistencia) and an Italian company (Mapfre Warranty) offering their French customer base the possibility to insure purchased second-hand motor vehicles against breakdown as well as other types of inconveniences. For this purpose, the companies partnered with professional second-hand motor vehicle dealers, by offering these latter's customers, at the time of purchasing a second-hand motor vehicle, additional insurance coverage. In this connection, the question put before the CJEU was whether the provision of such warranties by those companies constitutes an exempt supply of insurance services, within the meaning of Article 135(1)(a) of the VAT Directive - as argued by the French tax authorities, or rather a taxable transaction - as instead contended by the two affiliated companies. Notably, in their submission, the companies maintained that, although the supply in question consisted in the provision of insurance services,

---

83. IT: ECJ, 21 Feb. 2008, Case C-425/06, *Ministero dell'Economia e delle Finanze v. Part Service Srl.*
84. FR: ECJ, 16 Jul. 2015, Case C-584/13, *Directeur Général des Finances Publiques v. Mapfre Asistencia Compañia Internacional de Seguros y Reaseguros SA and Mapfre Warranty SpA v. Directeur Féněral des Finances Publiques*. H. van Kesteren, *Taxable and Non-Taxable Transactions*, in *CJEU - Recent Developments in Value Added Tax*, at 231-235 (M. Lang et al. eds, Linde 2016), includes also *Bookit* (UK: ECJ, 26 May 2016, Case C-607/14, *Bookit, Ltd v. Commissioners for Her Majesty's Revenue and Customs*) in the CJEU's line of decisions which, arguably, acknowledge the possibility to have a single composite supply made to the same customer by two distinct suppliers. Although admitting the existence of certain similarities with the two aforementioned cases, the author of this book, however, contends that *Bookit* concerned a quite peculiar situation, that is the situation of a company, affiliated to a group of companies, operating certain services, consisting in the processing of payments and booking via a call centre, two services which could hardly be seen on a stand-alone basis, inasmuch as those services are inextricably linked to the provision of the main service. By contrast, such linkage is less obvious in relation to the provision of insurance services, as it was both in *Part Service* and in *Mapfre Asistencia and Mapfre Warranty*. Lastly, it ought to be recalled that the possibility to have a single supply made to the same customer by two distinct suppliers was also envisaged by the Commission while discussing the situation of a joint supply of network's access and helpdesk services made to the same customer by two distinct suppliers. *See* European Commission, *Explanatory Notes on the EU VAT Changes to the Place of Supply of Telecommunications, Broadcasting and Electronic Services that Enter into Force in 2015 (Council Implementing Regulation (EU) No 1042/2013) published on 3 April 2014*, at 18-19, https://ec.europa.eu/taxation_customs/sites/taxation/files/resources/documents/taxation/vat/how_vat_works/telecom/explanatory_notes_2015_en.pdf (accessed 31 Mar. 2019).

which, taken in isolation, is exempt under EU VAT, such a supply was to be subject to the tax, as long as it was 'indissociably linked' with the sale of second-hand motor vehicles by partnered dealers, in a way that those two supplies constituted a single composite supply, which ought to receive the same treatment under EU VAT.[85]

Notwithstanding, ultimately, settling the case in favour of the tax authorities, the CJEU did not exclude, although only in an *obiter dictum*, that a single composite supply might also exist where more than a single supplier is involved in the provision of a good and/or a service to the same customer. Notably, in its decision, the CJEU reasoned that, despite the two supplies in question constituted, in principle, distinct and independent supplies for EU VAT purposes, it was ultimately for the referring court to determine whether, having regard to all the facts and circumstances of the case, the sale of a second-hand motor vehicle and the insurance coverage against breakdown, as well as other types of inconveniences provided by partnered dealers, were supplies so interconnected as to amount to a single composite supply.[86] Figure 6.1 below depicts graphically the scenario at which the CJEU hinted in *Mapfre Asistencia and Mapfre Warranty*.

Figure 6.1 Two Supplies for a Single Composite Supply: Mapfre Asistencia and Mapfre Warranty

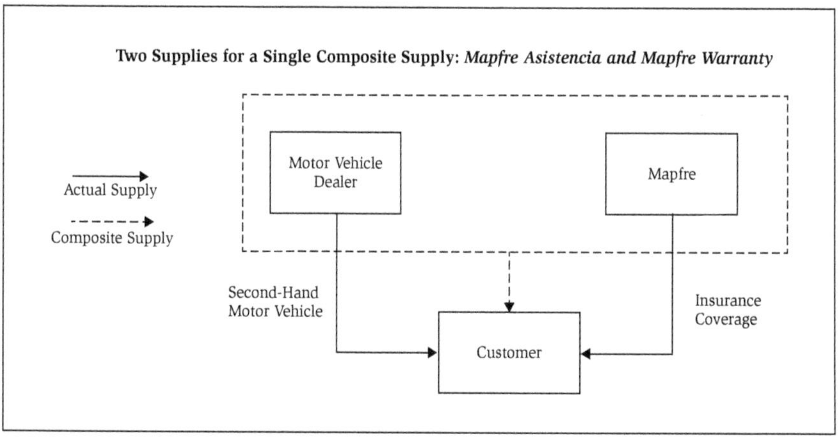

Apparently, in *Mapfre Asistencia and Mapfre Warranty*, the CJEU overruled some of its previous findings on this matter. Notably, in *Kerrutt*, with a reference to the supply of a building and of the land on which that building stood, the Court ruled that a single composite supply could not be envisaged, in so far as the two supplies in question were 'legally separate transactions', were not 'the subject of a single delivery' and, further,

85. Opinion *Mapfre Asistencia and Mapfre Warranty* (C-584/13), para. 39.
86. *Mapfre Asistencia and Mapfre Warranty* (C-584/13), paras 25-58.

were made by two distinct 'contractors'.[87] Further, the possibility to apply the doctrine on composite supplies to situations entailing the joint provision of a good and/or a service by more than a single supplier was expressly excluded by Advocate General Szpunar in *Mapfre Asistencia and Mapfre Warranty*.[88] A similarly preclusive stance was also taken by Advocate General Sharpston in *Klinikum Dortmund*, who, however, stipulated that, eventually, two supplies might amount to 'closely related activities' within the meaning of Article 132(1)(b) of the VAT Directive. The rationale for a distinction between 'a single composite supply' and 'closely related activities', however, was left completely unexplained by the same Advocate General.[89]

In truth, the possibility to apply the doctrine on composite supplies to situations entailing the joint provision of a good and/or a service by more than a single supplier had already been envisaged by the CJEU in *Part Service*, a case concerning two affiliated companies jointly providing motor vehicle leases to their customers. Nevertheless, in *Part Service*, the extension of the doctrine on composite supplies was limited to situations showing an abusive intent. Notably, in *Part Service*, evidence of the existence of an abuse was found, *inter alia*, in the fact that the two companies providing the lease were part of the same group and, further, that the leasing service, offered by one of the two affiliated companies, taken in isolation, was economically unprofitable, so that the viability of such business could not be ensured simply by means of contracts concluded by that company with its customers.[90] In a sense, the possibility to redefine the perimeter of two supplies by bundling them into a single composite supply, even if made by two distinct suppliers, was intended in that case by the CJEU, somehow, as a concrete application of the prohibition of abuse of law or '*fraus legis*' doctrine laid down by the Court, first, in *Emsland-Stärke* and, then, in *Halifax*.[91]

The possibility to apply the CJEU's doctrine on composite supplies, as extensively interpreted by the Court, first, in *Part Service* and, then, in *Mapfre Asistencia and Mapfre Warranty*, in relation to the joint provision of a good and/or a service to the same customer by more than a single undertaking, to transactions in the sharing economy is, indeed, quite promising. In certain instances, the relationship between a sharing economy platform and an individual supplier is, in fact, so strict that the two undertakings in question might well be considered as a single supplying party, which jointly enters into contractual arrangements with the individual customer for the carrying out of an overall activity toward him.[92] Notably, should Uber not be treated as

87. DE: ECJ, 8 Jul. 1986, Case C-73/85, *Hans-Dieter and Ute Kerrutt v. Finanzamt Mönchengladbach – Mitte*, paras 13-15.
88. Opinion *Mapfre Asistencia and Mapfre Warranty* (C-584/13), para. 42. Along the same lines, *see* Opinion *KPC Herning* (C-71/18), para. 31.
89. DE: Opinion of the Advocate General, 26 Sep. 2013, Case C-366/12, *Finanzamt Dortmund-West v. Klinikum Dortmund GmbH*, para. 49.
90. *Part Service* (C-425/06), para. 57.
91. DE: ECJ, 14 Dec. 2000, Case C-110/99, *Emsland-Stärke GmbH v. Hauptzollamt Hamburg-Jonas*, paras 46-59; UK: ECJ, 21 Feb. 2006, Case C-255/02, *Halifax plc, Leeds Permanent Development Services Ltd and County Wide Property Investments Ltd v. Commissioners of Customs & Excise*, paras 61-86.
92. *See* IT: ECJ, 18 Dec. 2014, Case C-434/13 P, *European Commission v. Parker Hannifin Manufacturing Srl and Parker-Hannifin Corp.*, para. 62, containing a formulation, relating to EU competition law, of the 'single economic entity' doctrine, i.e., the concept of two undertakings

the employer of its drivers, then the platform and the driver, as independent undertakings, could perhaps be regarded, for EU VAT purposes, as making a single composite supply toward the passenger.[93] Eventually, the same strand of reasoning might be applied to the situation of other sharing economy platforms like Airbnb and BlaBlaCar, which could well be seen as making a single composite supply toward their individual customers, as long as their supplies are indissociably linked with those made by their respective individual suppliers. The author instead submits that the case of HomeExchange is somehow different, in so far as this platform appears to be more akin to a mere promoter of the underlying activity carried out by its individual suppliers.[94]

Should the doctrine on composite supplies, as meant in the above, effectively apply to transactions in the sharing economy, then a question would arise on which of the two supplies concerned, one consisting in the intermediary service supplied by the platform, the other consisting in the underlying service supplied by the individual supplier, ought to be considered as the main supply. This is not indeed a theoretical exercise, rather it carries several implications for EU VAT purposes. It might, in fact, lead to the application of different rules as regards the place of supply, the chargeable event and chargeability of VAT, the taxable amount, the deduction of VAT, the applicable rates and exemptions, as well as the liability for payment of VAT. In order to make such a determination, it appears necessary to closely look at which of the two suppliers in question is, ultimately, responsible for making the economic operation as a whole toward the individual customer. Such determination seems contingent upon the concrete degree of control which is exercised by a platform over the activity of the individual supplier. In this connection, the rather restrictive contractual conditions imposed by a company like Uber upon its drivers might be problematic for the business model of that platform.[95] A different stance could eventually be taken considering the – perhaps – more 'liberal' approach adopted toward their individual suppliers users by

---

so closely linked to each other that they are capable of exerting a 'single competitive force' on the market. For a discussion of this doctrine in the specific field of the sharing economy, *see* J. Safron, *The Application of EU Competition Law to the Sharing Economy* (EU Law Working Papers No. 27, Stanford-Vienna Transatlantic Technology Law Forum 2018), at 1-42.

93. Noteworthy, in *Uber Systems Spain*, Advocate General Szpunar concluded that Uber's 'activity comprises a single supply of transport in a vehicle located and booked by means of the smartphone application and that this service is provided, from an economic standpoint, by Uber or on its behalf'. *See* Opinion *Uber Systems Spain* (C-434/15), para. 53.

94. Arguably, the phenomenon itself of the sharing economy, as a whole, has contributed to redefine the boundaries of the firm, by substituting the centralized coordination occurring within a traditional firm with the decentralized coordination occurring in a virtual marketplace. For a critical perspective in this regard, *see* J. Tomassetti, *Does Uber Redefine the Firm? The Post-industrial Corporation and Advanced Information Technology*, 34 Hofstra Lab. & Emp. L. J. 1 (2016), at 1-78.

95. *See* section §2.07[B]. Notably, in *Uber Systems Spain*, Advocate General Szpunar observed that 'it is undoubtedly the supply of transport which is the main supply and which gives the service economic meaning. Users look for drivers with one aim in mind: to be transported from A to B'. On the contrary, 'the supply whereby passengers and drivers are connected with one another is ... neither self-standing, nor the main supply, in relation to the supply of transport'. *See* Opinion *Uber Systems Spain* (C-434/15), paras 64-65.

platforms like Airbnb, HomeExchange, and BlaBlaCar.[96] Ultimately, the determination of which of the two supplies is to be regarded as the main supply depends on the concrete business model operated by a sharing economy platform and, further, on the kind of relationship which the platform in question actually maintains with its individual suppliers.

[C] Multiple Suppliers: The Need to Reconstruct the Supply Chain

The possibility to apply the doctrine on composite supplies to situations entailing the joint provision of a good and/or a service to the same customer by two distinct suppliers is, however, only available where each of the two suppliers in question has a direct relationship with that customer. Should this not be the case, then the doctrine on composite supplies, even in the loose interpretation at which the CJEU hinted, first, in *Part Service* and, then, in *Mapfre Asistencia and Mapfre Warranty*, could not be applied. This circumstance is, perhaps, best illustrated by the case of credit card services, where the consideration paid, through a credit card, by the customer to the supplier for the provision of a good and/or a service to him is reduced by a certain amount by the credit card company, such amount being retained by that company as remuneration for its payment processing services. Notably, in this situation, although, in fact, there is a point of contact between the customer and the credit card company, inasmuch as, in making the payment to the supplier, the customer actually interfaces with the credit card company only, no service instead is rendered by the company to the customer from an EU VAT perspective. The payment processing services are instead rendered by the credit card company solely to the supplier, from whom the company receives a consideration in return, although, in fact, directly deducted by the credit card company from the amount paid by the customer to the supplier. As for the relationships among the various parties within the supply chain, if, undoubtedly, there is a direct relationship between the supplier and the customer, the customer must instead be seen as a third party in relation to the provision of payment processing services by the credit card company to the supplier.[97] Figure 6.2 below depicts this scenario graphically.

96. *See* sections §2.07[A], §2.08[A], and §2.08[B].
97. *See* e.g., to that effect, BE: ECJ, 25 May 1993, Case C-18/92, *Chaussures Bally SA v. Belgian State, Minister for Finance*, para. 16; *Primback* (C-34/99), para. 29.

Figure 6.2 Direct Link: Credit Card Company's Case

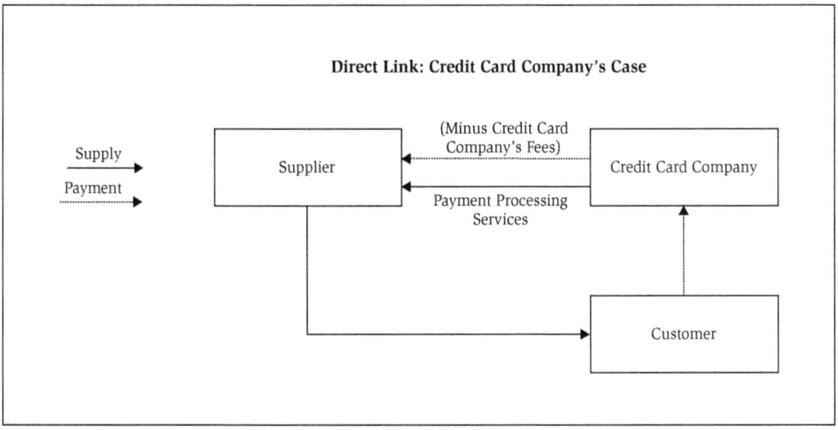

Apparently, the doctrine on composite supplies cannot also find an application in the case of two suppliers making two distinct supplies to the same customer from whom they receive separate considerations, if one of the two suppliers in question remits part of the amount received from the customer to the other supplier, as a remuneration for the services that the latter supplier renders to the customer only, but from which, nevertheless, the consideration for the services provided by the former supplier to the customer, somehow, depends. Notably, such rather intricate scenario was hypothesized by Advocate General Kokott in *Welmory*, although not specifically discussed by the CJEU in its decision. The case concerned a cooperation agreement between two companies, the Polish company Welmory and an affiliated Cypriot company. Notably, the Cypriot company operated an auction website on which Welmory offered and sold its own products. Importantly, customers could purchase the auctioned products only if they had previously acquired rights to submit a bid in the auction website from the Cypriot company. As a result, from the sale of auctioned products to customers, two different but interlinked streams of income resulted: an income was made by Welmory from the sale to customers, through its auction website, of its own products, whereas other income accrued to the Cypriot company from the sale to customers of rights to bid on its own auction website. However, Welmory also received payments from the Cypriot company in return for the sale of its own products and for services connected with them such as advertising. Based on the cooperation agreement in place and the flow of payments between the two affiliated companies, the Advocate General hypothesizes that, from an EU VAT perspective, Welmory did not supply any service to the Cypriot company, but rather it was the Cypriot company which made, in light of Article 73 of the VAT Directive[98], third-party payments to Welmory, as long as a 'direct link'

98. *See also* Art. 42 of the Implementing Regulation, stipulating that 'where a supplier of goods or services, as a condition of accepting payment by credit or debit card, requires the customer to pay an amount to himself or another undertaking, and where the total price payable by that

existed between the sale of auctioned products by Welmory to the customers and the income that the Cypriot company was able to obtain from the sale to the same customers of the right to submit bids in the auction site. Notably, such a direct link was found by the Advocate General in the circumstance that the amount of the income obtained by the Cypriot company depended on 'the number or the volume of product sales' by Welmory.[99] Figure 6.3 below depicts this scenario graphically.

Figure 6.3 Welmory*'s Alternative Hypothesis According to AG Kokott*

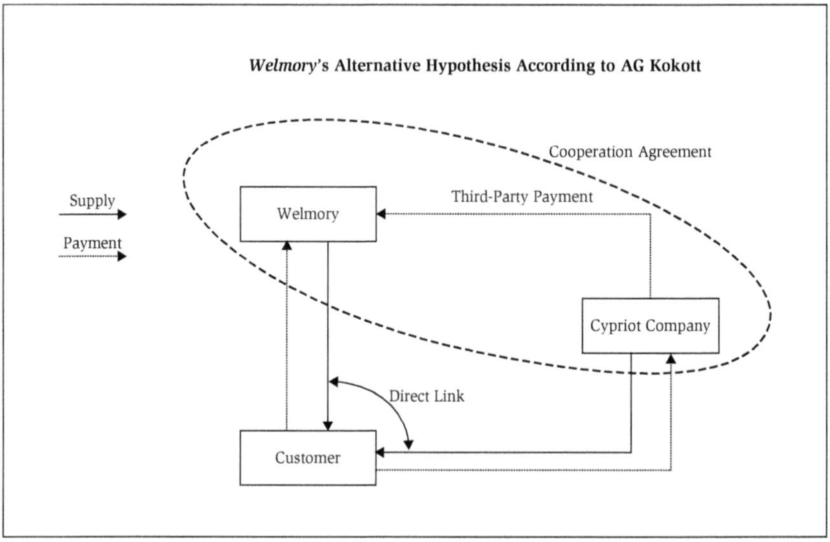

The determination of whether two or more suppliers involved in the joint provision of a good and/or a service to the same customer have, in effect, a point of contact with such customer, in the sense of directly supplying something to him, presupposes the factual reconstruction of the supply chain, i.e., of the relationships existing among the various parties taking part in the economic operation as a whole.[100] Admittedly, such an assessment is anything but an easy task. In fact, it presupposes a comprehensive examination of the case, which entails a legal - being premised on contractual obligations among parties - as well as economic - being based on factual evidences - analysis of the situation.[101] Indeed, it is settled in the CJEU's case law that, as to determine the treatment of transactions under EU VAT, it is necessary to look at their

customer is unaffected irrespective of how payment is accepted, that amount shall constitute an integral part of the taxable amount for the supply of the goods or services, under Articles 73 to 80 of Directive 2006/112/EC'.

99. PL: Opinion of the Advocate General, 15 May 2014, Case C-605/12, *Welmory sp. Z o.o. v. Dyrektor Izby Skarbowej w Gdańsku*, paras 59-64.

100. UK: Opinion of the Advocate General, 8 Dec. 2011, Case C-520/10, *Lebara Ltd v. Commissioners for Her Majesty's Revenue & Customs*, para. 38.

101. Opinion *Lebara* (C-520/10), para. 31.

'objective character'.[102] And yet, based on the same CJEU's case law, it is not entirely clear whether such an assessment must be primarily based on the juridical form of the transactions among parties or, instead, if greater relevance should be attributed to the economic purpose underlying an overall operation. Notably, the Court took the first view in *Cantor Fitzgerald International*, whereas it followed the latter approach in *SKF*.[103]

A proof of the difficulty to make such an assessment results from a comparison of two CJEU's decisions. The first case is *Elida Gibbs*. The factual background of the case can be summarized as follows. Elida Gibbs was a UK company selling toiletries either to wholesalers or retailers, who, in turn, resold those products to end consumers. For this purpose, the company operated a 'sales promotion scheme', on the basis of two distinct coupon systems, both enabling end consumers to receive a direct refund from the company. As a result of the operation of such sales promotion scheme, the company claimed repayment of its output VAT, on the ground that the discount which it conceded through the issuance of the coupons had factually reduced the consideration actually paid by end consumers. The UK tax authorities, however, denied the claimed refund of VAT, contending that, as a matter of evidence, there was no direct contact between the company and the end consumers. The findings of Advocate General Fennelly and the CJEU on this point, however, split. Notably, the Advocate General concluded that, in the case, there were two separate supplies, the first between Elida Gibbs and the wholesalers or retailers, whereas the second between those wholesalers or retailers and the end consumers, in respect of which the company was a mere third party.[104] The CJEU, however, found otherwise, contending that, in light of the 'basic principle' of the EU VAT system which intends to tax only the end consumer, it was not permissible for the tax authorities to collect an amount exceeding the tax actually paid by end consumers, even if the taxable person in question had no contractual relationship with them.[105] Figures 6.4 and 6.5 below depict graphically the supply chain in *Elida Gibbs*, as reconstructed by the Advocate General and the CJEU in their respective findings.

102. *See* e.g., UK: ECJ, 6 Apr. 1995, Case C-4/94, *BLP Group plc v. Commissioners of Customs & Excise*, para. 24.
103. UK: ECJ, 9 Oct. 2001, Case C-108/99, *Commissioners of Customs & Excise v. Cantor Fitzgerald International*, paras 17-34; SW: ECJ, 29 Oct. 2009, Case C-29/08, *Skatteverket v. AB SKF*, paras 26-41. For a discussion and comparison of these two cases, *see* A. van Doesum, *What Looks Like a Duck Is a Duck: Economic Purpose and Legal Reality in EU VAT Law*, 1 World J. VAT/GST L. 2 (2012), at 202-204.
104. UK: Opinion of the Advocate General, 27 Jun. 1996, Case C-317/94, *Elida Gibbs Ltd v. Commissioners of Customs and Excise*, paras 16-39.
105. UK: ECJ, 24 Oct. 1996, Case C-317/94, *Elida Gibbs Ltd v. Commissioners of Customs and Excise*, paras 18-35.

Figure 6.4 Elida Gibbs's *Supply Chain According to AG Fennelly*

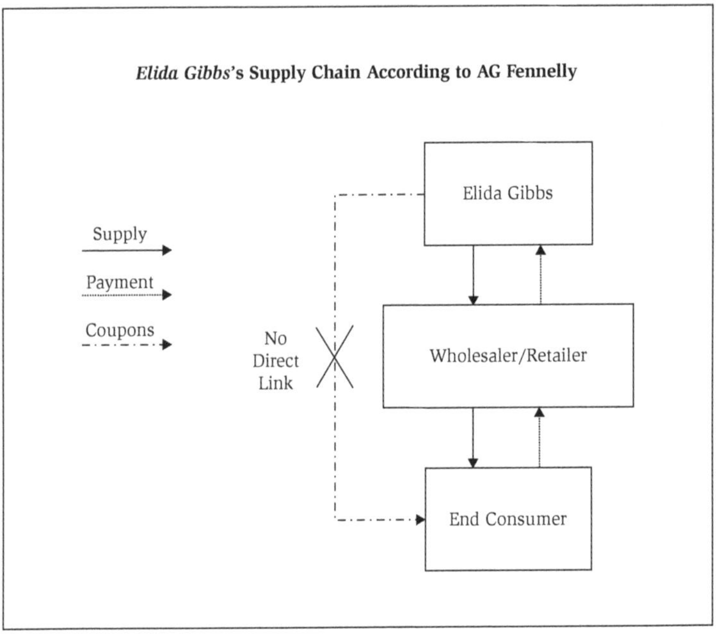

Figure 6.5 Elida Gibbs's *Supply Chain According to the CJEU*

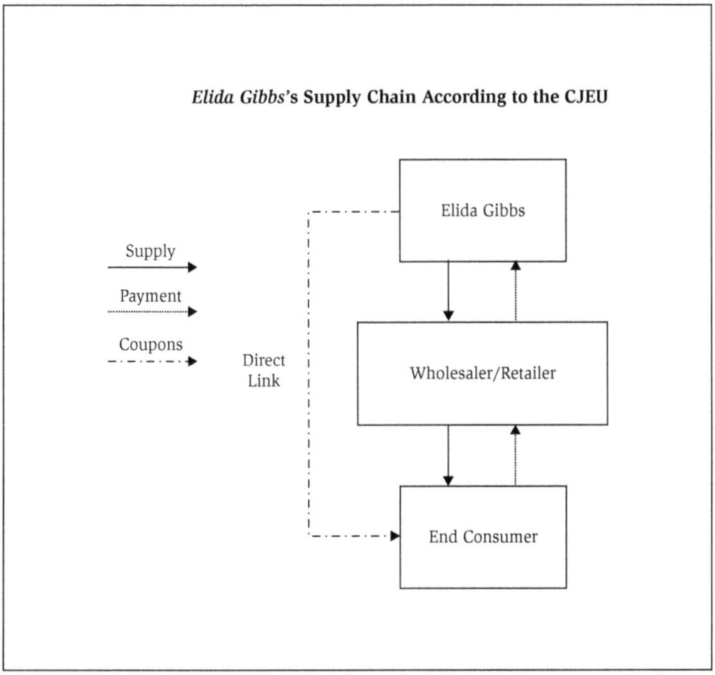

The second case is *Ibero Tours*. Ibero Tours was a German travel agent acting as an intermediary party between tour operators and end consumers. Pursuant to the special scheme for travel agents[106], the provision of various travel intermediation services by Ibero Tours was treated as a single supply. Notably, the activity of the company was remunerated through the payment of a commission by tour operators. In order to promote its own activity, however, Ibero Tours gave part of this commission away to end consumers (i.e., travellers), in the form of a reduction on the price paid by them in return for travel services. As a result, the amount received by the tour operators was always higher than that effectively paid by end consumers (i.e., travellers). Relying on the CJEU's findings in *Elida Gibbs,* Ibero Tours thus claimed a refund on its output VAT equal to the amount it had refunded to end consumers (i.e., travellers).

Once again, the findings of the Advocate General and the CJEU in the case split. Notably, taking the side of the Commission and, instead, dismissing the arguments raised by the intervening UK and German governments, Advocate General Wathelet found that arguing that Ibero Tours was not part of the supply chain terminating with the end consumer, but instead a mere supplier of intermediary services to the tour operator, simply 'ignores reality', as long as, 'even though, in very formalistic terms, a travel agent like Ibero Tours provides intermediary services to the tour operator in

106. Notably, the 'TOMS' is a special scheme included in Arts 306-310 of the VAT Directive.

return for a commission, it is the travel agent that offers the discount to the consumer and bears the financial burden'.[107] Although not clearly expressed in his reasonings, it seems that the Advocate General concluded that, as a matter of fact, Ibero Tours was at the head of a single supply chain, inasmuch as Elida Gibbs was in the eponymous case.[108] Noteworthy, for its part, the German government instead contended that Ibero Tours offered tour operators an intermediate service 'which disappears once it is supplied'. Further in this regard, according to the German government, the circumstance that, in *Ibero Tours*, the content of the supply consisted in a service was sufficient to distinguish that case from *Elida Gibbs*, concerning, instead, a supply of goods, which, almost by definition, cannot disappear after being supplied by the original supplier.[109]

The CJEU, however, made a different reconstruction of the supply chain compared with that of the Advocate General. In the Court's account, the two suppliers in question, i.e., Ibero Tours and the tour operator, did not take part in the same 'vertical' supply chain. Notably, the CJEU considered that the services provided by the tour operator to the end consumer constituted a single supply, as such 'totally separate' from the intermediary services provided by Ibero Tours to the tour operator. Based on such reconstruction of the supply chain, the Court eventually concluded that the principles established in *Elida Gibbs*, concerning the possibility to reduce the taxable amount in case of price discounts granted by the operator at the head of the supply chain to end consumers, were not applicable to the situation at hand. The ultimate result of such findings was that the financing of the price reduction, accorded by Ibero Tours to end consumers, was to be borne by this latter intermediary party only. Apparently, the Court took little notice of the fact that, in such a manner, the tax authorities received, by way of VAT, a sum greater than that actually paid by the end consumer and that, indeed, such a difference was entirely put at the expense of the taxable person (i.e., Ibero Tours).[110] Figures 6.6 and 6.7 below depict graphically the supply chain in *Ibero Tours*, as reconstructed by the Advocate General and the CJEU in their respective findings.

107. DE: Opinion of the Advocate General, 18 Jul. 2013, Case C-300/12, *Finanzamt Düsseldorf-Mitte v. Ibero Tours GmbH*, para. 26.
108. Notably, the circumstance that the Advocate General made a reconstruction of the supply chain similar to that operated in *Elida Gibbs* can be gleaned, first, from the fact that, in respect of the position occupied by Ibero Tours in the supply chain, he referred to a traveller as 'the consumer of a downstream service' and, further, from the fact that he considered Ibero Tours as the 'true' organizer of the whole supply made to the end consumer. *See* Opinion *Ibero Tours* (C-300/12), para. 33.
109. *See* Opinion *Ibero Tours* (C-300/12), para. 24.
110. DE: ECJ, 16 Jan. 2014, Case C-300/12, *Finanzamt Düsseldorf-Mitte v. Ibero Tours GmbH*, paras 23-33.

Figure 6.6 Ibero Tours*'s Supply Chain According to AG Wathelet*

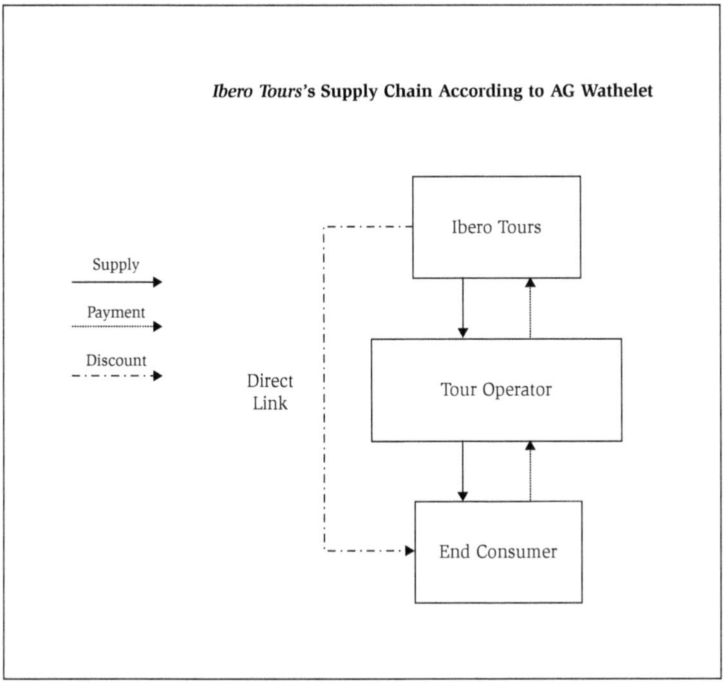

Figure 6.7 Ibero Tours*'s Supply Chain According to the CJEU*

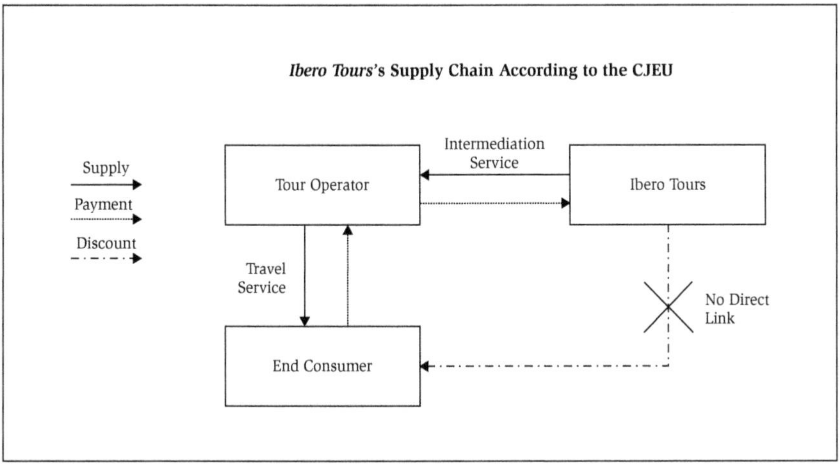

The reconstruction of the supply chain in the sharing economy, which presupposes a comprehensive examination of the actual role played by the various parties within it, essentially swings from the assessment that the CJEU made in *Elida Gibbs* to that provided by the Court in *Ibero Tours*. Notably, the relevant question attains to the actual possibility to establish, in a given situation, a direct link between the platform and the individual customer. Indeed, in foreseeable litigations on this matter, tax authorities are likely to argue based on *Elida Gibbs*'s findings, i.e., by contending that a platform is actually involved in the underlying supply toward the individual customer and, therefore, shall account for the related VAT, whereas a platform would likely approach the situation by relying on *Ibero Tours*'s reconstruction of the supply chain, i.e., by claiming to act as a mere intermediary toward the individual supplier, who, instead, is the sole party having a point of contact with the individual customer and, therefore, also the only one who makes the final supply to him. The possibility to rely on *Ibero Tours*'s findings, however, seems open to a platform only if it provides intermediary services solely to one of the underlying parties and not, instead, to both parties, i.e., both to the individual supplier and the individual customer. In this latter situation, it is in fact hard to maintain that the platform would have no point of contact with the individual customer. Notably, this is the case of Airbnb. Airbnb, in fact, charges both parties (i.e., hosts and guests) for its own services, although with commission fees calculated according to different percentages.[111] As seen, Uber instead charges only the individual supplier (i.e., driver) for its own services.[112] As for HomeExchange and BlaBlaCar, while, in their terms and conditions, those platforms claim to provide their own services to the individual customers only (i.e., respectively, guests and passengers), from whose payments those platforms indeed deduct their own commission fees, it is quite unclear whether, from an EU VAT perspective, those two platforms actually provide their own services to the individual customers, to the individual suppliers (i.e., respectively, hosts and drivers), or to both parties.[113] Moreover, as specifically regards HomeExchange, it should also be considered that, in case of reciprocal and simultaneous accommodation exchanges, both the underlying parties perform the role of host and guest, so that HomeExchange actually provides its own services to both those parties. In such event, the platforms in question might try to characterize their own services as mere 'input' services, i.e., services which 'disappear once they are supplied' and, therefore, which are to be kept distinct from the related underlying services. Obviously, the moot point is to ascertain whether a similar reconstruction of the supply chain, and of the relationships among the various parties within it, would not end up 'ignoring reality', as warned by Advocate General Wathelet in *Ibero Tours*. Although quite unlikely, an alternative scenario in this regard might even be the one hypothesized by Advocate General Kokott in *Welmory*, with those platforms not actually supplying any service to the individual suppliers, but only receiving third party payments from those suppliers based on a cooperation agreement in force with them. Nevertheless, this further scenario would eventually be applicable

111. *See* section §2.07[A].
112. *See* section §2.07[B].
113. *See* sections §2.08[A] and §2.08[B]. In this connection, it ought to be noted that even the concept of 'services', within the meaning of Art. 57 TFEU, does not necessarily require a service to be paid for by those toward whom it is performed. *See* e.g., NL: ECJ, 26 Apr. 1988, Case C-352/85, *Bond van Adverteerders and Others v. The Netherlands State*, para. 16.

only if no service is supplied by a platform to the individual suppliers, as instead it clearly occurs in the case of both Airbnb and Uber.

§6.04 ALL THE CHICKENS COME HOME TO ROOST: *LEBARA*

In the CJEU's jurisprudence, there is a case in which nearly all the issues discussed in the present chapter have been dealt with by the Advocate General and/or by the Court. This case is *Lebara*. Given the relevance of the various issues and the analysis of the supply chain contained therein, the case deserves the extensive examination which is provided in the following.

Lebara concerned a UK company (Lebara Ltd.) entrusted with routing telephone calls made by clients located all over the EU, first to its telephone switch situated in the UK, and then, from there, to a linked international telephone network, thus enabling those calls to progress toward the destinations desired by clients. Notably, three sets of contractual arrangements underpinned the functioning of Lebara's business model. The first entailed a cooperation agreement between the company and providers of international telephony. The second agreement, instead, related to a partnership between Lebara and phone operators located in various Member States, which were obliged to route local calls from their own clients toward Lebara's telephone switch situated in the UK. The third set of contractual agreements, finally, featured a collaboration between Lebara and local distributors established in various Member States. Notably, those agreements provided that Lebara was to sell phonecards, carrying its own brand, to local distributors at less than their face value, in return for which those distributors agreed to promote and sell the phonecards in question, each of these operators in its own Member State of establishment.

In a nutshell, the question put before the CJEU related to the factual reconstruction of the supply chain, as well as of the relationships among the various parties within it. In particular, the Court was asked to determine whether, through the sale of phonecards, representing for their purchasers the right to receive telecommunications services, to local distributors at less than their face value, Lebara was actually making two supplies for EU VAT purposes, the former at the time of the initial sale of those phonecards to local distributors, whereas the latter at the time of redemption of phonecards in question by purchasing clients.

Advocate General Jääskinen commenced his analysis by seeking to establish the actual nature of the supply made by Lebara. Notably, taking stock of the '"ultimate intention" of the end user when purchasing a phonecard', the Advocate General argued that Lebara, as a matter of fact, provided clients with 'a right of access to telecommunications services'. More precisely, the object of the supply in question was 'the right to access to international telephone calls that are cheaper than those available through the local telephone exchange in the Member State where the card is purchased, or indeed elsewhere'. According to the Advocate General, for clients, the possession of a phonecard was not, in fact, an aim in itself. Rather, of much greater interest to clients was 'the low-cost international phone calls which the card facilitates'. In the Advocate General's view, this circumstance, together with the need for purchasers of phonecards to dial a PIN code sent to them by Lebara in order to start making phone calls, was indeed able to create 'a direct link' between Lebara and the clients purchasing the phonecards in question.[114]

The Advocate General, then, went on to consider four possible alternative scenarios to reconstruct the supply chain, in light of the submissions made in this regard by the various parties intervening in the case. Notably, according to a first reconstruction proposed by the UK government, Lebara, by issuing phonecards, actually had made two consecutive supplies of services, one at the time of the initial sale of those phonecards to local distributors, whereas another at the time of redemption of the phonecards in question by purchasing clients. To put succinctly: two supplies made by the company to two different customers at two different points in time, the former made to local distributors, whereas the latter toward clients purchasing the phonecards in question. Such a reconstruction, however, was ultimately dismissed by the Advocate General, who reasoned, *inter alia*, that the notion of a 'double supply' for the same service was alien to the EU VAT system and, further, that, if adopted, this reconstruction would have created problems in terms of legal certainty and possible double taxation or non-taxation.[115] Figure 6.8 below depicts graphically the first possible reconstruction of the supply chain, as considered but rejected by Advocate General Jääskinen in *Lebara*.

Figure 6.8 Lebara*'s First Reconstruction of the Supply Chain According to AG Jääskinen*

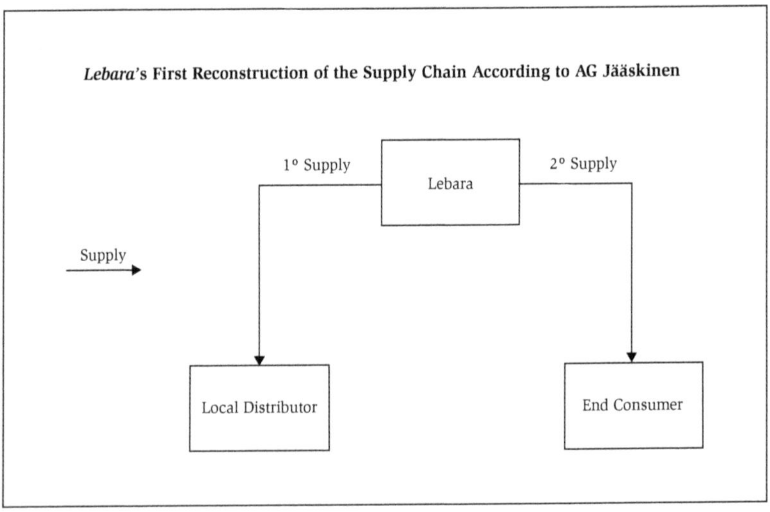

A second possible reconstruction of the supply chain was put forward by the Dutch government. As it was with the UK government's submission, the Netherlands argued

114. Opinion *Lebara* (C-520/10), paras 35-37.
115. *Id.*, paras 42-43.

in favour of the existence of two supplies in the case. However, only one of those two supplies was eventually made by Lebara. The other supply, instead, was solely operated by local distributors. More specifically, according to this reconstruction, Lebara had made a single supply of telecommunications services to its own clients. To such supply, it then accessed a separate but ancillary supply of distribution services made by local distributors to Lebara, whose taxable amount was constituted by the difference between, on the one hand, the price paid by clients to local distributors and, on the other hand, the sum paid by local distributors to Lebara. On the contrary, the supply of phonecards by Lebara to local distributors was not considered a taxable transaction in full EU VAT terms. Even this second cluster of assumptions, however, was ultimately dismissed by the Advocate General, who indeed observed that, actually, the local distributors had taken part in the supply chain and, further, that the solution proposed by the Dutch government did not quite accord with the fact that, under EU VAT, different rules apply depending on whether an intermediary makes a supply in his own name or, instead, in the name of the original supplier. While, in this latter case, the intermediary service constitutes an input supply for the original supplier, in the former situation, the intermediary is instead considered as fully taking part in the supply chain between the original supplier and the end consumer and, also, as the sole party making the final supply to him.[116] Figure 6.9 below depicts graphically the second possible reconstruction of the supply chain, as considered but rejected by Advocate General Jääskinen in *Lebara*.

Figure 6.9 Lebara*'s Second Reconstruction of the Supply Chain According to AG Jääskinen*

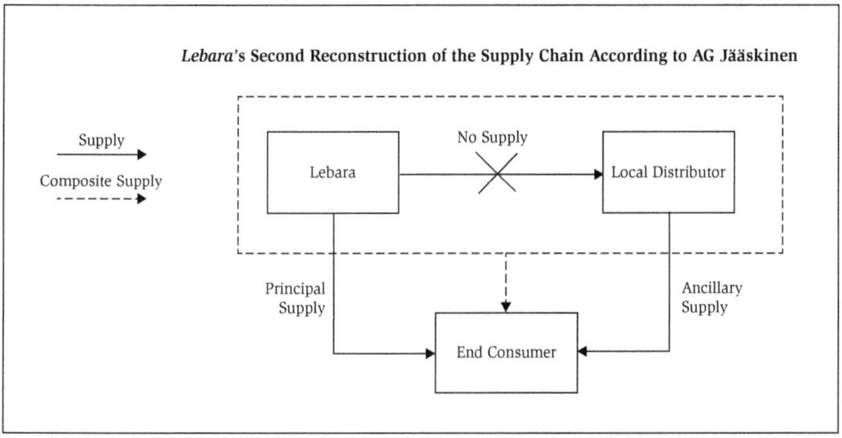

A third possible reconstruction of the supply chain was proposed by the Commission and, essentially, also shared by Lebara in its own submission. Under such scenario, all the transactions among parties were assumed to belong to a single supply chain. More

116. *Id.*, paras 46-55.

specifically, based on such reconstruction, Lebara, through the issuance of phonecards, had made a single supply of telecommunications services to local distributors, who, in turn, had carried out another identical supply to clients. To put succinctly: two distinct suppliers, two supplies, within a single chain of transactions. Even this third reconstruction, however, was ultimately dismissed by the Advocate General, who, indeed, considered the infeasibility of maintaining that the clients were actually purchasing the right to make telecommunications services from the local distributors, in so far as those services had never been completely transferred, in the first place, from Lebara to the local distributors. In this connection, the Advocate General further opined that, clearly, it was Lebara that actually rendered available to purchasing clients the telecommunication services, whereas the lack of a direct contractual (i.e., legal) relationship between Lebara and those clients was outrightly immaterial in this regard.[117] Figure 6.10 below depicts graphically the third possible reconstruction of the supply chain, as considered but rejected by Advocate General Jääskinen in *Lebara*.

Figure 6.10 Lebara*'s Third Reconstruction of the Supply Chain According to AG Jääskinen*

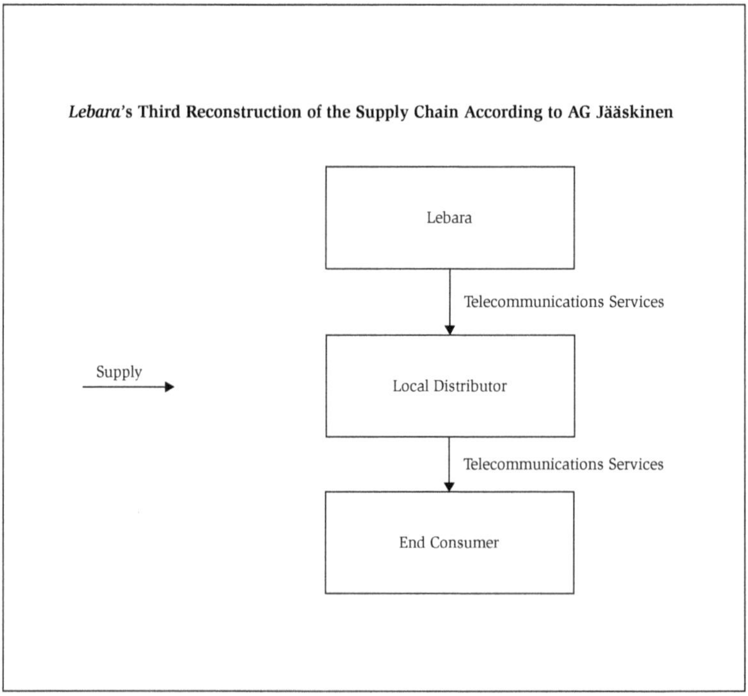

The fourth reconstruction, formulated in the alternative by the Commission, was eventually the one to which the Advocate General ultimately adhered. Notably, this

117. *Id.*, paras 56-67.

reconstruction is premised on Article 28 of the VAT Directive, which, for EU VAT purposes, creates the legal fiction of two identical supplies of services, provided consecutively by two distinct suppliers, the second acting as an agent of the first, who, instead, of a principal.[118] Based on such a legal fiction, the local distributors were considered as intermediaries, i.e., as agents, acting in their own name, but on behalf of Lebara, who, instead, performed the role of the principal. In practice, it was stipulated that the local distributors had received telecommunications services from Lebara, on behalf of whom they acted, and had then supplied services of identical nature to purchasing clients. Despite the undeniable similarities with the third scenario described above, the Advocate General regarded this fourth reconstruction as more appropriate in the case at hand. Notably, in his own view, this fourth reconstruction achieved the same result of the third scenario described above and, yet, without distorting the 'reality of the service', which entailed that the delivery of phonecards to the local distributors did not also imply that any 'economic risk' was transferred from Lebara, as demonstrated by the fact that the local distributors did not pay Lebara in case of non-activated phonecards. In this connection, it was also recalled that the local distributors took responsibility, in their own name but on behalf of Lebara, for the distribution of phonecards and for transferring the sums paid by the clients to Lebara, obviously, after deducting their own commission fees.[119] Figure 6.11 below depicts graphically the fourth possible reconstruction of the supply chain, as considered and agreed upon by Advocate General Jääskinen in *Lebara*.

118. For discussion of the provision contained in Art. 28 of the VAT Directive, *see* Chapters 7 and 8.
119. Opinion *Lebara* (C-520/10), paras 68-78.

Figure 6.11 Lebara's *Fourth Reconstruction of the Supply Chain According to AG Jääskinen*

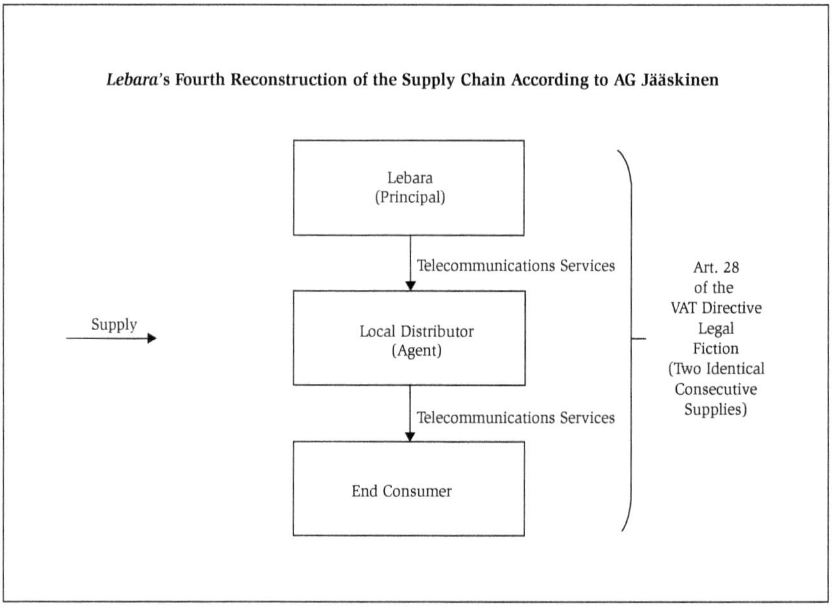

The assumption that the local distributors acted as intermediaries, i.e., as agents, in their own name and, yet, on behalf of their principal, i.e., Lebara, was precisely the point in which the findings of the Advocate General and the CJEU, otherwise quite similar, split. Notably, the Court concluded that, although a single supply chain existed, two distinct supplies were indeed made, the former by Lebara to the local distributors, whereas the latter by the local distributors to the clients. Although mentioned in passim, the provision of Article 28 of the VAT Directive, instead, was not specifically considered by the Court in its own decision. The CJEU, in fact, found that the local distributors had resold the phonecards to the clients in their own name *and on their behalf*, and not instead in their own name *but on behalf of Lebara*. According to the CJEU, in practice, Lebara had made a single supply of a complex service to the local distributors, by means of which the company had completely transferred to these latter parties the right to use the infrastructure necessary for making international phone calls. The CJEU also took stock of the fact that Lebara neither controlled the resale price charged by the local distributors to the clients, nor the company knew the identity of those clients at the time of the payment made to the company by the local distributors. For their own account, the local distributors had only committed to transfer to Lebara the remuneration paid by the clients, circumstance which was assumed not to create, by itself, a direct link between Lebara and those clients.[120] Figure 6.12 below depicts graphically the reconstruction of the supply chain considered and agreed upon by the CJEU in *Lebara*.

Figure 6.12 Lebara's *Reconstruction of the Supply Chain According to the CJEU*

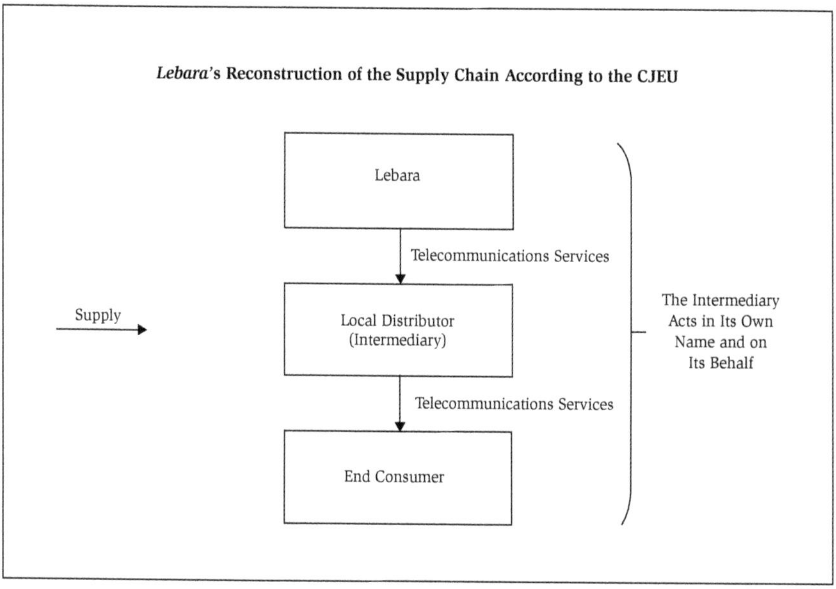

All the scenarios laid down by either the Advocate General or the CJEU in *Lebara* and summarized above could be applied, in principle, as to reconstruct the supply chain, and the relationships among the various parties within it, in the sharing economy. On closer inspection, however, some scenarios appear sounder than others. Notably, the first scenario recalled above, stipulating the provision of two distinct services to the same customer by the same supplier but at different points in time, i.e., the dubbed 'double supply' approach, hardly matches with the reality of most business models in the sharing economy, which indeed entails the provision of intermediary services by a platform to the individual supplier, whereas this first scenario completely disregards the transaction occurring between those two parties. Similar kinds of considerations

120. UK: ECJ, 3 May 2012, Case C-520/10, *Lebara Ltd v. Commissioners for Her Majesty's Revenue & Customs*, paras 33-43. Worth mentioning, the author notes that the reconstruction which the CJEU, ultimately, adhered to in the case is very similar to the one proposed jointly by the Commission and Lebara in their own submissions (i.e., the third alternative scenario delineated above). The only meaningful difference in this regard is constituted by the emphasis that the Court placed on the role of the local distributors as intermediary parties within the supply chain, although those parties acted both in their own name and on their behalf, whereas, in the reconstruction proposed by the Commission and Lebara, the role played by the local distributors within the supply chain was not quite specified.

could also be advanced to discard the second scenario recalled above, which, essentially, assumes the joint provision of a composite supply to the same customer by two distinct suppliers. The third scenario, stipulating the existence of two consecutive identical supplies made by two distinct suppliers, positioned vertically along a single supply chain, apparently looks closer to the structure of the supply chain in most sharing economy's business models. Nevertheless, in the author's opinion, this reconstruction fails to take into account that the services that the two undertakings in question, i.e., the platform and the individual supplier, respectively provide do not quite have the same nature and, as such, their own classification under EU VAT should differ. The same kind of contention could be raised against the fourth scenario, which relies on the deemed supply rule contained in Article 28 of the VAT Directive, thus creating the legal fiction of two supplies of services made consecutively by two distinct suppliers. Again, it could be maintained that the two supplies in question, although by way of a legal fiction deemed 'identical', are not really so in the context of the sharing economy.

In light of all the above, the author submits that the reconstruction which, in the context of the sharing economy, perhaps, best reflects the supply chain, as well as the relationships existing among the various parties within it, is ultimately the scenario considered and agreed upon by the CJEU in its findings in *Lebara*. Similar to the third and the fourth reconstructions assessed by the Advocate General in the case, this scenario assumes the existence of two distinct suppliers within a single 'vertical' supply chain, in which the final supply to the end consumer is operated only by the undertaking that is closer to him. Different from the aforementioned reconstructions, however, this scenario posits that the supplier positioned in the middle of the supply chain, i.e., the intermediary, acts in his own name and, also, on his own behalf.[121] Indeed, in the context of the sharing economy, platforms come to precisely fulfil such a role. As a matter of fact, platforms offer the individual customer an intermediary service aimed at facilitating the provision to him, by the individual supplier, of the underlying service, consisting in accommodation or passenger transport. Such intermediation service is, undoubtedly, carried out by the platform in its own name, as demonstrated by the circumstance that it is usually the platform's brand which is displayed to the individual customer. By all accounts, the role played by the platform in the supply chain is too prominent for considering such an intermediation service to be made only on behalf of the individual supplier. Indeed, quite the opposite. As Advocate General Szpunar contended in *Uber Systems Spain*, contrary to the company's claim, 'Uber actually does much more than match supply to demand: it created

121. In this connection, it ought to be observed that no provision in the VAT Directive specifically mentions the case of an intermediary party intervening in the supply toward the end consumer and acting both 'in his own name' and 'on his own behalf'. Nevertheless, such a possibility is expressly contemplated in the guidelines drafted by the VAT Committee. *See* European Commission, Value Added Tax Committee, *Guidelines resulting from the 93rd Meeting of 1 July 2011 – Document C* (taxud.c.1(2012)1410604 – 709). *See also* European Commission, Value Added Tax Committee, *Working Paper No. 814. Treatment of Online Supplies Made by a Travel Agent to Final Consumers*, at 8 (taxud.c.1(2014)2806510). Reference to an intermediary, acting both in his own name and on his own behalf, can also be found in *Mapfre Asistencia and Mapfre Warranty*. *See Mapfre Asistencia and Mapfre Warranty* (C-584/13), para. 38.

[*sic*] the supply itself. It also lays down rules concerning the essential characteristics of the supply and organizes how it works', as prominently shown by a reading of the terms and conditions set forth by the platform and with which its users must comply.[122] As seen, in the sharing economy, it is the platform the true 'market maker' within the supply chain.[123] Indeed, even from a purely economic perspective, with regard to the relationship between the platform and the individual supplier, the role of the principal is certainly played by the former, whereas the latter party appears, rather, as a mere 'agent', in so far as it economically depends on the former party.[124] Against this background, however, it might be contended that the 'meaningful supply', in the sense of being the relevant one from the perspective of the individual customer, is clearly that made by the agent/individual supplier, not certainly that made by the principal/platform. In light of all this, the reconstruction which the CJEU ultimately adhered to in *Lebara*, stipulating the existence of an intermediary party, who, however, acts with an extensive degree of autonomy from the original supplier, seems the best course to take in the context of the sharing economy. Nevertheless, it remains to be seen whether such an approach would be upheld by any future judicial appraisal - or not.[125]

§6.05 CHAPTER CONCLUSIONS AND RECOMMENDATIONS FOR IMPROVEMENT

[A] Main Findings

Although targeting final consumption, as stipulated by Article 1(2) Second Indent of the VAT Directive, EU VAT is administratively levied 'on each transaction'. The transaction is, in fact, the relevant tax object under EU VAT. Defining what exactly constitutes a transaction is therefore crucial, especially where a transaction is constituted by the joint provision to the same customer of several goods and/or services, possibly by different undertakings. The VAT Directive, however, does not contain any 'set' or 'absolute' rule on how to make such a determination. Some guidance in this regard has nevertheless been provided by the CJEU. Through the years, as from *Credit Protection Plan* on, the Court has in fact developed a specific doctrine on 'composite

122. Opinion *Uber Systems Spain* (C-434/15), para. 43.
123. *See* sections §1.03 and §4.02[B].
124. For a discussion, *see* section §8.03[E].
125. Apparently, Advocate General Szpunar hinted at a reconstruction of the supply chain similar to that proposed above in *Geelen*, by arguing that both 'the erotic sessions as such (i.e. the display of models) and their transmission over the Internet', on the one hand, and the 'provision of an interactive communication', on the other hand, are essential elements for 'the provision of interactive live erotic webcam sessions'. More to the point, it was reasoned that 'Mr. L.W. Geelen not only provides model displays, as such a service would have no value to his customers, given that the latter are in the Netherlands, while the models in the Philippines. Nor is he limited to mediation in the transmission of sessions, as he also organizes performances of models and provides them with the necessary equipment, and, as one can assume, pays them compensation' [author's unofficial translation]. *See* NL: Opinion of the Advocate General, 12 Feb. 2019, Case C-568/17, *Staatssecretaris van Financiën, L.W. Geelen*, paras 44-45.

supplies'. As a main rule, the doctrine on composite supplies mandates that every transaction shall be considered as fully distinct and independent. This main 'splitting' rule, however, has two relevant exceptions. Notably, two or more supplies need to be treated as a single, indivisible supply, (1) if they constitute 'a single supply from an economic point of view', or (2) if one supply is ancillary to the other.

As for the first exception to apply, it is relevant to consider the 'objective' economic purpose of a transaction as well as the 'subjective' intention shown by the individual customer. As regards the 'objective' economic purpose of a transaction, the way in which the services are presented on the market, especially in terms of commercial reality and practices, is a factor of particular importance. As regards the 'subjective' intention shown by the individual customer, the ability of a customer to determine his own level of consumption and make choices in relation to the products supplied to him, circumstances which could also be reflected in the contractual arrangements between the parties, is a factor of particular importance. The two approaches in question can eventually be reconciled where the economic purpose considered is that of the 'typical' or the 'average' customer.

As for the second exception to apply, which could be termed as 'ancillary principle' or 'principle of absorption', it is instead required that one or more elements of a transaction constitute a principle supply, whereas another or more elements constitute an ancillary supply, which, as such, must share the treatment of the principal supply. In particular, a supply must be regarded as ancillary to another principal supply if it does not constitute for a customer an end in itself, but simply a means of better enjoying the principal supply. In order to make such a determination, the CJEU usually refers both to the qualitative and quantitative contributions made by a supply to an economic operation as a whole, although, apparently, preference is granted by the Court for a qualitative-based approach.

The three rules, i.e., the main rule and its two exceptions, constituting the CJEU's doctrine on composite supply, however, do not exhaust the full spectrum of possible approaches in this regard.

One alternative approach to composite supplies relates to 'two-step' or 'preliminary' transactions, that is to situations in which two or more related supplies are made by a taxable person to the same customer at different points in time. Situations involving two-step transactions have indeed grown significantly in recent years, especially with the advent of the so-called 'subscription economy'. Notably, the most relevant and recent cases in this regard entail the payment of membership fees, i.e., situations in which customers are required to pay a price as a condition to enter into a market or to join a community. Although the CJEU's case law on this matter is not entirely consistent, apparently, payment of membership fees must be regarded as a consideration for a transaction fully distinct and independent from any subsequent – and indeed, merely eventual – transaction concluded on a market or inside a community.

Another alternative approach relates to the application of the CJEU's doctrine on composite supplies also to the situation in which two distinct undertakings jointly supply a good and/or a service to the same customer, as envisaged by the Court, first, in *Part Service* and, then, in *Mapfre Asistencia and Mapfre Warranty*, thus overruling some of its previous findings on this matter. Importantly, the possibility to apply the doctrine on composite supplies to situations entailing the joint provision of a good and/or a service to the same customer by two distinct suppliers is, however, only available where each of the two suppliers in question has a direct relationship with that customer.

Whichever approach is ultimately followed, it appears crucial to proceed to the factual reconstruction of the supply chain, i.e., of the relationships existing among the various parties taking part in the economic operation as a whole. Indeed, the CJEU's cases summarized above and, in particular, the various alternative reconstructions considered by either the Advocate General or the Court in *Lebara*, shows that such an assessment is, by no means, an easy task and that different reconstructions of the same supply chain, as well as of the relationships between the various parties within it, are equally possible.

Various conclusions of relevance in the context of the sharing economy can be drawn from the analysis summarized above. A first general conclusion is that, for defining what exactly constitutes a transaction, all the facts and circumstances of a sharing economy operation as a whole must be duly taken into account.

As regards the CJEU's doctrine on composite supplies, all the three rules constituting such a doctrine may well find an application in the context of the sharing economy. As a first possible scenario, a single sharing economy operation, which entails both the supply made by the platform and that made by the individual supplier, can be split into two or more supplies for EU VAT purposes. This scenario, however, might not ultimately hold up where the individual supplier is not 'truly' independent from the platform, as some courts might find especially in the case of Uber drivers.

As regards platform services, in general, the supplies in question can be viewed as a single composite supply from an economic point of view or, alternatively, as a single composite supply in which one supply is ancillary to the other. Notably, this seems to be the case of payment handling services, in so far as, clearly, a payment cannot be considered as independent from the service which it refers to. As regards services among platform users, the doctrine on composite supplies does not seem to come into prominence, as long as, in most instances, those services entail the provision to the individual customer of a 'unitary service', i.e., accommodation or passenger transport. Only with regard to services such as 'experiences' on Airbnb, the doctrine on composite supplies could eventually kick in.

The application of the CJEU's doctrine on composite supplies in the context of the sharing economy is not tenable in light of the five legal principles which compose the evaluation model as conceptualized in the present study. In particular, the bare circumstance that all the three rules constituting such a doctrine may well find an application in the context of the sharing economy does not consent to achieve sufficient equality and neutrality, in so far as this allows to treat similar situations in a different manner. Clearly, possible divergent interpretations and applications of such a doctrine neither serve the practical interest in simplicity of administration and collection. Moreover, although a flexible approach in drafting and interpreting legal provision is generally welcome, it is undoubted that too much flexibility, such as it occurs with the interpretation and application of the CJEU's doctrine on composite supplies, breeds legal instability.

As for other alternative approaches to composite supplies, in principle, the approach relating to 'two-step' or 'preliminary' transactions also comes into prominence in the context of the sharing economy. Despite this general assumption, the VAT Committee considered the grant of a right to participate in a virtual marketplace operated by a platform in return for payment of a membership fee as a fully distinct and independent service supplied by that platform to its users. Indeed, it is also hard to apply the doctrine on two-step or preliminary transactions to the case of HomeExchange, as long as this platform neither is involved in the provision of the underlying service of accommodation. Further, the author is not persuaded by the Commission's opinion which hints at the possibility to apply the doctrine on two-step or preliminary transactions to the provision of 'free' services by a digital company in return for user personal data, based on which VAT would not be levied immediately, i.e., when user personal data are obtained by the digital company, but only at a later moment, i.e., when the digital company sells those data to advertising businesses.

While considering the grant of a right to participate in a virtual marketplace operated by a platform in return for payment of a membership fee as a fully distinct and independent service supplied by that platform to its users is sound also from a principle-based perspective, the Commission's opinion which hints at the possibility to apply the doctrine on two-step or preliminary transactions to the provision of 'free' services by a digital company in return for user personal data, instead, does not meet the objectives of the five legal principles which compose the evaluation model as conceptualized in the present study. In particular, from the perspective of the equality and neutrality principles, it is not tenable to consider the provision of 'free' services by a digital company in return for user personal data as a transaction not to be immediately subject to EU VAT. Even if, arguably, such kinds of transactions only amount to inputs for a digital company, it is unquestionable that, in such event, a taxable transaction in full EU VAT terms takes place and, indeed, traditional businesses have their input transactions taxed as well. Thus, it is not clear for which given reason transactions entailing the provision of user personal data may be an exception to the above. Indeed, the author cannot find any reasonable justification in this regard, even in light of the simplicity and flexibility principles.

The possibility to apply the CJEU's doctrine on composite supplies, as extensively interpreted by the CJEU as to cover also situations in which two distinct undertakings jointly supply a good and/or a service to the same customer, to transactions in the sharing economy is, indeed, quite promising. In certain instances, the relationship between a sharing economy platform and an individual supplier is, in fact, so strict that the two undertakings in question might well be considered as a single supplying party, which jointly enters into contractual arrangements with the individual customer for the carrying out of an overall activity to him. More specifically, this line of reasoning could be maintained in the case of a platform like Uber and, possibly, also for Airbnb and BlaBlaCar, whereas HomeExchange appears to be more akin to a mere promoter of the activity carried out by its individual suppliers.

The possibility to apply the CJEU's doctrine on composite supplies, as extensively interpreted by the CJEU as to cover also situations in which two distinct undertakings jointly supply a good and/or a service to the same customer, to transactions in the sharing economy is also promising from a principle-based perspective. It is questionable, though. In particular, in light of the equality and neutrality principles, it not entirely clear whether a sharing economy platform and its individual suppliers should be considered as a single supplying party in the same way as a comparable and integrated more conventional business undoubtedly is. This is because it is not clear, in the first place, at which precise level the stage of comparison between the two above situations must be established. Notably, one may wonder whether traditional providers of accommodation and passenger transport services should be compared to sharing economy individual suppliers only or, rather, if the activities of the former should, more properly, be compared to the overall activity carried out by a sharing economy and, also, by its individual suppliers. Indeed, it is difficult to give an ultimate answer to such queries. In this connection, an assessment which takes into account the perspective of the individual customer, 'in terms of the satisfaction of his own needs'[126], could well be a promising course of action. Indeed, the principle of simplicity might also suggest considering a platform and its individual suppliers as a single supplying party. However, given the rapid evolution of business models in the context of the sharing economy, the validity of such cluster of assumptions needs to be constantly verified, as indeed it is mandated by the principle of flexibility.

Whichever approach is ultimately followed, it is necessary to proceed to the factual reconstruction of the supply chain, which inevitably presupposes a comprehensive examination of the actual role played by the various parties within it. Indeed, this is a very unsettled matter, as long as also determining 'who is supplying what to whom' is not, in itself, straightforward.[127]

A first possible reconstruction is that the platform is actually involved in the underlying supply toward the individual customer. An alternative reconstruction, instead, posits that the platform provides only intermediary services to the individual supplier, who is the sole party making the final supply to the individual customer. This latter possibility, however, seems open to a platform only if it provides its own services solely to one of the underlying parties and not, instead, to both parties, i.e., both the individual supplier and the individual customer, as certainly it is the case of Airbnb and, possibly, also of HomeExchange and BlaBlaCar. The scenario of a third-party payment made by the individual supplier to the platform in the context of a cooperation agreement among those parties, instead, seems quite unlikely. Ultimately, the author submits that the reconstruction that, perhaps, best reflects the supply chain, as well as the relationships among the various parties within it, in the context of the sharing economy is the scenario considered and agreed upon by the CJEU in *Lebara*, assuming

126. *Pro Med Logistik and Pongratz* (C-454/12 & C-455/12), para. 56. *See* section §6.02.
127. For similar issues in the framework of insurance arrangements, *see* M. Papis-Almansa, *Insurance in European VAT: Current and Preferred Treatment in the Light of the New Zealand and Australian GST Systems* at 277 (Kluwer Law International 2017), considering that, as to provide an answer to such dilemma, 'the *essentialia negotii* of an insurance contract and thus the actual risk transfer ought to be the decisive criterion' (emphases original).

that the platform – positioned in the middle of a single 'vertical' supply chain – offers the individual customer an intermediation service in its own name and, also, on its own behalf. It remains to be seen, however, whether such an approach would be upheld by any future judicial appraisal – or not.

As regards the factual reconstruction of the supply chain, as well as of the relationships among the various parties within it, reference to the principles underpinning EU VAT, and in particular to the five legal principles constituting the evaluation model as conceptualized in the present study, might eventually provide some help. In particular, for determining the relationship between the platform and the individual supplier in an individual case, the author submits that it would be useful to rely on the principle of neutrality, being it a principle which has inspired a purposive construction of the EU VAT system in several matters, through the adoption of an economic rather than a legal perspective.

[B] Recommendations

In terms of possible recommendations for improving the current EU VAT system in relation to the issues identified in this chapter, the author submits that, even if the various approaches for defining what exactly constitutes a transaction, inevitably, imply a case-by-case assessment, as long as, arguably, such determination does not permit any workable definitions[128], some interpretative clarification in relation to the application of the CJEU's doctrine on composite supplies is needed. Notably, some clarification in this respect might be offered in the guidelines drafted by the VAT Committee or in the explanatory notes issued by the Commission, both instruments which, although non-binding (for taxable persons, tax authorities, and courts), can still be a valid aid to interpretation, thus also serving the interests of simplicity and flexibility.[129] Indeed, the opportunity to lay down some guidelines in this matter has been acknowledged by the Commission itself. In the *Study on the Review of the VAT Special Scheme for Travel Agents and Options for Reform* instructed by the Commission, a proposal is, in fact, made to develop and render available to both Member States and taxable persons a series of detailed guidelines for determining the best course to

128. The author, indeed, does not believe in the possibility to adopt 'simple' and/or 'practical' rules for dealing with composite supplies, such as it might be considered a rule stipulating that, when a taxable person makes separate charges for the provision of various goods and/or services, then each good and/or service supplied is to be treated as a single and independent transaction. For a similar kind of suggestion, *see* D. Williams, *Ch. 6: Value-Added Tax*, in *Tax Law Design and Drafting*, at 27 (V. Thuronyi ed., International Monetary Fund 1996).

129. The author, indeed, submits that it would not be feasible, as to improve the application of the CJEU's doctrine on composite supplies, to lay down some binding provisions either in the VAT Directive or in the Implementing Regulation, as long as whether a transaction is a single composite supply – or not – must be specifically determined based on all the facts and circumstances of a case, whereas those rules would, inevitably, be formulated in abstract terms. Admittedly, in the past, the Commission planned the VAT Committee to be turned into a 'regulatory committee', endowed with the power to take measures to implement EU legislation, but the proposal did not ultimately follow through. *See* European Commission, *A Common System for VAT: A Programme for the Single Market*, at 19, COM(96) 328 final.

deal with the CJEU's doctrine on composite supplies.[130] It also ought to be recalled that some guidance on this point is already available at a national level. For instance, the UK tax authorities have laid down a list of indicators, extrapolated from both the CJEU's and domestic relevant case laws, to be used while dealing with composite supplies.[131] Notably, the guidelines and the list of indicators to be inserted in a dedicated document drafted by either the VAT Committee or the Commission might then read as follows:

> *COMPOSITE SUPPLIES*
>
> *European VAT is a general tax on consumption of all goods and services and its amount is exactly proportional to the final price of the goods and services. Administratively, the tax is levied on each transaction involving consumption of all goods and services. Under EU VAT, defining what exactly constitutes a transaction is of importance for several reasons, e.g., with regard to the classification of a transaction, the place of supply, the chargeable event and chargeability of VAT, the taxable amount, the deduction of VAT, the applicable rates and exemptions, as well as the liability for payment of VAT.*
>
> *The VAT Directive, however, does not contain any rule on how to deal with transactions, supplies, goods, or services composed of several elements, in short 'composite supplies'. As long as no set or absolute rule exists for determining the scope of a supply or a service under EU VAT, there will always be borderline cases. Despite the lack of any straightforward approach on how to make such a determination, so that this assessment would ultimately depend on an objective evaluation of all the facts and circumstances of a case, some useful indications can be gleaned from the case law of the Court of Justice of the European Union.*
>
> *As a main rule, every transaction shall be considered as fully distinct and independent. This entails that the VAT treatment accorded to each transaction must be kept separate. The same 'splitting' rule can also be applied, in principle, to the case of two or more related supplies made by a taxable person to the same customer at two different points in time, whether the first supply does not constitute, instead, a mere preliminary step toward the making of the second supply or, alternatively, the latter supply is necessary to the completion of the former supply.*
>
> *As a first exception to the foregoing main course, two or more supplies need to be considered as a single, indivisible composite supply, which should not be artificially split, so as not to distort the functioning of the EU VAT system, if the supplies in question constitute, from an economic point of view, a single supply having a distinct, self-contained, economic rationale. An example in this regard may be constituted by the lease of a residential property together with the provision of certain utilities, such as electricity, heating, and waste disposal, although not necessarily also including within it cleaning services. For the purpose of interpreting*

130. European Commission, *Study on the Review of the VAT Special Scheme for Travel Agents and Options for Reform* at 91 (2006), https://ec.europa.eu/taxation_customs/sites/taxation/files/travel_agents_special_vat_scheme_en.pdf (accessed 31 Mar. 2019).

131. Notably, the list of indicators compiled by the UK tax authorities makes specific reference to whether: (1) there is more than one supplier, (2) a typical customer considers that he is receiving two or more distinct and independent supplies, (3) both the terms of the contract and the 'economic reality' indicate the existence of more than a single supply, and (4) the existence of a composite supply is/was in the intention of the legislation/legislator. *See* UK: HMRC's Internal Manual, *Single and Multiple Supplies: HMRC's Approach: The General Approach* (2019), https://www.gov.uk/hmrc-internal-manuals/vat-supply-and-consideration/vatsc1 1113 (accessed 31 Mar. 2019).

the expression 'economic point of view', the 'objective' economic purpose of the transaction as well as the 'subjective' intention shown by the individual customer must be taken into account. In this connection, the following indicators of the existence of a composite supply can be extrapolated from the case law of the Court of Justice of the European Union:

(1) all the elements of a transaction are closely linked;
(2) all the elements of a transaction are necessary to its completion;
(3) all the elements of a transaction are part of a single supply under all commercial practices;
(4) all the services supplied are normally presented on the market as part of a single supply;
(5) splitting the transaction into two or more supplies would go against the economic reason for the individual customer;
(6) splitting the transaction into two or more supplies would go against contractual arrangements existing among the parties;
(7) splitting the transaction into two or more supplies would go against the use which the goods or services supplied are devoted to by the individual customer;
(8) the individual customer remains at all times free to determine his own level of consumption and to make choices in relation to the products supplied to him;
(9) splitting the transaction into two or more supplies would go against the economic intention of the typical or average customer;
(10) splitting the transaction into two or more supplies would create artificial distinctions based on insignificant differences.

As a second exception to the aforementioned main 'splitting' rule, a single composite supply shall also exist if one or more elements of a transaction constitute a principal supply, whereas another or more other elements constitute an ancillary supply, which, as such, must share the treatment of the principal supply. An example in this regard may be constituted by the provision by a company to airline passengers of a transport service connecting an 'off-airport' car park to the airport terminal. In particular, a supply must be regarded as ancillary to another principal supply if it does not constitute for a customer an end in itself, but simply a means of better enjoying the principal supply. In this connection, the following indicators of the existence of a composite supply can be extrapolated from the case law of the Court of Justice of the European Union:

(1) one or more elements of the supply are physically connected to one or more elements of the same supply;
(2) one or more of elements of the supply constitute the inevitable consequence of the supply of other elements of the same supply;
(3) the individual customer has no option but to receive the various services part of a composite supply in return for a single price;
(4) the price attributed to a specific service in the context of a composite supply constitutes the major part, in percentage, of the overall price paid by the individual customer for that supply;
(5) the price attributed to a specific service in the context of a composite supply has a substantial effect on the overall price paid by the individual customer for that supply.

All the above indicators concerning the existence of a composite supply can also be applied to the situation in which two distinct undertakings jointly supply a good and/or a service to the same customer, if the suppliers in question are related parties and an abusive intent is found, or if the supplies in question are so indissociably linked with one another as to constitute a single composite supply for EU VAT purposes.

As an additional or alternative measure, in case these or other guidelines and the list of indicators would not be considered either valid or sufficient to make a proper determination on a composite supply, especially in case of a cross-border transaction, the author suggests settling potential disagreements between taxable persons and tax authorities of two or more Member States through a decision released, upon a specific request made by one or all the taxable persons involved, under the framework of the VAT Cross-Border Rulings (CBRs), a pilot project started under the sponsorship of the EU VAT Forum in 2013, and which, in the author's opinion, should be institutionalized.[132] As a matter of fact, the CBR procedure has already been proved successful in relation to the assessment of a composite supply in at least one case, concerning a company which provided a series of cross-border services, some of which consisting, *inter alia*, in the storage, loading, and unloading of vessels/barges/trains/trucks, whereas some others attaining to the preparation of various types of documents, customs clearances, and representation. Indeed, by means of the CBR procedure, the competent authorities of the two Member States concerned (Netherlands and Belgium) eventually came to agree that the former string of services constituted as 'a single indivisible service which would be artificial to split', whereas the latter services did not 'form objectively a single indivisible service' with the former ones.[133] In order to render more effective such an instrument, mutual agreements reached under the CBR procedure should be collected and published systematically. Arguably, collection and publication of such mutual agreements would, in fact, contribute to avoid future litigations on similar issues. As a means to strengthen legal predictability and certainty, the CBR procedure would also consent to counterbalance possible detrimental effects entailed in the interpretation and application of the CJEU's doctrine on composite supplies in the context of the sharing economy.

---

132. Indeed, a proposal for establishing a permanent and online 'VAT dispute resolution mechanism' to settle disputes relating to EU VAT among Member States as from 1 June 2020 was made by the European Parliament in October 2018, but nevertheless rejected by the Commission in its later assessment in November 2018. *See* European Parliament, *Legislative Resolution of 3 October 2018 on the Proposal for a Council Directive amending Directive 2006/112/EC as Regards Harmonising and Simplifying Certain Rules in the Value Added Tax System and Introducing the Definitive System for the Taxation of Trade between Member States (COM(2017)0569 – C8-0363/2017 – 2017/0251(CNS))*, 3 Oct. 2018, T8-0366/2018; European Commission, *Follow Up to the European Legislative Resolution on the Proposal for a Council Directive amending Directive 2006/112/EC as regards Harmonising and Simplifying Certain Rules in the Value Added Tax System and Introducing the Definitive System for the Taxation of Trade between Member States*, SP(2018) 755.
133. European Commission, EU VAT Forum, *Cross-Border Rulings (update May 2017)* at 21 (taxud.c.4(2017)2926060). For preliminary considerations in relation to the CBR pilot project experience, *see* D. Raponi & F. Vitale, *Dispute Prevention: Advance (Cross-Border) Rulings: Experience of the Pilot Project and the Way Forward*, in *CJEU – Recent Developments in Value Added Tax 2016*, at 129-137 (M. Lang et al. eds, Linde 2017).

Whether there will be no enough consensus to support the introduction of a permanent dispute resolution mechanism under EU VAT, it might then be recommendable to rely on the 'double taxation dialogue' already in place between the tax authorities of some Member States, which enables a taxable person, in case of two or more Member States claiming VAT on the same transaction, to demand the tax authorities of the Member States concerned to enter into a dialogue with an aim of settling the subject matter among themselves by mutual agreement. Indeed, the instruction of a double taxation dialogue could be a means for two or more Member States to reach a common determination on a composite supply and, thus, to solve a dispute among themselves concerning the application of EU VAT on a cross-border transaction. Regrettably, at present, this procedure does not guarantee, however, that an agreement will ultimately be reached among the tax authorities of the Member States concerned, neither, indeed, the tax authorities in question are obliged to initiate any kind of arbitration procedure in case of a failure to reach an agreement.[134] Therefore, in order to render the procedure more appealing and effective for taxable persons, especially those involved in complex cross-border transactions, an obligation to initiate an arbitration procedure, together with a commitment to reach an agreement within a lead time (e.g., between six months and two years) and with no interest and penalties levied on the taxable persons for late payment of VAT, might be imposed upon the tax authorities of the Member States concerned. In this connection, if a convention for the avoidance of double taxation with respect to taxes on income and on capital is in force between the two Member States concerned, the arbitration procedure might eventually be started under the framework of Article 25(5) - or the corresponding article and paragraph - of such a treaty.[135] Similar to the case of the CBR procedure, mutual agreements reached through the double taxation dialogue by the tax authorities

134. European Commission, EU VAT Forum, *Information Note – VAT Double Taxation – Dialogue between Tax Administrations*, https://ec.europa.eu/taxation_customs/sites/taxation/files/resources/documents/taxation/vat/key_documents/eu_vat_forum/dialogue_tax_administrations_ms_en.pdf (accessed 31 Mar. 2019). For an examination of other possible measures in this field, *see* K. Spies, *Dispute Resolution in VAT: Status Quo under the EU VAT Directive and Room for Improvement*, in *CJEU – Recent Developments in Value Added Tax 2016*, at 91-127 (M. Lang et al. eds, Linde 2017).

135. It ought to be recalled, in fact, that Art. 25(3) of the OECD Model Tax Convention (MTC) provides that, besides the cases where taxation is not in accordance with the provisions of a tax treaty, the competent authorities 'may also consult together for the elimination of double taxation in cases not provided for in the Convention', provision which, as such, seems capable of covering also situations of double taxation occurring under EU VAT. For a discussion in this regard, *see* M. Bourgeois & A. Römer, *Effects of Existing Tax Treaties on VAT (Relevance of Arts. 24-27 OECD Model for VAT/GST)*, in *Value Added Tax and Direct Taxation: Similarities and Differences* (M. Lang, P. Melz & E. Kristoffersson eds, IBFD 2009); N.P. Eriksen & K. Haydl, *Avoidance of VAT/GST Double (Non-)Taxation: Recommendations and Other Types of Soft Law v. Legally Binding Instruments to Allocate Taxing Rights Between States (e.g. Bilateral Tax Treaties)*, in *Value Added Tax and Direct Taxation: Similarities and Differences* (M. Lang, P. Melz & E. Kristoffersson eds, IBFD 2009). Noteworthy, the existence of such a possibility, however, does not also seem to imply an extension of the mandatory arbitration process laid down in Art. 25(5) of a tax treaty to disputes concerning EU VAT. In the author's opinion, a similar option would, nevertheless, remain available if the Member States concerned relies on it on a voluntary basis. *See* OECD, *Model Tax Convention on Income and on Capital 2017 (Condensed Version)* (OECD Publishing 2017).

of different Member States should be collected and published systematically. Arguably, this would, in fact, contribute to avoid future litigations on similar issues and, thus, be a means to ensure legal certainty, although not in terms of predictability of legal provisions, as long as the double taxation dialogue is to take place only after the litigation phase has commenced.

As a last recommendation, it would be opportune to ensure that the CJEU's doctrine as well as other alternative approaches to composite supplies apply to transactions in the sharing economy in accordance with the principles underlying EU VAT. More to the point, the author submits that, given the rapid evolution of business models in the context of the sharing economy, continuous reliance on the fundamental principles underpinning EU VAT, such as those laid down in Chapter 3 and used as an evaluation model throughout the present study, i.e., the principles of equality, neutrality, simplicity, flexibility, and proportionality, would constitute a much more promising course of action for applying the CJEU's doctrine as well as other alternative approaches to composite supplies, rather than through the issuance of legislative and regulatory provisions, in so far as such detailed and prescriptive rules are likely to become obsolete in the span of few years.[136]

136. In this regard, *see* section §3.01, as well as footnotes n. 128-129 above in this chapter.

CHAPTER 7

Place of Supply

§7.01 INTRODUCTION

Nearly all tax laws, being either direct or indirect taxes, contain rules setting their territorial scope. Under EU VAT, this role is fulfilled by what the VAT Directive terms as 'place of supply' rules, although - precisely based on their ultimate function - perhaps a more accurate denomination would be 'place of taxation' rules.[1] The present chapter aims to filter out the main 'place of supply' rules applicable in the context of the sharing economy. More specifically, the ensuing analysis seeks to explore how supplies in the sharing economy, both those made by sharing economy platforms to their users and those made by users among themselves, shall be considered for place of supply purposes.

Under EU VAT, 'place of supply' rules are contained in Title V of the VAT Directive, which is entitled 'place of taxable transactions' (in French, *'lieu des operations imposables'*; in Italian, *'luogo delle operazioni imponibili'*). Title V is composed of four chapters. Notably, these four chapters are distinguished based on the types of taxable transactions in question, in particular whether they concern the supply of goods, the intra-Community acquisition of goods, the supply of services, or the importation of goods.[2] Of more interest to the present study, the rules relating to place of supply of services are laid down in Chapter 3 of Title V of the VAT Directive, from Articles 43-59a.

Place of supply rules, fundamentally, function as distributive rules[3], whose aim is to allocate taxing rights between two or more jurisdictions, by determining which

1. R. Millar, *Jurisdictional Reach of VAT*, in *VAT in Africa* at 175 (R. Krever ed., Pretoria University Law Press 2008).
2. *See* section §5.01.
3. *See* PL: Opinion of the Advocate General, 15 May 2014, Case C-605/12, *Welmory sp. Z o.o. v. Dyrektor Izby Skarbowej w Gdańsku*, para. 1, observing that 'a dispute about the place of supply of a service is also always a dispute about which Member State is entitled to impose tax'.

Member State shall have substantive jurisdiction to tax a cross-border transaction.[4] Their main purpose is, essentially, to avoid conflicts of jurisdiction[5], which may result in either double taxation or non-taxation.[6] And indeed, within the EU, avoidance of double taxation or non-taxation is also a means to ensure fair competition in the internal market.[7]

Although, in the context of indirect taxes, international double taxation and non-taxation have largely been underestimated[8], it appears that the same concepts operating in the field of direct taxation can thoroughly be applied also to an indirect tax such as EU VAT. Such an application, however, requires a certain degree of adaptation. Notably, the major adaptation entails a departure from the major distinction between international juridical and international economic double taxation or non-taxation. Contrary to direct taxes, under EU VAT, it is rather immaterial, in fact, whether double taxation affects a single taxable person, as it occurs when the person in question is not entitled to deduct his input VAT, or more than a single taxable person, as it happens when both the supplier and the customer are required to collect and remit VAT on the same transaction.[9] What counts, instead, is that both these situations ultimately lead to

4. As noted by B.J.M. Terra, *The Place of Supply in European VAT* at 1 (Kluwer Law International 1998), place of supply rules, instead, do not play any role in transactions which are confined to a single tax jurisdiction and to persons belonging to that jurisdiction only.
5. Noteworthy, the circumstance that the place of supply is located in a particular country does not also determine, by itself, the 'tax subject', i.e., the person liable for collection and remittance of the VAT due to the competent tax authorities of that country, and the 'collection point', i.e., 'the place where the liability to collect tax on a transaction is located'. *See* M. Senyk, *Territorial Allocation of VAT in the European Union* at 48 (Lund University 2018). Nevertheless, a linkage between these two issues may exist, especially whether the criteria that are used for determining the place of supply of a transaction – i.e., the 'substantive jurisdiction to tax' – are the very same of those used for determining liability for collection and remittance of VAT due in relation to that transaction – i.e., the 'enforcement jurisdiction to tax'. For a discussion, *see* W. Hellerstein, *Jurisdiction to Tax Income and Consumption in the New Economy: A Theoretical and Comparative Perspective*, 38 Ga. L. Rev. 1 (2003), at 1-70. For a discussion about liability regimes for collection and remittance of VAT, *see* Chapter 8.
6. DE: ECJ, 4 Jul. 1985, Case C-168/84, *Gunter Berkholz v. Finanzamt Hamburg-Mitte-Altstadt*, para. 14. Across different jurisdictions, double taxation or non-taxation in VAT/GST matters may be caused, in particular, by: (1) 'different principles as to approach to place of taxation', (2) 'different approaches and interpretation surrounding key proxies and concepts for determining place of taxation', (3) 'different approaches to the interaction of place of supply and time of supply', or (4) 'different approaches to bundled (mixed) supplies'. *See* OECD, *Report on the Application of Consumption Taxes to the Trade in International Services and Intangibles* at 18 (OECD Publishing 2004).
7. *See* points 19, 37, 51, and 62 of the Preamble of the VAT Directive. Noteworthy, the two objectives, i.e., that of avoiding double taxation or non-taxation and that of ensuring fair competition in the internal market, are not necessarily aligned under EU VAT. *See* e.g., Art. 273 of the VAT Directive, which allows Member States to 'impose other obligations which they deem necessary to ensure the correct collection of VAT and to prevent evasion', and yet this possibility is specifically made 'subject to the requirement of equal treatment as between domestic transactions and transactions carried out between Member States by taxable person and provided that such obligations do not, in trade between Member States, give rise to formalities connected with the crossing of frontiers'.
8. H.G. Ruppe, *General Report*, in *International Problems in the Field of General Taxes on Sales of Goods and Services*, at 121 (IFA Cahiers 1983 – 68B).
9. AT: Opinion of the Advocate General, 6 Sep. 2018, Case C-531/17, *Vetsch Int. Transporte GmbH Interveniente: Zollamt Feldkirch Wolfurt*, paras 3 and 40-41.

the imposition of a multiple tax burden in relation to the same economic operation. Thus, rather than focusing on whether double taxation occurs due to the application of the tax on one or more persons, under EU VAT, international double taxation requires taking into account the level of each single transaction, as long as double taxation is triggered by two or more jurisdictions claiming taxing rights over the same transaction.[10]

Despite no VAT/GST treaty against international double taxation and non-taxation has been concluded so far[11], the place of supply rules laid down in the VAT Directive do not exist completely in isolation. As recalled in Chapter 3, in fact, their application is assisted by two 'jurisdictional principles'[12], i.e., the territoriality and destination principles.[13] Under a perfectly designed set of jurisdictional rules which accord to these principles, the place of supply would correspond to the place where consumption actually takes place, of which expenditure made by the customer constitutes the most concrete manifestation.[14] Such considerations apply not only to B2C transactions, but also to B2B transactions, inasmuch as place of supply rules, in this latter context, are meant to facilitate the imposition of the tax burden on the end consumer, and although VAT revenues accrue only to the jurisdiction where the final supply, i.e., that made toward the end consumer, occurs.[15] Thus, for a country, being the place where consumption actually takes place does not automatically imply that the VAT due is to be remitted to the tax authorities of that country.

By their own nature, however, patterns of consumption are difficult to predict at the time when a transaction takes place, so that not always the place of supply of a good or a service would, indeed, match with the place of actual consumption of that good or

10. B.J.M. Terra, J. Kajus & O. Henkow, *Commentary on European VAT – Chapter 5: The Place of Supply* at para. 5.1.2. (IBFD Tax Research Platform 2019). *See also* Ruppe, *supra* n. 8, at 114, arguing that, 'in view of the special features of tax levied on goods it would therefore seem suitable to talk about international double taxation wherever an international transaction is subject to turnover tax ... regardless of whether it concerns the same taxpayer or not'. Against this line of reasoning, *see however* R. Ismer & K. Artinger, *International Double Taxation under VAT: Causes and Possible Solutions*, 45 Intertax 10 (2017), at 593-605, contending that the distinction between 'international juridical double taxation' and 'international economic double taxation' is also valid in the field of VAT/GST. Notably, the two authors point out that 'international juridical double taxation' is generally characterized by a doubling of the places of supply, whereas 'international economic double taxation' does not necessarily require a multiplication of places of supply, but it could also entail a mere divergent qualification of the same transaction by different countries, where one country refuses to grant input VAT credit while the other country levies output VAT.
11. Scholarly, a proposal for a VAT/GST Model Convention has nevertheless been made. *See* T. Ecker, *A VAT/GST Model Convention: Tax Treaties as Solution for Value Added Tax and Goods and Services Tax Double Taxation* (IBFD 2013). Some steps for applying VAT at the international level in a more coordinated fashion have been taken with the issuance of the International VAT/GST Guidelines by the OECD in 2015-17, which, although being a mere soft-law instrument, aim to be agreed standards for applying VAT/GST to cross-border supplies of services and intangibles. *See* OECD, *International VAT/GST Guidelines* (OECD Publishing 2017).
12. R. Millar, *The Destination Principle: Past Developments and Future Challenges*, in *GST in Australia: Looking Forward from the First Decade*, at 317 (C. Peacock ed., Thomson Reuters 2011).
13. *See* section §3.02.
14. Millar, *supra* n. 1, at 178.
15. OECD, *supra* n. 11, at 40.

service.[16] Further, although generally a country has substantive jurisdiction to tax the goods and services supplied within its own territory, there might be no consensus between different countries as to where such consumption actually takes place.[17] As a result of the difficulty to observe patterns of consumption, VAT/GST systems do not indeed tax 'material consumption', but instead use proxies for determining where consumption is deemed to take place. Proxies, which are anything but predictions of where actual consumption is likely to take place, indeed vary and may equally refer to the tangible and intangible aspects of a transaction[18], such as the supplier's, recipient's or another person's (e.g., an intermediary) place of establishment, the residence or location of those persons, the place of a transaction's physical performance, the location of a transaction's element as well as other elements to which the transaction relates, or even the place of use and enjoyment of a good or service.[19] Notably, EU VAT uses a combination of all these proxies, which are applied differently based on the nature and the characteristics of the transaction at stake that were known or knowable at the time when the supply took place.[20]

Given the definition of sharing economy as used in the present study[21], only the rules relating to place of supply of services as established under EU VAT are worth of examination. In particular, it is material to consider place of supply rules for those services which are most relevant in the context of the sharing economy sectors examined in the present study, i.e., accommodation and passenger transport services. In this connection, it should in fact be observed that, despite individual suppliers usually maintains a physical presence in the taxing jurisdiction, the cross-border dimension of those supplies of services cannot be entirely excluded. Notably, it is well possible for a guest resident - say - in France to book an accommodation on Airbnb or HomeExchange located - say - in Italy, which belongs to a host established or residing - say - in Spain. Likewise, a passenger transport service might be provided between parties established or residing in different countries and, especially in the case of

16. *Id.*, at 16.
17. *See* W. Hellerstein & M. Keen, *Interjurisdictional Issues in the Design of a VAT*, 63 Tax L. Rev. 2 (2010), at 372, pointing out that even the 'place of performance' of a service might ultimately be unclear, as it seems in the case of a laptop warranty belonging to a person located in the United States being operated by a person located in Bangalore. For a rather similar example, *see* OECD, *supra* n. 11, at 65-66. *See also* NL: Opinion of the Advocate General, 12 Feb. 2019, Case C-568/17, *Staatssecretaris van Financiën, L.W. Geelen*, essentially concerning whether services supplied at a distance by 'webcam models' are physically carried out at the place where those models perform in front of a web camera or, rather, where paying clients, connecting online with a fixed or mobile device, view 'in real time' those performances.
18. *See* R. Millar, *Intentional and Unintentional Double Non-taxation*, in *Value Added Tax and Direct Taxation: Similarities and Differences*, at para. 1.2. (M. Lang, P. Melz & E. Kristoffersson eds, IBFD 2009), equally referring to 'objective' - i.e., 'features of the physical world' - and 'subjective' - i.e., 'characteristics of the person intended to bear the incidence of the tax' - aspects, rather than 'tangible' and 'intangible' aspects.
19. Millar, *supra* n. 1, at 183.
20. As Millar, *supra* n. 1, at 178, observes, VATs/GSTs, contrary to income taxes, in fact 'are almost exclusively predictive. Their objective is to tax the consumption of goods and services, but they are applied at or before the time when the goods or services are first made available for use or consumption in the jurisdiction imposing the tax'.
21. *See* section §2.02.

BlaBlaCar, the service in question could well entail a cross-border journey.[22] As regards services provided by a platform to its users, the place of supply rules which most likely come into relevance, instead, relate to those for electronically supplied and intermediary services. Nevertheless, even the default place of supply rules for B2B and B2C transactions might potentially apply. A general overview of the place of supply rules for services is provided in the following section.

§7.02 PLACE OF SUPPLY OF SERVICES

At the time when services represented just a tiny fraction of overall cross-border trade, the place of supply rules governing their taxation under EU VAT were pretty much straightforward. Notably, while, under the Second Directive, the place of supply of services was based on the principle of 'effective use and enjoyment'[23], in the Sixth Directive, mainly with a view of simplifying tax compliance obligations for taxable persons, place of supply rules for services instead accorded with the origin principle.[24] In practice, under those rules, the supply of most services was located where the supplier was also established.[25] Nevertheless, as a result of the increasing importance of services in the worldwide economy, cross-border supplies of services have become far more common. In order to prevent distortions of competition caused by a potential divergent treatment of domestic and foreign supplies, as well as to simplify tax compliance obligations, especially due to the necessity for non-established suppliers to rely on the complex and time-consuming procedures laid down in the Eight and Thirteen Directives for obtaining a refund of their input VAT[26], countries commenced revisiting place of supplies rules for services as to accord with the destination principle, which leads to levy VAT where the customer is established.[27] Notably, after years of

22. Although quite rare, it might eventually be possible to conceive a cross-border trip in case of taxi services like those available on Uber, especially if the departure and destination points are located close to one another (e.g., an airport pickup in a country to reach a destination in another, nearby country).
23. Notably, Art. 6(3) of Second Directive mandated that 'the place of the provision of services shall, as a general rule, be regarded as being the place where the services provided, the right transferred or granted, or the object hired, is used or enjoyed'.
24. *See* European Commission, *Communication from the Commission to the Council, the European Parliament and the European Economic and Social Committee. Review and Update of VAT Strategy Priorities*, at 13 and 16, COM(2003) 614 final.
25. Notably, Art. 9(1) of the Sixth Directive prescribed that 'the place where a service is supplied shall be deemed to be the place where the supplier has established his business or has a fixed establishment from which the service is supplied or, in the absence of such a place of business or fixed establishment, the place where he has his permanent address or usually resides'. The exceptions to this rule, instead, were listed in Art. 9(2) of the Sixth Directive.
26. Council Directive 2008/9/EC of 12 February 2008 laying down Detailed Rules for the Refund of Value Added Tax, provided for in Directive 2006/112/EC, to Taxable Persons Not Established in the Member State of Refund but Established in Another Member State, OJ L 44/23 of 20 Feb. 2008; Thirteenth Council Directive 86/560/EEC of 17 November 1986 on the Harmonisation of the Laws of the Member States relating to Turnover Taxes – Arrangements for the Refund of Value Added Tax to Taxable Persons Not Established in Community Territory, OJ L 326/40 of 21 Nov. 1986.
27. *See* European Commission, *supra* n. 24, at 16-18; European Commission, *Proposal for a Council Directive amending Directive 77/388/EEC as regards the Place of Supply of Services*, COM(2003)

discussions at EU level[28], place of supply rules changed as from 1 January 2010.[29] Overall, this shift reflected the intention to tax services no longer based on where a business activity occurs, but instead based on where consumption of services actually takes place.[30]

Under EU VAT, place of supply rules for services primarily differ depending on the taxable status of the customer. It is therefore crucial to determine, in the first place, whether a customer is a taxable person or not and, in the former event, further verifying whether he is acting as such or not.[31] In so far as this piece of information is held by the transaction counterparty, certain measures have, opportunely, been introduced for simplifying investigative responsibilities on the side of the supplier. Notably, Article 43(1) of the VAT Directive mandates that a taxable person, who also carries out activities or transactions that are not considered as taxable supplies of goods or services in accordance with Article 2(1) of the VAT Directive, shall be regarded as a taxable person in respect of all the services rendered to him. This implies that, if the customer is a taxable person, the supply of services rendered to him is deemed to be located where that person is established, irrespective of the capacity in which that person effectively acts in the situation concerned and, further, unless one of the various exceptions to the default place of supply rule applies.[32] Another notable simplification rule is laid down in Article 43(2) of the VAT Directive, which stipulates that a non-taxable legal (!) person – then, a rule not to be extended to a natural person – who is identified for EU VAT purposes shall be regarded as a taxable person in the context of applying place of supply rules for services. This entails that, even if those legal persons are, in fact, non-taxable persons, the place of supply rules for B2B transactions, rather than those for B2C transactions, would apply to those parties.

Next to the taxable status of customer, place of supply rules differ based on certain aspects of the transactions concerned. Notably, the application of place of supply rules requires classifying and subdividing transactions into separate categories based on their own nature and characteristics. As will be explained in the following sections, with regard to underlying transactions among users of the sharing economy platforms examined in the present study, which concern accommodation and passenger transport services, special place of supply rules apply, both of which make

822 final; European Commission, *Amended Proposal for a Council Directive amending Directive 77/388/EEC as regards the Place of Supply of Services*, COM(2005) 334 final.

28. European Commission, *Consultation Paper: VAT – The Place of Supply of Services to Non-Taxable Persons*, D (2005).
29. Council Directive 2008/8/EC of 12 February 2008 amending Directive 2006/112/EC as regards the Place of Supply of Services, OJ L 44/11 of 20 Feb. 2008.
30. European Commission, *Green Paper on the Future of VAT: Toward a Simpler, More Robust and Efficient VAT System*, at 6-10, COM(2010) 695 final.
31. For a discussion, *see* Chapter 4.
32. The provision of Art. 43(1) of the VAT Directive can be seen, for the most part, as a codification of the CJEU's case-law in this regard. *See* SW: ECJ, 6 Nov. 2008, Case C-291/07, *Kollektivavtalsstiftelsen TRR Trygghetsrådet v. Skatteverket*, para. 35.

reference to the place where those services are physically carried out.[33] Such rules, indeed, constitute exceptions to the main ones for B2B and B2C transactions, which, respectively, make reference to the place where the customer or the supplier is established.[34] As clarified by the CJEU in *Dudda*, the kind of relationship between these and other special allocation rules and the default place of supply rules for B2B and B2C transactions reflects the one existing between *leges speciales* and *leges generales*. It follows that, as to determine the place of supply of a service, it must first be assessed whether the service in question is covered by any of those particular rules. Should this not be case, then the default rules for either B2B or B2C transactions would apply.[35] Further, as will be explained in the following sections, other special place of supply rules may apply with regard to transactions between the sharing economy platforms examined in the present study and their users, namely those for electronically supplied and intermediary services.[36]

As recalled above, the place of supply rules for services have undergone several changes through the years. Nevertheless, the place of supply rules for services connected with immovable property as well as those relating to passenger transport services have, remarkably, remained substantially unchanged.[37] The reason for such stalemate was, perhaps, best explained by Advocate General Poiares Maduro in *RAL (Channel Islands) and Others*. Notably, in that case, the Advocate General considered that the connecting factor of the place where those services are effectively provided out 'can without difficulty be physically identified and will coincide with the place of consumption' and, further, that those rules are 'far more in conformity with the general principle that VAT should be charged at the place of consumption'.[38] By contrast, several changes have interested the place of supply rules concerning electronically supplied and intermediary services, that is the other two main types of services which come into prominence in the sharing economy, as those made by a platform toward its users. An analysis of all these place of supply rules for services is provided in the following sections. Notably, sections §7.03 and §7.04 detail the general rules, respectively, for B2B and B2C transactions, that is the rules which apply by default in case no

---

33. *See Berkholz* (C-168/84), para. 14, considering that the VAT Directive 'sets out a number of specific instances of places where certain services are deemed to be supplied, whilst Article 9(1) [of the Sixth Directive, now Arts 44 and 45 of the VAT Directive] lays down the general rule on the matter'.
34. *See* sections §7.03 and §7.04 *infra*.
35. DE: ECJ, 26 Sep. 1996, Case C-327/94, *Jürgen Dudda v. Finanzgericht Bergisch Gladbach*, para. 21.
36. *See* sections §7.07 and §7.09 *infra*.
37. *See* sections §7.05 and §7.06 *infra*.
38. UK: Opinion of the Advocate General, 27 Jan. 2005, Case C-452/03, *RAL (Channel Islands) Ltd and Others v. Commissioners of Customs & Excise*, para. 30. Despite the unquestionable merits of allocating taxing rights over such kinds of transactions to the jurisdiction where the related services are physically carried out, it ought to be observed that this approach causes a non-negligible increase in the tax compliance burden for a non-established supplier, as long as that supplier has to register in the state in which the service is provided and entirely fulfils his own VAT obligations therein. On the other hand, in so far as no distinction exists with regard to whether the customer is a taxable or a non-taxable person, because the relevant place of supply rules equally apply to B2B and B2C transactions, the supplier is – at least – entirely relieved from the need to carry out any investigation concerning the taxable status of his customer.

other rule does. The subsequent sections, from §7.05 to §7.09, instead describe the special place of supply rules for services which are relevant in the context of the sharing economy, that is the various place of supply rules for, respectively, accommodation, passenger transport, electronically supplied, and intermediary services.

§7.03 DEFAULT RULE FOR B2B TRANSACTIONS

Both in the Second Directive and the Sixth Directive as until 1 January 2010, that is when Council Directive 2008/8/EC entered into force, the default place of supply rule for services was where the supplier had established his business or had a fixed establishment from which the service was supplied or, in case the former two references were not applicable, where the supplier has his permanent address or usually resided. Thus, pursuant to the default rule as applicable until 1 January 2010, the place of supply of – say – a 'call centre' service provided by a supplier established in Member State A to a taxable person established in Member B was where the supplier was established, i.e., Member State A. Figure 7.1 below depicts this scenario graphically.

Figure 7.1 Default Rule for B2B Transactions (as until 1 January 2010)

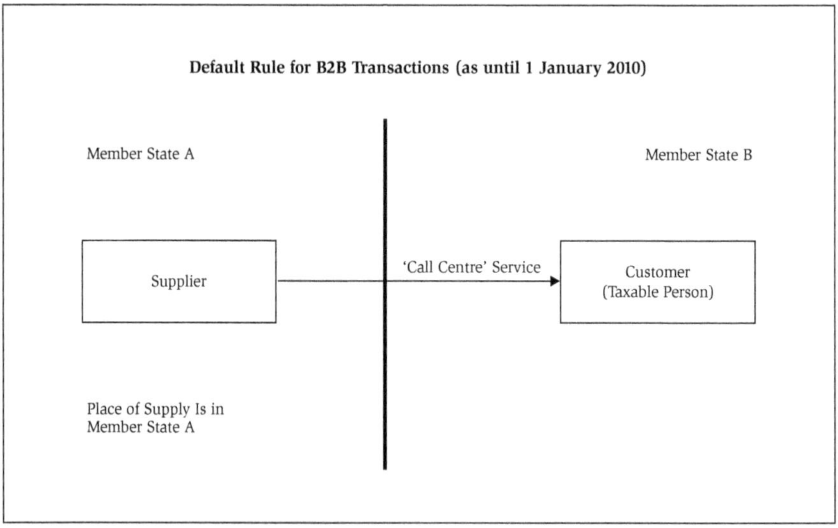

The new default rule, laid down in Article 44 of the VAT Directive and applicable as from 1 January 2010, instead mandates that the place of supply of services rendered to taxable persons shall be the place where the customer – who, in such situation, is required to account for VAT under the reverse charge or self-assessment mechanism[39]

39. For a description of the operation of the reverse charge mechanism, *see* Chapter 8.

– has established his own business. In this connection, Article 10(1) of the Implementing Regulation provides that this 'shall be the place where the functions of the business's central administration are carried out'. In its subsequent paragraphs, this article further specifies that, in order to make such a determination, 'the place where essential decisions concerning the general management of the business are taken, the place where the registered office of the business is located and the place where management meets' shall be jointly considered. Whether reference to these different sub-criteria yields unclear or mixed results, preference is to be given to a substantial criterion such as the place where essential business decisions are taken, whereas no importance should be attributed to a mere formal criterion such as a postal address.[40] As a further criterion, Article 44 of the VAT Directive stipulates that, if the services in question are provided to a fixed establishment of the taxable person located in a place other than the one in which he has established his own business, the place of supply of those services shall be the place where that fixed establishment is located. Under Article 11 of the Implementing Regulation, this is defined as a place 'other than the place of establishment of a business ... characterized by a sufficient degree of permanence and a suitable structure in terms of human and technical resources to enable it to receive and use the services supplied to it for its own needs'.[41] In the absence of either of these two establishments, reference is made to the place where the customer has his permanent address or usually resides. Worth mentioning, both these concepts are now defined in the Implementing Regulation. Notably, under Article 12 '"the "permanent address" of a natural person, whether or not a taxable person, shall be the address entered in the population or similar register, or the address indicated by that person to the relevant tax authorities, unless there is evidence that this address does not reflect reality'. Usual residence, instead, is defined by Article 13 of the Implementing Regulation as 'the place where that natural person usually lives as a result of personal and occupational ties'. The second paragraph of the aforementioned article further provides that, 'where the occupational ties are in a country different from that of the personal ties, or where no occupational ties exist, the place of usual residence shall be determined by personal ties which show close links between the natural person and a place where he is living'. Thus, pursuant to Article 44 of the VAT Directive, the place of supply of – say – a 'call centre' service provided by a supplier established in Member State A to a taxable person established in Member B is where the customer is established, i.e., Member State B. Figure 7.2 below depicts this scenario graphically.

---

40. The irrelevance, by itself, of a formal criterion such as a taxable person's 'letterbox address' was confirmed by the CJEU also in relation to the possibility for a taxable person to deduct his input VAT. *See* e.g., DE: ECJ, 15 Nov. 2017, Joined Cases C-374/16 and C-375/16, *Rochus Geissel v. Finanzamt Neuss and Finanzamt Bergisch Gladbach v. Igor Butin*, paras 29-50.
41. For a similar definition in the CJEU's case-law, *see, inter alia*, PL: ECJ, 16 Oct. 2014, Case C-605/12, *Welmory sp. z.o.o. Dyrektor Izby Skarbowej w Gdańsku*, para. 65; DE: ECJ, 28 Jun. 2007, Case C-73/06, *Planzer Luxembourg Sàrl v. Bundeszentralamt für Steuern*, para. 54; NL: ECJ, 17 Jul. 1997, Case C-190/95, *ARO Lease BV v. Inspecteur van de Belastingdienst Grote Ondernemingen te Amsterdam*, para. 15; UK: ECJ, 20 Feb. 1997, Case C-260/95, *Commissioners of Customs and Excise v. DFDS A/S*, para. 20; *Berkholz* (C-168/84), para. 18.

Figure 7.2 Default Rule for B2B Transactions (as from 1 January 2010)

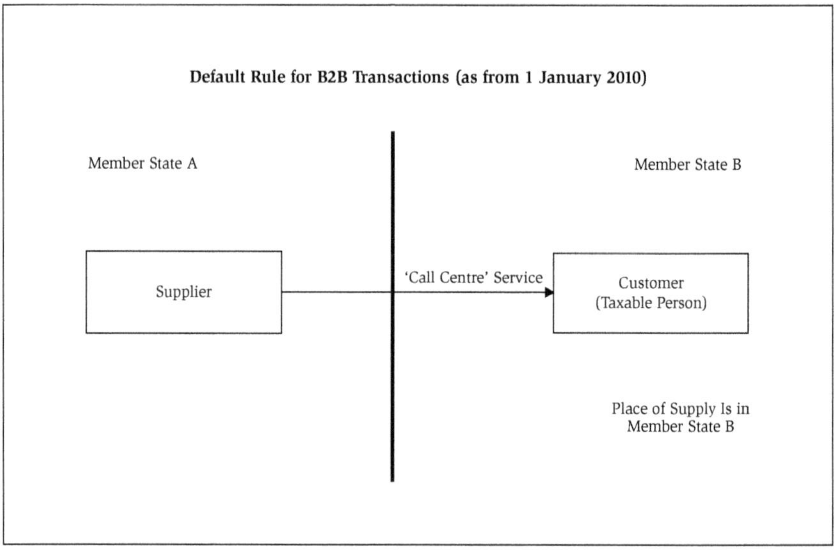

Although the default rule for B2B transactions has a very wide scope of application, services connected with immovable property and passenger transport services are among the few exceptions to this rule.[42] On the contrary, electronically supplied services and services made by intermediaries, whether rendered to taxable persons or persons identified as such equally follow the default rule for B2B transactions as laid down in Article 44 of the VAT Directive and explained above.

§7.04 DEFAULT RULE FOR B2C TRANSACTIONS

As from 1 January 2010, the VAT Directive also contains a default rule for B2C transactions. Notably, this rule is laid down in Article 45 of the VAT Directive. It stipulates that, where none of its many exceptions applies, the place of supply of services rendered to a non-taxable person shall be the place where the supplier has established his own business or, if the services in question are provided by a fixed establishment of the taxable person located in a place other than where such person has established his own business, the place of supply of those services shall be the

42. Indeed, already the Explanatory Memorandum attached to the Proposal for a Sixth Directive stipulated that, 'for all supplies of services, with the exception of services connected with immovable property and transport services, the place where the services are supplied is deemed to be the place where the supplier has established the seat of his business activities'. European Commission, *Proposal for a Sixth Council Directive on the Harmonization of Member States concerning Turnover Taxes Common System of Value Added Tax: Uniform Basis of Assessment (submitted to the Council by the Commission on 29 June 1973)*, at 11, COM(73) 950, Bulletin of the European Communities No. 11 (1973).

place where the fixed establishment of such person is located. In the absence of either of these two establishments, which, as seen, find a specification, respectively, in Articles 10 and 11 of the Implementing Regulation, reference is then made to the place where the supplier has his permanent address or usually resides, whose definitions, as seen, are laid down, respectively, in Articles 12 and 13 of the Implementing Regulation. As stated, the place of establishment of the supplier was the main rule also for B2B transactions as until 1 January 2010. Thus, pursuant to Article 45 of the VAT Directive, the place of supply of - say - a 'call centre' service provided by a supplier established in Member State A to a non-taxable person located in Member State B is the place where the supplier is established, i.e., Member State A. Figure 7.3 below depicts this scenario graphically.

Figure 7.3 Default Rule for B2C Transactions

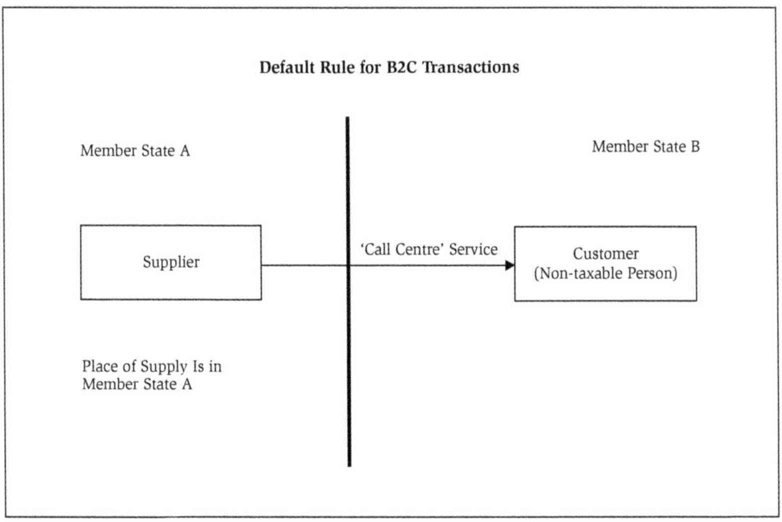

§7.05 SERVICES CONNECTED WITH IMMOVABLE PROPERTY

[A] Relevant Definitions and Rules

Immovable property has always received special attention in the context of allocating taxing rights across different jurisdictions. The primary reason for this spark of interest is that the concept of land, and of everything which is built upon it, is tightly clinched to the territory of a state. In a sense, the right to levy taxes on a real estate property is just the most prominent manifestation of the dominion of a sovereign state over its own territory.[43] Reflecting such an understanding, Article 47 of the VAT Directive provides that 'the place of supply of services connected with immovable property, including the services of experts and estate agents, the provision of accommodation in the hotel sector or in sectors with a similar function, such as holiday camps or sites developed for use as camping sites, the granting of rights to use immovable property and services for the preparation and coordination of construction work, such as the services of architects and of firms providing on-site supervision, shall be the place where the immovable property is located'.[44] Although Article 45 of the VAT Directive, as applicable until 1 January 2010, did not specifically mention either 'the provision of accommodation in the hotel sector or in sectors with a similar function' or 'the granting of rights to use immovable property', both these services were already considered as connected with immovable property.[45]

As stated, the special rule for services connected with immovable property applies irrespective of the taxable or non-taxable status of the recipient of the related services. A public consultation launched by the Commission in 2005, indeed, confirmed the general belief that taxation at the place where the immovable property is located is sound to most.[46] Nevertheless, one might still question the rationale behind having a separate place of supply rule for services connected with immovable property in relation to both B2B and B2C transactions.[47] A variety of reasons in this regard can be advanced. As stipulated by the explanatory notes on this matter issued by the Commission in 2015, the ultimate purpose of the special place of supply rule concerning services connected with immovable property is to ensure taxation at the presumed place of consumption of such services.[48] As a matter of fact, services connected with

43. For a discussion, *see* Tetłak K. & C. Kindl, *Taxing Rights in Relation to Immovable Property: VAT/GST v. Direct Taxation*, in *Value Added Tax and Direct Taxation: Similarities and Differences* (M. Lang, P. Melz & E. Kristoffersson eds, IBFD 2009).
44. Article 9(2)(a) of the Sixth Directive, by way of an exception to the main rule, stipulated that 'the place of the supply of services connected with immovable property, including the services of estate agents and experts, and of services for preparing and coordinating construction works, such as the services of architects and of firms providing on-site supervision, shall be the place where the property is situated'. With only a slightly modified wording, Art. 45 of the VAT Directive, as applicable until 1 January 2010, similarly provided that 'the place of supply of services connected with immovable property, including the services of estate agents and experts, and services *for the preparation and coordination* of construction work, such as the services of architects and of firms providing on-site supervision, shall be the place where the property is *located*' (emphases added to underline the few changes made to the previous text).
45. Notably, the Explanatory Memorandum to the 2003 Commission Proposal as regards the place of supply of services considered that the additions in question were made to 'give certainty' with regard to the fact that also these services should be included among those connected with immovable property. *See* European Commission, *Proposal for a Council Directive amending Directive 77/388/EEC as regards the Place of Supply of Services*, at 11, COM(2003) 822 final.
46. European Commission, *Summary Report on the Outcome of the Public Consultation from DG TAXUD, VAT – The Place of Supply of Services to Non-Taxable Persons*, at 7 (TAXUD-2005-00843).
47. Terra, Kajus & Henkow, *supra* n. 10, at para. 5.4.3.2.
48. European Commission, *Explanatory Notes on EU VAT Place of Supply Rules on Services Connected with Immovable Property that Enter into Force in 2017 (Council Implementing Regulation (EU) No 1042/2013)*, at 10 (2015), https://ec.europa.eu/taxation_customs/sites/taxation/files/resources/documents/taxation/vat/how_vat_works/explanatory_notes_new_en.pdf. (accessed 31 Mar. 2019)

immovable property are presumably consumed where the immovable property is located. Thus, for instance, in case of exchanges relating to timeshare usage rights, the CJEU considered that the services in question were not consumed at the place where the taxable person was established, but rather at the place where the immovable property in relation to which the timeshare usage rights were exchanged was located.[49] Another argument in favour of a special place of supply rule for services connected with immovable property rests on the fact that the 'situs' state, quite naturally, has all the supervision and tax collection powers in relation to the services in question. A further, obvious advantage entailed in the aforementioned special place of supply rule relates to the fact that the location of an immovable property can hardly be questioned, a circumstance that arguably renders the application of the place of supply rule concerned less susceptible to fraud.[50]

Taxation of services connected with immovable property at the place where the related property is located also serves to ensure neutrality with place of supply rules concerning the provision of goods, which, pursuant to Article 31 of the VAT Directive, is where the immovable property is located. Indeed, as clarified by the CJEU in *Shipping and Forwarding Enterprise Safe*, the concept of supply of goods does not only cover 'a transfer of ownership under procedures prescribed by the applicable national law', but it also relates to 'any transfer of tangible property by one party which empowers the other party actually to dispose of it as if he were the owner of the property'.[51]. In the absence of a special place of supply rule for services connected with immovable property, the default place of supply rules would have applied, which makes reference to either the place where the supplier – in the case of a B2B transaction – or the customer – in the case of a B2C transaction – is established. This might have induced a taxable person to characterize the transfer of ownership of an immovable property not as a supply of a good, but instead as a supply of a service.[52] By way of example, a taxable person might have tried to conclude a long-term lease of immovable property[53], instead of transferring a right in rem (e.g., usufruct, emphyteusis, or right of superficies) over the immovable property to another party[54], if the former was not to be considered as a service connected with immovable property under EU VAT, as such, taxed at the place where the immovable property concerned is located.

---

49. UK: ECJ, 3 Sep. 2009, Case C-37/08, *RCI Europe v. Commissioners for Her Majesty's Revenue and Customs*, para. 43. Along the same lines, *see* UK: ECJ, 16 Dec. 2010, Case C-270/09, *Macdonald Resorts Ltd v. The Commissioners for Her Majesty's Revenue & Customs*, para. 42.
50. European Commission, *supra* n. 48, at 10.
51. NL: ECJ, 8 Feb. 1990, Case C-320/88, *Staatssecretaris van Financiën v. Shipping and Forwarding Enterprise Safe BV*, para. 7. For a discussion, *see* section §5.02.
52. Noteworthy, the explanatory notes on this matter issued by the Commission consider that 'the leasing of immovable property can fall under Art. 47 of the VAT Directive only in so far as it qualifies as a supply of service and not as a supply of goods under the relevant national legislation'. *See* European Commission, *supra* n. 48, at 36. Along the same lines, *see also* European Commission, Value Added Tax Committee, *Guidelines resulting from the 93rd Meeting of 1 July 2011 – Document A* (taxud.c.1(2012)400557 – 707).
53. Articles 47 VAT Directive and 31(2)(h) Implementing Regulation.
54. Article 15(2)(b) VAT Directive.

[B] Sufficient Connection with Immovable Property

Undoubtedly, the most relevant question with regard to the type of services examined in the present section relates to which extent services need to be 'connected with' (in French, '*rattachant à*'; in Italian, '*relativi a*') an immovable property as to fall under the special rule laid down in Article 47 of the VAT Directive. Some guidelines on this matter have been offered by the CJEU in *Heger*. Notably, in that case, concerning whether the grant of fishing rights or a transfer of fishing permits constituted a supply of services connected with immovable property, the Court ruled that the services in question must be sufficiently connected with an immovable property for the special provision contained in Article 47 of the VAT Directive to apply, a statement which, however, by itself, is very vague, in so far as it does not obliterate the need to evaluate all the facts and circumstances of a case.[55] Indeed, such statement practically confirms only that it would run counter the rationale of the special rule in question to include every supply of services, provided that it has a connection, even a very tenuous one, with an immovable property, as long as a large number of services are, indeed, connected in a way or another with an immovable property.[56] In light of these observations, in *Heger*, the Court further reasoned that, as to establish a 'sufficiently direct connection' between a service and an immovable property, the immovable property in question shall constitute 'a central and essential element' of a supply of services.[57] As later specified in the explanatory notes on this matter issued by the Commission, the immovable property in question must also be clearly identified or, at least, identifiable.[58] Indeed, similar considerations are now included in Article 31a(1) of the Implementing Regulation, stipulating that 'services connected with immovable property ... shall include only those services that have a sufficiently direct connection with that property', which occurs 'in the following cases: (a) where they are derived from an immovable property and that property makes up a constituent element of the service[59] and is central to, and essential for, the services supplied[60]; (b) where they are provided to, or directed towards, an immovable property, having as their object the legal or

55. AT: ECJ, 7 Sep. 2006, Case C-166/05, *Heger Rudi GmbH v. Finanzamt Graz-Stadt*, para. 24. Also the OECD International VAT/GST Guidelines are, indeed, quite vague in this matter, as long as they only stipulate that a specific rule allocating the taxing rights to the jurisdiction where the immovable property is located might be appropriate where 'there is a close, clear and obvious link or association with the immovable property'. *See* OECD, *supra* n. 11, at 85.
56. As reasoned by Advocate General Sharpston in *Heger*, 'any service can ultimately be "connected" in one way or another with an immovable property, understood as a delimited space'. *See* AT: Opinion of the Advocate General, 7 Mar. 2006, Case C-166/05, *Heger Rudi GmbH v. Finanzamt Graz-Stadt*, para. 33. In favour of a narrow interpretation of Art. 47 of the VAT Directive, *see also* I. Lejeune, S. Kotanidis & S. Van Doninck, *The New EU Place-of-Supply Rules from a Business Perspective*, 20 Intl. VAT Monitor 2 (2009), Journals IBFD.
57. *Heger* (C-166/05), paras 23-25. Along the same lines, *see* OECD, *supra* n. 11, at 85.
58. European Commission, *supra* n. 48, at 12. Along the same lines, *see* OECD, *supra* n. 11, at 85.
59. In the CJEU's case-law, *see* ECJ, 27 Jun. 2013, Case C-155/12, *Minister Finansów v. RR Donnelley Global Turnkey Solutions Poland sp. z o.o.*, para. 35.
60. For example, 'the leasing or letting of immovable property'. *See* Art. 31a(2)(h) Implementing Regulation. In the CJEU's case-law, *see* BE: ECJ, 22 Jan. 2015, Case C-55/14, *Régie Communale Autonome du Stade Luc Varenne v. État Belge*, para. 34.

physical alteration of that property'[61]. Noteworthy, these two provisions are not cumulative, so that it sufficies that requirements from only one of the two points are met for a service to qualify as sufficiently connected with an immovable property.[62] It also ought to be recalled that a comprehensive - although purely indicative - list of services which shall be qualified as 'sufficiently' and 'directly' connected - or not - to an immovable property is provided, respectively, in Article 31a(2) and (3) of the Implementing Regulation. Noteworthy, among the types of services which should be seen as sufficiently connected with an immovable property, Article 31a(2)(p) of the Implementing Regulation lists 'intermediation in the sale, leasing or letting of immovable property and in the establishment or transfer of certain interests in immovable property or rights in rem over immovable property', thus extending, de facto, the scope of Article 47 beyond the services of experts and estate agents, two types of services expressly mentioned in the wording of that article and, as such, already regarded as sufficiently connected with an immovable property. Among the types of services which should not be seen as sufficiently connected with an immovable property, Article 31a(3)(d) of the Implementing Regulation, instead, lists 'intermediation in the provision of hotel accommodation or accommodation in sectors with a similar function, such as holiday camps or sites developed for use as camping sites, if the intermediary is acting in the name and on behalf of another person'. Where none of the two lists applies, it is instead necessary to verify the connection of the service in question with the immovable property, based on the general criteria laid down in Article 31(1) of the Implementing Regulation.[63]

[C] Leasing or Letting of Immovable Property

In the context of the sharing economy sectors examined in the present study, the most relevant types of services which fall within the scope of Article 47 of the VAT Directive undoubtedly relate to the leasing or letting of immovable property. Having specific regard to the transactions concluded among users on sharing economy platforms like Airbnb or HomeExchange, it is more accurate to affirm that the services in question consist in 'the provisions of accommodation in the hotel sector or in sectors with a similar function', situation which, indeed, the wording of Article 47 of the VAT Directive expressly mention. Notably, the leasing and letting of immovable property is specifically contemplated in Article 31a(2)(h) of the Implementing Regulation, whereas the provision of accommodation in the hotel sector or in sectors with a similar function, such as holiday camps or sites developed for use as camping sites, including the right to stay in a specific place resulting from the conversion of timeshare usage rights and the like, is included in Article 31a(2)(i) of the Implementing Regulation. The classification of a service as an 'ordinary' lease, which the former provision refers to, or, instead, as a 'short-term' lease, contemplated in the latter article, carries several

61. For example 'the maintenance, renovation and repair of a building or parts of a building'. *See* Art. 31a(2)(k) Implementing Regulation.
62. European Commission, *supra* n. 48, at 29.
63. European Commission, *supra* n. 48, at 26.

implications. Pursuant to Article 135(1)(l) of the VAT Directive, the leasing or letting of immovable property is, in fact, an activity exempt from EU VAT, whereas, according to Article 135(2)(a) of the VAT Directive, the same exemption does not apply to 'the provision of accommodation, as defined in the laws of the Member States, in the hotel sector or in sectors with a similar function'.[64]

The problem is that, neither the VAT Directive, nor the Implementing Regulation, provide a definition of either 'leasing or letting of immovable property' (in French, '*l'affermage et la location de biens immeubles*'; in Italian, '*l'affitto e la locazione di beni immobili*') or 'the provision of accommodation in the hotel sector or in sectors with a similar function' (in French, '*les opérations d'hébergement telles qui sont effectuées dans le cadre du secteur hôtelier ou de secteurs ayant une fonction similaire*'; in Italian, '*le prestazioni di alloggio effettuate nel settore alberghiero o in settori aventi funzioni analoghe*'). In order to determine the precise meaning of those expressions, it is therefore necessary to rely on the CJEU's case law.[65] As regards the former expression, some indications can be found, notably, in *Temco Europe,* where the Court defined the concept of leasing or letting of immovable property 'as essentially the conferring by a landlord on a tenant, for an agreed period and in return for payment, of the right to occupy property as if that person were the owner and to exclude any other person from enjoyment of such a right'.[66] Pursuant to such definition, the leasing or letting of immovable property, therefore, entails: (1) the right to occupy an immovable property as owner, (2) for an agreed period, (3) for consideration, and (4) to the exclusion of others. With specific regard to the latter point, the Court further considered that the existence of some restrictions on the right to occupy the let premises does not prevent that occupation being exclusive as regards all other persons not permitted by law or by the contract to exercise a right over the property which is the subject of the leasing or letting contract.[67] The CJEU has also explained that the definition of leasing or letting of immovable property in the VAT Directive is broader than the corresponding concept entailed under the various national laws and, indeed, it includes also a contract for a hotel room.[68] The provision of accommodation in the hotel sector or in sectors with a similar function is, therefore, to be plainly included in the concept of 'lease', although one of short duration[69] and, further, despite entailing a more active exploitation of

64. However, it ought to be recalled that Art. 137(1)(d) of the VAT Directive gives Member States the possibility to grant taxable persons the right to opt for taxation in respect of the leasing or letting of immovable property.
65. Noteworthy, both these expressions shall receive a definition based on EU law only. In this connection, with specific regard to the expression 'leasing and letting of immovable property', *see* SW: Opinion of the Advocate General, 26 Sep. 2000, Case C-150/99, *Svenska Staten (Swedish State) v. Stockholm Lindöpark AB and Stockholm Lindöpark AB v. Svenska staten (Swedish State)*, para. 29.
66. BE: ECJ, 18 Nov. 2004, Case C-284/03, *Belgian State v. Temco Europe SA*, para. 19.
67. *Temco Europe* (C-284/03), para. 25.
68. IR: ECJ, 12 Sep. 2000, Case C-358/97, *Commission of the European Communities v. Ireland*, para. 54; UK: ECJ, 12 Sep. 2000, Case C-359/97, *Commission of the European Communities v. United Kingdom of Great Britain and Northern Ireland*, para. 66.
69. For a similar appraisal, *see Macdonald Resorts* (C-270/09), paras 43-44. Against this contention, *see instead* Opinion *Stockholm Lindöpark* (C-150/99), at footnote 18, arguing that the exclusion of the provision of hotel or similar accommodation from the exemption for leasing or letting of

immovable property, in the sense that those kinds of leases might also include the provision of complementary services in addition to the supply of bare accommodation.[70]

As stated, pursuant to Article 135(2)(a) of the VAT Directive, such kinds of leases, however, are excluded from the exemption provided for in Article 135(1)(l) of VAT Directive. Notably, the applicability of EU VAT to services consisting in the provision of accommodation in the hotel sector or in sectors with a similar function was specifically confirmed by the CJEU in *Blasi*. In that case, the Court had to provide a concrete definition of the expression 'sectors with a similar function' and, in particular, it was asked to establish whether a lease of residential premises for less than six months could be included within such definition. In this connection, the Court reasoned that such a phrase cannot be interpreted strictly, but instead it must receive a 'broad construction', although, at the same time, the CJEU plainly admitted that Member States enjoy a certain 'margin of discretion' in this regard.[71] As observed by Advocate General Jacobs in that case, in fact, 'the words "sectors with a similar function" should be given a broad construction since their purpose is to ensure that the provision of temporary accommodation similar to, and hence in potential competition with, that provided in the hotel sector is subject to tax'.[72] The Advocate General further reasoned that 'it is true that the short-term letting of residential property may not entail all of the additional supplies of goods and services, such as the provision of meals and drinks, cleaning of rooms, provision of bed linen etc., normally provided in hotels. Nevertheless, there can be no doubt that a taxable person offering, for example, short-term holiday lets of residential property fulfils essentially the same function as – and is in a competitive relationship with – a taxable person in the hotel sector', thus concluding that 'the essential distinction between such lettings and exempt lettings of residential property is the temporary nature of the accommodation'.[73] The fact that Article 31a(2)(l) of the Implementing Regulation is to be interpreted broadly gains further confirmation in the explanatory notes on this matter issued by the Commission. In this connection, the explanatory notes in fact underline that 'any accommodation service subject to VAT (i.e., considered as a taxable supply) can qualify as connected

---

immovable property 'does not necessarily imply that the provision of *all* such accommodation would necessarily have fallen within the exemption; it may be that the Community [now EU] legislator merely sought to ensure that such accommodation was always treated in the same way, regardless of whether it fell with the definition of "leasing and letting" or not' (emphasis original).

70. NL: ECJ, 4 Oct. 2001, Case C-326/99, *Stichting 'Goed Wonen' v. Staatssecretaris van Financiën*, paras 52-53.
71. DE: ECJ, 12 Feb. 1998, Case C-346/95, *Elisabeth Blasi v. Finanzamt München I*, paras 17-27.
72. DE: Opinion of the Advocate General, 25 Sep. 1997, Case C-346/95, *Elisabeth Blasi v. Finanzamt München I*, para. 18.
73. Opinion *Blasi* (C-346/95), para. 19.

with immovable property under Article 31a(2)(1), regardless of the type of accommodation that is involved in the supply of the service (a room in a hotel, an apartment, a bungalow, a tree house, a yurt, a camping site, etc.)'.[74]

Ultimately, the decisive criterion in order to classify the leasing or letting of an immovable property as an 'ordinary lease', which is exempt under EU VAT, or rather as a lease consisting in the provision of accommodation in the hotel sector or in sectors with a similar function, which is a fully taxable transaction under EU VAT, relates to the nature and the characteristics of the supply at stake. Indeed, precisely the nature and the characteristics of the supply at stake, consisting in a long-term right to occupy a reserved residence, rather than the nature and the characteristics of the property itself, were decisive, in *Fortyseven Park Street*, for the UK Upper-Tier Tribunal to consider the supply in question as an 'ordinary' lease, as such, a supply to be exempt under EU VAT. Notably, despite the owner of the residential property in question received a number of hotel-style facilities (e.g., *conciergerie*, guest lounge, cloakrooms, in-room dining facilities), by examining the nature and the characteristics of the supply at stake, the UK Upper-Tier Tribunal found that such supply concerned a right entailing more than short-term accommodation and, further, it did not correspond to any supply which would typically be expected to be made in the hotel sector.[75]

[D] Services Connected with Immovable Property in the Sharing Economy

[1] Underlying Services in the Sharing Economy

The analysis made in the previous sections confirms that, precisely based on the nature and the characteristics of what is actually supplied, services provided by hosts to guests on sharing economy platforms like Airbnb and HomeExchange are to be seen as accommodation services akin to those provided by traditional hoteliers, to which the special place of supply rule contained in Article 47 of the VAT Directive applies and, further, which are subject to EU VAT pursuant to Article 135(2)(a) of the same Directive. The two services in question, i.e., the provision of short-term accommodation by users on sharing economy platforms and by traditional hoteliers, are in fact in competition with each other. Indeed, those two services essentially fulfil the same function, that is to provide short-term accommodation to travellers. The circumstance that the former type of lease might not also include the provision of additional goods and/or services, such as meals, drinks, daily room cleaning, or other kinds of amenities, as instead a hotel commonly offers to its own guests, is immaterial in this regard.

74. European Commission, *supra* n. 48, at 38. It also ought to be recalled that the CJEU has affirmed that, in some instances, even a houseboat can qualify as an immovable property. *See* DE: ECJ, 15 Nov. 2012, Case C-532/11, *Susanne Leichenich v. Ansbert Peffekoven and Ingo Horeis*, para. 29.

75. UK: Upper-Tier Tribunal, Tax and Chancery Chamber, 12 Feb. 2018, *HMRC v. Fortyseven Park Street Ltd* [2018] UKUT 0041 (TCC).

As for the distinction between hotel-like accommodation and an 'ordinary' lease of immovable property, the relevant criterion established for this purpose, first, by the CJEU in *Blasi* and, then, by the UK Upper-Tier Tribunal in *Fortyseven Park Street* relates to the duration of the rental. Transactions among users on sharing economy platform usually entail the provision of accommodation on a short-term duration. Accordingly, those services could not be seen as 'ordinary' leases of immovable property. It also ought to be considered that an 'ordinary' lease of immovable property usually entails a more 'passive activity' than accommodation services on Airbnb or HomeExchange, which, indeed, require a lessor to carry out a series of operations, such as listing and describing the property offered on the platform, updating availabilities, responding to booking requests and, presumably, cleaning the property before and after each rental. The same kinds of considerations apply even if the booked accommodation service does not ultimately take place, but the guest is nevertheless charged with a cancellation fee, as it occurs on Airbnb.[76]

[2] Particular Cases: 'Experiences' on Airbnb

A more challenging question arises in relation to additional services which might be offered, together with the provision of bare accommodation, by hosts to guests on a sharing economy platform. Notably, this is the case of 'experiences' (e.g., equitation lessons or wine-tasting itineraries) offered by hosts to guests on Airbnb, other than the provision of straight accommodation.[77] From the analysis made in the previous sections, it seems that those types of services shall be regarded as services connected with immovable property, which are subject to the special place of supply rule contained in Article 47 of the VAT Directive. As seen, the scope of Article 47 of the VAT Directive is, in fact, quite broad. As observed in the explanatory notes on this matter issued by the Commission, even 'the fact that a service is provided off-site, not directly to the owner of the immovable property or to a client located in a country different from the country where the immovable property is located is not decisive on its own when the service is assessed (as connected or not with immovable property)'.[78] And indeed, as further stipulated therein, 'each case must be judged objectively taking into account the factual circumstances at stake, the definition of immovable property provided by

76. *See* UK: ECJ, 15 Dec. 1993, Case C-63/92, *Lubbock Fine & Co. v. Commissioners of Customs and Excise*, para. 10, in which the CJEU reasoned that the term 'letting of immovable property' does also cover 'the case where a tenant surrenders his lease and returns the immovable property to his immediate landlord'. A similar consideration can be found in the explanatory notes issued on this matter by the Commission, stipulating that 'Article 31a(2)(p) will also apply even when the sale, leasing, letting, establishment of transfer of certain interests in immovable property or right in rem over immovable property does not finally take place'. *See* European Commission, *supra* n. 48, at 45.
77. *See* section §2.07[A].
78. European Commission, *supra* n. 48, at 12. In this regard, *see also* PT: ECJ, 28 Feb. 2019, Case C-278/18, *Manuel Jorge Sequeira Mesquita v. Fazenda Pública*, para. 35, where the Court concluded that the leasing or letting of immovable property also includes the transfer of the use of a land comprising vineyards for agricultural purposes to a company engaged in viticulture, despite such an activity, clearly, involves a more active use of the lent property rather than an ordinary lease of immovable property.

Article 13b and the provisions of Article 31a'.[79] Based on such broad understanding, it could be maintained that – say – even an 'experience' consisting in an equitation lesson provided by a host to a guest on Airbnb in the proximity of the leased property is to be considered as a service 'sufficiently connected' with the immovable property concerned. Figure 7.4 below depicts this scenario graphically.

Figure 7.4 'Experience' on Airbnb: Equitation Lesson

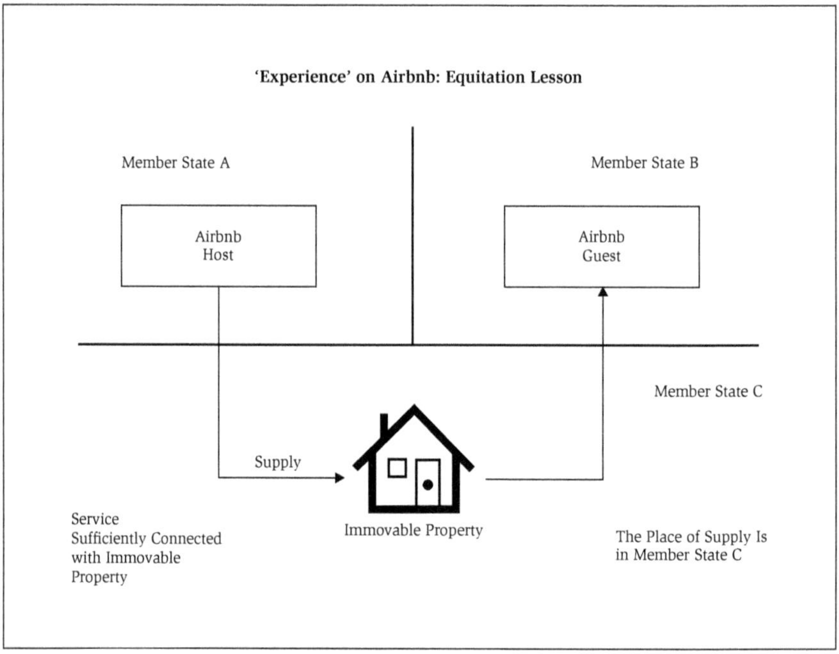

There are, however, a few instances which might eventually alter such an assessment. As reasoned by Advocate General Jacobs in *Stockholm Lindöpark*, for a service to be classified as a leasing or letting of immovable property, 'the characteristics of a lease should predominate in the contract' concluded between the supplier and the customer.[80] This circumstance presupposes a careful evaluation of both the number and the value of all the services offered, in particular whether the offering of additional services prevails over the provision of bare accommodation. Should, indeed, this be the case, then the services in question would no longer consist in the provision of accommodation, rather they would entail the supply of a 'complex' service, which, for EU VAT purposes, is to be assessed in light of the CJEU's doctrine on composite

79. European Commission, *supra* n. 48, at 27.
80. Opinion *Stockholm Lindöpark* (C-150/99), para. 36. *See also* UK: Opinion of the Advocate General, 27 Jan. 2000, Case C-359/97, *Commission of the European Communities v. United Kingdom of Great Britain and Northern Ireland*, para. 76.

supplies.[81] As a result, the services in question might receive, for EU VAT purposes, either a separate treatment, under the main 'splitting' rule, or the same treatment if, under the 'first exception' to the main rule, those services form a single supply from an economic point of view, or if, under the 'second exception' to the main rule, one of the two services is ancillary to the other. The intervention of the CJEU's doctrine on composite supplies or other alternative approaches to it might, ultimately, rule out the application of the special place of supply rule contained in Article 47 of the VAT Directive. By way of example, an 'experience' consisting in a wine-tasting itinerary offered by a host to a guest on Airbnb, whether its value is far greater than the provision of accommodation, so that the overall consideration paid is primarily made by the former rather than by the latter service, might lead to conclude that the service in question, in no event, is to be considered as connected with an immovable property, rather it relates to the supply of a more 'complex' service, which, in the light of the CJEU's doctrine on composite supplies, must be dealt with under other place of supply rules - in the example above, most likely Article 54 of the VAT Directive concerning, *inter alia*, services relating to 'educational, entertainment or similar activities', which stipulates that the place of supply of the services in question shall be the place where those activities actually take place.[82] Figure 7.5 below depicts this scenario graphically.

81. For a discussion of the CJEU's doctrine on composite supplies, *see* Chapter 6.
82. A quite illuminating example in this regard was provided by Advocate General Jacobs in *Stockholm Lindöpark* in relation to a golf course: '[i]f a person or entity were to pay for the exclusive use of a course for a specified period - say, in order to organize a tournament or championship - with a concomitant right to charge entrance fees for players and/or spectators, that would appear to partake fairly clearly of the nature of a lease or let. The same would not apply, however, to the casual golfer or group of golfers coming to play a round. Whilst it is obviously difficult to play golf without a course to play it on, the service provided in that case is the opportunity to play the game and not the opportunity to occupy the course. Indeed, a golfer may be thought of not as occupying the course in any sense but as traversing it. He or she has the right merely to move from one part of a golf course to the next, at a pace usually determined in part by other users of the course, for the sole purpose of enjoying the facilities provided at each stage. In that, the first 18 holes do not perhaps differ - in essence - from the 19th'. *See* Opinion *Stockholm Lindöpark* (C-150/99), para. 35.

Figure 7.5 'Experience' on Airbnb: Wine-Tasting Itinerary

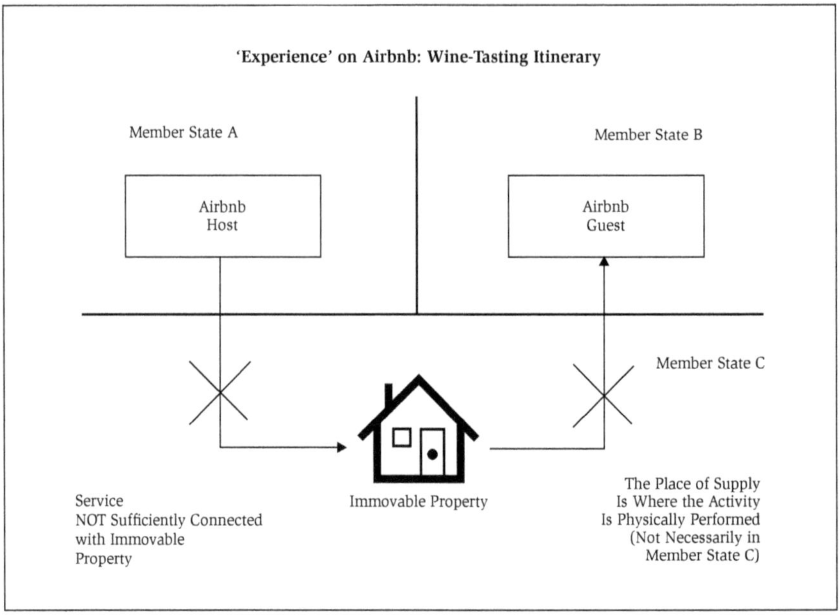

[3] Platform Services in the Sharing Economy

The treatment, for place of supply purposes, of services provided by sharing economy platforms like Airbnb and HomeExchange both to hosts and guests, instead, require a separate appraisal. In essence, those services aim to facilitate the provision of accommodation among platform users. Based on their ultimate function, the services in question can, therefore, be regarded as intermediary services. As stated, detailed rules concerning intermediary services relating to the provision of accommodation are contained in the Implementing Regulation. Notably, Article 31a(2)(p) of the Implementing Regulation stipulates that Article 47 of the VAT Directive also covers 'intermediation in the sale, leasing or letting of immovable property', thus extending the scope, de facto, of this latter article beyond the services of experts and estate agents, two types of services expressly mentioned in the wording of Article 47 and, as such, already regarded as services connected with immovable property.[83] By contrast, Article 31a(3)(d) of the Implementing Regulation stipulates that 'intermediation in the provision of hotel accommodation or accommodation in sectors with a similar function, such as holiday camps or sites developed for use as camping sites, if the intermediary

83. *See also* European Commission, *supra* n. 48, at 45.

is acting in the name and on behalf of another person' does not fall within the scope of Article 47 of the VAT Directive.[84]

In this latter situation, in practice, the intermediary is seen as supplying mediation rather than straight accommodation. The author submits that this is, indeed, the situation of services provided by sharing economy platforms like Airbnb and HomeExchange to their users. Such platform services, therefore, must be treated as intermediary services, to be dealt with, if relating to a B2B transaction, under the default place of supply rule of Article 44, which refers to the place where the customer has established his business, whereas, if relating to a B2C transaction, under the default place of supply rule of Article 46, which instead refers to the place of the underlying transaction.[85] In case of B2C transactions, the place of supply of those platform services, therefore, is the place where the immovable property in question is located, although not based on Article 47 of the VAT Directive, but pursuant to Article 46 of the same Directive. A confirmation of such an interpretation can eventually be gleaned from a reading of Article 31 of the Implementing Regulation and of the guidelines on this matter issued by the VAT Committee.[86] Figure 7.6 below depicts this scenario graphically, using, by way of example, services provided by Airbnb to its users.

Figure 7.6 Intermediary Services by Airbnb

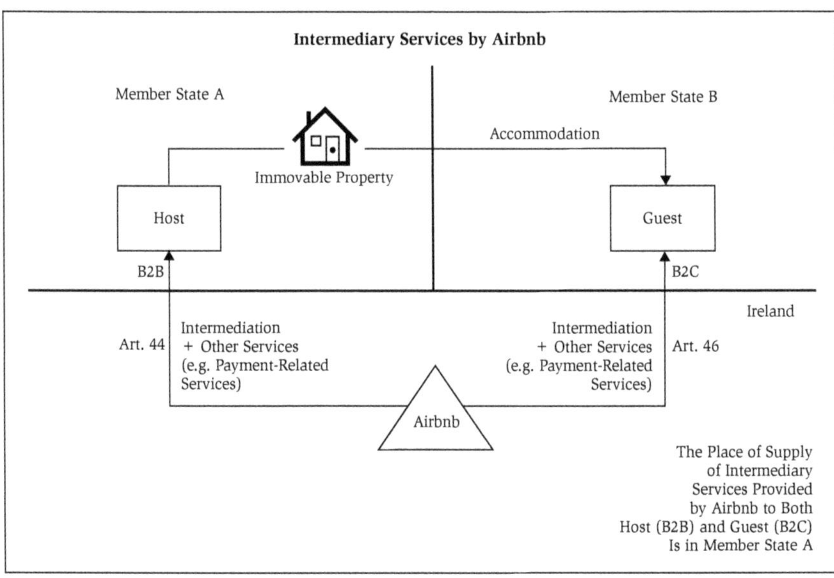

84. *See also* European Commission, Value Added Tax Committee, *Guidelines resulting from the 93rd Meeting of 1 July 2011 – Document A* (taxud.c.1(2012)400557 – 707).
85. *See* section §7.09[B].
86. European Commission, Value Added Tax Committee, *Guidelines resulting from the 88th Meeting of 30 Sept. 2009* (taxud.d.1(2009)405067 – 639).

What if, instead, the intermediary (i.e., the sharing economy platform) does not act in the name of another person but, instead, in his own name? Arguably, the services in question could no longer be regarded as intermediary services, which fall within the scope of either Article 44 or 46 of the VAT Directive, depending on whether they relate to B2B or B2C transactions. In such event, the services in question should, more properly, be characterized as 'ordinary' services, circumstance which triggers the application of the default place of supply rules laid down in Article 44 or 45 of the VAT Directive, again depending on whether the transaction is B2B or B2C. The same classification might also apply in the – in the author's opinion, unlikely – event that, based on their nature and characteristics, platform services could not be classified in any other manner.[87] Figure 7.7 below depicts this scenario graphically, using, by way of example, services provided by Airbnb to its users.

Figure 7.7 Intermediary (Airbnb) Acting in Its Own Name

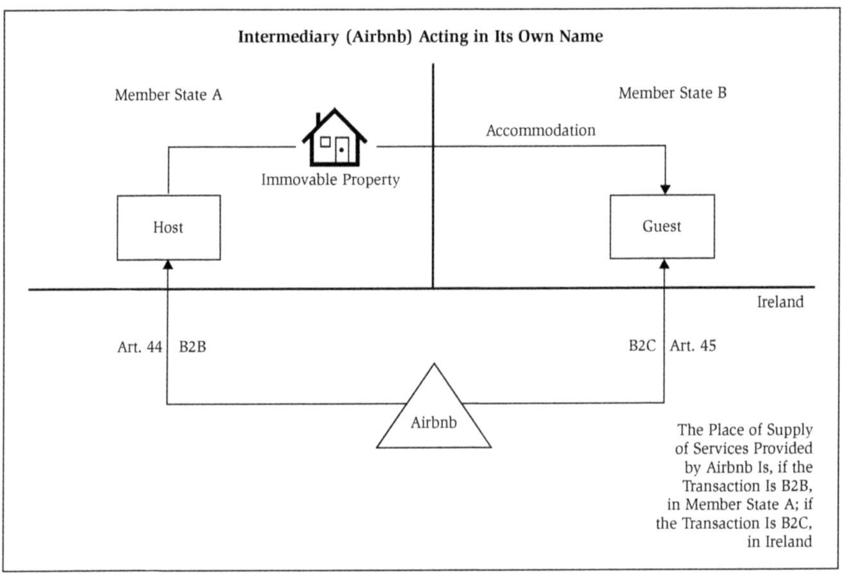

A different conclusion ought to be reached if the intermediary (i.e., the sharing economy platform) acts in his own name and, yet, on behalf of another person. In such event, the platform is no longer considered, for EU VAT purposes, based on the deemed

87. *See* European Commission, Value Added Tax Committee, *Working Paper No. 947, Services Provided by an Electronic Platform Connecting for Remuneration, by means of a Smartphone Application, a Driver Using His Own Vehicle with Persons Who Wish to Make Urban Journeys. The Significance of the VAT Identification Number*, at 14 (taxud.c.1(2018)1735106), considering that, indeed, this possibility exists where: (1) platform services do not meet the characteristics of any other service, (2) there is a composite supply by the platform and its main element is none of any other service, or (3) there is a composite supply by the platform and no main element can be ascertained, since all the component elements bear the same importance.

rule contained in Article 28 of the VAT Directive, as an intermediary, but rather as a 'full-fledged supplier' of the underlying service, concerning the provision of either accommodation or passenger transport. The intervention of the provision contained in Article 28 of the VAT Directive, in fact, extends the place of supply rule applicable to the underlying transaction also to the supply of the related services provided by the platform to its users. Thus, in case of services rendered to hosts and/or to guests by platforms like Airbnb and HomeExchange, these services are treated as accommodation services to which Article 47 of the VAT Directive applies. Indeed, such characterization is not expressly excluded either by the wording of Article 47 of the VAT Directive or by that of Article 31a(3)(d) of the Implementing Regulation, pursuant to which 'intermediation in the provision of hotel accommodation or accommodation in sectors with a similar function' does not fall within the scope of Article 47 of the VAT Directive only 'if the intermediary is acting *in the name and on behalf of another person*' and not, instead, also if the intermediary (i.e., the platform) is acting '*in his own name but on behalf of another person*', as expressly stipulated by Article 28 of the VAT Directive (emphases added). Figure 7.8 below depicts this scenario graphically, using, by way of example, services provided by Airbnb to its users.

Figure 7.8 Intermediary (Airbnb) Acting in Its Own Name and on Behalf of Another Person

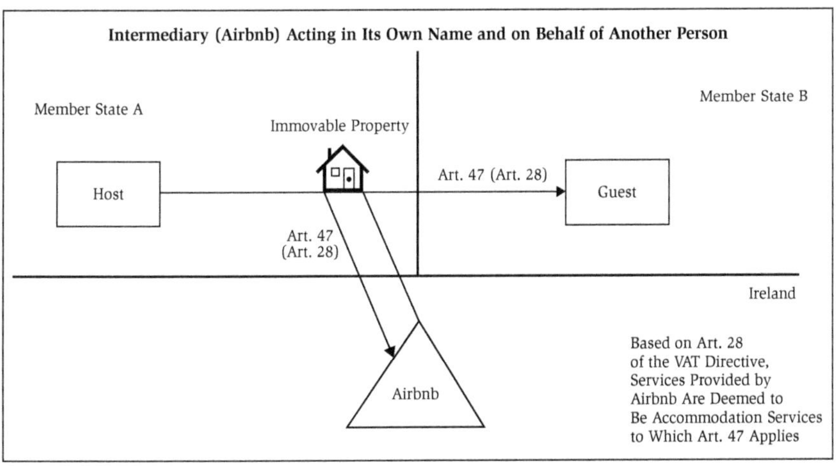

In case of B2C transactions, a further possibility indeed exists, i.e., that the services provided by a sharing economy platform to its users are characterized as electronically supplied services pursuant to Article 58 of the VAT Directive, stipulating that the place of supply is where the customer is established, has his permanent address, or usually resides. As observed by the explanatory notes on this matter issued by the Commission, 'indeed it cannot be excluded that, for example, thanks to modern technologies, some services connected with immovable property can be supplied not only on-site but also at a distance'.[88] In view of this eventuality, Article 31c of the Implementing Regulation thus prescribes that, 'for the purpose of determining the place of supply of telecommunications, broadcasting or electronically supplied services provided by a taxable person acting in his own name together with accommodation in the hotel sector or in sectors with a similar function, such as holiday camps or sites developed for use as camping sites, those services shall be regarded as being supplied at those locations'.[89] This statement accords with the fact that, as entailed in Article 7(3)(u) of the Implementing Regulation, the definition of electronically supplied services does not cover 'accommodation, car-hire, restaurant services, passenger transport or similar services booked online'. Arguably, the aforementioned provisions aim to clarify that those intermediary services, consisting in the booking of services having a 'tangible' nature and provided by disclosed agents[90], ought not to be seen as electronically supplied services. Indeed, this line of reasoning was also upheld by the VAT Committee, which observed that 'disconnecting an intermediation service from the underlying service puts at risk revenue of the Member State of consumption and artificially divides two very closely associated supplies'.[91] There are further reasons which might uphold this interpretation, such as the circumstance that taxing intermediary services at the place of supply of the related underlying services ensures that place of supply rules are applied in the simplest way possible as to accommodate the situation of a cross-border trade.[92] Should this reconstruction be confirmed, then these types of intermediary services, even if supplied via electronic means, would fall within the scope of the special place of supply rule for services connected with immovable property, since this is, indeed, the nature and the characteristics of the underlying transaction to which Article 46 of the VAT Directive concerning intermediary services makes reference. As a result, the place of supply of those intermediary services would be the place where the immovable property concerned is located. As will be explained later in this

88. European Commission, *supra* n. 48, at 11.
89. In this regard, the explanatory notes on electronically supplied services issued by the Commission further specify that 'for Article 31c to apply there must be a distinct supply of these services where the customer is required to pay separately'. *See* European Commission, *Explanatory Notes on the EU VAT Changes to the Place of Supply of Telecommunications, Broadcasting and Electronic Services that Enter into Force in 2015 (Council Implementing Regulation (EU) No 1042/2013)*, at 74 (2015), https://ec.europa.eu/taxation_customs/sites/taxation/files/resources/documents/taxation/vat/how_vat_works/telecom/explanatory_notes_2015_en.pdf (accessed 31 Mar. 2019).
90. In the sense of being linked with a 'tangible' proxy, like the location of a tangible property or to a specific location where the performance or event takes place. *See* Ecker, *supra* n. 11, at para. 17.3.3.3.1. Noteworthy, supplies made by undisclosed agents, being by statutory definition (i.e., pursuant to Art. 28 of the VAT Directive) of the same nature of the services that those agents themselves receive, instead, are certainly covered by Art. 7(3)(u) of the Implementing Regulation and, as such, excluded from the scope of electronically supplied services. *See* European Commission, Value Added Tax Committee, *Working Paper No. 906, VAT 2015: Interaction between Electronically Supplied Services and Intermediation Services and Initial Discussion on the Scope of the Concept of Intermediation Services when Taken in a Broader Context*, at 3 (taxud.c.1(2016)3297911). For a discussion in this regard, *see* section §7.09[C].
91. European Commission, Value Added Tax Committee, *supra* n. 90, at 5. *See also* European Commission, Value Added Tax Committee, *Working Paper No. 814, Treatment of Online Supplies Made by a Travel Agent to Final Consumers*, at 12 (taxud.c.1(2014)2806510).
92. European Commission, Value Added Tax Committee, *supra* n. 90, at 5.

chapter[93], the potential intersection, especially in case of B2C transactions, of different place of supply rules, namely, those contained in Articles 45, 46, 47, and 58 of the VAT Directive, may render the application of EU VAT rather complex in an individual case, with the risk of either double taxation or non-taxation, due to a cross-border service being considered by the Member States concerned under different place of supply rules.[94]

§7.06 PASSENGER TRANSPORT SERVICES

[A] Relevant Definitions and Rules

Already the Proposal for a Second Directive contained a special rule for transport services, which, indeed, concerned not only passengers but also goods. Notably, such special rule provided that 'transport services shall be deemed to be used or exploited within the territory of the Member State where the transport takes place, and, when transport takes place in the territory of two or more Member States, within the territories of these Member States in proportion to the respective distances covered in each'.[95]

Both the proposal and the wording of the Sixth Directive, as finally adopted, contained an almost identical rule. In particular, the wording of Article 9(2)(b) of the original Sixth Directive stipulated that 'the place where transport services are supplied shall be the place where transport takes place, having regard to the distances covered'.

Although a proposal was submitted by the Commission in 1992 for taxing supplies of all transport services in the Member State of departure[96], Article 48 of the VAT Directive did not change the 'territoriality rule'[97] relating to passenger transport services, which, therefore, continues being the place where transport actually takes place, proportionate to the distances covered. Notably, Article 48 of the VAT Directive reads as follows: 'the place of supply of passenger transport shall be the place where the transport takes place, proportionate to the distances covered'. Thus, pursuant to this rule, when passenger transport is carried out in the territories of various countries, VAT is due in every country where the transport actually takes place.

93. *See* sections §7.07–§7.09.
94. The risk of either double taxation or non-taxation in this regard was expressly mentioned in the proceedings of a public consultation launched by the Commission in 2007. *See* European Commission, *Report on the Outcome of the Consultation on 'Introduction of a Mechanism for Eliminating Double Imposition of VAT in Individual Cases'*, at 3 (TAXUD/D1/EWS/MAV D (2007) 15925).
95. European Commission, *Proposal for a Second Directive for the Harmonization among Member States of Turnover Tax Legislation, concerning the Form and Methods of Application of the Common System of Taxation on Value Added*, at Annex A 11 Third Indent, COM(65) 144 final, Supplement to the Bulletin of the European Economic Community No. 5 (1965).
96. European Commission, *Proposal for a Council Directive amending Directive 77/388/EEC as regards the Value Added Tax Arrangements Applicable to Passenger Transport*, COM(92) 416 final. However, due to a lack of the sufficient consensus to be adopted, the proposal in question was finally withdrawn in 1996.
97. *Id.*, at 1.

While discussing its proposal for changing the (then) applicable place of supply rules, which, however, maintained the 'territoriality rule' for passenger transport services, the Commission observed that the special place of supply rule for those services constitutes an exception to the default place of supply rules for both B2B and B2C transactions. As it was with the case of services connected with immovable property, the same rule, in fact, applies to both types of transactions. In this connection, the line of reasoning maintained by the Commission was that it is difficult, for interpretative and administrative reasons, to have different place of supply rules for B2B and B2C passenger transport services.[98]

Nevertheless, it is clear enough that the rule does not contribute in any meaningful way to a minimization of the administrative burden for a taxable person. A supplier of passenger transport services, in fact, needs to register for VAT and charge the tax to his customer in every country where the transport actually takes place, unless the reverse charge mechanism is applicable under a national VAT legislation.[99] Despite such a drawback, as emerged from a public consultation launched by the Commission in 2005, the general consensus is that, although existing rules governing the determination of the place of supply of passenger transport are difficult to apply, so that a shift in favour of taxation at the place of departure, undoubtedly, would represent a major simplification in this regard, the current rule is consistent with the objective to tax passenger transport services at the place of actual consumption.[100]

Importantly, the rule of Article 48 of the VAT Directive provides for the place where passenger transport services are to be taxed, but it does not also establish whether those services are actually taxed, as long as the services in question might be exempt with or without the right for the supplier to deduct his input VAT.[101] In this connection, in *Idéal Tourisme*, the CJEU considered that the principle of equal treatment does not preclude a legislation of a Member State which exempts international passenger transport by air, whereas it taxes international passenger transport by coach.[102] Further, although the rule does not concern, in principle, the method for determining the taxable amount in respect of the supply of transport services, its concrete operation inevitably affects the allocation to be made, when the taxable amount is determined on an all-inclusive basis, between the Member States in which

98. European Commission, *Proposal for a Council Directive amending Directive 77/388/EEC as regards the Place of Supply of Services*, at 7, COM(2003) 822 final.

99. In this connection, the OECD International VAT/GST Guidelines stipulates that 'the general rule based on the place of physical performance ... in respect of on-the-spot supplies of services and intangibles, might not lead to an appropriate result ... where the physical performance occurs in multiple jurisdictions because tax obligations could arise in multiple jurisdictions .... An example is the international transport of persons'. *See* OECD, *supra* n. 11, at 83.

100. European Commission, *supra* n. 46, at 4.

101. Notably, international passenger road transport services are generally exempt in Italy and in Luxembourg. France and the Netherlands, instead, subject those services to a reduced rate, whereas the standard national VAT rate normally applies in Bulgaria and in Germany. *See* European Commission, *VAT Rates Applied in the Member States of the European Union* (2019), https://ec.europa.eu/taxation_customs/sites/taxation/files/resources/documents/taxation/vat/how_vat_works/rates/vat_rates_en.pdf (accessed 31 Mar. 2019).

102. BE: ECJ, 13 Jul. 2000, Case C-36/99, *Idéal Tourisme SA v. Belgian State*, para. 40.

the supply is effected.[103] Lastly, as regards the apportionment according to the proportion of the distances covered, in *Reisebüro Binder*, the CJEU confirmed that the allocation on a pro-rata basis, having regard to the distances covered in each of the Member States concerned, is the only allowed method.[104]

[B] Passenger Transport Services in the Sharing Economy

[1] Underlying Services in the Sharing Economy

There is little or no doubt that services provided by users among themselves on sharing economy platforms like Uber and BlaBlaCar are to be characterized as passenger transport services. Therefore, for these services, the relevant place of supply rule is provided by Article 48 of the VAT Directive. Notably, pursuant to such a rule, the driver must charge the passenger with the VAT of the country where the transport actually takes place. Should a passenger transport be operated cross-border, then the driver would have to register (if not already established therein), collect, and remit the VAT due in every country where the transport actually takes place. More precisely, the VAT levied on the overall consideration that the driver receives from the passenger needs to be split and attributed to the tax authorities of every Member State in proportion to the distances covered in the territory of each country. However, if road transport services are exempt in one country, then no VAT would, in fact, be due by the driver in that country. Figure 7.9 below depicts this scenario graphically, using, by way of example, services provided by a BlaBlaCar driver.

103. DE: ECJ, 6 Nov. 1997, Case C-116/96, *Reisebüro Binder GmbH v. Finanzamt Stuttgart-Körperschaften*, para. 15.
104. *Id.*, para. 17.

Figure 7.9 Passenger Transport Services on BlaBlaCar

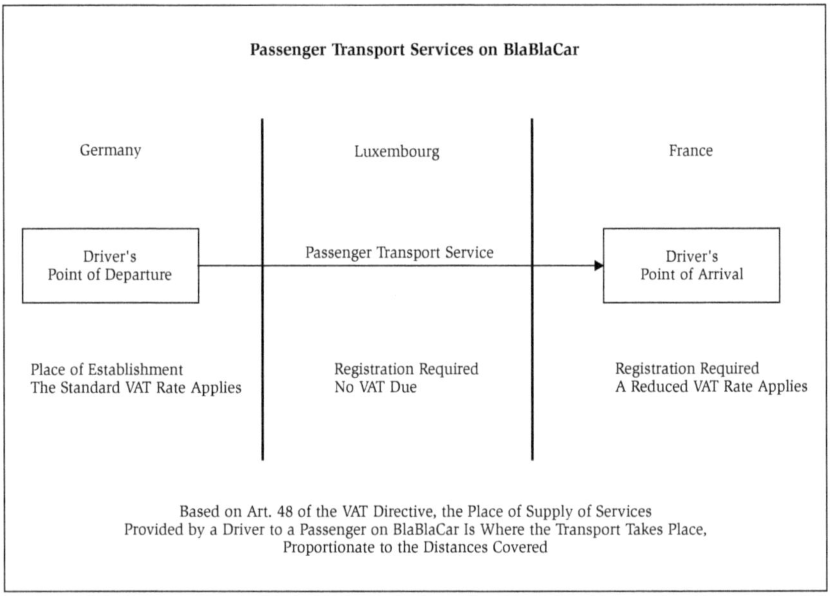

[2] Platform Services in the Sharing Economy

Services provided by sharing economy platforms like Uber and BlaBlaCar both to drivers and passengers are, instead, much more difficult to assess for place of supply purposes. Should, in fact, these services be characterized as intermediary services, then the rules of either Article 44, if the transaction is B2B, or Article 46 of the VAT Directive, if the transaction is B2C, would apply.[105] Indeed, the classification of a transaction as B2B or B2C would change in relation to the specific party, i.e., the driver or the passenger, toward which the services in question are provided. Notably, BlaBlaCar charges only the passenger for its own intermediary services. Nearly in all cases, the passenger is an end consumer, which means that the transaction in question is B2C and Article 46 of the VAT Directive, thus, applies.[106] Pursuant to the rule contained in that article, the place of supply of an intermediary service is to be found where the underlying transaction is supplied in accordance with the VAT Directive. Since, in this event, the underlying transaction consists in the supply of passenger transport services, for which the place of supply rule is where the transport takes place, proportionate to the distance covered, the same allocation mechanism would also

105. If Art. 28 of the VAT Directive applies, the considerations made above in section §7.05[D][3] would, instead, be valid, with the only difference that the relevant rule would not be that of Art. 47 but, obviously, that contained in Art. 48 of the VAT Directive.
106. *See* section §7.09[B].

apply in relation to the VAT due for the intermediary services provided by BlaBlaCar. Figure 7.10 below depicts this scenario graphically.

Figure 7.10 Intermediary Services by BlaBlaCar

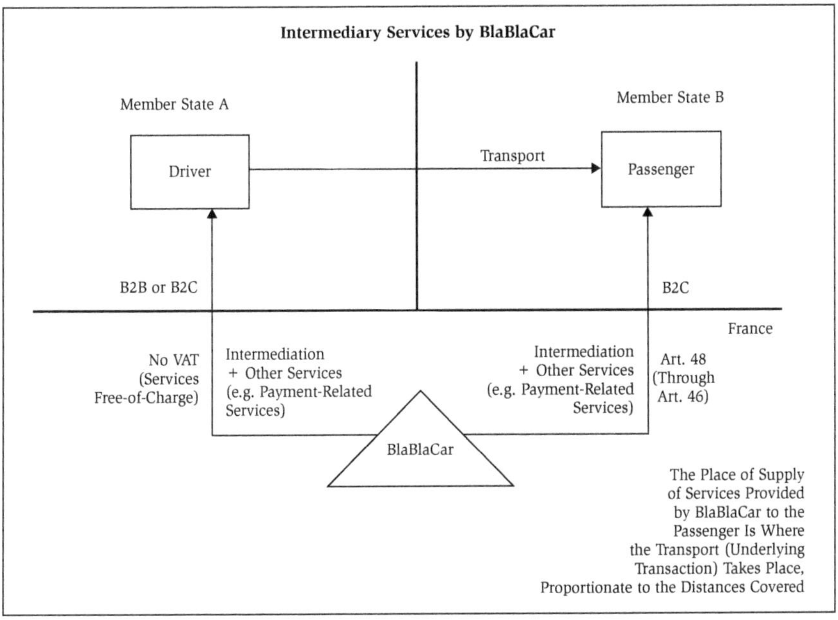

The situation of Uber is outright different, in so far as the company charges only the driver with a fee for its own services. Since, in nearly all cases, the driver is a taxable person[107], the transaction in question is B2B. Should the services provided by Uber be classified as intermediary services relating to passenger transport, then the relevant place of supply rule would be that of Article 44 of the VAT Directive, i.e., the default place of supply rule for B2B supplies, prescribing that the place of supply is where the customer has established his business, maintains a permanent establishment, has his permanent address, or usually resides. Noteworthy, pursuant to such a rule, Uber does not have to charge, in fact, any VAT. Instead, the mandatory reverse charge mechanism contained in Article 196 of the VAT Directive applies, meaning that the customer (i.e., the driver) has to account for the VAT due and remit it to the competent tax authorities.[108] Figure 7.11 below depicts this scenario graphically.

107. However, as seen in section §4.05, a driver might not actually be required to register for EU VAT purposes, in so far as his annual turnover remains below the registration threshold set by a national VAT legislation.
108. For a description of the operation of the reverse charge mechanism, *see* Chapter 8.

Figure 7.11 Intermediary Services by Uber

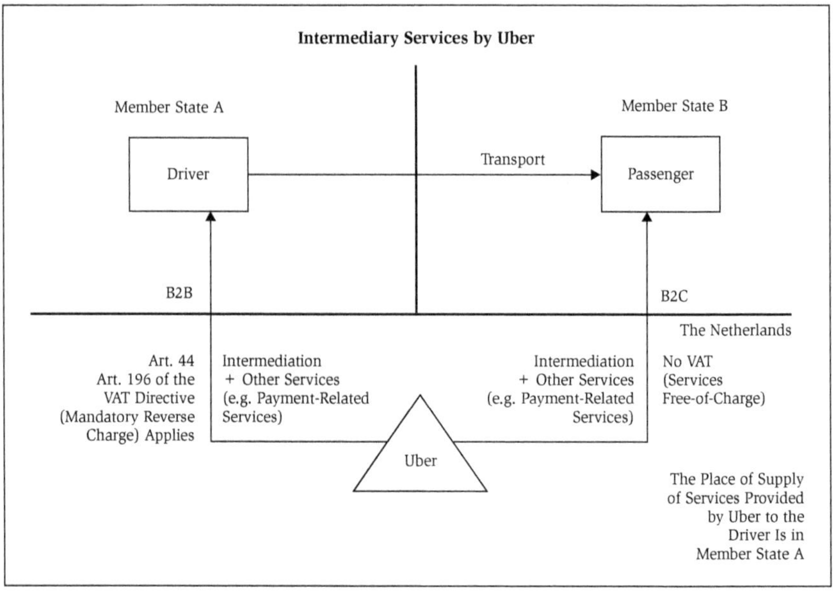

This situation is dissimilar if the driver is not considered independent from the platform, as some courts might find especially in the case of Uber drivers.[109] In such event, no supply for EU VAT purposes would, in fact, exist between the platform and the driver, the latter not being independent from the former. The platform would, then, account and charge the passenger for the transport services physically operated by the driver, in respect of which the place of supply rule contained in Article 48 of the VAT Directive applies. As a result, the platform must account and remit the VAT due for these services in every country where transport actually takes place, proportionate to the distances covered. Such state of play, however, could change substantially where the services provided by a platform in relation to passenger transport are not considered as intermediary services, but rather as electronically supplied services. An analysis in this regard is provided in the following sections.

§7.07 ELECTRONICALLY SUPPLIED SERVICES

[A] Relevant Definitions and Rules

As from 1 July 2003, a new Article 9(2)(f) was introduced in the text of the Sixth Directive (then Article 57 of the VAT Directive, as applicable until 2010), providing that the place of supply of services supplied electronically (commonly abbreviated as

109. *See* section §4.04.

e-services) by a taxable person outside the (then) Community to non-taxable persons established or resident in a Member State was the place where the non-taxable person resided.[110] Simplified procedures for registration and reporting obligations, enabling non-EU suppliers to deal with a single EU tax administration of their own choice, under the so-called OSS mechanism, were also introduced. The overarching purpose of the 2003 changes was to ensure effective taxation of electronically supplied services at place of consumption, thus arguably putting those services on a par with other intangible services, such as those supplied by consultants, engineers, consultancy bureau, lawyers, accountants, and other similar services, which, pursuant to Article 9(2)(e) of the Sixth Directive, were already taxed at the place where the customer was established, had his permanent address, or usually resided.[111]

As from 1 January 2015, the aforementioned rules were extended also to EU suppliers.[112] Accordingly, as from 1 January 2015, all electronically supplied services, concerning either B2B or B2C transactions, are subject to EU VAT in the Member State where the customer is established, has his permanent address, or usually resides. More precisely, if the transaction is B2B, the default place of supply rule contained in Article 44 of the VAT Directive applies. In case of B2C transactions, the relevant place of supply rule is, instead, contained in Article 58 of the VAT Directive. With an aim of simplifying the application of EU VAT for EU businesses supplying to non-taxable persons situated in another Member State, the so-called Mini-One-Stop-Shop (MOSS) scheme was also introduced, which, practically, enables those suppliers to account for the VAT due on their supplies via a web portal in the Member State of identification.[113]

Both the place of supply rules and the administrative obligations relating to electronically supplied services have been interested by a few more recent changes. As from 1 January 2019, paragraphs 2-5 were in fact added to Article 58 of the VAT Directive, providing that, if the total value, exclusive of VAT, of the supplies relating to electronically supplies services does not exceed EUR 10,000 (or the equivalent in national currency) per calendar year, the place of supply of such services rendered to non-taxable persons is where the supplier is established. However, in case the total value of the supplies concerned is below that threshold, suppliers have an option to shift the place of supply where the receiving non-taxable person is located.[114] A further

110. Notably, the provision in question was added to the wording of the Sixth Directive by Council Directive 2002/38/EC of 7 May 2002 amending and amending temporarily Directive 77/388/EEC as regards the Value Added Tax Arrangements Applicable to Radio and Television Broadcasting Services and Certain Electronically Supplied Services, OJ L 128/41 of 15 May 2002.
111. *See* European Commission, *Proposal for a Council Directive amending Council Directive 2002/38/EC as regards the Period of Application of the Value Added Tax Arrangements Applicable to Radio and Television Broadcasting Services and Certain Electronically Supplied Services*, at 2, COM(2006) 739 final.
112. Council Directive 2008/8/EC of 12 February 2008 amending Directive 2006/112/EC as regards the Place of Supply of Services, OJ L 44/11 of 20 Feb. 2008.
113. Notably, the Mini-One-Stop-Shop (MOSS) scheme is laid down in Art. 369a-369k of the VAT Directive.
114. Article 1 of Council Directive (EU) 2017/2455 of 5 December 2017 amending Directive 2006/112/EC and Directive 2009/132/EC as regards Certain Value Added Tax Obligations for Supplies of Services and Distance Sales of Goods, OJ L 348/7 of 29 Dec. 2017.

change is set to take place as from 1 January 2021, when the above paragraphs will be replaced by the new Article 59c of the VAT Directive, establishing a common threshold of EUR 10,000 (or the equivalent in national currency) per calendar year for taxable persons making distance sales of goods or services to non-taxable persons, in respect of which the place of supply will be where the supplier is established.[115]

As from 2011, a definition of electronically supplied services is contained in Article 7(1) of the Implementing Regulation. Notably, the definition reads as follows: '"[e]lectronically supplied services" as referred to in Directive 2006/112/EC shall include services which are delivered over the Internet or an electronic network and the nature of which renders their supply essentially automated and involving minimal human intervention, and impossible to ensure in the absence of information technology'. Based on such definition, four conditions must be fulfilled for a service to qualify as an electronically supplied service:

(1) the service in question must be delivered over the Internet or an electronic network;
(2) it must be essentially automated;
(3) it must involve minimal human intervention;
(4) it must be impossible to ensure in the absence of information technology.

Noteworthy, this definition is future oriented and, therefore, it also applies to all the new types of electronically services which are constantly being developed.[116] The second paragraph of Article 7 and Annex I of the Implementing Regulation also includes an illustrative list of electronically supplied services, which, *inter alia*, mentions: 'website hosting and webpage hosting', 'automated, online and distance maintenance of programmes', 'the supply of digitised products generally, including software and changes to or upgrades of software', or 'the transfer for consideration of the right to put goods or services up for sale on an Internet site operating as an online market on which potential buyers make their bids by an automated procedure and on which the parties are notified of a sale by electronic mail automatically generated from a computer'. However, as the definition of electronically supplied services itself, such a list is by no means exhaustive, so that future technological developments can well be taken into account.

[B] Minimal Human Intervention

Out of the aforementioned four conditions for a service to qualify as an electronically supplied service[117], the most critical one undoubtedly relates to the fact that the service

115. Article 2 of Council Directive 2017/2455/EU.
116. European Commission, Value Added Tax Committee, *Working Paper No. 843, VAT 2015: Scope of the Notion of Electronically Supplied Services*, at 5 (taxud.c.1(2015)694775).
117. In this connection, M. Lamensch, *European Value Added Tax in the Digital Era* at para. 2.2.3.1.2. (IBFD 2015), argues that the last part of the definition of electronically supplied

in question must only involve a 'minimal human intervention' (in French, '*accompagnée d'une intervention humaine minimale*'; in Italian, '*corredata di un intervento umano minimo*').[118] Notably, as underlined by the VAT Committee, this condition must be assessed only based on the relationship between the supplier and the customer and, further, in relation to the supply in question only. Moreover, it is solely the involvement on the side of the supplier and not also that on the side of the customer which is relevant.[119] Accordingly, back-office activities relating to the initial setting up and/or regular maintenance of a system used to supply services to customers do not prevent, by themselves, the services in question to qualify as electronically supplied services.[120] Indeed, inasmuch as a minimum of human intervention is admissible, human intervention does not need to be completely absent for a service to qualify as an electronically supplied service.[121] In this connection, however, the Commission submits that the possibility for the customer to obtain individual feedbacks, to ask questions, or to get tailored advices suffices for a service not to qualify as an e-service anymore, irrespective of whether or not that customer makes actual use of such a possibility.[122]

Nothing, in principle, prevents an intermediary from offering its own services via automated means. Should this indeed be the case, then the services in question would qualify as electronically supplied services. In such event, a classification issue would arise with regard to intermediary services rendered to non-taxable persons.[123] More to the point, a question would occur as to whether, in case of a supply to non-taxable persons of intermediary services, the delivery of which is automated and is made without the intervention of any human resource, the services in question are to be classified as services by intermediaries, which fall under the provision of Article 46 of

services 'seems redundant because information technology is core to the Internet and telecommunication and broadcasting networks, so that it is irrelevant to require that supplies made over the Internet be furthermore made with the use of information technology'.

118. For a discussion, *see* M.M.W.D. Merkx, *VAT and E-Services: When Human Intervention Is Minimal*, 29 Intl. VAT Monitor 1 (2018), Journals IBFD.
119. European Commission, Value Added Tax Committee, *Guidelines resulting from the 102nd Meeting of 30 March 2015 – Document D* (taxud.c.1(2015)4128689 – 862).
120. European Commission, Value Added Tax Committee, *Working Paper No. 843, VAT 2015: Scope of the Notion of Electronically Supplied Services*, at 5 (taxud.c.1(2015)694775).
121. And indeed, 'exceptional interventions' should normally be seen as staying within the minimum level of human intervention. *See* European Commission, Value Added Tax Committee, *Guidelines resulting from the 108th Meeting of 27-28 March 2017 – Document C* (taxud.c.1(2018)2397450 – 930).
122. European Commission, Value Added Tax Committee, *Working Paper No. 919. VAT 2015: Scope of the Notion of Electronically Supplied Services; Minimal Human Intervention (Second Follow-Up)*, at 6-7 (taxud.c.1(2017)1270284).
123. Noteworthy, only when the services in question are supplied to non-taxable persons, i.e., in case of a B2C transaction, an issue would arise with regard to the application of Arts 46 or 58 of the VAT Directive. In case of B2B transactions, for both intermediary and electronically supplied services Art. 44, in fact, applies. The only difference in this regard is that, for electronically supplied services, the supplier can report, at present, the VAT through the MOSS, whereas, for intermediary services, the supplier needs to file a regular VAT return. Nevertheless, as from 1 Jan. 2021, the MOSS will be extended also to intermediary services, pursuant to a redraft of Arts 359 and 369b of the VAT Directive. *See* Art. 2 of Council Directive 2017/2455/EU.

the VAT Directive, or, rather, as electronically supplied services, which are dealt with in Article 58 of the VAT Directive.

Indeed, both Articles 46 and 58 of the VAT Directive are special place of supply rules for which no specific ranking exists. Therefore, primacy between the two rules in question must be assessed only through interpretation, by carefully considering all the facts and circumstances of a case. Some guidance on this matter has nevertheless been provided by the VAT Committee. Notably, two clarifications have been issued in this regard. As a first thing, from a broad reading of Article 7(3)(u) of the Implementing Regulation mentioned in the previous sections, the Commission derives that, where a disclosed agent supplies services having a 'tangible' nature, such as accommodation and passenger transport services, the services in question cannot qualify as electronically supplied services.[124] Second, it is submitted that services requiring an 'active involvement' on the side of the intermediary, in the form of 'non-automated, human, distinct reactions' by that intermediary – which may well be an online platform – in the provision of the services in question, cannot qualify as electronically supplied services.[125] On the contrary, if the intermediary does not deal with individual requests made by customers, the services in question are considered as staying within the scope of a 'minimal human intervention' and, therefore, they qualify as electronically supplied services.[126]

Some discussion on this latter point also took place among representatives of Member States participating at the meetings of the VAT Committee. Notably, by referring to a provider of a platform where movable and immovable property is put on sale or is up for rent, a representative of a Member State distinguished two situations. He first contended that, if the price of the goods and/or services exchanged among users does not influence the price of the services rendered by the platform to its users, the services in question must be regarded as electronically supplied services. On the contrary, if there is an influence between the two supplies, the representative claimed that the services in question must be characterized as intermediary services, in respect of which either the place of supply rules of Article 44 or 46 of the VAT Directive apply, depending on the taxable status of the customer. A different criterion for distinguishing

124. *See* European Commission, Value Added Tax Committee, *Working Paper No. 814, Treatment of Online Supplies Made by a Travel Agent to Final Consumers*, at 11 (taxud.c.1(2014)2806510). Against this background, the author of this book submits that the explanation of Art. 7(3)(u) of the Implementing Regulation given by the Commission goes far beyond what such provision, indeed, stipulates. As a matter of fact, Art. 7(3)(u) of the Implementing Regulation only refers to the situation in which services of a 'tangible' nature, such as those consisting in the provision of accommodation and passenger transport, are 'booked online'. However, it is unclear whether the provision in question is also applicable to the case of intermediary services relating to accommodation and passenger transport carried out through – thus, not only 'booked online', as it may occur on a website like Booking.com – sharing economy platforms like Airbnb, Uber, HomeExchange, and BlaBlaCar.

125. European Commission, Value Added Tax Committee, *Guidelines resulting from the 107th Meeting of 8 July 2016 – Document D* (taxud.c.1(2017)1402399 – 914).

126. European Commission, Value Added Tax Committee, *Guidelines resulting from the 108th Meeting of 27-28 March 2017 – Document C* (taxud.c.1(2018)2397450 – 930). Overall, the VAT Committee seems to believe that, the more a service is customized, the less it ought to be considered as an electronically supplied service.

the two situations, instead, was put forward by a representative of another Member State. Notably, he drew a distinction between the situation in which a platform plays a 'deliberate role' in the underlying transaction, for instance by exerting an influence over the person making the underlying transaction or its pricing, from the case in which, instead, the platform only provides 'passive automated facilities', that is it operates only with a view of putting the two parties of the underlying transaction into contact. The representative then argued that, in the first case, the services in question must be seen as intermediary services, as such covered by Article 46 of the VAT Directive. In the second instance, in his opinion, the services in question must instead be considered as electronically supplied services, as such covered by Article 58 of the VAT Directive, if supplied to a non-taxable person. As pointed out by a representative of another Member State, this second scenario could, indeed, present itself in the case of 'an online marketplace where the potential buyers bid through an automatic procedure and the parties are notified of the conclusion of a purchase through an e-mail generated by a computer'.[127]

[C] Electronically Supplied Services in the Sharing Economy

[1] Underlying Services in the Sharing Economy

Based on the above exposition, it is rather clear that, in no event, services provided by users among themselves on sharing economy platforms, in case of either accommodation or passenger transport services, can qualify as electronically supplied services. Those services, in fact, have a 'tangible' nature, in the sense of involving the exploitation of a tangible property like a residential premise or a vehicle. More to the point, those services do not fall within the definition of electronically supplied services contained in Article 7(1) of the Implementing Regulation. In all evidence, the services in question are not delivered over the Internet or an electronic network, neither their supply is essentially automated, involves minimal human intervention, and is impossible to ensure in the absence of information technology. Indeed, the only possibility for those services to qualify as electronically supplied services occurs if the doctrine on composite supplies applies, so that the individual supplier and the platform are seen as jointly making a single composite supply to the same customer.[128]

Notably, this scenario would materialize either if platform services qualify as electronically supplied services and, further, those services constitute the principal supply to which the supply of the underlying service is ancillary, or, alternatively, if the two supplies in question are regarded as a single composite supply from an economic

127. European Commission, Value Added Tax Committee, *Working Paper No. 906, VAT 2015: Interaction between Electronically Supplied Services and Intermediation Services and Initial Discussion on the Scope of the Concept of Intermediation Services when Taken in a Broader Context*, at 6 (taxud.c.1(2016)3297911).
128. *See* section §6.03[B].

point of view and, further, such a single composite supply concerns electronically supplied services.[129] Figure 7.12 below depicts this scenario graphically.

Figure 7.12 Underlying Services in the Sharing Economy as Electronically Supplied Services

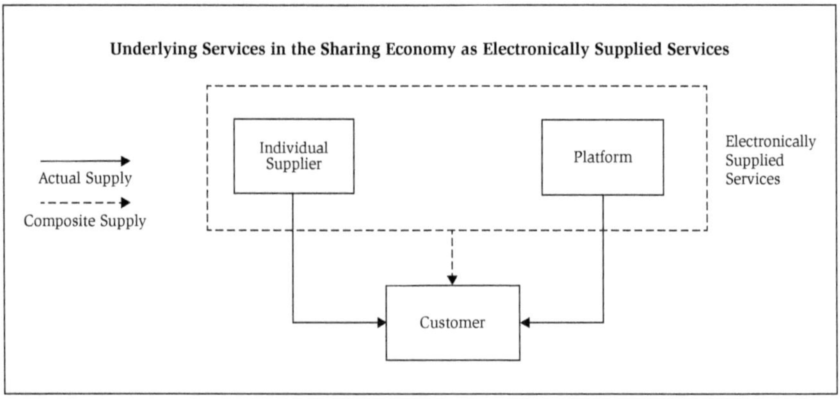

Nevertheless, the author submits that the scenario depicted above is highly improbable, given that, in the context of the sharing economy, the 'meaningful supply', in the sense of being the relevant supply from the perspective of the individual customer, clearly concerns services having a 'tangible' nature like accommodation or passenger transport services, not certainly dematerialized services like those provided by a sharing economy platform.[130]

[2] Platform Services in the Sharing Economy

Contrary to services provided by users on sharing economy platforms among themselves, the classification of services provided by a platform to its users as electronically supplied services entails a much more difficult assessment. The outcome of such assessment, essentially, depends on the level of involvement by a platform in the underlying services provided by its users among themselves.[131] On the one hand,

129. *See* European Commission, Value Added Tax Committee, *Working Paper No. 896, VAT 2015: Scope of the Notion of Electronically Supplied Services; Minimal Human Intervention (Follow-Up)*, at 6 (taxud.c.1(2016)922288), observing that 'where we are faced with a bundled supply the predominant element of this supply has to be identified and it should be verified whether this predominant element is fulfilling the conditions of the definition of electronically supplied services'.
130. *See* section §6.04.
131. Some criteria to assess the 'true' nature of the activity of a sharing economy platform have been laid down by the Commission in its Communication on *A European Agenda for the Collaborative Economy*, in the context of evaluating whether the services in question could be characterized as 'information society services' under EU law. Notably, for the purpose of such an assessment, the Commission mentioned three specific criteria, that is: (1) the platform sets

services provided by platforms to their users are capable of qualifying as electronically supplied services, to the extent that those services are delivered over the Internet or an electronic network, are essentially automated, involve minimal human intervention, and are impossible to ensure in the absence of information technology.[132] On the other hand, it is unquestionable that sharing economy platforms exert a certain degree – which indeed may vary from platform to platform, as well as from economic sector to economic sector – of influence and control over the underlying service, most notably by setting certain terms and conditions for performing the underlying services, by determining and adjusting the price of the underlying services, and by monitoring and enforcing user compliance with their own obligations.[133] In light of these latter considerations, it might be maintained that, as a matter of fact, the activity of a sharing economy platform does not consist merely in putting the two parties of the underlying transaction into contact, but rather it is more akin to that of a true organizer of the economic operation as a whole, so that the services provided by a platform to its users cannot quite be seen as electronically supplied services.[134]

---

the final price to be paid by users or merely recommends it, (2) it drafts all the key contractual terms which determine the contractual relationship between the individual suppliers and the recipients of the underlying services, and (3) it owns the key assets used to provide the underlying services. The Commission has further observed that, 'when these three criteria are all met, there are strong indications that the collaborative platform exercises significant influence or control over the provider of the underlying service, which may in turn indicate that it should be considered as also providing the underlying service (in addition to an information society service)'. *See* European Commission, *Communication from the Commission to the European Parliament, the Council, the European Economic and Social Committee and the Committee of the Regions on a European Agenda for the Collaborative Economy*, at 6, COM(2016) 356 final.

132. *See* European Commission, Value Added Tax Committee, *Working Paper No. 947, Services Provided by an Electronic Platform Connecting for Remuneration, by means of a Smartphone Application, a Driver Using His Own Vehicle with Persons Who Wish to Make Urban Journeys. The Significance of the VAT Identification Number*, at 11 (taxud.c.1(2018)1735106), considering that 'the platform sets up the system, monitors it, puts requirements, customizes, etc. but does not deal with individual supplies of services. i.e., requests coming from users and responses coming from the drivers'. Indeed, during a meeting of the VAT Committee, some representatives of Member States plainly admitted that 'when defining "electronic services", the means for providing a service had prevailed in the analysis without paying sufficient attention to the nature of the service'. *See* European Commission, Value Added Tax Committee, *Minutes 111th Meeting – 30 November 2018*, at 8 (taxud.c.1(2019)1709508).
133. *See* European Commission, Value Added Tax Committee, *Working Paper No. 947, Services Provided by an Electronic Platform Connecting for Remuneration, by means of a Smartphone Application, a Driver Using His Own Vehicle with Persons Who Wish to Make Urban Journeys. The Significance of the VAT Identification Number*, at 11 (taxud.c.1(2018)1735106), considering that the platform 'determines the standardised conditions under which the [underlying] services are provided and exercises prior control over access to the activity of the drivers as well as the users'.
134. *See* European Commission, Value Added Tax Committee, *Working Paper No. 882, VAT 2015: VAT Treatment of Online Gambling Services (Follow-Up)*, at 4, (taxud.c.1(2015)4459580), concerning a gambling operator who organizes a gambling activity, by setting up a platform on which players register, by establishing the rules of the game, by controlling their fulfilment, and by ensuring the operation of payments. For an opposite appraisal, *see* NL: ECJ, 12 May 2016, Case C-520/14, *Gemeente Borsele v. Staatssecretaris van Financiën and Staatssecretaris van Financiën v. Gemeente Borsele*, para. 35, where the CJEU found that a municipality was not the 'organizer', but rather a 'beneficiary' or a 'final consumer' of school transport services, which it acquired from transport undertakings and rendered them available to parents of pupils as

Admittedly, drawing a distinction between the two scenarios above is not an easy task. The case of Uber is illustrative in this regard. Is, indeed, Uber providing electronically supplied services or, rather, what the company offers ought to be seen as intermediary services relating to a passenger transport activity? Or both, in which case reliance must be placed upon the doctrine on composite supplies discussed in Chapter 6? In order to establish whether it is the driver or Uber that is actually 'steering the wheel' of the economic operation as a whole, it is necessary to closely examine the level of influence and control exerted by Uber over the underlying services rendered by the driver to the passenger.

The author submits that, ultimately, a comparison with a situation specifically examined by the VAT Committee might offer some clarifications in this regard. Notably, the case in question concerned an online gambling activity where a human dealer, employed by a digital company, spun the wheel of a roulette table in a casino at fixed intervals, every X minutes. During those intervals, players connected online with the dealer through the company's platform placed their bets or demanded cards. Asked to assess this situation from an EU VAT perspective, the VAT Committee reasoned that the possibility to qualify the service in question as an electronically supplied service depends on the actual degree of interaction existing between the dealer and the players. Thus, where the dealer keeps spinning the wheel at scheduled intervals, even if no bets are put or cards asked by customers playing online, the activity of the dealer and of the company which employs him shall be seen as completely disconnected from that of the players. In such event, the provision of the game service, in fact, is completely automated, as long as no significant level of human intervention is involved. Due to this circumstance, the service in question can qualify as an electronically supplied service. The assessment, instead, differs if the role of the dealer is more active, in the sense that the dealer is able to interact with customers playing online, so that his own activity varies depending on the inputs received from those players, or, even, if the betting activity odds are constantly updated during the game, so that those odds vary depending on the bets placed by individual players. In such event, the provision of the game service is no longer completely automated, inasmuch as the digital company is able to change pricing levels based on the bets placed by customers playing online. Due to these features, the service in question cannot qualify as an electronically supplied service any longer.[135]

Then, in which of the aforementioned two scenarios Uber fits best? Well, if one has to follow the analysis of the Uber's business model made both by Advocate General Szpunar and the CJEU, first, in *Uber Systems Spain* and, then, in *Uber France*, the second scenario, i.e., the case in which the degree of interaction exerted by the

---

part of its public service activities. In the author's opinion, the different appraisal made by the CJEU in *Gemeente Borsele*, however, is due to the peculiar nature of the activities (i.e., public service activities) in which the municipality was involved, so that the municipality could not be seen as a taxable person, inasmuch as it did not participate in any 'passenger transport market'. For a discussion in relation to the condition of 'market participation' for being a 'taxable person' under EU VAT, *see* section §4.02[B].

135. European Commission, Value Added Tax Committee, *Working Paper No. 882, VAT 2015: VAT Treatment of Online Gambling Services (Follow-Up)*, at 5-6 (taxud.c.1(2015)4459580).

platform over the underlying service is more than minimal, appears the most promising course of action.[136] Tellingly, in *Uber Systems Spain*, Advocate General Szpunar considered that, 'without exerting any formal constraints over drivers, Uber is able to tailor its supply to fluctuations in demand'.[137] In his own assessment, the Advocate General took particular notice of the fact that the ride fare is solely calculated by Uber's algorithm and that, further, the company's application is able to adjust the price of each ride to the intensity of the demand, notably by applying an appropriate multiplier to the basic fare when demand increases, for instance, as a result of an event or simply a change in the weather conditions, such as a storm.[138] Further, it was reasoned that Uber, especially through its embedded ratings function, as well as by presiding over accessibility of the transport supply, and by encouraging drivers to work when and where demand is high, is able to exert control - albeit indirectly - over the quality of the passenger transport services offered by the drivers.[139] Whether or not such assessment is indeed accurate, it ought to be observed out that, in any event, the classification of Uber services as electronically supplied services - or not - is not, actually, relevant. At present, the company in fact charges only the driver (with a 25% service fee calculated on the price of each ride), whereas, for passengers, the use of Uber app is free of any charge. Since, in most cases, the driver is a taxable person, the relevant place of supply rule is Article 44 of the VAT Directive, i.e., the default place of supply rule for B2B transactions, whether the services in question are classified as electronically supplied services or not.

As it is for Uber, the possibility that services provided by other sharing economy platforms qualify as electronically supplied services, ultimately, depends on the level of influence and control exerted by a platform over the underlying services provided by its users among themselves.[140] Starting with BlaBlaCar, despite claiming not to be a party to the underlying transactions, a certain level of influence and control is, undoubtedly, exerted by that platform over the ridesharing agreements among its users. First, the platform sets some standards for user interaction. Second, BlaBlaCar highlights the best ride and puts it at the top of search results. Third, user eligibility for a trip remains at the sole discretion of the company, which may even suspend a user account. Fourth, in case of a trip cancellation by either the driver or the passenger, the platform arranges for a refund to the other party and it also provides users with additional insurance coverage. Fifth and perhaps more importantly, BlaBlaCar requires drivers to limit the

136. *See* M. Álvarez Suso, *Comments on CJEU Case-Law on Taxable Transaction 2017: The Anti-Abuse Doctrine (Cussens) and the Sharing Economy (UBER)*, in *CJEU – Recent Developments in Value Added Tax*, at 249 (M. Lang et al. eds, Linde 2018), considering that, for EU VAT purposes, 'the services provided by Uber are to be qualified as urban transport of passengers ... and not as electronically supplied services'.
137. ES: Opinion of the Advocate General, 11 May 2017, Case C-434/15, *Asociación Profesional Elite Taxi v. Uber Systems Spain SL*, para. 47.
138. *Id.*, paras 49-50.
139. *Id.*, paras 48 and 51.
140. The author indeed submits that, not only the existence of some influence and control by a sharing economy platform over the provision of the underlying service is of importance as to determine the actual nature of the services rendered by that platform to its users, but also the intensity of such influence and control.

cost contribution asked to passengers to the costs actually incurred to provide the trip and an amount in this respect is even suggested by the company. The possibility for the driver to increase or decrease such an amount is, indeed, quite limited. Is this level of intervention more than minimal, so that BlaBlaCar services, even if operated by means of an algorithm, could not be regarded as electronically supplied services? Based on the way in which the company charges VAT on its own services, it seems that BlaBlaCar considers such services as electronically supplied services. In its terms and conditions, in fact, BlaBlaCar provides that VAT is to be charged based on the residence of the passenger. Previously, the company instead charged passengers with the VAT of every country in which the transport takes place, proportionate to the distances covered, i.e., based on the place of supply rule (i.e., Article 48 of the VAT Directive) of the underlying transaction to which Article 46 of the VAT Directive makes reference. Given the level of influence and control exerted by the platform over the ridesharing agreements among its users, the author submits that the current classification made by BlaBlaCar of its own services as electronically supplied services is not sound and that, as a matter of evidence, the services in question should rather be seen as intermediary services. Despite these latter considerations, a graphical representation of the situation in which BlaBlaCar's services are to qualify as electronically supplied services is provided in Figure 7.13 below.

Figure 7.13 BlaBlaCar Services as Electronically Supplied Services

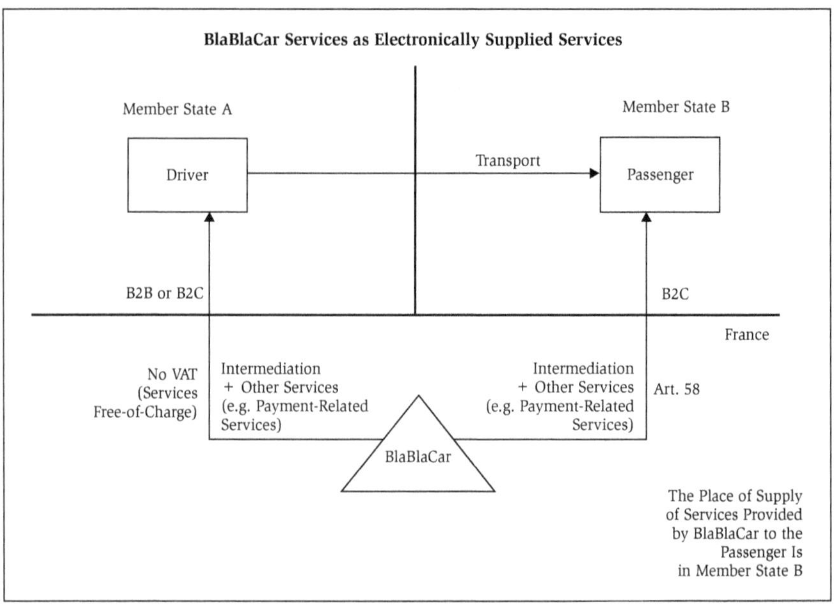

Determining the exact nature of the services provided by sharing economy platforms operating in the accommodation sector like Airbnb and HomeExchange is, equally, not clear-cut. Notably, in *Uber Systems Spain*, Advocate General Szpunar reasoned that, 'since the activity [of Uber] exists solely because of the platform ..., it is wrong to compare Uber to intermediation platforms such as those used to make hotel bookings or purchase flights'.[141] The same Advocate General further observed that, 'in contrast to the situation of Uber's drivers, both hotels and airlines are undertakings which function completely independently of any intermediary platform and for which such platforms are simply one of a number of ways of marketing their services. Furthermore, it is the hotels and airlines - and not the booking platforms - that determine the conditions under which their services are provided, starting with prices'.[142] Whether those considerations can seamlessly apply to the case of Airbnb and/or HomeExchange is very much open to discussion.[143] Eventually, some guidance in this regard could be offered by the CJEU quite soon.[144]

Contrary to the case of Uber, the classification issue is relevant in this case, in so far as, in most instances, the services in question are rendered to non-taxable persons, which means that, based on their different classification under EU VAT, also different place of supply rules would apply. Should, in fact, the services in question qualify as electronically supplied services, then Article 58 of the VAT Directive would apply and, therefore, the relevant place of supply would be where the customer is established, has his permanent address, or usually resides. If the services in question are classified otherwise - say - as intermediary services, then, pursuant to Article 46 of the VAT Directive, the place of supply would, instead, coincide with that of the underlying transaction, which, as long as this latter transaction consists in the provision of accommodation, would be where the rented immovable property is located. A graphical representation of the situation in which Airbnb's services qualify as electronically supplied services is provided in Figure 7.14 below.

141. Opinion *Uber Systems Spain* (C-434/15), paras 56-57.
142. *Id.*, para. 59.
143. For a discussion about the potential spill overs of the CJEU's decision in *Uber Systems Spain* in relation to the business model of other sharing economy platforms, in particular Airbnb, *see* C. Busch, *The Sharing Economy at the CJEU: Does Airbnb Pass the 'Uber Test'?*, 7 J. Eur. Cons. & Mkt L. 4 (2018), at 172-174. It also ought to be noted that certain digital companies like Booking.com are considerably expanding the range of their own activities, as to offer travellers even private holiday homes, so that it is becoming increasingly difficult to draw a neat line between the business model of those companies and that of Airbnb (and eventually, also that of HomeExchange). *See* D. Schaal, *Booking and Airbnb Are Now in a Homesharing Dead Heat*, Skyft (27 Feb. 2019). As seen, although some of its own services, such as the messaging and verification service, are essentially automated and, indeed, involve only a minimum human intervention, HomeExchange regards those services as 'ordinary' B2C services, to which Art. 45 of the VAT Directive applies. *See* section §2.08[A].
144. FR: *Request for a Preliminary Ruling from the Juge d'Instruction du Tribunal de Grande Instance de Paris (France) lodged on 13 June 2018 - Criminal Proceedings against YA and AIRBNB Ireland UC - Other Parties: Hotelière Turenne SAS, Pour un Hébergement et Tourisme Professionnel (AHTOP), Valhotel (Case C-390/18)*.

Figure 7.14 Airbnb Services as Electronically Supplied Services

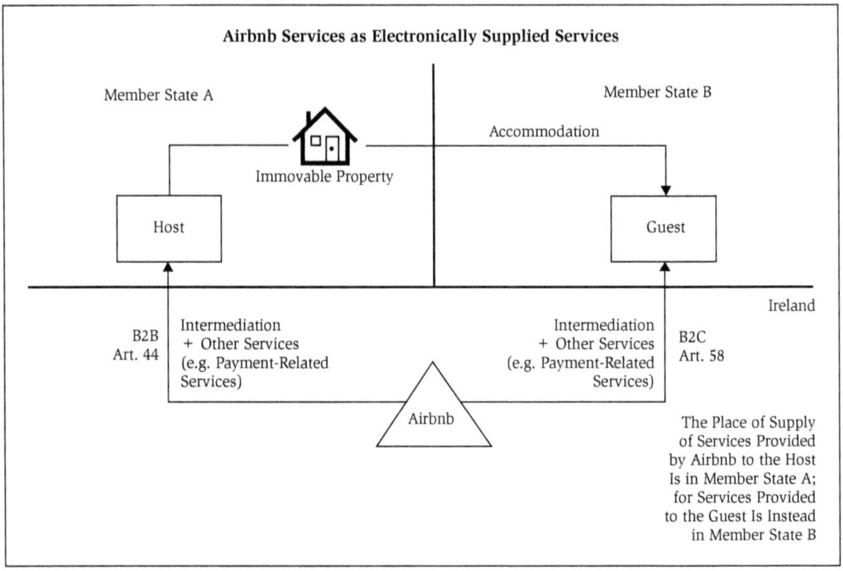

§7.08 USE AND ENJOYMENT RULE

Where services provided by a sharing economy platform to its users qualify as electronically supplied services and, further, those services are rendered to non-taxable persons, so that they fall within the scope of Article 58 of the VAT Directive, the effective use and enjoyment rule laid down in Article 59a of the VAT Directive could find an application.[145] Notably, Article 59a of the VAT Directive, introduced by Council Directive 2008/8/EC and applicable as from 1 January 2010, contains an optional mechanism to prevent double taxation, non-taxation, or distortion of competition caused by discrepancies existing between the place of supply rules of Member States and those of non-EU countries. This provision, however, is only applicable to certain types of services, among which electronically supplied services rendered to non-taxable persons. Fundamentally, whether implemented, the effective use and enjoyment rule enables a Member State to overrule the normal operation of place of supply

145. The exact meaning of the expression 'effective use and enjoyment' (in French, '*l'utilisation ou l'exploitation effectives*'; in Italian, '*l'effettiva utilizzazione e l'effettiva fruizione*') is not clear and, indeed, it has been left unexplained by both the VAT Directive and the Implementing Regulation. Apparently, the expression, however, is an EU law concept. *See* Terra, *supra* n. 4, at 222, arguing that 'it is time that this concept is explained in Community [now EU] legislation'. *See also* European Commission, Value Added Tax Committee, *Guidelines resulting from the 89th Meeting of 30 September 2009 – Document B* (taxud.d.1(2010)176579 – 645).

rules, as to rectify the place of actual consumption of a service, based on where the service in question is effectively used and enjoyed by the recipient.[146]

Notably, the rule encompasses two quite distinct scenarios. The first scenario, dealt with in Article 59a(a) of the VAT Directive, occurs when, on the basis of the place of supply rules contained in the VAT Directive, a service takes place within the EU and, yet, that service is effectively used and enjoyed outside the territories of any of the Member States. In this situation, the place of supply may shift outside the EU, i.e., where the service in question is effectively used and enjoyed. The second scenario, dealt with in Article 59a(b) of the VAT Directive, instead occurs when, on the basis of the place of supply rules contained in the VAT Directive, a service takes place outside the EU and, yet, that service is effectively used and enjoyed within the territory of a given Member State. In this situation, the Member State in question is allowed to consider the service as taking place within its own territory.[147]

Where a Member State has implemented the effective use and enjoyment rule, it could therefore occur that services provided in the context of the sharing economy, notably electronically supplied services provided by a sharing economy platform like Airbnb to a non-taxable person residing in the EU, but relating to the booking of an immovable property located in a non-EU country, would fall within the scope of this optional provision. If so, the operation of the effective use and enjoyment rule of Article 59a(a) would exclude the possibility for Airbnb to charge VAT on the services rendered to such non-taxable person.

Nevertheless, the operation of the effective use and enjoyment rule might lead to situations of double taxation or non-taxation, where the classification of a service under EU VAT does not ultimately reconcile with that made by another VAT/GST system.[148] Notably, in the context of the sharing economy, double taxation might occur in case of a Colombian resident who books accommodation in a Member State through Airbnb. Should, indeed, Airbnb services qualify as intermediary services for EU VAT purposes, then the place of supply rule of Article 46 of the VAT Directive would apply, which means that the Colombian resident is charged with VAT of the country in which the immovable property is located (as stipulated, an EU country). If, for Colombian

---

146. As it is implicit in the wording of Art. 59a of the VAT Directive, reference is to be made to the place where a service is used and enjoyed by the recipient, i.e., the person who uses the service, and not instead to the activity of the supplier. *See* European Commission, Value Added Tax Committee, *Working Paper No. 781, Application of the Effective Use and Enjoyment Rule to Market Research Studies*, at 3 (taxud.c.1(2014)195750).
147. Noteworthy, 'a Member State cannot, however, make use of this rule to tax the part of the service which is not effectively used and enjoyed within its territory. In those cases where the use and enjoyment takes place within more than one Member State it is necessary to determine a criterion of apportionment that allows each Member State to tax the part of that use that takes place in that Member State, and no more'. *See* European Commission, Value Added Tax Committee, *Working Paper No. 781, Application of the Effective Use and Enjoyment Rule to Market Research Studies*, at 5 (taxud.c.1(2014)195750).
148. As underlined by the VAT Committee, the exercise by a Member State of the optional provision of Art. 59a of the VAT Directive, in fact, does not depend on the tax treatment which is accorded to the service in question under the domestic tax law of a non-EU country. *See* European Commission, Value Added Tax Committee, *Guidelines resulting from the 89th Meeting of 30 September 2009 – Document B* (taxud.d.1(2010)176579 – 645).

VAT purposes, Airbnb services qualify as electronically supplied services, in respect of which, presumably, the relevant place of supply under Colombian VAT law is where the customer resides (Colombia), the Colombian resident is also charged with Colombian VAT. Double non-taxation might instead occur in the exactly reverse situation, i.e., where an EU resident books accommodation in Colombia through Airbnb, provided that, for both EU VAT and Colombian VAT purposes, Airbnb services qualify as electronically supplied services. Should the Member State where the customer resides implement the effective use and enjoyment rule of Article 59a(a) of the VAT Directive, then, pursuant to such rule, the place of supply would shift to Colombia, with the relevant consequence that the EU resident would be charged neither with EU VAT nor with Colombian VAT. A graphical representation of these two scenarios of double taxation and non-taxation is provided, respectively, in Figures 7.15 and 7.16 below.

Figure 7.15 Use and Enjoyment Rule Does Not Apply: Double Taxation

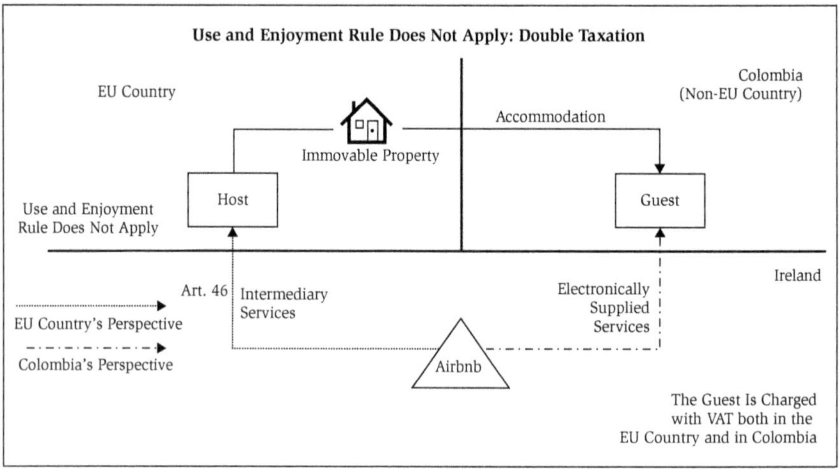

Figure 7.16 Use and Enjoyment Rule Applies: Double Non-taxation

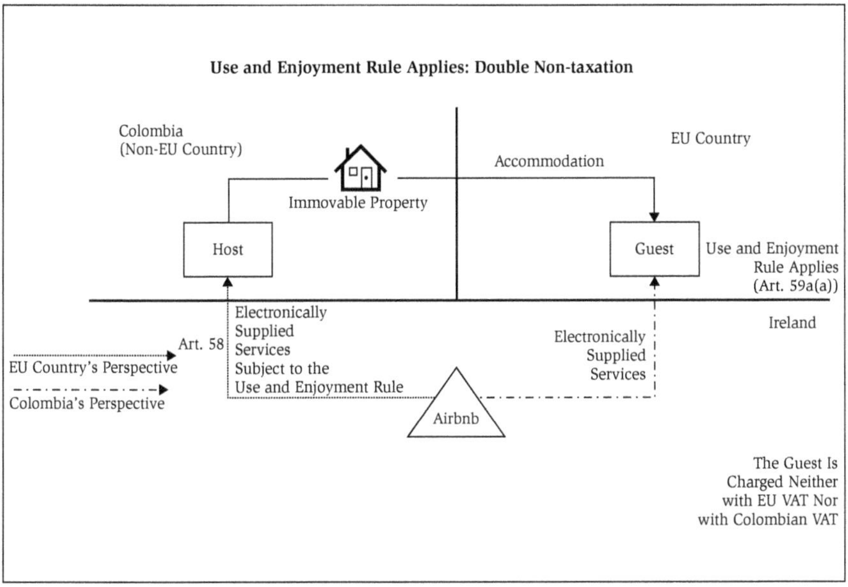

§7.09 SERVICES BY INTERMEDIARIES

[A] Types of Intermediaries under EU VAT

In today's economy, it is fairly common to have a supply chain entailing a series of transactions as well as involving a number of different undertakings, some of which may only perform the role of intermediaries. The term 'intermediary', by itself, is not defined anywhere in the VAT Directive or elsewhere in the Implementing Regulation. Neither the CJEU has, indeed, ever considered its precise meaning.[149] Despite the lack of any clue in this regard, the VAT Directive, apparently, seeks to distinguish two types of intermediaries, that is: (1) those who act in the name and on behalf of one or both parties to an underlying transaction, and (2) those who instead deal with customers in their own name and use the supplies provided to them by other taxable persons to make onward supplies to their customers. These two distinct categories of intermediaries are not only mutually exclusive, but also all-comprehensive, in the sense that an intermediary who intervenes in the supply chain must necessarily fall within one of the

149. In this connection, in *Alpenchalets Resorts*, Advocate General Bobek observed that, although 'the notion of intermediary, as used in Article 306 of the VAT Directive and its legal predecessors, has not been examined by the Court in any detail ... it would nonetheless appear that the Court effectively made the equation between "acting in its *own name*" and "*not being an intermediary*"' in *Van Ginkel Waddinxveen* (C-163/91) (emphases original). *See* DE: Opinion of the Advocate General, 5 Sep. 2018, Case C-552/17, *Alpenchalets Resorts GmbH v. Finanzamt München Abteilung Körperschaften*, at note 7. The author of this book, instead, contends that an intermediary, for EU VAT purposes, can well act 'in his own name'.

aforementioned two categories. The first type of intermediaries, i.e., those who act in the name and on behalf of their own principal, are indeed, from a contract law perspective, 'true agents', whereas, for EU VAT purposes, are generally referred to as 'disclosed agents'. For place of supply purposes, services rendered by this first type of intermediaries fall within the scope of Article 44 or 46 of the VAT Directive, depending on whether those services relate to, respectively, B2B or B2C transactions. The second type of intermediaries, i.e., those who act in their own name but on behalf of another person, are instead, from a contract law perspective, essentially 'commissionaires', whereas, for EU VAT purposes, are generally referred to as 'undisclosed agents'. For place of supply purposes, services rendered by this second type of intermediaries are dealt with in Article 28 of VAT Directive or, but only with regard to travel agents and tour operators, in Articles 306-310 of the Directive.[150] An analysis of these two distinct types of intermediaries is provided in the following sections. Notably, section §7.09[B] deals with the first type of intermediaries, i.e., disclosed agents, whereas the second type of intermediaries, i.e., undisclosed agents, is considered in section §7.09[C].

[B] Disclosed Agents

Intermediaries, as 'disclosed agents', were already considered for place of supply rules purposes in the Proposal for a Second Directive. The text of the Proposal for a Second Directive, in fact, stipulated that 'services performed by brokers, forwarding and other agents, and other intermediaries shall be deemed to be located at the place where the intermediary concerned wholly or mainly performs the service'.[151] Therefore, under the Second Directive, as well as in the wording of the Proposal for a Sixth Directive[152], the place of supply of services provided by disclosed agents was where that intermediary was established. Article 9(2)(e) Seventh Indent of the Sixth Directive, mentioning 'the services of agents who act in the name and for the account of another, when they

150. Notably, Arts 306-310 of the VAT Directive lay down the 'TOMS', which is one of the six special schemes included in the VAT Directive. Noteworthy, pursuant to the rules contained therein, if a travel agent acts in the name of another person, the travel agent is deemed to supply only intermediation and, as such, his own activity is left outside the special scheme for travel agents. *See* European Commission, Value Added Tax Committee, *Working Paper No. 814. Treatment of Online Supplies Made by a Travel Agent to Final Consumers*, at 10 (taxud.c.1(2014)2806510).
151. European Commission, *Proposal for a Second Directive for the Harmonization among Member States of Turnover Tax Legislation, concerning the Form and Methods of Application of the Common System of Taxation on Value Added*, at Annex A 11 Fourth Indent, COM(65) 144 final, Supplement to the Bulletin of the European Economic Community No. 5 (1965). With an aim of clarifying the ultimate rationale of this rule, the Explanatory Memorandum accompanying the proposal stipulated that, 'as regards brokers, etc., it is especially hard to lay down a uniform rule to locate their services at the place of use or exploitation, given the great diversity of the service rendered by these persons. Mainly with a view to ease tax collections, it seemed expedient to deem these services to be located at the place of the establishment where they are wholly or substantially performed'. *Id.*, at 22.
152. European Commission, *Proposal for a Sixth Council Directive on the Harmonization of Member States concerning Turnover Taxes Common System of Value Added Tax: Uniform Basis of Assessment (submitted to the Council by the Commission on 29 June 1973)*, at 11, COM(73) 950, Bulletin of the European Communities No. 11 (1973).

procure for their principal the services referred to in this point (e) [i.e. the aforementioned intangible services]', equated the place of supply of intermediary services relating to certain intangible services rendered by a disclosed agent with the place of supply of those intangible services. Accordingly, under the original Sixth Directive, the place of supply of services provided by a disclosed agent was where the customer had established his own business or had a fixed establishment to which the service was supplied or, in the absence of those places, where that customer had a permanent address or usually resided.

Following the 2003 Proposal of the Commission amending the Sixth Directive with regard to the place of supply of services[153], this rule was eventually changed in 2006. Notably, Article 44(1) of the Sixth Directive, as recast in 2006, provided that 'the place of supply of services by an intermediary acting in the name and on behalf of another person, other than those referred to in Articles 50 and 54 and in Article 56(1), shall be the place where the underlying transaction is supplied in accordance with this Directive'. Article 46 of the VAT Directive, as applicable from 1 January 2010, substantially maintained the same wording of the Sixth Directive as recast in 2006, but extended the application scope of the provision to all supplies of intermediary services to non-taxable persons, thus eliminating the exceptions to this rule mentioned in the previous wording.[154] As a result of this latter modification, Article 46 of the current VAT Directive provides that '[t]he place of supply of services rendered to a non-taxable person by an intermediary acting in the name and on behalf of another person shall be the place where the underlying transaction is supplied in accordance with this Directive'. The major change as from 1 January 2010 attains to the fact that, in case of B2B transactions, the place of supply of services made by an intermediary to a taxable person is no longer determined based on the place of supply rule applicable to the underlying transaction, rather it is always found where the customer is established. Accordingly, the special provision of Article 46 of the VAT Directive, currently, only covers services rendered to non-taxable persons, i.e., B2C transactions.

The rule has been made subject to some clarifications by means of secondary EU law and, also, from the CJEU. A first clarification, concerning the recipient of such intermediary services, is provided by Article 30 of the Implementing Regulation, pursuant to which 'the supply of services of intermediaries as referred to in Article 46 [of the VAT Directive] shall cover the services of intermediaries acting in the name and on behalf of the recipient of the services procured and the services performed by intermediaries acting in the name and on behalf of the provider of the services procured'.

153. Notably, Art. 9i ('Intermediary Services to Non-Taxable Persons') of the 2003 Commission's proposal stipulated that 'the place of supply of services rendered to non-taxable persons by intermediaries acting in the name and on behalf of other persons shall, where such services form part of transactions other than those referred to in Article 9e and Article 9j, be the place where those transactions are carried out'. *See* European Commission, *Proposal for a Council Directive amending Directive 77/388/EEC as regards the Place of Supply of Services*, at 20, COM(2003) 822 final.

154. Notably, Arts 50, 54, and 56(1)(l) of the Sixth Directive, as recast in 2006, provided special rules for intermediaries who, respectively, took part in an intra-Community transport of goods, performed ancillary services to it, or supplied services to customers established outside the EU.

A second clarification, instead, was offered by the CJEU in *Lipjes*. Notably, in that case, the Court explained that it is immaterial whether the party to which the intermediary services relate is a taxable person acting in that capacity or, instead, a non-taxable person. The wording of Article 46 of the VAT Directive, in fact, simply refers to 'another person', regardless of whether that person is a taxable person acting as such or not. Accordingly, Article 46 of the VAT Directive applies even if the underlying transaction is a non-taxable transaction, that is a transaction which falls outside the scope of EU VAT.[155]

A third clarification concerns the classification, for EU VAT purposes, of the underlying transaction to which the intermediary services relate. In this connection, it is stipulated that the intervention of an intermediary does not alter, anyhow, the classification for EU VAT purposes of the underlying transaction. This circumstance is, indeed, relevant as to assess whether a service operated by an intermediary must be placed within or outside the application scope of a provision, especially an exemption. Some clarification in this respect has been provided by the CJEU in a line of decisions. Particularly relevant it is the CJEU's decision in *SPI*, where the Court ruled that 'Article 9(2)(e) of the Sixth Directive [prescribing that the place of supply of advertising services was to be found where the customer was located] must be interpreted as applying not only to advertising services supplied directly and invoiced by the supplier to a taxable advertiser but also to services supplied indirectly to the advertiser and invoiced to a third party who in turn invoices them to the advertiser'.[156] And yet, a more rigorous stance was taken by the Court in other decisions, especially in situations where a provision demanded more stringent conditions for its own application. Notably, in *Taksatorringen*, the CJEU found that the expression 'insurance services' referred 'only to services provided by professionals who have a relationship with both the insurer and the insured party', thus concluding that, only in such event, the related exemption provided by the VAT Directive could eventually apply.[157]

Intermediary services, essentially, aim to render the consumption of the underlying transaction more feasible and convenient. From this perspective, it can fairly be maintained that an intermediary service is always consumed where also the underlying transaction is consumed. And yet, not necessarily this view ought to be upheld. Notably, it might be possible that a jurisdiction finds more appropriate and/or expedient to tax services provided by an intermediary at the place where such intermediary is located. Indeed, a public consultation launched by the Commission in 2005 highlighted divided opinions with regard to the best place of supply of services rendered by intermediaries. On the one hand, some respondents to this public consultation agreed with the Commission's proposal to tax those services at the place

155. NL: ECJ, 27 May 2004, Case C-68/03, *Staatssecretaris van Financiën v. D. Lipjes*, para. 23.
156. FR: ECJ, 15 Mar. 2001, Case C-108/00, *Syndicat des Producteurs Indépendants (SPI) v. Ministère de l'Economie, des Finances et de l'Industrie*, para. 22. *See also* LU: ECJ, 5 Jun. 2003, Case C-438/01, *Design Concept SA v. Flanders Expo SA*, para. 29; NL: ECJ, 3 Apr. 2008, Case C-124/07, *J.C.M. Beheer BV v. Staatssecretaris van Financiën*, para. 29
157. DK: ECJ, 20 Nov. 2003, Case C-8/01, *Assurandør-Societetet v. Skatteministeriet*, para. 44. Adopting a similarly strict approach, *see* NL: ECJ, 14 Dec. 2006, Case C-401/05, *VDP Dental Laboratory NV v. Staatssecretaris van Financiën*, paras 31-32 and 38-39.

where the intermediary was established and, further, independent from the characterization of the underlying transaction to which those services related, on the ground that such a rule is pretty straightforward and, thus, also simpler to implement. On the other hand, different respondents, mostly transport providers, travel agents, and tour operators, flagged a clear preference for applying the place of supply of the underlying transaction, based on the fact that such a rule consents to avoid potential distortions of competition between EU and non-EU intermediaries.[158]

[C] Undisclosed Agents

The second types of intermediaries considered under EU VAT are 'undisclosed agents', who, however, as Advocate Kokott rightly pointed out, might be better addressed as 'agent[s] of an undisclosed principal'[159], in so far as it is the principal and not the agent that, actually, remains undisclosed to the recipient of the supply. Those intermediaries are essentially 'commissionaires', i.e., undertakings acting on behalf of another person in the context of a principal-agent relationship.[160] The peculiarity of such a relationship is that, while, from a legal perspective, the supply to the customer shall be attributed to the agent, following an economic-based approach, that supply, instead, ought to be attributed to the principal. Indeed, principal-agent arrangements are fairly common in business practice. Nevertheless, contractual arrangements among parties, as such, are not determinative as to establish whether a principal-agent relationship exists for EU VAT purposes. Rather, the assessment of the various relationships among parties under civil and EU VAT laws is to be kept separate, with the relevant consequence that relationships among the persons concerned might have to be judged for civil law purposes differently than for EU VAT purposes.[161] Notably, in *Aspiro*, Advocate General Kokott considered sufficient, for the existence of a valid relationship under EU

158. European Commission, *Summary Report on the Outcome of the Public Consultation from DG TAXUD, VAT – The Place of Supply of Services to Non-Taxable Persons*, at 7-8 (TAXUD-2005-00843).
159. UK: Opinion of the Advocate General, 24 Feb. 2005, Case C-305/03, *Commission of the European Communities v. United Kingdom of Great Britain and Northern Ireland*, para. 41.
160. A consultation of the search database of the CJEU (up to 31 March 2019) shows that the term 'commissionaire', in relation to EU VAT, has never been used either by the Court or by the Advocates General. The CJEU, instead, has used the quite similar expression 'commission agent' in some of its decisions. *See* LU: ECJ, 4 May 2017, Case C-274/15, *European Commission v. Grand Duchy of Luxembourg*, para. 86; BE: ECJ, 14 Jul. 2011, Case C-464/10, *Belgian State v. Pierre Henfling and Others*, paras 27 and 35-38. As observed by J.F. Avery Jones, *What Is a 'Contract under which Commission Is Payable'?*, in *VAT in an EU and International Perspective: Essays in Honour of Han Kogels – Part I* (H. Van Arendonk, S. Jansen, R. Van der Paardt eds, IBFD 2011), the use of the English terms 'commissionaire' and 'commissions' is indeed a misnomer, given that common law does not have a concept such as a 'commission contract', which, in fact, is used only under civil law, as it derives, in particular, from the French '*contrat de commission*'.
161. UK: Opinion of the Advocate General, 24 Feb. 2005, Case C-305/03, *Commission of the European Communities v. United Kingdom of Great Britain and Northern Ireland*, para. 42.

VAT, even 'a merely *de facto* relationship' (emphasis original) between an insured agent and an insured party.[162]

The VAT Directive, indeed, contains special rules for undisclosed agents supplying goods or services on behalf of their principals. The existence of special rules for the activities of an undisclosed agent is motivated by the fact that, in order to be able to deduct their input VAT, taxable persons are required to have a proper invoice carrying their own name or denomination.[163] Such a requirement cannot be fulfilled, quite evidently, in the context of a principal-agent relationship, in which the original supplier is to remain unknown (i.e., 'undisclosed') to the customer and vice versa, because one of the two parties does not want to reveal itself to the other, or since non-disclosure is in the interest of the intermediary himself. Notably, undisclosed agents supplying goods to customers are dealt with in Artiicle 14(2)(c) of the VAT Directive, whereas the supply of services by undisclosed agents is considered in Article 28 of the VAT Directive.

Article 28 of the VAT Directive specifically provides that, 'where a taxable person acting in his own name but on behalf of another person takes part in a supply of services, he shall be deemed to have received and supplied those services himself'. While a specific rule for undisclosed agents supplying services was not included in the Second Directive[164], a provision in this respect was, instead, inserted in the Sixth Directive, whose wording was, indeed, quite similar to that of Article 28 of the current VAT Directive.[165] This provision creates the legal fiction of two identical supplies operated consecutively. More precisely, based on such a fiction, the undisclosed agent is 'deemed' (in French, '*il est reputé*'; in Italian, '*si ritiene che*') to have received from the original supplier (i.e., his own principal) the same services which he, then, supplies onward to his customer. Thus, for EU VAT purposes, the intermediary is equated to the original supplier, whereas the role of payer is assumed by the original supplier, which, ultimately, constitutes an inversion of their respective positions from the perspective of their contractual relations.

The meaning of the expressions 'takes part in a supply of services' (in French, '*s'entremet dans une prestation de services*'; in Italian, '*partecipi ad una prestazione di servizi*'), 'acting in his own name' (in French, '*agissant en son nom propre*'; in Italian, '*che agisca in nome proprio*'), 'but on behalf of another person' (in French, '*mais pour le compte d'autrui*'; in Italian, '*ma per conto terzi*'), while not defined in either the VAT Directive or the Implementing Regulation, has however found some specifications in

162. PL: Opinion of the Advocate General, 23 Dec. 2015, Case C-40/15, *Minister Finansów v. Aspiro SA*, para. 36.
163. Articles 178(1)(a) and 226(1) point (5) VAT Directive.
164. Nevertheless, the Second Directive contained a specific rule for a disclosed agent taking part in the supply of goods to the customer. *See* Art. 5(2)(c) of the Second Directive.
165. The provision in question was Art. 6(4) of the Sixth Directive, which read as follows: 'where a taxable person acting in his own name but on behalf of another takes part in a supply of services, he shall be considered to have received and supplied those services himself'. The difference with the wording of Art. 28 of the current VAT Directive rests in the fact that the latter uses the word 'deemed' rather than 'considered' and, further, that it adds the term 'person' with reference to 'another'.

the CJEU's case law, the VAT Committee's guidelines, and the Commission's explanatory notes. Their respective significance will be explained in greater detail in Chapter 8.[166] For the time being, it would suffice to underline that, in order to be regarded as an undisclosed agent, an intermediary must play an 'economic role' in the supply of services made by the supplier to the customer.[167] In this connection, according to the Commission, the user's perception of who, actually, is the provider of the service is of importance for an intermediary to be regarded as an undisclosed agent.[168]

When an intermediary takes part in the supply to a customer as an undisclosed agent of the supplier, there are two supplies which, ultimately, need to be considered. The first supply is between the supplier and the intermediary. The second supply, instead, is between the intermediary and the customer. Although these two supplies must be assessed separately for EU VAT purposes, their treatment under EU VAT is – to some extent – equated. By way of a legal fiction, the two supplies in question are, in fact, considered as having the same nature and, therefore, they receive the same classification under EU VAT. Indeed, this is done for a good reason. Without a similar legal fiction, a Member State might in fact classify those supplies differently and, therefore, also accord a different VAT treatment to them. Notably, this eventuality might have occurred where the first supply, but not also the second supply, had been considered by a Member State as falling within the scope of an exemption. A divergent characterization of the two supplies, instead, is not possible under the deemed provision of Article 28 of the VAT Directive. As reasoned by the CJEU in *Henfling and Others*, since the provision of Article 28 of the VAT Directive 'is couched in general terms, without containing restrictions as to its scope or its extent, the fiction created by that provision also concerns the application of VAT exemptions'.[169]

It ought to be noted, however, that the operation of the legal fiction contained in Article 28 of the VAT Directive does not also imply that, although having a similar characterization for EU VAT purposes, the same place of supply rule would seamlessly apply to the two supplies in question. For place of supply purposes, each transaction must in fact be gauged on its own merits.[170] Thus, for instance, if the first supply between the supplier and the undisclosed agent is a B2B transaction and it concerns electronically supplied services, Article 44 of the VAT Directive applies. Despite also being an electronically supplied service, the supply between the undisclosed agent and the end consumer, being a B2C transaction, instead falls within the scope of Article 58 of the VAT Directive, prescribing that the place of supply is where the customer is established, has his permanent address, or usually resides.

166. *See* section §8.03[C].
167. IT: ECJ, 19 Feb. 2009, Case C-1/08, *Athesia Druck Srl v. Ministero dell'Economia e delle Finanze and Agenzia delle Entrate*, para. 36.
168. European Commission, Value Added Tax Committee, *Working Paper No. 947, Services Provided by an Electronic Platform Connecting for Remuneration, by means of a Smartphone Application, a Driver Using His Own Vehicle with Persons Who Wish to Make Urban Journeys. The Significance of the VAT Identification Number*, at 13 (taxud.c.1(2018)1735106).
169. *Pierre Henfling and Others* (C-464/10), para. 36.
170. FI: ECJ, 4 May 2017, Case C-33/16, *Proceedings brought by A Oy*, para. 40.

[D] Intermediary Services in the Sharing Economy

In the context of the sharing economy, intermediary services come into prominence only in relation to services rendered by sharing economy platforms to their users. Clearly, platform users cannot, in fact, be seen as providing any type of intermediation. The place of supply rules relating to intermediary services provided by a platform, however, vary depending on which of the two types of intermediaries considered under EU VAT a sharing economy platform belongs to, that is whether the platform is regarded as a disclosed or an undisclosed agent. In this connection, the author submits there is no straightforward answer as to include a sharing economy platform in the former or the latter category of intermediaries/agents. Indeed, the specific criteria for distinguishing between the two types of intermediaries/agents will only be discussed later, in Chapter 8.[171] However, it must be underlined here that, based on the findings of both Advocate General Szpunar and the CJEU in *Uber Systems Spain*, the Commission is inclined to believe that Uber might ultimately be considered as acting as an undisclosed agent of the drivers and, therefore, that, for EU VAT purposes, there is a first supply of passenger transport services from the driver to that platform and, then, a second supply of passenger transport services from Uber to the passenger.[172] In a sense, according to the Commission, Uber, as an undisclosed agent, provides more than just an intermediation service. Notably, the relevant place of supply rules, resulting for each of the two possible classifications of a sharing economy platform as an intermediary under EU VAT, are considered separately in the following paragraphs.

Should a sharing economy platform assume the role of a disclosed agent, then the place of supply rules applicable to services carried out by such platform would be provided by Article 44 or 46 of the VAT Directive, depending on whether the recipient of those services is, respectively, a taxable person or not. Notably, where the customer is a taxable person, the default place of supply rule for B2B transactions contained in Article 44 of the VAT Directive applies, pursuant to which the place of supply is where the customer is established, maintains a fixed establishment toward which the services in question are provided, has his permanent address, or usually resides. On the contrary, in case of a B2C transaction, Article 46 of the VAT Directive requires making reference to the place of supply applicable to the underlying transaction, consisting in the provision of accommodation or passenger transport by the individual supplier. Notably, the detailed operation of the rules for those types of intermediary services, provided by sharing economy platforms to their users, have already been explained in the previous sections.[173]

---

171. *See* section §8.03[C].
172. *See* European Commission, Value Added Tax Committee, *Working Paper No. 947, Services Provided by an Electronic Platform Connecting for Remuneration, by means of a Smartphone Application, a Driver Using His Own Vehicle with Persons Who Wish to Make Urban Journeys. The Significance of the VAT Identification Number*, at 13 (taxud.c.1(2018)1735106), considering, in particular, the circumstance that passengers 'link the service with the platform itself and not with individual drivers'.
173. *See* sections §7.05–§7.07.

Should, instead, a sharing economy platform assume the role of an undisclosed agent, then the place of supply rules applicable to the services carried out by such platform would need to be assessed separately from those applicable to the underlying transaction. Nevertheless, due to the operation of the legal fiction contained in Article 28 of the VAT Directive, which deems the nature of the transaction made by the supplier to the undisclosed agent being the same as the onward supply by this latter party to the customer, a certain degree of influence by the underlying transaction over the services provided by the platform also exists in this situation. The legal fiction contained in Article 28 of the VAT Directive, in fact, prescribes that the classification of the two supplies in question is to be equated. This practically implies that the classification of the first supply, i.e., that between the supplier and the undisclosed agent, overhangs that of the second supply, i.e., the onward supply between the undisclosed agent and the customer. In other terms, the classification, for EU VAT purposes, of the first supply also determines the VAT treatment of the second supply. Since the underlying transaction in the sharing economy - which is the first of the two relevant supplies - consists in the provision of either accommodation or passenger transport, also the second supply, concerning the services provided by the platform to its users, ought to be classified the same as the first supply, i.e., as services consisting in the provision of either accommodation or passenger transport.[174]

Noteworthy, the application of Article 28 of the VAT Directive prevents potential conflicts in the classification of platform services, should those services meet the characteristics of other services - say - electronically supplied services and, thus, fall within the scope of other place of supply rules - say - Articles 44 and 58 of the VAT Directive. As will be explained later in Chapter 8[175], the legal fiction contained in Article 28 of the VAT Directive also prevents the application of the provision of Article 9a of the Implementing Regulation, as long as this rule is applicable only where both supplies - the former made by the supplier to the undisclosed agent, while the latter performed by the undisclosed agent to the customer - qualify as electronically supplied services. Indeed, this circumstance does not occur in the sharing economy, due to the fact that the underlying transaction - which is the first of the two supplies in question - does not relate to the provision of electronically supplied services, rather to the offering of services having a 'tangible' nature, such as accommodation or passenger transport. It is in fact true that, in principle, it is only the service supplied by a platform to its users - to one or both parties - that needs to be assessed with a view of determining whether or not such service qualifies as an electronically supplied service, whereas the underlying service of accommodation or passenger transport should, instead, remain outside the scope of such an assessment.[176] Nevertheless, since, pursuant to the legal

174. *See* European Commission, Value Added Tax Committee, *Working Paper No. 947, Services Provided by an Electronic Platform Connecting for Remuneration, by means of a Smartphone Application, a Driver Using His Own Vehicle with Persons Who Wish to Make Urban Journeys. The Significance of the VAT Identification Number,* at 13 (taxud.c.1(2018)1735106).
175. *See* section §8.03[D].
176. In a similar vein, *see* European Commission, Value Added Tax Committee, *Working Paper No. 882, VAT 2015: VAT Treatment of Online Gambling Services (Follow-Up),* at 5 (taxud.c.1(2015)4459580), considering that, in the case of a gambler operator, 'the requirement of

fiction entailed in Article 28 of the VAT Directive, the nature of the two supplies needs to be identical, the supply made by the sharing economy platform – which is the second of the two supplies in question – could not be classified for EU VAT purposes otherwise than the underlying supply, which, in no event, can be regarded as entailing the provision of an electronically supplied service. Accordingly, by way of the legal fiction entailed in Article 28 of the VAT Directive, the services provided by a platform would plainly fall within the scope of Article 7(3)(u) of the Implementing Regulation, stipulating that the definition of electronically supplied services does not cover 'accommodation, car-hire, restaurant services, passenger transport or similar services booked online', that is services having a 'tangible' nature.[177]

§7.10 CHAPTER CONCLUSIONS AND RECOMMENDATIONS FOR IMPROVEMENT

[A] Main Findings

'Place of supply' rules, with the assistance of the territoriality and destination principles, define the territorial scope of EU VAT. Place of supply rules, fundamentally, function as distributive rules, whose aim is to allocate taxing rights between two or more jurisdictions, by determining which Member State shall have substantive jurisdiction to tax a cross-border transaction. Their main purpose is, essentially, to avoid potential conflicts of jurisdictions, which may result in either double taxation or non-taxation. The place of supply generally corresponds to the place where consumption actually takes place, for the determination of which EU VAT uses a combination of various proxies, which are applied differently based on the nature and the characteristics of the transaction at stake that were known or knowable at the time when the supply took place. Place of supply rules for services, in particular, are contained in Articles 43-59a of the VAT Directive. They primarily differ depending on the taxable status of the customer and, next to that, based on certain aspects of the transaction concerned. Notably, with regard to the sharing economy services assessed in the present study, besides the two default place of supply rules for B2B and B2C transactions laid down, respectively, in Articles 44 and 45 of the VAT Directive, different special place of supply rules may apply. Several considerations can be advanced in this regard.

The first special 'place of supply rule' considered is contained in Article 47 of the VAT Directive, stipulating that the place of supply of services connected with an immovable property is where the immovable property concerned is located. The ultimate purpose of this special place of supply rule is to ensure taxation at the

minimal human intervention refers to the relationship between the gambler and the betting operator', whereas 'the sport event is outside that relationship, even though the winners or losers on the betting activity are determined by the outcome of that event'.

177. European Commission, Value Added Tax Committee, *Working Paper No. 906, VAT 2015: Interaction between Electronically Supplied Services and Intermediation Services and Initial Discussion on the Scope of the Concept of Intermediation Services when Taken in a Broader Context*, at 3 (taxud.c.1(2016)3297911); European Commission, Value Added Tax Committee, *Working Paper No. 814. Treatment of Online Supplies Made by a Travel Agent to Final Consumers*, at 11 (taxud.c.1(2014)2806510). *See* sections §7.05[D][3] and §7.07[B].

presumed place of consumption of such services. Notably, this special rule applies irrespective of the taxable or non-taxable status of the recipient of the related services. Undoubtedly, the most relevant question with regard to this type of services relates to which extent services need to be 'connected with' an immovable property as to fall under the special place of supply rule in question. Some guidelines on this matter have been offered by the CJEU and a series of specifications in this regard are contained in the Implementing Regulation. Noteworthy, although considering 'intermediation in the sale, leasing or letting of immovable property' as types of services sufficiently connected with an immovable property, the Implementing Regulation does not stipulate likewise with regard to 'intermediation in the provision of hotel accommodation or accommodation in sectors with a similar function'. Indeed, the CJEU has attributed to this latter expression a broad construction, by including within its scope even situations in which a short-term leasing or letting of residential property does not entail the provision of complementary services (e.g., meals and drinks, cleaning of rooms, bed linen) commonly offered by a hotel to its own guests. Ultimately, the decisive criterion in order to classify a leasing or letting of immovable property is the nature and the characteristics of the supply at stake, with particular regard to the length of the lease or letting in question.

The second special 'place of supply rule' considered is contained in Article 48 of the VAT Directive, stipulating that the place of supply of a passenger transport is where the transport concerned takes place, proportionate to the distances covered. Thus, pursuant to such rule, when passenger transport is carried out in the territories of various countries, VAT is due in every country where the transport actually takes place. Notably, this special rule applies irrespective of the taxable or non-taxable status of the recipient of the related services. Nevertheless, the rule does not contribute in any meaningful way to a minimization of the administrative burden for a taxable person. A supplier of passenger transport services, in fact, needs to register for VAT and charge the tax to his customer in every country where the transport actually takes place, unless a reverse charge mechanism is applicable under a national VAT legislation. Importantly, the rule provides for the place where passenger transport services are to be taxed, but it does not also establish whether those services are actually taxed, as long as the services in question may be exempt with or without the right for the supplier to deduct his input VAT. Further, although not concerning, in principle, the method for determining the taxable amount, the concrete operation of the rule inevitably affects the allocation to be made, when the taxable amount is determined on an all-inclusive basis, between the Member States in which the supply is effected.

The third special 'place of supply rule' considered is contained in Article 58 of the VAT Directive, stipulating that the place of supply of electronically supplied services to a non-taxable person is where the customer is established, has his permanent address, or usually resides, unless the total value of the supplies in question does not exceed EUR 10,000 (or the equivalent in national currency) per calendar year. Notably, the place of supply is the same also in case of B2B transactions, although not based on Article 58, but instead pursuant to the default place of supply rule contained in Article 44 of the VAT Directive. Importantly, businesses supplying to non-taxable persons situated in another Member State may rely on the MOSS scheme, which, practically, enables those suppliers to account for the VAT due on their supplies via a web portal in the Member State of identification. Out of the four conditions for a service to qualify as an electronically supplied service as laid down in Article 7(1) of the Implementing Regulation, the most critical one undoubtedly relates to the fact that the service in question must only involve a 'minimal human intervention'. Nothing, in principle, prevents an intermediary from offering its own services via automated means. Nevertheless, according to the Commission, services provided by intermediaries cannot qualify as electronically supplied services if they relate to services having a 'tangible' nature, such as accommodation and passenger transport services, or, further, if they require an active involvement on the side of the intermediary, in the form of non-automated, human, distinct reactions by that intermediary. In case the intermediary is a platform, this translates into the fact the platform must not exert an influence and control over the underlying transaction, but instead it must provide only passive automated facilities, that is it should operate only with a view of putting the two parties of the underlying transaction into contact.

The fourth special 'place of supply rule' considered is contained in Article 59a of the VAT Directive, stipulating that a Member State, in case a service qualify as an electronically supplied service and, further, it is rendered to non-taxable persons, may overrule the normal operation of place of supply rules, as to rectify the place of actual consumption of that service, based on where the service in question is effectively used and enjoyed by the recipient. Thus, pursuant to such optional mechanism, in order to prevent double taxation, non-taxation, or distortion of competition caused by discrepancies existing between the place of supply rules of Member States and those of non-EU countries, the place of supply of – *inter alia* – electronically supplied services rendered to non-taxable persons may shift either inside or outside the EU. Nevertheless, the operation of the effective use and enjoyment rule might lead to situations of double taxation or non-taxation, where the classification of a service under EU VAT does not ultimately reconcile with that made by another VAT/GST system.

The fifth special 'place of supply rules' considered relate to services provided by intermediaries. Notably, two types of intermediaries can be distinguished under EU VAT, that is: (1) disclosed agents, i.e., those who act in the name and on behalf of one or both parties to an underlying transaction, and (2) undisclosed agents, i.e., those who instead deal with customers in their own name and use the supplies provided to them by other taxable person to make onward supplies to their customers. The relevant place of supply rules relating to services provided by the first type of intermediaries are contained in Articles 44 and 46 of the VAT Directive, depending on whether those services relate to, respectively, B2B or B2C transactions. While, in the first case, the place of supply is where the customer is established, in the second case, the place of supply is where the underlying transaction is supplied. As clarified by means of secondary EU law and, also, by the CJEU, a disclosed agent may render the services in question to one or both parties to the underlying transaction, to either taxable or non-taxable persons, and without altering the classification for EU VAT purposes of the underlying transaction. The relevant place of supply rule relating to services provided by the second type of intermediaries is contained in Article 28 of the VAT Directive. Pursuant to such rule, which creates the legal fiction of two identical supplies operated consecutively, an undisclosed agent is deemed to have received from the supplier the same services which he, then, supplies onward to his customer. Importantly, for being regarded as an undisclosed agent, the intermediary must play an economic role in the supply of services made by the supplier to the customer. Moreover, the two supplies which this legal fiction creates, i.e., the first supply between the supplier and the intermediary and the second supply between the intermediary and the customer, are considered as having the same nature and, therefore, they receive the same classification under EU VAT, although not necessarily the same place of supply rules would seamlessly apply to the two supplies in question.

In light of all the above, there are indeed various place of supply rules which might potentially apply to services provided in the sharing economy, both between a platform and its users or among users themselves, as long as the cross-border dimension of those supplies of services cannot be entirely excluded.

As regards underlying transactions among users of the four sharing economy platforms examined in the present study, which concern accommodation and passenger transport services, special place of supply rules apply, both of which make reference to the place where those services are physically carried out.

More specifically, accommodation services, such as those provided by hosts to guests on sharing economy platforms like Airbnb and HomeExchange, must be seen as 'services connected with immovable property' pursuant to Article 47 of the VAT Directive, stipulating that the relevant place of supply is where the immovable property concerned is located. Mainly based on the duration of the rental, those services are, in fact, to be characterized as short-term leases akin to and in competition with those provided by traditional hoteliers, to which the special place of supply rule contained in Article 47 of the VAT Directive applies and, further, which are fully subject to EU VAT pursuant to Article 135(2)(a) of the same directive. A question might, eventually, arise with regard to additional services offered together with the provision of bare accommodation, such as it is in the case of 'experiences' offered by hosts to guests on Airbnb. In such event, it ought to be ascertained, in particular, whether the characteristics of a lease predominate, or if, instead, the services in question relate to the supply of a more 'complex' service.

Services provided by drivers to passengers on sharing economy platforms like Uber and BlaBlaCar are, instead, to be characterized as 'passenger transport' services pursuant to Article 48 of the VAT Directive, stipulating that the relevant place of supply is where the transport takes place, proportionate to the distances covered. Such classification implies that, in case of a cross-border journey, the driver has to register (if not already established therein), collect, and remit the VAT due in every country where the transport actually takes place. More precisely, the VAT levied on the overall consideration that the driver receives from the passenger needs to be split and attributed to the tax authorities of every Member State in proportion to the distances covered in the territory of each country.

The application of the aforementioned place of supply rules to services provided among platform users is, indeed, consistent with the five legal principles which compose the evaluation model as conceptualized in the present study. More specifically, in so far as, in the context of accommodation and passenger transport, the same place of supply rules apply to sharing economy and more conventional business activities, equality and neutrality are ensured. Simplicity and flexibility are also respected, although some compliance issues could not entirely be excluded in case of activities having a cross-border dimension, as it might be when the individual supplier and the immovable property are located in different jurisdictions or, further, in case of cross-border passenger transport services. Further, inasmuch as those rules constitute a 'clear, simple and practical criterion' for place of supply purposes, simplicity is ensured as well.[178] Also from the perspective of the flexibility principle, the innovative ways in which sharing economy services are provided, do not hold in favour of changing the current place of supply rules.

Undoubtedly, services provided by sharing economy platforms to their users, either to one or both parties, are much more difficult to assess for place of supply purposes. Indeed, various classifications of those services are possible under EU VAT.

A first possibility is that, based on their ultimate function, the services in question are regarded as intermediary services to which Article 44 or 46 of the VAT Directive apply, depending on whether the transaction in question is, respectively, B2B or B2C. While, in the first case, the place of supply is where the customer is established, in the second case, the place of supply is instead where the underlying transaction, consisting in either accommodation or passenger transport services, is supplied. Thus, based on this latter provision, in case a platform like Airbnb or HomeExchange supplies its own services to a non-taxable person, the place of supply of those services is where the immovable property used in the provision of accommodation services by the individual supplier is located. In case a platform like Uber or BlaBlaCar supplies its own services to a non-taxable person, the place of supply of those services is instead where the passenger transport service provided by the individual supplier actually takes place.

A second possibility is that a platform does not act in the name of another person, but instead in its own name. In such event, the services provided by the platform to its users could no longer be regarded as intermediary services, but instead must be characterized as 'ordinary' services, i.e., services to which Article 44 or 45 of the VAT Directive apply, depending on whether the transaction in question is, respectively, B2B or B2C. Notably, under those rules, the place of supply is, respectively, where the customer or the supplier is established. The same classification might also apply in the – in the author's opinion, unlikely – event that, in light of their nature and characteristics, platform services could not be classified in any other manner.

A third possibility is that the platform acts in its own name and, yet, on behalf of another person. In such event, based on the deemed rule contained in Article 28 of the VAT Directive, the platform is no longer considered as an intermediary, but rather as a full-fledged supplier of the underlying service, concerning the provision of either accommodation or passenger transport. The intervention of the provision contained in Article 28 of the VAT Directive, in fact, extends the place of supply rule applicable to the underlying transaction also to the supply of the related services provided by the platform to its users. Pursuant to such deemed rule, platform services would, thus, fall

178. NL: ECJ, 17 Jul. 1997, Case C-190/95, *ARO Lease BV v. Inspecteur van de Belastingdienst Grote Ondernemingen te Amsterdam*, paras 20 and 26.

within the scope of Article 47 or 48 of the VAT Directive, depending on whether the underlying transaction concerns, respectively, accommodation or passenger transport services.

A fourth possibility is that platform services are characterized as electronically supplied services, provided they are essentially automated and involve only a minimal human intervention, pursuant to the definition laid down in Article 7(1) of the Implementing Regulation. In such event, while, in case of a B2B transaction, the default rule contained in Article 44 of the VAT Directive applies, in case of a B2C transaction, the relevant place of supply rule is contained in Article 58 of the VAT Directive. Nevertheless, under both those rules, the place of supply is where the customer is established, has his permanent address, or usually resides. Ultimately, the possibility to qualify platform services as electronically supplied services essentially depends on the level of influence and control exerted by a platform over the underlying transaction. Based on the business model specifically adopted by each of the four sharing economy platforms examined in the present study, the author submits that Uber and BlaBlaCar are actively involved in the provision of the underlying services, whereas for Airbnb and HomeExchange the situation is less clear-cut.

A fifth and last possibility is that platform services are characterized as electronically supplied services, are rendered to non-taxable persons and, further, a Member State has implemented the effective use and enjoyment rule contained in Article 59a of the VAT Directive, pursuant to which the place of supply of those services may shift either inside or outside the EU, based on where the service in question is effectively used and enjoyed by the recipient. Noteworthy, the application of such optional provision might lead to situations of double taxation or non-taxation, where the classification of a platform service under EU VAT does not ultimately reconcile with that made by another VAT/GST system, as shown, respectively, by the case of a Colombian resident who books accommodation in a Member State, and the converse situation of an EU resident who books accommodation in Colombia through Airbnb.

The mere existence of so many different possibilities as regards the classification of platform services under place of supply rules, clearly, does not consent to meet the objectives entailed in the five legal principles which compose the evaluation model as conceptualized in the present study. In particular, the sheer circumstance that different sharing economy platforms, as well as various Member States, might classify, for place of supply purposes, platform services in a divergent manner wreaks havoc with the principles of equality and neutrality, in so far as it might create several inconsistencies in the interpretation and application of the same EU VAT provisions, lead to situations of double taxation or non-taxation, and generate significant distortions in the internal market. Moreover, uncertainties surrounding the classification, for place of supply purposes, of platform services might induce platforms to engage in purposive misclassifications of their own services or, even, simply to change their classification from time to time. As seen, BlaBlaCar currently regards its own services as electronically supplied services, whereas the company previously considered them as intermediary services.[179] Neutrality is also impaired from an international perspective, in so far as

179. *See* section §7.07[C][2].

the application of the effective use and enjoyment rule might lead to situations of double taxation or non-taxation. With specific regard to the equality principle, it also ought to be recalled that, for determining whether transactions are similar and therefore shall receive the same VAT treatment, the OECD International VAT/GST Guidelines make reference only to the characterization of the services supplied, whereas the way in which a transaction is made is, by itself, immaterial.[180] Obviously, any potential divergent interpretation and application of place of supply rules neither serves a practical interest in simplicity of administration and collection.[181] Moreover, although a flexible approach in drafting and interpreting legal provision is generally welcome, it is undoubted that too much flexibility, such, indeed, it occurs in the case in question, breeds legal uncertainty.

[B] Recommendations

In terms of possible recommendations for improving the current EU VAT system in relation to the issues identified in this chapter, the author submits that no change of the current place of supply rules for underlying services in the sharing economy, concerning the provision of either accommodation or passenger transport, is required. The relevant place of supply rules contained, respectively, in Articles 47 and 48 of the VAT Directive are, in fact, sound and consistent with the ultimate objective of EU VAT to locate the place of supply where consumption of those services actually takes place. Even the assessment conducted through the evaluation model as conceptualized in the present study, indeed, provides no ground for reviewing such place of supply rules.

Rather, the classification, for place of supply purposes, of services provided by sharing economy platforms to their users, either to one or both parties, is not crystal clear and, indeed, inconsistencies in the interpretation and application of the same rules by different sharing economy platforms, as well as by various Member States, are very much possible.[182] Some measures for clarifying the classification, for place of supply purposes, of platform services are therefore needed. Further, in order to avoid potential conflicts of jurisdiction among Member States, as well as purposive misclassifications by platforms of their own services, which might lead to situations of double taxation or non-taxation, a single, more straightforward proxy for determining the place of supply of those services ought to be laid down. Notably, the author submits that three alternative solutions might be implemented. Importantly, each of those three solutions is to be intended as a result of a mere policy decision, rather than reflecting the – supposedly – 'true' nature and characteristics of the services provided by sharing

180. *See* OECD, *supra* n. 11, at 30 and section §3.04.
181. DE: Opinion of the Advocate General, 25 Apr. 1996, Case C-327/94, *Jürgen Dudda v. Finanzgericht Bergisch Gladbach*, para. 35.
182. Notably, it appears that tax authorities of many Member States have not yet reached a formal position, neither firm views, on how to qualify, for EU VAT purposes, the relationships existent between a platform and its users. Presently, divergent interpretation and application of the rules in question by different Member States are, therefore, very much possible. *See* European Commission, Value Added Tax Committee, *Minutes 111th Meeting – 30 November 2018*, at 8 (taxud.c.1(2019)1709508).

economy platforms, circumstances which, as seen, are difficult – if feasible at all – to assess. In the author's view, the classification of a service under place of supply rules is, therefore, only a 'political' matter. Arguably, by ending the casuistic and rather confusing classification of platform services for place of supply purposes, the implementation of those three alternative solutions would also accord with the five legal principles which compose the evaluation model as conceptualized in the present study.

A first alternative solution is to treat platform services always as intermediary services, that is as services provided by a disclosed agent to one or both parties of the underlying transaction. In such event, while, in case of a B2B transaction, the default place of supply rule of Article 44 of the VAT Directive applies, in case of a B2C transaction, the relevant place of supply rule is contained in Article 46 of the VAT Directive. This solution has advantages but also drawbacks. The main advantage is that the classification of platform services as intermediary services accords with the broad reading of Article 7(3)(u) of the Implementation Regulation made by the Commission, pursuant to which, in no event, services having a 'tangible' nature, such as those relating to the provision of accommodation and passenger transport, can be regarded as electronically supplied services. The main drawback of this solution, instead, relates to the fact that whether the recipient of the services in question is a taxable or a non-taxable person is important, in so far as distinct place of supply rules are associated with the different taxable status of the customer. While in case of B2B transactions the place of supply is, in fact, where the customer is established, in case of B2C transactions the place of supply is, instead, where the underlying transaction, concerning the provision of either accommodation or passenger transport services, is supplied. Operatively, this first alternative solution might be implemented by inserting a clarification in the text of Article 7(3)(u) of the Implementing Regulation. The amended provision of Article 7(3)(u) of the Implementing Regulation might then read as follows (additions in italics):

> Article 7
>
> [...]
>
> 3. Paragraph 1 shall not cover the following:
>
> [...]
>
> u. accommodation, car-hire, restaurant services passenger transport or similar services booked online *or facilitated by collaborative platforms.*[183]

A second alternative solution is to treat platform services always as electronically supplied services, that is as services delivered over the Internet or an electronic network, which are essentially automated, involve minimal human intervention, and are impossible to ensure in the absence of information technology, as stipulated by Article 7(1) of the Implementing Regulation. In such event, while, in case of a B2B transaction, the default place of supply rule of Article 44 of the VAT Directive applies,

183. The author submits that the use of the term 'collaborative platforms', instead of 'sharing economy platforms', is preferable, given that such term is included in the Commission's Communication on *A European Agenda for the Collaborative Economy* and, hence, the use of such an expression is already established under EU law.

in case of a B2C transaction, the relevant place of supply rule is contained in Article 58 of the VAT Directive. This solution has several advantages. First, it consents to align the treatment, for place of supply purposes, of services provided by sharing economy platforms with those operated by other digital companies, such as Amazon, Apple, Facebook, Google, or Netflix. Second, this solution appears future oriented, in so far as, in the forthcoming years, an increasing number of services are likely to be provided by sharing economy platforms, even at a distance. Third, this solution renders quite unimportant whether the recipient of the services in question is a taxable person or not, as long as both the two relevant place of supply rules, contained, respectively, in Articles 44 and 58 of the VAT Directive, make reference to the place where the customer is established, has a permanent address, or usually resides. The main drawback of this solution, instead, relates to the fact the individual supplier and/or the individual customer, especially if they are non-taxable persons, might hold an incentive, as to avoid paying VAT on their own purchases, to falsely declare that the place of their usual residence is located outside the EU. Operatively, this second alternative solution might be implemented by amending the current definition of electronically supplied services laid down in Article 7(1) of the Implementing Regulation. In particular, the definition in question could be amended as no longer referring to the conditions of a service being essentially automated and involving minimal human intervention, but instead as only making reference to the circumstance that the service in question, due to its digital nature, can be provided at a distance. The amended definition of Article 7(1) of the Implementing Regulation might then read as follows (additions in italics):

> Article 7
>
> 1. 'Electronically supplied services' as referred to in Directive 2006/112/EC shall include services which are delivered over the Internet or an electronic network, *where the supplier and the recipient of the service, due to its digital nature, can be located in different places, and which* are impossible to ensure in the absence of information technology.[184]
>
> [...].

A third alternative solution is to treat platform services always the same as the underlying services to which they relate, that is as services connected with immovable property or concerning passenger transport. In such event, the very same place of supply rules for the underlying services equally apply to the services provided by the related sharing economy platform. In this way, the application scope of the place of supply for the underlying services is extended as to cover also the related platform services. The main advantage of this solution is that exactly the same place of supply rules applicable to the underlying services operate also with regard to the related

184. The author wishes to credit the prior formulation of a similar provision both to Lamensch, *supra* n. 117, at para. 4.2., and Merkx, *supra* n. 118. Ultimately, under the amended definition of 'electronically supplied services' proposed above, the classification of a service in that category would depend only on the medium for and the mode of delivery (i.e., over the Internet or an electronic network and, further, on a remote basis), rather than on its – supposedly – 'true' nature and characteristics.

supply made by the sharing economy platform, so that there is no need for a platform to determine whether the supplier and the customer is a taxable person or not. The main drawback, instead, relates to the fact that this solution entails a quite radical departure from the current EU VAT place of supply rules. Operatively, this third alternative solution might be implemented by inserting a specific reference to services provided by a sharing economy platform to its users in the text of Articles 47 and 48 of the VAT Directive. The amended provisions of Articles 47 and 48 of the VAT Directive might then read as follows (additions in italics):

> Article 47
>
> The place of supply of services connected with immovable property, including the services of experts and estate agents, the provision *and the facilitation, even by a collaborative platform,* of accommodation in the hotel sector or in sectors with a similar function, such as holiday camps or sites developed for use as camping sites, the granting of rights to use immovable property and services for the preparation and coordination of construction work, such as the services of architects and of firms providing on-site supervision, shall be the place where the immovable property is located.
>
> Article 48
>
> The place of supply of passenger transport, *including the facilitation, even by a collaborative platform, of passenger transport,* shall be the place where the transport takes place, proportionate to the distances covered.

In the alternative, this third solution might be implemented, operatively, by means of specific provisions to be inserted in the Implementing Regulation. The amended provision of Article 31a(2), which contains a list of services to be considered as sufficiently connected with an immovable property, and a new and renumbered Article 32 of the Implementing Regulation might then read as follows (additions in italics):

> Article 31a
>
> [...]
>
> 2. Paragraph 1 shall cover, in particular, the following:
>
> [...]
>
> i. the provision *and the facilitation, even by a collaborative platform,* of accommodation in the hotel sector or in sectors with a similar function, such as holiday camps or sites developed for use as camping sites, including the right to stay in a specific place resulting from the conversion of time-share usage rights and the like;
>
> [...]
>
> *Article 32*
>
> *Services in respect of passenger transport as referred to in Article 48 of Directive 2006/112/EC shall include the facilitation, even by a collaborative platform, of the supply of passenger transport.*

Table 7.1 below provides a schematic summary concerning the presumed classification, for place of supply purposes, of sharing economy services under the current place of supply rules, as laid down in the VAT Directive.

Table 7.1 Classification for Place of Supply Purposes of Sharing Economy Services under the Current Place of Supply Rules

Type of Service	*Classification*	*Transaction*	*Article*	*Place of Supply*
Host's service on Airbnb	Service connected with immovable property	B2B	Article 47	Place where the immovable property is located
Host's service on Airbnb	Service connected with immovable property	B2C	Article 47	Place where the immovable property is located
Host's service on HomeExchange	Service connected with immovable property	B2B	Article 47	Place where the immovable property is located
Host's service on HomeExchange	Service connected with immovable property	B2C	Article 47	Place where the immovable property is located
Driver's service on Uber	Passenger transport service	B2B	Article 48	Place where the transport takes place, proportionate to the distances covered
Driver's service on Uber	Passenger transport service	B2C	Article 48	Place where the transport takes place, proportionate to the distances covered
Driver's service on BlaBlaCar	Passenger transport service	B2B	Article 48	Place where the transport takes place, proportionate to the distances covered
Driver's service on BlaBlaCar	Passenger transport service	B2C	Article 48	Place where the transport takes place, proportionate to the distances covered
Airbnb's service (1)	Intermediary service	B2B	Article 44	Place where the customer is established
Airbnb's service (1)	Intermediary service	B2C	Article 46 (Article 47)	Place of supply of the underlying transaction (accommodation services)

Airbnb's service (2)	Electronically supplied service	B2B	Article 44	Place where the customer is established
Airbnb's service (2)	Electronically supplied service	B2C	Article 58 (*)	Place where the customer usually resides
HomeExchange's service (1)	Intermediary service	B2B (**)	Article 44	Place where the customer is established
HomeExchange's service (1)	Intermediary service	B2C	Article 46 (Article 47)	Place of supply of the underlying transaction (accommodation services)
HomeExchange's service (2)	Electronically supplied service	B2B (**)	Article 44	Place where the customer is established
HomeExchange's service (2)	Electronically supplied service	B2C	Article 58 (*)	Place where the customer usually resides
Uber's service (1)	Intermediary service	B2B	Article 44	Place where the customer is established
Uber's service (1)	Intermediary service	B2C (**)	Article 46 (Article 48)	Place of supply of the underlying transaction (passenger transport services)
Uber's service (2)	Electronically supplied service	B2B	Article 44	Place where the customer is established
Uber's service (2)	Electronically supplied service	B2C (**)	Article 58 (*)	Place where the customer usually resides
BlaBlaCar's service (1)	Intermediary service	B2B	Article 44	Place where the customer is established
BlaBlaCar's service (1)	Intermediary service	B2C	Article 46 (Article 48)	Place of supply of the underlying transaction (passenger transport services)

Type of Service	*Classification*	*Transaction*	*Article*	*Place of Supply*
BlaBlaCar's service (2)	Electronically supplied service	B2B	Article 44	Place where the customer is established
BlaBlaCar's service (2)	Electronically supplied service	B2C	Article 58 (*)	Place where the customer usually resides

(*) Article 59a (a) and (b) may also apply

(**) Quite unlikely

Tables 7.2, 7.3, and 7.4 below provide a schematic summary concerning the classification, for place of supply purposes, of sharing economy services, as suggested, respectively, in the first, second, and third alternative solutions laid down above.

Table 7.2 Classification for Place of Supply Purposes of Sharing Economy Services as Proposed in the First Alternative Solution

Type of Service	*Classification*	*Transaction*	*Article*	*Place of Supply*
Host's service on Airbnb	Service connected with immovable property	B2B	Article 47	Place where the immovable property is located
Host's service on Airbnb	Service connected with immovable property	B2C	Article 47	Place where the immovable property is located
Host's service on HomeExchange	Service connected with immovable property	B2B	Article 47	Place where the immovable property is located
Host's service on HomeExchange	Service connected with immovable property	B2C	Article 47	Place where the immovable property is located
Driver's service on Uber	Passenger transport service	B2B	Article 48	Place where the transport takes place, proportionate to the distances covered
Driver's service on Uber	Passenger transport service	B2C	Article 48	Place where the transport takes place, proportionate to the distances covered
Driver's service on BlaBlaCar	Passenger transport service	B2B	Article 48	Place where the transport takes place, proportionate to the distances covered
Driver's service on BlaBlaCar	Passenger transport service	B2C	Article 48	Place where the transport takes place, proportionate to the distances covered
Airbnb's service	Intermediary service	B2B	Article 44	Place where the customer is established
Airbnb's service	Intermediary service	B2C	Article 46 (Article 47)	Place of supply of the underlying transaction (accommodation services)

Type of Service	*Classification*	*Transaction*	*Article*	*Place of Supply*
HomeExchange's service	Intermediary service	B2B (**)	Article 44	Place where the customer is established
HomeExchange's service	Intermediary service	B2C	Article 46 (Article 47)	Place of supply of the underlying transaction (accommodation services)
Uber's service	Intermediary service	B2B	Article 44	Place where the customer is established
Uber's service	Intermediary service	B2C (**)	Article 46 (Article 48)	Place of supply of the underlying transaction (passenger transport services)
BlaBlaCar's service	Intermediary service	B2B	Article 44	Place where the customer is established
BlaBlaCar's service	Intermediary service	B2C	Article 46 (Article 48)	Place of supply of the underlying transaction (passenger transport services)

(**) Quite unlikely

Table 7.3 Classification for Place of Supply Purposes of Sharing Economy Services as Proposed in the Second Alternative Solution

Type of Service	*Classification*	*Transaction*	*Article*	*Place of Supply*
Host's service on Airbnb	Service connected with immovable property	B2B	Article 47	Place where the immovable property is located
Host's service on Airbnb	Service connected with immovable property	B2C	Article 47	Place where the immovable property is located
Host's service on HomeExchange	Service connected with immovable property	B2B	Article 47	Place where the immovable property is located
Host's service on HomeExchange	Service connected with immovable property	B2C	Article 47	Place where the immovable property is located
Driver's service on Uber	Passenger transport service	B2B	Article 48	Place where the transport takes place, proportionate to the distances covered
Driver's service on Uber	Passenger transport service	B2C	Article 48	Place where the transport takes place, proportionate to the distances covered
Driver's service on BlaBlaCar	Passenger transport service	B2B	Article 48	Place where the transport takes place, proportionate to the distances covered
Driver's service on BlaBlaCar	Passenger transport service	B2C	Article 48	Place where the transport takes place, proportionate to the distances covered
Airbnb's service	Electronically supplied service	B2B	Article 44	Place where the customer is established
Airbnb's service	Electronically supplied service	B2C	Article 58 (*)	Place where the customer usually resides
HomeExchange's service	Electronically supplied service	B2B (**)	Article 44	Place where the customer is established

Type of Service	*Classification*	*Transaction*	*Article*	*Place of Supply*
HomeExchange's service	Electronically supplied service	B2C	Article 58 (*)	Place where the customer usually resides
Uber's service	Electronically supplied service	B2B	Article 44	Place where the customer is established
Uber's service	Electronically supplied service	B2C (**)	Article 58 (*)	Place where the customer usually resides
BlaBlaCar's service	Electronically supplied service	B2B	Article 44	Place where the customer is established
BlaBlaCar's service	Electronically supplied service	B2C	Article 58 (*)	Place where the customer usually resides

(*) Article 59a (a) and (b) may also apply

(** Quite unlikely

Table 7.4 Classification for Place of Supply Purposes of Sharing Economy Services as Proposed in the Third Alternative Solution

Type of Service	*Classification*	*Transaction*	*Article*	*Place of Supply*
Host's service on Airbnb	Service connected with immovable property	B2B	Article 47	Place where the immovable property is located
Host's service on Airbnb	Service connected with immovable property	B2C	Article 47	Place where the immovable property is located
Host's service on HomeExchange	Service connected with immovable property	B2B	Article 47	Place where the immovable property is located
Host's service on HomeExchange	Service connected with immovable property	B2C	Article 47	Place where the immovable property is located
Driver's service on Uber	Passenger transport service	B2B	Article 48	Place where the transport takes place, proportionate to the distances covered
Driver's service on Uber	Passenger transport service	B2C	Article 48	Place where the transport takes place, proportionate to the distances covered
Driver's service on BlaBlaCar	Passenger transport service	B2B	Article 48	Place where the transport takes place, proportionate to the distances covered
Driver's service on BlaBlaCar	Passenger transport service	B2C	Article 48	Place where the transport takes place, proportionate to the distances covered
Airbnb's service	Service connected with immovable property (simplification provision)	B2B	Article 47	Place where the immovable property is located
Airbnb's service	Service connected with immovable property (simplification provision)	B2C	Article 47	Place where the immovable property is located

Type of Service	*Classification*	*Transaction*	*Article*	*Place of Supply*
HomeExchange's service	Service connected with immovable property (simplification provision)	B2B (**)	Article 47	Place where the immovable property is located
HomeExchange's service	Service connected with immovable property (simplification provision)	B2C	Article 47	Place where the immovable property is located
Uber's service	Passenger transport service (simplification provision)	B2B	Article 48	Place where the transport takes place, proportionate to the distances covered
Uber's service	Passenger transport service (simplification provision)	B2C (**)	Article 48	Place where the transport takes place, proportionate to the distances covered
BlaBlaCar's service	Passenger transport service (simplification provision)	B2B	Article 48	Place where the transport takes place, proportionate to the distances covered
BlaBlaCar's service	Passenger transport service (simplification provision)	B2C	Article 48	Place where the transport takes place, proportionate to the distances covered

(**) Quite unlikely

CHAPTER 8

Liability for Collection and Remittance of VAT

§8.01 INTRODUCTION

Collection and remittance to the competent authorities of the amount due is crucial to the functioning of every tax system. Under EU VAT, other than in a single-stage tax such as the RST, collection and remittance to the competent authorities of the amount due occur at each stage of the supply chain, from the original supplier till the end consumer.[1] The present chapter aims to filter out the main regimes in relation to a 'liability for collection and remittance of VAT' applicable in the context of the sharing economy. More specifically, the ensuing analysis seeks to explore whether and, eventually, to which extent a 'liability for collection and remittance of VAT' may be imposed upon sharing economy platforms in lieu of individual suppliers.

Collection and remittance of VAT can be secured through a variety of approaches. Notably, the obligation to collect and remit VAT can be imposed, individually or in some combination, respectively, on: (1) the supplier, (2) the customer, or (3) an intermediary.[2] Attribution of a liability for collection and remittance of VAT to one or more persons is, ultimately, a mere policy decision, in respect of which every jurisdiction is fully sovereign, although, under EU VAT, each Member State must exercise such sovereignty within the boundaries established by the VAT Directive. Under EU VAT, liability regimes for collection and remittance of VAT are numerous and, in particular, can be found in Articles 193-205 of the VAT Directive. A sort of liability regime is also entailed in Article 28 of the VAT Directive, considering the

1. *See* section §1.02.
2. OECD, *Mechanisms for the Effective Collection of VAT/GST When the Supplier Is Not Located in the Jurisdiction of Taxation* at 12 and 17 (OECD Publishing 2017).

situation of an undisclosed agent, i.e., a taxable person who, acting in his own name but on behalf of another person, takes part in a supply of services to a customer.[3]

From a tax design perspective, various persons can, in principle, be held liable for collecting and remitting VAT. The most straightforward approach is to impose such kind of liability upon the supplier. Under this approach, usually referred to as 'supplier collection model', obligations resulting from concepts as different as 'taxable person' and 'tax liability' are attributed to the same person, i.e., the person making the taxable transaction.

Although, in general, it is desirable that VAT is collected and remitted by the taxable person who also makes the taxable transaction, there are situations which suggest operating otherwise and considering, instead, another person as the one liable for collection and remittance of the amount due.[4] The most expeditious approach in this regard is that the other party to a transaction, i.e., the customer, assumes such kind of liability, especially where only that party is established in the jurisdiction where VAT is due.[5] Under this approach, usually referred to as 'customer collection model', which, indeed, subverts the basic functioning of VAT, as long as this tax entails invoicing by the supplier and deduction by the customer, VAT is effectively transformed into a 'purchase tax'.[6] The best known example of customer collection model is the so-called 'reverse charge' or 'self-assessment' mechanism, which, indeed, the OECD recommends as the most suitable approach for B2B transactions.[7] The 'reverse charge' or 'self-assessment' mechanism, instead, is not equally endorsed for B2C transactions, as long as this approach is considered largely ineffectual, since end consumers are not entitled to claim any input tax deduction and, hence, they usually do not also have any incentive to report their own transactions[8], unless an external inducement is provided to them in order to solve this 'last mile' problem (e.g., in the form of monetary rewards to reporting end consumers).[9]

3. *See* sections §7.09[C] and §8.03[C].
4. Notably, in case of a supplier 'not located in the jurisdiction of taxation'. For a discussion, *see* W. Hellerstein, S. Buydens & D. Koulouri, *Simplified Registration and Collection Mechanisms for Taxpayers That Are Not Located in the Jurisdiction of Taxation: A Review and Assessment* (OECD Publishing 2018).
5. A valid alternative approach may consist in the introduction of 'simplified registration and compliance regimes' for non-established suppliers. For a discussion, *see* OECD, *supra* n. 2, at 35-51.
6. European Commission, *Common System of Value Added Tax: Arrangements for Taxing Transactions Carried Out by Non-Established Taxable Persons. Communication and Report from the Commission to the Council and the European Parliament*, at 63, COM(94) 471 final.
7. OECD, *supra* n. 2, at 23-24.
8. D. Pomeranz, *No Taxation Without Information: Deterrence and Self-Enforcement in the Value Added Tax*, 105 Amer. Econ. Rev. 8 (2015), at 2540. Indeed, a tax reporting obligation imposed upon end consumers is sometimes dubbed as a 'tax on honesty'. *See* W. Hellerstein, *A Hitchhiker's Guide to the OECD's International VAT/GST Guidelines*, 18 Flo. Tax Rev. 10 (2016), at 621.
9. For an example in this regard, J. Naritomi, *Consumers as Tax Auditors* (2018), papers.ssrn.com (accessed 31 Mar. 2019).

A third category of persons can also be held liable for collecting and remitting VAT. Those persons are intermediaries.[10] Under this approach, usually referred to as 'intermediary collection model', collection and remittance of VAT, instead of being imposed upon the supplier or the customer, is trusted to another party which intervenes in the supply chain. The main advantage associated with such liability regime is that intermediaries are, normally, fewer and, thus, also easier to monitor than customers, especially if those latter happen to be end consumers. Moreover, intermediaries are usually endowed with all the necessary resources, in terms of information and means, to comply with obligations resulting from the imposition of a liability for collection and remittance of VAT upon them. This circumstance is further magnified in the context of C2C transactions, where the monitoring of those transactions by tax authorities is, indeed, far more difficult, due to the non-business nature of undertakings taking part in those transactions.[11] The following sections focus on liability regimes designed for intermediaries and, in particular, digital platforms, which, indeed, constitute the most relevant approach for ensuring collection and remittance of VAT in the context of the sharing economy.

The term 'intermediary' is an umbrella concept, which may well include a wide array of persons, being either financial and payment institutions, redelivers, importers, transporters, and fulfilment houses (in case of supplies of goods), or, indeed, digital platforms. As a matter of fact, in all advanced economies, presently most taxes are collected through the intervention of third parties, being either private or public institutions, which, practically, are forced to act as agents for the government.[12] And indeed, actual data reveal that tax enforcement is excellent whenever a system of third party withholding or reporting is put in place.[13] Scholarly, withholding taxation is also

10. The author submits that the term 'intermediaries', rather than 'third parties', ought to be preferred in this context, inasmuch as third parties may fulfil a role even under a supplier or customer collection model, especially in terms of reducing administrative and routine tasks for VAT-liable persons, such as those concerning registration, tax calculation and remittance, invoicing, filing and submission of returns and recapitulative statements, as well as record keeping. Notably, specialized third-party providers like Amazon offers services at a budget price which help small businesses comply with their own VAT obligations. *See Save Time and Money with VAT Services on Amazon*, https://services.amazon.co.uk/services/vat-services-on-amazon/faq.html (accessed 31 Mar. 2019).
11. Indeed, the OECD has acknowledged the potential role that intermediaries could play in simplifying compliance, not only for non-established suppliers, but, more broadly, in relation to the fulfilment of the obligations by SMEs, as early as 2000. *See* OECD, *Report by the Technology Technical Advisory Group (TAG)* at 15 (OECD Publishing 2000). Notably, the OECD has expressed a similar view even more recently, while evaluating the role of intermediaries intervening in the supply of products over the Internet and, in particular, the role of digital platforms in this regard. *See* OECD, *supra* n. 2, at 25-27.
12. For a perspective on this, *see* e.g., H.J. Kleven, C.T. Kreiner & E. Saez, *Why Can Modern Governments Tax So Much? An Agency Model of Firms as Fiscal Intermediaries*, 83 Economica 330 (2016), at 219-246.
13. OECD, *Tax Administration 2015: Comparative Information on OECD and Other Advanced and Emerging Economies* at 297-312 (OECD Publishing 2015). Nevertheless, even tax collection and remittance by a third party may be tilted if this party, ultimately, colludes with the taxpayer. For a discussion, *see* L. Lederman, *Statutory Speed Bumps: The Roles Third Parties Play in Tax Compliance*, 60 Stan. L. Rev. 3 (2007), at 695-743.

proposed as a viable solution against a series of tax issues arising in the digital economy.[14]

Notably, the OECD distinguishes two broad approaches based on which a liability for collection and remittance of VAT can be imposed upon an intermediary. The first approach is the 'contractual approach', pursuant to which a liability for collection and remittance of VAT is attributed to an intermediary if, and to the extent that, it is so established by contractual or other legal arrangements between the various parties intervening in the supply chain. The second approach, instead, is the 'deemed supplier approach', pursuant to which an intermediary is, by means of a legal fiction, statutorily designated as the supplier upon whom a liability for collection and remittance of VAT is imposed.[15] Indeed, this latter approach has been adopted by an increasing number of jurisdictions, in relation to cross-border supplies of digital services and intangibles as well as for importation of low-value goods made through digital platforms.[16]

Ultimately, nothing seems to prevent the attribution of a liability for collection and remittance of VAT to digital platforms even in the narrower context of the sharing economy. Indeed, this circumstance was plainly recognized even by the OECD, which, in 2019, has commenced a groundwork examination of the potential role that sharing economy platforms may fulfil in the context of collection and remittance of VAT in lieu of individual suppliers.[17] The present chapter, fundamentally, seeks to answer to the same query, by establishing whether and, eventually, to which extent, it is feasible and also desirable to impose a liability for collection and remittance of VAT upon sharing economy platforms in lieu of individual suppliers. Nevertheless, inasmuch as such liability may be developed in parallel to other kinds of liabilities, further possibilities in this regard are equally explored. In this connection, an analysis of the main liability

14. A. Báez & Y. Brauner, *Taxing the Digital Economy Post BEPS ... Seriously* (2019), https://papers.ssrn.com (accessed 31 Mar. 2019).
15. OECD, *supra* n. 2, at 25-27.
16. OECD, *The Role of Digital Platforms in the Collection of VAT/GST on Online Sales* at 15-17 (OECD Publishing 2019). Notably, in the last few years, liability regimes for digital platforms, besides under EU VAT (*see* section §8.03[B]), have been introduced or proposed under Australian, Canadian, Indian, New Zealand, and Singaporean VAT/GST laws. For a high-level overview of some of these regimes, *see* KPMG, *VAT/GST Treatment of Cross-Border Services. 2017 Survey* (2017), https://assets.kpmg.com/content/dam/kpmg/xx/pdf/2017/11/ess-survey-13-nov-17.pdf (accessed 31 Mar. 2019). Indeed, the problem for a jurisdiction to enforce its own taxing rights over foreign or non-established taxpayers is not limited to the field of VAT/GST, but instead it is also of interest to the collection and remittance of other taxes, such as the RST in the US subnational context. In this regard, *see* US: Supreme Court, 21 Jun. 2018, *South Dakota v. Wayfair Inc.*, No. 17-494, 138 S. Ct. 2080 (2018), reversing prior US constitutional case law, which inhibited US subnational states from requiring taxpayers that were not physically present in a subnational state to collect the RST on sales made in their own territory.
17. The examination of the potential role which sharing economy platforms could play in the context of collection and remittance of VAT, instead, was carved out from discussions concerning the potential role played in this regard by other digital platforms. *See* OECD, *supra* n. 16, at 19, considering that supplies in the sharing economy 'have specific characteristics' compared with other digital supplies and that, for this reason, the OECD Working Party No. 9 on Consumption Taxes (WP9) 'has decided to develop work in this area as a separate work stream'.

regimes for collection and remittance of VAT contained in the VAT Directive is provided in the following section.[18]

§8.02 MAIN LIABILITY REGIMES UNDER EU VAT

Under EU VAT, liability for collection and remittance of the amount due to the tax authorities of the Member State having jurisdiction to tax a certain transaction is, in principle, attributed to the supplier, i.e., the taxable person making the taxable transaction. Notably, in such event, the concept of 'taxable person', contained in Article 9 of the VAT Directive, fully matches with the 'taxable person' mentioned in Article 193 of the VAT Directive, which lays down the general rule relating to a liability for collection and remittance of VAT. One of the reasons for imposing, as a general rule, a liability for collection and remittance of VAT upon the supplier is that there are much fewer suppliers than customers to monitor and audit. Importantly, this approach functions well only if the supplier is located in the jurisdiction having taxing rights over a certain transaction, given that, only in such event, a country has both substantive and enforcement jurisdiction to tax the supplier. Figure 8.1 below provides a diagrammatic example of the functioning of the main liability regime for collection and remittance of VAT on a cross-border supply of services, in relation to the situation of a non-established supplier.

18. Noteworthy, under EU VAT, attribution of a VAT liability is, normally, the precondition for imposing upon a person all or, at least, some of the administrative obligations laid down in Title XI of the VAT Directive. In particular, a person who is appointed as the person liable for collecting and remitting the VAT due to the tax authorities of the Member State where a supply takes place, may be obliged to register (Arts 213-216 VAT Directive), to issue invoices (Arts 217-240 VAT Directive), to keep financial accounts (Arts 241-249 VAT Directive), to submit VAT returns (Arts 250-261 VAT Directive), to file recapitulative statements (Arts 262-271 VAT Directive), to remit the VAT due to the competent tax authorities (Arts 206-212 VAT Directive), and, even, to comply with all the other obligations which could eventually be imposed by a Member State on taxable persons (Art. 273 VAT Directive), or those relating to certain importations or exportations (Arts 274-280 VAT Directive). Notably, the detailed content of such provisions, although relevant for the application of EU VAT, is neither examined in this chapter nor discussed elsewhere in the present study.

Figure 8.1 Main Liability Regime for Collection and Remittance of VAT (Article 193 VAT Directive)

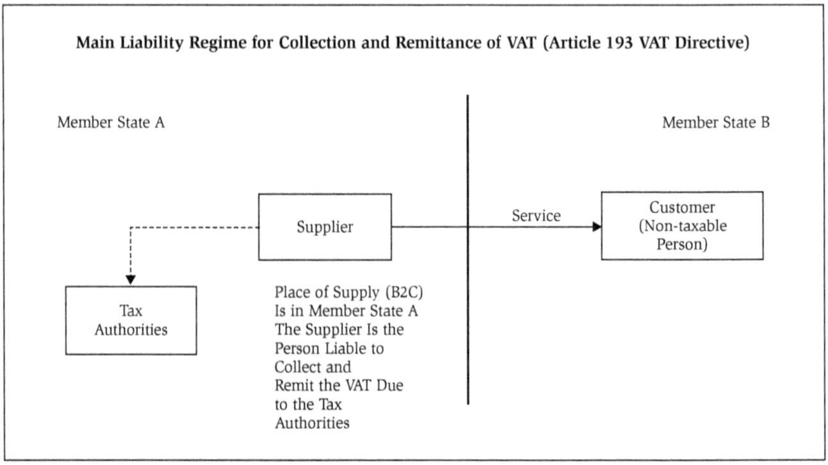

Exceptions to this general rule, however, are numerous and, in particular, can be found in Articles 194-199b, 202, 204, and 205 of the VAT Directive.[19] These exceptions mainly concern cases where the transaction is carried out by a non-established supplier[20], situation which, indeed, requires the application of the general reverse charge mechanism[21] provided for goods and services, respectively, in Articles 194 and 196 of the VAT Directive.[22] The main difference between the provisions of Articles 194 and 196 relates

19. Noteworthy, the Second Directive did not contain any provision for distinguishing taxable persons from persons liable to pay VAT. A specific provision in this regard was, in fact, introduced only in the text of the original Sixth Directive. *See* Art. 21 of the Sixth Directive, entitled 'persons liable to pay tax to the authorities'.
20. *See* DE: ECJ, 6 Oct. 2011, Case C-421/10, *Finanzamt Deggendorf v. Markus Stoppelkamp*, para. 36, considering that, for a supplier, in order to be considered a 'taxable person who is not established within the territory of the country', it is sufficient that he has established the seat of his own economic activity outside that country.
21. Importantly, the reverse charge mechanism in question must not be confused with the optional reverse charge mechanism specifically detailed in Arts 199, 199a, and 199b of the VAT Directive.
22. Article 195 of the VAT Directive, instead, provides a special reverse charge mechanism for supplies of electricity and gas, whereas Arts 197 and 198 of the VAT Directive deal with the reverse charge, respectively, in cases of simplified triangulations and transactions relating to investment gold. Noteworthy, in 2018, a proposal was filed by the Commission, pursuant to which both Arts 195 and 197 of the current VAT Directive will be repealed. As a result, the applicable rule for supplies of electricity and gas and simplified triangulation will be Art. 194 of the VAT Directive. Further, the introduction of a new Art. 194a has been proposed, according to which VAT shall be payable by the person to whom the goods are supplied, in so far he is a 'certified taxable person' [concept to be defined, by new Art. 13a of the VAT Directive, as a particularly qualified person in terms of VAT compliance], if the goods are supplied by a taxable person not established within the territory of the Member State in which the VAT is due. *See* European Commission, *Proposal for a Council Directive amending Directive 2006/112/EC as regards the Introduction of the Detailed Technical Measures for the Operation of the Definitive VAT System for the Taxation of Trade between Member States*, COM(2018) 329 final.

to the fact that the application for a Member State of the reverse charge mechanism is, in the former case, a mere option, whereas it is mandatory in the latter case.[23]

Notably, pursuant to the reverse charge mechanism laid down in Articles 194 and 196 of the VAT Directive, liability for collection and remittance of VAT shifts between the two parties to a transaction, i.e., from the supplier to the customer. Thus, when the reverse charge mechanism applies, the status of person liable for collection and remittance of VAT is entirely transferred from the supplier to the customer. In the elegant words of the CJEU, the reverse charge provides for a 'transfer mechanism of the tax obligation' between the two parties to a transaction.[24] This implies that all the obligations associated with a taxable transaction are to be met by the recipient of that transaction only. As such, the reverse charge mechanism wreaks havoc with the fractional collection system, throughout the entire supply chain, which underpins the EU VAT system. Figure 8.2 below provides a diagrammatic example of the functioning of the reverse charge mechanism, in relation to collection and remittance of the VAT due on a cross-border supply of services.

Figure 8.2 Mandatory Reverse Charge Mechanism (Article 196 VAT Directive)

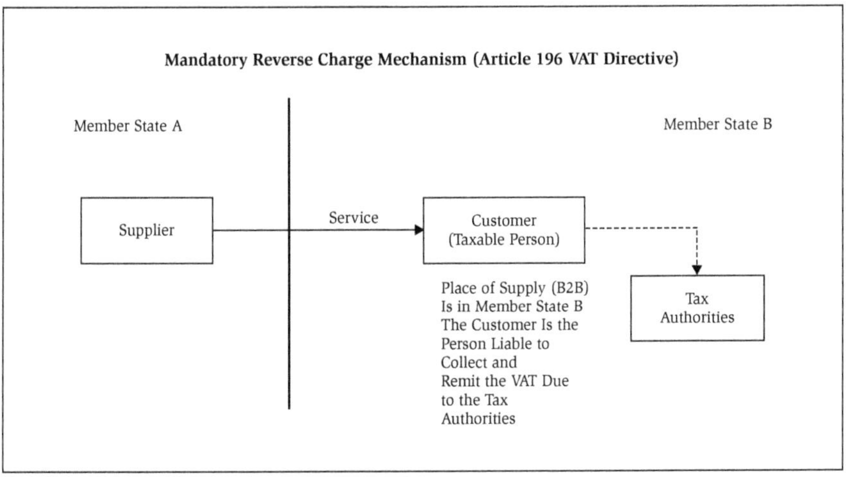

All the exceptions - either optional or mandatory - to the main liability regime contained in Article 193 of the VAT Directive, essentially, aim to reconcile situations in

23. Notably, these two distinct provisions reflect the different wording of point (a) and (b) of Art. 21(1) of the Sixth Directive, as amended by the Council Directive 91/680/EEC, providing a compulsory reverse charge mechanism, *inter alia*, in case of certain intangible services listed in the Sixth Directive (e.g., advertising services, banking and insurance services, and services of consultants, lawyers, and accountants). *See* Council Directive 91/680/EEC of 16 December 1991 supplementing the Common System of Value Added Tax and amending Directive 77/388/EEC with a view to the Abolition of Fiscal Frontiers, OJ L 376/1 of 31 Dec. 1991.
24. IT: ECJ, 15 Mar. 2007, Case C-35/05, *Reemtsma Cigarettenfabriken GmbH v. Ministero delle Finanze*, para. 32.

which the country having substantial jurisdiction to tax does not possess, at the same time, enforcement jurisdiction to tax, circumstance which, indeed, is capable of creating a jurisdictional break in the staged collection and remittance process of VAT that, instead, works quite smoothly and seamlessly in a purely domestic scenario.[25]

Nevertheless, other situations may equally be conceived. Notably, one is specifically envisaged by Article 205 of the VAT Directive, which enables Member States to 'provide that a person other than the person liable for payment of VAT is to be held jointly and severally liable for the payment of VAT'. The designation of a person as 'jointly and severally liable' (in French, '*solidairement tenue*'; in Italian, '*responsabile in solido*') is, indeed, a mere option for Member States, which, apparently, must exercise it by enacting specific legislation.[26] By holding another person liable to pay in case the primary debtor fails to comply with his own obligations, joint and several liability essentially aims to ensure that the amount due would ultimately be collected and remitted to the competent tax authorities.[27] Notably, there are two distinct categories of persons upon whom a joint and several liability may be imposed. Where the supplier is liable for collection and remittance of VAT, any other person may be held jointly and severally liable with him. Where, instead, the person liable for collection and remittance of VAT is not the supplier, this latter may eventually be held liable for payment of VAT, together with the former and for the entire amount due.[28] Noteworthy, the obligation on that co-debtor is only limited to payment of the amount due, whereas other types of obligations, such as those concerning submission of VAT returns or keeping of VAT records, fall exclusively upon the person who is primarily liable.

Under EU VAT, joint and several liability is an independent or stand-alone liability regime, which applies next to those contained in Article 193 of the VAT Directive or in other provisions derogating to such general rule. And indeed, the

25. For a discussion, *see* W. Hellerstein, *Jurisdiction to Tax Income and Consumption in the New Economy: A Theoretical and Comparative Perspective*, 38 Georgia L. Rev. 1 (2003), at 1-70.
26. NL: Opinion of the Advocate General, 14 Mar. 1989, Case C-342/87, *Genius Holding BV v. Staatssecretaris van Financiën*, para. 18. *See however* R. de la Feria & R. Foy, *Italmoda: The Birth of the Principle of Third-Party Liability for VAT Fraud*, Brit. Tax Rev. 3 (2016), at 270-281, who contend that, based on the CJEU's decision in *Schoenimport 'Italmoda' Mariano Previti* (NL: ECJ, 18 Dec. 2014, Joined Cases C-131/13, C-163/13 and C-164/13, *Staatssecretaris van Financiën v. Schoenimport 'Italmoda' Mariano Previti vof and Turbu.com BV and Turbu.com Mobile Phone's BV v. Staatssecretaris van Financiën*, para. 62), third-party liability can well arise even in the absence of a national legislation providing for it and, therefore, such kind of liability has been transformed, in effect, 'from a rule, into a principle'.
27. Noteworthy, in 2008, the Commission laid down a proposal to amend the VAT Directive and to introduce the possibility to hold, in case of an intra-Community acquisition of goods, a non-established supplier jointly and severally liable for the VAT due when certain obligations were not fulfilled by him, thus implicitly contributing to a VAT loss in the Member State where the intra-Community acquisition takes place. Nevertheless, such proposal has not yet been adopted. *See* European Commission, *Proposal for a Council Directive amending Directive 2006/112/EC on the Common System of Value Added Tax as regards Tax Evasion Linked to Import and Other Cross-Border Transactions*, COM(2008) 805 final.
28. *See* LT: ECJ, 18 May 2017, Case C-154/16, *'Latvijas Dzelzceļš' VAS v. Valsts ieņemumu dienests*, para. 85, considering that 'it follows from the very nature of joint and several liability that each debtor is liable for the total amount of the debt and the creditor remains, in principle, free to request the payment of that debt by one or several debtors as he chooses'.

provision contained in Article 205 of the VAT Directive differs substantially from the main liability rule, as well as from its various exceptions. While, under all the other liability regimes, one person only - either the supplier or the customer - ranks as the person liable for the VAT due on a given taxable transaction, under a joint and several liability regime, the liability for payment of VAT - but not, also, for other obligations associated with the carrying out of a taxable transaction (e.g., the obligation to declare VAT) - is, instead, attributed to more than a single person. Further, Article 205 of the VAT Directive does not impose any limitation with regard to either the identification of the person to be made jointly and severally liable for payment of VAT, the type of transactions to be included, or its territorial scope. Nevertheless, the CJEU has clarified in several occasions that the imposition of a joint and several liability is subject to the general principles of EU law and, in particular, to the principles of legal certainty and proportionality.[29] The Court has also warned that a joint and several liability cannot translate into 'a system of strict liability', thus 'going beyond what is necessary to preserve the public exchequer's rights'.[30] Figure 8.3 below provides a diagrammatic example of the functioning of the joint and several liability regime, in relation to collection and remittance of the VAT due on a cross-border supply of services.

29. UK: ECJ, 11 May 2006, Case C-384/04, *Commissioners of Customs & Excise and Attorney General v. Federation of Technological Industries and Others*, para. 35. For a discussion, *see* I. Lejeune, S. Vandenberghe & T. Racquet, *Limited Third-Party Liability in EU VAT Matters*, 23 Intl. VAT Monitor 6 (2012), Journals IBFD.

30. *Federation of Technological Industries and Others* (C-384/04), para. 32. *See also* UK: Opinion of the Advocate General, 7 Dec. 2005, Case C-384/04, *Commissioners of Customs & Excise and Attorney General v. Federation of Technological Industries and Others*, para. 30, where Advocate General Poiares Maduro considered that establishing a liability system, based on a non-rebuttable legal presumption, 'would be tantamount to introducing strict liability through the backdoor'.

Figure 8.3 Joint and Several Liability (Article 205 VAT Directive)

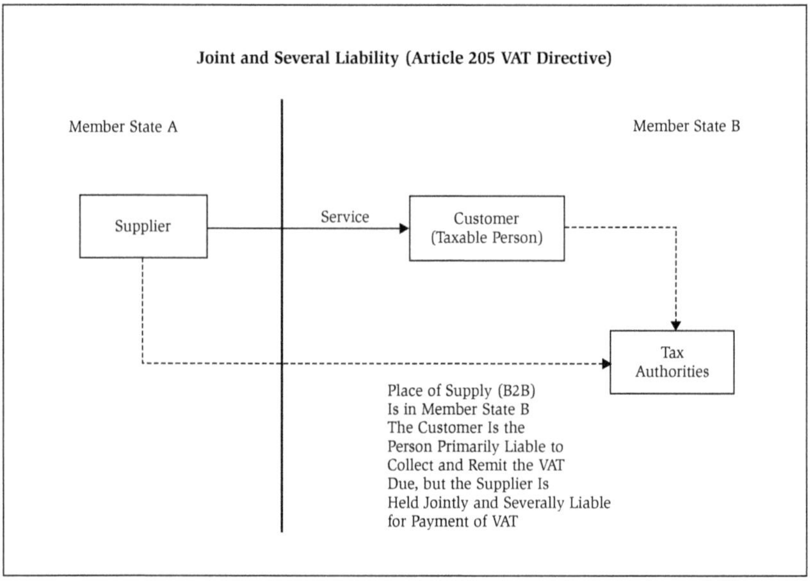

As observed by the CJEU in *Pactor Vastgoed*, the designation of a person as the one liable for collection and remittance of VAT does not amount to a procedural rule, which, as such, may find proper specification in a national VAT legislation. Rather, it does constitute a substantive rule underpinning the whole EU VAT system.[31] As a substantive rule, however, the possibility for a Member State to make such designation encounters a few limitations. Accordingly, even the imposition of a liability for collection and remittance of VAT upon an intermediary or a digital platform requires the fulfilment of a series of conditions. An analysis of the various liability regimes for intermediaries and digital platforms contained in the VAT Directive is provided in the following sections.

§8.03 LIABILITY REGIMES FOR INTERMEDIARIES AND PLATFORMS UNDER EU VAT

[A] Historical Overview of Liability Regimes for Intermediaries

The potential role of intermediaries in the collection and remittance of VAT has come into prominence in the legislative history of EU VAT quite early on. Article 21 of the proposed Sixth Directive, in fact, stipulated that not only 'taxable persons who carry out taxable transaction', but also 'agents of taxable persons established in another

31 NL: ECJ, 10 Oct. 2013, Case C-622/11, *Staatssecretaris van Financiën tegen Pactor Vastgoed BV* paras 31-32.

country who carry out taxable transactions' were to be held liable to pay VAT. Rather, the problem was to define, with sufficient degree of precision, the types of 'agents' that could be held liable for payment of VAT. The text of Article 21 of the proposed Sixth Directive did not provide any indication in this regard, so that it might have been maintained that every agent, potentially, could have fallen within the scope of such provision. Concerns with regard to the broad extension of VAT liability, in the sense of including too many intermediaries, were in fact raised during the legislative process by both the European Parliament and the European Economic and Social Committee, which, for this purpose, proposed a series of amendments to the text released by the Commission. The text of the Sixth Directive, as finally adopted, essentially reflected those amendments and, ultimately, their rationale was equally shared by the Commission, which plainly admitted that the original text of the provision was 'too widely drafted since the agent of a taxable person established in another country is not necessarily in a position to determine the amount of the tax due where the taxable person himself carries out operations in another country, of which the agent is not informed', so that it was eventually found more appropriate 'to limit the scope of the text in order to avoid systematic recourse to a tax agent, by specifying that this provision only applies to the agent where the taxable transaction is carried out through him or with his assistance'.[32]

Among the intermediaries who may be regarded as agents of a non-established supplier, Article 204 of the VAT Directive lists tax representatives.[33] Notably, a 'tax representative' (in French, '*représentant fiscal*'; in Italian, '*rappresentante fiscale*') is a person, not predetermined by legislation, but instead designated as his local representative by a non-established supplier, who acts for and complies with certain tax obligations, such as invoicing, accounting, submitting returns or recapitulative statements, in that country on behalf of this latter party. Originally, tax representation was conceived in the Sixth Directive as a mere possibility available to Member States, which could require a non-established supplier to appoint a representative established in their territory to deal with his own VAT obligations therein.[34] The measure in question, essentially, aimed to make it easier, for a non-established supplier, the fulfilment of his own VAT obligations and, for Member States, the monitoring and recovery of the VAT due.

32. For a more detailed historical account of the legislative history of the EU VAT system in this regard, *see* B.J.M. Terra & J. Kajus, *Commentary on European VAT* at para. 11.2.1.2 (IBFD Tax Research Platform 2019).
33. European Commission, *supra* n. 6, at 57, in fact, defines a 'tax representative' as 'an intermediary with knowledge of the language and the procedures' of the Member State having taxing rights over a transaction. Nevertheless, it ought to be noted that not necessarily a tax representative is also an intermediary of a non-established supplier. As observed by the CJEU in *Athesia Duck*, this only occurs where 'the tax representative plays an economic role in the supply of services in question'. However, in this event – the Court reasoned – 'it is on account of that role and not his capacity as tax representative that the transactions entered into by him are subject to tax'. *See* IT: ECJ, 19 Feb. 2009, Case C-1/08, *Athesia Druck Srl v. Ministero dell'Economia e delle Finanze and Agenzia delle Entrate*, para. 35.
34. Article 21(1) of the Sixth Directive.

Nevertheless, the designation of a local representative, endowed with sufficient financial means to guarantee for the VAT due, presented several administrative hurdles, which, indeed, amounted to an actual impediment to the free movements of goods and services within the EU. Notably, a report prepared by the Commission in 1994 highlighted a number of difficulties for a non-established supplier and, in particular, for a small business to find a person willing to perform the role of fiscal representative and, further, considerable costs associated with such designation, circumstance which could, ultimately, induce a non-established supplier not to trade in a Member State for avoiding such kinds of hindrances. Other issues related to the fact that the tax representative, inevitably, depended on the information supplied to him by the non-established supplier, to the nature and extent of the obligations imposed upon the person liable for payment, as well as to the fact that considerable differences existed in the interpretation, from one Member State to another, of the expression 'tax representative'. Moreover, the extent of a tax representative's responsibility was not specified in the VAT Directive or elsewhere.[35] Due to these and other shortcomings, and with a view of simplifying and harmonizing the whole system of liability regimes, tax representation was eventually reformed by Council Directive 2000/65/EC.[36] As a result of the enacted amendments, under Article 204 of the current VAT Directive, the designation of a tax representative is a mere option for a foreign supplier, unless the supplier is established in a country with which no legal instrument, providing administrative cooperation and mutual assistance[37], exists and, further, such designation is required under the laws of the Member State concerned.

[B] Liability Regimes for Intermediaries and Platforms

As stated, the VAT Directive contains specific rules for intermediaries intervening in the supply chain from the original supplier till the end consumer.[38] Those rules, however, differ substantially, based on the role actually fulfilled by the intermediary within the supply chain. Notably, the VAT Directive distinguishes between disclosed and undisclosed agents. The first category, expressly contemplated in Article 46 of the VAT Directive[39], is composed of those intermediaries who act in the name and on behalf of another person, this latter being considered, for EU VAT purposes, as the sole party making the supply to the customer. By acting in the name of another person,

35. European Commission, *supra* n. 6, at 4-8 and 55-58.
36. Council Directive 2000/65/EC of 17 October 2000 amending Directive 77/388/EEC as regards the Determination of the Person Liable for Payment of Value Added Tax, OJ L 269/44 of 21 Oct. 2000.
37. Council Directive 2010/24/EU of 16 March 2010 concerning Mutual Assistance for the Recovery of Claims relating to Taxes, Duties and Other Measures, OJ L 84/1 of 31 Mar. 2010; Council Regulation (EU) No. 904/2010 of 7 October 2010 on Administrative Cooperation and Combating Fraud in the Field of Value Added Tax, OJ L 268/1 of 12 Oct. 2010.
38. *See* section §7.09.
39. Notably, Art. 46 of the VAT Directive reads as follows: 'the place of supply of services rendered to a non-taxable person by an intermediary, acting in the name and on behalf of another person shall be the place where the underlying transaction is supplied in accordance with this Directive'.

those intermediaries are in fact regarded as providing mediation to either the supplier, the customer, or both parties. The second category, referred to in Articles 14(2)(c)[40] and 28[41] of the VAT Directive, is instead composed of those intermediaries who, in the supply chain, act in their own name but on behalf of another person. By acting in their own name, those intermediaries are in fact regarded not as providing mediation, but instead as directly supplying goods or services to the customer.

More recent changes to the text of the VAT Directive are of specific interest to digital platforms. Notably, as from 1 January 2021, a platform facilitating distance sales of goods imported from third territories or third countries[42] in consignments of an intrinsic value not exceeding EUR 150 (i.e., low-value goods) will be deemed as the supplier of those goods to the customer. A similar deemed provision will also apply to platforms facilitating the supply of goods from a non-EU supplier within the EU.[43] Accordingly, when the requirements laid down in those new provisions are met, a digital platform will be liable for collecting and remitting to the competent tax authorities the VAT due on the sales of goods it facilitates. Notably, the new rules aim to ensure effective and efficient collection of VAT, as well as to reduce the overall administrative burden for non-established suppliers, tax administrations, and customers alike.[44]

Although, in principle, imposing a liability for collection and remittance of VAT upon digital platforms presents great potential, as long as, presently, most cross-border supplies are channelled via digital platforms[45], the new provisions do not, ultimately, appear easy to implement, neither their actual extension is, indeed, crystal clear. The use of the term 'facilitates' (in French, '*facilite*'; in Italian, '*facilita*'), in fact, suggests

---

40. Article 14(2)(c) of the VAT Directive contains specific rules with regard to intermediaries intervening in the supply of goods to customers. Notably, Art. 14(2)(c) stipulates that, 'in addition to the transaction referred to in paragraph 1 [i.e. the transfer of the right to dispose of tangible property as owner], each of the following shall be regarded as a supply of goods: ... c. the transfer of goods pursuant to a contract under which commission is payable on purchase or sale'.
41. *See* section §8.03[C].
42. The definitions of 'third territories' and 'third countries' are provided, respectively, in points 3 and 4 of Art. 5 of the VAT Directive. While the latter concept indicates all the countries outside the EU, the former instead includes the territories specifically listed in Art. 6 of the VAT Directive (some of which, nevertheless, form part of the Customs Union).
43. *See* Art. 14a of the VAT Directive, introduced, as from 1 January 2021, by Art. 2 of Council Directive (EU) 2017/2455 of 5 December 2017 amending Directive 2006/112/EC and Directive 2009/132/EC as regards Certain Value Added Tax Obligations for Supplies of Services and Distance Sales of Goods, OJ L 348/7 of 29 Dec. 2017. Noteworthy, both those deemed provisions apply irrespective of whether the platform is established or not in the EU.
44. Point 7 of the Preamble of Directive 2017/2455/EU.
45. Notably, a 2018 survey conducted by the International Post Corporation found that the four world largest platforms, i.e., Alibaba, Amazon, eBay, and Wish account for approximately 64% of the cross-border e-commerce items purchased. *See* International Post Corporation (IPC), *Cross-Border E-Commerce Shopper Survey 2018* at 12 (2018), https://www.ipc.be/services/markets-and-regulations/cross-border-shopper-survey (accessed 31 Mar. 2019). Another study has estimated that around 60% of private consumption and 30% of public consumption of goods and services related to the total digital economy are transacted via online intermediaries. *See* Copenhagen Economics, *Online Intermediaries: Impact on the EU Economy* at 9 (2015), https://www.copenhageneconomics.com/dyn/resources/Publication/publicationPDF/2/342/1454501505/edima-online-intermediaries-eu-growth-engines.pdf (accessed 31 Mar. 2019).

that the scope of a platform's intervention in the supply is broad, arguably broader than as meant in the comparable expression 'taking part' used in Article 28 of the VAT Directive. If so intended, then it is hard to conceive a digital platform which, in a way or another, does not 'facilitate' the supply to a customer, even in case of platforms operating as pure marketplaces or, further, which do not handle any payment on behalf of either party to the underlying transaction.[46] A proposal to better determine the scope of the term 'facilitates' was eventually tabled by the Commission in December 2018. The proposal, in particular, aims to set the minimum level of intervention required to a platform as to be considered 'facilitating' an underlying transaction among the supplier and the customer of a good or a service. Notably, under the proposed new Article 54b of the Implementing Regulation, specifically concerning the obligation imposed upon a platform to keep records of distance supply of services, it is prescribed that the term 'facilitates' shall not cover a supply of services where the platform is not, either directly or indirectly, involved in: (1) setting the general terms of the underlying transaction, (2) charging the customer in respect of the payment made, (3) ordering or delivering the goods, or (4) providing the services concerned. Moreover, it is stipulated that the term 'facilitates' shall not cover instances where a platform provides only for: (1) processing payment in relation to the supply, (2) listing or advertising the services concerned, or (3) redirecting or transferring customers to other electronic interfaces where services are offered, without any further intervention in the supply.[47]

[C] Liability Regimes for Undisclosed Agents

Given the definition of sharing economy as used in the present study[48], which concerns only the provision of services and does not also entail the supply of goods, the ensuing analysis merely concentrates on cases in which an intermediary intervenes in the supply of services to a customer. In this connection, the relevant provision is Article 28 of the VAT Directive. As stated, Article 28 of the VAT Directive stipulates that, 'where a taxable person acting in his own name but on behalf of another person takes part in a supply of services, he shall be deemed to have received and supplied those services himself'.[49] A legal fiction of two identical supplies of services provided consecutively

46. For a perspective on this and other possible shortcomings of the new rules, *see* M. Lamensch, *Rendering Platforms Liable to Collect and Pay VAT on B2C Imports: A Silver Bullet?*, 29 Intl. VAT Monitor 2 (2018), Journals IBFD.

47. European Commission, *Proposal for a Council Implementing Regulation amending Implementing Regulation (EU) No 282/2011 as Regards Supplies of Goods or Services Facilitated by Electronic Interfaces and the Special Schemes for Taxable Persons Supplying Services to Non-Taxable Persons, Making Distance Sales of Goods and Certain Domestic Supplies of Goods*, COM(2018) 821 final.

48. *See* section §2.02.

49. *See* section §7.09[C]. Notably, the Sixth Directive contained a provision with an almost identical wording, i.e., Art. 6(4) of the Sixth Directive, which read as follows: 'where a taxable person acting in his own name but on behalf of another takes part in a supply of services, he shall be considered to have received and supplied those services himself'. The only differences with the wording of Art. 28 of the VAT Directive relate to the fact that the latter uses the word 'deemed', rather than 'considered', and that it adds the term 'person' with reference to 'another'. Noteworthy, Art. 28(3)(e) of the Sixth Directive allowed Member States to derogate from the

is, thus, created. Pursuant to such legal fiction, the intermediary, who acts in his own name, is considered for EU VAT purposes to have, first, received the services in question from the supplier on behalf of whom he acts and, then, to supply them onward to the customer. The intermediary is therefore considered, for EU VAT purposes, as the person making the supply to the customer. He is, in fact, a 'deemed supplier'. And indeed, such a 'deemed supplier' approach amounts to imposing, de facto, a liability for collection and remittance of VAT upon intermediaries taking part in the supply to the customer.

For this legal fiction to apply, however, three sets of requirements need to be fulfilled. Notably, the intermediary must: (1) take part in the supply to the customer, (2) act in his own name, but (3) on behalf of another person. Should even only one of those three general requirements not be fulfilled, then the deemed provision of Article 28 of the VAT Directive would not apply. Such an eventuality might occur, for instance, because the intermediary does not act in his own name, but instead in the name of another party. In such event, the intermediary is, in fact, regarded as a disclosed agent. Alternatively, the intermediary, instead of acting on behalf of another party, could also act in his own behalf. In such event, the taxable person in question is no longer considered as an intermediary, but rather as a 'full-fledged supplier' (thus, not even a 'deemed supplier'). In order to assess whether those three sets of general requirements are indeed fulfilled in a given situation, it is crucial to accurately check the contractual obligations agreed upon by parties to a supply chain and, next to that, to carefully verify whether those obligations are effectively fulfilled by the parties in question.[50] In this connection, it is stipulated that, where, on the one hand, contractual obligations and, on the other hand, economic and commercial reality do not match, the latter should prevail.[51] As affirmed by the CJEU in several occasions, 'economic and commercial reality' is, in fact, a fundamental criterion for the application of the EU VAT system.[52]

The first requirement entails that the intermediary effectively 'takes part' in the supply to the customer. For the legal fiction of Article 28 of the VAT Directive to apply, it is in fact required that the intermediary is involved in the supply chain toward the

deemed rule in question, so as not to consider certain persons taking part in a supply of services as having received and supplied those services themselves.

50. BE: ECJ, 14 Jul. 2011, Case C-464/10, *Belgian State v. Pierre Henfling and Others*, para. 40.

51. European Commission, *Explanatory Notes on the EU VAT Changes to the Place of Supply of Telecommunications, Broadcasting and Electronic Services that Enter into Force in 2015 (Council Implementing Regulation (EU) No 1042/2013) published on 3 April 2014* at 27-28 (2015), https://ec.europa.eu/taxation_customs/sites/taxation/files/resources/documents/taxation/vat/how_vat_works/telecom/explanatory_notes_2015_en.pdf (accessed 31 Mar. 2019). In the CJEU's case-law, *see* UK: ECJ, 20 Jun. 2013, Case C-653/11, *Her Majesty's Commissioners of Revenue and Customs v. Paul Newey*, para. 46. Importantly, the CJEU acknowledges that the examination of contractual obligations must remain the starting point for the analysis of the transaction. *See* PL: ECJ, 17 Jan. 2013, Case C-224/11, *BGŻ Leasing sp. z o.o. v. Dyrektor Izby Skarbowej w Warszawie*, para. 47. In the VAT Committee's working papers, *see* e.g., European Commission, Value Added Tax Committee, *Working Paper No. 885, VAT 2015: Harmonised Application of the Presumption*, at 4 (taxud.c.1(2015)4659331).

52. UK: ECJ, 5 July 2018, Case C-544/16, *Marcandi Limited, Agissant Sous le Nom Commercial 'Madbid' v. Commissioners for Her Majesty's Revenue & Customs*, para. 45.

customer. To be more precise: the intermediary must take part in the *same* supply chain to which both the supplier and the customer belong. As seen in Chapter 6, reconstructing the supply chain can, indeed, be a difficult exercise, in so far as the role played by each party within it is often unclear. Notably, the intermediary does not take part in in the supply to the customer when he only supplies an 'input' service, i.e., an intermediate service 'which disappears once it is supplied' to the original supplier, as stipulated in *Ibero Tours*.[53]

The second requirement, which demands an intermediary to act 'in his own name', is, undoubtedly, the most important and, also, difficult condition to assess. The fulfilment of such requirement is, in fact, decisive for considering an intermediary as an undisclosed rather than as a disclosed agent. Notably, this requirement seeks to establish whether, for EU VAT purposes, the relationship between the supplier and the intermediary is that of agency, i.e., that occurring between a principal and his agent, or if, instead, two consecutive supplies exist, i.e., there is, first, a supply from the supplier to the intermediary and, then, a second supply from the intermediary to the customer. In this latter event, the intermediary is no longer treated for EU VAT purposes as an 'agent', but rather as a 'principal'. As observed by Advocate General Trstenjak in *RCI Europe*, 'the definitive criterion for this classification is whether the applicant is simply putting two members in touch with one another for the purpose of enabling them to agree contractually', in which event 'the act in question would be one of agency', or if, instead, 'the members were to effect that exchange without knowing who the beneficiary was to be', because the taxable person 'itself takes responsibility for the coordination and the supply to the end consumer, so that the taxable person 'would be acting in its own name' and would be considered as the principal for EU VAT purposes.[54]

For considering an intermediary as an undisclosed rather than a disclosed agent, reference ought to be made both to contractual documentation and economic reality. More specifically, as observed by the CJEU in *Van Ginkel Waddinxveen*, the contractual arrangements existing between the various parties must be examined first.[55] Such line of reasoning was later upheld by the CJEU in *ISt*.[56] In this connection, it appears that, while labels used in a contract by the parties to describe their own relationships are by no means conclusive[57], an examination of the contractual obligations still remains the necessary starting point for identifying the relationships among the various parties within a supply chain.[58] Noteworthy, contractual documentation might not be

53. DE: Opinion of the Advocate General, 18 Jul. 2013, Case C-300/12, *Finanzamt Düsseldorf-Mitte v. Ibero Tours GmbH*, para. 24. For a discussion of this case, *see* section §6.03[C].
54. UK: Opinion of the Advocate General, 2 Apr. 2009, Case C-37/08, *RCI Europe v. Commissioners for Her Majesty's Revenue and Customs*, para. 102.
55. NL: ECJ, 12 Nov. 1992, Case C-163/91, *Van Ginkel Waddinxveen BV, Reis- en Passagebureau Van Ginkel BV and others v. Inspecteur der Omzetbelasting Utrecht*, para. 21.
56. DE: ECJ, 13 Oct. 2005, Case C-200/04, *Finanzamt Heidelberg v. ISt internationale Sprach- und Studienreisen GmbH*, para. 20.
57. BE: Opinion of the Advocate General, 4 May 2004, Case C-284/03, *Belgian State v. Temco Europe SA.*, paras 17-37.
58. See BE: ECJ, 18 Nov. 2004, Case C-284/03, *Belgian State v. Temco Europe SA.*, para. 22, where, besides the initial will of the parties, as crystallized in a contract, the agreements between the

included in a single legal paper, so that an examination of different legal sources could, perhaps, be required. Moreover, contractual documentation needs to be assessed in light of EU VAT only. This implies that the qualification of legal rights and obligations under contract law might not ultimately match with that provided under EU VAT. As a result of all this, the examination of contractual documentation may not be as easy as it could appear at first glance.

Even more difficult it is to assess economic reality as a criterion, since the concept itself is quite vague and, indeed, a variety of different factors may well be taken into account for this purpose. A few clarifications in this regard, however, were laid down by the CJEU in *Henfling and Others,* a case concerning local agents, called 'buralistes', taking bets in the territory of Belgium on behalf of a foreign company. Notably, in assessing the role of those buralistes and, in particular, whether they were to be considered as undisclosed or disclosed agents of the foreign company, the CJEU found as relevant criteria, *inter alia,* whether or not the activity of those intermediaries mentioned the name and carried the signs of the company (i.e., the principal) and, further, if the regulations which customers had committed to adhere were those established by that company only.[59] A series of criteria were also laid down by UK courts in *Secret Hotels2,* a case litigated at various stages in the UK between 2010 and 2014. Notably, the case concerned whether a UK-based company (Secret Hotels2, formerly Med Hotels), operating a website through which the company marketed hotel accommodation, in the sale of foreign hotel accommodation to holidaymakers, acted as a principal, i.e., in its own name and on behalf of those hoteliers, and therefore was obliged to pay UK VAT on its margin under the Tour Operators' Margin Scheme (TOMS) laid down in Articles 306-310 of the VAT Directive - the position of the UK tax authorities, or whether the company acted as a disclosed agent of the hoteliers, in which case, pursuant to either Article 44 or 46 of the VAT Directive, no UK VAT was in fact due - the position of Med Hotels. Notably, the factors taken into account, by the UK courts, for making such determination related to the fact that the company, *inter alia*: (1) drafted the legal arrangements applicable to its relationship with the other parties, (2) established policies related to booking cancellation and set related charges, (3) dealt with customer in its own name in respect of the use of its website and in the services of its local handling agents, (4) provided customers with alternative accommodation in case of booking issues, (5) offered customers compensation and complaint handling services, and (6) used the resources of hoteliers in the provision of travel facilities marketed through its own website.[60]

---

stipulating parties which could have intervened at a later stage, notably during the performance of the contract, were also taken into account by the Court. In this connection, it also ought to be considered the possibility that certain clauses, inserted by the parties into a contract, may be subject to limitations or mandatory extensions under civil or public law, so that the original will of the parties is, ultimately, altered. *See* DE: ECJ, 12 Feb. 1998, Case C-346/95, *Elisabeth Blasi v. Finanzamt München I,* para. 26.

59. *Henfling and Others* (C-464/10), para. 43.
60. Most of these factors can be found listed in UK: Supreme Court, 5 Mar. 2014, *The Commissioners for Her Majesty's Revenue and Customs v. Secret Hotels2 Limited (Formerly Med Hotels Limited)* [2014] UKSC 16, at paras 45-50.

A consultation of the search database of the CJEU's case law reveals that the expression 'on behalf of', which, indeed, is the third requirement for an intermediary to be considered as an undisclosed agent under EU VAT, has not been analysed by the Court so far and, therefore, the issue can by no means be seen as '*acte clair*'.[61] Nevertheless, it should be recalled that, in late 2018, a reference to the CJEU was made by the UK First-Tier Tribunal, seeking a clarification of the quite similar expression 'on behalf of the supplier' contained in Article 33 of the VAT Directive. Notably, the referral asks the Court to assess whether goods are, indeed, transported 'on behalf of the supplier', where, *inter alia*, 'the customer has no practical alternative but to use the delivery company' and/or 'the customer has contact only with the supplier and not with the delivery company'.[62]

The expression, instead, has already been considered – to some extent – by UK courts in *Secret Hotels2*. Notably, the UK Upper Tribunal reasoned that, for a taxable person to act 'on behalf of' another person, the former must have the authority to conclude contracts which are also binding on the latter party.[63] The author, indeed, submits that the same kinds of considerations can be applied in the context of EU VAT. The author also assumes that, as maintained by the CJEU in *Lipjes* in relation to the specific situation of a disclosed agent[64], even with regard to an undisclosed agent, it is, in fact, irrelevant whether the person on behalf of which the intermediary acts in the supply of services to a customer is a taxable person or not, and, next to that, if the supply received by the intermediary is a taxable transaction or not. While no specific clarification in this regard can be found in the Implementing Regulation, as instead provided by Article 30 of the Implementing Regulation in case of a disclosed agent, this assumption gains confirmation from the bare wording of Article 28 of the VAT Directive, which, indeed, requires the intermediary being only a 'taxable person', whereas the person on behalf of which the intermediary acts is merely referred to as 'another person', without any further regard to his taxable status under EU VAT. Likewise, the provision of Article 28 of the VAT Directive only refers to the need that the intermediary takes part in a supply of service to the customer, without any further regard to whether the transaction in question is taxable or not.[65]

61. For a similar conclusion, *see* UK: First-Tier Tribunal, 27 Apr. 2018, *Healthspan Limited v. Commissioners for Her Majesty's Revenue and Customs* [2018] UKFTT 0241 (TC), paras 265-267.
62. UK: *Reference for a Preliminary Ruling from the First-Tier Tribunal (Tax Chamber) (United Kingdom) Made on 12 November 2018 – Healthspan Limited v. Commissioners for Her Majesty's Revenue and Customs (Case C-703/18)*. Notably, the issue arises from the elusive practice of some businesses to split the supply of goods from their transport and delivery, with the intention to avoid accounting and paying VAT in the Member State of destination of the goods as mandated by Art. 33 of the VAT Directive, since, following a 'literal' rather than 'substantial' interpretation of that provision, in this way, the transport of the goods would not be made 'on behalf of the supplier'. For a discussion in this regard, *see* European Commission, Value Added Tax Committee, *Working Paper No. 855, Distance Selling* (taxud.c.1(2015)2158321).
63. UK: Upper Tribunal, Tax and Chancery Chamber, 29 July 2011, *Secret Hotels 2 Ltd (Formerly Med Hotels Ltd) v. The Commissioners for HM Revenue and Customs* [2011] UKUT 308 (TCC), at paras 124, 126, and 128.
64. NL: ECJ, 27 May 2004, Case C-68/03, *Staatssecretaris van Financiën v. D. Lipjes*, para. 23.
65. For a similar appraisal, *see* M. Lamensch, *The Scope of the EU VAT System: Traditional & Digital Economy Related Questions*, in *CJEU – Recent Developments in Value Added Tax*, at 123 (M. Lang et al. eds, Linde 2018).

[D] Digital Platforms as Undisclosed Agents

More detailed rules concerning a digital platform, which acts in its own name but on behalf of another person, that is as undisclosed agent of its own principal, can be found in the Implementing Regulation. Notably, Article 9a of the Implementing Regulation provides that, where electronic services - including telephone services rendered through the Internet and Voice over Internet Protocol (VoIP) services - are supplied through a telecommunications network, an interface[66], or a portal[67], such as a marketplace for applications, 'a taxable person taking part in that supply shall be presumed to be acting in his own name but on behalf of the provider of those services unless that provider is explicitly indicated as the supplier by that taxable person and that is reflected in the contractual arrangements between the parties'. Indeed, the legal construction of Article 9a of the Implementing Regulation is broad enough as to make difficult a rebuttal by an intermediary taking part in the supply chain. As observed by the VAT Committee, Article 9a of the Implementing Regulation must, in fact, be applied 'as widely as possible in the interest of simplicity'.[68] Further, as Article 9a of the Implementing Regulation itself clarifies, a rebuttal is, indeed, only possible if the service 'provider is explicitly indicated as the supplier by that taxable person and this is reflected in the contractual arrangements between the parties'. Article 9a of the Implementing Regulation goes on to specify that, for such condition to be fulfilled and, thus, as to exclude the application of the 'deemed supplier' rule contained in Article 28 of the VAT Directive, two cumulative conditions must exist, that is: (1) 'the invoice issued or made available by each taxable person taking part in the supply of the electronically supplied services must identify such services and the supplier thereof', and (2) 'the bill or receipt issued or made available to the customer must identify the electronically supplied services and the supplier thereof'. Even if both those conditions are indeed fulfilled, the actual possibility for a digital platform to opt-out from the

66. A definition of a 'portal' can be found in the explanatory notes on this matter issued by the Commission. Notably, it is stipulated therein that 'a "portal" is any type of electronic shop, website or similar environment that offers electronic services directly to the consumer without diverting them to another supplier's website, portal etc. to conclude the transaction. Common examples of this include app stores, electronic marketplaces and websites offering e-services for sale'. *See* European Commission, *supra* n. 51, at 13.
67. According to the explanatory notes on this matter issued by the Commission, 'an "interface" includes a portal but it is a wider concept. In computing it should be understand as a device or a program which allows two independent systems or the system or the end user to communicate'. *See* European Commission, *supra* n. 51, at 13.
68. European Commission, Value Added Tax Committee, *Working Paper No. 885, VAT 2015: Harmonised Application of the Presumption*, at 3 (taxud.c.1(2015)4659331). Despite a commitment to simplicity, a public survey prepared on behalf of the Commission in 2016 found that, actually, most businesses struggle with applying the provision of Art. 9a of the VAT Directive, due to different interpretations of this legal fiction by Member States, and, indeed, further clarification and a common interpretation across all Member States were put forward as viable solutions to that effect. *See* Deloitte, *VAT Aspects of Cross-Border e-Commerce – Options for Modernization, Final Report – Lot 3: Assessment of the Implementation of the 2015 Place of Supply Rules and the Mini-One Stop Shop* at 195-204 (2016), https://ec.europa.eu/taxation_customs/sites/taxation/files/vat_aspects_cross-border_e-commerce_final_report_lot3.pdf (accessed 31 Mar. 2019).

application of such deemed provision remains quite constrained. Article 9a of the Implementing Regulation, in fact, stipulates that a digital platform who, 'with regard to a supply of electronically supplied services, authorises the charge to the customer or the delivery of the services, or sets the general terms and conditions of the supply, shall not be permitted to explicitly indicate another person as the supplier of those services'.

As observed by the VAT Committee, all these conditions are essentially designed to ensure that 'economic actors having a stronger position on the market do not force taxable persons placed earlier in the supply chain to take responsibility for B2C supplies'.[69] In this connection, the phrase 'authorises the charge to the customer' specifically refers to the situation where the taxable person can influence whether, at what time, or under which preconditions, the customers pay. As for the expression 'authorises the delivery of the services', indeed, it entails a broader concept than simply 'makes the delivery', and it also includes the situation where the taxable person can influence whether, at what time, or under which preconditions, the delivery in question is operated. Lastly, the phrase 'general terms and conditions of the supply' covers any general terms and conditions set by a taxable person taking part in the supply, and with which a customer must agree before purchasing the service in question. As such, it might include the terms and conditions for maintaining an account on a platform, as well as the licence agreement to have access to a service.[70] The deemed rules contained in Articles 28 of the VAT Directive and 9a of the Implementing Regulation, instead, are not applicable in case of a platform merely processing payments (e.g., a credit card company) or only providing telephone services through the Internet (e.g., a phone network company). Among the activities related to payment processing and, thus, excluded from the scope of the deemed rule, the Commission initially inserted also accepting bad debt risk and providing first line customer care.[71] A more restrictive approach in this regard, which only excluded taxable persons processing payment from the scope of the deemed rule, was instead proposed by the Commission later on.[72]

As a result of the broad construction attributed to Article 9a of the Implementing Regulation, a digital platform taking part in the supply chain toward a customer is usually considered as the person supplying electronically supplied services to the customer. Notably, the explanatory notes on this matter issued by the Commission consider that, based on the analysis of all the facts and circumstances of a given situation, an indication exists that a taxable person takes part in the supply to the customer when that person: (1) owns or manages the technical platform over which the services are delivered, (2) is responsible for the actual delivery, (3) is responsible for collecting payment unless the only involvement of the taxable person is the processing of payment, (4) controls or exerts influence over the pricing, (5) is the one legally required to issue a VAT invoice, receipt or bill to the end user in respect of the

69. European Commission, Value Added Tax Committee, *Working Paper No. 885, VAT 2015: Harmonised Application of the Presumption*, at 4 (taxud.c.1(2015)4659331).
70. European Commission, *supra* n. 51, at 34-35.
71. European Commission, *supra* n. 51, at 32.
72. European Commission, Value Added Tax Committee, *Working Paper No. 885, VAT 2015: Harmonised Application of the Presumption*, at 3 (taxud.c.1(2015)4659331).

supply, (6) provides customer support in relation to queries about or problems with the service itself, (7) exerts control or influence over the presentation and format of the virtual marketplace (such as app stores or websites), such that the brand and identity of the taxable person are significantly more prominent than those of other persons involved in the supply, (8) has legal obligations or liabilities in relation to the service provided, (9) owns the customer data related to the supply in question, and (10) is in a position to credit a sale without the supplier's permission or prior approval in cases where the supply was not properly received.[73]

[E] Sharing Economy Platforms as Undisclosed Agents

The specific rules detailed in Article 9a of the Implementing Regulation and summarized above, however, are not applicable in the context of the sharing economy, as the concept is intended in the present study. This is due to the circumstance that, under the provision of Article 9a of the Implementing Regulation, the types of services which a digital platform is deemed, first, to receive from the supplier and, then, to supply onward to the customer must necessarily be 'electronically supplied services'. However, in the context of the sharing economy, only the services provided by a platform to its users could qualify as such for EU VAT purposes.[74] On the contrary, underlying services operated by individual suppliers – which constitute the first of the two supplies to be considered, pursuant to the legal fiction contained in Article 28 of the VAT Directive – do not fulfil all the four conditions laid down in Article 7(1) of the Implementing Regulation for being characterized as 'electronically supplied services'. As explained in Chapter 7, services provided by individual suppliers, in fact, have a 'tangible' nature, inasmuch as those services entail the exploitation of a tangible property like a residential premise or a vehicle. Indeed, the only possibility for those services to qualify as electronically supplied services occurs if the doctrine on composite supplies applies, so that the platform and the individual supplier are seen as jointly making a single composite supply to the same customer. And yet, the application of the composite supply doctrine, besides being highly improbable, would inevitably lead to exclude the intervention of the deemed rule contained in Article 28 of the VAT Directive, as long as, under that doctrine, the two supplies made, respectively, by the platform and by the individual supplier are seen as a single composite supply.[75]

It follows that a sharing economy platform might, ultimately, be considered as a deemed supplier, that is as the person supplying, for EU VAT purposes, the services to the individual customer, and, as such, be held liable for collecting and remitting the VAT due in lieu of the individual supplier, only based on the three general requirements laid down in Article 28 of the VAT Directive.[76] On the contrary, the specific rules detailed in Article 9a of the Implementing Regulation and summarized above are not applicable to sharing economy platforms. Therefore, in the context of the sharing

73. European Commission, *supra* n. 51, at 28-29.
74. *See* section §7.07[C][2].
75. *See* section §7.07[C][1].
76. *See* section §8.03[C].

economy, it is crucial to assess whether, pursuant to Article 28 of the VAT Directive, a platform, acting in its own name but on behalf of an individual supplier, effectively takes part in the supply of services having a 'tangible' nature, concerning the provision of either accommodation or passenger transport, to the individual customer. As seen, such an assessment must be conducted on a case-by-case basis and, further, by making reference both to contractual documentation and economic reality. Accordingly, the related assessment might well diverge based on the type of the underlying services that a platform facilitates, the business model as resulting from the contractual documentation, as well as the way in which a platform actually carries out its own business. Drawing inspiration from the case law considered in the previous sections, the author has identified a series of conditions which might help conduct such an assessment and has tried to relate them to the specific business model of each of the four sharing economy platforms examined in the present study, i.e., Airbnb, Uber, HomeExchange, and BlaBlaCar. The results of such tentative assessment are displayed in Table 8.1 below. Notably, 'v' indicates that the specific condition under assessment, showing a certain level of intervention by the platform in the underlying supply, is met by the platform concerned, whereas 'x' states that the condition assessed is not, or not entirely, fulfilled by that platform. Where the majority of the conditions are met, the author submits that an assumption can be made that the platform in question effectively takes part in the supply toward the individual customer and, therefore, that it operates as an undisclosed agent of the individual supplier for EU VAT purposes.

Table 8.1 Conditions to Check for a Sharing Economy Platform to Effectively Take Part in the Supply of the Underlying Service Pursuant to Article 28 of the VAT Directive

Conditions	*Airbnb*	*Uber*	*HomeExchange*	*BlaBlaCar*
The platform provides its users with access to its website and/or its app services in its own name	v	v	v	v
The platform drafts the relevant contractual documentation and sets standards for user interaction	v	v	v	v
The platform marketizes the underlying services under its own brand	v	v	x	v
The platform shares – other than in a limited way – contact details of each party to the underlying transaction with the other one	x	x	v	v

Conditions	*Airbnb*	*Uber*	*HomeExchange*	*BlaBlaCar*
The platform controls or exerts influence over the pricing of the underlying transaction	x	v	v	v
The platform uses its own resources in the provision of the underlying services	x	x	x	x
The platform commits to arrange alternative accommodation/passenger transport and/or to operate refunds in case the individual supplier is unable to provide the requested service	v	x	v	v
The platform sets cancellation policies and determines the related charges	x	v	x	v
The platform deals with VAT invoicing and accounting on behalf of the individual supplier	v	v	x	x
The platform acts as a payment collection agent on behalf of its users	v	v	v	v
The platform reserves itself the right to remove and/or suspend a user's account in case of poor ratings and reviews and/or multiple cancellations of booking requests	v	v	v	v
The platform engages in complaints and compensation handling	v	v	v	x

Table 8.1 above reveals the existence of some commonalities among the four sharing economy platforms examined in the present study. Notably, a few of the conditions listed in the table are, indeed, fulfilled by all the platforms under assessment, such as the circumstance that every platform provides its users with access to its website and/or its app services in its own name, drafts the relevant contractual documentation and sets standards for user interaction, does not use its own resources in the provision of the underlying services, acts as a payment collection agent on behalf of its users, as well as reserves itself the right to remove and/or suspend a user's account in case of poor ratings and reviews and/or multiple cancellations of booking requests.

Apart from these commonalities, however, several differences exist among the four sharing economy platforms examined in the present study. Notably, Uber meets most of the conditions laid down in the table above. Particularly striking is the fact that the US-based company controls or exerts influence over the pricing of the underlying transaction, as well as the circumstance that the platform deals with VAT invoicing and accounting on behalf of the individual supplier. The same kinds of considerations apply to BlaBlaCar. Particularly striking is the fact that the French-based company controls or exerts influence over the pricing of the underlying transaction, as well as the circumstance that the platform shares – other than in a limited way – contact details of each party to the underlying transaction with the other one. Airbnb and HomeExchange, instead, meet a fewer number of conditions. Notably, Airbnb is the sole platform which does not control or exert influence over the pricing of the underlying transaction. Also, the platform does not share – other than in a limited way – contact details of each party to the underlying transaction with the other one, neither it sets cancellation policies and determines the related charges. On the contrary, Airbnb commits to arrange alternative accommodation and/or to operate refunds in case the individual supplier is unable to provide the requested service, deals with VAT invoicing and accounting on behalf of the individual supplier, and engages in complaints and compensation handling. HomeExchange, instead, is the sole platform which does not marketize the underlying services under its own brand. Also, the platform neither sets cancellation policies and determines the related charges, nor it deals with VAT invoicing and accounting on behalf of the individual supplier. On the contrary, HomeExchange shares – other than in a limited way – contact details of each party to the underlying transaction with the other one, commits to arrange alternative accommodation and/or to operate refunds in case the individual supplier is unable to provide the requested service, and engages in complaints and compensation handling.

At this juncture, the relevant question is whether these or, even, other conditions, making reference to the way in which a platform effectively carries out its own business, indeed provide valid grounds for establishing the actual role played by a sharing economy platform in the supply chain for EU VAT purposes. Arguably, what the assessment of those conditions has revealed, in fact, is simply that, in the context of the sharing economy, there is a party, i.e., the platform, which, although contractually characterized as the agent, is economically dominant over another party, i.e., the individual supplier, who, legally speaking, is instead considered as the principal. One may wonder whether this circumstance is, by itself, sufficient to overturn the principal-agent relationship, so that, for EU VAT purposes, who is the agent becomes the principal and vice versa. As a matter of fact, such a possibility was explicitly rejected by the UK Supreme Court in *Secret Hotels2*. Notably, in that case, the Court found that a one-sided bargain – even if entailing a very one-sided deal, as it was in *Secret Hotels2* – is not, per se, incompatible with the structure of an agency arrangement, that is with the fact that an intermediary playing a dominant role in the supply chain can, ultimately, be a disclosed agent for EU VAT purposes.[77] In particular, as the Upper Tribunal (Morgan J.) in the case reasoned (it is indeed a long quotation, but in the author's opinion the passage deserves to be cited in full):

77. UK: Supreme Court, 5 Mar. 2014, *The Commissioners for Her Majesty's Revenue and Customs v. Secret Hotels2 Limited (formerly Med Hotels Limited)* [2014] UKSC 16, at paras 36-44.

> [i]t is quite possible in a case like the present for the relevant parties to adopt different legal structures to produce similar (but not identical) economic results. Thus, it would be possible for the hotel operators, Med and the holidaymakers to adopt a legal structure of sale and sub-sale with Med buying hotel accommodation from the hotel operators and then supplying the same to holidaymakers. Conversely, it is possible for the parties to adopt a different legal structure whereby the hotel operators through the agency of Med supply hotel accommodation to holiday makers. In both cases, matters could be arranged whereby the hotel operators receive the net sum of £X for the accommodation and the holidaymaker pays £X plus a mark-up, so that in each case Med benefits to the extent of the mark up. The different legal structures will nonetheless have different legal and different economic consequences. I do not see how it can be said that the sale and sub-sale structure is economically real and the agency structure is economically unreal. It might even be argued that the agency structure is more apposite rather than the reverse. After all, the party who provides the hotel accommodation is the hotel operator and the person who uses the hotel accommodation is the holidaymaker. If the hotel operator and the holidaymaker adopt a legal structure where the hotel accommodation is provided to the holidaymaker through an intermediary, I do not see how that legal structure should be regarded as lacking economic reality so that it must for the purposes of VAT be analysed as if it were a different legal structure which the parties have chosen not to use.[78]

The author of this book concurs with this statement. Indeed, it is settled in the CJEU's case law that a taxable person is generally free to choose the organizational structures and the form of transactions which he considers as the most appropriate for his own economic activities and for the purposes of limiting his own tax burdens.[79] Accordingly, the business model specifically adopted by a sharing economy platform cannot be considered as 'economically unreal', simply because the 'sale and sub-sale structure' is perceived, economically speaking, as more appropriate than the 'agency structure' used by most sharing economy platforms.

All in all, the analysis made above confirms that the attribution to a sharing economy platform of a liability for collection and remittance of VAT, as meant in the deemed rule contained in Article 28 of the VAT Directive, necessarily presupposes, against any sweeping conclusion, a case-by-case assessment, which must take into account both contractual documentation and economic reality. Ultimately, in order to simplify such an assessment, as well as to attribute to a sharing economy platform a liability for collection and remittance of VAT in a larger number of cases and, arguably, with greater legal certainty, it might be convenient to introduce a new liability regime specific to sharing economy platforms in the EU VAT system. An analysis in this regard is provided in the following sections.

78. UK: Upper Tribunal, Tax and Chancery Chamber, 29 Jul. 2011, *Secret Hotels 2 Ltd (Formerly Med Hotels Ltd) v. The Commissioners for HM Revenue and Customs* [2011] UKUT 308 (TCC), at para. 112.
79. *See* e.g., UK: ECJ, 22 Dec. 2010, Case C-277/09, *The Commissioners for Her Majesty's Revenue & Customs v. RBS Deutschland Holdings GmbH*, para. 53.

§8.04 A NEW LIABILITY REGIME FOR SHARING ECONOMY PLATFORMS

[A] A New Liability Regime: Which Platforms?

Should a new liability regime specific to sharing economy platforms be introduced in the EU VAT system, then the first question which, from a policy design perspective, needs to be answered would relate to the platforms to enlist under that regime. For this purpose, it seems convenient to lay down a series of features which a sharing economy must possess. Those features should consider, in particular, the ability of a platform to exert a certain level of influence and control over the underlying transaction.

In this connection, two features appear of critical importance. The first is that the platform should possess sufficient and accurate information to assess the amount of VAT due. The second, instead, relates to the fact that the platform should have effective means to collect and remit the tax by obtaining the amount due from the individual supplier.[80] Notably, as for the first feature, a platform should possess, or – at least – be able to obtain, sufficient and accurate information over: (1) the status of the supplier and whether or not he is required to register for VAT, (2) the status of the customer, (3) the nature of the supply, (4) the elements to determine the place of taxation and the applicable collection regime, (5) the value of the supply, and (6) the taxing point of the supply.[81] Indeed, all these pieces of information are necessary to make a proper determination of the VAT due in relation to the underlying transaction. Should these pieces of information not be available or, further, not be easily obtained by a platform from the individual supplier without radically changing its own business model, then a liability for collection and remittance of VAT in lieu of individual suppliers could not, reasonably, be imposed upon such a platform.[82]

As for the second feature, that is the possession by a platform of effective means to collect and remit the amount of VAT due, it entails that a platform should have effective access to the sums transferred from the individual customer to the individual supplier in the context of the underlying transaction taking place between those parties. Indeed, all the platforms examined in the present study, i.e., Airbnb, Uber, HomeExchange, and BlaBlaCar, are involved in receiving and processing payments made by the individual customer to the individual supplier. As such, it could be maintained that all these platforms have effective means to extract VAT from the sum paid by users through them and remit it to the tax authorities. In order to prevent tax

80. For a similar approach, *see* OECD, *supra* n. 16, at 26.
81. *Id.*, at 33.
82. Indeed, with regard to the possession, by a third party, of all the necessary information to charge VAT on a supply, as early as 2000 the OECD acknowledged that financial institutions did not possess the essential information to be involved in collection and remittance of VAT, as long as the payment authorization process operated by those parties did not 'involve access to customer's address, telephone number, e-mail address, and description of product and catalogue product number'. In this connection, the OECD also worried that 'change in the authorization process would require fundamental systems modifications affecting issuing banks, merchant banks, credit card associations, credit card holders and other parties'. *See* OECD, *supra* n. 11, at 18.

arbitrage opportunities by platforms, it is important, however, that the condition that a platform actually possesses the sums transferred receives a broader understanding, as to cover also situations in which the platform has only indirect access to the sums transferred from the individual customer to the individual supplier, such as it occurs in the case in which the sums transferred are in the material availability of a third party, whether this third party is affiliated to the platform or, even, if this third party is bound by contractual obligations toward the latter, thanks to which the platform can have effective access to the sums transferred.[83]

Rather than focusing on information and means at a disposal of a platform, whose actual availability by a platform, in an individual case, might be difficult to ascertain for tax authorities, a better course of action could, perhaps, be envisaged. In particular, such approach would require focusing on the types of services which a sharing economy platform actually provides to its users and, in particular, to the individual supplier. In the context of the sharing economy, this practically entails assessing the degree of 'facilitation' effectively provided by a platform in matching supply and demand of the underlying services. Based on such evaluation, it might be possible to establish whether or not the platform in question has sufficient and accurate information, as well as effective means, to fulfil VAT obligations in lieu of individual suppliers. Some guidance might eventually be provided in this regard. Notably, such guidance could consist in a list of services, as those contained in the explanatory notes issued by the Commission in relation to the application of Article 9a of the Implementing Regulation.[84] Not every single service offered by a digital platform and listed therein, however, is also relevant in the context of the sharing economy. As seen, the actual delivery of the underlying service, in fact, is never operated by a sharing economy platform, but instead it is always rendered by the individual supplier. Other facilitation services, such as the exercise of control or influence over the pricing of the underlying transaction, the issuance of invoices, receipts or bills to users, or the provision of customer support, are instead provided also by sharing economy platforms. An approach based on the services effectively operated by a platform, with a view of imposing a liability for VAT upon it, was also put forward by the OECD Working Party No. 9 on Consumption Taxes (WP9) in its March 2019 report on *The Role of Digital Platforms in the Collection of VAT/GST on Online Sales*. Notably, for the purpose of such assessment, the WP9 singled out the following services offered by a digital platform to its users: (1) setting up the terms and conditions of the underlying transaction (e.g., price, payment, and delivery conditions), (2) processing payments, (3) supervising the delivery of the underlying supply, and (4) providing customer support services. The mere performance by a platform of other services, such as

83. According to the OECD, the obligation for a platform to collect and remit the VAT due by the individual supplier also extends to the situation in which payment for the underlying supply is made by the individual customer directly to the individual supplier, without the platform having the material availability of the sums transferred. In such event, the OECD stipulates that 'the digital platform will need to recover the VAT/GST component from the underlying supplier in order to remit it to the tax authorities in the jurisdiction of taxation'. *See* OECD, *supra* n. 16, at 25.
84. *See* section §8.03[D].

carrying content via the Internet or listing advert offers, was not instead considered, by itself, sufficient to justify the imposition of a liability regime upon a digital platform.[85]

The real difficulty entailed in such assessment is, however, to ascertain which types of services could indeed justify a liability shift from the individual supplier to the sharing economy platform. It does not appear, in fact, possible to single out a 'killer' service capable of indicating, by itself, the ability of a sharing economy platform to assume a VAT liability. Thus, the only feasible approach in this regard would consist in drawing up a list of services, to be inserted in the Implementing Regulation, which might indicate that a platform actually takes part or facilitates the underlying transaction and, therefore, that the imposition of a liability upon such platform is reasonable. Notably, this list could include all or only some of the services singled out in Table 8.1 above, especially those revealing a certain level of influence and control exerted by a platform over the underlying transaction, for instance in terms of price setting, invoicing, payment, and refund processing. In this connection, it is important that the list would be regularly reviewed and constantly updated, so as to remain flexible enough to accommodate other services which sharing economy platforms might eventually operate in the near future and, further, that platforms would be informed and consulted in the process of updating and amending such a list.[86] Instead, it does not appear equally convenient to compile a negative list – such as that provided by the OECD in its aforementioned report delivered in March 2019[87] or by the Implementing Regulation in relation to both electronically supplied services[88] and services connected with immovable property[89] – of services which, if performed by a platform, would indicate the inability of that platform to meet the obligations associated with the imposition of a VAT liability, as long as the performance of those services is not sufficient to exclude the actual capability of a platform to fulfil that role in the near future, given the rapid evolution of business models in the context of the sharing economy.

The inclusion of a positive list in the Implementing Regulation would, arguably, consent to achieve a sufficient degree of legal certainty, especially in terms of who, i.e., the individual supplier or the platform, shall be held liable for VAT in a given situation, thus ensuring a minimum level of harmonization in the interpretation and application of EU VAT across different Member States. With an aim of increasing compliance and information accessibility by platforms, the list and subsequent changes to it could, perhaps, be rendered available online. Eventually, the possibility for sharing economy platforms to rely on an advance ruling procedure, such as the CBR procedure operated under the sponsorship of the EU VAT Forum, might contribute to further enhance legal

85. OECD, *supra* n. 16, at 73-74 (Annex I).
86. For a similar approach, *see* OECD, *supra* n. 16, at 27-28. Notably, in that document, the OECD recommends tax authorities to adopt a flexible approach in compiling a list of services to be deemed as relevant, since 'a platform may for instance be eligible for the application of a full VAT/GST liability regime on the basis of the functions it performs, whereas the application of this regime would in fact result in disproportionate compliance burden given the platform's technological or financial capabilities'. *Id.*, at 27.
87. *Id.*, at 73-74 (Annex I).
88. Article 7(3) Implementing Regulation.
89. Article 31a(3) Implementing Regulation.

certainty. Moreover, a *de minimis* rule could be introduced, based on which a platform, whose annual turnover remains under a certain threshold, would not be required to collect and remit to the competent tax authorities the VAT due on the underlying transaction in lieu of individual suppliers.[90] Lastly, as a means to reduce compliance risks for a platform which can prove to have acted in good faith or has made reasonable efforts to ensure compliance from its own individual suppliers, certain safe harbours might be introduced, especially in cases where the sums transferred are not in the material availability of that platform.[91]

[B] A New Liability Regime: Which Transactions?

A second set of policy design questions, subsequent to the determination of which sharing economy platforms ought to be included in the envisaged liability regime, concerns the transactions to be covered. In this connection, it is quite evident that reference is to be made to transactions among platform users only, without any further reference to the provision of services by the platform to its users. Accordingly, it is of little or no importance whether a platform is established or not in the jurisdiction having taxing rights over the underlying transaction. Hence, it follows that a liability regime should be equally imposed upon domestic and foreign platforms. Indeed, neither the rules for electronically supplied services contained in Articles 28 of the VAT Directive and 9a of the Implementing Regulation, nor the new rules for distance sales of goods contained in Article 14a of the VAT Directive, draw any sort of distinction based on whether the digital platform taking part or facilitating the underlying transaction is established or not in the Member State concerned. Eventually, as a sole measure to simplify compliance for non-established platforms, the possibility to rely on the MOSS scheme, as to fulfil obligations related to the assumption of a VAT liability, should be extended to those platforms.[92]

Due to the circumstance that underlying transactions in the sharing economy platforms examined in the present study relate to accommodation or passenger transport services, in respect of which the relevant place of supply rules make reference to the place where those services are physically carried out[93], it is quite evident that also the VAT liability associated with those transactions would arise in the country were those services are physically carried out. Accordingly, it is irrelevant whether the supplier is established in the jurisdiction claiming taxing rights over the underlying transaction, or, instead, if the transaction is operated by a foreign supplier. Indeed, this latter eventuality is more likely to occur in case of accommodation services, such as those provided on sharing economy platforms like Airbnb and HomeExchange, where the supplier can well be established in a country other than where the rented property

90. For a similar approach, *see* OECD, *supra* n. 16, at 38.
91. *Id.*, at 24.
92. Noteworthy, Art. 359 of the VAT Directive, as amended by Council Directive 2017/2455/EU, provides, as from 1 January 2021, an extension of the MOSS scheme to all services supplied at a distance.
93. *See* sections §7.02, §7.05, and §7.06.

is located. It is more difficult, instead, that this scenario would materialize in case of passenger transport services, such as those provided on sharing economy platforms like Uber and BlaBlaCar, as long as, in those situations, it is likely that the driver is also a resident of the country where the transport takes place. The related assessment, however, may change in case of a cross-border journey operated by a driver on BlaBlaCar. Based on such considerations, it can fairly be maintained that a shift of VAT liability from the individual supplier to the platform should occur even in case where the underlying transaction is carried out by a domestic supplier. Indeed, this view gains force from the fact that holding otherwise would require platforms and tax authorities to make whimsical distinctions between domestic and foreign supplies, a circumstance which is very much capable of causing legal uncertainty in the application of the envisaged liability regime. Notably, this might occur in relation to the VAT liability associated with a cross-border passenger transport service, where a platform faces a VAT liability only in the jurisdictions in which the individual supplier (i.e., the driver) is not established, with a subsequent split of liabilities among the individual supplier and the platform, depending on the jurisdiction concerned.[94]

As seen in Chapter 7, the special place of supply rules for accommodation and passenger transport services contained, respectively, in Articles 47 and 48 of the VAT Directive, apply regardless of whether the transaction in question is B2B or B2C.[95] Accordingly, it is quite impractical to require a platform, as to determine the extent of its own VAT liability and obligations over the supply made by the individual supplier, to draw a similar kind of distinction, especially considering the difficulty to determine the status of both the individual supplier and the individual customer in the sharing economy.[96] As a matter of fact, the application of the envisaged liability regime to both B2B and B2C transactions does render much easier, for a sharing economy platform, to comply with the obligations related to the assumption of a VAT liability. Indeed, this circumstance further contributes to reduce the wealth of information which a platform must possess for a liability regime to be reasonably imposed upon it, in so far as the platform is entirely relieved from collecting and assessing a series of indicia in order to determine the actual status of a customer (e.g., his VAT number, records of previous transactions, certificates, or other credentials).

94. Apparently, such kinds of compliance complexities have not been quite evaluated – and, in any event, were left to a separate future report – by the OECD WP9 in its report on *The Role of Digital Platforms in the Collection of VAT/GST on Online Sales* released in March 2019. In that document, the WP9 has in fact maintained – although only in passim – that 'broadening the scope of this regime [the liability regime for digital platforms] to cover other types of services (such as transport or accommodation services as well as other "on-the-spot" supplies, i.e., non-remotely delivered supplied) appears theoretically possible. It requires, however, a careful balancing of a number of considerations including the potential disadvantage of applying this regime for supplies where there may be no need to deviate from the full VAT/GST liability at the level of the underlying supplier'. *See* OECD, *supra* n. 16, at 30.

95. *See* sections §7.05 and §7.06.

96. *See* section §4.02[D]. *See*, however, OECD, *supra* n. 16, at 32-33, considering that, for digital services and intangibles, distinguishing between B2B and B2C transactions is indeed crucial, as long as the liability regime for digital platforms envisaged therein applies only in relation to the latter type of transactions.

Lastly, the need to simplify compliance matters for platforms also suggests deeming irrelevant, for the purpose of establishing the VAT liability of a platform over a transaction made by an individual supplier, whether the annual turnover of such individual supplier falls below or above the registration threshold established in a country. Various considerations can be advanced in favour of this position. For one thing, requiring a platform to distinguish between businesses obliged to register or not would considerably increase the costs for that platform to comply with the EU VAT system, thus potentially undermining legal certainty. Indeed, it may be quite hard for a platform to monitor thresholds fixed at the level of each individual supplier, inasmuch as an individual supplier could eventually perform his own activities using multiple platforms and/or different channels of sales.[97] Second, given that registration thresholds are anything but harmonized across the EU[98], a platform might face a variable degree of liability based on the Member State in which the individual supplier operates and, should a registration threshold set by a Member State be too high or too low, the platform in question might even decide not to operate in that country. Third, it could be argued that the individual supplier, by operating through a platform rather than following more conventional business routes, has chosen – at least implicitly – to be a 'full-fledged' supplier, who, as such, should face the related tax obligations, namely the fact that VAT is imposed on his output supplies. Fourth, it could be maintained that the benefits, for an individual supplier, to use the technological, commercial, and legal infrastructure provided by a platform far exceed tax disadvantages vis-à-vis a comparable traditional business, who, instead, is not required to charge any VAT on his output supplies.

[C] A New Liability Regime: Which Relationship Between Individual Suppliers and Platforms?

The implementation of a liability regime, pursuant to which a sharing economy platform is held responsible for collecting and remitting to the competent tax authorities the VAT due on an underlying transaction carried out by an individual supplier, brings the question of how to characterize, for EU VAT purposes, the relationship between the individual supplier and the platform concerned.

A first possibility in this regard is to treat such kind of relationship as an 'ordinary' B2B transaction, as similarly provided under the deemed rule contained in Article 28 of the VAT Directive. In such event, the individual supplier is required to charge VAT on his output transactions, whereas he is entitled to deduct the VAT paid on his inputs.[99] Although this approach – which might hereinafter be referred to as 'taxation regime' – follows the normal operation of EU VAT, its application does not contribute anyhow to obviate one of the most ticklish problems which motivates the

97. For similar considerations, *see* OECD, *supra* n. 16, at 38.
98. *See* section §4.05.
99. Noteworthy, this approach is also the one favoured by the OECD WP9 in its report on *The Role of Digital Platforms in the Collection of VAT/GST on Online Sales* released in March 2019. *See* OECD, *supra* n. 16, at 24.

shift of VAT liability from the individual supplier to the platform, that is the need to reduce the overall VAT compliance costs for the former party. And indeed, those compliance costs are likely to be substantial, especially recalling that individual suppliers need to properly apportion between deductible and non-deductible VAT, based on the extent to which inputs are used for carrying out their output transactions. Neither the envisaged regime, indeed, spares costs for tax authorities, as long as the tax administration is required to verify that the cost deduction and the apportionment operation are made by individual suppliers in an appropriate manner.

A more appealing alternative might then consist in relieving entirely the individual suppliers from the need to account for any VAT, either on their output or input transactions. Accordingly, based on this approach – which might eventually be referred to as 'exemption regime' – the individual supplier neither has to charge any VAT on his outputs nor has the right to deduct any VAT on his inputs. Nevertheless, an option ought to be rendered available to individual suppliers, especially for those with a significant annual turnover, to register and account for VAT under normal rules. In such event, the application of VAT follows its regular course, with individual suppliers charging VAT on their outputs and deducting VAT on their inputs, except for the notable fact that their output transactions are treated not as directly made to individual customers, but instead as carried out toward the platform, which, then, is deemed to operate a second supply to the individual customers, as similarly provided under the deemed rule contained in Article 28 of the VAT Directive.

Nevertheless, exempting transactions between the individual supplier and the platform creates a series of hurdles.[100] The major issue in this regard relates to the fact that the VAT which the individual supplier has paid on his inputs cannot be deducted either by himself, as long as, under the envisaged liability regime, the individual supplier is – de facto – removed from the EU VAT system, or by the platform, since such input VAT relates to expenses which were borne not by the platform, but by the individual supplier alone. This circumstance leads to VAT cascading, in so far as the VAT paid by the individual supplier on his inputs is likely to be passed on the price finally charged to the individual customer or, alternatively, it reduces the profit margins of the individual supplier, the platform, or both parties.[101] As seen in Chapter 1, VAT cascading runs counter a central premise of EU VAT, that is to be a tax neutral for businesses, in the sense of not constituting a cost for them, but only for end consumers.[102] It also ought to be considered that VAT cascading puts supplies of accommodation and passenger transport services in the sharing economy at a disadvantage vis-à-vis traditional businesses operating in the same economic sectors, inasmuch as these latter businesses are able – contrary to the former – to deduct their

100. The existence of several difficulties in this respect was also recognized by the OECD. *See* OECD, *supra* n. 16, at 24.
101. Importantly, the amount of 'hidden' VAT cannot be exactly measured, in so far as the extent to which the supplier is able to shift his non-deductible input VAT on to the customer depends on various economic factors, most notably price elasticity. Further, it could be foreseen that platforms and individual suppliers might be willing to put commercial arrangements in place, which are most likely to take any VAT-associated costs into account.
102. *See* section §1.02.

input VAT in full. An effort should then be made to remove the amount of non-deductible VAT paid by individual suppliers on their inputs.

A variety of strategies can be developed to that effect. A first solution is to allow individual suppliers to deduct their input VAT, although not requiring them to charge any VAT on their inputs. This, in effect, implies zero-rating transactions carried out by those suppliers. Although, in principle, this solution avoids VAT cascading, the related benefits come at a considerable cost for the public exchequer, inasmuch as tax authorities do not receive any VAT on transactions carried out by the individual suppliers in question. This undesirable result could, ultimately, be obliterated if the VAT payable on transactions that are deemed to be carried out by the platform is levied on the overall amount finally charged to the individual customer, which ought to include the consideration for the services materially operated by both the platform and the individual supplier. At a closer inspection, however, such an option is not desirable either, as long as it requires the platform to charge the individual customer with VAT without having, at the same time, the possibility to claim any VAT on the inputs used by the individual supplier in providing the services in question, whereas the individual supplier is left with the not insignificant problem to claim refund for the VAT on his inputs, with all the difficulties associated with apportionment of mixed-used assets already recalled above. It is not conceivable, in fact, that the individual supplier provides a platform with all the necessary information for deducting VAT on his inputs, as long as this circumstance, quite evidently, washes out any benefits, in terms of compliance costs, associated with the envisaged liability shift.

A second solution is to allow platforms to charge a reduced rate on their output transactions, as a means to compensate those parties for the impossibility to deduct any VAT on the inputs used by the individual supplier in the provision of accommodation or passenger transport services. There are, however, a number of detrimental effects associated with this solution. From a theoretical standpoint, the introduction of reduced rates represents a major departure from the ideal design of EU VAT, pursuant to which every good and service shall be subject to the very same rate. From a practical perspective, the application of a reduced VAT rate on services made by a platform entails a more favourable treatment accorded to those services vis-à-vis comparable business activities. Moreover, the introduction of reduced rates leads to a significant increase in administrative and compliance costs, inasmuch as platforms are required to account separately for the VAT charged to individual customers in respect of the underlying services - indeed, subject to a reduced rate - and for the VAT concerning the provision to individual customers of their own services - instead, subject to the standard rate. Application of different rates further requires additional audit oversight by tax authorities, which must carefully ensure that platforms do not engage in purposive misclassification of the charges related to the two types of services in question.

A third solution is to allow platforms to deduct a predetermined amount of input VAT, which is set to exactly correspond to the foreseeable amount of non-deductible VAT paid by individual suppliers on their inputs. This presumptive amount of deductible VAT, practically, is meant to partially compensate a platform for the non-deductible VAT faced by the individual supplier and that the supplier in question, arguably, is able to pass on in the price of his own services. Operatively, this flat-rate input VAT compensation scheme might be calculated on the basis of account statistics for the specific sector considered, i.e., accommodation or passenger transport, averaged for a certain number of years. Admittedly, the proposed system resembles very closely the common flat-rate scheme for farmers included in Articles 295-305 of the VAT Directive. In terms of advantages, the implementation of such compensation scheme represents a practical solution against the problem of VAT cascading highlighted above. Further, the use of fixed quotas for the determination of the deductible input VAT consents to better align the treatment of sharing economy activities with traditional economic activities, as long as the presumptive amount of deductible VAT is calculated on the basis of the average percentage of deductible VAT for businesses operating in the same economic sector. Nevertheless, even this solution has several drawbacks. Besides representing a major departure from the normal levying of VAT, the first drawback relates to the sheer difficulty to determine, in an individual case, the presumptive amount of deductible input VAT, circumstance which may lead to arbitrary over-taxation or under-taxation of sharing economy platforms, depending on the size of the platform concerned. Moreover, it is not clear which inputs, in concrete, ought to be made eligible for inclusion in the fixed deduction scheme (indeed: residential premises, vehicles, and what else?).[103] The end result is that the envisaged flat-rate compensation scheme may turn into a rather arbitrary way to remove the amount of non-deductible VAT on inputs, thus ultimately failing to restore the (ac)claimed neutrality of EU VAT.

[D] Alternative Liability Regimes for Sharing Economy Platforms

A regime which entails a complete liability shift from the individual supplier to the sharing economy platform, however, is neither the sole nor necessarily the best solution for ensuring collection and remittance to the competent tax authorities of the VAT due on the underlying transaction. In the following, two alternative liability regimes for sharing economy platforms are, in particular, illustrated: (1) joint and several liability regimes, and (2) formal agreements for collaboration between platforms and tax authorities.

Under the first alternative liability regime, a platform is held jointly and severally liable with the individual supplier for payment of the VAT due on the transaction made by the latter party. As explained previously, the attribution of a joint and several

103. Interestingly, with specific regard to the common flat-rate scheme for farmers, the Explanatory Memorandum attached to the Proposal for a Sixth Directive stipulated, in a quite similar vein, that, 'because of the technical difficulties in drawing up an exhaustive list of agricultural products from European farms, it seemed preferable to abandon the idea of such a list and to lay down criteria whereby a common definition of agricultural products may be formulated which will be of value having regard to the fiscal aims pursued'. *See* European Commission, *Proposal for a Sixth Council Directive on the Harmonization of Member States concerning Turnover Taxes Common System of Value Added Tax: Uniform Basis of Assessment (submitted to the Council by the Commission on 29 June 1973)*, at 25, COM(73) 950, Bulletin of the European Communities No. 11 (1973).

liability upon a person for payment of the VAT due by another person, essentially, aims to ensure that the amount due would ultimately be collected and remitted to the competent tax authorities, which, under this regime, are thus able to enforce their taxing rights over another person in case the primary debtor fails to comply with his own VAT obligations. In a sense, such liability regime aims to assist a jurisdiction in ensuring compliance and enforcing its taxing rights over a supplier. More to the point, joint and several liability is a 'secondary' or 'vicarious' type of liability, i.e., a liability that is attributed to a person for an infringement committed by another person, due to a special relationship existing between these two parties.[104]

As stated, under current EU VAT, there is no mandatory provision for introducing a joint and several liability for payment of the tax due on a transaction.[105] Pursuant to Article 205 of the VAT Directive, the designation of a person as jointly and severally liable, in fact, is a mere option available to each Member State. Notably, a joint and several liability regime specifically designed for digital platforms was introduced in the UK in 2016-2017. The liability regime enacted by the UK presupposes the existence of a faulty or negligent behaviour by a platform. In other terms, under the legislated regime, a platform can be held responsible if it fails to take proper action against non-fulfilment, by the supplier, of his own VAT obligations.[106] More precisely, the liability of a platform arises in two distinct situations. The first situation occurs where a platform has 'actual knowledge' that a violation was committed by the supplier, in particular after it receives a notice by the tax authorities signalling a non-compliant behaviour by the supplier, and yet, notwithstanding such a warning, it takes no action to secure compliance from him (as such, it is a sort of 'forward-looking liability'). The second situation, instead, is premised on a 'constructive knowledge' by the platform, i.e., on the legal presumption that, in a given situation, a platform should have reasonably known that the supplier was infringing his own VAT obligations (as such, it is a sort of 'past liability').[107] Noteworthy, with regard to the participation of a person

104. Forms of vicarious liability are often employed in the context of principal-agent relationships. Indeed, the concept can be traced back to the Latin maxims '*respondeat superior*' (i.e., 'let the master answer') and '*qui facit per alium facit per se*' (i.e., 'he who acts through another acts himself'). *See* W.J. Stewart, *Collins Dictionary of Law. 'Vicarious Liability'*. 3rd ed. (Collins 2006).
105. *See* section §8.02.
106. Notably, the joint and several liability regime for digital platforms was introduced in the UK, first, by Finance Bill 2016, and, then, extended by Finance Bill 2017-18. *See* UK: HMRC, *VAT: Overseas Businesses and Joint and Several Liability for Online Marketplaces* (2016), https://www.gov.uk/government/publications/vat-overseas-businesses-and-joint-and-several-liability-for-online-marketplaces/vat-overseas-businesses-and-joint-and-several-liability-for-online-marketplaces (accessed 31 Mar. 2019); HMRC, *VAT: Extending Joint and Several Liability for Online Marketplaces and Displaying VAT Numbers Online – Guidance Note* (2017), https://www.gov.uk/government/publications/vat-extending-joint-and-several-liability-for-online-marketplaces-and-displaying-vat-numbers-online-guidance-note (accessed 31 Mar. 2019).
107. For a perspective on these two approaches, in relation to the attribution of a joint and several liability to digital platforms, *see* OECD, *supra* n. 16, at 63-64.

to a VAT fraud, a 'knowledge test' was laid down by the CJEU in the joined cases *Kittel and Recolta Recycling*.[108]

Indeed, uncertainties might arise on whether a platform actually had sufficient knowledge or, at least, it ought to have known the existence of a violation committed by the individual supplier, but nevertheless it failed to take any appropriate action against him. In this connection, the author submits that, in no event, a mere assumption or supposition of a breach should be considered enough to hold a platform responsible.[109] This is even truer in the situation at hand, which envisages a vicarious liability imposed upon a party (i.e., the platform) for a violation committed by another – although related – party (i.e., the individual supplier). As stipulated with regard to the full liability regime illustrated in the previous sections, it is in fact crucial to ensure that the platform held jointly and severally liable is sufficiently involved in the supply to the individual customer and that the platform does not play, instead, only a marginal role within the supply chain.[110] Fulfilment of such condition is, indeed, material to consider the imposition of this type of liability as fully compliant with the principles of legal certainty and proportionality underpinning EU VAT.[111] From another perspective, it is also worth noting that, apparently, EU institutions consider joint and several liability insufficient to ensure effective and efficient collection of VAT.[112]

The second alternative, fundamentally, consists in putting in place a system of cooperative tax compliance between sharing economy platforms and tax authorities.[113] A similar approach was explored in the UK. Notably, in early 2018, the UK tax

108. BE: ECJ, 6 Jul. 2006, Joined Cases C-439/04 and C-440/04, *Axel Kittel v. Belgian State and Belgian State v. Recolta Recycling SPRL*, paras 39-61.
109. For a similar perspective, in the CJEU's case law, *see* HU: ECJ, 21 Jun. 2012, Joined Cases C-80/11 and C-142/11, *Mahagében Kft v. Nemzeti Adó- és Vámhivatal Dél-dunántúli Regionális Adó Főigazgatósága and Péter Dávid v. Nemzeti Adó- és Vámhivatal Észak-alföldi Regionális Adó Főigazgatósága*, paras 61 and 65. At the same time, however, it ought to be highlighted that the CJEU requires a certain behavioural standard from the taxable person. In this connection, *see* IT: ECJ, 15 Dec. 2011, Case C-427/10, *Banca Antoniana Popolare Veneta SpA v. Ministero dell'Economia e delle Finanze and Agenzia delle Entrate*, paras 37 and 39, making reference to a taxable person as a 'prudent and alert economic operator'.
110. In this connection, *see* BE: ECJ, 21 Dec. 2011, Case C-499/10, *Vlaamse Oliemaatschappij NV v. FOD Financiën*, para. 15, in which a warehouse keeper, who was held jointly and severally liable under a national VAT, claimed playing only 'a passive role in the VAT arrangements applicable to warehouses', due to the circumstance that he merely made 'his warehouse available to his customers to allow goods to be stored' and, further, that he had 'no legal or fiscal means at his disposal to monitor or enforce the effective payment of VAT by his customers'.
111. *Federation of Technological Industries and Others* (C-384/04), paras 29 and 35.
112. Point 7 of the Preamble of Council Directive 2017/2455/EU.
113. In this connection, *see* OECD, *Co-operative Compliance: A Framework: From Enhanced Relationship to Co-operative Compliance* (OECD Publishing 2013). For a scholarly approach to cooperative compliance, *see* K. Bronzewska, *Acknowledgements in Cooperative Compliance: A New Approach to Managing Taxpayer Relations* (IBFD 2016). Noteworthy, a guide for creating a best practice framework for effective cooperation between tax administrations and businesses was issued by the EU VAT Forum in 2016. *See* European Commission, EU VAT Forum, *Guide on Enhanced Cooperation between Member States and Business in the Field of Fighting VAT Fraud* (2016), https://ec.europa.eu/taxation_customs/sites/taxation/files/resources/documents/taxation/tax_cooperation/vat_gap/2016-03_guide-on-adm-cooperation_en.pdf (accessed 31 Mar. 2019).

authorities issued a consultation document featuring a survey on the potential role of digital platforms – including those 'that facilitate the sharing economy' – in ensuring and enhancing tax compliance by their users.[114] In this consultation document, the UK tax authorities highlighted, in particular, that, since 'there is a wide range of different models for the ways platforms engage with their users', 'understanding more about how they interact with people and businesses who earn money through them will be helpful for building a picture of what interventions might be appropriate and proportionate to support tax compliance'.[115] Notably, an agreement to help build a collaborative relationship between tax authorities and online marketplaces, as well as to promote VAT compliance by users of those marketplaces, has been open to signature in the UK as from 25 April 2018.[116] At time of writing (March 2019), the agreement has been signed, *inter alia*, by Amazon, eBay, and Etsy.[117] Commitments taken by online marketplaces under this agreement include, in particular, the provision to UK tax authorities of information concerning businesses operating on their platforms and transactions concluded therein, the education of suppliers through dedicated guidelines, videos, webinars, and online forums, as well as the obligation to take appropriate action whenever presented with evidence of potential non-compliance by their users.[118]

In the context of the present inquiry on the potential role of sharing economy platforms with regard to collection and remittance of VAT in lieu of individual suppliers, formal agreements – better if rendered public, as to increase their overall transparency and effectiveness – between platforms and tax authorities can represent a viable solution, especially where the business model adopted by a platform does not enable that platform to collect and remit to the competent tax authorities the VAT due from the individual suppliers. And indeed, due to the low initiative of individual suppliers to report their own taxes independently, sharing economy platforms can play a pivotal role in supporting compliance by those parties. In this connection, besides education and communication strategies[119], implementation of a specific requirement for sharing economy platforms to provide either on a regular basis, upon request, or spontaneously, tax authorities with information about users and transactions occurring on their marketplaces might be particularly helpful in targeting non-compliance by

114. UK: HMRC, *The Role of Online Platforms in Ensuring Tax Compliance by Their Users* at 5 (2018), https://assets.publishing.service.gov.uk/government/uploads/system/uploads/attachment_data/file/687363/The_role_of_online_platforms_in_ensuring_tax_compliance_by_their_users.pdf (accessed 31 Mar. 2019).
115. *Id.*, at 10.
116. UK: HMRC, *Tackling Online VAT Fraud and Error – The Role of Online Marketplaces in Co-operating with HMRC – The Agreement* (2018), https://www.gov.uk/government/publications/hmrc-and-online-marketplaces-agreement-to-promote-vat-compliance/tackling-online-vat-fraud-and-error-the-role-of-online-marketplaces-in-co-operating-with-hmrc-the-agreement (accessed 31 Mar. 2019).
117. UK: HMRC, *Tackling Online VAT Fraud and Error – The Role of Online Marketplaces in Co-operating with HMRC: List of Signatories* (2018), https://assets.publishing.service.gov.uk/government/uploads/system/uploads/attachment_data/file/719795/List_of_signatories.pdf (accessed 31 Mar. 2019).
118. HMRC, *supra* n. 116.
119. For a similar approach, *see* OECD, *supra* n. 16, at 55-56.

individual suppliers.[120] Eventually, an electronic interface could also be developed, where information about users and transactions can be uploaded by platforms and shared with tax authorities in real time.[121]

As it is with the case of a joint and several liability regime, formal agreements for collaboration between platforms and tax authorities could well entail the attribution to a platform of certain enforcement obligations, which, indeed, may span from blocking and removing a non-compliant business from its online marketplace to the publication, on its own website, of a name-and-shame list of non-compliant individual suppliers. In this connection, however, it is important to identify clearly and in advance which types of information (e.g., name, address, and tax identification number of individual suppliers, number and types of transactions in a year, amounts received/paid during a year) can be reasonably[122] and, also, lawfully[123] expected from a sharing economy platform to be reported to tax authorities, especially taking into account that information available to a sharing economy platform might well differ depending on the platform concerned. It is also crucial to strike an appropriate balance between requiring platforms to collect all the relevant information and avoiding imposing a disproportionate burden upon them, circumstance which might eventually occur if various types of information are required for those platforms by different Member States.[124] In this connection, given the multi-jurisdictional level at which most sharing economy platforms operate, it is also crucial to set up appropriate administrative cooperation arrangements between tax authorities of different Member States.[125] Last but not least, besides helping secure a mutually beneficial and trustable collaboration between platforms and tax authorities, formal agreements may also represent the foundation

---

120. OECD, *supra* n. 16, at 51-54. *See also*, with regard to the fulfilment of income tax obligations by users, OECD, *The Sharing and Gig Economy: Effective Taxation of Platform Sellers: Forum on Tax Administration* at 38 (OECD Publishing 2019). Indeed, the potential fulfilment of a compliance and policing role by online platforms has plainly been recognized by representatives of governments and businesses gathering at the EU VAT Forum. *See* European Commission, EU VAT Forum, *Consolidated Report on Cooperation between Member States and Businesses in the Field of e-Commerce/Modern Commerce* at 8 (taxud.c.4(2018) 1507602), https://ec.europa.eu/taxation_customs/sites/taxation/files/d-1507602_report_consolidated_en.pdf (accessed 31 Mar. 2019).
121. For a similar proposal in the C2C e-commerce industry, *see* W. Huang, Y. Liao & S. Li, *C2C Electronic Commerce Tax Management Based on Big Data*, in *Proceedings of the Third International Conference on Economic and Business Management (FEBM 2018)* (Atlantis Press 2018).
122. Especially in terms of information availability, that is whether the platform can be expected to have the requested information readily at hand. In this connection, it can be maintained that information sharing should be limited to those information/data which are available to a platform in the normal course of its own business activities.
123. Notably, in the EU, limitations may exist with regard to privacy and data security under the General Data Protection Regulation (EU) 2016/679 (GDPR), as well as under national laws and internal regulations. *See* Regulation (EU) 2016/679 of the European Parliament and of the Council of 27 April 2016 on the Protection of Natural Persons with regard to the Processing of Personal Data and on the Free Movement of Such Data, and repealing Directive 95/46/EC (General Data Protection Regulation), OJ L 119/1 of 4 May 2016.
124. For similar considerations, *see* OECD, *supra* n. 16, at 54.
125. *Id.*, at 52.

stone, or even a transitional measure, toward the introduction of a full liability regime into the EU VAT system.[126]

§8.05 CHAPTER CONCLUSIONS AND RECOMMENDATIONS FOR IMPROVEMENT

[A] Main Findings

Collection and remittance to the competent tax authorities of the amount due is crucial to the functioning of EU VAT. Under EU VAT, liability regimes for collection and remittance of VAT are numerous and, in particular, can be found in Articles 193-205 of the VAT Directive. Notably, pursuant to the main liability regime contained in Article 193 of the VAT Directive, liability for collection and remittance of VAT is attributed to the supplier. The main exception to this general rule concerns the reverse charge mechanism laid down in Articles 194 and 196 of the VAT Directive, pursuant to which the liability for collection and remittance of VAT shifts from the supplier to the customer. Other situations relate to tax representation, under Article 204 of the VAT Directive, and joint and several liability, under Article 205 of the same directive. Among the categories of persons that can be held liable for collecting and remitting VAT, there are also intermediaries and, in particular, digital platforms. Ultimately, nothing seems to prevent the attribution of a liability for collection and remittance of VAT to digital platforms even in the narrower context of the sharing economy and, indeed, in 2019, the OECD has commenced a groundwork examination of the potential role that sharing economy platforms may fulfil in the context of collection and remittance of VAT in lieu of individual suppliers.

A sort of liability regime is also entailed in Article 28 of the VAT Directive, considering the situation of an undisclosed agent, that is a taxable person who, acting in his own name but on behalf of another person, takes part in a supply of services to a customer. A legal fiction of two identical supplies of services provided consecutively is, thus, created. Notably, pursuant to such legal fiction, an intermediary, who acts in his own name, is considered, for EU VAT purposes, to have, first, received the services in question from the supplier on behalf of whom he acts and, then, to supply them onward to the customer. The intermediary is therefore considered, for EU VAT purposes, as the person making the supply to the customer. He is, in fact, a 'deemed supplier'. And indeed, such a 'deemed supplier' approach amounts to imposing, de facto, a liability for collection and remittance of VAT upon intermediaries taking part in the supply to the customer.

For this legal presumption to apply, however, three sets of requirements need to be fulfilled. Notably, the intermediary must: (1) take part in the supply to the customer, (2) act in his own name, but (3) on behalf of another person. In order to assess whether these three sets of requirements are indeed fulfilled in a given situation, it is crucial to accurately check the contractual obligations agreed upon by parties to a supply chain

126. *Id.*, at 57.

and, next to that, to carefully verify whether those obligations are effectively fulfilled by the parties in question. However, in case of a mismatch between the two, economic and commercial reality must take precedence over contractual obligations. More specifically, the first requirement entails that the intermediary effectively 'takes part' in the same supply chain to which both the supplier and the customer belong. As for the second requirement, the definitive criterion is whether the intermediary is simply putting two parties into contact, in which event the intermediary is a disclosed agent, or, instead, if the intermediary takes responsibility for the coordination and the supply to the customer, in which event the intermediary is an undisclosed agent. As for the third requirement, for a taxable person to act 'on behalf of' another person, it seems that the former must have the authority to conclude contracts which are also binding on the latter party.

More detailed rules concerning a digital platform, which acts in its own name but on behalf of another person, that is as an undisclosed agent of its own principal, are laid down in Article 9a of the Implementing Regulation, pursuant to which a digital platform taking part in the supply of electronic services to a customer is deemed to have received and supplied those services itself. Indeed, the legal construction of Article 9a of the Implementing Regulation is broad enough as to make difficult a rebuttal by an intermediary taking part in the supply chain. A rebuttal, in fact, is only possible if the service provider is explicitly indicated as the supplier by the digital platform and, further, this is reflected in the contractual arrangements between the parties. In any event, where a digital platform, with regard to a supply of electronically supplied services, authorizes the charge to the customer or the delivery of the services, or sets the general terms and conditions of the supply, that platform is not permitted to explicitly indicate another person as the supplier of those services. On the contrary, the deemed rules contained in Articles 28 of the VAT Directive and 9a of the Implementing Regulation are not applicable in case of a platform merely processing payments and, possibly, also where a platform only provides telephone services through the Internet.

The specific rules detailed in Article 9a of the Implementing Regulation, however, are not applicable in the context of the sharing economy, since the provision in question concerns only electronically supplied services, whereas underlying services operated by individual suppliers in the sharing economy have a 'tangible' nature, inasmuch as those services entail the exploitation of a tangible property like a residential premise or a vehicle. It follows that a sharing economy platform might be held liable for collecting and remitting the VAT due in lieu of the individual supplier, only based on the general requirements laid down in Article 28 of the VAT Directive, whose assessment must be conducted on a case-by-case basis and, further, by making reference both to contractual documentation and economic reality. Accordingly, the related assessment might well diverge based on the type of the underlying services that a platform facilitates, the business model as resulting from the contractual documentation, as well as the way in which a platform actually carries out its own business. An identification and examination of a series of conditions, as tentatively made in Table 8.1 above, might help conduct such an assessment. And yet, a similar kind of examination, by no means, can be held conclusive. Notably, the business model of a sharing economy platform cannot be considered as 'economically unreal', simply because the 'sale and sub-sale structure' is perceived, economically speaking, as more appropriate than the 'agency structure' used by most sharing economy platforms, given that, under EU VAT, a taxable person is generally free to choose the organizational structures and the form of transactions which he considers as the most appropriate for his own economic activities and for the purposes of limiting his own tax burdens.

And indeed, this latter consideration plainly accords with the five legal principles which compose the evaluation model as conceptualized in the present study. As a first thing, the possibility for a taxable person to choose the organizational structures and the form of transactions which he considers as the most appropriate for his own economic activities and for the purposes of limiting his own tax burdens is consistent with the principle of neutrality, in so far as this principle would be frustrated if a 'sale and sub-sale' structure was, in all events, to be preferred over an 'agency structure'. Compliance with the principle of equality is also ensured, in so far as, according to this principle, only the characterization of a transaction should matter, whereas the way in which a transaction is made, that is through a sale and sub-sale structure rather than by means of an agency structure, is, by itself, immaterial.[127] Indeed, a limitation with regard to the possibility to recharacterize, *ex post*, the organizational structure of a taxable person would also be a measure to achieve simplicity, in so far as it is likely to lower compliance and administrative costs for taxable persons and tax authorities alike. Lastly, from the perspective of the flexibility principle, such an approach would eventually enable to accommodate new ways of conducting business alternative to more conventional business routes, such as those which are constantly being developed in the sharing economy.

In order to attribute a liability for collection and remittance of VAT to a sharing economy platform in a larger number of cases and, arguably, with greater legal certainty, a new liability regime specific to sharing economy platforms could be introduced in the EU VAT system. From a policy design perspective, however, various questions need to be answered before such liability regime might be enacted.

A first question attains to the sharing economy platforms to enlist under that regime. In this connection, it is crucial to ensure that the platform possesses sufficient and accurate information to assess the amount of VAT due as well as effective means to collect and remit the tax by obtaining the amount due from the individual supplier. Both these features, indeed, are necessary for the liability regime to accord with the five legal principles which compose the evaluation model as conceptualized in the present study, especially recalling the need to ensure a proportion between the obligations entailed in the regime and the actual capabilities of a platform. Rather than focusing on the information and means at a disposal of a platform, a better course of action might then consist in assessing the degree of 'facilitation' effectively provided by a platform in matching supply and demand of the underlying services. To give guidance in this regard, a positive list of facilitation services might be compiled, which should be regularly reviewed and constantly updated, so as to comply also with the principle of

127. *See* OECD, *International VAT/GST Guidelines* at 30 (OECD Publishing 2017) and section §3.04.

flexibility. Further, in terms of simplification measures, it might be evaluated the possibility for sharing economy platforms to rely on an advance ruling procedure, such as the CBR procedure operated under the sponsorship of the EU VAT Forum, the enactment of a *de minimis* rule, based on which a platform whose annual turnover remains under a certain threshold is not required to collect and remit to the competent tax authorities the VAT due on the underlying transaction in lieu of individual suppliers, as well as the introduction of certain safe harbours, as a means to reduce compliance risks for a platform, especially in cases where the sums transferred are not in the material availability of that platform.

A second question attains to the transactions to be covered by the envisaged liability regime. In this connection, it is quite evident that reference is to be made to transactions among platform users only, without any further reference to the provision of services by the platform to its users. Hence, it follows that the liability regime should be equally imposed on domestic and foreign platforms, arise irrespective of whether the individual supplier is established or not in the jurisdiction having taxing rights over the underlying transaction, and apply regardless of whether the transaction in question is B2B or B2C and, further, of whether the supplier is required to register for VAT or not. Noteworthy, in the author's opinion, such a generalized application of the regime, besides being consistent with the principles of equality and neutrality, also contributes to simplify the application of the liability regime, in so far as a platform is not required to obtain a series of information concerning the individual supplier from whom it derives a liability for collection and remittance of VAT (e.g., his taxable status, place of establishment or usual residence, and annual turnover).

A third question attains to the characterization, for EU VAT purposes, of the relationship between the individual supplier and the sharing economy platform. Various possibilities can be conceived in this regard. A first possibility is to treat such kind of relationship as an 'ordinary' B2B transaction. The problem with this approach is that it does not contribute anyhow to reduce the overall VAT compliance costs for the individual supplier, thus ultimately failing to comply with the principle of simplicity. A more appealing alternative might then consist in exempting the transaction between these two parties. The introduction of an exemption from VAT, by itself, is however problematic from the perspective of the neutrality principle underpinning EU VAT. Moreover, the impossibility to deduct the VAT which the individual supplier has paid on his inputs leads to VAT cascading. As to remove the amount of non-deductible input VAT and, thus, avoid VAT cascading, a variety of strategies can be developed, that is: (1) the underlying transaction can be zero-rated, i.e., exempt but with the possibility for the individual supplier to deduct his input VAT, (2) a reduced rate can be introduced for output transactions made by platforms, as a means to compensate them for the impossibility to deduct any VAT on the inputs used by the individual suppliers in the provision of accommodation or passenger transport services, or (3) a flat-rate input VAT compensation scheme can be enacted, pursuant to which platform can deduct a predetermined amount of input VAT calculated on the basis of account statistics for the specific sector considered, averaged for a certain number of years. Noteworthy, none of these strategies is deprived of some drawbacks, also from a principle-based perspective.

A regime which entails a complete liability shift from the individual supplier to the sharing economy platform, however, is neither the sole nor necessarily the best solution for ensuring collection and remittance to the competent tax authorities of the VAT due on the underlying transaction. Two alternative liability regimes can, in particular, be envisaged. Under the first alternative liability regime, a platform is held jointly and severally liable with the individual supplier for payment of the VAT due on the transaction made by the latter party. Joint and several liability is a 'secondary' or 'vicarious' type of liability, which may arise either where a platform has 'actual knowledge' of a violation committed by the individual supplier and, yet, it takes no action to secure compliance from him, or where the platform should have reasonably known that the individual supplier was infringing his own VAT obligations. And indeed, in so far as there are uncertainties in relation to these two conditions, concerns might arise from the perspective of the simplicity principle. The second alternative liability regime, fundamentally, consists in putting in place a system of cooperative tax compliance between sharing economy platforms and tax authorities. Under this regime, sharing economy platforms may support compliance by individual suppliers, through the provision to tax authorities of information about users and transactions occurring on their marketplaces and/or by adopting measures to enforce tax obligations upon individual suppliers. From a principle-based perspective, however, it is important to observe a proportionality rule when establishing the types of information and enforcement obligations for sharing economy platforms.

[B] Recommendations

In terms of possible recommendations for improving the current EU VAT system in relation to the issues identified in this chapter, the author submits that, given the pivotal role fulfilled by sharing economy platforms in relation to the supply of services by the individual supplier to the individual customer, the attribution of a liability for collection and remittance of the VAT due on the underlying transactions to these types of intermediaries is, indeed, very much welcome. However, taking into account the multi-jurisdictional level at which most sharing economy platforms operate, it might be convenient to develop some internationally agreed principles and standards for imposing such a liability upon those platforms. This would also ensure a coherent implementation of liability regimes and, thus, contribute to a minimization of inconsistencies in this regard across different VAT/GST systems.[128] Perhaps, such aims could be better fulfilled by a supranational institution like the OECD, first, through the identification of best practices in the field and, then, by issuing specific guidelines, to be implemented on a stand-alone basis or to be added to the text of the current OECD International VAT/GST Guidelines. As a matter of fact, a minimization of inconsistencies in this regard across different VAT/GST systems is crucial to ensure neutrality in

128. For a similar approach, *see* OECD, *supra* n. 16, at 36, considering, in particular, that 'consistency among country approaches is key in achieving high compliance levels, notably by reducing compliance costs and improving the quality and performance of compliance processes'.

a cross-border context, which is precisely the declared intention set forth in the OECD International VAT/GST Guidelines.[129]

As regards more specifically EU VAT, a first recommendation is to leave the current rules unchanged. In such event, the liability of a sharing economy platform for the VAT due by the individual supplier is to be evaluated only based on the three general requirements laid down in Article 28 of the VAT Directive, which, notably, apply where the platform takes part in the supply to the individual customer, acts in its own name, but on behalf of the individual supplier. As seen, such an assessment, which must be conducted on a case-by-case basis and, further, by making reference to both contractual documentation and economic reality, is rather casuistic and, thus, problematic from the perspective of the simplicity principle. Further, although entailing a flexible approach, in so far as such an assessment might well diverge, issues arise also from the perspective of the equality and neutrality principles. Eventually, in order to apply the provision in question 'as widely as possible in the interest of simplicity'[130], the term 'facilitates' might be added to the wording of Article 28 of the VAT Directive. Accordingly, the deemed rule contained therein would be applicable where a taxable person either takes part in or facilitates a supply of services. The amended provision of Article 28 of the VAT Directive might then read as follows (additions in italics):

> Article 28
>
> Where a taxable person acting in his own name but on behalf of another person takes part in *or facilitates* a supply of services, he shall be deemed to have received and supplied those services himself.

Moreover, with a view of simplifying such an assessment, which, as stated, is to be conducted otherwise on a case-by-case basis and, further, by making reference both to contractual documentation and economic reality, a positive list of facilitation services offered by sharing economy platforms to their users might be compiled and inserted in the explanatory notes on this matter issued by the Commission. More to the point, it could be stipulated that the provision by a platform of a certain number of those services indicates that the platform in question actually takes part in or facilitates the provision of the underlying services and, therefore, that the platform in question is to be held liable for collecting and remitting to the competent tax authorities the VAT due on the underlying transaction in lieu of the individual supplier, as provided under Article 28 of the VAT Directive. In order to be sufficiently future oriented and, thus, to ensure compliance with the principle of flexibility, it is important that the explanatory notes and the proposed list would be regularly reviewed and constantly updated, possibly through an involvement of platforms in the process. Also, with an aim of increasing compliance and information accessibility by platforms, the list and the subsequent changes to it could, perhaps, be rendered available online. Operatively, based on the services currently provided by sharing economy platforms and, further,

129. *See* OECD, *supra* n. 127, at 3.

130. *See* European Commission, Value Added Tax Committee, *Working Paper No. 885, VAT 2015: Harmonized Application of the Presumption; Article 9a of the VAT Implementing Regulation*, at 3 (taxud.c.1(2015)4659331), and sections §3.06 and §8.03[D].

drawing inspiration from the services listed in Table 8.1 above, the list to be inserted in the explanatory notes on this matter issued by the Commission might then read as follows:

> *APPLICATION OF ARTICLE 28 OF THE VAT DIRECTIVE TO COLLABORATIVE PLATFORMS – DETAILED INDICATORS*
>
> *The deemed rule contained in Article 28 of the VAT Directive applies when a taxable person takes part in or facilitates the supply to the customer, acts in his own name, but on behalf of another person.*
>
> *In order to assess whether these three sets of requirements are indeed fulfilled in a given situation, it is crucial to accurately check the contractual obligations agreed upon by the various parties to the supply chain and, next to that, to carefully verify whether those obligations are effectively fulfilled by the parties in question. If there is a contradiction between, on the one hand, contractual obligations and, on the other hand, economic and commercial reality, then the latter should prevail.*
>
> *In the context of the collaborative economy, various elements can be indicative of a collaborative platform taking part in or facilitating the underlying transaction, which may then be captured by the deemed rule contained in Article 28 of the VAT Directive.*
>
> *Some indicators suggesting that a collaborative platform takes part in or facilitates the provision of the underlying services are listed below:*
>
> (1) *the platform provides its users with access to its website and/or its app services in its own name;*
> (2) *the platform drafts the relevant contractual documentation and sets standards for user interaction;*
> (3) *the platform marketizes the underlying services under its own brand;*
> (4) *the platform shares – other than in a limited way – contact details of each party to the underlying transaction with the other one;*
> (5) *the platform controls or exerts influence over the pricing of the underlying transaction;*
> (6) *the platform uses its own resources in the provision of the underlying services;*
> (7) *the platform commits to arrange alternative accommodation/passenger transport and/or to operate refunds in case the individual supplier is unable to provide the requested service;*
> (8) *the platform sets cancellation policies and determines the related charges;*
> (9) *the platform deals with VAT invoicing and accounting on behalf of the individual supplier;*
> (10) *the platform acts as a payment collection agent on behalf of its users;*
> (11) *the platform reserves itself the right to remove and/or suspend a user's account in case of poor ratings and reviews and/or multiple cancellations of booking requests;*
> (12) *the platform engages in complaints and compensation handling.*
>
> *Where a collaborative platform performs at least* … [number] *of the aforementioned services, an indication exists that the platform in question takes part in or facilitates the provision of the underlying services.*[131]

131. The author submits that the use of the term 'collaborative platforms', instead of 'sharing economy platforms', is preferable, given that such term is included in the Commission's Communication on *A European Agenda for the Collaborative Economy* and, hence, the use of such an expression is already established under EU law.

A second recommendation consists in introducing a specific liability regime, along the lines of the one discussed in this chapter. Under this regime, by means of a legal fiction, a sharing economy platform is statutorily designated as the supplier, upon whom a liability for collection and remittance to the competent tax authorities of the VAT due on the underlying transactions in which it takes part or which it facilitates is imposed. In so far as the introduction of such a liability regime provides enough clarity on the types of obligations for a sharing economy platform in relation to the VAT due on the underlying supplies, this solution would also achieve simplicity and legal certainty. Whether the principles of equality and neutrality are also respected, instead, is very much open to discussion, inasmuch as the imposition upon sharing economy platforms of a liability for collection and remittance of VAT in lieu of individual suppliers might give leeway to potential distortions in the internal market. Even from the perspective of the flexibility principle, there is indeed the problem to keep such liability regime in line with technological and commercial developments which are likely to affect sharing economy platforms in the forthcoming years. Operatively, this new liability regime could be inserted in the text of the VAT Directive, as a fully stand-alone regime in parallel to the liability regime for undisclosed agents contained in Article 28 of the VAT Directive. This provision - to be inserted in a new Article 28a of the VAT Directive - might then read as follows (additions in italics):

> *Article 28a*
>
> *1. Where a collaborative platform acting in its own name but on behalf of the individual supplier takes part in or facilitates the supply of the underlying service, it shall be deemed to have received and supplied that service itself.*

Eventually, the text of such new provision might continue by detailing the treatment to be accorded to the transaction between the individual supplier and the sharing economy platform. The relevant paragraph might then read as follows (additions in italics):

> *2. For the purposes of paragraph 1, Member States shall exempt the transaction between the individual supplier and the collaborative platform.*

If, instead, it is decided to zero-rate, rather than to exempt, the transaction in question, a provision to that effect could be inserted in the wording of Article 169 of the VAT Directive, notably at point (d) - or (e), should the specific recommendation made at the end of Chapter 5 be pursued. The new point (e) of Article 169 of the VAT Directive might then read as follows (additions in italics):

> Article 169
>
> In addition to the deduction referred to in Article 168, the taxable person shall be entitled to deduct the VAT referred to therein in so far as the goods and services are used for the purposes of the following:
>
> [....]
>
> *d. (or e). transactions which are exempt pursuant to Article 28a(2).*

In the alternative, a reduced rate for output transactions made by sharing economic platforms could be introduced. Operatively, the application of a reduced rate on such transactions can be secured by inserting a new point (22) in Annex III to the VAT Directive ('List of supplies of goods and services to which the reduced rates referred to in Article 98 may be applied'), to which Article 98(2) of the VAT Directive - indeed, concerning reduced rates - makes reference. The new point (22) in Annex III to the VAT Directive might then read as follows (additions in italics):

> Annex III
>
> List of supplies of goods and services to which the reduced rates referred to in Article 98 may be applied
>
> [...]
>
> *(22) Transactions between the individual supplier and the collaborative platform, where Article 28a(1) applies.*

As a last alternative, a flat-rate input VAT compensation scheme might be enacted. Operatively, the enactment of such a scheme, as a means to compensate sharing economy platforms for the impossibility to deduct any VAT on the inputs used by individual suppliers in the provision of the underlying services, can be secured by adding a second paragraph to the text of Article 28a of the VAT Directive. The new paragraph (2) of Article 28a of the VAT Directive might then read as follows (additions in italics):

> *Article 28a*
>
> [...]
>
> *2. For the purposes of paragraph 1, Member States shall allow a collaborative platform to deduct a flat-rate percentage to its turnover as a compensation for the input VAT charged to it by the individual supplier that is not deductible by that collaborative platform. The flat-rate compensation percentages shall be calculated on the basis of macro-economic statistics related to the economic sector in which the collaborative platform operates for the preceding ...* [number] *years.*

If, instead, it is decided not to operate a complete liability shift from the individual supplier to the sharing economy platform, a provision might be inserted in the text of the Implementing Regulation, to build upon the deemed rule contained in Article 28 of the VAT Directive and, further, to be worded along the lines of Article 9a of the Implementing Regulation. This provision, which could, perhaps, be numbered as Article 9b of the Implementing Regulation, might then read as follows (additions in italics):

> *Article 9b*
>
> *1. For the application of Article 28, where a service is supplied through a collaborative platform, the collaborative platform taking part in or facilitating that supply shall be presumed to be acting in its own name but on behalf of the individual provider of that service, unless that provider is explicitly indicated as the supplier by that collaborative platform and that is reflected in the contractual arrangements between the parties.*

In order to regard the supplier of the underlying service as being explicitly indicated as the supplier of that service by the collaborative platform, the following conditions shall be met:

(a) the invoice issued or made available by each taxable person taking part in or facilitating the supply of the service in question must identify such service and the supplier thereof;
(b) the bill or receipt issued or made available to the individual customer must identify the underlying service supplied and the supplier thereof.

For the purposes of this paragraph, a collaborative platform which, with regard to an underlying service, authorises the charge to the individual customer or the delivery of that service, or sets the general terms and conditions of the underlying transaction, shall not be permitted to explicitly indicate another person as the supplier of that service.

2. This Article shall not apply to a collaborative platform which only provides for processing of payments in respect of the underlying service and which does not take part in or facilitates the supply of that service.

As a third recommendation, one might pledge for the introduction of an alternative liability regime specific to sharing economy platforms. The author, however, does not endorse this suggestion. Indeed, with specific regard to a joint and several liability, a provision to that effect is already included in Article 205 of the VAT Directive, which, eventually, could apply also to the situation of a sharing economy platform, so that, arguably, there would be no need to insert another provision to the same effect in the text of either the VAT Directive or the Implementing Regulation. Moreover, the author believes that, indeed, rendering such provision mandatory for Member States would not represent a viable and, also, desirable course of action, given the uncertainties which might arise on whether a platform, effectively, had sufficient knowledge or, at least, it ought to have known the existence of a violation committed by the individual supplier. As stated, legal uncertainties in this regard would be matter of concern from the perspective of the simplicity principle. As regards a system of cooperative tax compliance between sharing economy platforms and tax authorities, those formal agreements, indeed, involve procedural matters and, thus, under EU law, are to be dealt with by national legislations only. Accordingly, no change would be needed at the level of either the VAT Directive or the Implementing Regulation. Certainly, the possibility that the various procedural rules enacted by Member States in this regard might eventually diverge could not be considered as consistent with the five legal principles which compose the evaluation model as conceptualized in the present study.

Part IV Summary and Conclusions

CHAPTER 9

Main Findings, Recommendations and Overall Conclusions

§9.01 INTRODUCTION

The aim of this book was to understand whether the current EU VAT system is sufficiently equipped to deal with the ongoing transformation of the supply chain as well as the increasing digitalization of the economy ushered in by the rise of multisided digital platforms. In particular, the present contribution intended to examine and evaluate some of the main issues that the sharing economy poses to the EU VAT system, as well as to advance solutions wherever and in so far relevant shortcomings in the application of the current EU VAT provisions to the sharing economy were found. The existence of a gap in the literature, besides the keen interest of the author as well as of the general public on this topic, is what motivated the present research.[1]

After providing a definition as well as a general background of the main features of the sharing economy, the research specifically examined the business models of four sharing economy platforms, two operating in the accommodation sector, i.e., Airbnb and HomeExchange, whereas the other two active in the passenger transport industry, i.e., Uber and BlaBlaCar, which, however, differ significantly among each other in terms of business structure and market orientation.[2]

The current treatment under EU VAT of these four sharing economy platforms was presented using the dogmatic method of legal analysis, based on the *travaux preparatoires* publicly available, as well as the interpretation of the relevant EU VAT propositions by the CJEU, the Advocates General to the Court, the VAT Committee, the Commission, and the VAT doctrine. Reflecting an increasing need for a more adaptable legal thinking, the research further sought to test the current treatment under EU VAT of these four sharing economy platforms against a framework of selected legal

1. *See* Chapter 1.
2. *See* Chapter 2.

principles, i.e., the principles of equality, neutrality, simplicity, flexibility, and proportionality.[3]

In particular, following the VAT Determination scheme, whose steps reflect the structure of the VAT Directive, the research focused on five legal propositions underpinning the EU VAT system, i.e., the concepts of 'taxable persons'[4] and 'taxable transactions'[5], the CJEU's doctrine on 'composite supplies' and other alternative approaches to it[6], the interpretation and application of 'place of supply' rules[7], as well as the current and potential role of sharing economy platforms in relation to a 'liability for collection and remittance of VAT' in lieu of individual suppliers[8].

Building upon the legal analysis conducted through such compounded rule-based and principle-based approach, a series of tentative solutions and possible recommendations for improving the current EU VAT system in relation to the main issues identified throughout the study were formulated at the end of each chapter. The exploratory purpose of this study was, however, limited. Tentative solutions and possible recommendations, in fact, were only advanced with an aim of reforming the current EU VAT system, without the (false?) pretence to revolutionize its theoretical design.

A summary of the main findings and recommendations for improving the current EU VAT system is provided in the following sections.

§9.02 MAIN FINDINGS

Overall, the rise of the sharing economy presents two types of challenges to the current EU VAT system.

A first type of challenges relates to the ability of the sharing economy to disrupt, in tax law as well as in different areas of the law, foundational dichotomous categories and, thus, to create new legal 'hybrids'. As seen, foundational dichotomous categories, such as those between suppliers and customers, business and private spheres, employees and self-employed, are largely no longer viable as organizational legal structures in the sharing economy. In a sense, as vividly explained by Judge Chhabria, applying the existing legal categories to the business models featuring the sharing economy is like trying to fit a 'square peg' into 'round holes'.[9]

A second type of challenges relates to the business model according to which sharing economy platforms operate. As seen, rather than along a linear supply chain, where value is created aggregately by several businesses which transform inputs into outputs, sharing economy platforms generate value by building virtual marketplaces and facilitating transactions among two groups of users, i.e., individual suppliers and individual customers, who, otherwise, would fail to interact by their own forces mainly

3. *See* Chapter 3.
4. *See* Chapter 4.
5. *See* Chapter 5.
6. *See* Chapter 6.
7. *See* Chapter 7.
8. *See* Chapter 8.
9. *See* section §1.01.

due to high transaction costs. In a sense, by transforming otherwise economically inconvenient activities into fully feasible and profitable services, sharing economy platforms have pushed the 'digital frontier' farther and farther.[10]

These two types of challenges, indeed, pose a series of hurdles, first, in relation to the application of the current EU VAT categories and, second, in relation to the factual reconstruction, for EU VAT purposes, of the supply chain and of the relationships among the various parties within it.

A summary of the main issues in this regard, as identified in each chapter of the present study, is provided in the following subsections.

[A] Taxable Persons

The concept of 'taxable persons' was discussed in Chapter 4.

The legal analysis has shown that the concept of 'taxable person' has a wide scope and that, indeed, its interpretation receives a broad understanding. As a matter of fact, it does not take that much for a person to qualify as a taxable person under EU VAT. This was confirmed by several findings. First, for being a taxable person, a person neither needs to make a profit from an economic activity, nor it is relevant the subjective intention of the person carrying out such an activity. Second, an economic activity can also entail the mere exploitation of tangible or intangible property and, further, be concluded even in a single day. Third, a person is not required to mobilize so many resources to become a taxable person and, indeed, the application scope of private activities under EU VAT is quite narrow. Fourth, even a person under some disciplinary control, subject to limitations as for his own remuneration and responsibility, or acting under a cooperation agreement with other persons, can still act 'independently' and, thus, qualify as a taxable person under EU VAT.

From the aforementioned considerations, it follows that both sharing economy platforms and individual suppliers generally qualify as taxable person under EU VAT. Essentially, only platforms and individual suppliers who, exclusively, carry out free-of-charge activities or act in a private capacity are excluded from the subjective or personal scope of EU VAT. In this connection, it was found, however, that the provision of services by a platform in return for user personal data is not to be regarded as a free-of-charge activity. As for individual suppliers, instead, it was established that no carveout exists for occasional activities and, further, that the possibility for a person to act in a private capacity is quite narrow. Equally narrow it appeared the possibility to recharacterize for EU VAT purposes, looking at economic reality rather than contractual documentation, individual suppliers as employees of a sharing economy platform. Lastly, from a principle-based perspective, it was submitted that the circumstance that, nearly in all situations, both sharing economy platforms and individual suppliers qualify as taxable persons under EU VAT is consistent with the five legal principles which compose the evaluation model as conceptualized in the present study.

10. *See* section §1.03.

Two main issues were identified from the legal analysis of the concept of 'taxable persons', as conducted in the context of the sharing economy.

The first issue relates to the difficulty to determine the amount of input VAT that an individual supplier shall be effectively entitled to deduct, given that distinguishing between business and private spheres is not always feasible in the sharing economy and, further, than an individual supplier may even decide to use a privately acquired asset in the furtherance of his own economic activities only on a later date. This is also problematic from the perspective of the simplicity and flexibility principles.

The second issue relates to opportunities that platforms and their users have to erode their own VAT liabilities and obligations, as a result of the circumstance that an individual supplier may not charge any VAT on his supplies, due to his annual turnover remaining below the registration threshold for EU VAT purposes, especially where a registration threshold is set particularly high by a Member State. Further, the lack of any harmonization of registration thresholds across different Member States is capable of creating significant distortions in the internal market. This is also problematic from the perspective of the equality and neutrality principles.

The overall conclusion from the legal analysis of the concept of 'taxable persons', as conducted in the context of the sharing economy, is that, although the interpretation and application of such concept is generally sound, solutions need to be found as to determine the amount of input VAT that an individual supplier shall be effectively entitled to deduct and, further, with regard to the operation of registration thresholds, especially across different Member States.[11]

[B] Taxable Transactions

The concept of 'taxable transactions' was discussed in Chapter 5.

The legal analysis – which, in particular, focused on the supply of goods and the supply of services – has shown that a transaction must meet two general conditions to be subject to EU VAT. As a first general condition, a consideration in return for which the supply is made shall exist. Although not defined in the VAT Directive or elsewhere, the expression 'for consideration' was interpreted broadly by the CJEU, as entailing everything received in return for a supply, provided it is capable of being expressed in money. Indeed, a consideration may also be provided for a lower price than the cost price, consist in a mere reimbursement of expenses, or be paid in the form of a subscription fee. As a second general condition, a direct link between the supply and the consideration for it needs to be established. The concept of 'direct link' has a subjective and an objective dimension, in the sense that there must be, first, a legal relationship between the supplier and the customer and, second, a direct reciprocity between the service provided and the consideration received in return. Barter transactions are also subject to EU VAT, although, in a barter transaction, there are two supplies for EU VAT purposes and, further, two different methods exist for attributing a value to the consideration in kind.

11. *See* section §4.06[A].

From the aforementioned considerations, it follows that both transactions made between a sharing economy platform and its users and among users themselves, generally, qualify as taxable transactions under EU VAT. It is, in fact, indisputable that both sharing economy platforms and individual suppliers provide their own services for consideration, in so far as also payments by means of an annual subscription, cancellation fees, personal data, those made in kind, or mere reimbursements of expenses amount to a consideration for EU VAT purposes. Also, it does not appear a difficult exercise to establish a direct link either between the services provided by a platform and the consideration paid in return by its users and, further, between the services provided and the consideration received in case of transactions among users themselves. Only if the benefits provided by users among each other are not evenly balanced or, further, in case of non-reciprocal and deferred exchanges, a direct link might, ultimately, be considered as missing and, therefore, the transactions in question are to be excluded from the objective or substantive scope of EU VAT. As regards barter transactions, both those occurring between a platform and its users in return for user personal data and those taking place among users themselves, it was established the need to split those transactions into separate supplies for EU VAT purposes. Lastly, from a principle-based perspective, it was submitted that the circumstance that both transactions made between a sharing economy platform and its users and among users themselves, generally, qualify as taxable transactions under EU VAT is consistent with the five legal principles which compose the evaluation model as conceptualized in the present study.

Three main issues were identified from the legal analysis of the concept of 'taxable transactions', as conducted in the context of the sharing economy.

The first issue relates to the expression 'for consideration'. Although a broad understanding of this expression is in line with the theoretical design as well as with the principles underpinning EU VAT, the application of EU VAT to certain transactions in the sharing economy, such as those entailing the provision of a service in return for a mere reimbursement of expenses, may ultimately discourage the carrying out of those activities. As a means to simplify the application of EU VAT, it might then be convenient to relieve those transactions entirely from VAT.

The second issue relates to the concept of 'direct link', which might ultimately be broken where the benefits provided by users to each other are clearly unrelated, as it is in the case of a holiday exchange relating to homes for which the market renting fees clearly do not match. Further, a direct link might also be considered as missing, due to the lack of a legal relationship between the individual supplier and the individual customer, in case of non-reciprocal and deferred exchanges. Indeed, excluding the application of EU VAT to those kinds of transactions is also problematic from the perspective of the equality and neutrality principles.

The third issue relates to barter transactions, either between a platform and its users or among users themselves. VAT cascading, in fact, arises where one of the two parties to a barter transaction is a non-taxable person, as a result of the circumstance that the taxable person neither can charge VAT on his outputs nor can deduct VAT on his inputs. Further, the value to be attributed to the consideration paid in kind is not straightforward to determine and, indeed, the two different methods developed by the

CJEU in this regard, relying on a market valuation and a cost price approach, appear fairly inadequate in the context of the sharing economy. In light of the simplicity and flexibility principles, it might then be useful to introduce appropriate derogations and simplification measures for valuation purposes.

The overall conclusion from the legal analysis of the concept of 'taxable transactions', as conducted in the context of the sharing economy, is that, although the interpretation and application of such concept is generally sound, solutions need to be found in certain instances, notably as to exclude from the objective or substantive scope of EU VAT transactions entailing the provision of a service in return for a mere reimbursement of expenses, to establish when a direct link between the supply and the consideration exists, to limit the application of EU VAT in case of barter transaction where one of the two parties is a non-taxable person, as well as to develop a single, more straightforward method to attribute a value to a consideration paid in kind.[12]

[C] Composite Supplies

The CJEU's doctrine on 'composite supplies' and other alternative approaches to it were discussed in Chapter 6.

The legal analysis has shown that various approaches exist in relation to 'composite supplies', that is supplies entailing the joint provision to the same customer of several goods and/or services, possibly by different undertakings. As a main rule, the doctrine on 'composite supplies', developed by the CJEU through the years, as from *Credit Protection Plan* on, mandates that every transaction shall be considered as fully distinct and independent. This main 'splitting' rule, however, has two relevant exceptions. Notably, two or more supplies need to be treated as a single, indivisible supply, (1) if they constitute 'a single supply from an economic point of view', or (2) if one supply is ancillary to the other. As for the first exception to apply, it is relevant to consider the 'objective' economic purpose of a transaction as well as the 'subjective' intention shown by the individual customer. As for the second exception to apply, instead, it is required that one or more elements of a transaction constitute a principal supply, whereas another or more elements constitute an ancillary supply, which, as such, must share the treatment of the principal supply. It was established that, however, other alternative approaches exist in relation to 'composite supplies'. One alternative approach relates to 'two-step' or 'preliminary' transactions, i.e., situations in which two or more related supplies are made by a taxable person to the same customer at different points in time. Another alternative approach relates to the application of the CJEU's doctrine on composite supplies also to the situation in which two distinct undertakings jointly supply a good and/or a service to the same customer. Whichever approach is ultimately followed, it is crucial to proceed to the factual reconstruction of the supply chain, i.e., of the relationships existing among the various parties taking part in the economic operation as a whole.

12. *See* section §5.06[A].

From the aforementioned considerations, it follows that all the three rules constituting the CJEU's doctrine on 'composite supplies' may well find an application in the context of the sharing economy. Notably, other than in cases where the main 'splitting' rule applies, platform services such as payment handling services can be viewed as a single composite supply from an economic point of view or, alternatively, as a single composite supply in which one supply is ancillary to the other. On the contrary, besides the case of 'experiences' on Airbnb, the doctrine on composite supply does not seem to come into prominence with regard to services among platform users, as long as, in most instances, those services entail the provision to the individual customer of a 'unitary service'. As for other alternative approaches to composite supplies, the author indeed is not persuaded by the Commission's opinion which hints at the possibility to apply the doctrine on two-step or preliminary transactions to the provision of 'free' services by a digital company in return for user personal data. The author, instead, submits that the CJEU's doctrine on composite supplies, as extensively interpreted by the CJEU as to cover also the situation in which two distinct undertakings jointly supply a good and/or a service to the same customer, might find an application in the sharing economy, in so far as a sharing economy platform and an individual supplier can well be considered as a single supplying party. A different factual reconstruction of the supply chain, as well as of the actual role played by the various parties within it, are equally possible. A first possible reconstruction is that the platform is actually involved in the underlying supply toward the individual customer. An alternative reconstruction, which, however, is open to a platform only if it provides its own services solely to one of the underlying parties and not, instead, to both parties, is that the platform offers only intermediary services to the individual supplier, who is the sole party making the final supply to the individual customer. Ultimately, the author submits that the reconstruction that, perhaps, best reflects the supply chain, as well as the relationships among the various parties within it, in the context of the sharing economy is the scenario considered and agreed upon by the CJEU in *Lebara*, assuming that the platform – positioned in the middle of a single 'vertical' supply chain – offers the individual customer an intermediation service in its own name and, also, on its own behalf. Lastly, from a principle-based perspective, it was submitted that the bare circumstance that various approaches to composite supplies may well find an application in the context of the sharing economy, as well as the possibility to proceed to different reconstructions of the same supply chain and of the relationships among the various parties within it, is not tenable in light of the five legal principles which compose the evaluation model as conceptualized in the present study.

The main issue identified from the legal analysis of the doctrine on 'composite supplies' and other alternative approaches to it, as conducted in the context of the sharing economy, relates to the definition of what exactly constitutes a transaction, especially where a transaction is constituted by the joint provision to the same customer of several goods and/or services, possibly by different undertakings. Indeed, as long as such determination does not permit any workable definitions, a case-by-case assessment, which entails the need to carefully assess all the facts and circumstances of a sharing economy operation as whole, is unavoidable. In this connection, the bare circumstance that all the various approaches on 'composite supplies' may well find an application in the context of the sharing economy is not tenable, in so far as it can lead to treat similar situations in a different manner, which, clearly, is also problematic from the perspective of the principles underpinning EU VAT and which compose the evaluation model as conceptualized in the present study.

The overall conclusion from the legal analysis of the doctrine on 'composite supplies' and other alternative approaches to it, as conducted in the context of the sharing economy, is that, even if the various approaches for defining what exactly constitutes a transaction, inevitably, imply a case-by-case assessment, there is a need, in relation to 'composite supplies', of some interpretative clarification as well as of appropriate instruments for settling potential disagreements between taxable persons and tax authorities of two or more Member States.[13]

[D] Place of Supply

'Place of supply' rules, along with the territoriality and destination principles, were discussed in Chapter 7.

The legal analysis – besides the two default place of supply rules for B2B and B2C transactions – focused on the special place of supply rules which are of importance in the sharing economy. The first rule considered relates to services connected with immovable property, stipulating that, for both B2B and B2C transactions, the place of supply is where the immovable property concerned is located. In this connection, it was shown that 'the provision of hotel accommodation or accommodation in sectors with a similar function' – expression to which the CJEU has indeed given a broad construction – falls under such rule, whereas intermediation relating to those services does not. The second rule considered relates to passenger transport services, stipulating that, for both B2B and B2C transactions, the place of supply is where the transport takes place, proportionate to the distances covered. In this connection, it was shown that, in case of a cross-border journey, VAT is due in every country where the transport actually takes place, a rule which, however, does not contribute in any meaningful way to a minimization of the administrative burden for a taxable person. The third rule considered relates to electronically supplied services, stipulating that, for both B2B and B2C transactions, although based on different provisions, the place of supply is where the customer is established, has his permanent address, or usually resides. The most critical condition for a service to qualify as an electronically supplied service, undoubtedly, concerns the fact that the service in question must only involve a 'minimal human intervention'. In this connection, it was shown that services provided by intermediaries do not qualify as electronically supplied services if they relate to services having a 'tangible' nature, such as accommodation and passenger transport services, or, further, if they require an active involvement on the side of the intermediary, in the form of non-automated, human, distinct reactions by that intermediary. The fourth rule considered relates to the optional provision which enables a Member State, in case a service qualifies as an electronically supplied service and, further, it is rendered to a

13. *See* section §6.05[A].

non-taxable person, to rectify the place of actual consumption of that service, based on where the service in question is effectively used and enjoyed by the recipient. In this connection, it was shown that the operation of such a rule might lead to situations of double taxation or non-taxation, where the classification of a service under EU VAT does not ultimately reconcile with that made by another VAT/GST system. The fifth rule considered relates to services provided by intermediaries, being either disclosed or undisclosed agents. Notably, disclosed agents are those who act in the name and on behalf of one or both parties to an underlying transaction, whereas undisclosed agents are those who deal with customers in their own name and use the supplies provided to them by other taxable persons to make onward supplies to their customers. In this connection, it was shown that, as regards services provided by disclosed agents, depending on whether the transaction is B2B or B2C, the place of supply is, respectively, where the customer is established or where the underlying transaction is supplied. Instead, as regards services provided by undisclosed agents, based on a legal fiction, an undisclosed agent is deemed to have received from the supplier the same services which he, then, supplies onward to the customer, with the relevant consequence that the two supplies in question receive the same classification under EU VAT.

From the aforementioned considerations, it follows that the place of supply of services provided by users among themselves is where those services are physically carried out. More precisely, accommodation services, such as those provided by hosts to guests on sharing economy platforms like Airbnb and HomeExchange, constitute services connected with immovable property, for which the relevant place of supply is where the immovable property concerned is located. A question might, eventually, arise only with regard to additional services offered together with the provision of bare accommodation, such as in case of 'experiences' offered by hosts to guests on Airbnb. Services provided by drivers to passengers on sharing economy platforms like Uber and BlaBlaCar, instead, constitute passenger transport services, for which the relevant place of supply is where the transport takes place, proportionate to the distances covered. From a principle-based perspective, it was submitted that the application of the aforementioned place of supply rules to services among platform users is, indeed, consistent with the five legal principles which compose the evaluation model as conceptualized in the present study. Undoubtedly, services provided by sharing economy platforms to their users are much more difficult to assess for place of supply purposes. Indeed, various classifications of those services are possible under EU VAT. A first possibility is that platform services are regarded as services made by a disclosed agent, for which, depending on whether the transaction in question is B2B or B2C, the place of supply is, respectively, where the customer is established or where the underlying transaction, consisting in either accommodation or passenger transport services, is supplied. A second possibility is that platform services are characterized as 'ordinary' services, for which, depending on whether the transaction in question is B2B or B2C, the place of supply is, respectively, where the customer or the supplier is established. A third possibility is that platform services constitute services made by an undisclosed agent, with the relevant consequence that the platform is no longer considered as an intermediary, but rather as a full-fledged supplier of the underlying service, concerning the provision of either accommodation or passenger transport. A fourth possibility is that platform services are characterized as electronically supplied services, for which the place of supply is where the customer is established, has his permanent address, or usually resides. The fifth and last possibility is that platform services are characterized as electronically supplied services and the effective use and enjoyment rule applies, based on which the place of supply of those services may shift either inside or outside the EU. From a principle-based perspective, it was submitted that the mere existence of so many different possibilities as regards the classification of platform services under place of supply rules, clearly, does not consent to meet the objectives entailed in the five legal principles which compose the evaluation model as conceptualized in the present study.

The main issue identified from the legal analysis of 'place of supply' rules, as applied to the sharing economy, relates to the classification, for place of supply purposes, of services provided by platforms to their users. As seen, the classification for place of supply purposes of platform services is not crystal clear and, indeed, inconsistencies in the interpretation and application of the same rules by different sharing economy platforms, as well as by various Member States, are very much possible.

The overall conclusion from the legal analysis of 'place of supply' rules, as applied to the sharing economy, is that some measures for clarifying the classification, for place of supply purposes, of platform services are needed and, further, that, in order to avoid potential conflicts of jurisdiction among Member States, as well as purposive misclassification by platforms of their own services, which might lead to situations of double taxation or non-taxation, a single, more straightforward proxy for determining the place of supply of those services ought to be laid down.[14]

[E] Liability for Collection and Remittance of VAT

Regimes entailing a 'liability for collection and remittance of VAT' were discussed in Chapter 8.

The legal analysis – after a concise illustration of the main liability regimes for collection and remittance of VAT contained in the VAT Directive – focused on liability regimes for intermediaries and, in particular, digital platforms. In this connection, it was shown that a liability regime for collection and remittance of VAT applies to an intermediary who, acting in his own name but on behalf of another person, takes part in a supply of services to a customer. For this legal presumption to apply, however, the intermediary must: (1) take part in the supply to the customer, (2) act in his own name, but (3) on behalf of another person. In order to assess whether these three sets of requirements are indeed fulfilled in a given situation, reference is to be made both to contractual obligations and economic and commercial reality, with precedence taken by this latter in case of a mismatch between the two. More detailed rules and, also, a broader legal construction in relation to such liability regime, which makes more difficult a rebuttal, are provided in the Implementing Regulation with regard to a digital

14. *See* section §7.10[A].

platform, which, acting in its own name but on behalf of another person, takes part in the supply of electronically supplied services to a customer.

From the aforementioned considerations, it follows that the liability regime for collection and remittance of VAT contained in the Implementing Regulation, with regard to a digital platform which acts in its own name but on behalf of another person, is not applicable in the context of the sharing economy, since it concerns only electronically supplied services, whereas underlying services operated by individual suppliers in the sharing economy cannot qualify as such. Accordingly, it was shown that a sharing economy platform might be held liable for collecting and remitting the VAT due in lieu of the individual supplier, only based on the general requirements laid down in Article 28 of the VAT Directive, whose assessment must be conducted on a case-by-case basis and, further, by making reference to both contractual documentation and economic reality. In order to attribute a liability for collection and remittance of VAT to a sharing economy platform in a larger number of cases and, arguably, with greater legal certainty, it was submitted that a new liability regime specific to sharing economy platforms could be introduced in the EU VAT system. From a policy design perspective, however, various questions need to be answered before such liability regime might be enacted. A first question attains to the sharing economy platforms to enlist under that regime. A second question attains to the transactions to be covered by the envisaged liability regime. A third question attains to the characterization, for EU VAT purposes, of the relationship between the individual supplier and the sharing economy platform. Two alternative liability regimes, other than the one entailing a complete liability shift from the individual supplier to the sharing economy platform, can also be envisaged. Under the first alternative liability regime, a platform is held jointly and severally liable with the individual supplier for payment of the VAT due on the transaction made by the latter party. The second alternative liability regime, instead, consists in putting in place a system of cooperative tax compliance between sharing economy platforms and tax authorities. From a principle-based perspective, it was submitted that, while there must be a limitation with regard to the possibility to recharacterize, *ex post*, the organizational structure of a taxable person, the introduction and implementation of a new liability regime specific to sharing economy platforms should, instead, be made in light of the five legal principles which compose the evaluation model as conceptualized in the present study.

The main issue identified from the legal analysis of the various regimes entailing a 'liability for collection and remittance of VAT', as conducted in the context of the sharing economy, relates to whether it is preferable to apply to sharing economy platforms the liability regimes currently contained in the VAT Directive, or if, instead, a new liability regime specific to sharing economy platforms is to be introduced in the EU VAT system. Under the first option, the problem relates to assessing whether, in a given situation, a platform indeed fulfils the three general requirements entailed in the liability regime for intermediaries, which, notably, applies only if the platform takes part in the supply to the individual customer, acts in his own name, but on behalf of the individual supplier. Under the second option, instead, the problem relates to which type of liability regime to introduce and, further, its concrete design, in particular with regard to the platforms to enlist, the transactions to be covered, as well as the characterization, for EU VAT purposes, of the relationship between the individual supplier and the platform.

The overall conclusion from the legal analysis of the various regimes entailing a 'liability for collection and remittance of VAT', as conducted in the context of the sharing economy, is that, given the pivotal role fulfilled by sharing economy platforms in relation to the supply of services by the individual supplier to the individual customer, the attribution of a liability for collection and remittance of the VAT due on the underlying transactions to such types of intermediaries is, indeed, very much welcome. There are, however, various strategies in this regard and, further, it is submitted that advantages and drawbacks of each policy option ought to be carefully evaluated in light of the five legal principles which compose the evaluation model as conceptualized in the present study.[15]

§9.03 RECOMMENDATIONS

Overall, there are various, and often competing, ways for improving the current EU VAT system in relation to the main issues as identified, in the context of the sharing economy, throughout the present study.

Indeed, tentative solutions and possible recommendations, advanced in each chapter of the present study, equally relate to a policy, legislative, or interpretative level. In particular, suggested measures consist either in the development of a set of policies by different VAT/GST systems, especially in the form of internationally agreed principles and standards, in the introduction or amendment of certain legislative provisions, such as those contained in the VAT Directive and in the Implementing Regulation, or in the adoption of some interpretative instruments, notably in the form of the guidelines drafted by the VAT Committee or the explanatory notes issued by the Commission. Importantly, whether relating to a policy, legislative, or interpretative level, the tentative solutions and possible recommendations advanced in each chapter of the present study are not conceived in vacuum. Rather, their formulation is directly linked to the main issues identified in the context of interpreting and applying the five EU VAT propositions examined in the present study to the sharing economy, and whose main findings were illustrated in the previous sections.

A summary of all the tentative solutions and possible recommendations for improving the current EU VAT system, as advanced in each chapter of the present study, is provided in the following subsections.

[A] Taxable Persons

In view of the main issues identified in relation to the concept of 'taxable persons', tentative solutions and possible recommendations for improving the current EU VAT system were formulated as follows:

15. *See* section §8.05[A].

(1) The definition of 'taxable person', as laid down in Articles 9-12 of the VAT Directive, should be left unchanged. The application scope of this concept and its understanding are, in fact, broad enough as to include within it both sharing economy platforms and individual suppliers.
(2) The determination of the amount of input VAT that an individual supplier shall be effectively entitled to deduct should be simplified, recalling that, in the sharing economy, assets are frequently and seamlessly used by an individual supplier for both business and private purposes. In this connection, two specific recommendations were advanced:
   (i) A first recommendation is to compile an EU-common list of assets normally utilized in the provision of accommodation and passenger transport services (e.g., a residential property and a car), and, for each of those assets, to establish a fixed percentage of deductible input VAT, eventually variable depending on the effective use of that asset in the furtherance, by a taxable person, of his own economic activity. Importantly, those fixed percentage should be the same for all businesses in the same industry and be calculated on the basis of macro-economic statistics related to the specific economic sector concerned, averaged for a certain number of years. A possibility for an individual supplier to opt-out from such flat-rate compensation scheme, however, ought to be rendered available, in so far as that person may find financially more convenient to account for VAT under normal rules.
   (ii) A second recommendation is to insert a specification in the text of Article 187(2) of the VAT Directive, as to clarify that a person is entitled to an adjustment of his initial deduction of input VAT, even if it relates to an asset that the person in question did not initially intend to expressly use in the furtherance of his own business activities, but it was used for such purpose only at a later date.
(3) In order to establish a sufficiently level playing field in the internal market, the current prohibition for SMEs to benefit from the exemption regime in a Member State other than the country in which the VAT is due should be removed. Further, the Commission's current proposal to introduce an EU-wide maximum registration threshold of EUR 85,000 or the equivalent in national currency should be implemented. In this connection, it is also suggested to make the introduction of a registration threshold mandatory for each Member State and, further, to introduce also a minimum registration threshold, below which no business would be required to account for any VAT. From an administrative standpoint, an online portal through which SMEs can complete VAT registration as well as an OSS mechanism available to SMEs for complying with their cross-border VAT obligations should be set up. The current possibility for an individual supplier to opt out and account

for VAT under normal rules should nevertheless be retained, if this is favourable to that person from a financial point of view.[16]

[B] Taxable Transactions

In view of the main issues identified in relation to the concept of 'taxable transactions', tentative solutions and possible recommendations for improving the current EU VAT system were formulated as follows:

(1) The expression 'for consideration', as laid down in Article 2(1) of the VAT Directive, should neither specified nor clarified. Although not defined in the VAT Directive or elsewhere, the application scope of this expression and its understanding are, in fact, broad enough as to include within it both transactions between a sharing economy platform and its users and those among users themselves.

(2) A provision might eventually be inserted in the wording of the VAT Directive and/or in the Implementing Regulation (perhaps in Article 132(1) of the VAT Directive, notably at point (f-*bis*)), containing a carveout, in the form of an exemption from VAT, for transactions among sharing economy users where a mere reimbursement of expenses is paid by the individual customer to the individual supplier, provided the individual customer is a non-taxable person and, further, that such exemption is not likely to cause distortion of competition. A right of option for taxation in respect of those transactions should however be rendered available, in so far as that person finds financially more convenient to deduct the VAT paid on the inputs used in the furtherance of his own economic activity, even if, conversely, he must charge VAT on output supplies for which he obtains a mere reimbursement of expenses.

(3) Some guidelines should be developed for making the determination of the existence of a direct link between a supply and the consideration for it easier. Notably, specific indications in this regard, as derived from the CJEU's decisions, could be inserted in the guidelines drafted by the VAT Committee or in the explanatory notes issued by the Commission.

(4) As a solution against VAT cascading, a provision might be inserted in the VAT Directive (perhaps in Article 169 of the VAT Directive, notably at point (d)) to exempt (*rectius*: zero-rate) certain barter transactions made by a taxable person to a non-taxable person, provided the application scope of such exemption is maintained sufficiently narrow, so as to have negligible effects.

(5) With an aim of ensuring equal treatment between transactions concluded in money and those made in kind, a provision might be inserted in the VAT Directive (perhaps in Article 77(2) of the VAT Directive), stipulating that, in case of certain barter exchanges, the value of the services supplied shall be set

16. *See* section §4.06[B].

equal to the open market value and be determined according to a series of fixed, predetermined and, possibly, objective criteria and indices to be laid down in the text of the Implementing Regulation.[17]

[C] Composite Supplies

In view of the main issues identified in relation to the CJEU's doctrine on 'composite supplies' and other alternative approaches to it, tentative solutions and possible recommendations for improving the current EU VAT system were formulated as follows:

(1) Even if the various approaches for defining what exactly constitutes a transaction, inevitably, imply a case-by-case assessment, some interpretative clarification in relation to the application of the CJEU's doctrine on 'composite supplies' might be offered. For this purpose, a series of detailed guidelines and a list of indicators, to be used while dealing with composite supplies, might be inserted in a dedicated document drafted by either the VAT Committee or the Commission.

(2) As an additional or alternative measure, the pilot project concerning a VAT CBR procedure should be institutionalized as an instrument upon which taxable persons and tax authorities of two or more Member States may rely to settle potential disagreements in relation to the assessment of a composite supply. In order to render more effective such an instrument and, arguably, avoid future litigations on similar issues, mutual agreements reached under the CBR procedure should be collected and published systematically.

(3) Whether there will be no enough consensus to support the introduction of a permanent dispute resolution mechanism under EU VAT, the double taxation dialogue already in place between the tax authorities of some Member States should be institutionalized as an instrument upon which taxable persons and tax authorities of two or more Member States may rely to reach a common determination on a composite supply. In order to render the procedure more appealing and effective for taxable persons, an obligation to initiate an arbitration procedure, together with a commitment to reach an agreement within a lead time and with no interest and penalties levied on taxable persons for late payment of VAT, might be imposed upon the tax authorities of the Member States concerned. In order to avoid future litigations on similar issues, mutual agreements reached through the double taxation dialogue by the tax authorities of different Member States should be collected and published systematically.

(4) Given the rapid evolution of business models in the context of the sharing economy, for applying the CJEU's doctrine as well as other alternative

17. *See* section §5.06[B].

approaches to composite supplies, continuous reliance should be placed upon the fundamental principles underpinning EU VAT, rather than on the legislative and regulatory provisions which might be issued on this matter.[18]

[D] Place of Supply

In view of the main issues identified in relation to the interpretation and application of 'place of supply' rules, tentative solutions and possible recommendations for improving the current EU VAT system were formulated as follows:

(1) 'Place of supply' rules for underlying services in the sharing economy, concerning the provision of either accommodation or passenger transport, should be left unchanged. The relevant place of supply rules contained, respectively, in Articles 47 and 48 of the VAT Directive, are, in fact, sound and consistent with the ultimate objective of EU VAT to locate the place of supply where consumption of those services actually takes place.

(2) The classification, for place of supply purposes, of services provided by sharing economy platforms to their users should instead be clarified and, further, a single, more straightforward proxy for determining the place of supply of those services ought to be laid down. As a result of a mere policy decision, three alternative solutions might be implemented:

   (i) a first alternative solution is to treat platform services always as intermediary services, that is as services provided to its users by a platform acting as a disclosed agent, so as to apply to them Article 44 or 46 of the VAT Directive, depending on whether the transaction in question is, respectively, B2B or B2C.

   (ii) a second alternative solution is to treat platform services always as electronically supplied services in light of the definition contained in Article 7(1) of the Implementing Regulation, so as to apply to them Article 44 or 58 of the VAT Directive, depending on whether the transaction in question is, respectively, B2B or B2C.

   (iii) a third alternative solution is to treat platform services always the same as the underlying services to which they relate, that is as services connected with immovable property or concerning passenger transport, either by amending the text of Articles 47 and 48 of the VAT Directive or by inserting specific provisions in the Implementing Regulation (perhaps in Articles 31a and 32), so as to include within their scope also services consisting in the facilitation, even by a sharing economy platform, of accommodation and passenger transport activities.[19]

18. *See* section §6.05[B].
19. *See* section §7.10[B].

[E] Liability for Collection and Remittance of VAT

In view of the main issues identified in relation to the current and potential role of sharing economy platforms with regard to a 'liability for collection and remittance of VAT' in lieu of individual suppliers, tentative solutions and possible recommendations for improving the current EU VAT system were formulated as follows:

(1) Taking into account the multi-jurisdictional level at which most sharing economy platforms operate, internationally agreed principles and standards for the attribution of a liability for collection and remittance of the VAT due on the underlying transactions upon those platforms should be developed. With an aim of ensuring a coherent implementation of liability regimes and contributing to a minimization of inconsistencies in this regard across different VAT/GST systems, it is also suggested that a supranational institution like the OECD, first, identifies best practices in the field and, then, issues specific guidelines, to be implemented on a stand-alone basis or to be added to the text of the current OECD International VAT/GST Guidelines;

(2) As regards more specifically EU VAT, a first recommendation is to leave the current rules unchanged, so that the liability of a sharing economy platform for collection and remittance of the VAT due by the individual supplier is to be evaluated only based on the three general requirements laid down in Article 28 of the VAT Directive. In order to apply the provision in question as widely as possible in the interest of simplicity, the term 'facilitates' might eventually be added to the wording of that provision. Moreover, with a view of simplifying the related assessment, a positive list of facilitation services offered by sharing economy platforms to their users might be compiled and inserted in the explanatory notes on this matter issued by the Commission. In this connection, it could be stipulated that the provision by a platform of a certain number of those services indicates that the platform in question actually takes part in or facilitates the provision of the underlying services. In order to be sufficiently future oriented, the explanatory notes and the proposed list should be regularly reviewed and constantly updated, possibly through an involvement of platforms in the process. Also, with an aim of increasing compliance and information accessibility by platforms, the list and the subsequent changes to it ought to be rendered available online.

(3) A second recommendation consists in introducing a new liability regime specific to sharing economy platforms in the text of the VAT Directive (perhaps in Article 28a) or of the Implementing Regulation (perhaps in Article 9b), pursuant to which, by means of a legal fiction, a sharing economy platform is statutorily designated as the supplier, upon whom a liability for collection and remittance to the competent tax authorities of the VAT due on the underlying transactions in which it takes part or facilitates is imposed. As regards treatment of transactions between the individual supplier and the sharing economy platform, four different treatments are possible:
   (i) the transactions in question is to be exempt;
   (ii) the transactions in question is to be zero-rated;
   (iii) the transactions in question is to be exempt, but a reduced rate should apply to output transactions made by sharing economy platforms;
   (iv) the transactions in question is to be exempt, but a flat-rate input VAT compensation scheme should be enacted as a means to compensate sharing economy platforms for the impossibility to deduct any VAT on

the inputs used by individual suppliers in the provision of the underlying services;

(4) A third recommendation is to avoid introducing any alternative liability regime specific to sharing economy platforms, either in the form of a joint and several liability or by putting in place a system of cooperative tax compliance between sharing economy platforms and tax authorities, as long as those solutions are neither viable nor desirable and, further, no change at the level of either the VAT Directive or the Implementing Regulation is needed.[20]

Table 9.1 below provides a schematic summary of the main issues and recommendations, in relation to each of the five EU VAT propositions examined in the present study.

Table 9.1 Schematic Summary of the Main Issues and Recommendations in Relation to Each of the Five EU VAT Propositions Examined in the Present Study

Proposition	*Issue*	*Recommendation*
Taxable Persons	Definition of the concept 'taxable person'	No change
	Deduction of input VAT	Simplification measures: - EU-common list of assets with a fixed percentage of deductible input VAT (with an opt-out possibility) - more leeway for temporal adjustments to input VAT deductions
	Registration thresholds and special scheme for SMEs	Harmonization and simplification measures: - extension of SMEs to cross-border transactions - EU-wide maximum registration threshold of EUR 85,000 or the equivalent in national currency - mandatory minimum registration threshold - online portal for VAT registration and OSS mechanism

20. *See* section §8.05[B].

Proposition	*Issue*	*Recommendation*
Taxable Transactions	Definition of the expression 'for consideration'	No change
	Mere reimbursement of expenses	Exemption from VAT (with limitations, safeguards, and opt-out possibility)
	Existence of a 'direct link' between a supply and the consideration for it	Specific indications through VAT Committee's guidelines or Commission's explanatory notes
	Barter transactions between taxable and non-taxable persons	Zero-rating (with limitations and safeguards)
	Value of the consideration in kind in case of barter transactions	Open market value established through fixed, pre-determined and, possibly, objective criteria and indices
Composite Supplies	Interpretation and application of the CJEU's doctrine and other various approaches to composite supplies	Case-by-case assessment, but also: - detailed guidelines and a list of indicators drafted by the VAT Committee or the Commission - VAT CBR procedure - double taxation dialogue - continuous reliance on EU VAT principles
Place of Supply	Classification of services among platform users for place of supply purposes	No change
	Classification of services provided by sharing economy platforms to their users for place of supply purposes	Three alternative solutions: - classification as always intermediary services - classification as always electronically supplied services - classification always the same as services connected with immovable property or concerning passenger transport

Proposition	*Issue*	*Recommendation*
Liability for Collection and Remittance of VAT	Minimization of inconsistencies in relation to liability regimes across different VAT/GST systems	Internationally agreed principles and standards to be implemented on a stand-alone basis or to be added to the OECD International VAT/GST Guidelines
	Attribution to sharing economy platforms of a liability for collection and remittance of the VAT due on the underlying transactions in lieu of individual suppliers	Three alternative options: - current liability regime, insertion of the word 'facilitates', plus a positive list of facilitation services offered by platforms to be drafted by the Commission - new and specific liability regime for sharing economy platforms - alternative liability regimes (not endorsed)
	Treatment of transactions between individual suppliers and sharing economy platforms in case of a new liability regime	Four alternative approaches: - exemption - zero-rating - exemption, but reduced rate on output transactions made by platforms - exemption, but flat-rate input VAT compensation scheme for platforms

§9.04 OVERALL CONCLUSIONS

The aim of this book was to understand whether the current EU VAT system is sufficiently equipped to deal with the ongoing transformation of the supply chain as well as the increasing digitalization of the economy ushered in by the rise of multisided digital platforms. In particular, the present contribution intended to examine and evaluate some of the main issues that the sharing economy poses to the EU VAT system, as well as to advance solutions wherever and in so far relevant shortcomings in the application of the current EU VAT provisions to the sharing economy were found. Remarkably, the legal analysis, conducted through a compounded rule-based and principle-based approach, has not provided a single, straightforward answer to the research queries, but rather it has yielded patchwork and mixed results.

The research, in fact, has shown that the current EU VAT treatment of the sharing economy is sound only in a limited number of cases, notably with regard to the concept of 'taxable persons' and the expression 'for consideration', as well as in relation to the classification, for place of supply purposes, of accommodation and passenger transport services. On the contrary, the current EU VAT treatment of the sharing economy needs some 'fixes' in a series of other situations, notably in relation to the determination of the amount of input VAT to be deducted, the operation, in a cross-border scenario, of registration thresholds and of the special scheme for SMEs, the provision of a mere reimbursement of expenses in return for a service, the application of VAT to certain barter transactions made by a taxable person to a non-taxable person, as well as the classification, for place of supply purposes, of services provided by sharing economy platforms to their users. Lastly, in other circumstances, notably with regard to the existence of a direct link between a supply and the consideration for it, the determination of the value of the consideration in kind in case of barter transactions, the interpretation and application of the CJEU's doctrine and other alternative approaches to composite supplies, the current EU VAT treatment of the sharing economy, although not altogether faulty, is not consistent either, also from the perspective of the principles underpinning EU VAT and which compose the evaluation model as conceptualized in the present study. Indeed, in the author's view, the same principles should also guide the potential attribution, to a sharing economy platform, of a liability for collection and remittance of the VAT due on the underlying transactions in lieu of individual suppliers.

Despite the absence of a one-fits-all solution against the various issues that the sharing economy poses to the application of the five EU VAT propositions examined in the present study, the author submits that, in light of the ongoing transformation of the supply chain as well as the increasing digitalization of the economy ushered in by the rise of multisided digital platforms, some reform of the current EU VAT system is, ultimately, needed. In this connection, tentative solutions and possible recommendations, advanced in each chapter of the present study, whether relating to a policy, legislative, or interpretative level, might indeed provide options for incremental and targeted amendments to the current EU VAT provisions.

Overall, this book has revealed that the seeds of change have already been sown. Indeed, the twenty-first century economic and social landscapes are evolving at a fast pace, whereas the sharing economy – which is part of such ongoing shift – is set to stay. Even VAT pundits, then, had better prepare themselves and watch closely this – growing – space.

Bibliography

Articles, Books and Book Chapters

Alexy R., *On the Structure of Legal Principles*, 13 Ratio Juris 3 (2000), 294-304.

Alley C. & D. Bentley, *A Remodelling of Adam Smith's Tax Design Principles*, 20 Australian Tax Forum 4 (2005), 579-624.

Álvarez Suso M., *Comments on CJEU Case-Law on Taxable Transaction 2017: The Anti-abuse Doctrine (Cussens) and the Sharing Economy (UBER)*, in *CJEU – Recent Developments in Value Added Tax* (M. Lang et al. eds, Linde 2018), 233-249.

Amand C., *VAT Neutrality: A Principle of EU Law or a Principle of the VAT System?*, 2 World Journal of VAT/GST Law 3 (2013), 163-181.

Amand C., *When Is a Link Direct?*, 7 International VAT Monitor 1 (1996), Journals IBFD.

Annacondia F., *VAT Registration Thresholds in Europe*, 29 International VAT Monitor 6 (2018), Journals IBFD.

Avery Jones J.F., *Tax Law: Rules or Principles?*, 17 Institute for Fiscal Studies 3 (1996), 63-89.

Avery Jones J.F., *What Is a 'Contract under Which Commission Is Payable'?*, in *VAT in an EU and International Perspective: Essays in Honour of Han Kogels – Part I* (H. Van Arendonk, S. Jansen & R. Van der Paardt eds, IBFD 2011).

Azam R. & O. Mazur, *Cloudy with a Chance of Taxation*, 22 Florida Tax Review 2 (2019), 500-570.

Báez A. & Y. Brauner, *Taxing the Digital Economy Post BEPS ... Seriously* (2019), https://papers.ssrn.com (accessed 31 March 2019).

Bal A.M., *The Vague Concept of 'Taxable Person' in EU VAT Law*, 24 International VAT Monitor 5 (2013), Journals IBFD.

Bauwens M., *Peer to Peer and Human Evolution. On 'the P2P Relational Dynamic' as the Premise of the Next Civilizational Stage* (2005), http://z.agoravox.fr/IMG/P2PandHumanEvolV2.pdf (accessed 31 March 2019).

Belk R., *Sharing*, 36 Journal of Consumer Research 5 (2010), 715-734.

Benkler Y., *'Sharing Nicely': On Sharable Goods and the Emergence of Sharing as a Modality of Economic Production*, 114 Yale Law Journal 2 (2004), 273-358.

Beretta G., *Il Regime Fiscale delle Locazioni Brevi*, Diritto e Pratica Tributaria 3 (2018), 1011-1056.

Beretta G., *The Taxation of the 'Sharing Economy'*, 70 Bulletin of International Taxation 11 (2016), Journals IBFD.

Blank J.D. & L. Osofsky, *Simplexity: Plain Language and the Tax Law*, 66 Emory Law Journal 2 (2016), 189-264.

Botsman R. & R. Rogers, *What's Mine Is Yours. How Collaborative Consumption Is Changing the Way We Live* (HarperCollinsPublishers 2010).

Botsman R., *The Sharing Economy: Dictionary of Commonly Used Terms*, https://rachelbotsman.com/blog/the-sharing-economy-dictionary-of-commonly-used-terms/ (accessed 31 March 2019).

Botsman R., *The Sharing Economy Lacks a Shared Definition* (21 November 2013), http://www.fastcoexist.com/3022028/the-sharing-economy-lacks-a-shared-definition#8 (accessed 31 March 2019).

Bourgeois M. & A. Römer, *Effects of Existing Tax Treaties on VAT (Relevance of Arts. 24-27 OECD Model for VAT/GST)*, in *Value Added Tax and Direct Taxation: Similarities and Differences* (M. Lang, P. Melz & E. Kristoffersson eds, IBFD 2009).

Braithwaite J., *Rules and Principles: A Theory of Legal Certainty*, 27 Australian Journal of Legal Philosophy (2002), 47-82.

Brauner Y. & A. Báez, *Withholding Taxes in the Service of BEPS Action 1: Address the Tax Challenges of the Digital Economy* (IBFD White Paper 2015).

Brokelind C., *Chapter 1: Introduction*, in *Principles of Law: Function, Status and Impact in EU Tax Law* (C. Brokelind ed., IBFD 2014).

Bronżewska K., *Acknowledgements in Cooperative Compliance: A New Approach to Managing Taxpayer Relations* (IBFD 2016).

Busch C. et al., *The Rise of the Platform Economy: A New Challenge for EU Consumer Law?*, 5 Journal of European Consumer and Market Law 1 (2016), 3-10.

Busch C., *The Sharing Economy at the CJEU: Does Airbnb Pass the 'Uber Test'?*, 7 Journal of European Consumer and Market Law 4 (2018), 172-174.

Butler D., *The Usefulness of the 'Direct Link' Test in Determining Consideration for VAT Purposes*, 13 EC Tax Review 3 (2004), 92-102.

Cairncross F., *The Death of Distance: How the Communications Revolution Is Changing Our Lives* (Harvard Business Press 1997).

Calo R. & A. Rosenblat, *The Taking Economy: Uber, Information, and Power*, 117 Columbia Law Review 6 (2017), 1623-1690.

Campanella T., *Aforismi Politici* (1601).

Cannas F., *Sharing Economy: Everyone Can Be an Entrepreneur for Two Days ... but What about a VAT Taxable Person?*, 6 World Journal of VAT/GST Law 2 (2018), 82-99.

Carlson G.N. & M.K. Patrick, *Addressing the Regressivity of a Value-Added Tax*, 42 National Tax Journal 3 (1989), 339-351.

Cheal D., *The Gift Economy* (Routledge 2015).

Cherry M.A., *The Gamification of Work*, 40 Hofstra Law Review 4 (2012), 851-858.
Chynoweth P., *Legal Research*, in *Methodologies of Legal Research: Which Kind of Method for What Kind of Discipline?* (M. van Hoecke ed., Hart Publishing 2011), 28-37.
Cnossen S., *Global Trends and Issues in Value Added Taxation*, 5 International Tax & Public Finance 3 (1998), 399-428.
Cnossen S., *The Value-Added Tax: Key to a Better Tax Mix*, 6 Australian Tax Forum 3 (1989), 265-282.
Coase, R.H. *The Nature of the Firm*, 16 Economica New Series 4 (1937), 386-405.
Creedy J., *Indirect Tax Reform and the Role of Exemptions*, 22 Fiscal Studies 4 (2001), 457-486.
Dagan T., *Itemizing Personhood*, 29 Virginia Tax Review 1 (2009), 93-136.
Das A., *An Introduction to Operations Management: The Joy of Operations* (Routledge 2015).
De la Feria R. & R. Foy, *Italmoda: The Birth of the Principle of Third-Party Liability for VAT Fraud*, British Tax Review 3 (2016), 270-281.
De la Feria R. & R. Krever, *Ending VAT Exemptions: Toward a Post-Modern VAT*, in *VAT Exemptions: Consequences and Design Alternatives* (R. de la Feria ed., Kluwer Law International 2013), 3-36.
De la Feria R., *EU VAT System as Interpretative Aids to EU VAT Rules*, in *CJEU – Recent Developments in Value Added Tax 2015* (M. Lang, et al. eds, Linde 2016), 1-17.
De la Feria R., *Place Where the Supply/Activity Is Effectively Carried Out as an Allocation Rule: VAT v. Direct Taxation*, in *Value Added Tax and Direct Taxation: Similarities and Differences* (M. Lang, P. Melz & E. Kristoffersson eds, IBFD 2009).
De la Feria R., *Tax Fraud and the Rule of Law* (Working Paper Series, University of Oxford 2018), 1-32.
De la Feria R., *The EU VAT System and the Internal Market* (IBFD 2009).
De la Feria R., *The EU VAT Treatment of Public Sector Bodies: Slowly Moving in the Wrong Direction*, 37 Intertax 3 (2009), 148-165.
De la Feria R., *VAT and the EC Internal Market: The Shortcomings of Harmonization* (Working Paper Series, University of Oxford 2009), 1-36.
De la Feria R., *Chapter 12 – VAT and the EU Internal Market: The Paradoxes of Harmonization*, in *Traditional and Alternative Routes to European Tax Integration: Primary Law, Secondary Law, Soft Law, Coordination, Comitology and Their Relationship* (D. (Dennis) Weber ed., IBFD 2010).
De Stefano V., *The Rise of the 'Just-in-Time Workforce': On-Demand Work, Crowdwork and Labour Protection in the 'Gig Economy'*, International Labour Office, Condition of Work and Employment Series, No. 71 (2016), 1-35.
Due J.F., *Government Finance: An Economic Analysis* (RD Irwin 1963).
Dworkin R., *Taking Rights Seriously* (Harvard University Press 1977).
Dyal-Chand R., *Regulating Sharing: The Sharing Economy as an Alternative Capitalist System*, 90 Tulane Law Review 2 (2015), 241-309.
Ebrill L. et al. (eds), *The Modern VAT* (International Monetary Fund 2001).

Ecker T., *A VAT/GST Model Convention: Tax Treaties as Solution for Value Added Tax and Goods and Services Tax Double Taxation* (IBFD 2013).

Egholm Elgaard K.K., *The Impact of the Charter of Fundamental Rights of the European Union on VAT Law*, 2 World Journal of VAT/GST Law 2 (2016), 63-91.

Eisenmann T., G. Parker & M.W. van Alstyne, *Strategies for Two-Sided Markets*, 84 Harvard Business Review 10 (2006), 92-101.

Englisch J., *Chapter 11 – VAT and General Principles of EU Law*, in *Traditional and Alternative Routes to European Tax Integration: Primary Law, Secondary Law, Soft Law, Coordination, Comitology and Their Relationship* (D. (Dennis) Weber ed., IBFD 2010).

Englisch J., *EU Perspectives on VAT Exemptions* (Working Paper Series, University of Oxford 2011).

Englisch J., *VAT/GST and Direct Taxes: Different Purposes*, in *Value Added Tax and Direct Taxation – Similarities and Differences* (M. Lang, P. Melz & E. Kristoffersson eds, IBFD 2009).

Eriksen N.P. & K. Haydl, *Avoidance of VAT/GST Double (Non-)Taxation: Recommendations and Other Types of Soft Law v. Legally Binding Instruments to Allocate Taxing Rights Between States (e.g. Bilateral Tax Treaties)*, in *Value Added Tax and Direct Taxation: Similarities and Differences* (M. Lang, P. Melz & E. Kristoffersson eds, IBFD 2009).

Evans C., *Taxation Compliance and Administrative Costs: An Overview*, in *Tax Compliance Costs for Companies in an Enlarged European Community* (M. Lang et al. eds, Kluwer Law International 2008), 447-470.

Evans D.S. (ed.), *Platform Economics: Essays on Multi-Sided Businesses* (Competition Policy International 2011).

Evans D.S. & M. Noel, *Defining Antitrust Markets When Firms Operate Two-Sided Platforms*, Columbia Business Law Review 3 (2005), 667-702.

Evans D.S. & R. Schmalensee, *Failure to Launch: Critical Mass in Platform Businesses*, 9 Review of Network Economics 4 (2010), 1-26.

Evans D.S. & R. Schmalensee, *Matchmakers: The New Economics of Multisided Platforms* (Harvard Business School 2016).

Farmer P. & R. Lyal, *EC Tax Law* (Clarendon Press 1994).

Freyer D., *The Proportionality Principle under EU Tax Law: General and Practical Problems Caused by Its Extensive Application – Part 1*, 57 European Taxation 9 (2017), Journals IBFD.

Freyer D., *The Proportionality Principle under EU Tax Law: General and Practical Problems Caused by Its Extensive Application – Part 2*, 57 European Taxation 10 (2017), Journals IBFD.

Friedman G., *Workers Without Employers: Shadow Corporations and the Rise of the Gig Economy*, 2 Review of Keynesian Economics 2 (2014), 171-188.

Gallagher L., *The Airbnb Story: How Three Ordinary Guys Disrupted an Industry, Made Billions, and Created Plenty of Controversy* (Houghton Mifflin Harcourt 2017).

Gansky L., *The Mesh: Why the Future of Business Is Sharing* (Penguin 2010).

Grinberg I., *User Participation in Value Creation*, British Tax Review 4 (2018), 407-421.

Grlica I., *How the Sharing Economy Is Challenging the EU VAT System*, 28 International VAT Monitor 2 (2017), Journals IBFD.

Gupta S. & C.F. Mela, *What Is a Free Customer Worth? Armchair Calculations of Non-paying Customers' Value Can Lead to Flawed Strategies*, 86 Harvard Business Review 11 (2008), 102-109.

Hacker P. & B. Petkova, *Reining in the Big Promise of Big Data: Transparency, Inequality, and New Regulatory Frontiers*, 15 North-Western Journal of Technology and Intellectual Property 1 (2017), 1-42.

Hamari J., M. Sjöklint & A. Ukkonen. *The Sharing Economy: Why People Participate in Collaborative Consumption*, 67 Journal of the Association for Information Science and Technology 9 (2015), 2047-2059.

Hart H.L.A, *The Concept of Law. 3rd Ed.* (Clarendon Law Series 2012).

Hatzopoulos V., *The Collaborative Economy and EU Law* (Hart Publishing 2018).

Heber C., *Recent CJEU Case-Law on Public Bodies – A Comment*, in *ECJ – Recent Developments in Value Added Tax 2016* (M. Lang. et al. eds, Linde 2017), 187-216.

Hellerstein W. & M. Keen, *Interjurisdictional Issues in the Design of a VAT*, 63 Tax Law Review 2 (2010), 359-408.

Hellerstein W., *A Hitchhiker's Guide to the OECD's International VAT/GST Guidelines*, 18 Florida Tax Review 10 (2016), 589-637.

Hellerstein W., *Jurisdiction to Tax Income and Consumption in the New Economy: A Theoretical and Comparative Perspective*, 38 Georgia Law Review 1 (2003), 1-70.

Hellerstein W., S. Buydens & D. Koulouri, *Simplified Registration and Collection Mechanisms for Taxpayers That Are Not Located in the Jurisdiction of Taxation: A Review and Assessment* (OECD Publishing 2018).

Henkow O., *Chapter 15: Accessorium Sequitur Principale – The Issue of Defining the Tax Object for VAT Purposes*, in *Principles of Law: Function, Status and Impact in EU Tax Law* (C. Brokelind ed., IBFD 2014).

Henkow O., *Financial Activities in European VAT: A Theoretical and Legal Research of the European VAT System* (Kluwer Law International 2008).

Herbain C., *VAT Neutrality* (Larcier Promoculture 2015).

Huang W., Y. Liao & S. Li, *C2C Electronic Commerce Tax Management Based on Big Data*, in *Proceedings of the Third International Conference on Economic and Business Management (FEBM 2018)* (Atlantis Press 2018).

Ismer R. & K. Artinger, *International Double Taxation under VAT: Causes and Possible Solutions*, 45 Intertax 10 (2017), 593-605.

Ivanov D., A. Tsipoulanidis & J. Schönberger, *Global Supply Chain and Operations Management in Business and Economics: A Decision-Oriented Introduction to the Creation of Value* (Springer 2017).

James S., *The Complexity of Tax Simplification: The UK Experience*, in *The Complexity of Tax Simplification* (S. James, A. Sawyer, T. Budak eds, Palgrave Macmillan 2016), 229-246.

Kaldor N., *An Expenditure Tax* (Allen & Unwin 1955).

Kant I., *Critique of Practical Reason* (Hackett Publishing 2002).

Keen M. & J. Mintz, *The Optimal Tax Threshold for Value-Added Tax*, 88 Journal of Public Economics 3 (2004), 559-576.

Keller R.I., *The Taxation of Barter Transactions*, 67 Minnesota Law Review 2 (1983), 441-512.

Kingston C.I., *Taxing the Future*, 51 Tax Law Review 4 (1996), 641-653.

Kleven H.J., C.T. Kreiner & E. Saez, *Why Can Modern Governments Tax So Much? An Agency Model of Firms as Fiscal Intermediaries*, 83 Economica 330 (2016), 219-246.

Kocourek A. & J.H. Wigmore, *Primitive and Ancient Legal Institutions* (Little, Brown & C. 1915).

Kogels H.A. & M.E. van Hilten, *Never a Dull Moment*, 28 International VAT Monitor 2 (2017), Journals IBFD.

Kollmann J., *Taxable Supplies and Their Consideration in European VAT - With Selected Examples of the Digital Economy* (IBFD 2018).

Koopman T., *Judicial Activism and Procedural Law*, 1 European Review of Private Law 1/2 (1993), 67-82.

Kreiczer-Levy S., *Consumption Property in the Sharing Economy*, 43 Pepperdine Law Review 1 (2015), 61-124.

Kumar V., *Making 'Freemium' Work*, 92 Harvard Business Review 5 (2014), 27-29.

Kuneva M. (European Consumer Commissioner), *Keynote Speech. Roundtable on Online Data Collection, Targeting and Profiling* (31 March 2009), http://europa.eu/rapid/press-release_SPEECH-09-156_en.htm (accessed 31 March 2019).

Lamensch M., *European Value Added Tax in the Digital Era* (IBFD 2015).

Lamensch M., *Rendering Platforms Liable to Collect and Pay VAT on B2C Imports: A Silver Bullet?*, 29 International VAT Monitor 2 (2018), Journals IBFD.

Lamensch M., *The Scope of the EU VAT System: Traditional & Digital Economy Related Questions*, in *CJEU – Recent Developments in Value Added Tax* (M. Lang et al. eds, Linde 2018), 105-131.

Lamensch M., *The Use of Soft Law by the European VAT Legislator, and What the CJEU Makes of It*, in *CJEU – Recent Developments in Value Added Tax 2015* (M. Lang et al. eds, Linde 2016), 21-50.

Lashinsky A., *Wild Ride: Inside Uber's Quest for World Domination* (Portfolio 2017).

Lauré M., *Au Secours de la TVA* (Presses Universitaires de France 1957).

Lederman L., *Statutory Speed Bumps: The Roles Third Parties Play in Tax Compliance*, 60 Stanford Law Review 3 (2007), 695-743.

Lejeune I. & E. Peters, *Trends in the VAT Case-Law of the CJEU (2017)*, in *CJEU – Recent Developments in Value Added Tax 2017* (M. Lang et al. eds, Linde 2018), 363-381.

Lejeune I., E. Cortvriend & D. Accorsi, *Implementing Measures Relating to EU Place-of-Supply Rules: Are Business Issues Solved and Is Certainty Provided?*, 22 International VAT Monitor 3 (2011), Journals IBFD.

Lejeune I., S. Kotanidis & S. Van Doninck, *The New EU Place-of-Supply Rules from a Business Perspective*, 20 International VAT Monitor 2 (2009), Journals IBFD.

Lejeune I., S. Vandenberghe & T. Racquet, *Limited Third-Party Liability in EU VAT Matters*, 23 International VAT Monitor 6 (2012), Journals IBFD.

Lenaerts K. & J.A. Gutiérrez-Fons, *The Constitutional Allocation of Powers and General Principles of EU Law*, 47 Common Market Law Review 6 (2010), 1629-1670.
Lessig L., *Remix: Making Art and Commerce Thrive in the Hybrid Economy* (Penguin 2008).
Lobel O., *The Law of the Platform*, 101 Minnesota Law Review 1 (2016), 87-166.
Lodin S-O., *Progressive Expenditure Tax – An Alternative? A Report of the 1972 Government Commission on Taxation* (LiberFörlag 1978).
MacCormick N., *Reconstruction after Deconstruction: A Response to CLS*, 10 Oxford Journal of Legal Studies 4 (1990), 539-558.
Malgieri G. & B. Custers, *Pricing Privacy – The Right to Know the Value of Your Personal Data*, 34 Computer Law and Security Review 2 (2018), 289-303.
Martin C.J., *The Sharing Economy: A Pathway to Sustainability or a Nightmarish Form of Neoliberal Capitalism?*, Ecological Economics 121 (2016), at 149-159.
Meade J., *The Structure and Reform of Direct Taxation* (Institute for Fiscal Studies 1978).
Melz P., *Who Is a Taxable Person to VAT?*, in *International Studies in Taxation, Liber Amicorum Sven-Olof Lodin* (K. Andersson, P. Melz & C. Silfverberg eds, Kluwer London 1991), 158-172.
Merkx M.M.W.D., *The VAT Consequences of Crowdfunding*, 27 International VAT Monitor 1 (2016), Journals IBFD.
Merkx M.M.W.D., *VAT and E-Services: When Human Intervention Is Minimal*, 29 International VAT Monitor 1 (2018), Journals IBFD.
Messere K.C., *Tax Policy in OECD Countries: Choices and Conflicts* (IBFD 1993).
Millar R., *Illusory Supplies and Unacknowledged Discounts: VAT and Valuation in Consumer Transaction*, British Tax Review 2 (2003), 153-184.
Millar R., *Intentional and Unintentional Double Non-taxation*, in *Value Added Tax and Direct Taxation: Similarities and Differences* (M. Lang, P. Melz & E. Kristoffersson eds, IBFD 2009).
Millar R., *Jurisdictional Reach of VAT*, in *VAT in Africa* (R. Krever ed., Pretoria University Press Law), 175-214.
Millar R., *The Destination Principle: Past Developments and Future Challenges*, in *GST in Australia: Looking Forward from the First Decade* (C. Peacock ed., Thomson Reuters 2011), 313-341.
Millar R., *UberX Drivers Supply Taxi Travel and So Must Be Registered for GST*, 6 World Journal of VAT/GST Law 1 (2017), 47-54.
Mirlees J. et al., *Tax by Design* (Oxford University Press 2011).
Morse G., *Identifying the Taxable Amount for Value Added Tax of a Supply of Goods at a Reduced Cash Price: A Question of Analysis or Principle*, British Tax Review 3 (2002), 179-211.
Muñiz J.R., *Legal Principles and Legal Theory*, 10 Ratio Juris 3 (2010), 267-287.
Naritomi J., *Consumers as Tax Auditors* (2018), papers.ssrn.com (accessed 31 March 2019).
Nellen F.J.G., *Information Asymmetries in EU VAT* (Kluwer Law International 2017).
Owyang J. & A. Samuel, *The New Rules of the Collaborative Economy: 2015 Data on the Growth of Sharing* (2015), http://www.web-strategist.com/blog/2015/10/05/

report-the-new-rules-of-the-collaborative-economy-2015-data-on-the-rise-of-sharing/ (accessed 31 March 2019).

Owyang J., *Honeycomb 3.0: The Collaborative Economy Market Expansion* (2016), http://www.web-strategist.com/blog/2016/03/10/honeycomb-3-0-the-collaborative-economy-market-expansion-sxsw/ (accessed 31 March 2019).

Papis-Almansa M., *Insurance in European VAT: Current and Preferred Treatment in the Light of the New Zealand and Australian GST Systems* (Kluwer Law International 2017).

Parker G.G., M.W. Van Alstyne & S.P. Choudary, *Platform Revolution: How Networked Markets Are Transforming the Economy and How to Make Them Work for You* (W.W. Norton & Company 2016).

Pfeiffer S., *Comment on 'Free' Internet Services*, in *CJEU – Recent Developments in Value Added Tax* (M. Lang et al. eds, Linde 2018), 133-139.

Pfeiffer S., *VAT on 'Free' Electronic Services?*, 27 International VAT Monitor 3 (2016), Journals IBFD.

Pincher R., *Is There a Link?*, British Tax Review 3 (1995), 306-316.

Pistone P., *Soft Tax Coordination: A Suitable Path for the OECD and the European Union to Address the Challenges of International Double (Non-)Taxation in VAT/GST Systems*, in *Value Added Tax and Direct Taxation: Similarities and Differences* (M. Lang, P. Melz & E. Kristoffersson eds, IBFD 2009).

Pomeranz D., *No Taxation Without Information: Deterrence and Self-Enforcement in the Value Added Tax*, 105 American Economic Review 8 (2015), 2539-2569.

Prassl J. & M. Risak, *Uber TaskRabbit, & Co: Platforms as Employers? Rethinking the Legal Analysis of Crowdwork*, 37 Comparative Labour Law and Policy Journal 3 (2016), 604-619.

Raponi D. & F. Vitale, *Dispute Prevention: Advance (Cross-Border) Rulings: Experience of the Pilot Project and the Way Forward*, in *CJEU – Recent Developments in Value Added Tax 2016* (M. Lang et al. eds, Linde 2017), 129-137.

Raz J., *Legal Principles and the Limits of Law*, 81 Yale Law Journal 5 (1972), 823-854.

Rendahl P., *Cross-Border Consumption Taxation of Digital Supplies* (IBFD 2009).

Reugebrink J. & M.E. van Hilten, *Omzetbelasting* (Deventer 1997).

Reugebrink J., *The Sixth Directive for Harmonization of Value Added Tax*, 15 Common Market Law Review 3 (1978), 309-319.

Rifkin J., *The Age of Access: The New Culture of Hypercapitalism* (Penguin 2001).

Rochet J.C. & J. Tirole, *Platform Competition in Two-Sided Markets*, 1 Journal of the European Economic Association 4 (2003), 990-1029.

Rolim J.D., *Proportionality and Fair Taxation*, 43 Intertax 5 (2015), 405-409.

Ruppe H.G., *General Report*, in *International Problems in the Field of General Taxes on Sales of Goods and Services* (IFA Cahiers 1983 – 68B), 109-148.

Safron J., *The Application of EU Competition Law to the Sharing Economy* (EU Law Working Papers No. 27, Stanford-Vienna Transatlantic Technology Law Forum 2018), 1-42.

Sandel M.J., *What Money Can't Buy: The Moral Limits of Markets* (Macmillan 2012).

Schenk A., V. Thuronyi & W. Cui, *Value Added Tax: A Comparative Approach* (Cambridge University Press 2015).

Schneider H., *Creative Destruction and the Sharing Economy* (Edward Elgar Publishing 2017).

Schor J., *Debating the Sharing Economy*, 4 Journal of Self-Governance and Management Economics 3 (2016), 7-22.

Schumpeter J.A., *Capitalism, Socialism, and Democracy* (Routledge 2010).

Schwarze J., *European Administrative Law* (Sweet & Maxwell 1992).

Senyk M., *Territorial Allocation of VAT in the European Union* (Lund University 2018).

Shelton J.R., *Emerging Issues in Taxing Business in a Global Economy*, in *Taxing International Business. Emerging Trends in APEC and OECD Economies* (R. Venn ed., OECD Publishing 1997).

Simon P., *The Age of the Platform: How Amazon, Apple, Facebook, and Google Have Redefined Business* (BookBaby 2011).

Simons A.L.C., *Neutrality in VAT and the Organ-Grinder*, 3 EC Tax Review 2 (1994), 44-45.

Slemrod J. & J. Bakija. *Taxing Ourselves: A Citizen's Guide to the Debate over Taxes* (MIT Press 2008).

Smith A., *An Inquiry into the Nature and Causes of the Wealth of Nations* (R.H. Campbell, A.S. Skinner & W.B. Todd eds, Oxford University Press 1976).

Soler Roch M.T., *The Principle of Proportionality and the Prevention of Fraud in VAT*, in *VAT in an EU and International Perspective: Essays in Honor of Han Kogels* (H. van Arendonk, S. Jansen, R. van der Paardt eds, IBFD 2011), 81-90.

Spies K., *Dispute Resolution in VAT: Status Quo under the EU VAT Directive and Room for Improvement*, in *CJEU – Recent Developments in Value Added Tax* (M. Lang, et al. eds, Linde 2016), 91-127.

Stewart W.J., *Collins Dictionary of Law. 'Vicarious Liability' 3rd Ed.* (Collins 2006).

Stiglitz J.E., *Economics of the Public Sector. 3rd Ed.* (W.W. Norton & Company Inc. 2000).

Stone B., *The Upstarts. How Uber, Airbnb and the Killer Companies of the New Silicon Valley Are Changing the World* (Little, Brown & Co. 2017).

Sundararajan A., *The End of Employment and the Rise of Crowd-Based Capitalism* (MIT Press 2016).

Swinkels J., *Cancellation Charges and Compensations under EU VAT*, 19 International VAT Monitor 6 (2008), Journals IBFD.

Tait A.A., *Value Added Tax – International Practice and Problems* (International Monetary Fund 1988).

Tapscott D., *The Digital Economy: Promise and Peril in the Age of Networked Intelligence* (McGraw-Hill 1996).

Taylor F.W., *The Principles of Scientific Management* (Harper & Brothers 1919).

Terra B.J.M. & J. Kajus, *Commentary on European VAT* (IBFD Tax Research Platform 2019).

Terra B.J.M. & J. Kajus, *Introduction to European VAT (Recast)* (IBFD Tax Research Platform 2019).

Terra B.J.M., *Sales Taxation. The Case of Value Added Tax in the European Community* (Kluwer Law International 1988).

Terra B.J.M., *The Place of Supply in European VAT* (Kluwer Law International 1998).

Tetłak K. & C. Kindl, *Taxing Rights in Relation to Immovable Property: VAT/GST v. Direct Taxation*, in *Value Added Tax and Direct Taxation: Similarities and Differences* (M. Lang, P. Melz & E. Kristoffersson eds, IBFD 2009).

Tomassetti J., *Does Uber Redefine the Firm? The Postindustrial Corporation and Advanced Information Technology*, 34 Hofstra Labour & Employment Law Journal 1 (2016), 1-78.

Trenta C., *Rethinking EU VAT for P2P Distribution* (Kluwer Law International 2015).

Tridimas T., *The General Principles of EU Law. 3rd Ed.* (Oxford University Press 2013).

Tridimas T., *The Principle of Proportionality*, in *Oxford Principles of European Union Law* (R. Schütze & T. Tridimas eds, Oxford University Press 2018), 243-264.

Turina A., *Which 'Source' Taxation for the Digital Economy?*, 46 Intertax 6&7 (2018), 495-519.

US Tax Foundation, *Ten Principles of Sound Tax Policy* (2005).

Van Alstyne M.W., G.G. Parker & S.P. Choudary, *Pipelines, Platforms, and the New Rules of Strategy*, 94 Harvard Business Review 4 (2016), 54-62.

Van de Leur M., *Watch Out, You May Be a Taxable Person!*, 24 International VAT Monitor 5 (2013), Journals IBFD.

Van Doesum A., H.W.M. van Kesteren, & G.J. van Norden, *Fundamentals of EU VAT Law* (Kluwer Law International 2016).

Van Doesum A., *Taxable Amount*, in *CJEU – Recent Developments in Value Added Tax* (M. Lang, et al. eds, Linde 2014), 177-222.

Van Doesum A., *What Looks Like a Duck Is a Duck: Economic Purpose and Legal Reality in EU VAT Law*, 1 World Journal of VAT/GST Law 2 (2012), 202-204.

Van Hilten M.E., *Over Neutraliteit van de Omzetbelasting en Het Hellend Vlak van de Uitzonderingen* (Kluwer Deventer 2010).

Van Hilten M.E., *The Legal Character of VAT*, in *Selected Issues in European Tax Law: The Legal Character of VAT and the Application of General Principles of Justice: Summary of an EFS Seminar in Honour of Fons Simons* (D. Albregtse & H. Kogels eds, Kluwer Law International 1999), 3-8.

Van Kesteren H., *Taxable and Non-Taxable Transactions*, in *CJEU – Recent Developments in Value Added Tax* (M. Lang et al. eds, Linde 2016), 209-240.

Van Kesteren H., *Taxable Transactions*, in *CJEU – Recent Developments in Value Added Tax 2017* (M. Lang et al. eds, Linde 2018), 205-231.

Vanistendael F., *Chapter 3: The Role of (Legal) Principles in EU Tax Law*, in *Principles of Law: Function, Status and Impact in EU Tax Law* (C. Brokelind ed., IBFD 2014).

Vanistendael F., *Neutrality and the Limits of VAT*, in *Selected Issues in European Tax Law: The Legal Character of VAT and the Application of General Principles of Justice: Summary of an EFS Seminar in Honour of Fons Simons* (D. Albregtse & H. Kogels eds, Kluwer Law International 1999), 13-18.

Vann R., *Improving Tax Law Improvement: An International Perspective*, 12 Australian Tax Forum 2 (1995), 193-246.

Weber D. (Dennis) & T. Sirithaporn, *Chapter 11: Legal Certainty, Legitimate Expectations, Legislative Drafting, Harmonization and Legal Enforcement in EU Tax Law*, in *Principles of Law: Function, Status and Impact in EU Tax Law* (C. Brokelind ed., IBFD 2014).

Westberg B., *Cross-Border Taxation of E-Commerce* (IBFD 2002).
Williams D., *Ch. 6: Value-Added Tax*, in *Tax Law Design and Drafting* (V. Thuronyi ed., International Monetary Fund 1996).
Zawodsky F.S., *Value Added Taxation in the Digital Economy*, British Tax Review 5 (2018), 606-627.

Newspaper Articles

Barinka A. & E. Newcomer, *Uber Valued at $120 Billion in an IPO?*, Bloomberg (17 October 2018).
Bergin T., *Exclusive – Loophole Allows Uber to Avoid UK Tax, Undercut Rivals*, Reuters (7 June 2017).
Croft J. & M. Murgia, *Uber Faces Legal Challenge on Paying VAT*, Financial Times (20 March 2017).
Freeman S., *'Uberization' of Everything Is Happening, but Not Every 'Uber' Will Succeed*, Huffington Post (1 April 2015).
Friedman T.L., *Welcome to the 'Sharing Economy'*, The New York Times (20 July 2013).
Gmelich K., *Airbnb Says It Made a Profit Again in 2018*, Bloomberg (15 January 2019).
Greenhouse S., *The Whatchamacallit Economy*, New York Times (16 December 2016).
Houlder V., *Airbnb's Edge on Room Prices Depends on Tax Advantages*, Financial Times (2 January 2017).
O'Keefe B. & M. Jones, *How Uber Plays the Tax Shell Game*, Fortune (22 October 2015).
Scanlon S., *Peer-to-Peer Rental: The Rise of the Sharing Economy*, The Economist (9 March 2013).
Schaal D., *Booking and Airbnb Are Now in a Homesharing Dead Heat*, Skyft (27 February 2019).
Sharing Economy Shows Up Outdated Tax Rules, Financial Times (3 January 2017)
Subscribers Are the New, New Thing in Business, The Economist (7 April 2018).
Thomson A., *BlaBlaCar Value Hits $1.6 Billion after Latest Funding Round*, Bloomberg (17 September 2015).
Transcript of Mark Zuckerberg's Senate Hearing, The Washington Post (10 April 2018).
Walsh B., *Today's Smart Choice: Don't Own. Share*, Time Magazine (17 March 2011).
Worstall T., *Reuters' Tom Bergin Wrong Again – Uber Does Not Avoid VAT, Rather It Does Not Charge VAT*, Forbes (8 June 2017).

Official Documents

Australia

Australian Taxation Office (ATO), *The Sharing Economy and Tax*, https://www.ato.gov.au/General/The-sharing-economy-and-tax/ (accessed 31 March 2019).

Canada

Revenu Québec, *Uber Drivers*, https://www.revenuquebec.ca/en/businesses/sector-specific-measures/uber-drivers/ (accessed 31 March 2019).

European Union (EU)

European Commission

European Commission, *Proposal for a Second Directive for the Harmonisation among Member States of Turnover Tax Legislation, concerning the Form and Methods of Application of the Common System of Taxation on Value Added*, COM(65) 144 final, Supplement to the Bulletin of the European Economic Community No. 5 (1965).

European Commission, *Proposal for a Sixth Council Directive on the Harmonisation of Member States concerning Turnover Taxes Common System of Value Added Tax: Uniform Basis of Assessment (submitted to the Council by the Commission on 29 June 1973)*, COM(73) 950, Bulletin of the European Communities No. 11 (1973).

European Commission, *Proposal for a Council Directive amending Directive 77/388/EEC as regards the Value Added Tax Arrangements Applicable to Passenger Transport*, COM(92) 416 final.

European Commission, *Common System of Value Added Tax: Arrangements for Taxing Transactions Carried Out by Non-Established Taxable Persons. Communication and Report from the Commission to the Council and the European Parliament*, COM(94) 471 final.

European Commission, *A Common System for VAT: A Programme for the Single Market*, COM(96) 328 final.

European Commission, *Communication from the Commission to the Council, the European Parliament and the European Economic and Social Committee. Review and Update of VAT Strategy Priorities*, COM(2003) 614 final.

European Commission, *Proposal for a Council Directive amending Directive 77/388/EEC as regards the Place of Supply of Services*, COM(2003) 822 final.

European Commission, *Amended Proposal for a Council Directive amending Directive 77/388/EEC as regards the Place of Supply of Services*, COM(2005) 334 final.

European Commission, *Consultation Paper: VAT – The Place of Supply of Services to Non-Taxable Persons*, D(2005).

European Commission, *Summary Report on the Outcome of the Public Consultation from DG TAXUD, VAT – The Place of Supply of Services to Non-Taxable Persons* (TAXUD-2005-00843).

European Commission, *Proposal for a Council Directive amending Council Directive 2002/38/EC as regards the Period of Application of the Value Added Tax Arrangements Applicable to Radio and Television Broadcasting Services and Certain Electronically Supplied Services*, COM(2006) 739 final.

European Commission, *Report on the Outcome of the Consultation on 'Introduction of a Mechanism for Eliminating Double Imposition of VAT in Individual Cases'* (TAXUD/D1/EWS/Mav D(2007) 15925).

European Commission, *Proposal for a Council Directive amending Directive 2006/112/EC on the Common System of Value Added Tax as regards Tax Evasion Linked to Import and Other Cross-Border Transactions*, COM(2008) 805 final

European Commission, *Green Paper on the Future of VAT: Toward a Simpler, More Robust and Efficient VAT System*, COM(2010) 695 final.

European Commission, *Communication from the Commission to the European Parliament, the Council and the European Economic and Social Committee on the Future of VAT: Toward a Simpler, More Robust and Efficient VAT System Tailored to the Single Market*, COM(2011) 851 final.

European Commission, *Explanatory Notes on the EU VAT Changes to the Place of Supply of Telecommunications, Broadcasting and Electronic Services That Enter into Force in 2015 (Council Implementing Regulation (EU) No 1042/2013)* (2015), https://ec.europa.eu/taxation_customs/sites/taxation/files/resources/documents/taxation/vat/how_vat_works/telecom/explanatory_notes_2015_en.pdf (accessed 31 March 2019).

European Commission, *Explanatory Notes on EU VAT Place of Supply Rules on Services Connected with Immovable Property that Enter into Force in 2017 (Council Implementing Regulation (EU) No 1042/2013)* (2015), https://ec.europa.eu/taxation_customs/sites/taxation/files/resources/documents/taxation/vat/how_vat_works/explanatory_notes_new_en.pdf (accessed 31 March 2019).

European Commission, *Proposal for a Directive of the European Parliament and of the Council on Certain Aspects Concerning Contracts for the Supply of Digital Content*, COM(2015) 634 final.

European Commission, *Communication from the Commission to the European Parliament, the Council, The European Economic and Social Committee and the Committee of the Regions. Online Platforms and the Digital Single Market Opportunities and Challenges for Europe*, COM(2016) 288 final.

European Commission, *Communication from the Commission to the European Parliament, the Council, the European Economic and Social Committee and the Committee of the Regions on a European Agenda for the Collaborative Economy*, COM(2016) 356 final.

European Commission, *Study on the Review of the VAT Special Scheme for Travel Agents and Options for Reform Final Report* (2016), https://ec.europa.eu/taxation_customs/sites/taxation/files/travel_agents_special_vat_scheme_en.pdf (accessed 31 March 2019).

European Commission, *Proposal for a Directive of the European Parliament and of the Council on Transparent and Predictable Working Conditions in the European Union*, COM(2017) 797 final.

European Commission, *Questions and Answers – Data Protection Reform Package* (2017), http://europa.eu/rapid/press-release_MEMO-17-1441_en.htm (accessed 31 March 2019).

European Commission, *Proposal for a Council Directive amending Directive 2006/112/EC on the Common System of Value Added Tax as regards the Special Scheme for Small Enterprises*, COM(2018) 21 final.

European Commission, *Commission Staff Working Document. Impact Assessment accompanying the Document Proposal for a Council Directive amending Directive 2006/112/EC on the Common System of Value Added Tax as regards the Special Scheme for Small Enterprises*, SWD (2018) 9 final.

European Commission, *Proposal for a Council Directive on the Common System of a Digital Services Tax on Revenues resulting from the Provision of Certain Digital Services*, COM(2018) 148 final.

European Commission, Commission Staff Working Document, *Impact Assessment accompanying the Document Proposal for a Council Directive laying down Rules relating to the Corporate Taxation of a Significant Digital Presence and Proposal for a Council Directive on the Common System of a Digital Services Tax on Revenues resulting from the Provision of Certain Digital Services*, SWD (2018) 81 final.

European Commission, *Proposal for a Council Directive amending Directive 2006/112/EC as regards the Introduction of the Detailed Technical Measures for the Operation of the Definitive VAT System for the Taxation of Trade between Member States*, COM(2018) 329 final.

European Commission, *Proposal for a Council Implementing Regulation amending Implementing Regulation (EU) No 282/2011 as Regards Supplies of Goods or Services Facilitated by Electronic Interfaces and the Special Schemes for Taxable Persons Supplying Services to Non-Taxable Persons, Making Distance Sales of Goods and Certain Domestic Supplies of Goods*, COM(2018) 821 final.

European Commission, *Follow Up to the European Legislative Resolution on the Proposal for a Council Directive amending Directive 2006/112/EC as regards Harmonising and Simplifying Certain Rules in the Value Added Tax System and Introducing the Definitive System for the Taxation of Trade between Member States*, SP (2018) 755.

European Commission, *Information Notice. Test Case for Private Ruling Requests relating to Cross-Border Situations* (2018), https://ec.europa.eu/taxation_customs/sites/taxation/files/cbr_info-notice-to-the-public_en.pdf (accessed 31 March 2019).

European Commission, *Report: The Use of the Collaborative Economy. Survey Requested by the European Commission, Directorate-General for Internal Market, Industry, Entrepreneurship and SMEs and Co-ordinated by the Directorate-General for Communication* (2018), Flash Eurobarometer 467 – TNS Political & Social.

European Commission, *VAT Rates Applied in the Member States of the European Union* (2019), https://ec.europa.eu/taxation_customs/sites/taxation/files/resources/documents/taxation/vat/how_vat_works/rates/vat_rates_en.pdf (accessed 31 March 2019).

European Economic and Social Committee

European Economic and Social Committee, *Taxation of the Collaborative Economy – Analysis of Possible Tax Policies Faced with the Growth of the Collaborative Economy (Exploratory Opinion Requested by the Estonian Presidency)*, ECO/434-EESC-2017-02946-00-00-ac-tra.

European Parliament

European Parliament, *Report on the Proposal for a Council Directive amending Directive 2006/112/EC on the Common System of Value Added Tax as regards the Special Scheme for Small Enterprises*, COM(2018) 0021 - C8-0022/2018 - 2018/0006(CNS), A8-0260/2018.

European Parliament, *Legislative Resolution of 3 October 2018 on the Proposal for a Council Directive amending Directive 2006/112/EC as Regards Harmonising and Simplifying Certain Rules in the Value Added Tax System and Introducing the Definitive System for the Taxation of Trade between Member States* (COM(2017)0569 - C8-0363/2017 - 2017/0251(CNS)), 3 October 2018 (T8-0366/2018).

EU VAT Forum

European Commission, EU VAT Forum, *Guide on Enhanced Cooperation between Member States and Business in the Field of Fighting VAT Fraud* (2016), https://ec.europa.eu/taxation_customs/sites/taxation/files/resources/documents/taxation/tax_cooperation/vat_gap/2016-03_guide-on-adm-cooperation_en.pdf (accessed 31 March 2019).

European Commission, EU VAT Forum, *Cross-Border Rulings (update May 2017)* (taxud.c.4(2017)2926060).

European Commission, EU VAT Forum, *Consolidated Report on Cooperation between Member States and Businesses in the Field of e-Commerce/Modern Commerce* (taxud.c.4(2018) 1507602), https://ec.europa.eu/taxation_customs/sites/taxation/files/d-1507602_report_consolidated_en.pdf (accessed 31 March 2019).

European Commission, EU VAT Forum, *Information Note – VAT Double Taxation – Dialogue between Tax Administrations*, https://ec.europa.eu/taxation_customs/sites/taxation/files/resources/documents/taxation/vat/key_documents/eu_vat_forum/dialogue_tax_administrations_ms_en.pdf (accessed 31 March 2019).

Value Added Tax Committee

European Commission, Value Added Tax Committee, *Guidelines resulting from the 52nd Meeting of 28-29 May 1997 (XXI/97/1.566).*

European Commission, Value Added Tax Committee, *Guidelines resulting from the 88th Meeting of 13-14 July 2009 (taxud.d.1(2009)358416 – 634).*

European Commission, Value Added Tax Committee, *Guidelines resulting from the 89th Meeting of 30 September 2009 (taxud.d.1(2009)405067 – 639).*

European Commission, Value Added Tax Committee, *Guidelines resulting from the 89th Meeting of 30 September 2009 – Document B (taxud.d.1(2010)176579 – 645).*

European Commission, Value Added Tax Committee, *Guidelines resulting from the 93rd Meeting of 1 July 2011 - Document A (taxud.c.1(2012)400557 – 707).*

European Commission, Value Added Tax Committee, *Guidelines resulting from the 93rd Meeting of 1 July 2011 – Document C (taxud.c.1(2012)1410604 – 709).*

European Commission, Value Added Tax Committee, *Guidelines resulting from the 102nd Meeting of 30 March 2015 – Document D (taxud.c.1(2015)4128689 – 862).*

European Commission, Value Added Tax Committee, *Guidelines resulting from the 107th Meeting of 8 July 2016 – Document D (taxud.c.1(2017)1402399 – 914).*

European Commission, Value Added Tax Committee, *Guidelines resulting from the 108th Meeting of 27-28 March 2017 – Document C (taxud.c.1(2018)2397450 – 930).*

European Commission, Value Added Tax Committee, *Working Paper No. 781, Application of the Effective Use and Enjoyment Rule to Market Research Studies (taxud.c.1(2014)195750).*

European Commission, Value Added Tax Committee, *Working Paper No. 786, Services Provided to Companies by Their Shareholders (taxud.c.1(2014)201835).*

European Commission, Value Added Tax Committee, *Working Paper No. 814, Treatment of Online Supplies Made by a Travel Agent to Final Consumers (taxud.c.1(2014)2806510).*

European Commission, Value Added Tax Committee, *Working Paper No. 836, VAT Treatment of Crowdfunding (taxud.c.1(2015)576037).*

European Commission, Value Added Tax Committee, *Working Paper No. 843, VAT 2015: Scope of the Notion of Electronically Supplied Services (taxud.c.1(2015)694775).*

European Commission, Value Added Tax Committee, *Working Paper No. 855, Distance Selling (taxud.c.1(2015)2158321).*

European Commission, Value Added Tax Committee, *Working Paper No. 878, VAT Treatment of Sharing Economy (taxud.c.1(2015)4370160).*

European Commission, Value Added Tax Committee, *Working Paper No. 882, VAT 2015: VAT Treatment of Online Gambling Services (Follow-Up) (taxud.c.1(2015)4459580).*

European Commission, Value Added Tax Committee, *Working Paper No. 885, VAT 2015: Harmonised Application of the Presumption (taxud.c.1(2015)4659331).*

European Commission, Value Added Tax Committee, *Working Paper No. 896, VAT 2015: Scope of the Notion of Electronically Supplied Services; Minimal Human Intervention (Follow-Up) (taxud.c.1(2016)922288).*

European Commission, Value Added Tax Committee, *Working Paper No. 906, VAT 2015: Interaction between Electronically Supplied Services and Intermediation Services and Initial Discussion on the Scope of the Concept of Intermediation Services when Taken in a Broader Context (taxud.c.1(2016)3297911).*

European Commission, Value Added Tax Committee, *Working Paper No. 919, VAT 2015: Scope of the Notion of Electronically Supplied Services; Minimal Human Intervention (Second Follow-Up) (taxud.c.1(2017)1270284).*

European Commission, Value Added Tax Committee, *Working Paper No. 947, Services Provided by an Electronic Platform Connecting for Remuneration, by means of a Smartphone Application, a Driver Using His Own Vehicle with Persons Who Wish to Make Urban Journeys. The Significance of the VAT Identification Number (taxud.c.1(2018)1735106).*

European Commission, Value Added Tax Committee, *Working Paper No. 958. Conditions for There Being a Taxable Transaction When Internet Services Are Provided in Exchange for User Data (taxud.c.1(2018)6248826).*
European Commission, Value Added Tax Committee, *Minutes 111th Meeting – 30 November 2018 (taxud.c.1(2019)1709508).*

Organisation for Economic Co-operation and Development (OECD)

OECD, *Electronic Commerce: Taxation Framework Conditions. A Report by the OECD Committee on Fiscal Affairs, as presented to Ministers at the OECD Ministerial Conference 'A Borderless World: Realizing the Potential of Electronic Commerce' on 8 October 1998* (OECD Publishing 1998).
OECD, *Report by the Technology Technical Advisory Group (TAG)* (OECD Publishing 2000).
OECD, *Consumption Taxation of Cross-Border Services and Intangible Property in the Context of E-Commerce* (OECD Publishing 2001).
OECD, *Report on the Application of Consumption Taxes to the Trade in International Services and Intangibles* (OECD Publishing 2004).
OECD, *The Application of Consumption Taxes to the International Trade in Services and Intangibles: Progress Report and Draft Principles* (OECD Publishing 2005).
OECD, *Co-operative Compliance: A Framework: From Enhanced Relationship to Co-operative Compliance* (OECD Publishing 2013).
OECD, *Exploring the Economics of Personal Data: A Survey of Methodologies for Measuring Monetary Value* (OECD Publishing 2013).
OECD, *The Distributional Effects of Consumption Taxes in OECD Countries* (OECD Publishing 2014).
OECD/G20, *Addressing the Tax Challenges of the Digital Economy, Action 1: 2015 Final Report* (OECD Publishing 2015).
OECD, *Tax Administration 2015: Comparative Information on OECD and Other Advanced and Emerging Economies* (OECD Publishing 2015).
OECD, *Protecting Consumers in Peer Platform Markets. Exploring the Issues* (OECD Publishing 2016).
OECD, *International VAT/GST Guidelines* (OECD Publishing 2017).
OECD, *Mechanisms for the Effective Collection of VAT/GST When the Supplier Is Not Located in the Jurisdiction of Taxation* (OECD Publishing 2017).
OECD, *Model Tax Convention on Income and on Capital 2017 (Condensed Version)* (OECD Publishing 2017).
OECD, *Consumption Tax Trends 2018* (OECD Publishing 2018).
OECD/G20, *Tax Challenges Arising from Digitalisation – Interim Report 2018* (OECD Publishing 2018).
OECD, *Public Comments Received on the Possible Solutions to the Tax Challenges of Digitalisation* (2019), http://www.oecd.org/tax/beps/public-comments-received-on-the-possible-solutions-to-the-tax-challenges-of-digitalisation.htm (accessed 31 March 2019).

OECD, *The Role of Digital Platforms in the Collection of VAT/GST on Online Sales* (OECD Publishing 2019).

OECD, *The Sharing and Gig Economy: Effective Taxation of Platform Sellers: Forum on Tax Administration* (OECD Publishing 2019).

United Kingdom (UK)

Her Majesty's Revenue and Customs (HMRC), *VAT: Overseas Businesses and Joint and Several Liability for Online Marketplaces* (2016), https://www.gov.uk/government/publications/vat-overseas-businesses-and-joint-and-several-liability-for-online-marketplaces/vat-overseas-businesses-and-joint-and-several-liability-for-online-marketplaces (accessed 31 March 2019).

Her Majesty's Revenue and Customs (HMRC), *Alternative Method of VAT Collection. Summary of Responses* (2017), https://assets.publishing.service.gov.uk/government/uploads/system/uploads/attachment_data/file/663989/Alternative_method_of_VAT_collection_-_summary_of_responses.pdf (accessed 31 March 2019).

Her Majesty's Revenue and Customs (HMRC), *VAT: Extending Joint and Several Liability for Online Marketplaces and Displaying VAT Numbers Online – Guidance Note* (2017), https://www.gov.uk/government/publications/vat-extending-joint-and-several-liability-for-online-marketplaces-and-displaying-vat-numbers-online-guidance-note (accessed 31 March 2019).

Her Majesty's Revenue and Customs (HMRC), *Tackling Online VAT Fraud and Error – The Role of Online Marketplaces in Co-operating with HMRC – The Agreement* (2018), https://www.gov.uk/government/publications/hmrc-and-online-marketplaces-agreement-to-promote-vat-compliance/tackling-online-vat-fraud-and-error-the-role-of-online-marketplaces-in-co-operating-with-hmrc-the-agreement (accessed 31 March 2019).

Her Majesty's Revenue and Customs (HMRC), *Tackling Online VAT Fraud and Error – The Role of Online Marketplaces in Co-operating with HMRC: List of Signatories* (2018), https://assets.publishing.service.gov.uk/government/uploads/system/uploads/attachment_data/file/719795/List_of_signatories.pdf (accessed 31 March 2019).

Her Majesty's Revenue and Customs (HMRC), *The Role of Online Platforms in Ensuring Tax Compliance by Their Users* (2018), https://assets.publishing.service.gov.uk/government/uploads/system/uploads/attachment_data/file/687363/The_role_of_online_platforms_in_ensuring_tax_compliance_by_their_users.pdf (accessed 31 March 2019).

Her Majesty's Revenue and Customs (HMRC), *Internal Manual. Single and Multiple Supplies: HMRC's Approach: The General Approach* (2019), https://www.gov.uk/hmrc-internal-manuals/vat-supply-and-consideration/vatsc11113 (accessed 31 March 2019).

Office of Tax Simplification, *Value Added Tax: Routes to Simplification. Presented to Parliament pursuant to Section 186(4)(b) of Finance Act 2016* (2017), https://www.gov.uk/government/uploads/system/uploads/attachment_data/file/657215/Value_added_tax_routes_to_simplification_web.pdf (accessed 31 March 2019).

United States (US)

New York State. Department of Taxation and Finance, *Transportation Network Company Assessment*, https://www.tax.ny.gov/bus/tnc/assessment.htm (accessed 31 March 2019).

Surveys and Empirical Studies

Copenhagen Economics, *Online Intermediaries: Impact on the EU Economy* (2015), https://www.copenhageneconomics.com/dyn/resources/Publication/publicationPDF/2/342/1454501505/edima-online-intermediaries-eu-growth-engines.pdf (accessed 31 March 2019).

Deloitte, *VAT Aspects of Cross-Border e-Commerce – Options for Modernization, Final Report – Lot 3: Assessment of the Implementation of the 2015 Place of Supply Rules and the Mini-One Stop Shop* (2016), https://ec.europa.eu/taxation_customs/sites/taxation/files/vat_aspects_cross-border_e-commerce_final_report_lot3.pdf (accessed 31 March 2019).

Donovan S.A., D.H. Bradley & J.O. Shimabukuru, *What Does the Gig Economy Mean for Workers?* (2016), https://digitalcommons.ilr.cornell.edu/cgi/viewcontent.cgi?article=2512&context=key_workplace (accessed 31 March 2019).

Dourado E. & C. Koopman, *Evaluating the Growth of the 1099 Workforce* (Mercatus Center, George Mason University 2015), https://www.mercatus.org/publication/evaluating-growth-1099-workforce (accessed 31 March 2019).

Ernst & Young (EY), *Key Indirect Tax Issues in the Sharing Economy*, http://www.ey.com/gl/en/services/tax/vat--gst-and-other-sales-taxes/ey-managing-indirect-taxes-in-the-digital-age-ch7-key-indirect-tax-issues-in-the-sharing-economy (accessed 31 March 2019).

Evans P.C. & A. Gawer, *The Rise of the Platform Enterprise: A Global Survey* (2016), https://www.thecge.net/app/uploads/2016/01/PDF-WEB-Platform-Survey_01_12.pdf (accessed 31 March 2019).

Farrell D. & F. Greig, *Paychecks, Paydays and the On-Demand Platform Economy: Big Data on Income Volatility* (JP Morgan Chase Institute 2016).

International Post Corporation (IPC), *Cross-Border E-Commerce Shopper Survey 2018* (2018), https://www.ipc.be/services/markets-and-regulations/cross-border-shopper-survey (accessed 31 March 2019).

Koopman C., M. Mitchell & A.D. Thierer, *The Sharing Economy: Issues Facing Platforms, Participants, and Regulators* (2015), https://papers.ssrn.com/sol3/papers.cfm?abstract_id=2610875 (accessed 31 March 2019).

KPMG, *VAT/GST Treatment of Cross-Border Services. 2017 Survey* (2017), https://assets.kpmg.com/content/dam/kpmg/xx/pdf/2017/11/ess-survey-13-nov-17.pdf (accessed 31 March 2019).

PricewaterhouseCoopers (PwC), *The Sharing Economy: How Will It Disrupt Your Business* (2014), http://pwc.blogs.com/files/sharing-economy-final_0814.pdf (accessed 31 March 2019).

URL Resources

About Us – BlaBlaCar, https://www.blablacar.com/about-us (accessed 31 March 2019).

Airbnb Fast Facts, https://press.airbnb.com/fast-facts/ (accessed 31 March 2019).

Airbnb Privacy Policy, https://www.airbnb.com/terms/privacy_policy (accessed 31 March. 2019).

Airbnb's Host Guarantee, https://www.airbnb.com/guarantee (accessed 31 March 2019).

BlaBlaCar Privacy and Data Protection Policy, https://blog.blablacar.co.uk/about-us/privacy-policy (accessed 31 March 2019).

Can I Offer a Ride on BlaBlaCar with My Company Car?, https://www.blablacar.co.uk/faq/question/my-car-is-a-professional-a-company-or-a-service-vehicle-can-i-offer-trips-on-blablacar-using-that-vehicle (accessed 31 March 2019).

Can I Purchase GuestPoints?, https://homeexchangehelp.zendesk.com/hc/en-us/articles/360000622018-Can-I-purchase-GuestPoints- (accessed 31 March 2019).

Can I Redeem My GuestPoints for Cash?, https://homeexchangehelp.zendesk.com/hc/en-us/articles/360000631297-Can-I-redeem-my-GuestPoints-for-cash- (accessed 31 March 2019).

Can I Tip My Driver with the App?, https://help.uber.com/riders/article/can-i-tip-my-driver-with-the-app--?nodeId = 8459a496-5ed2-4f9d-b15c-d8afd9ccf34f (accessed 31 March 2019).

Cancelling an Uber Ride, https://help.uber.com/riders/article/cancelling-an-uber-ride-?nodeId = 56270015-1d1d-4c08-a460-3b94a090de23 (accessed 31 March 2019).

Conditions and Details of HomeExchange's Guarantees, https://www.homeexchange.com/p/service-plus-termsofuse-en (accessed 31 March 2019).

Do GuestPoints Expire?, https://homeexchangehelp.zendesk.com/hc/en-us/articles/360001062358-Do-GuestPoints-expire- (accessed 31 March 2019).

Does Airbnb Provide Professional Photography Services?, https://www.airbnb.com/help/article/297/does-airbnb-provide-professional-photography-services?q = photo (accessed 31 March 2019).

English Oxford Dictionary, *Ancillary*, https://en.oxforddictionaries.com/definition/ancillary (accessed 31 March 2019).

Getting a Trip Receipt, https://help.uber.com/riders/article/getting-a-trip-receipt?nodeId = 846f6cad-6f27-492a-9e0b-d2f056e1298e (accessed 31 March 2019)

GuestPoints, https://www.homeexchange.com/p/guestpoints-en (accessed 31 March 2019).

HomeExchange Acquires HomeExchange, https://www.homeexchange.com/blog/guesttoguest-acquires-homeexchange/ (accessed 31 March 2019).

HomeExchange Privacy Policy, https://www.homeexchange.com/p/privacy-policy (accessed 31 March. 2019).

How Are Fares Calculated?, https://help.uber.com/riders/article/how-are-fares-calculated?nodeId = d2d43bbc-f4bb-4882-b8bb-4bd8acf03a9d (accessed 31 March 2019).

How Do I Cancel a Ride?, https://www.blablacar.co.uk/faq/question/how-do-i-cancel-a-ride (accessed 31 March 2019).

How Do I Set the Passenger Contribution for My Ride?, https://www.blablacar.co.uk/faq/question/how-do-i-set-my-price (accessed 31 March 2019).
How Do I Turn Smart Pricing On or Off?, https://www.airbnb.com/help/article/1168/how-do-i-turn-smart-pricing-on-or-off (accessed 31 March 2019).
How Do Taxes Work for Hosts?, https://www.airbnb.com/help/article/481/how-do-taxes-work-for-hosts (accessed 31 March 2019).
How Do Taxes Work for Guests?, https://www.airbnb.com/help/article/318/how-do-taxes-work-for-guests (accessed 31 March 2019).
How Do We Order Rides in the Search Results?, https://www.blablacar.co.uk/faq/question/how-do-we-order-rides-in-the-search-results (accessed 31 March 2019).
How Does My Experience's Rating or Reviews Affect My Ability to Host?, https://www.airbnb.com/help/article/2159/how-does-my-experience-s-rating-or-reviews-affect-my-ability-to-host (accessed 31 March 2019).
How Much Is Your Personal Data Worth, https://ig.ft.com/how-much-is-your-personal-data-worth/ (accessed 31 March 2019).
How to Do Your VAT Registration, https://www.uber.com/en-GB/drive/tax-information/ (accessed 31 March 2019).
In What Areas Is Occupancy Tax Collection and Remittance by Airbnb Available, https://www.airbnb.com/help/article/2509/in-what-areas-is-occupancy-tax-collection-and-remittance-by-airbnb-available (accessed 31 March 2019).
Legal Notice, https://www.homeexchange.com/p/legal-notice (accessed 31 March 2019).
My Fare Was Adjusted, https://help.uber.com/partners/article/my-fare-was-adjusted-?nodeId=5f9a6dc9-0357-41b7-be1b-912cb883ee46 (accessed 31 March 2019).
New Agreements Make Host Income Tax Simple, https://press.airbnb.com/new-agreements-make-host-income-tax-simple/ (accessed 31 March 2019).
Pass e Abbonamento: Ecco le Tariffe, https://blog.blablacar.it/blablalife/lp/costo-servizio (accessed 31 March 2019).
Payments and Earnings, https://www.uber.com/en-GH/drive/resources/payments/ (accessed 31 March 2019).
Pricing, https://www.homeexchange.com/choose-plan (accessed 31 March 2019).
Ratings, https://www.blablacar.co.uk/member-ratings (accessed 31 March 2019).
Reciprocal and Non-Reciprocal Exchanges, https://homeexchangehelp.zendesk.com/hc/en-us/articles/360000601998-Reciprocal-and-non-reciprocal-exchanges (accessed 31 March 2019).
Save Time and Money with VAT Services on Amazon, https://services.amazon.co.uk/services/vat-services-on-amazon/faq.html (accessed 31 March 2019).
Service Fees, https://blog.blablacar.co.uk/blablalife/lp/service-fees (accessed 31 March 2019).
Terms of Service, https://www.airbnb.com/terms (accessed 31 March 2019).
Uber – Company Info, https://www.uber.com/en-IT/newsroom/company-info/ (accessed 31 March 2019).
Uber Privacy Policy, https://privacy.uber.com/policy (accessed 31 March. 2019).

UK Tax Strategy, https://www.uber.com/legal/other/uk-tax/ (accessed 31 March 2019).

Understanding Ratings, https://help.uber.com/partners/article/understanding-ratings?nodeId=fa1eb77f-ad79-4607-9651-72b932be30b7 (accessed 31 March 2019).

United Kingdom – Uber Community Guidelines, https://www.uber.com/legal/community-guidelines/uk-en/ (accessed 31 March 2019).

United States – Uber Community Guidelines, https://www.uber.com/legal/community-guidelines/us-en/ (accessed 31 March 2019).

We Are Home-Exchangers, https://www.homeexchange.com/p/about-us (accessed 31 March 2019).

Welcome to the HomeExchange Community, https://www.homeexchange.com/p/community (accessed 31 March 2019).

What Happens if My Host Cancels?, https://homeexchangehelp.zendesk.com/hc/en-us/articles/360000609918-What-happens-if-my-host-cancels- (accessed 31 March 2019).

What Happens in the Case of Damages or Disagreements?, https://homeexchangehelp.zendesk.com/hc/en-us/articles/360000626478-What-happens-in-the-case-of-damages-or-disagreements- (accessed 31 March 2019).

What If a Passenger Cancels Before Departure or Doesn't Show Up?, https://www.blablacar.co.uk/faq/question/what-if-a-passenger-cancels-before-departure-or-doesn-t-show-up (accessed 31 March 2019).

What Is Airbnb's Guest Refund Policy for Homes?, https://www.airbnb.com/help/article/544/what-is-airbnb-s-guest-refund-policy-for-homes?q=Airbnb%20Guest%20Refund%20Policy (accessed 31 March 2019).

What Is Instant Book?, https://www.airbnb.com/help/article/523/what-is-instant-book (accessed 31 March 2019).

What Is the Airbnb Service Fee, https://www.airbnb.com/help/article/1857/what-is-the-airbnb-service-fee (accessed 31 March 2019).

What Is the Order that the Listings Appear in Search Results?, https://homeexchangehelp.zendesk.com/hc/en-us/articles/360000730577-What-is-the-order-that-the-listings-appear-in-search-results- (accessed 31 March 2019).

What Is VAT and How Does It Apply to Me?, https://www.airbnb.com/help/article/436/what-is-vat-and-how-does-it-apply-to-me (accessed 31 March 2019).

Who Is Covered by the Free of Charge Additional Insurance Cover Offered by BlaBlaCar?, https://www.blablacar.co.uk/faq/question/who-is-covered-by-the-free-of-charge-additional-insurance-offered-by-blablacar (accessed 31 March 2019).

Why Is There a Fixed Price per Passenger?, https://www.blablacar.co.uk/faq/question/why-is-there-a-fixed-price-per-passenger (accessed 31 March 2019).

Why Was My Listing Deactivated?, https://www.airbnb.com/help/article/489/why-was-my-listing-deactivated (accessed 31 March 2019).

Why Was My Listing Paused or Suspended?, https://www.airbnb.com/help/article/1303/why-was-my-listing-paused-or-suspended (accessed 31 March 2019).

Table of Cases

Australia

European Union (EU)

France

Spain

United Kingdom (UK)

United States (US)

Table of Legislation

European Union (EU)

Index

B

C

D

J

M

N

P

Q

R

T

U

W

Z

EUCOTAX Series on European Taxation

(1) Peter HJ Essers, Guido JME de Bont & Eric CCM Kemmeren (eds), *The Compatibility of Anti-Abuse Provisions in Tax Treaties with EC Law,* 1998 (ISBN 90-411-9678-1).
(2) Gerard TK Meussen (ed.), *The Principle of Equality in European Taxation,* 1999 (ISBN 90-411-9693-5).
(3) Michael Lang (ed.), *Tax Treaty Interpretation,* 2001 (ISBN 90-411-9857-1).
(4) Pasquale Pistone, *The Impact of Community Law on Tax Treaties: Issues and Solutions,* 2002 (ISBN 90-411-9860-1).
(5) René Offermanns, *The Entrepreneurship Concept in a European Comparative Tax Law Perspective,* 2002 (ISBN 90-411-9887-3).
(6) Michael Lang & Mario Züger, *Settlement of Disputes in Tax Treaty Law,* 2002 (ISBN 90-411-9904-7).
(7) Carlo Pinto, *Tax Competition and EU Law,* 2003 (ISBN 90-411-9913-6).
(8) Michael Lang, Hans-Jörgen Aigner, Ulrich Scheuerle & Markus *Stefaner, CFC Legislation, Tax Treaties and EC Law,* 2004 (ISBN 90-411-2284-2).
(9) Mattias Dahlberg, *Direct Taxation in Relation to the Freedom of Establishment and the Free Movement of Capital,* 2005 (ISBN 90-411-2363-6).
(10) Michael Lang, Judith Herdin & Ines Hofbauer, *WTO and Direct Taxation,* 2005 (ISBN 90-411-2371-7).
(11) Dennis Weber, *Tax Avoidance and the EC Tray Freedoms: A Study of the Limitations under European Law for the Prevention of Tax Avoidance,* 2005 (ISBN 90-411-2402-0).
(12) Félix Alberto Vega Borrego, *Limitations on Benefits Clauses on Double Taxation Conventions,* 2005 (ISBN 90-411-2370-9).
(13) Michael Lang, Josef Schuch & Claus Staringer, *ECJ-Recent Developments in Direct Taxation,* 2006 (ISBN 90-411-2509-4).
(14) Reuven S. Avi-Yonah, James R. Hines Jr. & Michael Lang, *Comparative Fiscal Federalism. Comparing the European Court of Justice and the US Supreme Court's Tax Jurisprudence,* 2007 (ISBN 978-90-411-2552-1).
(15) Christiana HJI Panayi, *Double Taxation, Tax Treaties, Treaty-Shopping and the European Community,* 2007 (ISBN 978-90-411-2658-0).
(16) Dennis Weber, *The Influence of European Law on Direct Taxation: Recent and Future Developments,* 2007 (ISBN 978-90-411-2667-2).
(17) Michael Lang & Pasquale Pistone, *The EU and Third Countries: Direct Taxation,* 2007 (ISBN 978-90-411-2665-8).
(18) Oskar Henkow, *Financial Activities in European VAT: A Theoretical and Legal Research of the European VAT System and Preferred Treatment of Financial Activities,* 2007 (ISBN 978-90-411-2703-7).
(19) Michael Lang (ed.), *Tax Compliance Costs for Companies in an Enlarged European Community,* 2008 (ISBN 978-90-411-2666-5).

(20) Michael Lang (ed.), *Source versus Residence. Problems Arising from the Allocation of Taxing Rights in Tax Treaty Law and Possible Alternatives*, 2008 (ISBN 978-90-411-2763-1).
(21) Ioanna Mitroyanni, *Integration Approaches to Group Taxation in the European Internal Market*, 2008 (ISBN 978-90-411-2779-2).
(22) Rolf Eicke, *Tax Planning with Holding Companies. Repatriation of US Profits from Europe:Concepts, Strategies, Structures*, 2008 (ISBN978-90-411-2794-5).
(23) Peter Essers et al. (ed.), *The Influence of IAS/IFRS on the CCCTB, Tax Accounting, Disclosure and Corporate Law Accounting Concepts: 'A Clash of Cultures'*, 2008 (ISBN 978-90-411-2819-5).
(24) Tonny Schenk-Geers, *International Exchange of Information and the Protection of Taxpayers*, 2009 (ISBN 978-90-411-3142-3).
(25) Raymond Adema, *UCITS and Taxation: Towards Harmonization of the Taxation of UCITS*, 2009 (ISBN 978-90-411-2839-3).
(26) Michael Lang, Jianwen Liu & Gongliang Tang (eds), *Europe–China Tax Treaties*, 2010 (ISBN 978-90-411-3216-1).
(27) Michael Lang, Pasquale Pistone, Josef Schuch & Claus Staringer (eds), *Procedural Rules in Tax Law in the Context of European Union and Domestic Law*, 2010 (ISBN 978-90-411-3376-2).
(28) Sjaak J.J.M. Jansen, *Fiscal Sovereignty of the Member States in an Internal Market: Past and Future*, 2011 (ISBN 978-90-411-3403-5).
(29) Dennis Weber & Bruno da Silva, *From Marks & Spencer to X Holding: The Future of Cross-Border Group Taxation*, 2011 (ISBN 978-90-411-3399-1).
(30) Claus Bohn Jespersen, *Intermediation of Insurance and Financial Services in European VAT*, 2011 (ISBN 978-90-411-3732-6).
(31) Sabine Heidenbauer, *Charity Crossing Borders: The Fundamental Freedoms' Influence on Charity and Donor Taxation in Europe*, 2011 (ISBN 978-90-411-3813-2).
(32) Michael Lang, et al., *The Future of Indirect Taxation: Recent Trends in VAT and GST Systems around the World*, 2012 (ISBN 978-90-411-3797-5).
(33) Harm van den Broek, *Cross-Border Mergers within the EU: Proposals to Remove the Remaining Tax Obstacles*, 2012 (ISBN 978-90-411-3824-8).
(34) Michael Lang, et al. (eds), *Tax Treaty Case Law around the Globe – 2011*, 2012 (ISBN 978-90-411-3876-7).
(35) Dennis Weber (ed.), *CCCTB: Selected Issues*, 2012 (ISBN 978-90-411-3872-9).
(36) Daniël Smit, *EU Freedoms, Non-EU Countries and Company Taxation*, 2012 (ISBN 978-90-411-4041-8).
(37) Rita de la Feria, *VAT Exemptions: Consequences and Design Alternatives*, 2013 (ISBN 978-90-411-3276-5).
(38) Karin Simader, *Withholding Taxes and the Fundamental Freedoms*, 2013 (ISBN 978-90-411-4842-1).
(39) Madeleine Merkx, *Establishments in European VAT*, 2013 (ISBN 978-90-411-4554-3).
(40) Carla De Pietro, *Tax Treaty Override*, 2014 (ISBN 978-90-411-5406-4).

(41) G.K. Fibbe & A.J.A. Stevens (eds), *Hybrid Entities and the EU Direct Tax Directives*, 2015 (ISBN 978-90-411-5942-7).
(42) Gerard Staats, *Personal Pensions in the EU*, 2015 (ISBN 978-90-411-5953-3).
(43) Michael Lang & Ine Lejeune (eds), *VAT/GST in a Global Digital Economy*, 2015 (ISBN 978-90-411-5952-6).
(44) Massimo Basilavecchia, Lorenzo del Federico & Pietro Mastellone (eds), *Tax Implications of Environmental Disasters and Pollution*, 2015 (ISBN 978-90-411-5611-2).
(45) Cristina Trenta, *Rethinking EU VAT for P2P Distribution*, 2015 (ISBN 978-90-411-6137-6).
(46) Marie Lamensch, Edoardo Traversa & Servaas van Thiel (eds), *Value Added Tax and the Digital Economy: The 2015 EU Rules and Broader Issues*, 2016 (ISBN 978-90-411-6612-8).
(47) Raffaele Petruzzi, *Transfer Pricing Aspects of Intra-Group Financing*, 2016 (ISBN 978-90-411-6732-3).
(48) Mario Grandinetti (ed.), *Corporate Tax Base in the Light of the IAS/IFRS and EU Directive 2013/34: A Comparative Approach*, 2016 (ISBN 978-90-411-6745-3).
(49) Bruno da Silva, *The Impact of Tax Treaties and EU Law on Group Taxation Regimes*, 2016 (ISBN 978-90-411-6905-1).
(50) Michael Lang, Alfred Storck & Raffaele Petruzzi (eds), *Transfer Pricing in a Post-BEPS World*, 2016 (ISBN 978-90-411-6710-1).
(51) Marta Papis-Almansa, *Insurance in European VAT: Current and Preferred Treatment in the Light of the New Zealand and Australian GST Systems*, 2017 (ISBN 978-90-411-8360-6).
(52) Wolfgang Speckhahn, *Real Estate Investment Trusts In Europe: Europeanising Tax Regimes*, 2017 (ISBN 978-90-411-8360-6).
(53) Frank J.G. Nellen, *Information Asymmetries in EU VAT*, 2017 (ISBN 978-90-411-8837-3).
(54) Erik Ros, *EU Citizenship and Direct Taxation*, 2017 (ISBN 978-90-411-8584-6).
(55) Werner Haslehner, Georg Kofler & Alexander Rust (eds), *EU Tax Law and Policy in the 21st Century*, 2017 (ISBN 978-90-411-8815-1).
(56) Claudia Sanò, *National Legal Presumptions and European Tax Law*, 2018 (ISBN 978-90-411-6613-5).
(57) Christoph Marchgraber, *Double (Non-)Taxation and EU Law*, 2018 (ISBN 978-90-411-9410-7).
(58) Dennis Weber & Jan van de Streek (eds), *The EU Common Consolidated Corporate Tax Base: Critical Analysis*, 2018 (ISBN 978-90-411-9233-2).
(59) Werner Haslehner (ed.), *Investment Fund Taxation: Domestic Law, EU Law, and Double Taxation Treaties*, 2018 (ISBN 978-90-411-9669-9).
(60) Jérôme Monsenego, *Selectivity in State Aid Law and the Methods for the Allocation of the Corporate Tax Base*, 2018 (ISBN 978-90-411-9413-8).
(61) José Manuel Almudí Cid, Jorge A. Ferreras Gutiérrez & Pablo A. Hernández González-Barreda (eds), *Combating Tax Avoidance in the EU: Harmonization and Cooperation in Direct Taxation*, 2019 (ISBN 978-94-035-0154-3).

(62) Werner Haslehner, Georg Kofler & Alexander Rust (eds), *Time and Tax: Issues in International, EU, and Constitutional Law*, 2019 (ISBN 978-94-035-0354-7).

(63) Nathalie Wittock, *Sales Promotion Techniques and VAT in the EU*, 2019 (ISBN 978-94-035-0861-0).

(64) Carla De Pietro (ed.), *New Perspectives on Fiscal State Aid: Legitimacy and Effectiveness of Fiscal State Aid Control*, 2019 (ISBN 978-94-035-1415-4).

(65) Giorgio Beretta, *European VAT and the Sharing Economy*, 2019 (ISBN 978-94-035-1435-2).

www.ingramcontent.com/pod-product-compliance
Ingram Content Group UK Ltd.
Pitfield, Milton Keynes, MK11 3LW, UK
UKHW020229290926
15470UKWH00001B/428

9 789403 51435